Contemporary Problems in Personnel

St. Clair Press titles
in Management and Organizations

**ORGANIZATIONAL BEHAVIOR AND MANAGEMENT:
A Contingency Approach, rev. ed.**
    Henry L. Tosi and W. Clay Hamner, eds.

CONTEMPORARY PROBLEMS IN PERSONNEL, rev. ed.
    W. Clay Hamner and Frank L. Schmidt, eds.

MANAGEMENT: Contingencies, Structure, and Process
    Henry L. Tosi and Stephen J. Carroll

**READINGS IN MANAGEMENT: Contingencies, Structure,
and Process**
    Henry L. Tosi, ed.

**EXPERIENCES IN MANAGEMENT
AND ORGANIZATIONAL BEHAVIOR**
    Douglas T. Hall, Roy J. Lewicki, Donald D. Bowen,
    and Francine S. Hall

THEORIES OF ORGANIZATION
    Henry L. Tosi, ed.

ORGANIZATIONAL BEHAVIOR
    Stephen J. Carroll and Henry L. Tosi

NEW DIRECTIONS IN ORGANIZATIONAL BEHAVIOR
    Barry M. Staw and Gerald R. Salancik, eds.

revised edition

Contemporary Problems in Personnel

Edited by

W. Clay Hamner
Duke University

Frank L. Schmidt
U.S. Civil Service Commission
and George Washington University

St. Clair Press
4 East Huron Street
Chicago, Illinois 60611

To Ellen and Betty

First Printing, July, 1977
Second Printing, January 1978

Contemporary Problems in Personnel
Revised Edition

Contemporary Problems in Personnel, Revised Edition
Copyright © 1974, 1977 by St. Clair Press
All rights reserved. Printed in the United States of America

No part of this publication may be reproduced, stored in a retrieval system, or transmitted in any form or by any means, electronic, mechanical, photocopying, recording, or otherwise, without the prior written permission of the publisher.

Library of Congress Catalog Card Number 77-70939

ISBN 0-914292-10-2

Cover design by H. B. Smith

St. Clair Press
4 East Huron Street
Chicago, Illinois 60611

Preface to the Revised Edition

When we organized the first edition of this book in 1974, we were convinced that the problems faced by personnel managers were more complex and needed more sophisticated solutions than we, as academics, were then presenting in the college classroom. The response to the first edition indicated that many of you shared our evaluation. Since 1974, many changes have occurred as a result of government rules and regulations, Supreme Court decisions, and changes in the work environment. In this edition, we have attempted to recognize these changes and anticipate future changes so that the student who has mastered the material in this text will be well prepared to understand the importance of sound personnel policies and practices in today's organizations.

We have replaced or updated a number of readings found in the first edition, and on those topics for which no in-print articles seemed quite adequate, we commissioned articles by authorities in the areas so that those topics would be covered. We have maintained the same organization found in the first edition, however; changes have been made solely to make the book more readable and current. This feature should allow the instructor who has a favorite text which is a little dated to continue to use that text while employing this reader as a supplement. Finally, because we consider them significant, the "Federal Executive Agency Guidelines on Employee Selection Procedures" have been included as an appendix.

We would like to thank Stephen J. Carroll, Don Hellriegel, Herbert Heneman III, Hilton Jarrett, Michael Keeley, and Kendrith M. Rowland for their advice and suggestions on the planning for this book. We also would like to thank Robert St. Clair and Curt Johnson for their outstanding editorial help.

W. C. H.
F. L. S.

Contents

Chapter 1 Contemporary Personnel: A Blending of the Needs of the Individual with the Needs of the Organization   1

Readings **Herbert E. Meyers**
Personnel Directors Are the New Corporate Heroes   2
Rossall J. Johnson
The Personnel Administrator of the 1970s   8

Chapter 2 Selection Methods: The Interview, Testing, Assessment Centers, and Work Sampling   18

Section A Introduction   21

Readings **Leona E. Tyler**
Variability Among Individuals—A Universal Phenomenon   21
L. C. Megginson
Manpower Planning and Forecasting   25
A. K. Korman
Personnel Selection: The Basic Models   31

Section B The Interview as a Selection Technique   44

Readings **John B. Miner**
The Selection Interview   44
Robert E. Carlson, Paul W. Thayer, Eugene C. Mayfield, and Donald Peterson
Improvements in the Selection Interview   51

Section C Testing for Selection   60

Readings **Anne Anastasi**
Nature and Use of Psychological Tests   60
John B. Miner
Psychological Testing and Fair Employment Practices: A Testing Program that Does Not Discriminate   67
William H. Mobley
Meeting Government Guidelines on Testing and Selection   75

	Professional Affairs Committee, Division 14, American Psychological Association Guidelines for Choosing Consultants for Psychological Selection Validation Research and Implementation 82
Section D	**The Assessment Center as a Selection Technique** 85
Readings	**William Byham** The Assessment Center as an Aid in Management Development 85 **Allen I. Kraut** A Hard Look at Management Assessment Centers and their Future 100
Section E	**Work Sampling as a Selection Technique** 111
Readings	**Paul F. Wernimont and John P. Campbell** Signs, Samples, and Criteria 111 **James E. Campion** Work Sampling for Personnel Selection 117 **Frank L. Schmidt, Alan L. Greenthal, John E. Hunter, John G. Berner, and Felecia W. Seaton** Job-Sample vs. Paper-and-Pencil Trades and Technical Tests: Adverse Impact and Examinee Attitudes 123
Chapter 3	**Personnel Decisions: Legal Constraints** 132
Readings	**Colquitt L. Meacham** Sex Discrimination in Employment—The Law: Where It Is and Where It's Going 134 **William Brown III** The Equal Employment Opportunity Act of 1972 142 **Thaddeus Holt** Personnel Selection and the Supreme Court 147 **William A. Gorham** Political, Ethical, and Emotional Aspects of Federal Guidelines on Employee Selection Procedures 159
Chapter 4	**The Impact of Training on Future Performance** 175
Readings	**John P. Campbell, Marvin D. Dunnette, E. E. Lawler, and K. E. Weick** Training and Development: Methods and Techniques 176 **Stephen J. Carroll, Frank T. Paine, and John J. Ivancevich** The Relative Effectiveness of Training Methods—Expert Opinion and Research 193
Chapter 5	**Development Problems: The Individual's Career** 204
Reading	**Douglas T. Hall and Marilyn A. Morgan** Career Development and Planning 205

Chapter 6	**Performance Evaluation and Human Resource Accounting** 227	
Readings	**John B. Miner** Management Appraisal: A Review of Procedures and Practices 228 **Robert I. Lazer** The "Discrimination" Danger in Performance Appraisal 239 **James Goodale** Behaviorally-based Rating Scales: Toward an Integrated Approach to Performance Appraisal 246	
Chapter 7	**Motivating Performance in Organizational Settings** 255	
Section A	**Applied Motivation Programs** 256	
Readings	**W. Clay Hamner** Worker Motivation Programs: Importance of Climate, Structure, and Performance Consequences 256 **W. Clay Hamner and Ellen P. Hamner** Behavior Modification on the Bottom Line 284 **William F. Dowling** Job Redesign on the Assembly Line: Farewell to Blue Collar Blues? 298 **Michael Beer and Edgar F. Huse** A Systems Approach to Organization Development 312 **Henry L. Tosi and Stephen J. Carroll** Management by Objectives 326	
Section B	**Compensation and Reward Systems** 332	
Readings	**W. Clay Hamner** How to Ruin Motivation with Pay 332 **Fred G. LeSieur and Elbridge S. Puckett** The Scanlon Plan Has Proved Itself 340	
Chapter 8	**Job and Work Satisfaction** 352	
Readings	**E. E. Lawler** Satisfaction and Behavior 352 **Lyman W. Porter and Richard M. Steers** Organizational, Work, and Personal Factors in Employee Turnover and Absenteeism 362	
Chapter 9	**Union Constraints on Personnel Action** 377	
Readings	**D. C. Bok and J. T. Dunlop** Collective Bargaining in the United States: An Overview 378 **R. Stagner and H. Rosen** Forms and Methods of Settling Industrial Disputes 393	

	Archie Kleingartner Collective Bargaining Between Salaried Professionals and Public Sector Management 412
Chapter 10	**Current Issues in Personnel:** **Women, Minorities, and the Disadvantaged** 423
Section A	**Minorities and the Disadvantaged in Personnel Decisions** 425
Readings	**Charles E. Silberman** Black Economic Gains: Impressive but Precarious 425 **Lester C. Thurow** The Economic Progress of Minority Groups 430 **Grace Hall and Alan Saltzstein** Equal Employment in Urban Governments: The Potential Problem of Interminority Competition 438
Section B	**Women and Personnel Decisions** 445
Readings	**Sandra L. Bem and Daryl J. Bem** Does Sex-bias Job Advertising "Aid and Abet" Sex Discrimination? 445 **Benson Rosen and Thomas H. Jerdee** Sex Stereotyping in the Executive Suite 456 **Bertrand B. Pogrebin** Who Shall Work? 469 **Maureen Kempton** All We Want for Christmas Is Our Jobs Back 476
Chapter 11	**Current Problems in Personnel:** **Employee Well-Being in the World of Work** 478
Readings	**U.S. News and World Report** Protecting People on the Job: ABC's of a Controversial Law 479 **Rick King** In the Sanding Booth at Ford 483 **Harry Levinson** On Executive Suicide 491 **Harrison M. Trice** Alcoholism and the Work World 496
Chapter 12	**A Look into the Future** 503
Readings	**William A. Steiger** Can We Legislate the Humanization of Work? 503 **Marvin D. Dunnette, Leatta Hough, Henry Rosett,** **Emily Mumford, and Sidney A. Fine** Work and Nonwork: Merging Human and Societal Needs 508
Appendix	**Federal Executive Agency Guidelines on Employee Selection Procedures** 517

CHAPTER 1

Contemporary Personnel: A Blending of the Needs of the Individual with the Needs of the Organization

Personnel as a discipline today is concerned with the application of psychological research and research methods to the problems of human resource utilization in organizational settings. As we move toward the 1980s, the personnel function has taken on a much broader role in both public and private organizations. It is our intention in this first chapter to provide the reader with an appreciation of this broader role and to emphasize to the reader the reason why an understanding of the topics presented in this book will enhance his or her managerial talents.

In the early 1960s, personnel was seen by many as a "dead-end" job which, to quote from our first reading, attracted "a bunch of drones whose apparent missions in life were to create paperwork, recruit secretaries who couldn't type, and send around memos whose impertinence was exceeded only by their irrelevance."

As Meyer notes in this first reading, the image was unfortunately accurate in many cases. Organizations had been long noted for using personnel as a dumping ground for executive misfits. However, during the past 15 years, beginning with the passage of Title VII of the Civil Rights Act (see chap. 3), the personnel function has been elevated to a key position in the organization. The personnel executive today must be a hard-driving business manager. He or she is charged with increasing the productivity and the quality of work life of the members of the organization. In the first reading Meyer discusses how the personnel executives at such companies as I.B.M., Delta Airlines, and Citibank are now power-wielding members of their companies' management teams. The importance that companies are placing on the personnel director is seen in the compensation they pay these directors. In 1975, for example, the average personnel manager in large business earned an average of $61,000 per year and in many cases, directors are earning more than $100,000 per year.

In the second article, Johnson (1971) says that changes occuring in the 1970s are demanding changes in the duties and responsibilities of the personnel administrator. In order to become, as he or she must, the director of human resources, the personnel major in college should have a well-grounded background in organizational behavior and applied psychology. Johnson says that the reason this background is needed is because of the added responsibility and demands placed on the personnel manager from inside and outside the organization. The personnel manager must have both upward as well as downward influence in the organization and must be able to advise top management on "people" programs (see the article "Worker Motivation Programs" by Hamner, chap. 7, for examples), and represent the employees of the organization. Johnson emphasizes the necessity for the possession of both statistical and accounting skills by personnel directors.

This chapter, then, sets the stage for the reader of this book. We have attempted in it to give the rationale for our belief that personnel is critical as a subject and to give an understanding of the importance of each article selected. Students who gain a thorough grasp of the topics covered in this book should have no trouble with advanced courses in personnel and related courses.

Personnel Directors Are the New Corporate Heroes

HERBERT E. MEYER

The personnel department has been represented on many a corporate organization chart as an orphaned box—one that came from nowhere and didn't seem to fit anywhere. To many businessmen, including many chief executives, the people who worked in "personnel" appeared to be a bunch of drones whose apparent missions in life were to create paperwork, recruit secretaries who couldn't type, and send around memos whose impertinence was exceeded only by their irrelevance. As a result of this perception, personnel directors, whatever their individual competence, suffered the *sui generis* image of being good-old-Joe types—harmless chaps who spent their careers worshiping files, arranging company picnics, and generally accomplishing nothing whatsoever of any fundamental importance.

In some cases, this depressing image was accurate. Companies *have* been known to use their personnel departments as a sort of dumping ground for executive misfits, or for burned-out vice presidents who needed just a little while longer on the payroll to be eligible for their pensions. But there have always been some personnel directors who found the job a springboard to higher corporate office, and in some companies the executive in charge of personnel management has traditionally been regarded not as an outcast but as an heir apparent.

The current chairman and chief executive of Delta Airlines, W. T. Beebe, was once Delta's senior vice president for personnel. Both Richard D. Wood, the chairman of Eli Lilly & Co., and one of his predecessors as chief executive served as corporate personnel directors on their way to the top—and a former president had followed the same route. Right now, the top Lilly executive responsible for personnel, Harold M. Wisely, holds the rank of executive vice president and has a seat on the company's board of directors.

Reprinted from *Fortune*, February 1976, with permission.

A Step Toward the Top

In the last few years, many companies have joined Delta and Lilly in putting their personnel departments in the hands of powerful senior executives. That old chestnut about a transfer to personnel being a one-way ticket to oblivion is no longer true. Absolutely no one at First National City Bank viewed it as a setback for Lawrence M. Small when he was transferred from the commercial-banking division to head the personnel division in August, 1974. Indeed, it was universally regarded as one very impressive step up the ladder: the job carries the title of senior vice president, and Small was only thirty-two years old at the time. And at I.B.M., to cite just one other example, the former director of personnel resources, David E. McKinney, is now president of the Information Records Division, an important marketing and manufacturing unit.

Those good-old-Joes of yesteryear would be stunned by the amount of power and prestige today's personnel directors can claim within their companies. At Dow Chemical Co., for example, the man in charge of personnel, Herbert Lyon, reports directly to President Ben Branch, the chief executive. Lyon is a member of Dow's board of directors, and is responsible for, among other things, global product planning and corporate administration. At Warnaco Inc., most of the executives promoted to jobs in top management during the last three years were singled out for advancement by John Limpitlaw, the company's vice president for personnel.

The executives who are being put in charge of personnel departments today are hard-driving business managers who speak what they call "bottom-line language"; they are as interested in profits as any other executives. George A. Rieder, senior vice president for personnel at Indiana National Bank in Indianapolis, provides an almost textbook example of how today's personnel executives perceive their role. "I'm not a personnel manager," Rieder says, in a tone of voice conveying scorn for that traditional title. "I'm a business manager with responsibilities for personnel."

Rieder quickly adds that this difference is much more than merely semantic. "It's a difference of style, scope, and approach. I view myself as a businessman first, whose job has as much of an impact on the bottom line around here as anybody else's. To be effective I have got to understand every aspect of my company's business, and I have got to participate actively in major management decisions before they're made." As a senior vice president, Rieder reports to John R. Benbow, the bank's president, and participates actively in day-to-day management of the business.

"Good ones are worth a lot"

Salary scales provide a measure of the growing importance of personnel. When the average salaries of executives in different specialties are compared—manufacturing, finance, and so on—personnel directors come out as the lowest paid. But they've begun catching up, because they are getting bigger raises than other executives. According to the American Management Association, the average compensation for personnel directors of industrial companies with sales of $500 million to $1 billion was $61,400 in 1975. Executives in charge of manufacturing for those companies got an average of $83,400, chief financial officers got $103,400, and chief executives $225,700. But since 1970, the average compensation of personnel directors has increased by 20 percent, compared with just 13.5 percent for chief financial officers, 15 percent for manufacturing executives, and 18 percent for chief executives.

It's likely that personnel directors will continue to receive larger raises than other kinds of executives, according to Pearl Meyer, a compensation expert who is executive vice president of Handy Associates. "These poor guys in personnel won't be at the bottom of the scale for too much longer," Mrs. Meyer predicts. "Companies are recognizing that good ones are worth a lot." Last year, when Chase Manhattan Bank went looking for an executive to head its human-resources division (modern corporations don't have personnel departments anymore), the bank put out word that for the right man, it would pay up to $120,000. Chase was obviously not in the market for a mere picnic planner. (The right man turned out to be Alan Lafley, from General Electric.)

Clearly, things are not at all what they used to be in the once dull world of personnel or, if you please, human-resource management. And just as clearly, much of the pressure for change came from the economic environment in which corporations have been operating. As Warnaco's John Limpitlaw points out, "The business climate out there today is a whole lot different from what it was ten years ago." In the economy of the 1970s, just about everybody has found the going tough and profits hard to come by. The cost of labor—union contracts, executive salaries, pension plans, and so on—keeps moving up.

Furthermore, many companies that had expanded geometrically during the 1960s discovered that their acquisition programs had left them with a tangle of incompatible compensation plans, and with scores of highly paid executives who now seemed to be in the wrong jobs or, worse, were superfluous. And with the stock market remaining in the doldrums, stock-option plans that had looked like money machines during the 1960s suddenly seemed most unsatisfactory; new compensation plans had to be devised to keep key executives contented. The job of personnel director took on new dimensions—especially as chief executives began scrambling to minimize the adverse effects of the recession.

Companies eager to increase their workers' productivity—and which were not?—discovered that an alert personnel director was in a unique position to contribute to the company's welfare. For example, George Sherman, the vice president of industrial relations at Cleveland's Midland-Ross Corp., got to wondering just why productivity rates in Japanese factories were so high. He flew to Japan, visited some factories, and concluded that part of the answer lay in the use of committees, made up of both workers and supervisors, that met regularly to hear suggestions for meeting production goals. On his return to the U.S., Sherman got clearance to form Japanese-style committees of workers and supervisors at the company's electrical-equipment plant in Athens, Tennessee. One modification of the Japanese plan involved the offer of a cash bonus to both workers and managers if productivity really did increase beyond the goal set by Midland-Ross. One year and 400 suggestions later, productivity at the Athens plant was up by 15 percent. The company was able to cancel plans to invest $250,000 in added manufacturing capacity, because output increased without it. Now Sherman expects to set up similar committees at other plants.

Time off When It Counts

An idea developed by I.B.M.'s vice president for personnel, Walton Burdick, further illustrates how a personnel executive can help his company, and its workers, through a difficult economic period. Burdick developed a policy allowing I.B.M.'s employees to defer vacation time for as long as they wanted. Postponement was actively urged during years of booming business activity, thus keeping a lid on the number of employees. The payoff for both I.B.M. and its employees came during the past year, when the recession took a bite out of I.B.M.'s production. Workers who had saved up weeks or even months of vacation time were encouraged (rather firmly, one gathers) to use it.

I.B.M. Chairman Frank Cary credits the policy of deferred time off for helping the company get through a rough period without any layoffs. "You can't put a dollar sign on this sort of thing," Cary says. "The real benefit is in terms of morale. Our people know our policies are designed to keep them on the payroll. It makes them a lot more willing to go along with organizational changes we propose from time to time."

Pressure on American corporations from their not-so-silent partner, Uncle Sam, has done a great deal to add luster to the job of personnel director. In the last twenty years, there have been more than a hundred individual pieces of federal legislation directly affecting the relationship between corporations and their employees—e.g., the Work Hours Act of 1962, the Occupational Safety and Health Act of 1970, and the Employees Retirement Income Security Act of 1974. There has been a whole basket of laws and regulations to outlaw discrimination, including the Civil Rights Act of 1960, the Equal Pay Act of 1963, and the Age Discrimination in Employment Act of 1967.

Suits that Concentrate the Mind

Personnel directors complain that the federal rules and regulations are poorly conceived, sloppily written, and almost impossible to comply with because they change so rapidly. But many of those same personnel directors concede that the federal government's antidiscrimination activities have done wonders for their own prestige and power. To paraphrase Samuel Johnson, there is something about being sued for a lot of money that concentrates a chief executive's mind wonderfully. While some antidiscrimination suits involve just one aggrieved person and not much money, there have also been some class-action suits whose costs to corporations have been considerable. American Telephone & Telegraph Co. has settled two antidiscrimination suits—one for $38 million and another for $25 million—and nine steel companies settled one for a total of $31 million. The threat of class-action suits by aggrieved employees or disgruntled job applicants has made chief executives very much interested in having their personnel directors come up with ways to avoid even the appearance of discrimination. "Boy, do they listen to us now," says one personnel expert rather cheerfully.

In addition to setting affirmative-action goals, such as for the number of women and blacks to be hired during the coming year, and the number to be promoted into various levels of management, personnel directors develop procedures to make sure the goals are reached. That may involve new hiring systems or special training programs for those already hired and marked for fast promotion. Personnel directors must spend a lot of time these days with supervisors at all levels, helping them to meet their targets.

At Chemetron Corp., Melvin Shulman, corporate director of human resources, works directly with Chief Executive John P. Gallagher to set the affirmative-action goals and develop the procedures for reaching them. Then he works with Chemetron's line executives to make sure they understand what those goals are, and also that they understand how serious could be the consequences of failing to reach them. Says Shulman: "I tell them of the possible damage to the company, but in a sense I'm making sure they realize that their own careers here are involved. When they understand how directly the chief executive is involved, and that in effect I'm representing him, they're more than willing to get cracking."

Personnel directors probably would have come in from the cold even without the help of a topsy-turvy economy or a flood of legislation. It would have happened because attitudes within the American corporation itself have been changing steadily for at least a generation—the attitude of chief executives toward their subordinates as well as the attitude of employees at all levels toward the companies for which they work.

It is so commonplace now for chief executives to deliver speeches extolling "people" as their companies' most important resource that one tends to dismiss the phrase as cant. For some chief executives, of course, it may be. But a growing number of them really do realize that the quality and morale of their employees can make the difference between success and failure for their companies. One chief executive who is especially articulate on the importance of a company's human resources is Delta Airlines' Tom Beebe. "The name of the game in business today is personnel," he says emphatically. "You can't hope to show a good financial or operating report unless your personnel relations are in order, and I don't care what kind of a company you're running. A chief executive is nothing without his people. You've got to have the right ones in the right jobs for them, and you've got to be sure employees at every level are being paid fairly and being given opportunities for promotion. You can't fool them, and any chief executive who tries is going to hurt himself and his company."

Since Beebe is a former personnel man, there is some temptation to pooh-pooh his views as those of a man loyal to his old specialty. But one cannot argue with success. Delta hasn't had a strike in twenty years, and as airlines go, it is uncommonly profitable.

Courses for the Comers

Every chief executive has to be especially concerned about bringing along capable successors. One company that is justifiably famous for the breadth and quality of its management-training programs is I.B.M. Frank Cary works closely with Walton Burdick, the vice president for personnel, to develop those programs and to assign the executive "graduates" to appropriate jobs within I.B.M. "It's the chief executive's responsibility to make sure the company has personnel policies and practices that can select the best people, then train them for management positions," says Cary.

Dresser Industries' senior vice president for industrial relations, Thomas Raleigh, spends a lot of time with President John V. James developing and administering the company's executive-training programs. At the recently established Dresser Leadership Center, a campus-like training center near the company's Dallas headquarters, executives enroll for courses lasting one to four weeks. They take courses in business management, and also study aspects of Dresser's energy-related business that may be unconnected to their immediate assignments. And Raleigh gets a chance to size up Dresser officials who work far from Dallas.

Few personnel managers work only with executives, of course, and the changed attitudes of employees toward their companies present a constant flow of new challenges. Today's blue- and white-collar workers want more from their jobs than just a paycheck; they want satisfaction, and they want to be treated fairly. Specifically, they want a salary that's fair in relation to their co-workers' salaries, and they want a fair chance for promotion that's based on an objective evaluation of their performances rather than the subjective whims of their immediate supervisors, or on their sex or skin color.

When Harold Johnson joined Philadelphia's INA Corp. as vice president for personnel a few months ago—he was formerly with American Medicorp Inc.—the insurance company did not have a fully developed system for setting the salaries of new employees. Nor were there clear ground rules for awarding raises, or for evaluating employee performance. "Things worked pretty much according to the whims of individual supervisors," says Johnson. "There were no company-wide standards at all. The employees were unhappy because they felt their salaries were sometimes unfair, and because they felt top management wasn't aware of the quality work they were doing. And top management needed a tool to help identify the high performers so they could be promoted, or selected for advanced training."

INA Chairman Ralph Saul has ordered Johnson to develop a system to identify the company's most promising executives, and to establish corporate salary scales so that employees in similar jobs will be paid within an established range. Johnson is also devising an evaluation system to assure that raises will be awarded in a consistent way, based on individual performance. Once the system is in effect, Johnson will be responsible for getting supervisors to use it. Saul has told Johnson that the latter's own job performance will be measured in part by how quickly he can get the new pay and evaluation system working.

Power for the Team

In many companies, the personnel director's responsibilities have become so complex that they can only be shouldered by topflight business managers who have the backing of the chief executive. The people who do the job like to say that in the years to come, a tour of duty in the personnel department (more likely the division of human resources) will be mandatory for any executive who aims to be chairman. Though that may prove to be an exaggeration, it is true that more companies are transferring up-and-coming executives into personnel for a while, en route to greater things. Dow Chemical's Herbert Lyon says it's a good thing for personnel departments to have a mix of professional experts, who have worked exclusively in personnel, and generalists who are brought in for a tour of duty from other parts of the company. I.B.M.'s Walton Burdick agrees, and adds that in his view the professional personnel types—of whom he is one—benefit even more than the generalists from having a mix. "It gives the specialists a better sense of what's really going on out there," he explains.

Citibank's Larry Small reflects a perspective common to executives who have moved into personnel but who do not expect to remain in it forever. "I'm not a personnel guy," he says carefully, displaying the annoyance of a man who has explained this to others before and who knows he'll have to explain it again to somebody else. "I'm a businessman—a manager. I just happen to be handling personnel at the moment, because it's a very important part of managing a business today."

As more and more personnel departments become populated with managers like Small, what were once enclaves will increasingly be seen as key corporate divisions. And the executives who run them, whether they are called personnel directors or executive vice presidents for human resources, will finally be recognized for what they now are and what in retrospect they always should have been—power-wielding members of their companies' management teams.

The Personnel Administrator of the 1970s

ROSSALL J. JOHNSON

Stated in broad terms, personnel management as it is known today is too narrow and must be expanded to a point where the function requires that there be intervention in the day-to-day operations of an organization in order to protect the investment in human resources. In other words, a positive posture is needed.

To indicate a new role for the personnel manager, a change in name seems to be appropriate. Somewhat arbitrarily, the title of Director of Human Resources Management has been selected. This Director is not a Personnel Administrator with a new title, but an executive with training in information systems programming, budgeting, and organization theory, as well as the basis of psychology, sociology, and economics. Such a director can be thought of as a controller of human resources. There is an analogy in a way—the Controller of Finances is concerned with money aspects of an organization, while the Director of Human Resources Management is concerned with people. One should establish budgets for people and set up people reserves just as one must set up reserves of money. And finally there must be an evaluation for the use of people just as there is for money. The reason for drawing this analogy is that very few organizations give as much consideration to their investment in people as they do to their money investments.

It is becoming more and more apparent that the mobilization and allocation of human resources is of greater concern and import to organizations than the management of financial and physical resources. There is no dispute that a business enterprise cannot get off the ground without financial backing and that for certain types of operations there is no business without the physical resources. But the prevailing thought should be that these resources are less valuable if they are misused, and it is people who will determine the fate of these resources.

The above, of course, is obvious and has been a well-known fact of life for some time. What is not so evident and what has been given less than adequate attention is the management of the people who are working with the money and the facilities. Much attention has been given to the structuring of the organizational pyramid, but little to the impact of individual development or change on the personnel.

A survey of some 70 companies in the Chicago area revealed that the planning of human resources is done only on a short range basis. Less than ten of these companies indicated plans for projecting people requirements for more than one or two years. There was little evidence that any of these companies had the necessary information for developing a long range manpower budget.

Traditionally, the personnel department has been viewed as a staff or service department, and traditionally, its role has been to engage in activities connected with:

Employment
Training
Wage and Salaries
Labor Relations

Various Fringe Activities
  Safety
  First Aid
  Recreation
  Insurance
  Cafeterias

The proposal here is not to do away with or neglect these areas but rather, to incorporate them into a model that will allow the people problems in industry to be considered in a more systematic way. This means that the area of personnel administration will be expanded and the *staff* orientation will be shifted to a control orientation.

Basically, the idea is to view people as a resource which must be managed with as much care as a corporation manages its funds. This means that there is a controller of people resources, and this also means that there is a people budget, a people audit, and control mechanisms to ensure that the people are being used as budgeted. Here the similarity stops because people are not dollars, and where dollar A equals dollar B, person A does not equal person B. The control mechanism must recognize individual rights and differences. It is at this point that the complexities of human resources management begin to become evident.

To examine this problem a simple over-all systemic approach will be introduced. Human resource management means that there is an appropriate selection of people who will implement the inputs into an organization so that the desired outputs result.

The following comments will start with the outputs, jump back to the inputs and then look at the implementation. Since basically there is a money input and a profit output, a program planning, and budget system would be appropriate.

Outputs

The desired output is reaching the organization objectives. In operational terms the objectives can be stated according to activities, markets, profits, product or service, that is, something that is operational in nature and something that the Director of Human Resources Management can interpret in terms of people requirements. The director is not taking a passive, advisory role in this planning stage; he is directing the thinking of management rather than sitting back and waiting for personnel requisitions to come in. He is not waiting; he is agitating. A key to the success of human resources management is that the attitudes of all executives be changed to expect the role of the human resources director to be control-oriented.

The director is first of all demanding *operational* objectives and then asking what talents are needed now and tomorrow so that the objectives can be met. He is also asking what changes need to be made in the organization structure now or in the future. This applies to an ongoing corporation or organization, where objectives change over a period of time. These objectives need to be clarified so that appropriate skills can be acquired, maintained, or developed. If the corporation is considering a change in objectives, the impact on the people budget should be reviewed *before* the decision is made. The emphasis on the phrase "before the decision is made" is another important point: in the past many corporations have completed a merger arrangement, shifted production facilities, opened new plants, etc., without considering the people problem. For instance, the lack of appropriate integration of the people in a number of mergers and acquisitions has been the cause of less than expected earnings and even resulted in failures to reach objectives. The Penn Central Railroad would be an example of an organization that failed to live up to its expectations because of the lack of integration of the two organizations.

The director of human resources must be in on the initial stages of most decisions. This means that his position must be at the vice-president level, and it also means that he should be an active member of the planning committee and in frequent consultation with the president. The director must be in a position to head off the dissipation of human resources and must be able to anticipate future demands for people talents. This requires the centralization of the function of human resources management. These are budgeting problems that should be in constant control. In summary then, the output of an organization is the target, and the shifting of the objective—gradual as it may be—is a necessary part of the control information. To reach these objectives, the inputs must be appropriate.

Inputs

One of the inputs required in a corporation is, of course, people activity. As indicated, the input must be appropriate if the output target is to be met. Here, again, there should be active participation on the part of the Human Resources Management department. It is at this stage that skills are being specified.

Not only should there be budget information for today, there must also be information for next year and the year after and for the next ten years. Unlike dollars and machines, people cannot be put into the bank or stored or sold for scrap or junked. People *now* make demands for security, and when a person is separated, a charge is made to the company. The separation cost may, in part, be in monetary terms such as increased premiums on unemployment insurance, or separation pay, or it may be a cost in terms of negative reputation, so that the best workers do not apply for jobs with the corporation, or it may be a cost in terms of poor employee relations, or a cost in terms of work disruption. And it is conceivable that in the not too distant future it may be that an employee cannot be separated without government approval. With these kinds of costs and restrictions facing the corporation, the days of trial and error are limited, and corporations need to sharpen the skill of budgetary control over human resources now. It should be recognized however, that all human resources needs cannot be satisfied; thus a trade-off must be made, a trade-off in terms of efficiencies versus desired skills and knowledge.

The input is in terms of the skills needed for the output. But the determination of the needed skills is dependent not only on the output but what is available in the organization. The term *skill* has a very broad definition and means not only achievement but also potential, and it means both ability in a technical sense and in the interpersonal behavior sense. To determine what is available in an organization and what is needed requires a sophisticated information system that will allow intelligent evaluations and decisions. There is no question, for instance, that, when a human resource need arises, the present manpower inventory of an organization should be thoroughly and quickly searched and evaluated before turning to external sources.

Implementation

Up to this point there have been comments on the output and the input. The core of the problem lies in the way in which inputs of the organization are transferred into outputs. That is, implementation is the necessary link between the two.

Keeping in mind that the concern is with an on-going organization, it must be remembered that nothing stops and that decisions are made continuously, even though the executives may choose not to make a decision, for that in itself is a decision, and the organization continues with its progress either toward the objective or off in another direction. Because implementation is on-going and because there is no stopping point, control mechanisms are used to govern the disposition of money, so it is necessary to have a systematic allocation of human resources.

Financial budgets are based on estimates, usually of revenue and in terms of what is needed to get the job done. The human resource budget is no different except that a much longer time factor is involved. A one-year human resource budget is mandatory, while a ten-year projection is also vital to maintain high efficiency and position attitudes as well as organizational continuity.

One might question the realism of a ten-year budget. There is no doubt that such a long projection will be subject to considerable revision as time goes on, but this is true of all budgeting processes. While ten years was arbitrarily selected, for some industries an eight or twelve-year budget might be more appropriate. The basic purposes of the long-range budget are to bring about a rethinking of organizational goals, an analysis of the human resources, implications of current trends in technology and an evaluation of the present manpower inventory in terms of future requirements. If an organization is unable to establish a long-range budget, then there should be a questioning of the adequacies of the current information; probably the whole information system needs to be overhauled with new inputs supplementing or displacing old ones.

The recent economic downtrend is a case in point. While the extent of the business setback could not be predicted, the need to plan for such an eventuality should have been recognized. Many organizations are now trimming their people requirements so as to reduce costs. While some reduction in the work force may be a direct result of loss of sales, some of it was based on an edict from above: cut your personnel by 10 percent or 15 percent or some other set figure. No thought was given, no investigation was made as to the long-term impact. There was a need to cut costs, and the consequences of wholesale discharge are to be faced later. Unless an organization is on the verge of bankruptcy, such across-the-board reduction in personnel is a very costly approach to the problem. If there are excesses of personnel in various departments, it probably is not 10 percent in each section. Some may be overstaffed by 50 percent and others by 2 percent or 15 percent or even understaffed. One should ask: if a company has extra staff, why did it wait until financial problems developed before reducing the staff and why not do it in an orderly manner at the time the excesses arise? To ask the question in a different way: what have the various corporations done about the internal environment on a continuous basis so that external factors will have a reduced impact?

Is there an implication that these mass layoffs and panic cost-cutting procedures needn't have taken place? It would seem so. All too frequently management is pressured into emergency situations which may relieve the immediate crisis, but which, over an extended period, year in and year out, may cause heavy losses.

It is imperative that the human resources be controlled and that control be centralized so that consistency and flexibility are not lost. The human resources budget requires considerable information, and the gathering processes and interpreting of this information require the efforts of many people. This is not a nose counting operation; it is a planning, programming, and budgeting procedure that is stated in terms of the work requirement, when it is to be done, and what kinds of skills are required. But its complexities are many. Perhaps a broad outline of some of the information will indicate the job to be done.

There are at least seven areas where information is needed for the implementation of effective control and use of the human resources. They are:

1. Evolution of the Organization

An organization goes through an evolutionary process from its inception to a period of rapid growth, to a plateau, to a decline or another growth period. Each step in the evolutionary process means changes in personnel, changes in the decision making process, changes in information system or, broadly speaking, changes in the organization structure and procedures.

For instance, in a new organization the main thrust may be on selling of ideas and objectives and in establishing role relationships. Later, the selling of objectives may be routine and the roles may be well coordinated. Those who are the specialists in the management of human resources should be observing to see that the appropriate changes in thrust come about because of the evolutionary processes and that the organization adjusts to the changes in emphasis.

There are any number of examples of organizations which entered a market with specific quality of goods or services only to find that later, when an attempt was made to change the quality in order to be more competitive, some people in the organization evidently didn't understand the need to change with time and refused to adjust. Or perhaps the owner-manager makes decisions today with 5,000 employees in the same manner as he did when there were only 50. The human resources manager needs to stand to one side and observe this evolutionary process so that he may make the appropriate recommendations and decisions.

2. Flow of People

What are the causes of the flow of people through the organization and in and out of the organization? Death, illness, retirement, obsolescence, involuntary separation, advancement and transfer, and voluntary separation. How many of these can be predicted? Perhaps all except the last one—voluntary separation—and even this may be predicted at times.

Actuary figures will not pinpoint the specific individual who will die, but it will indicate how many probably will die before reaching retirement and how many will be incapacitated by illness. Do companies make use of this available information in estimating manpower needs in five years or ten years? Everyone knows when his boss is going to reach retirement age, but is good use made of retirement information when forecasting people needs? Few companies use such information.

Obsolescence is a tough one, but in some cases the signs are quite obvious if one is trained to look for them. Here the director of human resources and his staff can make a unique contribution since it should be part of their job to anticipate obsolescence before it arrives. Those employees with obsolete skills should be alerted to the condition well before the fact. Such timing allows for planned retraining or planned early retirement. When pinpointed early a valuable employee (valuable in terms of attitudes and reliability) may be transferred to another job.

Discharge—defined here as leaving the organization at the request of the organization—involuntary. It may be because of unacceptable performance or because of reduction of work-force, etc. Within certain time constraints this can be anticipated, but over an extended period of time it is an unanticipated change unless a pattern can be established. While it is acknowledged that there will be some involuntary separations, in most organizations there are far too many. Here is an area where the human resources department can be useful in reducing turnover.

Voluntary separation is frequently the cause of an unpredictable void in an organization. This is a costly type of separation because it not only leads to less efficient operations, but frequently results in the vacancy being quickly filled by an unqualified person who must be trained on the job by an individual who is not completely acquainted with the job.

There have been studies on the probability of an individual advancing in the organization and how long he can expect to remain in any one position. This type of information can be useful in career planning for selected individuals, and it can be helpful in determining problem areas in the developing system. Blind alleys in the flow of personnel can be opened up and favored avenues for advancement can be reexamined. Undesirable voluntary separations can be reduced by regulating the avenues to advancement.

3. Role Establishment

Role Establishment refers to a process where individuals understand role relationships so that behavior may be predicted more accurately. There may be a difference, for instance, in view of the role of an engineer. He may look upon himself as a professional person and, therefore, behaves in a "professional manner," while the production manager sees the engineer's role as that of "any other employee" and refuses to accept the professional role behavior. While this type of information does not directly affect the number of people in a budget, it does allow for the full utilization of those in the work force. This, then, is a new and important dimension that is part of the job of the people budget director—the human resources manager. He must be observant of those potential points of friction that will reduce the efficiency of the organization. This leads directly into the area of interrelationships.

4. Interrelationships

Manpower requirements are increased or decreased according to effectiveness of interrelationships. These relationships can be at the interpersonal level or interdepartmental or interdivisional level. For the sake of brevity, these can be classified as intra-organizational relationships. In the past, the effectiveness of such relationships was dealt with at the local level. However, the inefficiencies and frictions and even sabotage that results from inappropriate intra-organizational relationships are too expensive to tolerate over extended periods of time. If the human resources are to be utilized efficiently and the budget is to be held to minimum requirements, the director of human resources must pinpoint inappropriate relationships. This is especially important at the levels above the interpersonal level. It may mean a direct intervention by the director of human resources, but hopefully, a correction will be encouraged from within. In effect, the director has taken on the role of change agent.

5. Change and Time

Change frequently causes people to feel threatened. The director of human resources can reduce the feelings of insecurity if he is able to anticipate change and send out the appropriate information or establish programs to meet the changing conditions.

A time factor is involved because most changes can be anticipated. The need is to identify those things which are going to disturb people—perhaps a new automatic machine, a different technique in packaging, a computerized operation, or the dropping of a line of goods. All of these have a lead time before the change becomes a reality, and it is during this time that action should take place to relieve anxieties.

6. *Evaluation and Reward*

Evaluation should be considered an on-going process at different levels. The job of the director of human resources management is to see that it is a continuous process and that the various levels are evaluated. While productivity may be one factor in evaluation, the organizational effectiveness of a group of people should also be included. At the individual level, some form of equity theory should be incorporated so that the relationships between perceived contribution and reward can be balanced with "actual" contribution and reward. Much more information must be processed more efficiently so that evaluations have greater validity and acceptance and thus, rewards may be more equitable.

7. *Will to Work*

Considerable research work has been carried out in the areas of the measurement of attitudes and the elucidation of motivating factors. To date there has been only limited success in pinpointing causes for poor work performance. Close supervision has been found to have caused both high and low productivity. The authoritarian leader has been shown to be more efficient, while the democratic leader has happier subordinates. On the other hand, there have been unhappy but efficient subordinates under a democratic leader. The director of human resources must be in the main stream of information flow so that he can make an analysis and recommendations on the will to work.

Centralized Control and Auditing

Considerable stress has been placed on control of human resources in the implementation comments. The term "control" is one of the words that is frowned upon by rights groups because it implies using workers as puppets. Here the term "control" is used to imply that people are operating in an organization with set objectives and that their talents are utilized to meet these objectives. At the same time, the organization has obligations to the individual in terms of compensation, job satisfaction, etc. Supposedly, there is a mutual advantage which can only be attained when controls are instituted.

Organizations are dynamic systems where the characteristics are continually changing. Because of the dynamic aspects, fixed rules and regulations, fixed policies and procedures, as well as the organization structure are outdated rather quickly. Some one person should be responsible for noting the conditions which have an impact on the human resources and then "recommend" changes that should be made.

The term "recommend" may imply a passive role, but the intent here is to indicate that the changes recommended will be adopted in most instances because the director is responsible for the management of the human resources.

It is the thesis here that the total human resources be controlled through a central point via the vehicle of the human resources programming, planning, and budgeting. In addition, it is recommended that the director of human resources management be given a major role in guiding the structuring of the organization and control of the people aspects.

There is a fine line to be walked by the director of human resources in this dominant role, for it is all too easy for him to undermine superior-subordinate relationships. There is no intention of disrupting the rapport of supervisors with subordinates. It is anticipated that the control mechanisms would strengthen the ties by the very fact that there is consistency, there is planning, there is increased flow of pertinent information, and there is more appropriate selection and training of supervisors. The director of human resources is one man with a staff, and he is in no position to know of or contend with all of the interpersonal contacts. This is not his function. His job is to see to it that through the placement of people, the flow of information, and the development programs, dysfunctional interpersonal and intra-organizational interactions are reduced. The supervisor is still the key to appropriate management of the human resources.

The inputs of people into an organizational effort are so critical that they must be controlled in a positive way and from a central point. It is no longer an acceptable practice to allow the supervisors, department heads, or division vice-presidents to set independent policy or make independent decisions concerning the disposition of people.

While the trend is toward decentralization in industry, the purse strings in financial management are held in the home office. The management of human resources should be under even greater control because of the long range implications. Not only should the human resources "purse strings" be centralized, but some basic policies should be adhered to in all parts of the organization.

Human Resources Audit

The audit of human resources management should be an integral and on-going function of the centralized control mechanism. This type of audit opens up a new facet to the control of the use of people. Some examples of the function may clarify the position.

First, there is the routine part which checks budgeted personnel against actual. As indicated before, this is not a numbers game but an audit of talents, skills, and potential. The computer can be very useful in maintaining a continuous audit of this type. There is also the evaluation of new employees in terms of the ability to handle the position they have been hired to fill, and also in terms of potential to be useful employees five years from now and ten years from now.

There are more complex issues to audit. For instance, the effectiveness of an organization is determined in part by an understanding by everyone of the objectives and goals. When there are multiple goals or objectives, there is a need to weight them. Question: Do all employees weight them the same? How do you motivate people toward the same goals or objectives and at the same time, how do you get them to give the same weights?

Simple example: What are the objectives of the fire department?
1. To put out fires
2. To reduce property damage
3. To save lives
4. To prevent fires

Do all firemen weight these the same? Which has the top priority?

The area of interpersonal or intraorganizational conflict should be subjected to audit. One should start with the assumption that not all conflict can be avoided and also that some conflict may be desirable. The problem then comes down to judging what is desirable and/or unavoidable conflict. While the fine differences may not be definable, there are conflicts which are so gross that there is no question but that the conflict is detrimental to the organization. It is these situations where the director of human resources can use his office to reduce or eliminate the friction. . . .

The basis for human resources decisions should also be incorporated into the audit process. The guiding question is: are the people decisions based on an open or closed system of information? "Closed system of information" means that only a limited amount of information within the organization is available as a basis for the decision. "Open system" means that both internal and external sources of unrestricted information are referred to. Generally speaking, the tendency is to use the closed system, and frequently this is acceptable. But when the open system should be used and is not used, some very poor decisions can result.

An example: Take a situation where a supervisor comes to work intoxicated and as a result creates a number of embarrassing incidents. The policy is quite clear in this company on dealing with inebriated employees. (1) The employee shall immediately be sent home. (2) The employee should not report back to work until a disposition has been made of his case and the penalty established. (3) Reporting for work in an intoxicated condition is considered sufficient grounds for immediate discharge.

A closed system approach could easily occur in the above situation, and in all probability the supervisor would be discharged. An open system approach might reveal that the supervisor:

1. Had been with the company for thirty years with no record of intoxication.
2. Is two years away from retirement.
3. Is physically deteriorating to the point where he is approaching senility.
4. A tragedy in his personal life had occurred prior to the date of his offense.

Now, after additional information is available, one might ask if a decision other than discharge should be made. Although the above type of incident may be appropriately handled right now in many organizations, there is a nagging question of, "Do we catch all of the closed system type of decisions which should have been based on an open system type of information?" It is up to the director of human resources management to audit this and to see that adequate information is used as a basis for people decisions.

To sum it up, the role of the personnel director must be expanded; his image must be changed. The staff position of personnel director as an advisor to line personnel should be set aside and in its place there should be a director of human resources who guards the people investment through centralized control and inspection. The director of human resources management must report directly to the chief executive officer and be a party to all planning from the beginning.

The chief occupation of the director of human resources, then, is to:

1. Establish and manage a human resources planning, programming, and budgeting mechanism and auditing system.
2. Review and revise the information system so that adequate decision information is available.
3. Identify critical people areas and critical people problems.
4. Interpret events and situations in terms of impact on human resources.
5. Analyze the effectiveness of the organization today, recommend action, and plan for tomorrow.

Such a director needs to have expertise in the planning, programming, budgeting systems approach, and he must be capable of establishing an appropriate information system and control mechanism. Basic to the job is a working knowledge of organization theory, psychology, sociology, and economics. A professional with these qualifications is a necessity. Conditions of the 1970s will not allow anything else.

CHAPTER 2

Selection Methods: The Interview, Testing, Assessment Centers, and Work Sampling

The basis of all selection and placement work is the bedrock fact of human differences. Obviously, if individuals were all identical in abilities, skills, traits, and potentialities, personnel selection would be unnecessary and superfluous. It would not matter who was assigned to which job. Tyler presents rather dramatic evidence that differences between individuals are a universal phenomenon, extending from man down the hierarchy of life to even the single-cell organisms. She indicates that scientific personnel selection is indeed based on a solid foundation.

But even if we understand the magnitude of human differences and succeed in developing accurate methods of assessing them, in many real-life situations individuals with the desired "profile" of characteristics may not be available, either from inside or outside the organization, when organizational needs require them. Thus, the need for manpower planning—for a built-in organizational system which anticipates future needs for individuals with various trait and potential profiles. In his brief article, Megginson explains why manpower planning is important not only to the organization but also to the nation. He presents the general objectives of this function, including a brief introduction to the new and important area of human resource accounting.

Over the years, industrial psychologists have developed a number of procedures and techniques that can be used to accurately identify and measure the traits and abilities needed for success on different jobs. Such measurements can then be used in selection and placement decisions. Korman's article provides a step-by-step discussion of these techniques, pointing out their limitations as well as their strengths.

In summary, individual differences are universal and ineradicable. They must not only be recognized, they must be taken into account in organizational and manpower planning. Industrial psychology has provided organizations with procedures for the determination and measurement of work-related traits and dimensions which can be used to improve personnel decisions.

The interview is a virtually universally used selection technique. In his article, Miner points out that it is indeed useful for many of the purposes for which it is employed, but its major purpose in most selection settings is probably to predict future job performance, and for this purpose it is usually invalid. Starting with this basic fact, Carlson, Thayer, Mayfield, and Peterson describe a program of research carried out on the interview by one organization. The results of this research led to changes in the way the interview was used and a new training program for interviewers. From a more general point of view, this article illustrates how behavioral science research can lead directly to improvements in personnel operations.

It is essential in any discussion of personnel testing, especially at the introductory level, to work from a clear definition of just what a psychological test is. Misconceptions and erroneous ideas are extremely common in this area. Anastasi's definition goes a long way toward clarification: a psychological test—any psychological test—is simply a sample of behavior used to predict future behavior. Within the context of this simple but accurate definition, she provides a lucid discussion of the psychometric concepts of standardization, test difficulty, reliability, and validity. Her article thus provides a basis for understanding of the other readings in section C of this chapter.

As Thaddeus Holt and William Gorham point out in chapter 3, the use of psychological tests in the selection and placement of personnel has come under legal scrutiny in recent years. Confusion has developed among employers as to what technical and legal standards tests or other selection procedures must meet under the Civil Rights Act of 1964. The article by William Mobley clarifies these questions where it is possible to do so, and points up some of the remaining ambiguities and difficulties which must be resolved in the future.

Until recently, the trend in court cases involving selection had been so strongly against employers that many had almost concluded that no test or other selection procedure could successfully meet the requirements laid down by the Equal Employment Opportunity Commission. In his article describing selection testing at AT&T, John Miner demonstrates that this conclusion is unwarranted. Taken together with the change in direction shown by the Supreme Court in the *Davis* decision (see the article by Thaddeus Holt in chap. 3), the fact that the AT&T program successfully survived intense scrutiny by EEOC may portend a brighter future for job-related selection procedures than many had previously envisioned.

Government requirements that selection procedures must be demonstrated to be job-related has created a heavy demand by business organizations for outside consultants with the training and skills necessary to carry out validation studies. In order to protect organizations from charlatans and the unqualified, the Professional Affairs Committee of division 14 of the American Psychological Association (the division of Industrial and Organizational Psychology) has drawn up a set of guidelines for the selection of validation consultants, which we here reprint. (Thus, the ubiquitous selection problem extends even into the selection of selection researchers. An interesting tongue-in-check question here is whether or not these selection procedures meet EEOC legal requirements.)

Next to government intervention designed to insure selection fairness, the most important development in personnel selection in the past decade or so is probably the rise of assessment centers. In reading the articles by Byham and Kraut, keep in mind Anastasi's definition of a psychological or personnel test as a sample of behavior used to predict future behavior. It is obvious that most assessment center exercises are behavior samples from the universe of managerial behaviors. (Section E of this chapter is devoted to the principles of work sampling and performance testing.) Because of this, Byham can state that they have content validity and thus meet EEOC validation requirements. In addition, many validity studies have been carried out using the principles described by Korman (section A of this chapter), and these indicate that assessment center evaluations show substantial correlations with subsequent managerial success.

As both Byham and Kraut point out, the assessment center is a development technique as well as a selection technique, and is often used in combination with training programs.

In recent years, there has been somewhat of a trend away from aptitude tests (which supposedly measure basic potential and have connotations of fixedness) to achievement tests (which attempt to measure currently developed skills and knowledges and which suggest the possibility of individual improvement in the areas measured). The relevance of the content of most achievement tests is more obvious to most testees, and, thus, the test is more likely to be accepted as fair. In addition, achievement tests often have obvious content validity. They are less likely to be challenged by EEOC or OFCC (Office of Federal Contract Compliance), and they may actually be better predictors of future performance than aptitude measures.

One of the principal differences between aptitude and achievement tests is that the behavior measured by achievement tests is more similar to the behavior actually required on the job. Wernimont and Campbell suggest that this should be a basic principle of performance prediction: Make the behaviors sampled by the predictor or test as similar as possible to the job behaviors to be predicted. Their article thus points in the direction of work-sample or performance tests. Campion's study then provides a description of the successful construction and use of a work-sample selection test. Performance tests similar to Campion's are now being used by the New Jersey, New York, and Michigan Civil Service Commissions.

Although the hypothesis that work sample tests might show smaller majority-minority score differences has been around for a number of years, the study by Frank Schmidt and his colleagues is the first to put this hypothesis to the test. Not only did they find smaller adverse impact for the job-sample test, but they also found that both minority and majority group members preferred the job-sample test to the written test. This study may point to an increased emphasis in the future on work-sample tests as a means of meeting equal employment objectives while at the same time improving the quality of the workforce.

Section A
Introduction

Variability among Individuals—A Universal Phenomenon

LEONA E. TYLER

This [article] is about *human* differences. But before we examine these human differences in detail, it may be instructive to consider briefly what we know about variability in other forms of animal life. Ordinary observation demonstrates again and again that one animal of a species differs in many ways—in behavior as well as appearance—from other animals of the same species. Dog-lovers never tire of stories about some dog's unusual intelligence, resourcefulness, or devotion. Farmers recognize and deal appropriately with temperamental differences in cows. Horses differ in intellectual achievements as well as running speed.

As experimental psychologists have observed animals in their laboratories, a body of scientific knowledge about individual differences has accumulated. It can be concluded with some certainty that individual variability characterizes all species—from the highest to the lowest.

It is not surprising that monkeys differ in behavioral characteristics. Any zoo visitor can observe this for himself. A study by Fjeld (1934) contributes some quantitative evidence as to just how marked the differences between individual monkeys are in a kind of problem-solving capacity somewhat analogous to what we call intelligence in human beings. Figure 1 shows the sort of performance required.

To get the food box open, each animal was required to depress one or more of the plates in the floor. In Problem 1, the easiest problem, all he had to do was to depress Plate 1 and the door would open. In Problem 2, he must depress Plates 1 and 2 in turn, then the door opened; in Problem 3, Plates 1, 2, and 3. Problem 4 required him to depress 1, 2, and 3, reverse his direction, and step on 2 again. In Problem 7 the order was Plate 1, 2, 3, 2, 1, 2, 3. Out of a group of fifteen rhesus monkeys who served as subjects through the whole experiment, one was unable to learn more than 2 problems, whereas one learned 22. The rest varied all the way from 3 to 13. A similar study by Koch (1935) on Cebus monkeys gave similar results with somewhat less variability in performance from animal to animal.

From *The Psychology of Human Differences*. Copyright © 1965. Reprinted by permission of Prentice-Hall, Inc., Englewood Cliffs, New Jersey.

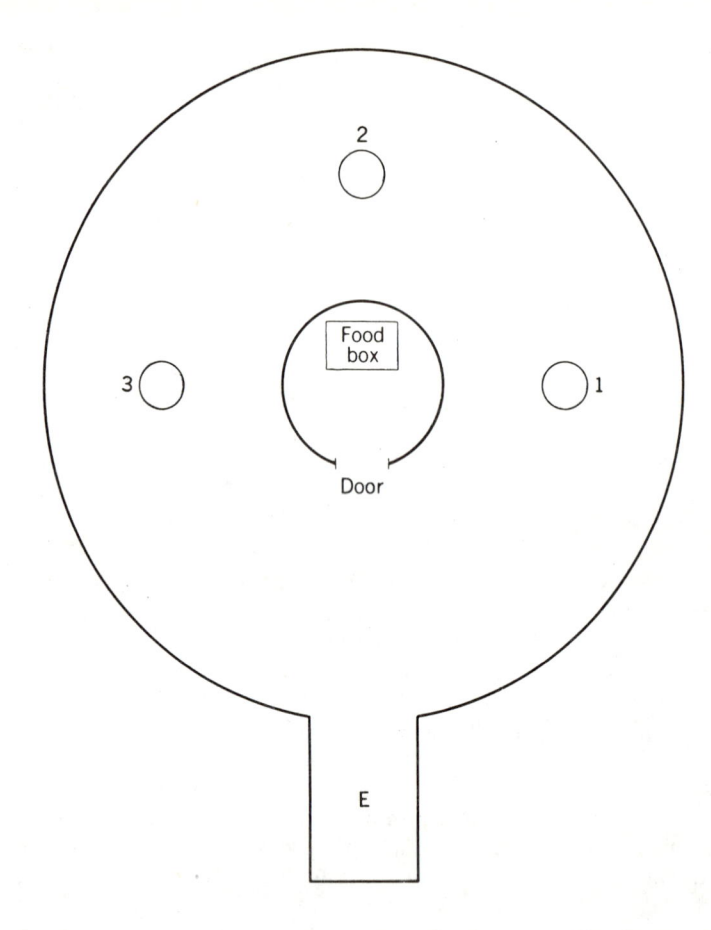

Figure 1. Design of Problem Box Used in Fjeld Experiment (Fjeld, 1934)

A good demonstration of individual differences in cats is a study by Warren (1961). What he required each animal to do in order to obtain food in this kind of experiment was to choose one of two small objects presented to him simultaneously. The "right" object was distinguished from the "wrong" one in different ways in different experiments. In some experiments, it was the *position* that mattered—for example, the left-hand one was always correct. In other experiments it was the shape of the object that was the clue, and the animal had to notice whether it was a square, triangle, circle, trapezoid, or some other geometrical form. The problem was made more difficult for the animal by arranging things in such a way that he must take *size*, as well as position or shape, into consideration. Thus in the position experiments, he was rewarded for choosing the left-hand object when the stimuli were small and for choosing the right-hand object when the stimuli were large. In the shape discrimination experiments, he was to choose one of the pair (e.g., square) when the stimuli were large and the other (e.g., semicircle) when the stimuli were small. It was the task of each cat to discover through a series of trials just what he was expected to do. Once he "caught on" he would choose correctly every time.

It turned out that discriminations on the basis of shape were more difficult than discriminations on the basis of position, but that there were very large differences between animals. The most "brilliant" of the 21 cats Warren tested required only 54 trials to solve the shape-size problem. The "dullest" one required 760 trials. The others ranged somewhere in between.

Because rats have been a favorite kind of experimental subject in psychological laboratories, a considerable amount of information about individual differences in this species has accumulated. They differ widely in maze-running ability (Tryon, 1942), and in temperamental traits such as wildness (C. S. Hall, 1951). Geier, Levin, and Tolman (1941) carried out an elaborate study in which they identified four different traits upon which their rat subjects differed from one another, two of them "intellectual" traits and two "emotional" or "motivational" traits.

What is more surprising than these findings, however, is the report by J. Hirsch that there are individual differences in the behavior of fruit flies (Hirsch, 1962). The object of Hirsch's research program has been to find out more about the genetic bases of behavior.... But it is worth noting here that individual differences have been demonstrated in what biologists call *taxes*, such as phototaxes and geotaxes—the tendency to approach or to withdraw from light, and the tendency to move upward (against gravity) or to move downward (with gravity). Figure 2 shows graphically the percentages of trials on which different individuals in one experimental population moved *up* in an ingeniously contrived geotactic maze (Hirsch, 1959). Its resemblance to the kind of distribution we often obtain from testing human subjects is obvious.

But individual differences in behavior have been found in species lower than the fruit fly, even in one-celled animals. There is evidence, for instance, that protozoa show changes in behavior with continued experience in a situation, a form of learning that seems to be an elementary sort of conditioned response. Razran (1933) reported that whereas the average protozoon took 138.5 trials to "learn" this, the range from

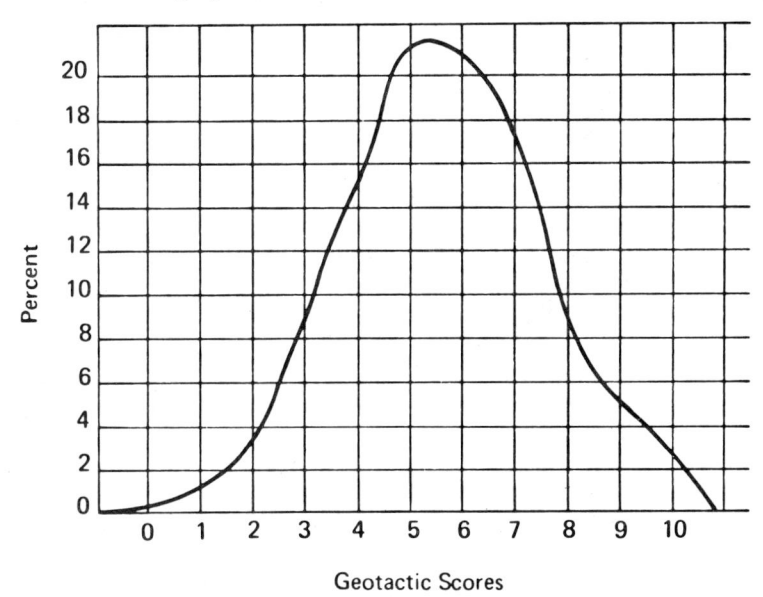

Figure 2. Distribution of Geotactic Scores for Male Fruit Flies in a Particular Breeding Population (Hirsch, J., 1959)

fastest to slowest was from 79 to 284 trials. Some experiments by French (1940), using paramecia as subjects, supplied evidence on two other traits or characteristics. One is the tendency to form groups. By an ingenious method, French separated the "groupers" from the "free-swimmers," kept them separate and in clear water for a half hour, and then put them back into separate food solutions to see if the grouping tendency persisted. It did, to a striking extent. Similar experiments were run to see whether tendencies to enter or not to enter solutions in which a small amount of some foreign chemical had been placed would persist. Again, differences turned out to be fairly large in some of the experiments and statistically significant in all.

Examples based on many other types of performance in many other species might be given, but enough have probably been cited to convince the student of human psychology that variation in mental characteristics is far from being an exclusively human phenomenon. Such studies are important for us in that they suggest that differences are universal and usually ineradicable. If this is the case we must learn to understand them, accept them, and use them in the building of our common society.

Human Characteristics in Which Differences Have Been Measured

Many types of measurement have been made on human beings. First, it is obvious to all of us that human individuals are not the same in size and shape. We have learned to expect and to make at least some provision for this kind of variation, though the army still sometimes has trouble fitting out the new recruit whose shoes are size 13, and women find that both the 8's and the 46's are sometimes hard to obtain at dress shops. Much first-rate work has been done in the field of anthropometric measurements. Not only gross height and weight, but the exact sizes of most of the individual parts of the body have been measured. Second, measurements have been made of the physiological processes, or the way various organ systems of the body function. Basal metabolism, the amount of calcium, sugar, acid, and hemoglobin in the blood, respiratory rate, pulse rate, and concentrations of acid and of urea in the urine are physiological characteristics in which individuals have been found to show definite, measurable differences.

The extensive research work of Williams (1956) has provided an impressive amount of evidence about this variability in physical and physiological characteristics. The organs of the body, such as the stomach and the heart, differ markedly in size and shape. The chemical composition of the various fluids of the body show a similar variability. Take saliva, for example (Williams, 1956, p. 59). The amount of uric acid secreted in saliva by nine different individual subjects varied from 2.5 μg. per ml. in one case to 150 μg. per ml. in another. The amino acids, serine, glycine, alanine, and lysine, were not present at all in some cases but occurred in appreciable amounts in others. Each person's saliva is probably as unique as his appearance, voice, or disposition.

In successive chapters, Williams summarizes evidence with regard to individual differences in enzymic patterns, endocrine activities, excretion patterns, pharmacological manifestations, and nutrition, all of which he considers to be genetically determined. . . .

There is even more abundant evidence for individual differences in all sorts of psychological characteristics. There is much variability with regard to motor capacities, such as reaction time, speed of tapping, steadiness, and swiftness of blow.

Individuals differ markedly in sensory and perceptual characteristics such as keenness of vision, hearing, and sense of smell. Some are better than others at analyzing and remembering complex patterns of lines, colors, or sounds. Differences in intelligence and the more narrowly defined intellectual processes, such as memory, judgment, and problem solving, have been demonstrated in hundreds of surveys at all age levels. Among persons who have had equal amounts of schooling there are wide discrepancies in how much they know. People differ in aptitudes and talents, in interests, values, and attitudes, in personality assets and liabilities. In short, research on human beings corroborates the conclusion from animal studies—individual differences in measurable characteristics constitute a universal phenomenon. . . .

References

Fjeld, H. A., "The Limits of Learning in the Rhesus Monkeys," *Genet. Psychol. Monogr.*, 1934, 15, 369-537.

French, J. W., "Individual Differences Paramecium," *J. Comp. Psychol.*, 1940, 30, 451-456.

Geir, F. M., Levin, M. and Tolman, E. C., "Individual Differences in Emotionality, Hypothesis Formation, Vicarious Trial and Error and Visual Discrimination Learning in Rats," *Comp. Psychol. Monogr.*, 1941, 17, No. 3.

Hall, C. S., Individual Differences. In C. P. Stone, *Comparative Psychology* (3rd edition), Englewood Cliffs, New Jersey: Prentice-Hall, 1951.

Hirsch, J., "Individual Differences in Behavior and Their Genetic Basis. In E. L. Bliss (Ed.), *Roots of Behavior*, New York: Hoeber-Harper, 1962, Ch. 1.

Koch, A. M., "The Limits of Learning Ability in Cebus Monkeys," *Genet. Psychol. Monogr.*, 1935, 17, 164-234.

Razran, G. H. S., "Conditional Responses in Animals Other Than Dogs." *Psychol. Bull.*, 1933, 30, 261-324.

Tryon, R. C. Individual Differences. In F. A. Moss (Ed.), *Comparative Psychology* (rev. edition), Englewood Cliffs, New Jersey: Prentice-Hall, 1942, Ch. 13.

Warren, J. M., "Individual Differences in Discrimination Learning by Cats," *J. Genet. Psychol.*, 1961, 98, 89-93.

Williams, R. J., *Biochemical Individuality*, New York: Wiley, 1956.

Manpower Planning and Forecasting

L. C. MEGGINSON

A basic aspiration of most owners and managers is to perpetuate the organization with which they are involved. To achieve this objective, the chief executive officer must find a successor to himself, and qualified people must be selected to fill the

Reprinted with permission from Megginson, *Personnel: A Behavioral Approach* (rev. ed.; Homewood, Ill.: Richard D. Irwin, Inc.), pp. 197-203.

vacancies that periodically occur throughout all levels of the organization. Thus, it is probably an understatement to say that an organization's manpower planning function constitutes one of its most important personnel responsibilities. The results obtained from recruiting, selecting, placing, training, developing, and motivating employees, depend directly for their success upon the effectiveness of the planning and forecasting phase of manpower development.

However, because of the systems concept, manpower planning cannot be studied in isolation, organizational planning and manpower planning are interrelated and interacting. Organizational planning, by its nature, takes precedence over, and provides direction to, manpower planning. The latter, in turn, can be most effectively done within the framework of properly structured organizational relationships and predetermined positions.

Futhermore, if the concept of organizational development is to be utilized by a firm, meaningful plans for providing structural units with sufficient qualified personnel cannot even be established, much less implemented, unless anticipated organizational requirements have been established. These requirements, in turn, are based upon the dynamic concept of an outgoing organizational flow.[1] Finally, to be most effective, manpower planning must be considered as an integrated approach to organizational development, with plans being formulated and implemented at all levels, and in all units, of the enterprise. . . .

Why Manpower Planning Is Important

The paramount problem in manpower planning is searching for individuals with the potential for development, for if the prospective employee is capable and is not hired, he does not enter the promotional stream of employees from which supervisory and managerial employees are obtained. If he is incapable and hired anyway, he enters the upward-flowing stream and may become an incapable manager through the inexorable workings of the seniority system.

Although a work team is a group in action, it is composed of a number of individual members with unique personalities. The only way to strengthen the group is to improve the caliber of individuals hired, for it is impossible to improve the collective group except through improving the abilities of its component members.

Importance to the Nation

A principal reason for the economic supremacy of the United States has been its fortunate selection and development of employees to staff its business enterprises. It has been tacitly assumed that this supply of personnel would automatically be replenished, both quantitatively and qualitatively, as the need arose, thus assuring a continuous supply of producers and leaders to meet the ever-increasing demands made upon the nation's productive capacity. It is becoming increasingly apparent that this is not a valid assumption, as it becomes evident that producers and leaders are in scarce supply. One of the great limitations placed upon our productive capability is the lack of an available supply of adequately trained and developed personnel for the rapidly expanding activities associated with technological advancement.

The economic slack in the early 1970s has served to hide this tendency. Now, though, with industry, commerce, and government expanding their activities, personnel officers are discovering that men in the prime working ages with the right skills and experience are increasingly hard to find. If the United States is to remain preeminent in the economic realm, it must somehow perpetuate the supply of managerial, technical, and skilled employees to meet the growing needs for increased productivity and social responsibility.

Importance to Organizations

National interest in effective planning is equaled by the concern of individual organizations. The judicious recruitment and hiring of a sufficient number of qualified individuals is significant in that these individuals provide the basic productive resource of which an organization is composed. They furnish the source for present and future managerial talent in the organization, since most organizations follow the policy of promoting from within. Only when there are capable employees in the lower levels are there potential managers to promote into the higher organizational echelons.

Although automation is making progress, people are still needed to run the companies. The future of business organizations depends upon these employees, the work they perform, and the ideas they contribute toward improving operations. People remain the greatest asset; though all companies can buy the same materials and equipment, people make the difference in what that equipment produces.

Although effective employment is important to all organizations, it is especially important to expanding companies. It is axiomatic that these enterprises continually look for the one resource for which there is no substitute, namely "talent," or personnel with the mental ability, creativity, and initiative needed for meeting the requirements of these growing concerns. Previously, the need for these talents focused on the research and development function, but now this type of talent is just as urgently needed in production, sales, finance, and every other organizational area. This need is not confined to the company's top echelons, for such personnel are required at every level where the capacity for independent action spells the difference between success and failure.

The main function of a manager is to assemble individuals into a productive organization. Through selective employment, employee cooperation, and coordination of managerial and employee efforts, productive activity can be accomplished. The "pragmatic test of practicality" is that the successful manager is able to assemble a productive organization while the unsuccessful one is not.

Manpower Planning Objectives

Organizations can no longer rely upon finding talented manpower just when they need it. Systematic steps must be taken in order to assure that a reservoir of talent is available when vacancies occur. Consequently, planning and searching for qualified talent must be continuous. Therefore, the overall objectives of manpower planning are to: relate human resource needs to the overall activity of the enterprise; make long-range estimations of the firm's specific and general needs; and maximize the return on investment in human resources.

Relating Human Resources to Enterprise Needs

The human resources of a business are an integral part of all of its activities. It should be recognized that development of those resources is dependent upon other organizational resources; consequently, selecting, developing, and utilizing human resources must be considered as one integrated process designed to incorporate both present and future needs of the firm. Therefore, organizational goals should be clearly defined and established so that selection can be based upon finding personnel capable of realizing those goals.

As an organization grows and develops, its need for manpower with special skills, knowledge, and expertise [increases]. Usually, this increasing need tends to coincide with a shortage of such personnel because of the lead time needed to educate and train people to use the new technology. Thus, long-range manpower plans are needed to adjust to this imbalance. Also, other planning activities become involved.[2]

The cost of recruiting this short-supply, high-talent personnel then poses a problem. So, wages and benefit systems require planning in order to provide internal consistency and external competitiveness.

The problem of integrating this elite group into the organizational framework of statuses and emotional webs must be planned for. The training and development of these personnel, as well as the upgrading of present employees pose a related problem.

The efficient matching of people and jobs, as well as the removal of barriers to flexibility in moving people within the firm, create related problems. The introduction of new technologies and managerial techniques enhance the need for planning how to use the talents, enthusiasm, and dedication of less talented people so their objectives, as well as those of the firm, will be achieved.

Finally, the problems associated with motivating all these individuals need planning for in order to encourage high productivity and employee satisfaction.

Estimating Long-range Manpower Needs

While most forward-looking managers now recognize the crucial importance of maintaining a pool of talented personnel, there is no agreement on how best to develop a reserve of this resource. It is becoming increasingly clear that the adjustment of the work force on an immediate need basis has certain weaknesses. Among these weaknesses are: hurried and indiscriminate selection, which prevents a thorough survey of available talent; a rapidly accumulating backlog of work; and inadequate training of new employees.

There is frequently an excessive demand for immediately available personnel during certain periods of the business cycle, during emergency periods, and in areas with a shortage of personnel. In such cases, an otherwise unacceptable candidate will often be employed in order just to have someone to fill the position. Conversely, when the company has a sufficiently high reputation, or when there is an abundant supply of workers relative to the demands, a company may "hoard" personnel in anticipation of future needs.

Even though there is no uniformity in defining manpower planning or in determining how to create a "pool" of qualified personnel, there is general unanimity concerning the problems manpower planning is concerned with. These objectives can be classified as: planning future manpower needs as a whole, that is, ascertaining how many people from both a qualitative and a quantitative point of view will the firm need in order to operate its business in future periods; planning the future manpower balance within the firm, or establishing how many of those presently employed by the organization will stay with it in future periods; planning for those recruiting and selecting activities required to provide the enterprise with the required personnel, and in case manpower needs are smaller than the present manpower balance within the firm; planning for laying off of the manpower surplus.[3]

In estimating long-range needs, a distinction needs to be made between planning and forecasting. Forecasting implies a passive process, whereas, planning involves not only forecasting but other active decisions regarding manpower requirements and how they can be met.

A company's manpower needs are influenced by external, as well as internal, factors. Among others, the external factors consist of the political situation, the nation's level of production as indicated by the GNP, the level of overall technological development, actions of competing companies, and the development of substitute products and changed uses of the firm's own products.

Manpower planning is basically derived out of other plans. Manpower needs are not autonomous, so planning for these needs must take into account various other internal factors which will influence manpower requirements. Some of those factors are expected sales, production plans, and labor productivity.

Maximizing Return on Investment in Human Resources

A new concept in manpower planning is developing whereby the human resources are treated as capital assets in much the same way that plant and equipment are presently treated. In essence, this system attempts through an accounting model to measure the cost of the resources, what it would cost to replace the resources, and what their value would be based upon their potential earning ability.

This new system emphasizes that man is a unique entity requiring individualized consideration. Thus, managers are becoming more concerned with *accounting for the human resources,* both in terms of the cost involved and in terms of general information to be used in long-range manpower planning and for decision-making purposes. The new system would supply management with a management audit to forecast requirements, to acquire the necessary human resources, and then to develop the human asset to its optimum capacity.

If employees were viewed as a capital asset, several changes would probably occur in the management of the resource. Higher management would insist upon recruiting and selecting the best people; more emphasis would be placed upon the completion of human development programs; greater devotion would be given to an individual's developmental activities; and time and consideration would be given to matching employees with jobs in order to ensure that they were placed in challenging positions which would effectively utilize their capabilities. The aim of the firm would be to ensure a maximum return on investment on their human resources.[4] In attempting to achieve this goal, managers would strive to expand the span of responsibility of employees who would be construed to represent major investments even when formal positions of advancement are not available. Management would also become more selective in making its initial investments in human resources.

This form of accounting could provide management with an additional indicator of an employee's potential growth before advancement is made in his position. This system would focus attention on the employee as a valuable *investment* which enhances earning power rather than as an *operating expense* which acts to drain the organization's financial resources.

Paradoxically, accounting for man as a capital asset should restore the personality of each individual and pave the way to more humanistic treatment of employees. Greater attention would be given to an individual's selection, development, placement, advancement, motivation, and redevelopment. Finally, the dangers of overextending an individual, underutilizing his talents, and allowing for managerial obsolescence, would probably be avoided.

The basic premise underlying this new system is that the analytical and conceptual frameworks designed for the management of physical and financial assets can be applied to the management of human resources.[5] Also, any decision based only upon the physical and financial considerations and which ignores the value of the key personnel factor is likely to lead the executive to a nonoptimal conclusion.

The personnel manager is prone to "deal" his way through a series of familiar activities without questioning how the cost of his actions compares with the value derived from them. Often, he is unable to have projects accepted by higher management because he cannot provide them with a practical and cost-oriented value judgment. As the function of the personnel manager focuses on the most important and valuable asset of an organization, and while this element is seemingly subjective and highly intangible, the personnel man must be value conscious, and this leads to the need to quantify his actions. Thus, *human value accounting* has unlimited possibilities for making future decisions and evaluating past commitments.

According to the vice president of personnel and public affairs, Caterpillar Tractor Company, his firm spent $8.5 million for personnel training and development in 1966.[6] He proposed that in this day of electronic data processing there must be some way to "quantify" the personnel function in an accounting fashion by measuring its value in relation to its cost.

The R. G. Barry Corporation has conducted an experiment in accounting for human resources whereby it uses the process for human resource planning and reporting.[7] Investment in human resources is contained in a pro forma balance sheet and income statement in an effort to capitalize the company's cost of acquisition, development, maintenance, and utilization of its human resources. While the system in no way attempts to reflect adequately the underlying value of the human resources, a cost analysis approach does present a beginning point from which other systems can be developed. . . .

Notes

1. George Steiner, "Rise of the Corporate Planner," *Harvard Business Review*, Vol. 48, No. 5 (September-October, 1970), pp. 133-39.

2. Frank H. Cassell, "Manpower Planning: The Basic Policies," *Personnel*, Vol. 42, No. 6 (November-December, 1965), pp. 55-61.

3. Burckhardt Wenzel, "Planning for Manpower Utilization," *The Personnel Administrator*, Vol. 15, No. 3 (May-June, 1970), pp. 36-40.

4. Robert Wright, "Managing Man as a Capital Asset," *Personnel Journal*, Vol. 49, No. 4 (April, 1970), pp. 290-98.

5. James S. Hekimian and Curtis H. Jones, "Put People on Your Balance Sheet," *Harvard Business Review*, Vol. 45, No. 1 (January-February, 1967), pp. 105-13.

6. Roger T. Kelley, "Accounting in Personnel Administration," *Industrial Relations*, Vol. 7, No. 2 (February, 1968), pp. 24-28.

7. William C. Pyle, "Human Resource Accounting," *Financial Analysts Journal*, Vol. 26, No. 5 (September-October, 1970), pp. 69-78.

Personnel Selection:
The Basic Models

A. K. KORMAN

The Traditional Personnel Selection Model: Predictive Validity

The major contributions which industrial psychology has made to the personnel selection process have been in two areas. One has been the development of psychological measures which predict job performance and which are available to the employing company prior to the time of hiring or rejecting, while the second has concerned itself with the development of appropriate methodologies for evaluating whether or not a given predictor is actually operating effectively, i.e., whether it is predicting the behavior which it should be predicting. Information relating to these two questions has then generally been reported to management, to be used by them in their judgment and decision making in the way they see most fit. . . .

Step 1–The Job Analysis

The traditional personnel selection model has as its first step the study of the characteristics and required behaviors of the job for which the selection process is being undertaken. It is obvious, of course, that one must have some understanding of the nature of the job that one wishes to select for, since not to know this would reduce all selection to a purely random, chance basis. The procedure for finding out this information (which also has value for various other organizational functions such as training, job transfer, and performance appraisal) is known as a "job analysis," and it consists, usually, of a description of the various behaviors, characteristics, and abilities required of the occupant of that job. The ways in which this information is obtained varies with the company, the job, the occupant, etc., but in essence there are two major procedures.

One way is to ask the current job occupant to describe what he does, either subjectively or along some defined dimensions. This method has some advantages. It elicits worker cooperation by bringing him in on the decision making and possibly enhances his self-esteem (with consequent implications for performance) at the same time. A second advantage is, of course, that the job occupant probably knows the job better than anybody else. At the same time, however, there is the disadvantage that the job occupant will probably be most motivated to distort, either consciously or unconsciously, his description in a favored direction. Furthermore, there is another disadvantage to this procedure in that the occupant may not be psychologically, educationally, or emotionally equipped to write an accurate description of his job duties.

Similar advantages and disadvantages attach themselves to the other major job analysis method, that of "observation." Analyzing a job by observation has the advantage of eliminating "faking" to a great extent since an observer should generally be more objective. Furthermore, the observer will also usually be a "qualified" recorder.

Abraham K. Korman, *Industrial and Organizational Psychology*, © 1971. Reprinted by permission of Prentice-Hall, Inc., Englewood Cliffs, N. J.

However, the first advantage could be illusory in that the job occupant may fake his performance, either consciously or subconsciously, if someone is watching him. In addition, a second possible disadvantage is that this procedure is completely inappropriate for mental "thinking" jobs and for jobs which involve a long period of time before a specific job activity is finished. (The analogy here is between the division manager who might be working on a decentralization plan taking five years as opposed to the mechanical repetitive job.) Since these "long-cycle" types of jobs are becoming increasingly the norm in our society, we might expect to see a decrease in the method of "observation" in job analysis as time goes on.

Besides the advantages and disadvantages of each of these procedures, there are problems in job analysis which are common to both (and, in fact, to any observational system involving the rating of such social objects as jobs and people, as we shall point out in our later discussion on performance appraisal methods). One set of these problems has been called the "judgment" errors and can be summarized as follows:

1. *The "halo" error:* This is the tendency to allow one characteristic of a rating object to dominate ratings along other dimensions of the object being rated. An example of this is when we are more likely to attribute intellectual qualities to a person who wears glasses than a person who does not.

2. *The "central tendency" error:* This is the tendency to rate all rating objects around the "middle" or mean of a rating continuum and not to use the extremes.

3. *The "leniency" error:* This is the tendency to rate all social objects in a relatively favorable manner and not to attribute negative aspects to them.

While there are other kinds of judgment errors besides these, these are probably the most important. How one overcomes them is a different problem, however, and about this there is little agreement. In fact there are some who argue that these may not be errors at all and that one of the only reasons they are considered as such is due to the stubborn refusal of psychologists to admit that (1) some kinds of human behavior may not be distributed according to the normal bell-shaped curve (i.e., in some cases, all people might be "good") and (2) some people may actually have all their characteristics integrally a function of their main characteristic (i.e., the halo error is not an error). This seems an extreme position to take, however. Suffice to say for our purposes here that these behaviors are probably "errors" in the traditional sense but their importance and possible remedial actions will probably vary according to the given situation. . . .

A second problem of perhaps more serious import in job analysis is how one incorporates into a description of a job's characteristics some recognition of the fact that jobs are becoming increasingly of the type whereby the behaviors that are engaged in cannot be specified in advance but result from the characteristics of the person who happens to fulfill the role at that particular time. For example, let us look at the differences between a management role and the role of a sewing-machine operator in a dress factory. It is much simpler to specify in advance what the behavior of the latter should be than the former. In fact, it is probably very much the case that the essence of the managerial role is success in the ability to handle problems which cannot be specified or "programmed" in advance. While this difference in potential specificity of roles was always a problem for job analysts, its signficance is increasing greatly because more jobs in our automated society are becoming increasingly like that of the manager and increasingly less like that of the sewing-machine operator.

It should be emphasized that we are not suggesting that we do away with the job analysis as an aid in the selection (and other manpower utilization) program. This is clearly an impossibility, since the alternative is chaos. However, it is to suggest that this is a significant problem which must be taken into account in future job analysis research.

Step 2–Hypothesis Development

The second step in the traditional model is derived from the job analysis, with this step consisting, essentially, of hypothesis generation as to the kinds of individuals who would be most likely to fit the behavioral demands of the job. This step can be a subjective one based on a subjective appraisal on the job analysis information. Hence, it can be highly dependent on the cognitive characteristics of the person developing the hypotheses. Unfortunately, we know little about the kinds of people who would be particularly good at this type of thing. Such recognition of this situation is, undoubtedly, one of the reasons the more common procedure in job analysis has been to describe jobs in terms of more objective psychological dimensions and then to verify such descriptions by either (1) testing job occupants with unambiguous tests of these dimensions or (2) getting qualified interjudge agreement as to the importance of the dimensions for the given job. Due to the difficulty of getting tests which are unambiguous measures of simple psychological dimensions, particularly in nonability areas, the latter verification procedure is the more common one today.

A good example of the kinds of dimensions by which jobs may be described and compared to one another in terms of the requirements they call for is seen in Table 1. This summarizes some recent work by McCormick and his co-workers (cf. McCormick, Cunningham, and Gordon, 1967). Since these dimensions can be used in varying quantities to describe a variety of different jobs, it is obvious that this project has great potential for assisting in such personnel activities as selection, job promotions, transfers, training, etc.

TABLE 1
DIMENSIONS OF JOB BEHAVIOR AND EXAMPLES

1. *Decision making and communication activities:*
   Develops budgets; supervises management personnel; verbal presentations; forecasts needs; variety of communications; personnel decisions
2. *Hierarchical person-to-person interaction:*
   Instructs; supervises students, trainees, patients, subordinates, etc.; issues directives; schedules work of others; interchanges information with prospective employees, students, or trainees
3. *Skilled physical activities:*
   Skill of hand tool usage; number of hand tools used; finger manipulation; estimates size
4. *Mental vs. physical activities:*
   Positive loadings—deals with data; interprets information; intelligence; uses mathematics; clerical tasks
   Negative loadings—manual force; moves objects by hand; deals with things
5. *Responsible personal contact:*
   Persuades; interchanges information with customers, clients, patients, etc.; distractions from people seeking or giving information
6. *General physical activities:*
   Adjustment to the vertical; climbing; balancing; general physical coordination
7. *Unpleasant vs. pleasant working conditions:*
   Uncomfortable atmosphere; unclean environment
8. *Decisions affecting people:*
   Personnel decisions (promotions, transfers, hiring, etc.)

9. *Varied intellectual vs. structured activities:*
   Positive loadings—interpretation of information; intelligence; usage of mathematics; occupation prestige
   Negative loadings—high job structure; repetitiveness; deals with things
10. *Supervisory activities:*
    Supervises others; issues directives; number of people supervised
11. *Man-machine control activities:*
    Control operations; monitors work process; interpretation of information; responsible for physical assets
12. *Planning and decision making:*
    Uniqueness of decisions; time span of decisions; forecasts needs; develops methods
13. *Skilled manual activities:*
    Skill of hand tool usage; finger manipulation; number of hand tools used
14. *Intellectual vs. physical activities*
    Positive loadings—"thinking" (vs. "doing"); occupation prestige
    Negative loadings—activity domain—things; repetitiveness; job structure
15. *Body-balancing activities:*
    Adjustment to the vertical; balancing; climbing
16. *Physical vs. sedentary activities:*
    Positive loadings—standing; general force; manual force
    Negative loadings—activity domain—data
17. *Clerical activities:*
    Clerical tasks (filing, typing, shorthand, etc.)
18. *Knee-bending activities:*
    Crawling; kneeling; stooping
19. *Informative communications:*
    Giving information; instructing; issuing directives; verbal communications
20. *Communication of data:*
    Reporting; activity domain—data; interchange of information; written communication
21. *Persuasive communications:*
    Persuading; verbal presentations; negotiating
22. *Public contact activites:*
    Publicizing; information interchange with public
23. *White- vs. blue-collar situations:*
    Positive loadings—wearing presentable clothing; social obligations; occupational prestige
    Negative loadings—receiving hourly and/or overtime pay; receives close supervision
24. *Job security vs. performance-dependent income:*
    Positive loadings—job security; occupational prestige
    Negative loadings—receives tips; commissions, hourly pay, and/or overtime pay
25. *Apparel: Optional vs. work clothes:*
    Positive loading—wears special working clothes
    Negative loading—dress left to incumbent's discretion
26. *Apparel: Formal vs. optional:*
    Positive loadings—wears presentable clothing; social obligations; occupational prestige
    Negative loading—dress left to incumbent's discretion
27. *Apparel: Specific uniform:*
    Wears specific uniform
28. *Hourly pay vs. salary:*
    Positive loading—regular salary
    Negative loading—hourly pay; overtime pay
29. *Annoying environment:*
    Noise; uncomfortable atmosphere; poor illumination; cramped work space

---

Source: E. J. McCormick, J. W. Cunningham, C. G. Gordon: Job dimensions based on factorial analyses of worker-oriented job variables. *Personnel Psychology,* 1967, *20,* 417-30.

Step 3–Predictor Development

Once the relevant psychological and behavior variables have been hypothesized, it is time for the third step. This consists of deciding how one is to measure individual differences in job applicants on the relevant variables. The most important problem is that it is important that one choose a measure which actually measures the relevant psychological variable which one is proposing as being demanded by the job. The reasons for this are simple. If the chosen measure is not an actual measure of the relevant variable, two possible problems develop, depending on whether or not the measure is actually related to job performance. First, we may reject a good hypothesis as to the cause of good job performance in a given job and not know it. Hence, whatever else we eventually learn about the job in terms of selection and training, such knowledge must always be incomplete, perhaps seriously so. Suppose, however, that the "mistake" works; i.e., suppose we have hypothesized "sociability" as an important variable but have measured "anxiety" by mistake (without knowing it) and "anxiety" does actually predict job performance. It does not matter, the "practical" man says, that it does not measure what it is supposed to measure, since it predicts job performance and hence can be used for selection. The answer to this is that this is a wasteful, shortsighted, uneconomical attitude. One reason that is so can be seen if we assume that the relevant important psychological variable is "sociability" (when it is really "anxiety"). First, of all the recommendations for managerial action in training, development, appraisal, and promotion which would follow from such a successful prediction would be based on a mistaken, erroneous belief. A second reason this attitude is an impractical one relates to the fact that jobs do change, and sometimes a variable which used to predict performance no longer does. Hence, if we find that our measure of sociability (which is really anxiety) no longer predicts job performance, we shall start looking for new predictors eliminating sociability, although a good measure of sociability might now be a good predictor on the changed job.

How does one decide, then, when a measure is actually a measure of the desired variable? The best process for this is a procedure known as "construct validity," consisting basically of looking at all the relationships which the proposed measure of the variable has with other measured variables and then deciding whether or not these observed relationships are consistent with what they should be if the measure was really measuring what it says it is. (The judgment is, of course, a subjective one and hence must be a result of the knowledge and skills of the person making the judgment.) . . .

It should be noted that the process of establishing the construct validity of an instrument is a never-ending one and that we must continually be concerned with obtaining new information on the construct validity of our instrument since the more we know about it, the more we can have confidence that we are actually measuring what we claim we are measuring. In this sense, then, the development of the construct validity of an instrument is similar to the testing of the utility of a theory. In both cases, however, as we have emphasized throughout this [article], great practical benefits ensue.

What kinds of predictors are typically chosen? As indicated above, . . . the development of measures of characteristics that will be good predictors of performance has been a primary concern of industrial psychologists with the result that a wide variety of different measures may be used. Briefly, we may summarize them into the following categories (others besides these are possible):

1. *Ability tests:* These consist of measures of verbal and other abilities. . . .
2. *Objective personality tests:* These are measures of personality characteristics

which have a relatively structured format; i.e., the individual respondent describes himself along dimensions defined by the test constructor rather than along dimensions defined by himself.

3. *Projective personality tests:* These are measures of personality characteristics which have an unstructured format and which allow the individual to respond along any dimension which he wishes and which he constructs.

4. *Objective life-history items:* These consist of questions concerning relatively objective characteristics of a person's school, work, and personal background; the rationale for these is that they are measures of various attitudinal and personal characteristics of the individual which are not measured by other means.

5. *Interviews and other judgmental assessments:* These consist of judgments by various individuals as to the extent to which the individual possesses the behavioral characteristics which are felt to be necessary for adequate job performance.

Which of these are the best? . . . This is a multidimensional question, with the answer depending on the criteria used, the occupations involved, various ethical problems, theoretical measurement problems, etc. To some extent, it is even a meaningless question since such a question implies that one may have a choice in the given situation. Yet, this may not be the case.

For example, the best predictors of job performance have consistently been ability tests. However, just as consistently, it has also been shown that their predictive effectiveness will reach only a certain point and that it is necessary to use personality test variables if one wishes to predict performance more accurately above this point, even though personality tests are generally not as effective predictors as ability tests (Guion and Gottier, 1965).

For these reasons, then, our later procedure will be not to bother to make any comparative claims as to the relative fruitfulness of these kinds of measures, since all have their uses in given situations and all must be improved to the greatest extent possible. Their usefulness depends on the given prediction situation and the given prediction problem, and they must be evaluated as such, a procedure which constitutes the basis for our discussion here. . . .

Step 4–Administration of Predictors to Applicant Sample

Once the measures of the relevant behaviors have been decided upon, they are administered to the applicants for the job in question. However, the measures are *not* used as a basis for selection at this time. Rather, the applicants are then selected for the job in question on the basis of whatever procedures for this process are existing at that time. The scores on the hypothesized predictor measures are filed away at this time, to be utilized in connection with step 5.

The reasoning behind this procedure can be explained quite simply. Thus, if we use the hypothesized measure as a basis for hiring, then we shall never know what the job performance would have been of those individuals with the predictor scores who were not hired. That is, if the company were to take in only those with high scores, then we would not know the eventual performance of those with low scores and vice versa. The problem is, of course, that the unselected group might have been better in job performance than the selected; something we could not know unless we gave them the opportunity.

Step 5–Relate Predictor Test Scores to Measure of Job Performance

After the applicants have been hired and been on the job for a long enough period of time to get some meaningful measure of differences in job performance, the first critical point in this process is reached. This is to relate scores on the predictor variable to the measure of job performance, i.e., the criterion.

There are two major problems which are of concern here. First, what measures of relationship should be used, and what are the advantages and disadvantages of each of these measures? Second, how shall we interpret the results found in terms of their practical significance for organizational action? These are the questions we shall attempt to answer here, discussing both where we have only *one* predictor variable for each applicant and where we have more than one predictor variable for each person.

1. The correlation coefficient. Undoubtedly, the most popular method for describing the relationship between two variables that has been utilized in personnel selection research has been the correlation coefficient, or *r*, . . . The reasons for this are several. First, there is the element of familiarity, i.e., most industrial psychologists are quite familiar with it, having studied it as part of their graduate training. Second, it is a convenient way of summarizing a relationship into one general descriptive term. Hence, when we say that a correlation is .60, it is agreed that this means something different than when we say a correlation is .10 or − .35. A third reason for the great utilization of the correlation coefficient is that there is a considerable amount of theory developed around it, theory concerned with how much confidence we can have in certain obtained results, given certain assumptions. Thus, because the theory concerning the correlation coefficient is well developed, we are able to specify, given certain assumptions, the likelihood that our results are not due to "chance" or "unstable" factors and we can also estimate the degree to which our specifications will be in error. Related to both this reason and the second is a fourth advantage of using the correlation coefficient as a measure of a relationship and that is that the actual *r* obtained is directly convertible into a measure of predictive accuracy, the purpose of the whole selection mechanism process. . . .

These advantages hold whether we are concerned with the situation when we have only one predictor variable for each applicant or, the far more common case, when we are concerned with more than one predictor in a given selection situation. In the latter situation, the correlation coefficient which is used is called the multiple correlation coefficient, as opposed to the "simple *r*," the measure used in the case where there is only one predictor variable. The two can be distinguished in this way:

1. For the case of one predictor—one criterion, we correlate the two variables X (the predictor) and Y (the criterion) using the appropriate formula.[1]

2. For the case of multiple predictors—one criterion, the procedure can be outlined conceptually as follows:[2]

    a. Assume four predictor variables, X_1, X_2, X_3, and X_4, and one criterion variable Y.

    b. All the predictor variables are correlated with the criterion variable and with each other.

    c. Each predictor variable is then weighted by a statistical procedure according to the degree of its intercorrelations with the criterion and with the other predictor variables; the higher the correlation with the criterion and the lower the correlation with the other predictors, the greater the weight that specific variable has for predicting that criterion.

    d. The absolute sum of these weights are then converted, again statistically, into a correlation coefficient called the multiple *r* which is then interpretable along the *same* scale as the regular *r*. In other words it has the same range from −1.00 to +1.00, an *r* of 0.00 means no relationship between the two variables, and so on. In this case, of course, the X or predictor variable is not a single variable, but a weighted composite of the four predictor variables, with each individual's score on this composite being the average of his scores on each of the predictor variables, corrected by the weight for the variables. An example of this procedure is given in Figure 3.

The last statement does point to one difference between the simple and multiple r which the reader should keep in mind and which does limit to an extent the general equating of the two we have made here. This difference results because the weighting system used in developing the multiple correlation is based on *maximizing* the correlation between the predictors and criterion and all variables are weighted on this basis, whether the scores that are being weighted are based on real, valid differences between people or on chance, accidental influences on the scores. The problem is that these chance, accidental scores are counted only if they add to the level of the correlation coefficient. They are *not* counted if they decrease this level; rather, they are ignored. It is for this reason that the multiple r has a general tendency to be too high, given the nature of the scores involved. Hence, it is even more necessary in the case where the multiple r is used that the step we have called "cross-validation," which we shall discuss later, be employed. . . . [Editor's note: Because chance does to some extent affect the computed weights, the multiple correlation technique of combining tests into a composite is often no more effective—and sometimes less effective—than simply adding up scores on the different tests with no weighting. See Frank Schmidt, "The Relative Efficiency of Regression and Simple Unit Predictor Weights in Applied Differential Psychology." *Educational and Psychological Measurement,* 1971, 31, 699-714. This is especially true when there is a small sample involved. See W. Clay Hamner, "The importance of Sample Size, Cut-off Techniques, and Cross-validation in Multiple Regression Analysis, *Proceedings, Midwest American Institute for Decision Sciences* meeting, East Lansing, Michigan, April, 1973.]

Perhaps the only way of . . . approaching some kind of meaningful judgment as to whether a given correlation is of practical significance is to view it in terms of the specifics of a given situation since it is these specifics which may play an important part in determining whether or not to use selection instruments at all. . . .

Let us assume that we do not have any selection instruments at all and we hire all people who apply for each job; that is, we predict that *all* will succeed. The number of mistakes in prediction we shall make are as follows:

Situation A = 10% (the base rate of success is 90%)
Situation B = 55% (the base rate of success is 45%)
Situation C = 90% (the base rate of success is 10%)

Hence, if a test is to be of practical usefulness, its correlation coefficient must be higher in situation A than in situation B and much higher than in Situation C, since our accuracy of prediction is so much higher in the former than the latter without the use of any selection instruments at all. (It is for this reason that selection instruments are often utilized in managerial and high-level selection which would be considered to be too low to be of practical usefulness when dealing with lower-level employees.) This, then, is one factor which enables us to interpret when a correlation coefficient is practically useful.

A second factor of significance is the selection ratio. Consider the situation where we need select only 1 of 100 applicants for a job, as opposed to one where we must select 50 of 100. Since in the first case we can take only the best, a selection instrument does not have to be very accurate in increasing our ability to predict job behavior over chance levels. It only has to be a little bit better than chance in order to help us in picking out the best person for the job. On the other hand, this is not the case in the latter situation, where we must pick out 50 and where, hence, the selection instrument must be high in validity to be useful. The former case is called a "low selection ratio" situation and the latter, of course, a "high selection ratio" situation.

These two factors, then, the "base rate of success" (or "difficulty level" of the job) and the selection ratio in the given situation, are the major guides we have in determining the practical usefulness of a given selection instrument for any given selection question. . . .

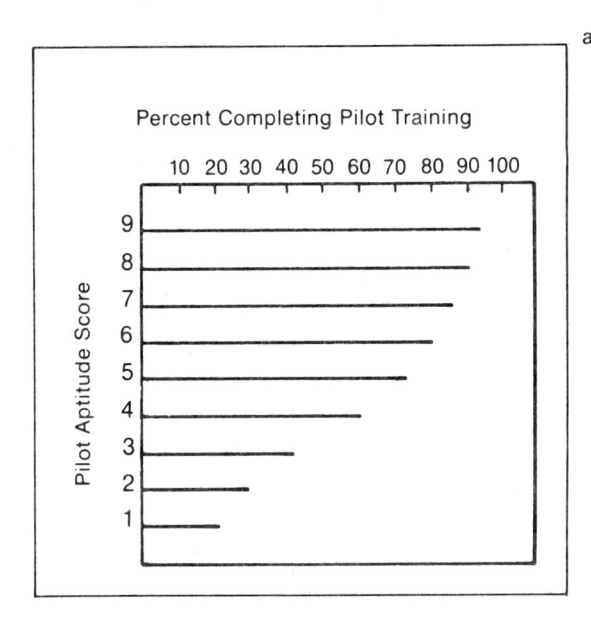

a

Percent Completing Pilot Training

Pilot Aptitude Score	Percent (10-100)	Number with this score	Approximate odds of success
9		14,682	9 in 10
8		15,286	9 in 10
7		24,367	8 in 10
6		30,066	8 in 10
5		31,091	7 in 10
4		22,827	6 in 10
3		11,471	4 in 10
2		2,239	3 in 10
1		904	2 in 10

b

Percent Staying with Company over 1½ Years

Scored Application Score	Percent (10-100)	Number scoring in this range	Approximate odds of staying with firm 1½ years or more
20 and above		18	9 in 10
15-19		20	6 in 10
10-14		21	4 in 10
9 and below		24	1 in 10

Figure 1. Examples of simple cut-off systems relating test scores to job behavior. (a) Chart showing relation between pilot aptitude score and successful completion of pilot training ("Psychological Activities in Training Command AAF," *Psychological Bulletin*, 1945, *42*, (b) Chart showing relation between biographical "score" and length of service for female office employees ("Development of a Weighted Application Blank to Aid in the Selection of Office Employees," *Research Report No. 7*, Personnel Research, 3M Co., 1956). (Source: M. D. Dunnette and W. Kirchner: *Psychology Applied to Business and Industry*. New York: Appleton-Century-Crofts, 1965.)

2. *Simple and multiple cut-off systems.* To overcome some of the weaknesses of the correlation coefficient as a way of describing the relationship between the hypothesized predictors of job behavior and actual job behavior, an increasing number of psychologists have suggested the use of simple and multiple cut-off systems. These, in essence, are expectancy charts and/or tables which depict the level of job performance which is to be expected from any given level of predictor scores; cut-offs can then be developed both for simple and multiple predictors which will maximize the level of performance. . . .

Although the cut-off methods do not provide convenient summary figures for describing the obtained relationships, a look at this chart indicates the obvious advantages which account for its increasing usage. It is clear and easy to interpret, thus overcoming the resistance to the correlation coefficient as a medium of communication which is frequently found among nonpsychologically trained people. A second advantage is perhaps a more technically important one in that it can be keyed to any type of relationship, linear or curvilinear, better than the correlation coefficient. Consider the example given in Figure 2.

Predictor X	Criterion Y
10	25
9	25
8	25
7	25
Acceptable performance	Unacceptable performance
6	20
5	18
4	16
3	14

Figure 2.

If we were to compute the correlation coefficient between these variables, it would probably not be a high one due to the lack of variation in criterion performance for all those with predictor scores of 7 or above. Hence, we might discard this predictor if we were using correlation analysis. On the other hand, if we were using a cut-off system, we would have perfect prediction if we selected all those with predictor scores of 7 or more and rejected those with scores of 6 or less.

The comparative discussion is somewhat analogous but does get more complex when we talk about situations where there are multiple predictors. To review our previous comments, the reader will recall that in the multiple r situation the various predictor variables are weighted in terms of their relationships to the criterion. In essence, each individual is then assigned a score based on his scores on the predictor variables, corrected by the weights for each variable. Consider Figure 3, taken from our example in Figure 1.

One aspect which is immediately apparent and which is crucial to our discussion is that there is a variety of ways by which a person may derive a given X score on the composite variable. Hence, person A gets a score of 62 by being high on variables 2 and 3, even though he is only medium on variable 1. On the other hand, individual E is high on variable 1 but he is considerably lower on variables 2 and 3. In other words, E has "compensated" for being low on variable 2 by being higher on variable 1. This principle of "compensation" and of there being alternative ways to derive high predictor scores is the essence of the multiple correlation system.

Suppose, now, that we wanted to use a multiple cut-off system. How would this operate? Using the same sample, suppose we found that the following cut-offs for each of the variables led to the highest level of predicted performance:

Cut-off Levels
Variable X_1 = 9 or more
Variable X_2 = 6 or more
Variable X_3 = 3 or more

According to these levels, using our previous examples, the following decisions would be made:

Individual A = Hire
Individual B = Reject
Individual C = Reject
Individual D = Hire
Individual E = Hire

Hence, we see that requiring each individual to be above a given level on all predictors, as in the multiple cut-off system, leads to different decisions than when we allow a person to compensate for being low on one predictor by being extra high on the other.

Which system is a better one? There is, of course, no simple answer to this. It depends on the situation. In some prediction situations it would seem that we can safely allow compensation and use the multiple *r* method, given the other advantages we have previously mentioned. However, it is also apparent that cut-offs may be necessary on some variables in that a low score on that given predictor cannot be compensated for by high scores on any other predictor. An example of this concerns the necessity of visual acuity for being a dentist. Unless the dentist has a high level of visual acuity, any other ability of his, verbal, manipulative, or otherwise, is not likely to be of use or value to him.

Hence, perhaps the best approach to use in the multiple predictor situation is a combination of the multiple cut-off and multiple correlation methods. The first step would be to use the multiple cut-off method for those variables where a minimum level is considered necessary and select people on that basis. After this is done, the multiple *r* method should be used with the remaining predictors in order to select from those remaining after the initial cut-off is made.

Step 6–Cross-validation

The next step in the traditional personnel selection model depends on whether or not the results in step 5 look promising. Assuming that they do, the next step is to *repeat the entire procedure*, utilizing the same job, same measure of performance, same kinds of applicants, etc. The reason for this kind of procedure relates to the essentially conservative nature of the scientific endeavor in that it is felt that despite proper precautions of the type we have discussed, it is always conceivable that a single obtained result, no matter how positive the relationship, could always occur on the basis of chance factors alone. Hence, to have greater confidence in the results, one should always replicate or repeat the study. This is the purpose of the cross-validation step.

Unfortunately, it is often the case that the results of step 5 are not promising enough to continue to the cross-validation attempt. In this case, there is nothing else to do according to the traditional personnel selection model but start all over again.

Step 7–Recommendation for Selection
Finally, the last step in the procedure, assuming that step 6 works out, is to make recommendations for selection. The essential problem here is to develop a procedure as to the kinds of scores which will be acceptable for selection and to set up guidelines for the administration of such recommendations. . . .

Predictors		Variables					
	X_1	X_2	X_3	X_4	Composite predictor		Level necessary
Individual weights	3	2	1	0	score (i.e., the X variable in the multiple		for hiring
Applicants					correlation equation)		decision = 55
A	10	12	8	9	62		Hire
B	6	7	15	9	47		Reject
C	13	3	11	15	56		Hire
D	9	6	8	4	47		Reject
E	13	10	3	8	62		Hire

Figure 3.

The Concurrent Validity Model

The first major revision to be made in the traditional personnel selection model is, in some respects, not a revision at all, since its historical antecedents are at least as old. In addition, it is probably more commonly used in the industrial situation than is the traditional selection model. The reason for this is that its major purpose is to eliminate what is practically the most frustrating aspect of the traditional model, the delay between the administration of the predictor measures and the collection of job behavior measures. In essence, the concurrent validity model differs from the traditional model (which we call "predictive validity") in that it utilizes present, already working groups on employees as test groups upon which to determine whether given variables are related to job performance. In other words the procedure is very much the same as the traditional approach except that the hypothesized predictors of successful job performance are administered to those already on the job for whom job performance data are immediately available. If the expected relationships occur and are replicated in a cross-validation relationship and so on, then the measures are recommended for administrative use in selection procedures.

There is little doubt that it is because this procedure overcomes the time problem inherent in the traditional model that it became the most popular method for developing selection instruments in industrial situations. Yet, there are some who feel that despite this enormous benefit of the concurrent validity model, this advantage, when weighed in the balance, does not compensate for the very serious disadvantages entailed, disadvantages which include almost all of those in the traditional model plus several that are unique to it alone. These additional disadvantages, we shall see, are so serious that some have argued the concurrent validity procedure should be used only as a hypothesis generator, not as a hypothesis tester (Guion, 1965).

[Now], this procedure also makes the following crucial assumptions:

1. The motivational determinants of responding to a possible selection instrument such as personality tests, attitude questionnaires, etc., are the same for those already on the job as for those applying for the job.

2. Scores on a potential predictor of job behavior are not related in any systematic manner to experience on the job.

It is quite obvious that these are two very important assumptions, violations of which would destroy the validity of this whole procedure. How often are they violated? There is little systematic evidence available, but it would appear that this would depend to a great extent on the instruments being studied. For example, there are studies on record where various kinds of leadership attitudes have been studied via a concurrent validity procedure and then recommended for administrative use in selection. It seems hard to believe that attitudes in this area are not reflecting organizational experience to a great extent. Similarly, when a person with union security is asked about his motivational characteristics, it is hard to believe that the psychological determinants of his answers are similar to those of a person who has been out of work for several months.

There is a third problem associated with the concurrent validity procedure, and that is a technical one. Consider the situation where an organization has a job category involving 40 positions but which now has 5 available openings. Who are the 35 currently on the job? Technically, they are a subgroup of those who were originally hired for that position, differing from the 5 who left in that they remained on the job. Now if we assume, that in general, the person who stays on the job or who is not fired is more competent than the one who quits or is fired, then the 35 now on the job would, in general, show less variation in job performance than the original unrestricted group of 40. If this were so, then it would be harder to find any correlation between predictor and job performance, since a correlation measures the similarity in variation between two variables and one of the variables does not have much variation. This, in turn, would depress the level of the correlation to a level perhaps lower than it would be if we had used it in a predictive validity situation. . . .

References

Dunnette, M. and Kirchner, W., *Psychology Applied to Business and Industry*, New York: Appleton, 1965.

Ghiselle, E. and Brown, C., *Personnel and Industrial Psychology*, 2nd edition, New York: McGraw-Hill, 1955.

Guion, R. M., *Personnel Testing*. New York: McGraw-Hill, 1965.

Guion, R. and Gottier, R. F., "Validity of Personnel Measures in Personnel Selection," *Personnel Psychology*, 1965, 18, 135-64.

McCormick, E. J., Cunningham, J. W. and Gordon, C. E., "Job Dimensions Based on Factorial Analysis of Worker-Oriented Variables," *Personnel Psychology*, 1967, 20, 417-430.

Section B
The Interview as a Selection Technique

The Selection Interview

JOHN B. MINER

. . . Although it should be evident that interview procedures are widely used for a variety of purposes, the primary concern here is with specific applications in the evaluation of human inputs to a business organization. Thus, applications in such areas as marketing research, employee counseling, managment appraisal, attitude surveys, and so on will receive very little attention.

Even within the input context, the interview serves a number of purposes. It is much more than a selection device. Probably this is why it has survived and even thrived in the face of extended attacks by industrial psychologists and others and of considerable evidence that as commonly used it is often not a very effective selection technique.

There are, in fact a number of requirements connected with the input process that at present cannot be accomplished in any other way, although telephone and written communication might be substituted in certain instances. Interviews are used as often to sell the company and thus recruit candidates for employment as to select. A single interview frequently involves both selection and recruiting aspects. Furthermore, terms of employment characteristically are negotiated in the interview situation, and an important public relations function is performed. Rejected applicants are particularly likely to leave with very negative attitudes toward the company, if they have not talked with a responsible representative.

Even when the focus is directly on the selection process, the interview appears to possess certain unique values, which may account for its continued widespread use. For one thing, the great flexibility of the technique, which can contribute to limited validity in some selection situations, may represent a major asset at other times. The interview is the method *par excellence* for filling in the gaps between other selection techniques—gaps that could not have been foreseen until the other techniques were actually applied. Responses on the application blank may make it clear that further information regarding the circumstances surrounding certain previous employment and separation decisions is needed. An interview can be of considerable help in providing such information.

Reprinted with permission of Macmillan Publishing Co., Inc., from *Personnel Psychology*. Copyright © 1969 by Macmillan Publishing Co., Inc.

It is also clear that the interview is widely used to determine whether an applicant is the type of person who can be expected to fit in and get along in the particular firm. Its use with reference to such organizational maintenance considerations is probably much more widespread than its use in predicting productivity. This is not to imply that other selection techniques cannot be used to predict maintenance criteria, but that, for various reasons, they often are not given the same emphasis as the interview. Something about the process of personal judgment produces a strong feeling of validity, even when validity is not present. It is not surprising, therefore, that many companies place heavy emphasis on interviewing when attempting to predict whether a man will be a source of conflict, will have a negative impact on others, or will be an extremely unhappy employee.

Finally, there are situations, especially when managerial and professional positions are involved, where the interview is the only major selection technique that realistically can be used. When a man who already has a good job, who gives every evidence of being a good prospect, and who does not have a strong initial incentive to make a move is faced with extensive psychological testing, a physical exam, and an application blank (above and beyond the resume he has already submitted), he may shy away. If this seems likely, it is often wiser to rely on the interview, reference checks, and the like, in spite of their shortcomings, than to face the prospect of losing the man entirely.

What Is Known about the Selection Interview

A great deal has been written regarding the techniques of interviewing for various purposes (1, 3, 5, 6). Much of this, however, derives from the expertise and opinion of specific individuals. What is really known, in the sense that it is based on studies using selection models . . . and on other scientific research procedures, is considerably less.

The discussion here will be restricted to that which is known in this scientific sense. Unfortunately, when this is done, a great deal is left to the discretion of the individual interviewer. Yet there is little point in continuing to perpetuate much of the existing lore, which in many instances has been developed out of situations far removed from the company employment office, and which may therefore be quite erroneous when applied to a selection interview in the business world.

Consistency of Interviewer Judgments

There is considerable evidence that, although an interviewer will himself exhibit consistency in successive evaluations of the same individual, different interviewers are likely to come to quite disparate conclusions (7). When two employment interviewers utilize their idiosyncratic interview procedures on the same applicant, the probability is that they will come to different decisions. They normally will elicit information on different matters, and even when the topics covered do overlap, one man will weigh the applicant's responses in a way that varies considerably from that employed by the other.

These problems can be overcome. Interviewers can be trained to follow similar patterns in their questioning and to evaluate responses using the same standards. When more structured interview techniques are used, when the questions asked are standardized and responses are recorded systematically, the consistency of the judgmental process increases markedly. Within limits, it does not matter which interviewer is used; the results tend to be similar. Unfortunately, however, structuring of a kind that will increase the consistency of judgments appears to be the exception rather than the rule in most personnel offices. Where strong reliance is placed on the interview, the final selection decision often depends as much on which interviewer is used as on the characteristics of the applicant. On the other hand, agreement does not guarantee accuracy of prediction; there can be great consistency in picking the wrong people.

Accuracy of Interview Information

Studies aimed at determining the accuracy of statements regarding work history made in the interview indicate that reporting errors may occur. In one instance, when a check was made with employers, information given by the interviewees regarding job titles was found to be invalid in 24 percent of the cases. Job duties were incorrectly reported by 10 percent, and pay by 22 percent (11). In general, the tendency was to upgrade rather than downgrade prior work experience.

Other research suggests that, in most employment situations, interview distortion is probably not so prevalent as the preceding figures suggest (9). Yet, in any given instance an interviewer may be faced with an applicant who deliberately, or perhaps unconsciously, falsifies his report. The tendency is for the man to make his record look better than it is. It can be assumed, also, that many applicants will avoid discussing previous instances of ineffective work performance. Where valid data are essential, it is usually desirable to check interview statements against outside sources.

Accuracy of Interviewer Judgments

The inevitable conclusion derived from a number of investigations is that interview judgments, as they are usually made in the employment situation, are not closely related to independent measures of the characteristics judged nor to measures of success on the job. In an over-all sense, the evidence regarding the validity of the selection interview yields a distinctly disappointing picture (7).

There are conditions under which the interview exhibits considerable strength as a selection device, and there are some characteristics capable of being judged more effectively than others. Studies dealing with the relationship between interview estimates of intelligence and test scores indicate that the interview can be quite valid in this area. In addition, the interview would appear to have good potential as a predictor of self-confidence, the effectiveness with which a man can express himself, certain types of attitudes, sociability, and a variety of mental abilities. Such characteristics as dependability, creativity, honesty, and loyalty seem more difficult to estimate correctly in the normal interview situation.

The evidence regarding the value of the interview as a selection procedure is certainly not all negative. Where the interview approach is planned in advance and a relatively structured format is followed, so that much the same questions are asked of all interviewees, relatively good validities have been obtained against job performance criteria (4, 12). The results of one such study, which utilized the concurrent model, are presented in Table 1. Clearly these interview judgments constitute quite adequate predictors in certain instances. Others among the attitude estimates are considerably less effective.

In another series of studies, rather sizable predictive validities were reported for over-all interviewer estimates of suitability for employment, when a highly structured, patterned interview approach was followed (8). When validated against duration of employment for the 587 people who left the company within an eighteen-month period, the interviews yielded a correlation of .43. The men rated higher initially in the employment interview stayed longer. The 407 employees who were still on the job eighteen months after hiring were rated for performance effectiveness by their superiors, and the results were compared with the earlier interview judgments. A predictive validity coefficient of .68 was obtained. Subsequent studies using the same patterned interview format produced correlations with success criteria consistently in the .60's.

TABLE 1

CORRELATIONS BETWEEN ATTITUDE EVALUATIONS FROM INTERVIEWS AND SUPERVISORS' PERFORMANCE RATINGS

Attitudes	Group 1 (N = 12)	Group 2 (N = 14)
Formulation of goal	.14	.60
Strength of job interest	—.13	.40
Strength of general interests	.42	.85
Self-regard	.67	.63
Acquisitive perseverance	—.13	—.30
All five attitudes combined	.45	.71
Formulation of goal, strength of general interests, and self-regard combined	.54	.66

Source: Adapted from K.A. Yonge, "The Value of the Interview: An Orientation and a Pilot Study," *Journal of Applied Psychology*, Vol. 40 (1956), p. 29.

It is evident that when the selection interview is used in a relatively standardized manner and individualized interviewer approaches and biases are controlled, the interview can be quite effective. Under such standardized conditions, the interview takes on certain characteristics of the application blank or a psychological test. It becomes in many respects an oral version of the common written selection procedures, although still with greater flexibility. There is nothing in what has been said to imply that less structured (and less directive) interviews may not yield equally good validities under certain circumstances and with certain interviewers, but without further research it is not possible to specify exactly what these requisite conditions are.

The McGill University Studies

Certain other conclusions regarding the decision-making process in the interview are derived from a series of studies carried out at McGill University over a 10-year period (10). As a result of this research, it is now clear that in the actual employment situation most interviewers tend to make an accept-reject decision early in the interview. They do not wait until all the information is in. Rather, a bias is developed and stabilized shortly after the discussion starts. This bias serves to color the remainder of the interview and is not usually reversed.

Second, interviewers are much more influenced by unfavorable than by favorable data. If any shift in viewpoint occurs during the interview, it is much more likely to be in the direction of rejection. Apparently, selection interviewers tend to maintain rather clear-cut conceptions regarding the role requirements of the jobs for which they are interviewing. They compare candidates against these stereotypes in the sense of looking for deviant characteristics, and thus for negative evidence with regard to hiring. Positive evidence is given much less weight.

These findings suggest certain guidelines for maximizing the effectiveness of employment interviewing. For one thing, if it is intended that the interview should make a *unique* contribution to the selection process, the interviewing ought to be done with relatively little foreknowledge of the candidate. Contrary to common practice, application blanks, test scores, and the like should be withheld until after the initial selection interview. Personal history data should be obtained directly from the candidate in oral form even if written versions are available. This approach will serve to delay decision-making in the interview with the result that information obtained during the latter part of the discussion can be effectively utilized in reaching a judgment. If data are needed to fill in the gaps between the various selection techniques, these can be obtained from a second interview. Thus, the interview as an independent selection tool should be clearly differentiated from the interview as a means of following up on leads provided by other devices. The interviewer should be clear in his own mind as to which objective he is seeking.

When the interview is used as an independent procedure, information obtained from the various sources should be combined and evaluated subsequently to reach a final selection decision, rather than during the interview proper. When the interview is used to supplement application blank, medical history, and psychological test data, it should be as an information-gathering device only, not as an ideally constituted selection procedure. In neither case should it assume the proportions of a final arbiter superseding all other techniques and sources of information.

Types of Employment Interviews

It is evident that the content of the selection interview may be varied. Different interviewers may ask different questions, concentrate on different parts of the man's prior experience, and attempt to develop estimates of different characteristics. It is also true, however, that the basic technique or procedure may be varied.

Patterned, or Structured, Interviews

The patterned, or structured, interview already has been noted in connection with the discussions of the consistency and accuracy of interviewer judgments. Often a detailed form is used, with the specific questions to be asked noted and space provided for the answers. The form is completed either during the interview or immediately afterward, from memory. In other cases, only the areas to be covered are established in advance, the order of coverage and actual question wording being left to the interviewer. Either way the more structured approach offers distinct advantages over the usual procedure, where different interviewers may go off in completely different directions depending on their own and the candidate's predilections. On the other hand, it should be recognized that information loss may occur because of a lack of flexibility.

Nondirective Procedures

The nondirective approach derives originally from psychotherapy and counseling. It permits the person being interviewed considerable leeway in determining the topics to be covered. The basic role of the interviewer is to reflect the feelings of the other person and to restate or repeat key words and phrases. This tends to elicit more detailed information from the interviewee, especially with reference to his emotional reactions, attitudes, and opinions. Because the candidate actually controls the content of the interview, this procedure may take the discussion far afield. It frequently yields a great deal of information about the prior experiences, early family life, and interpersonal relationships of the individual, but much of this often has no clear relationship to the employment decision. For this reason, the nondirective technique is usually mixed with a more directive, questioning approach when it is used in the selection interview.

Multiple and Group Interviews

Another procedure, which has proved to yield good validity (7), involves the use of more than one interviewer. Either the candidate spends time talking to several different people separately or he meets with a panel or board whose members alternate in asking him questions. This latter approach can easily be integrated into a patterned or structured format, and when this is done the resulting decisions and evaluations appear to maximize prediction of subsequent performance. Normally, the group evaluation is derived after discussion among the various interviewers, but independent estimates can be obtained from each man, and these then are averaged to achieve a final decision. The major disadvantage of any multiple interviewer procedure, of course, is that it can become very costly in terms of the total number of man-hours required. For this reason, it is usually reserved for use in selecting people for the higher level positions.

Stress Interviews

The stress approach achieved some acceptance in the business world after World War II as a result of its use during the war to select men for espionage work with the Office of Strategic Services. As used in industry, this procedure usually involves the induction of failure stress. The interviewer rather suddenly becomes quite aggressive, belittles the candidate, and throws him on the defensive. Reactions to this type of treatment are then observed.

Because it utilizes a sample of present behavior to formulate predictions, rather than focusing on past behavior, the stress interview is in many ways more a situational test than a selection interview. It has the disadvantage that rejected candidates who are subjected to this process can leave with a very negative image of the company, and even those whom the company may wish to hire can become so embittered that they will not accept an offer. This does not happen often, and usually a subsequent explanation can eradicate any bad feelings. When the fact that there is little positive evidence on the predictive power of the stress interview is added to these considerations, it seems very difficult to justify its use under normal circumstances. The selection situation itself appears to be anxiety-provoking enough for most people.

The Interview and Selection Models

It seems absolutely essential, if a company is to make effective use of the selection interview, for the interviewer to receive some systematic feedback on the validity of his decisions. In order to accomplish this, written evaluations of each candidate must be recorded at the conclusion of the interview. These interview ratings can then be compared at a later date with criterion information provided by the man's immediate superior or derived from some other source. In this way, the interviewer can modify his technique over time to maximize his predictive validity (2).

This approach suffers in that no follow-up can be made on those applicants who are not hired. However, in most companies, personnel recommendations are not followed religiously. For various reasons, those recommended for rejection are hired on occasion. In addition, other selection procedures may outweigh an original negative interview impression. Thus, there will be individuals in the follow-up group who have received rather low ratings, although the preponderant number will have had generally favorable evaluations in the interview.

One should not expect perfect success from these studies, of course. Yet, an interview should contribute something above what might be obtained by chance alone, and from the use of other techniques. Also, if a standardized interview form is used, individual questions can be analyzed to see if they discriminate between effective and ineffective employees. If certain questions appear not to be contributing to the predictive process, others can be substituted and evaluated in a similar manner.

References

1. Bellows, R. M., and M. F. Estep, *Employment Psychology: The Interview*. New York: Holt, Rinehart & Winston, 1961.
2. England, G. W., and D. G. Paterson, "Selection and Placement—The Past Ten Years," in H. G. Heneman et al. (eds.), *Employment Relations Research*. New York: Harper & Row, 1960, pp. 43-72.
3. Fear, R. A., *The Evaluation Interview*. New York: McGraw-Hill, 1958.
4. Ghiselli, E. E., "The Validity of a Personnel Interview," *Personnel Psychology*, Vol. 19 (1966), 389-394.
5. Kahn, R. L., and G. F. Cannell, *The Dynamics of Interviewing*. New York: Wiley, 1957.
6. Lopez, F. M., *Personnel Interviewing–Theory and Practice*. McGraw-Hill, 1965.
7. Mayfield, E. C., "The Selection Interview—A Re-evaluation of Published Research," *Personnel Psychology*, Vol. 17 (1964), 239-260.
8. McMurry, R. N., "Validating the Patterned Interview," *Personnel*, Vol. 23 (1947), 263-272.
9. Tiffin, J., and E. J. McCormick, *Industrial Psychology*, 5th ed., Englewood Cliffs, N.J.: Prentice-Hall, 1965.
10. Webster, E. C., *Decision-Making in the Employment Interview*. Montreal, Can.: Industrial Relations Centre, McGill Univ., 1964.
11. Weiss, D. J., and R. V. Dawis, "An Objective Validation of Factual Interview Data,"*Journal of Applied Psychology*, Vol. 44 (1960), 381-385.
12. Yonge, K. A. "The Value of the Interview: An Orientation and a Pilot Study," *Journal of Applied Psychology*, Vol. 49 (1956), 25-31.

Improvements in The Selection Interview

ROBERT E. CARLSON
PAUL W. THAYER
EUGENE C. MAYFIELD
DONALD A. PETERSON

The effectiveness and utility of the selection interview has again been seriously questioned as a result of several comprehensive reviews of the research literature.[1] Not one of these classic summary reviews of the interview research literature arrived at conclusions that could be classed as optimistic when viewed from an applied standpoint. Yet none of this is new information. As early as 1915, the validity of the selection interview was empirically questioned.[1] Despite the fact that it is common knowledge that the selection interview probably contributes little in the way of validity to the selection decision, it continues to be used. It is clear that no amount of additional evidence on the lack of validity will alter the role of the interview in selection. Future research should obviously be directed at understanding the mechanism of the interview and improving interview technology. As Schwab has stated, "Companies are not likely to abandon the use of the employment interview, nor is it necessarily desirable that they do so. But it is grossly premature to sit back comfortably and assume that employment interviews are satisfactory. It is even too early to dash off unsupported recommendations for their improvement. A great deal of research work remains, research which companies must be willing to sponsor before we can count the interview as a prime weapon in our selection arsenal."[3] This was essentially the conclusion that the Life Insurance Agency Management Association reached some six years ago. In addition, the life insurance industry, through LIAMA, took action and sponsored basic research on the selection interview.

The research reported here is an attempt to improve the use of the selection interview in the life insurance industry. The role of the interview in selection presented a particularly difficult problem for the life insurance industry where each agency manager is responsible for many of the traditional personnel management functions. In addition, these agencies are scattered across the U.S. and Canada and make centralizing the selection process difficult. In order to strengthen the role of the selection interview in each manager's selection system, LIAMA has been doing basic research on the selection interview for the past six years.

The research reported here is part of a long-run research program concerned with how interviewers make employment decisions. Its purpose is to try to determine the limits of an interviewer's capability in extending his judgment into the future. This summary covers the early studies in a program of research to develop interim tools and the training necessary to make the selection interview a useful selection instrument.

The first step in the interview research program was to observe and record numerous interviews, to interview in depth the interviewers on their decision process, to conduct group decision conferences where the interviewers discussed their percep-

Reprinted by permission of the authors and the publisher from *Personnel Journal,* vol. 50 (April 1971), no. 4, pp. 268-75, 317.

tion of their decision process for a given taped interview, and to examine the published research on the selection interview. Based upon this information, a model of the selection interview was constructed that specified as many of the influences operating during the interview as could be determined. Initially, there appeared to be four main classes of influences operating to affect/limit the decision of the interviewer. They were:
- The physical and psychological properties of the interviewee
- The physical and psychological properties of the interviewer
- The situation/environment in which the interviewer works
- The task or type of judgment the interviewer must make

The research strategy has been to systematically manipulate and control the variables specified in the model, trying to eliminate variables that do not have any influence, trying to assess the magnitude of those variables that have an influence, and adding variables that other research has shown to be promising. The first section of this article will describe some of the research findings; the second section will describe some of the materials that have been developed; and the third section will describe the interviewer training that has been developed.

What Are Some Findings?

Structured vs. Unstructured Interviews

One question that has often been asked is, "What kind of interview is best?" What interview style—structured, where the interviewer follows a set procedure; or unstructured, where the interviewer has no set procedure and where he follows the interviewee's lead—results in more effective decisions? In this study, live interviews were used. Each interviewee was interviewed three times. Interviewers used the following three types of interviewing strategies: structured, where the interviewer asked questions only from an interview guide; semistructured, where the interviewer followed an interview guide, but could ask questions about any other areas he wished; and unstructured, where the interviewer had no interview guide and could do as he wished. The basic question involved was the consistency with which people interviewing the same interviewee could agree with each other. If the interviewers' judgments were not consistent—one interviewer saying the applicant was good and the other saying he was bad—no valid prediction of job performance could be made from interview data. Agreement among interviewers is essential if one is to say that the procedure used has the potential for validity.

The results indicated that only the structured interview generated information that enabled interviewers to agree with each other. Under structured conditions, the interviewer knew what to ask and what to do with the information he received. Moreover, the interviewer applied the same frame of reference to each applicant, since he covered the same areas for each. In the less-structured interviews, the managers received additional information, but it seemed to be unorganized and made their evaluation task more difficult. Thus, a highly-structured interview has the greatest potential for valid selection.[4]

Effect of Interviewer Experience

In the past it had been assumed that one way to become an effective interviewer was through experience. In fact, it has been hypothesized that interviewers who have had the same amount of experience would evaluate a job applicant similarly.[5] To determine whether this was indeed the case, a study was done that involved managers who had conducted differing numbers of interviews over the same period. Managers were then compared who had similar as well as differing concentrations of interviewing experience. It was found that when evaluating the same recruits, interviewers with similar experiences did not agree with each other to any greater degree than did interviewers with differing experiences. It was concluded that interviewers benefit very little from day-to-day interviewing experience and apparently the conditions necessary for learning are not present in the day-to-day interviewer's job situation.[6] This implied that systematic training is needed, with some feedback mechanism built into the selection procedure, to enable interviewers to learn from their experiences; the job performance predictions made by the interviewer must be compared with how the recruit actually performs on the job.

Situational Pressures

One of the situational variables studied was how pressure for results affected the evaluation of a new recruit. One large group of managers was told to assume that they were behind their recruiting quota, that it was October, and that the home office had just called. Another group was ahead of quota; for a third group, no quota situation existed. All three groups of managers evaluated descriptions of the same job applicants. It was found that being behind recruiting quota impaired the judgment of those managers. They evaluated the same recruits as actually having greater potential and said they would hire more of them than did the other two groups of managers.[7]

One more highly significant question was raised: Are all managers, regardless of experience, equally vulnerable to this kind of pressure? Managers were asked how frequently they conducted interviews. Regardless of how long the person had been a manager, those who had had a high rate of interviewing experience—many interviews in a given period of time—were less susceptible to pressures than were those with a low interviewing rate. The interviewers with less interviewing experience relied more on subjective information and reached a decision with less information. It was concluded that one way to overcome this problem of lack of concentrated interviewing experience was through the general use of a standardized interview procedure and intensive training in its use.

Standard of Comparison

Another condition studied was the standards managers applied in evaluating recruits. It was found, for example, that if a manager evaluated a candidate who was just average after evaluating three or four very unfavorable candidates in a row, the average one would be evaluated very favorably.[8] When managers were evaluating more than one recruit at a time, they used other recruits as a standard.[9] Each recruit was compared to all other recruits. Thus, managers did not have an absolute standard —who they thought looked good was partly determined by the persons with whom they were comparing the recruit. This indicated that some system was necessary to aid a manager in evaluating a recruit. The same system should be applicable to each recruit. This implied that some standardized evaluation system was necessary to reduce the large amount of information developed from an interview to a manageable number of constant dimensions.

Effect of Appearance

Some of the early studies utilized photographs to try to determine how much of an effect appearance had on the manager's decision. A favorably rated photograph was paired with a favorably rated personal history description and also with an unfavorably rated personal history. It was found that appearance had its greatest effect on the interviewer's final rating when it complemented the personal history information.[10] Even when appearance and personal history information were the same (both favorable or both unfavorable), the personal history information was given twice as much weight as appearance. However, the relationship is not a simple one and only emphasized the need for a more complete system to aid the manager in selection decision-making.

Effect of Interview Information on Valid Test Results

In many selection situations, valid selection tests are used in conjunction with the interview data in arriving at a selection decision. Two recent studies have investigated how the emphasis placed on valid test results (*Aptitude Index Battery*) is altered by the more subjective interview data. Managers do place great emphasis on the AIB knowing that the score does generate a valid prediction.

However, how much weight is given to the score depends on other conditions; e.g., a low-scoring applicant is judged better if preceded by a number of poor applicants, unfavorable information is given much greater weight if it is uncovered just prior to ending the interview, etc. This finding suggested that what is needed is some system that places the interview information and other selection information in their proper perspective.[11]

Interview Accuracy

A recent study tried to determine how accurately managers can recall what an applicant says during an interview. Prior to the interview the managers were given the interview guide, pencils, and paper, and were told to perform as if *they* were conducting the interview. A 20-minute video tape of a selection interview was played for a group of 40 managers. Following the video tape presentation, the managers were given a 20-question test. All questions were straightforward and factual. Some managers missed none, while some missed as many as 15 out of 20 items. The average number was 10 wrong. In a short 20-minute interview, half the managers could not report accurately on the information produced during the interview! On the other hand, those managers who had been following the interview guide and taking notes were quite accurate on the test; note-taking in conjunction with a guide appears to be essential.

Given that interviewers differed in the accuracy with which they were able to report what they heard, the next question appeared to be "How does this affect their evaluation?" In general it was found that those interviewers who were least accurate in their recollections rated the interviewee higher and with less variability, while the more accurate interviewers rated the interviewee average or lower and with greater variability. Thus, those interviewers who did not have the factual information at their disposal assumed that the interview was generally favorable and rated the interviewee more favorable in all areas. Those interviewers who were able to reproduce more of the factual information rated the interviewee lower and recognized his intra-individual differences by using more of the rating scale. This implied that the less accurate interviewers selected a "halo strategy" when evaluating the interviewee, while the more accurate interviewers used an individual differences strategy. Whether this is peculiar to the individual interviewer or due to the fact that the interviewer did or didn't have accurate information at his disposal is, of course, unanswerable from this data.

Can Interviewers Predict?

The ultimate purpose of the selection interview is to collect factual and attitudinal information that will enable the interviewer to make accurate and valid job behavior predictions for the interviewee. The interviewer does this by recording the factual information for an applicant, evaluating the meaning of the information in terms of what the interviewee will be able to do on the job in question, and extending these evaluations into the future in the form of job behavior predictions. The question is, "How reliably can a group of interviewers make predictions for a given interviewee?" Without high inter-interviewer agreement, the potential for interview validity is limited to a few interviewers and cannot be found in the interview process itself.

In this study, a combination of movies and audio tapes were played simulating an interview. In addition, each of the 42 manager-interviewers was given a detailed written summary of the interview. The total interview lasted almost three hours and covered the interviewee's work history, work experience, education and military experience, life insurance holdings, attitude toward the life insurance career, family life, financial soundness, social life and social mobility, and future goals and aspirations. After hearing and seeing the interview and after studying a 20-page written summary, each interviewer was asked to make a decision either to continue the selection process or to terminate negotiations. In addition, each interviewer was asked to make a list of all the factual information he considered while making his decision. Also, the interviewer was to rate the interviewee in 31 different areas. The ratings were descriptive of the interviewee's past accomplishments, such as his job success pattern, the quantity and quality of his education, his family situation, financial knowledge and soundness, etc. Finally, the interviewers were asked to make job behavior predictions in 28 different job specific activities such as, Could he use the telephone for business purposes? Could he make cold calls? Would he keep records? Would he take direction? What about his market?

The interviewers agreed quite well with each other on which facts they reportedly considered in making their employment decision. Almost 70 percent of the factual statements were recorded by all the interviewers. The remaining 30 percent of the factual statements were specific to interviewers. This tended to confirm a hypothesis of Mayfield and Carlson where they postulate that the stereotypes held by interviewers consist of general as well as specific content.[12] It was concluded that interviewers do record and use similar factual information with agreement.

The interviewers agreed less well with each other on the evaluation or value placed on the facts. The median inter-interviewer correlation was .62, with a low of .07 and a high of .82. This means that the interviewers still agreed reasonably well on the evaluation—good vs. bad—quality of the information they received. They would make similar selection-rejection decisions.

The job behavior predictions of the interviewers, however, were not nearly as high in agreement. The median inter-interviewer correlation was .33 with a low of —.21 and a high of .67. This means that the interviewers do not agree with each other on how well the interviewee will perform the job of a life insurance agent in 28 different areas. In addition, those predictions that required the interviewer to extend his judgment further into the future had significantly greater inter-interviewer variability than did those predictions that could be verified in a shorter period of time. Thus, interviewers can agree more with each other's predictions if the job behavior is of a more immediate nature.

These findings imply that although interviewers probably use much the same information in making a decision, they will evaluate it somewhat differently. Furthermore, the interviewers are not able to agree on how well the individual will perform on the job.

Thus, it was concluded that interviewers evaluate essentially similar things in an applicant; they agree reasonably well whether an applicant's past record is good or bad, but they cannot agree on good or bad for what. Yet here, and only here, is where the clinical function of the interviewer is difficult to replace with a scoring system. In being able to make accurate and valid job behavior predictions, the interview can pay for itself in terms of planning an applicant's early job training and as a mechanism whereby a supervisor can learn early how to manage an applicant. In order for the interviewer to be able to make accurate and valid job behavior predictions, it follows that he must have a feedback system whereby he can learn from his past experiences. Only through accurate feedback in language similar to the behavior predictions can the interviewer learn to make job behavior predictions. The results further imply that the interviewer must be equipped with a complete selection system that coordinates all the selection steps and provides the interviewer with as relevant and complete information as possible when he makes job behavior predictions.

Conclusions

These early studies in LIAMA's interview research program provided little in the way of optimism for the traditional approach to the selection interview. However, this research did indicate specific areas where improvements in selection and interview technology could be made. It did indicate where interim improvements could be tried and evaluated while the long-term research on the interview continued.

Two major applied implications may be derived from the interview research to date. First, the selection interview should be made an integral part of an over-all selection procedure, and to accomplish this, new and additional materials are needed. The new materials should include a broad-gauge, comprehensive, structured interview guide; standardized evaluation and prediction forms that aid the interviewer in summarizing information from all steps in the selection process; and an evaluation system that provides feedback to the interviewer in language similar to the preemployment job behavior predictions he must make. The second major applied implication is that an intensive training program for interviewers is necessary if interviewers are to initially learn enough in common to increase the probability of obtaining general validity from the selection interview. Thus, the early studies have provided specific information that has been used to change the way selection is carried out in the insurance industry.

Implementation: Development of a Selection Process

As a result of and based upon the early interview research, LIAMA constructed the *Agent Selection Kit*. This is a complete agent selection procedure to be used by agency branch managers and general agents in the field. Selection begins when the agency head secures the name of a prospective recruit and ends when the new agent has been selling for six months or when negotiations or employment is terminated. Because research demonstrated the necessity of formally taking into consideration each step in the selection process, each step in the procedure is carefully placed to maximize the potential of succeeding and following steps. The *Agent Selection Kit* introduced the following new ideas to the insurance industry:

(1) *Selection should more properly be viewed as manpower development*. The *Agent Selection Kit* is a completely integrated process, more properly described as

manpower development; it goes beyond just selection. The assumption is that if industry is really going to have an appreciable effect on the manpower problem, it will have to think of recruiting, selection, training, and supervision as parts of a total manpower development process and not as entities by themselves. Quantity and quality of recruiting have an impact on selection—selection affects training—training capabilities, in turn, should affect selection. Unless viewed as a continuous, dependent process, maximum use cannot be made of the information the tools provide. If viewed as a complete process, the information gained from each step is carried forward to make future steps and the final decision more powerful.

(2) *Organizational differences must be taken into consideration in selection.* Because the *Agent Selection Kit* is a complete selection process, it can be modified to meet company and agency differences. By clearly spelling out the philosophy and principles behind the steps in the *Agent Selection Kit,* the company and the agency head are able to evaluate what is being gained or lost by altering the steps in selection. Further, because the agency head is forced to make job behavior predictions, he can begin to consider each recruit in terms of his particular agency needs, style, and strengths. Agency differences as well as individual differences enter into the employment decision in a systematic manner.

(3) *A career with any company should be entered into based on realistic job expectations.*[13] The company should know what the job recruit expects from his association with the company. Under such a condition, the manager can make a manpower development decision that properly considers selection, early training, motivation, and supervision practices of the applicant in question. The job recruit should know what the company expects of him, how the company is going to help him accomplish these goals, and the difficulties and benefits he may encounter in undertaking the job. With such knowledge, the recruit can make more than a job decision. He can make a career decision. The creation of realistic expectations further implies that the employment decision be one of "mutual consent." Professional management of the future will not be able to rely on a slanted job presentation to attract recruits to a career in hopes that one or two applicants will succeed. Manpower development decisions will replace selection decisions. The *Agent Selection Kit* is built around the concept of "mutual consent" with respect to a career decision. There are already indications that the recruit of the future will respond to a "mutual exploration" theme, where together he and the manager will examine the individual's future in an industry. The *Agent Selection Kit* provides a systematic fact-finding procedure that appeals to the recruit.

(4) *The selection interview should proceed according to a highly-structured format.* The *Agent Selection Kit* contains two self-contained structured interview guides. The first interview guide is to be used with applicants who have had extensive prior work history and concentrates on this work experience. The alternate interview guide is to be used with applicants just completing their education or military experiences and without any work experience. In addition, both interview guides cover the recruit's education, military experience, attitude toward insurance and toward the insurance agent's job, family commitments, finances, social mobility, social life, and future goals and aspirations. The interview guides present the initial series of questions and several alternative probes. Experience and pretesting have indicated that recruits are receptive to a structured approach and that interviewers can learn to use the guides after brief, but intensive, training.

(5) *Employment decisions should be based on predictions of future job behavior.* The *Agent Selection Kit* considers decision-making from the point of view of a prediction of future behavior, rather than from vague, over-all impressions of potential or

character. The manager manages the agent's activity, use of the telephone, record-keeping, prospecting, etc. The *Agent Selection Kit* enables the manager to make predictions about such job behaviors.

(6) *The manager should be able to learn from and correct his selection system.* The *Agent Selection Kit* procedure contains a built-in "feedback system" that enables the manager to learn from and correct his selection process. LIAMA interview research has shown that managers do not learn from the traditional approach to selection interviewing. To correct this, the *Agent Selection Kit* includes an Agent Performance Rating Form that the manager uses to compare to his final decision ratings. Discrepancies between his prediction and results point to areas in his selection and early training process that need extra effort.

Implementation: Training in Selection and Interviewing

To ensure at least uniform initial introduction to the material, LIAMA designed a three-day skill-building workshop. Three general training objectives and 16 specific behavioral objectives served as guides in setting up the training program. The first general goal was to develop in each trainee *knowledge* of selection and interview techniques; the second goal was to create favorable *attitudes* in the managers toward selection and self-confidence in their ability to conduct a technically good selection interview; and third, to develop *skill* in actually using the selection and interview materials. As a result of participating in the training, the agency heads are to actually be better at selection and interviewing than they were prior to training, to know they are better, and to be able to immediately use the new material with some skill. Thus, the goals of the training are to change attitudes as well as to develop knowledge and skill. These specifications dictated that the workshops be built around small-sized classes, class participation, and practice with standardized case material and controlled feedback.

To accomplish the goals of the training program, the first step in the workshop is to help the agency manager to understand and accept the principles behind the steps in the selection process. This helps to make the trainees receptive to discarding their current approach to selection and to accepting the new approach. Once the agency head accepts the logic of the principles on which the *Agent Selection Kit* is based, the next step is to get the trainee to recognize and question how he is currently conducting his selection process. This is accomplished through the use of edited tapes that demonstrate some of the effects of violating the selection principles. At the end of this first phase of the training, the agency heads are receptive to a new procedure and are aware of what a good procedure should contain.

The skill training that follows is designed to make the agency head more proficient in the use of the interview and evaluation procedures. The interview technique training includes taped examples, practice, and critique. The final evaluation practice sessions are extremely important to agency heads. Here the manager is asked to combine information from all the selection methods he has utilized—the interview, reference checks, credit reports, interview with the wife, precontract training, etc. The manager practices making job behavior predictions in areas such as use of the telephone, night work, markets, prospecting activities, etc. For the first time, managers recognize that they will not be managing the recruit's character or how impressive he looks, but rather they recognize that they must manage his work activities. Managers begin to recognize that selection should try to predict the recruit's performance in these activities.

During the workshops, the participants' attitudes swing from skepticism to receptivity, from impatience with the training detail to complete acceptance. These swings in attitude are built into the schedule, since early experimental workshops showed that they were necessary to modify and solidify managers' attitudes.

The managers leave their workshop with greater knowledge, with a skill that is well along in development, and with much greater self-confidence in their selection and early training procedure that they can put into practice immediately.

The Future

The *Agent Selection Kit* was introduced to LIAMA's 300-plus member companies in 1969. By mid-1970, 40 major life insurance companies had introduced it to their general agents and managers. Obviously, at this time it is much too early to evaluate its effectiveness. However, it is currently being evaluated as part of LIAMA's research program on the selection interview. In addition, it also provides a natural field setting for further pure research on the selection interview. Thus, LIAMA's research on the interview is an example of pure research generating an improved product, which, in turn, furthers the pure research effort.

Notes

1. See, for example, R. Wagner, "The Employment Interview: A Critical Summary," *Personnel Psychology*, Vol. 2 (1949), pp. 17-46.

G. W. England and D. G. Paterson, "Selection and Placement—The Past Ten Years," in H. G. Henneman, Jr., et al. (Editors), *Employment Relations Research: A Summary and Appraisal*, New York: Harper, 1960, pp. 43-72.

E. C. Mayfield, "The Selection Interview: A Reevaluation of Published Research," *Personnel Psychology*, Vol. 17 (1964), pp. 239-260.

L. Ulrich and D. Trumbo, "The Selection Interview Since 1949," *Psychological Bulletin*, Vol. 63 (1965), pp. 100-116.

2. W. D. Scott, "The Scientific Selection of Salesmen," *Advertising and Selling*, Vol. 25 (1915), pp. 5-6 and 94-96.

3. D. P. Schwab, "Why Interview? A Critique," *Personnel Journal*, Vol. 48, No. 2 (1969), p. 129.

4. R. E. Carlson, D. P. Schwab, and H. G. Henneman III, "Agreement Among Selection Interview Styles," *Journal of Industrial Psychology*, Vol. 5, No. 1 (1970), pp. 8-17.

5. P. M. Rowe, "Individual Differences in Assessment Decisions," Unpublished doctoral thesis, McGill University, 1960.

6. R. E. Carlson, "Selection Interview Decisions: The Effect of Interviewer Experience, Relative Quota Situation, and Applicant Sample on Interviewer Decisions," *Personnel Psychology*, Vol. 20 (1967), pp. 259-280.

7. Ibid.

8. R. E. Carlson, "Effects of Applicant Sample on Ratings of Valid Information in an Employment Setting," *Journal of Applied Psychology*, Vol. 54 (1970), pp. 217-222.

9. R. E. Carlson, "Selection Interview Decisions: The Effect of Mode of Applicant Presentation on Some Outcome Measures," *Personnel Psychology*, Vol. 21 (1968), pp.193-207.

10. R. E. Carlson, "The Relative Influence of Appearance and Factual Written Information on an Interviewer's Final Rating," *Journal of Applied Psychology*, Vol. 51 (1967), pp. 461-468.

11. R. E. Carlson, "The Effect of Interview Information in Altering Valid Impressions," *Journal of Applied Psychology*, In Press.

12. E. C. Mayfield and R. E. Carlson, "Selection Interview Decisions: First Results from a Long-Term Research Project," *Personnel Psychology*, Vol. 19 (1966), pp. 41-53.

13. Life Insurance Agency Management Association, *"Realistic" Job Expectations and Survival*, Research Report 1964-2 (File 432).

Section C
Testing for Selection

Nature and Use of Psychological Tests

ANNE ANASTASI

... Although the general public may still associate psychological tests most closely with "IQ tests" and with tests designed to detect emotional disorders, these tests represent only a small proportion of the available types of instruments. The major categories of psychological tests [are] tests of general intellectual level, traditionally called intelligence tests: tests of separate abilities, including multiple aptitude batteries, tests of special aptitudes, and achievement tests; and personality tests, concerned with measures of emotional and motivational traits, interpersonal behavior, interests, attitudes, and other nonintellectual characteristics.

In the face of such diversity in nature and purpose, what are the common differentiating characteristics of psychological tests? How do psychological tests differ from other methods of gathering information about individuals? The answer is to be found in certain fundamental features of both the construction and use of tests. It is with these features that the present [article] is concerned.

What Is a Psychological Test?

A psychological test is essentially an objective and standardized measure of a sample of behavior. Psychological tests are like tests in any other science, insofar as observations are made on a small but carefully chosen *sample* of an individual's behavior. In this respect, the psychologist proceeds in much the same way as the chemist who tests a patient's blood or a community's water supply by analyzing one or more samples of it. If the psychologist wishes to test the extent of a child's vocabulary, a clerk's ability to perform arithmetic computations, or a pilot's eye-hand coordination, he examines their performance with a representative set of words, arithmetic problems, or motor tests. Whether or not the test adequately covers the behavior under consideration obviously depends on the number and nature of items in the sample. For

Reprinted with permission of MacMillan Publishing Co., Inc., from *Psychological Patterns* (3rd ed.), by Anne Anastasi. Copyright © 1968 by Anne Anastasi.

example, an arithmetic test consisting of only five problems, or one including only multiplication items, would be a poor measure of the individual's computational skill. A vocabulary test composed entirely of baseball terms would hardly provide a dependable estimate of a child's total range of vocabulary.

The *diagnostic* or *predictive value* of a psychological test depends on the degree to which it serves as an indicator of a relatively broad and significant area of behavior. Measurement of the behavior sample directly covered by the test is rarely, if ever, the goal of psychological testing. The child's knowledge of a particular list of 50 words is not, in itself, of great interest. Nor is the job applicant's performance on a specific set of 20 arithmetic problems of much importance. If, however, it can be demonstrated that there is a close correspondence between the child's knowledge of the word list and his total mastery of vocabulary, or between the applicant's score on the arithmetic problems and his computational performance on the job, then the tests are serving their purpose.

It should be noted in this connection that the test items need not resemble closely the behavior the test is to predict. It is only necessary that an empirical correspondence be demonstrated between the two. The degree of similarity between the test sample and the predicted behavior may vary widely. At one extreme, the test may coincide completely with a part of the behavior to be predicted. An example might be a foreign vocabulary test in which the students are examined on 20 of the 50 new words they have studied; another example is provided by the road test taken prior to obtaining a driver's license. A lesser degree of similarity is illustrated by many vocational aptitude tests administered prior to job training, in which there is only a moderate resemblance between the tasks performed on the job and those incorporated in the test. At the other extreme one finds projective personality tests such as the Rorschach inkblot test, in which an attempt is made to predict from the subject's associations to inkblots how he will react to other people, to emotionally toned stimuli, and to other complex, every-day-life situations. Despite their superficial differences, all these tests consist of samples of the individual's behavior. And each must prove its worth by an empirically demonstrated correspondence between the subject's performance on the test and in other situations.

Whether the term "diagnosis" or the term "prediction" is employed in this connection also represents a minor distinction. Prediction commonly connotes a temporal estimate, the individual's future performance on a job, for example, being forecast from his present test performance. In a broader sense, however, even the diagnosis of present condition, such as mental retardation or emotional disorder, implies a prediction of what the individual will do in situations other than the present test. It is logically simpler to consider all tests as behavior samples from which predictions regarding other behavior can be made. Different types of tests can then be characterized as variants of this basic pattern.

Another point that should be considered at the outset pertains to the concept of *capacity*. It is entirely possible, for example, to devise a test for predicting how well an individual can learn French before he has even begun the study of French. Such a test would involve a sample of the types of behavior required to learn the new language, but would in itself presuppose no knowledge of French. It could then be said that this test measures the individual's "capacity" or "potentiality" for learning French. Such terms should, however, be used with caution in reference to psychological tests. Only in the sense that a present behavior sample can be used as an indicator of other, future behavior can we speak of a test measuring "capacity." No psychological test can do more than measure behavior. Whether such behavior can serve as an effective index of other behavior can be determined only by empirical try-out.

Standardization

It will be recalled that in the initial definition a psychological test was described as a standardized measure. Standardization implies *uniformity of procedure* in administering and scoring the test. If the scores obtained by different individuals are to be comparable, testing conditions must obviously be the same for all. Such a requirement is only a special application of the need for controlled conditions in all scientific observations. In a test situation, the single independent variable is usually the individual being tested.

In order to secure uniformity of testing conditions, the test constructor provides detailed directions for administering each newly developed test. The formulation of such directions is a major part of the standardization of a new test. Such standardization extends to the exact materials employed, time limits, oral instructions to subjects, preliminary demonstrations, ways of handling queries from subjects, and every other detail of the testing situation. Many other, more subtle factors may influence the subject's performance on certain tests. Thus, in giving instructions or presenting problems orally, consideration must be given to the rate of speaking, tone of voice, inflection, pauses, and facial expression. In a test involving the detection of absurdities, for example, the correct answer may be given away by smiling or pausing when the crucial word is read. . . .

Another important step in the standardization of a test is the establishment of *norms*. Without norms, test scores cannot be interpreted. Psychological tests have no predetermined standards of passing or failing. An individual's score can be evaluated only by comparing it with the scores obtained by others. As its name implies, a norm is the normal or average performance. Thus, if normal eight-year-old children complete 12 out of 50 problems correctly on a particular arithmetic reasoning test, then the eight-year-old norm on this test corresponds to a score of 12. The latter is known as the raw score on the test. It may be expressed as number of correct items, time required to complete a task, number of errors, or some other objective measure appropriate to the content of the test. Such a raw score is meaningless until evaluated in terms of a suitable set of norms.

In the process of standardizing a test, it must be administered to a large, representative sample of the type of subjects for whom it is designed. This group, known as the standardization sample, serves to establish the norms. Such norms indicate not only the average performance but also the relative frequency of varying degrees of deviation above and below the average. It is thus possible to evaluate different degrees of superiority and inferiority. . . .

It might also be noted that norms are established for personality tests in essentially the same way as for aptitude tests. The norm on a personality test is not necessarily the most desirable or "ideal" performance, any more than a perfect or errorless score is the norm on an aptitude test. On both types of tests, the norm corresponds to the performance of typical or average individuals. On dominance-submission tests, for example, the norm falls at an intermediate point representing the degree of dominance or submission manifested by the average individual. Similarly, in an emotional adjustment inventory, the norm does not ordinarily correspond to a complete absence of unfavorable or maladaptive responses, since a few such responses occur in the majority of "normal" individuals in the standardization sample. It is thus apparent that psychological tests, of whatever type, are based on empirically established norms.

Objective Measurement Of Difficulty

Reference to the definition of a psychological test with which this discussion opened will show that such a test was characterized as an objective as well as a standardized measure. In what specific ways are such tests objective? Some aspects of the objectivity of psychological tests have already been touched on in the discussion of standardization. Thus, the administration, scoring, and interpretation of scores are objective insofar as they are independent of the subjective judgment of the individual examiner. Any one individual should theoretically obtain the identical score on a test regardless of who happens to be his examiner. This is not entirely so, of course, since perfect standardization and objectivity have not been attained in practice. But at least such objectivity is the goal of test construction and has been achieved to a reasonably high degree in most tests.

There are other major ways in which psychological tests can be properly described as objective. The determination of the difficulty level of an item or of a whole test, and the measurement of test reliability and validity, are based on objective, empirical procedures. The concepts of reliability and validity will be considered in subsequent sections. We shall turn our attention first to the concept of difficulty.

When Binet and Simon prepared their original, 1905 scale for the measurement of intelligence, they arranged the 30 items of the scale in order of increasing difficulty. Such difficulty, it will be recalled, was determined by trying out the items on 50 normal and a few mentally retarded children. The items correctly solved by the largest number of children were, *ipso facto,* taken to be the easiest; those passed by relatively few children were regarded as more difficult items. By this procedure, an empirical order difficulty was established. This early example typifies the objective measurement of difficulty level, which is now common practice in psychological test construction.

Not only the arrangement but also the selection of items for inclusion in a test can be determined by the proportion of subjects in the trial samples who pass each item. Thus, if there is a bunching of items at the easy or difficult end of the scale, some items can be discarded. Similarly, if items are sparse in certain portions of the difficulty range, new items can be added to fill the gaps. . . .

The difficulty level of the test as a whole is, of course, directly dependent on the difficulty of the items that make up the test. A comprehensive check of the difficulty of the total test for the population for which it is designed is provided by the distribution of total scores. If the standardization sample is a representative cross section of such a population, then it is generally expected that the scores will fall roughly into a *normal distribution curve.* In other words, there should be a clustering of individuals near the center of the range and a gradual tapering off as the extremes are approached. A theoretical normal curve, with all irregularities eliminated, is shown in Figure 1. In plotting such a frequency distribution, scores are indicated on the baseline, and frequencies, or number of persons obtaining each score, on the vertical axis. A smooth curve like the one illustrated is closely approximated when very large samples are tested.

Let us suppose, however, that the obtained distribution curve is not normal but clearly skewed, as illustrated in Figures 2A and 2B. The first of these distributions, with a piling of scores at the low end, suggests that the test has too high a floor for the group under consideration, lacking a sufficient number of easy items to discriminate properly at the lower end of the range. The result is that persons who would normally scatter over a considerable range obtain zero or near-zero scores on this test. A peak at the low end of the scale is therefore obtained. This artificial piling of scores is illustrated schematically in Figure 3, in which a normally distributed group yields a skewed distribution on a particular test. The opposite skewness is illustrated in Figure 2B, with the scores piled up at the upper end, a finding that suggests insufficient test ceiling. Administering a test designed for the general population to selected samples of college or graduate students will usually yield such a skewed distribution, a number of students obtaining nearly perfect scores. With such a test, it is impossible to measure individual differences among the more able subjects in the group. If more difficult items had been included in the test, some individuals would undoubtedly have scored higher than the present test permits.

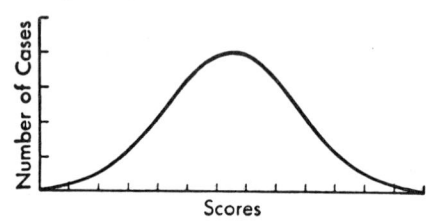

Figure 1. A Normal Distribution Curve

When the standardization sample yields a markedly nonnormal distribution on a test, the difficulty level of the test is ordinarily modified until a normal curve is approximated. Depending on the type of deviation from normality that appears, easier or more difficult items may be added, other items eliminated or modified, the position of items in the scale altered, or the scoring weights assigned to certain responses revised.

A. Piling at Lower End of the Scale   B. Piling at Upper End of the Scale

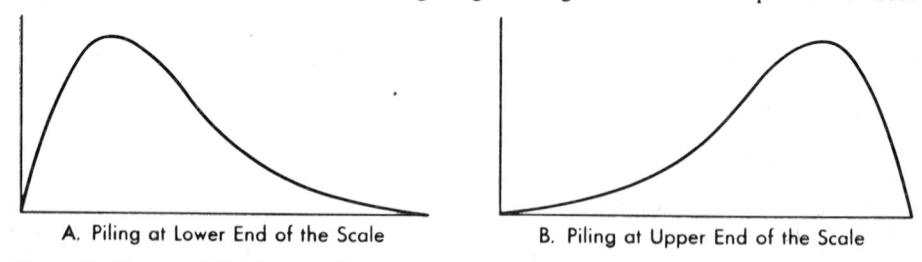

Figure 2. Skewed Distribution Curves

Such adjustments are continued until the distribution becomes at least roughly normal. Under these conditions, the most likely score, obtained by the largest number of subjects, usually corresponds to about 50 percent correct items. To the laymen who is unfamiliar with the methods of psychological test construction, a 50 percent score may seem shockingly low. It is sometimes objected, on this basis, that the examiner has set too low a standard of passing on the test. Or the inference is drawn that the group tested is a particularly poor one. Both conclusions, of course, are totally meaningless when viewed in the light of the procedures followed in developing psychological tests. Such tests are deliberately constructed and specifically modified so as to yield a mean score of approximately 50 percent correct. Only in this way can the maximum differentiation between individuals at all ability levels be obtained with the test. With a mean of approximately 50 percent correct items, there is the maximum opportunity for a normal distribution, with individual scores spreading widely at both extremes.[1]

Reliability

How good is this test? Does it really work? These questions could—and occasionally do—result in long hours of futile discussion. Subjective opinions, hunches, and personal biases may lead, on the one hand, to extravagant claims regarding what a particular test can accomplish and, on the other hand, to stubborn rejection. The only way in which questions such as these can be conclusively answered is by empirical trial. The *objective evaluation* of psychological tests involves primarily the determination of the reliability and the validity of the test in specified situations.

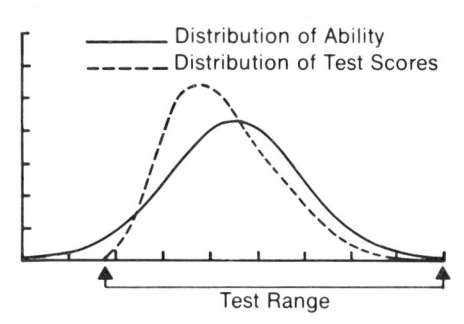

Figure 3. Skewness Resulting from Insufficient "Test Floor"

As used in psychometrics, the term reliability always means consistency. Test reliability is the consistency of scores obtained by the same persons when retested with the identical test or with an equivalent form of the test. If a child receives an IQ of 110 on Monday and an IQ of 80 when retested on Friday, it is obvious that little or no confidence can be put in either score. Similarly, if in one set of 50 words an individual identifies 40 correctly, whereas in another, supposedly equivalent set he gets a score of only 20 right, then neither score can be taken as a dependable index of his verbal comprehension. To be sure, in both illustrations it is possible that only one of the two scores is in error, but this could be demonstrated only by further retests. From the given data, we can conclude only that both scores cannot be right. Whether one or neither is an adequate estimate of the individual's ability in vocabulary cannot be established without additional information.

Before a psychological test is released for general use, a thorough, objective check of its reliability must be carried out. . . . Reliability can be checked with reference to temporal fluctuations, the particular selection of items or behavior sample constituting the test, the role of different examiners or scorers, and other aspects of the testing situation. It is essential to specify the type of reliability and the method employed to determine it, because the same test may vary in these different aspects. The number and nature of individuals on whom reliability was checked should likewise be reported. With such information, the test user can predict whether the test will be about equally reliable for the group with which he expects to use it, or whether it is likely to be more reliable or less reliable.

Validity

Undoubtedly the most important question to be asked about any psychological test concerns its validity, i.e., the degree to which the test actually measures what it purports to measure. Validity provides a direct check on how well the test fulfills its function. The determination of validity usually requires independent, external *criteria* of whatever the test is designed to measure. For example, if a medical aptitude test is to be used in selecting promising applicants for medical school, ultimate success in medical school would be a criterion. In the process of validating such a test, it would be administered to a large group of students at the time of their admission to medical school. Some measure of performance in medical school would eventually be obtained for each student on the basis of grades, ratings by instructors, success or failure in completing training, and the like. Such a composite measure constitutes the criterion with which each student's initial test score is to be correlated. A high correlation, or *validity coefficient,* would signify that those individuals who scored high on the test had been relatively successful in medical school, whereas those scoring low on the test had done poorly in medical school. A low correlation would indicate little correspondence between test score and criterion measure and hence poor validity for the test. The validity coefficient enables us to determine how closely the criterion performance could have been predicted from the test scores.

In a similar manner, tests designed for other purposes can be validated against appropriate criteria. A vocational aptitude test, for example, can be validated against on-the-job success of a trial group of new employees. A pilot aptitude battery can be validated against achievement in flight training. Tests designed for broader and more varied uses are validated against a number of criteria and their validity can be established only by the gradual accumulation of data from many different kinds of investigations.

The reader may have noticed an apparent paradox in the concept of test validity. If it is necessary to follow up the subjects or in other ways to obtain independent measures of what the test is trying to predict, why not dispense with the test? The answer to this riddle is to be found in the distinction between the validation group on the one hand and the groups on which the test will eventually be employed for operational purposes on the other. Before the test is ready for use, its validity must be established on a representative sample of subjects. The scores of these persons are not themselves employed for operational purposes but serve only in the process of testing the test. If the test proves valid by this method, it can then be used on other samples in the absence of criterion measures.

It might still be argued that we would only need to wait for the criterion measure to mature, or become available, on *any* group in order to obtain the information that the test is trying to predict. But such a procedure would be so wasteful of time and energy as to be prohibitive in most instances. Thus, we could determine which applicants will succeed on a job or which students will satisfactorily complete college by admitting all who apply and waiting for subsequent developments! It is the very wastefulness of such a procedure that tests are designed to reduce. By means of tests, the individual's eventual performance in such situations can be predicted with a determinable margin of error. The more valid the test, of course, the smaller will be this margin of error. . . .

Validity tells us more than the degree to which the test is fulfilling its function. It actually tells us *what* the test is measuring. By examining the criterion data, together with the validity coefficients of the test, we can objectively determine what the test is measuring. It would thus be more accurate to define validity as the extent to which we know what the test measures. The interpretation of test scores would undoubtedly be clearer and less ambiguous if tests were regularly named in terms of the criteria against which they had been validated. A tendency in this direction can be recognized in such test labels as "scholastic aptitude test" and "personnel classification test" in place of the vague title "intelligence test."

Note

1. Actually, the normal curve provides finer discrimination at the ends than at the middle of the scale. Equal discrimination at all points of the scale would require a rectangular distribution. The normal curve, however, has an advantage if subsequent statistical analyses of scores are to be conducted, because many current statistical techniques assume approximate normality of distribution. For this and other reasons, it is likely that most tests designed for general use will continue to follow a normal-curve pattern for some time to come. In the construction of custom-made tests to serve clearly defined purposes, however, the form of the distribution of scores should depend on the type of discrimination desired.

Psychological Testing and Fair Employment Practices: A Testing Program that Does Not Discriminate

JOHN B. MINER

In the past few years a number of employing organizations have discontinued psychological testing programs or failed to initiate planned programs as a result of fair employment practices legislation and enforcement efforts by the Equal Employment Opportunity Commission (EEOC) and by the Office of Federal Contract Compliance (OFCC) (Bureau of National Affairs, 1971). Given the uncertainties of the current situation these employers have decided that testing for purposes of hiring and promotion is not worth the risk involved. Although this kind of reasoning has been applied primarily to the testing aspects of the selection process, it is being extended to application blanks and interviews as well. The result appears to be that some organizations are moving precipitously close to random hiring, with all the implications for subsequent performance failure that such an approach involves (Miner and Brewer, 1974).

Increasingly psychologists, lawyers, and personnel specialists are being asked to provide opinions as to whether testing programs will be acceptable to EEOC and/or OFCC. Both of these federal organizations have published guidelines and other documents in an effort to reduce uncertainty and assist employers to comply with legislation and executive orders bearing on testing. Yet, nothing has been published to date that would provide a sure guide to employer action; many uncertainties and ambiguities remain. Faced with the prospects of terminated federal contracts, sizable awards for damages, and restrictions on earnings by regulatory bodies it is not surprising that some companies have decided to forego further testing until the present situation clears.

Such a strategy may require a long wait. The reason is that both EEOC and OFCC have taken the position that they will not approve individual testing programs as being fair and nondiscriminatory. They argue in part that they lack the manpower to carry out the

Reprinted from *Personnel Psychology*, Vol. 27 (Spring) 1974, with permission.

many investigations this would require. Even more important, however, is the government's position that under existing law it is up to the employer to establish that employment practices do not discriminate, and that government certification of testing programs would be wholly inconsistent with this particular legal strategy.

If there is a sizable disparity between the distribution of women or minorities in the labor force of the geographical area as compared with any major job category of an employer, this is in and of itself sufficient basis to warrant a charge of discrimination. It is then up to the organization involved to show that the disparity exists for some reason other than outright discrimination, if it can. To certify testing programs or any other selection procedures in advance would serve to undermine the government's legal position in such cases. As a result it seems clear that a full interpretation of fair employment practices legislation will emerge only after a series of court tests and hearings before the semi-judicial federal regulatory bodies.

Decisions of this kind such as *Griggs* v. *Duke Power Company, United States* v. *Georgia Power Company, et al.*, and *Moody, et al.* v. *Albemarle Paper Company* (see the Holt article in chap. 3) have had a great deal more to say regarding types of procedures that are not acceptable, than about what is fair employment practice; the testing programs questioned in these cases have not emerged from the judicial process unscathed. Yet what is needed if adequate guides for action are to be developed are examples of testing programs which have been subjected to intensive federal scrutiny, and have survived intact. The first instance of this kind occurred . . . in the case of charges brought by EEOC and certain civil rights groups against the American Telephone and Telegraph Company before the Federal Communications Commission.

It is particularly important that psychologists and others concerned with testing be fully aware of the details of this case because, in view of the nature and monetary value of the final settlement, the exoneration of AT&T testing procedures could easily be overlooked. . . .

The AT&T Testing Program

What . . . are the characteristics of the testing program which has elicited . . . approval, or at least lack of disapproval, in the final analysis from governmental agencies concerned with fair employment practices and equal opportunity? What is the specific nature of the model thus presented to other employing organizations?[1]

A total of 31 validity studies were submitted to EEOC and reviewed by the author. Of these eight were multi-company studies utilizing data from widely dispersed geographical locations, 12 were conducted within the Pacific Telephone and Telegraph Company, six within the Southern and/or South Central Bell Companies, three within the New Jersey company, and two within the Michigan company. All the multi-company studies and one each from the Pacific Coast and the South were carried out by AT&T's personnel research unit; the remainder were conducted by the individual operating companies. Although the magnitude of this research may seem overwhelming, it should be remembered that AT&T is a very large, nationwide employer with many occupational groups.

Of the 10 studies by AT&T's personnel research unit seven reported results for training criteria only and no subsequent job performance relationships. These studies involved primarily those employee groups which were of greatest concern to EEOC— operators, clerks, plant craft employees, and service representatives. The remaining three studies which did utilize subsequent job performance criteria had salesmen and managers as subjects, jobs which were less focal for the EEOC investigation. In six of the seven cases where only training criteria were used the measures were specially devised job simulations and were not standard training evaluation procedures. Examples are described by Grant and Bray (1970) and Gael and Grant (1972). Only in one study involving computer programmers did the AT&T personnel researchers use standard training criteria based on instructor's ratings. Thus, it is clear that the basic validation strategy was to use indexes such as simulations, work samples, and specially developed job knowledge measures with those occupational groups which were of greatest concern to EEOC.

A question arises as to whether such special post-training criteria might not have been devised for the specific purpose of yielding high correlations with the predictors, irrespective of their relation either to actual training success or to subsequent job performance. These criteria place strong emphasis on intellectual or scholastic ability (learning ability) and the measures are obtained under conditions of maximal rather than typical motivation. Both of these conditions are inherent in the initial testing situation as well (the most consistently used predictor was the School and College Ability Test published by Educational Testing Service).

One approach to testing this hypothesis involves a comparison of results obtained with regular training criteria such as course grades, instructor's ratings, pass-fail decisions, performance on quizzes, and retention-separation during training with results obtained when the special post-training criteria are used. Of the nine analyses using regular criteria, three were conducted by AT&T personnel research (two of these used job performance criteria as well) and six by individual operating companies. Of the eight studies using specialized criteria, six were conducted by AT&T personnel research and two by operating companies. Data on the extent to which statistically significant validity coefficients ($p < .05$) were obtained using the two types of training criteria are given in Table 1.

TABLE 1
FINDINGS FROM VALIDATION STUDIES CONDUCTED USING VARIOUS TYPES OF TRAINING CRITERIA

Type of Criterion Measure	Valid ($p<.05$)	Not Valid ($p>.05$)	Validity Level Not Indicated
Regular Training Criteria	7 (78%)	1 (11%)	1 (11%)
Special Post-Training Criteria	8 (100%)	0	0
	($x^2=.44$, N.S.; $df=1$)		

TABLE 2
FINDINGS FROM VALIDATION STUDIES CONDUCTED USING TRAINING AND PERFORMANCE CRITERIA

Type of Criterion Measure	Valid ($p<.05$)	Not Valid ($p>.05$)	Validity Level Not Indicated
Training Criteria	15 (88%)	1 (6%)	1 (6%)
Job Performance Criteria	11 (65%)	5 (29%)	1 (6%)
	($x^2=1.46$, N.S.; $df=1$)		

Note—Three studies utilized both types of criterion measures.

On the record it appears that the specially devised post-training criteria have no particular proclivity for yielding validity, thus the hypothesis of biased selection of criterion measures is not supported. In subsequent analyses the two types of training criteria are treated as a single class.

From the data of Table 1 it would appear that the training criteria used in all 17 studies are closely related to the actual content of training. It remains to be demonstrated, however, that the training (and the training criteria) are associated with subsequent job performance. How, for instance, does the incidence of validity vary as between training criteria and job performance criteria such as supervisory ratings, field review ratings, promotion rates, and hard measures of productivity? Data are given in Table 2.

Although there is a tendency for the incidence of nonvalid results to increase as one moves from training to later job performance, the shift is not sufficient to yield anything approaching statistical significance. Thus, it cannot be said that validity is obtained less frequently when actual job performance criteria are used. Given the fact that the validity analyses using performance data are based on predictions over longer periods of time (and thus permit greater opportunities for real changes in the individuals to intervene) than those based on training data, the comparisons of Table 2 might even be viewed as overstating the criterion differences.

There are three studies in which both training criteria and job performance criteria are used. In one instance the relationship between the two is not reported, in another it is not significant, and in the third it is a highly significant $+.75$. Where the two are negatively correlated, one could argue that the training is detrimental to ultimate objectives, and thus validation against training criteria is unwarranted. Where the two are uncorrelated, the use of training criteria must be justified in its own right—effective selection saves the cost of training. Where the two are positively correlated, validation using training criteria can be justified both in its own right and as it contributes to the prediction of a less than ultimate index of job performance. Based on these interpretations there is nothing in the data reported by AT&T that would lead one to reject the findings obtained using training criteria; there are no negative correlations between training and performance measures.

On the other hand it is entirely possible that in selecting those who will succeed in training, the company contributes to a higher turnover rate (and thus is burdened with greater replacement costs). The only data available related to this point derive from an incompletely described 1970 force loss study conducted in New York. In this instance, the separation rate was reported to be 24.7 percent per year for those with high test scores and 26.6 percent for those with lower scores. The difference is described as not significant, but tends to favor those with higher scores. Thus, again there is nothing to indicate that the findings obtained with training criteria should be rejected.

Taken as a whole this line of analysis tends to support the various criteria used in the AT&T studies. On the other hand, there are points at which the data become uncomfortably sparse. More information on relationships between various training criteria and indexes of subsequent job performance, especially retention, would make it easier to interpret the results that are reported. In many locations turnover appears to be quite high in the entry level jobs; yet little evidence is provided relating predictors to this criterion.

Another approach to criterion analysis involves consideration of minority group members separately. If, for instance, a criterion relationship is statistically significant for whites, but not blacks, there is a possibility that the mere fact that an individual is black may have had an impact on the criterion measurement process such as to eliminate any possibility of validity. This effect seems most likely when ratings are used, but it can occur with other criteria as well.

There are nine studies in which validities were calculated separately for blacks and whites. The results are given in Table 3.

TABLE 3
Findings from Validation Studies Using Both Black and White Subjects

Type of Criterion Measure	Valid ($p<.05$) for Both	Valid ($p<.05$) for Whites Only
Special Post-Training Criteria	6 (100%)	0
Job Performance Criteria	2 (67%)	1 (33%)

Generally, significant correlations occur somewhat less frequently among blacks than whites, but they do occur in both groups for all studies except one. In this one instance the criterion measure used was a direct index of output or productivity, and thus least vulnerable to any bias which would tend to obliterate validity; yet the validity coefficients were +.32 for whites and −.04 for blacks.

Inspection of the scatter plots given in Table 4 indicates a restriction of range at the lower end of the test score distributions in both the black and white samples; 25 has been used as a cutting score in both instances. The source of the differential validity, however, appears to be the similar limitation at the upper end of the test score distribution for blacks. This compression does not occur among the whites, and in fact it is the relationship demonstrated in cells where there are practically no blacks represented at all that accounts in large part for the significant correlation among whites. This analysis suggests that the failure to obtain validity for blacks in this instance is a function of the *test score* distribution in the sample much more than of the *criterion* distribution.

TABLE 4
Relationships between Test Scores and Criterion Performance for Blacks and Whites

Blacks
Criterion Performance

Test Scores	Low	Medium	High	Totals
40 and over	0	0	1	1
35-39	2	3	1	6
30-34	3	0	1	4
25-29	6	5	4	15
				$N=26$

Whites
Criterion Performance

Test Scores	Low	Medium	High	Totals
40 and over	1	5	11	17
35-39	11	4	14	29
30-34	13	9	9	31
25-29	13	13	10	36
				$N=113$

There is only one study where validities were computed separately for males and females and significance was obtained for both groups. In addition there are three studies utilizing Spanish surname subjects, although only two of these are reported in sufficient detail to determine whether statistical significance was obtained. In these latter instances validity was in fact established, using supervisory ratings and a post-training simulation as criteria.

Taken as a whole the studies of minority group members do not provide a basis for concluding that the criterion measures used introduce any special bias against minorities. Where the minority samples are lower on the criterion they tend to have lower test scores as well.

With only a few exceptions the 31 studies are predictive, rather than concurrent in nature; also there is a heavy reliance on ability tests, primarily mental ability. There are only four instances where validities are reported for other types of measures—a standardized interview including role playing, an assessment center evaluation covering many aspects of the individual, a stenographic test, and a typing test. A comparison of validities obtained with these measures as against those obtained with the mental ability tests is given in Table 5. On the evidence it would appear that wider use of tests other than those of mental ability could have been made without any sacrifice in validity.

TABLE 5
FINDINGS FROM VALIDATION STUDIES USING VARIOUS TYPES OF TESTS AS PREDICTORS

Type of Test	Valid ($p<.05$)	Not Valid ($p>.05$)	Validity Level Not Indicated
Mental Ability	23 (82%)	3 (11%)	2 (7%)
Other	3 (75%)	1 (25%)	0
	($x^2=.11$, N.S.; $df=1$)		

Note—One study utilized both types of tests.

Overall, in spite of the deficiencies of individual analyses, the results obtained from this series of 31 studies are very impressive in terms of the extent to which validity has been demonstrated.

Implications and Conclusions

In the final analysis when all the evidence was in, EEOC did not continue to press on the matter of psychological testing, and accepted a settlement which left AT&T's existing testing program intact. This represented a major change in position from the one taken by EEOC at the time when the initial charges were filed. With full access to validity information, which they did not have in December, 1970, the government lawyers concluded that their case against AT&T's testing practices was not sufficiently strong to warrant pursuing this particular aspect of the case further.

On the other hand AT&T did agree not to "rely upon the minimum scores required or preferred on its pre-employment aptitude test batteries as justification for its failure to meet its intermediate targets for any job classification." What does this mean?

In agreeing to this provision, AT&T committed itself to one, or both, of two possible strategies, assuming that lower average test scores continue to characterize minority applicants as they have in the past. One approach involves a differential investment in recruiting such that a much greater proportion of minority group members are induced to apply for jobs. Under this strategy the minimum test scores are held at the same level for all, and targets for hiring are met by locating more qualified minority group members and inducing them to join the company by offering attractive salaries, benefits and working conditions. In this instance the tests remain just as useful in identifying future effective performers among minorities as among whites.

An alternative to differential recruiting is differential selection. This involves establishing different minimum scores for different groups as required to meet the hiring targets. In the case of blacks at the present time, for instance, it would require a lower cutting score than for whites.

This approach does produce lower recruiting costs, but the savings may well be dissipated over time by increased training expenditures; further, there is greater risk of performance failure, assuming constant performance standards, and perhaps also certain problems, when it comes time for upgrading and promotion. Yet, even with the difficulties inherent in this approach tests continue to be useful; there is no basis for concluding that testing would make no contribution and, therefore, should be suspended for minority applicants. Tests can still be used to select those with the *highest* probability of effective performance *within* each group—white male, black, white female, Spanish surname, or whatever—even though differential cutting scores are used. Minimum scores need be set only as low as required to meet hiring targets. Furthermore, the test scores can prove useful in making post-hiring assignments and placement decisions.

Whatever strategy AT&T adopts, it will be able to retain many, if not the full, benefits of its testing program. On the other hand it is not entirely clear that the law does in fact require that hiring targets be given priority over the use of validated performance-related tests in making selection decisions. The AT&T case was settled by consent decree and AT&T agreed to this provision; no court required it. There is some feeling among lawyers who are active in the fair employment practices area that employing organizations have yielded on points that might have been decided in their favor had they been considered by the courts; and that there have been far too many consent decrees (Bureau of National Affairs, 1972). It is entirely possible the AT&T settlement represents a case in point.

In any event the clear implication of the final settlement is that testing programs can survive close government scrutiny and that psychological testing need not be abandoned in these times of increased governmental surveillance of all aspects of employment. In fact to follow the route of abandonment, as some personnel managers have advocated, may be an invitation to disaster. There are two reasons for this conclusion.

If some employing organizations, such as AT&T, continue to use valid tests these organizations are in a position to skim the top of a local labor force—male and female, black and white. Those who abandon testing will tend to abandon other selection procedures also as pressure for validation increases there too; inevitably they will move eventually to random hiring. But random hiring where everyone is employing randomly is one thing; random hiring in a labor market where a number of employers are actively selecting on a scientific basis is quite different. Under the latter conditions there may well be so little of the type of talent needed remaining in a local labor force that performance and productivity are seriously hampered. The situation is not unlike that occuring with the use of advertising, where if some companies invest, others in the industry are under strong pressure to follow suit, merely to remain in competition.

Another consideration in any decision regarding abandoning testing relates to the basic position taken by EEOC and other government enforcement agencies—"if an employer doesn't have a proper distribution of minorities in its workforce, he is guilty unless he can prove the imbalance is job-related." (Bureau of National Affairs, 1972). The way to show that an imbalance is job-related is to demonstrate that qualities needed for effective job performance are lacking in a segment of the labor force with which fair employment laws are concerned—a sex, racial, color, national origin, or religious group. If a psychological test can be shown to be valid (performance-related), and the quality measured is not in balance as between men and women, blacks and whites, or whatever, then the imbalance in an employer's workforce can be said to be job-related. With the use of psychological tests (plus acceptable validation and normative research) this response to a charge of discrimination can be readily advanced. Thus, discontinuing testing rather than providing protection against charges may well serve to eliminate the possibility of an effective and entirely justified defense; a charge of discrimination may accordingly be upheld for lack of test data.

It should be emphasized that AT&T, although apparently in a position to make this defense with regard to many of its installations and local labor markets, did not do so; rather it accepted the indicated hiring targets. The reasoning behind this outcome is not known to the author. In any event there is every indication from statements by EEOC lawyers and psychologists that such a line of defense could be substantiated through proper psychological research; thus, that psychological testing can be used to show that a workforce imbalance is a function of job requirements rather than either intentional or unintentional discrimination.

Note

1. The following discussion draws primarily on a memorandum written by the author for the EEOC on October 31, 1971. This memorandum contains a review of all validity information which had been provided to EEOC by AT&T up to that time. It was prepared while the author was serving as a consultant to EEOC, but was not submitted in evidence before the FCC. Permission to publish this material has been given by David Copus of EEOC and Douglas W. Bray of AT&T. The contributions of both of these individuals to this article are gratefully acknowledged.

In addition to the above mentioned memorandum, the following discussion also draws upon updating information provided in the testimony of Donald L. Grant and Douglas W. Bray of AT&T before the FCC (dated August 1, 1972).

References

Bray, D. W. and Grant, D. L. The assessment center in the measurement of potential for business management. *Psychological Monographs,* 1966, 80, 1-27.

Bureau of National Affairs, Inc. ASPA-BNA survey: Personnel testing. *Bulletin to Management,* September 9, 1971, 1-8.

Bureau of National Affairs, Inc. EEOC urges employers use job-related tests. *Daily Labor Report,* November 7, 1972, A9-10.

Gael, S. and Grant, D. L. Employment test validation for minority and non-minority telephone company service representatives. *Journal of Applied Psychology,* 1972, 56, 135-139.

Grant, D. L. and Bray D. W. Validation of employment tests for telephone company installation and repair occupations. *Journal of Applied Psychology,* 1969, 53, 24-34.

Miner, J. B. and Brewer, J. F. The management of ineffective performance. In M. D. Dunnette (ed.), *Handbook of Industrial and Organizational Psychology.* Chicago: Rand, McNally, 1974.

Meeting Government Guidelines on Testing and Selection

WILLIAM H. MOBLEY

The use of tests for personnel selection and upgrading continues to be a focal point for controversy, especially as related to equal opportunity employment. The controversy has been stimulated and intensified by at least six related factors:

1. The significance of the basic issues involved; the unquestionable right of individuals to be considered for jobs on the basis of qualification and not race, color, age, sex, religion or national origin; the rightful concern of industry for employing individuals who are likely to work safely and productively.

2. The complexity of the evaluation of test validity in situations which are heterogeneous with respect to groups covered by government selection guidelines.

3. The fact that various commentators on the testing issue are speaking from different vantage points and at differing levels of discourse.

4. The ambiguity inherent in professional and government guidelines on test usage as they are presently constituted. This ambiguity, predictably, has led to differences in interpretation. . . .

5. Until recently the relative lack of research on some of the critical issues involved; e.g., the differential prediction hypothesis; content validity; generalizing validity findings from one setting to another; the *why* underlying observed ethnic/racial average differences on some tests and criteria.

6. A tendency to confound what are essentially two distinguishable questions: (a) the question of valid selection based on predicted or demonstrated job performance and (b) the question of what activities, programs or procedures can and should be undertaken to develop and utilize *individuals* for whom, at present, predicted job success is low.

Given the controversial, complex and frequently confusing nature of the testing question, this article has attempted to narrow the domain by selecting five issues for closer examination. These issues are: (1) The legality and utility of testing. (2) The "adverse effect" criterion. (3) Evidence of validity. (4) The differential prediction hypothesis. (5) Where to go from here.

Legality and Utility of Testing

There is little question that standardized testing has been singled out for close scrutiny by the various government agencies involved in monitoring equal employment opportunity. This scrutiny has had both positive and negative effects. On the positive side, it has forced many organizations to validate their testing procedures, a step psychologists have recommended (with limited success) for years. As the result of the validation process, some organizations have documented the validity of some tests, have installed new tests where needed and where validity could be established and/or have dropped tests which could not be validated or which did not possess sufficient utility in a given situation.

Reprinted from *The Personnel Administrator*, November-December 1974, with permission.

On the negative side, many organizations have abandoned testing for such reasons as: the unwillingness to expend the resources necessary to conduct validation research; the hope that abandonment of testing would make their selection and upgrading procedures immune from criticism by government compliance agencies; or the belief, fostered by some government officials, that testing is illegal. These are the wrong reasons for abandoning testing.

To abandon testing because of the mistaken belief that testing is illegal, in an attempt to avoid pressure from compliance investigators, or because validation research is difficult and costly, ignores that fact that properly validated standardized tests may, in the words of both the EEOC and OFCC testing guidelines: ". . . Significantly aid in the development and maintenance of an efficient work force and, indeed, aid in the utilization and conservation of human resources generally." From: 1607.1 of EEOC Selection Guidelines (1970), 60-3.1 of OFCC Selection Guidelines (1971).

Neither the Civil Rights Act, the subsequent interpretive guidelines nor any subsequent court case have declared testing *or any particular test* to be inherently illegal. The most the courts have said is that if a test has an adverse effect on minorities, the test must be demonstrably related to job performance (see *Griggs* v. *Duke Power, Supreme Court Reporter*, 1971).

Just as the illegality of testing is a misconception, so is the belief that abandonment of standardized testing will avoid the need to validate, will ensure nondiscriminatory selection and upgrading and/or will avoid scrutiny of employment process by compliance agencies. Both the EEOC and OFCC guidelines (and the government's . . . "Uniform Guidelines on Employee Selection Procedures") cover *any* standard used in employment or promotion, including personal histories, education and interviews. To the extent any of these standards result in adverse effect, they too must be validated. The abandonment of standardized testing does not eliminate the need to validate.

More fundamental is the probability that non-test selection procedures, such as the interview, are not only more difficult to validate, but also may be less effective in accurately assessing and predicting future performance and thus in minimizing discrimination. In fact, Wallace, Kissinger and Reynolds stated, in an EEOC research report: "We have . . . concluded that careful selection and administering of tests and validation of the testing instrument within an industrial setting may be the most desirable means to achieve the goal of full utilitzation of the nation's human resources" (Wallace, et. al., EEOC, 1966).

The paradox, as I see it is that in response to the Civil Rights Act and subsequent guidelines, some companies may have abandoned the use and/or search for valid or validatable standardized tests, when in the final analysis, such standardized tests may well be the most effective tool in ensuring selection and and upgrading on the basis of legitimate qualification, rather than race, color, religion, sex or national origin.

Adverse Effect Criterion

The next issue is the "adverse effect" criterion of discrimination. From the standpoint of validation falling within the domain of the government guidelines the key phrase is "adversely effects." If the tests used by an organization do *not* have an adverse impact, they are *not* subject to the government validation requirements. However, organizations should certainly seek to assess the validity of their tests as good business and professional practice even if not required by a goverment compliance agency.

What does adverse effect mean? One definition is based on a comparison of the percentage of minority applicants and percentage of non-minority applicants who qualify on the particular test in question. This might be called the "qualification rate" definition of adverse effect. If the average score for minorities on certain tests is lower than the average score for non-minorities, the percentage of minorities meeting any given qualifying score generally will be lower than the percentage of non-minorities meeting that qualifying score for these tests.

The question then becomes, how much of a difference results in a judgment of adverse effect. There are statistical tools available for assessing the statistical significance of differences in proportions of percentages. Employers would be well advised to run these statistical analyses to see if in fact the tests (and non-test standards) being used are disqualifying a statistically significant greater percentage of minorities. If not, the government guidelines do not require submission of evidence of validity.

While qualification rate is a frequently cited basis for evaluating adverse effect, it would seem critical that those responsible for equal employment opportunity, both company and government compliance investigators, look beyond qualification rate to *hiring* experience.

Given that a goal of equal employment opportunity is to ensure the employment (and promotion) of qualified minorities, reliance on qualification rate with no deference to minority hiring experience could result in the following paradoxical situation. An employer who is making a good faith effort to hire more minorities may in fact seek out and test many applicants who otherwise might not apply or who could be screened out prior to testing for other reasons. A possible result of this good faith effort may be an increase in the apparent discrepancy between the proportion of minorities and non-minorities who fail to exceed the test standards. Conversely, the employer who tests many non-minorities who could otherwise be screened out and tests only a select group of minorities, may in fact reduce the apparent test-related adverse effect.

The paradox is that the qualification rate definition of adverse effect is a somewhat elastic and incomplete criterion that may be counterproductive to affirmative action. More emphasis on the proportion of minorities and non-minorities actually *hired* would seem justified.

Evidence of Validity

The third issue deals with a series of questions concerning the generation and presentation of evidence of validity. Since this issue is complex and involves a number of statistical considerations, I will simply comment on some of the problems rather than discuss them in detail.

The government guidelines on employee selection indicate that given an adverse effect, an employer must have available evidence of a test's validity and that such evidence should consist of data demonstrating that the test is predicative of, or significantly correlated with, important elements of work behavior which comprise, or are relevant, to the job or jobs for which candidates are being evaluated.

There should be little argument with the need to demonstrate the relationship between the test and important aspects of work behavior. The problems which arise are basically related to the ambiguity in certain passages of the guidelines. Examples of this ambiguity include the following:

1. The guidelines refer to the American Psychological Association's 1966 *Standards*

for Educational and Psychological Tests as the source for generally accepted procedures for determining validity. The 1966 APA standards were intended primarily as a guide for test developers and publishers. However, APA recently published a revised set of standards which is more definitive from the viewpoint of test users. This revised document should help reduce some of the ambiguity inherent in satisfying the government guidelines.

2. The term *technically feasible* is used in several passages of the guidelines and is defined as: having or obtaining sufficient sample sizes to achieve findings of statistical and practical significance, the opportunity to obtain unbiased job performance criteria, etc. What constitutes sufficient sample size and opportunity to collect unbiased criteria are obviously open to interpretation.[1]

3. The guidelines provide that validity findings from one unit of a company or from other companies may be applied to other units, provided that *no significant differences* exist between units, jobs, applicant populations and other contextual variables. What constitutes *significant differences* in units, jobs, applicant populations and contextual variables are open to interpretation.

4. The guidelines provide that an employer may *continue to use a test that is not presently fully supported by the required evidence of validity,* provided he can cite evidence of validity in similar situations and that he has in progress validation procedures which are designed to produce, within a reasonable time, the additional data required. The guidelines also suggest that the employer "may have to alter or suspend test cutoff scores so that score ranges broad enough to permit the identification of criterion-related validity will be obtained." What constitutes "a reasonable period of time" and under what conditions an employer "may have to alter *or* suspend" cutoff scores are open to interpretation.

In listing these various examples of ambiguity (and there are many more) in the guidelines, I am not advocating that all areas of ambiguity can or should be eliminated. No set of guidelines could adequately anticipate the variety of contexts and conditions which would bear on the question what evidence and action would be adequate. On the other hand, it is clear that some of the ambiguity could be reduced by a clearer statement from compliance agencies on how they propose to interpret their guidelines in various contexts. Such a statement would help ensure that all parties have clearer perceptions of what the groundrules actually are.

A related question concerns *who evaluates submitted validation* evidence. Given the ambiguity in the guidelines and the complexity of some of the issues and statistical procedures involved, professionally developed validation research would seem to warrant review and evaluation by testing and validation experts rather than placing this burden on field compliance investigators whose expertise may be in areas other than test validation.

Just as no organization should accept the validity of its tests without professionally-developed supporting evidence, one would hope that field compliance officials would seek *professional evaluation* of the submitted evidence without rejecting, before the fact, the guidelines' statement of purpose and in some cases without making automatic demands that all testing be abolished.

Another problem is the lack of feedback on evidence of validity submitted to various compliance agencies. Given the alternative interpretations in certain sections of the guidelines, the growing body of recently published research relevant to the issues involved and the need to make operating and administrative decisions based on submitted evidence, the company or organization that is making a good faith effort to comply with the guidelines, to be responsive to the issues involved, is left in somewhat of a quandary when feedback from the professional (or even non-professional) evaluation is not forthcoming.

Differential Prediction Hypothesis

The next issue concerns the differential prediction hypothesis. Although an attempt has been made to avoid statistical language up to this point, it will be necessary to introduce some statistical language in what follows.

The passage from the guidelines dealing with differential prediction raises important issues related to equal opportunity employment. As noted earlier, the guidelines require that any adverse impact based on a test must be job-related.

The key issue in differential prediction is whether or not a given test score predicts the same level of success for different racial ethnic or other protected groups as it does for other groups. The fact that the guidelines devote considerable attention to the need for separate and differential prediction studies indicated that they were written with the belief that differential prediction was a probable hypothesis; i.e., that given test scores would be related to performance in *different and unfair* ways for minority as contrasted with non-minority subgroups.

There should be no quarrel with the need to conduct differential prediction studies where technically feasible nor with the need to make appropriate adjustments if a given test clearly predicts different performance scores for different protected subgroups.

A primary restraint on technical feasibility is sample size. Sample size is intimately related to the statistical significance of validity coefficients. If, for example, you had a non-minority sample of 40 and a minority sample of 20, the non-minority validity coefficient would have to be .30 to be statistically significant while the minority validity coefficient would have to be .43 to be significant. Suppose the validity coefficient is .30 in both groups. This sort of finding does *not* substantiate the claim of differential prediction, only the lack of statistical significance in a smaller sample. The differential prediction hypothesis can be adequately evaluated only where there are adequate sample sizes.[2]

Since the validity of industrial testing for selection and placement has typically been criterion referenced, evaluation of the question of bias and unfairness must go beyond comparisons of mean test performance. Unfairness in selection testing can be empirically evaluated only when one considers group differences in test performance, criterion measures and how the two relate. (Statistical techniques for evaluating the differences have been presented by Gulliksen and Wilks, 1950, and others.)

How viable is this hypothesized need for differential prediction based on racial subgroups? While there has been too little strong research relevant to this point, there would appear to be a growing body of evidence suggesting that differential prediction may not be as prevalent as once thought and that in many cases it does not work to the disadvantage of minorities. (See e.g. Boehm, 1972; Crooks, L.A., 1972; Gael and Grant, 1972; Guinn, Tupes, and Allen, 1970; Ruch, 1972; Grant and Bray, 1971; Bray and Moses, 1972.) This body of evidence would seem to argue against the abolishment of testing until differential prediction is technically feasible, an action frequently demanded by some compliance officers.

There is certainly a need for additional strong research on the differential prediction question. Hopefully this research will be of the quality of the . . . Educational Testing Service-Civil Service Commission Six-Year Study (Crooks, 1972), which should be read by all parties interested in the testing question. . . .

Where to from Here?

From the government, one would hope to see: a reduction of certain crucial ambiguities in *testing guidelines;* a recognition of the need for *professional review* and *feedback* on submitted validation research; and the *conduct and financial* support of additional strong professional research on such issues as differential prediction, new predictors, the *why* underlying observed ethnic mean differences in some predictors and criteria and strategies for developing individuals for whom successful performance cannot at present be predicted.

From professionals one would hope to see: *a sound and comprehensive set of standards* on both test development and test usage; *development of general principles*[3] dealing with relationships among various job behaviors and measures of various skills, aptitudes and abilities rather than the promulgation of situation-specific non-cumulative prediction studies; and the conduct of *strong research* in such areas as are mentioned in the preceding paragraph.

From test publishers one would hope to see more emphasis on *validation research* for their tests, the previously mentioned Education Testing Service-Civil Service Six-Year Study being a good model; more emphasis of compilation and *publication of both normative data and validity studies* by job, minority group, geographic location, etc., and a continued search for improved predictors.

Finally, from companies, one would hope to see a recognition of the value of developing better procedures for job analysis as a requirement for test selection and development, criterion development and generalizability studies; a continued search for *improved* valid predictors; exploration of *work samples*[4] and other predictors based on *content validity; cooperative industry-wide validation research studies* designed to meet the problems of "technical feasibility"; development of *multiple performance criteria* including behaviorally anchored ratings, job knowledge tests and work samples.

In the final analysis, the issue of the ability of tests to aid in the selection (and promotion) of qualified *individuals* without regard to race, color, sex, age, religion or national origin will be resolved by sound reasoning and good research. In the pursuit of sound, non-discriminatory selection practices, it is important that we keep two issues clear. The issue of valid selection based on predicted or demonstrated job performance must be distinguished from the equally important issue of what activities, programs or procedures can be effectively undertaken to develop and utilize individuals for whom predicted job success is low. To assume that a good solution to the second issue is elimination of valid testing is clearly simplistic and not in the best interest of individuals, organizations or the nation. To assume that validated selection procedures relieve organizations of the need to explore activities, programs and procedures to develop and utilize individuals for whom success at present is improbable, is also simplistic and not in the best interest of individuals, organizations or the nation.

In summary, I am suggesting the need to progress on two fronts. The continued application and development for valid predictors *and* the search for better ways to develop and utilize individuals for whom success is less likely. The creative and cooperative efforts of all parties, industry, academe and government are required to make progress on both fronts.

Notes

1. The question of how many study participants are necessary to make a criterion validity study technically feasible was addressed in a recent research study by Schmidt, Hunter, and Urry *(Journal of Applied Psychology,* 1976,*61,* 473-485). Psychologists had previously believed that about 30 or so subjects was an adequate number, but the findings in this research study indicate that the required number is much larger—often 300 or more.

2. Humphreys has pointed out that it is bad statistics to assess black-white differences in test validity by testing to determine whether the validity coefficient is statistically significant for one race but not the other. The proper test is one which assesses the significance of the *difference* between the two validities. (See, Humphreys, L. G. Statistical definitions of test validity for minority groups, *Journal of Applied Psychology,* 1973,*58,* 1-4.) This test, however, requires relatively large numbers of blacks and whites in order to detect any differences that might exist. Fortunately, recent research indicates that such differences probably do not occur any more frequently than would be expected on the basis of chance alone (Hunter, J. E., Schmidt, F. L., and Hunter, R. The differential validity hypothesis: A disconfirmation. Manuscript to be submitted for publication to *Journal of Applied Psychology).* Research findings such as these may lead to the elimination of the requirement for differential validation. See also Schmidt, F. L., Berner, J. G., and Hunter, J. E. Racial differences in employment test validities: Reality or illusion? *Journal of Applied Psychology,* 1973, *58,* 5-9 and O'Connor, E. J., Wexley, K. N., and Alexander, R. A. Single group validity: Fact or fallacy? *Journal of Applied Psychology,* 1975, *60,* 352-355.

3. Recent research in validity generalization indicates that it may be possible, after all, to develop such general principles. This research shows that test validity may not be situationally specific, as has long been believed. Instead, general test-types valid for a given job in one setting may be equally valid for the same general job-type in other organizations and settings. As a result, the method developed in this research may make many criterion validity studies unnecessary in the future. (Schmidt, F. L., and Hunter, J. E. Development of a General Solution to the Problem of Validity Generalization. Winning paper, 1976, James McKeen Cattell Research Design Contest.)

4. Section E of this chapter is devoted to work sample testing.

References

Crooks, L. A. (ed.) An investigation of sources of bias in the prediction of job performance: A six-year study. Princeton, N. J.: Educational Testing Service, 1972.

Boehm, V. R. Negro-White differences in validity of employment and training selection procedures. *Journal of Applied Psychology,* 1972, 56, 33-39.

Gael, S., and Grant, D. L. Employment test validation for minority and nonminority telephone company representatives. *Journal of Applied Psychology,* 1972, 56, 135-39.

Grant, D. L., and Bray, D. W. Validation of employment tests for telephone company installation and repair occupations. *Journal of Applied Psychology,* 1970, 54, 7-14.

Bray, D. W., and Moses, J. L. Personnel selection. *Annual Review of Psychology,* 1972, 23, 545-76.

Guidelines for Choosing Consultants for Psychological Selection Validation Research and Implementation

PROFESSIONAL AFFAIRS COMMITTEE
DIVISION 14
AMERICAN PSYCHOLOGICAL ASSOCIATION

The proper use of procedures in selection and placement of people in organizations is not only desirable, but in most instances, it is required by law. It is necessary that any selection device (tests, interviews, application forms, etc.) be used in a manner that does not select unfairly among individuals. In order to satisfy legal requirements in most situations, the selection tests or other procedures must be properly "validated." "Validation" is the term commonly employed to describe the determination of the value of personnel selection procedures.

Validation of psychological tests and other selection tools requires a high degree of specialized competency and experience which is not always available within organizations, particularly smaller ones. Nevertheless, it is necessary that all organizations meet the requirements of various state and federal laws and it is often necessary to seek the professional services of persons or firms qualified to validate selection procedures.

The Industrial and Organizational Division (Division 14) of the American Psychological Association (APA) has prepared the following guidelines to assist organizations in the determination of qualified individuals or firms seeking professional help in selection validation procedures. There is not a single standard upon which a judgment about qualification for selection validation can be made (e.g., special validation license, list of recommended or acceptable persons, etc.). Therefore, the standards are termed guidelines in recognition of the fact that the burden for deciding upon candidates for validation work rests within the organization seeking such services.

Some judgment must be exercised by the person or firm having to select a qualified selection validation consultant and, to some degree, the problem is no different than that of selecting a consultant of any kind. Most consultants (individuals or firms) with sufficient competence and experience to perform psychological test validation would fulfill the requirements of the guidelines.

Certification

Most states require that persons who offer psychological services to the public, including test validation, must be certified or licensed. Requirements vary state by state, but such certification or licensing should be considered as a minimum requirement. Proof of certification or licensing may be demanded because official documents are provided to persons having passed the examination and other requirements for state certification or licensing.

Reprinted by permission of the Professional Affairs Committee, Division 14, American Psychological Association.

Professional Membership

Generally, persons engaged in test validation work belong to the American Psychological Association (APA). Membership is probable in Division 14 of the American Psychological Association (Division of Industrial and Organizational Psychology) or Division 5 (Division of Evaluation and Measurement). Although membership in either the APA or Divisions 14 or 5 is not crucial, it indicates that the person subscribes to the principles and ethics of this professional organization. Thus, membership in the APA is strongly recommended.

A very desirable additional qualification is the possession of diplomate status from the American Board of Professional Psychology (ABPP) with a speciality in industrial and organizational psychology.

Education

Most industrial and organizational psychologists hold the Ph.D. degree. Some competent persons do not, but in these cases, the experience of the person should be explored very carefully. A Bachelor's Degree is not sufficient. Regardless of degree, the individual's training should have included heavy emphasis on statistics and behavioral sciences.

Knowledge and Experience

A potential consultant should be able to provide evidence of similar work and experience in business, industry, government, etc. in the area of test validation including, if possible, reprints or reports of his researches. In the case of test validation, a minimum requirement should be that the consultant demonstrate familiarity with existing federal and state laws and regulations that are applicable (e.g., Uniform Guidelines on Employee Selection Procedures, etc.). Similarly, the potential candidate should be familiar with the Standards for Educational and Psychological Tests and Manuals published by the APA.

In cases where individuals may not have had the time to build a repository of experience, then evidence of specific graduate training in test and measurement theory, statistics, and behavioral science should be sought (preferably from a transcript from an accredited college or university).

Recent Clients

The names of previous clients should be provided in order that they may be verified. Questions about the consultant's specific tasks performed, integrity, promptness, and fulfillment of obligations could be answered in this manner.

Claims Made

Normally, a competent professional will *not* make any claims for extraordinary results nor guarantee certain positive outcomes. Such claims, if made, should be grounds for discontinuing further consideration of the potential consultant. Exaggerated claims, whether made verbally or in a brochure, are unethical and would not be made by acceptable consultants. Further, the potential consultant should not be interested in selling or promoting a unique method or device that only he can perform. Acceptable procedures are available to all qualified professionals.

Fees

No generally agreed upon standard fee or fee rate is established. The nature of the task and experience of the person(s) will figure in determining the fee to be charged. The firm seeking the services of the consultant should negotiate a fee satisfactory to each party. However, the fee should be for services performed and, in no case, should be dependent upon provisions of some "positive" or "guaranteed" results.

Section D
The Assessment Center as a Selection Technique

The Assessment Center as an Aid in Management Development

WILLIAM C. BYHAM

Assessment centers can aid an organization in the early identification of management potential and in the diagnosis of individual management development needs so that training and development effort can be invested most efficiently. Centers can also act as a powerful stimulant to management development, providing self-insight into problem areas and identifying possible development actions. In addition, the method can increase the accuracy of initial selection of potential managers or salesmen, which will give the management development practitioner better material with which to work. More than one hundred large and small organizations are presently using this relatively new method; some of these are AT&T, IBM, Standard Oil (Ohio), Sears Roebuck, Olin, Cummins Engine, Department of Agriculture, G.E., J. C. Penney, Ford, Steinberg's, Northern Electric, Kodak and Merrill Lynch, Pierce, Fenner and Smith. Hundreds more are actively implementing applications. Reasons for the increasing interest in the technique are three-fold:

1. Accuracy of the technique has been proven in studies conducted by AT&T, IBM, Sears Roebuck and Standard Oil (Ohio). Candidates chosen by the method have been found to be two to three times more likely to be successful at higher management levels than those promoted on the basis of supervisory judgement.

2. Time and money are saved by combining assessment and development in the same procedure. Participation in the program is an extremely powerful learning experience for both participants and the higher management assessors who observe and record the participants' behavior.

3. Management acceptance is high because the assessment center looks valid and makes sense to management. Management is impressed by the simulations of the challenges an employee will face as he or she moves up in management and by the fact that

Reprinted by special permission from the December 1971 *Training and Development Journal.* Copyright 1971 by the American Society for Training and Development, Inc.

line managers usually make the judgment of potential and management development needs.

Assessment centers differ greatly in length, cost, contents, staffing and administration, depending on the objectives of the center, the dimensions to be assessed and the employee population. Basically an assessment center is a formal procedure incorporating group and individual exercises for the identification of dimensions of managerial or sales success identified as important for a particular position or level of management. It differs from other techniques in that a number of individuals are processed at the same time, trained managers who are usually not in a direct supervisory capacity conduct and evaluate the assessment, and multiple exercises are used to evaluate behavior.

Typical Center

In a typical center aimed at identifying the potential of first-level managers for middle-level management positions, 12 participants are nominated by their immediate supervisors as having potential based on their current job performance. For two days, participants take part in exercises developed to expose behaviors deemed important in the particular organization. A participant may play a business game, complete an in-basket exercise, participate in two group discussions and in an individual exercise, and be interviewed. Six assessors observe the participants' behavior and take notes on special observation forms. After the two days of exercises, participants go back to their jobs and the assessors spend two more days comparing their observations and making a final evaluation of each participant. A summary report is developed on each participant, outlining his or her potential and defining development action appropriate for both the organization and the individual. (See Appendix A for a description of a typical two-day center.)

The level of candidate assessment usually dictates the length of the center. Centers for identifying potential in non-management candidates for foreman positions often last only one day while middle management and higher management centers can last as long as two and a half days.

Assessment centers are most popular and seem to be most valid when the position for which the individuals are being considered is quite different from their current positions, for instance, the promotion of salesmen or technicians into management or from direct supervision to middle management where he or she must manage through others. Because the new job requires different skills and abilities than the present job, it is difficult for managers to assess the candidates' managerial aptitude prior to promotion. Thus, many failures result. By simulating in an assessment center the problems and challenges of the level of management for which the individual is being considered, it is possible for management to determine the potential of the individual for the higher level position.

Early Identification

Because of the difficulty of determining supervisory skills in most non-management jobs, the greatest use of assessment centers is the identification of potential for first-level supervision. AT&T alone has assessed more than 70,000 candidates for the first-level management, and about one-half of the assessment center operations in the United States are aimed at identifying supervisory potential.

Another increasing use of assessment centers is in the *early* identification of potential. There are many situations in which management potential must be identified at an early stage so various administrative actions can be taken. For example, AT&T has a program of identifying management potential in blacks and women during their second year of employment so various compensatory training and development activities can be planned to speed them toward management. Another example is found in firms with a commission-sales salary structure which forces them to identify potential early in order to get the salesman on a track into management before high sales income makes movement impossible. Several organizations are using assessment centers for this purpose.

Increasingly, assessment centers are being used at higher levels of management; and it is in these applications that the full potential of centers for management development is achieved. There are numerous middle management assessment centers in operation and a few centers aimed at top management positions.

Individual Management Development Needs

Assessment center summary reports are not usually go—no-go documents. Rather they detail the strengths and weaknesses of participants on the dimensions the organization has previously identified as important to success. Examples of specific behavior at the center are provided as an aid to problem diagnosis and in the later feedback of performance to the participant. Frequently the manager/assessors will make specific developmental recommendations which are also included in the report. . . . This may go directly to management or to staff experts who add additional developmental suggestions based on the needs identified.

Most assessment centers above the bottom level of management have as their primary or strong secondary objective the building of individual development plans. This is not true at bottom-level management because many of those assessed at that level will not reach management; thus, an investment in diagnosing development needs is questionable. While some developmental diagnosis may be possible for those recommended for advancement, it is not generally a prime objective in such programs.

After a number of candidates have been processed, it is possible to use assessment data as an aid in allocating training and development expenditures and in planning new development programs. An extremely useful development needs audit can be obtained by summarizing the needs of a number of assessed participants. Common areas of need can be identified for special priority. Information from multiple assessments can also aid in designing new programs. For instance, Kodak recently developed a new pre-foreman training program based on its early assessment experience. Insights from assessments of candidates for the position of product service center manager by the J. C. Penney Company resulted in the development of a totally new development plan. So few technically-trained candidates were found to have the necessary management potential that the company decided to change its whole approach to filling the position and developed a program to give technical training to people of proven managerial competence.

Stimulation of Self-Development

Participation in an assessment center is a developmental experience As can be quickly recognized, many assessment exercises such as the in-basket, management games and leaderless group discussions also are training exercises. Thus, to the extent that performance feedback is provided, participation in an assessment center is a developmental experience. In most centers above the lowest level of management, considerable performance feedback is provided during the assessment program. A good example of the kinds of feedback provided is the assessment center program of the Autolite Division of the Ford Motor Company. Participants take part in professionally led critiques of their performance in group activities, and they watch their performance in groups by means of videotape. After individually taking the in-basket for assessment purposes, they meet in small groups to share their decisions and actions with each other, to evaluate their reasoning and to broaden their repertory of responses.

Even without special feedback opportunities built in, there is a great deal of evidence that most participants gain in self-insight from participating in assessment exercises and that this insight is fairly accurate. The evidence comes from comparing participant responses on self-evaluation questionnaires given after exercises with assessor evaluations. Correlations of .6 and higher based on large samples from several organizations have been found.

While self-insight gained from taking part in assessment center exercises is important, it is secondary to the insights gained from receiving feedback of the assessor observations. Almost all assessment centers provide feedback to participants. The amount and detail of the feedback vary greatly but are largely related to organizational level. Higher-level participants get much more information than lower-level participants. Career counseling and planning discussions are often combined with assessor feedback for higher-level participants. Most feedback interviewing ends in a written commitment to action on the part of the participant and sometimes the organization.

Combined Assessment and Training

Still another important way the assessment center can stimulate development is to combine physically an assessment program with a training program. This is sometimes done because of the sheer economics of the combination. Junior Achievement Incorporated was able to put an assessment program into the beginning of an existing two-week training program with little loss in training impact. The Huyck Corporation recently completed a series of centers in which an entire level of upper middle management was assessed. Since it is an international company, this entailed bringing in participants from Australia, South America and Europe in addition to participants from throughout the United States. Rather than have the participants leave after two and a half days as would be normal, they followed the regular center activities with two and a half days of training exercises. The economics of travel and facilities was such that these additional days of training could be added at slight increase in expense.

But most important as an argument for combining or closely associating training and assessment is the "unfreezing" process that occurs with assessment. As indicated above, even without formal feedback from assessors, center participants are greatly sensitized to their own shortcomings and open to development ideas and training. A number of companies have recognized the advantages of integrating training and assessment because of this unfreezing process. Most have chosen to follow the assessment with training designed to correct common problems such as group efficiency, sensitivity to others, public speaking, management skills and decision making. The ideal situation is for assessor observations to be fed back during the training period to maximize development.

Assessor Training

An assessor in an assessment center benefits more than the participant in terms of direct training. Between assessor training and participation as an assessor in a center, the assessor benefits in the following ways:
1. Improvement in interviewing skills
2. Broadening of observation skills
3. Increased appreciation of group dynamics and leadership styles
4. New insights into behavior
5. Strengthening of management skills through repeated working with in-basket case problems and other simulations
6. Broadening of repertory of responses to problems
7. Establishment of normative standards by which to evaluate performance
8. Development of a more precise vocabulary with which to describe behavior

While many on-the-job uses can be made of these improved skills, perhaps the greatest impact is in performance appraisal interviewing. Extensive self-report data from assessors indicate a vast improvement in both accuracy and success of appraisal interviewing. Organizations such as G.E. feel so strongly about the many benefits from assessor training that they have increased the ratio of assessors to participants in their programs in order to expose more assessors to the experience.

Assessor training comes from a formal training program prior to the center, but principally from application of the procedures as an assessor in an assessment center. It is a unique opportunity for managers to focus on observing behavior without the normal interruptions associated with business. After observing the behavior, the assessors can compare their observations with those of other assessors and sometimes have the opportunity to repeat the observation via videotape recording. The procedures learned in assessor training are put into practice and thus stamped into the assessor's memory.

The principal focus of assessor training is usually on interviewing, observing behavior and handling the in-basket. All exercises in an assessment center usually call for some combination of these skills. In addition, practice on all the exercises to be observed in assessment centers is usually provided. Any number of assessors can be trained at once, with assessor training for as many as 25 individuals not uncommon. Many organizations starting assessment centers initially train large numbers of managers as assessors to establish a pool from which to draw assessors. This plan has a number of other benefits which include providing a large number of management people with a quick orientation to the program so that they can most effectively use the reports generated. It also allows the opportunity for a rough screening of the assessors so that the most skilled assessors can be used in the assessment center program.

In most centers run by large corporations, assessors serve only once. The exception is AT&T centers where assessors work on six-month assignments. In smaller companies assessors must, by necessity, be used more often. In all situations assessors must be trained, but naturally more training is committed to the person who will serve for 20 weeks than for one week. Training for new, short-service assessors usually takes from two to five days, depending upon the complexity of the center, the importance of the assessment decision and the importance management gives to assessor training. A few organizations have cut assessor training to the point that it is more orientation than training, but this is not advisable. Training is important both for accurate results and for the assessors themselves.

Assessor Level

Assessors are usually line managers two or more levels above the participants nominated by their supervisors for the task. Line managers are used because:

1. They are familiar with the jobs for which the participant is being assessed and can therefore better judge the participant's aptitude.

2. Participation as an assessor is a developmental experience.

3. The involvement of the line management greatly increases the acceptance of the program by other managers and by the participants themselves.

4. Exposure as an assessor increases familiarity with the program, assuring most effective use of the results.

Providing broad familiarity with an assessment program is an extremely important result. Take, for instance, the common situation found in the use of psychological test results by managers. Managers usually over-rely or under-rely on test results. They have difficulty determining the correct emphasis because they are not familiar with the tests, tester or intent of the program. While the same lack of understanding can happen relative to an assessment center report, the involvement of line managers both in the development of the program and as assessors in the program gives a much wider basis of understanding. When a manager who has been an assessor gets the assessment report, he knows the basis for the observations and judgments and can more accurately weigh them against data on job performance and other available information.

A few organizations mix line managers and personnel department or other staff people. This decision usually results from a difficulty recruiting assessors or as a means of decreasing assessor training (the trained staff people lead the line managers in completing forms, etc.).

Even less frequently are professional psychologists used as assessors. AT&T has made occasional use of academic psychologists hired for the summer as assessors in their research centers and in the evaluation of very high levels of management. A few other organizations have done similar experimentation with professional psychologists as assessors but have discontinued the process. The little research available indicates that professionals do no better than *trained* line managers in performing their tasks. While the professional psychologists may have some superior observational skills, this is probably negated by their lack of company knowledge. A few organizations use a single professional assessor to do certain kinds of testing and interpreting of results.

Validity and Relation to EEOC Guidelines

To insure that they are getting what they have paid for, practitioners have always been concerned with the validity of selection, appraisal and training techniques. Since the *Griggs et al. vs. Duke Power* Supreme Court Case (1971), which affirmed the guidelines on employee selection and promotion promulgated by the Equal Employment Opportunity Commission, organizations must be prepared to prove that their standards for selection and appraisal are job-related. This includes assessment centers.

Assessment centers can be shown to be job-related through their content. To the extent the center's dimensions resulted from an accurate and complete job analysis and to the extent that the exercises and procedures used accurately measured the dimensions, the procedure is valid. Center exercises often are forms of job samples just as a typing test is a job sample of a typist's job and thus possess rational validity; they make sense. An in-basket exercise obviously meets most of the criteria for a job sample but so also does an exercise measuring group effectiveness if given to executives who must spend a great deal of their time in meetings. Perhaps because of the reasonableness of the assessment center method to both participants and observers, no known charges of discrimination resulting from applying the assessment center method have been filed anywhere in the United States.

To prove a center job-related through its content, particular care must be taken in establishing the dimensions through a complete job analysis and in choosing the proper exercises and procedures to be sure that the desired dimensions are brought out. Research relating dimensions to individual assessment center exercises conducted by Standard Oil (Ohio)[1] and AT&T[2] will help in the latter step.

The superior way of establishing job-relatedness is through statistically relating job criterion such as performance ratings or advancement in the organization with assessment center ratings. An organization adopting the assessment center method should set up procedures to collect data so such relationships can be investigated. In the meantime there is strong evidence from organizations more experienced with the method that the procedure is, in general, extremely valid. While validity in one organization does not necessarily mean the procedure is valid in another, the existence of these studies would be an important consideration in any court case involving assessment centers.

There are 22 published research studies attempting to evaluate the overall validity of assessment centers applications. Fifteen show positive results, six have such small samples as to show no results, and one study based on a very small sample indicates the assessment center process is not effective. While 15 positive studies may not seem like a massive research finding, it becomes more impressive when the extremely high quality and scientific rigor of many of the studies are considered and when the research is compared with research attempting to establish results of other management selection or development programs. Even given its recent adoption by most organizations as a management development tool, far more is known about the assessment center method than most other procedures with the exception of tests.

Pure Research Studies

Two excellent research studies have been conducted under conditions that meet the most rigorous experimental specifications. Both conducted by AT&T, they involve situations in which employees were processed through centers, the results not used in any way, and later progress and performance followed up. The first study involved 123 new college hires and 144 non-college first-level managers.[3] After a period of eight years, 82 percent of the college assessees and 75 percent of the noncollege assessees who reached middle-level management were accurately identified by the center. Equally important, 88 percent of the college assessees and 95 percent of the noncollege assessees who were never promoted out of the first-level management were identified. Thus the assessment center was found to be valid at choosing both "comers" and "losers." This study differs from all other studies to be discussed in that AT&T used, in the main, professional psychologists as assessors and supplemented the usual assessment exercises with a number of clinical techniques.

The second study rating the title of "pure research" was conducted to validate

AT&T's salesman selection assessment centers.[4] Seventy-eight newly-hired system salesmen were assessed right after being hired, but management had no access to the assessment data. Later on, an experienced field review team having no knowledge of assessment center reports observed the assessees during actual sales calls and rated their performance. The validity results were particularly impressive. The assessment panel predicted that nearly one-half of the assessees would not be acceptable, and only 24 percent of those gave acceptable sales calls compared to 68 percent of the "acceptable" group and 100 percent of the "more than acceptable" group. The correlation between the assessment panel global rating and the field review rating was .51, a substantial increase in prediction compared to the multiple correlation of .33 between four paper and pencil tests and the criteria. Also indicating the importance of the assessment center prediction was the finding that supervisor and trainer ratings were unrelated to job performance.

Operational Studies

Most of the large organizations that have operated centers for any significant length of time have some validity data on their ongoing centers. To various extents, these studies all suffer from methodological flaws caused by the fact that use was made of the data in the organization. To the extent that good performance in a center affected the criterion used, e.g., promotion, use of the criterion as a measure of validity is impaired. The extent of this contamination remains a mystery; but through various statistical and experimental design methods, most of the reported studies have minimized the effect.

Being the first to apply the technique, AT&T has also conducted the most impressive operational validity studies. An early study conducted by Michigan Bell compared an assessed group promoted to management with a group promoted before the assessment center program.[5] But unfortunately, the groups were not matched. Results revealed nearly twice as many high performance and potential men at first-level management in assessed as in non-assessed groups. Another study conducted by New England Bell Company compared "acceptable" and "non-acceptable" assessed groups consisting of craftsmen promoted to first-level management and first-level managers promoted to second level. The acceptable group was "definitely superior" to the non-acceptable group according to the researchers.[6] A large follow-up study,[7] using four other Bell companies, compared three groups (N = 223) of first-level candidates assessed "acceptable," "questionable" and "not acceptable" and subsequently promoted to management to non-assessed groups (N = 283) promoted before and after the assessment program. As in the other follow-up studies, this study was also limited to recently promoted managers in the assessed group; but unlike the other studies, by denoting a "not acceptable" assessed group of those promoted, the false negative rate could be determined. Moreover, by studying the two non-assessed groups, possible halo bias due to promotion before versus after the assessment center could be determined. An attempt was made to match assessed and non-assessed groups but it was not entirely successful.

While use of assessment centers obviously improved selection odds, it was by no means perfect as indicated by the fact that nearly 50 percent of those thought to be non-acceptable actually succeeded on the job. This research and most other research indicate that assessment centers are better at predicting ratings of management potential and actual advancement than performance at first level. This is probably caused by the increasing importance of the management component of jobs as individuals rise in an organization. It is this management component that is most commonly and accurately measured in an assessment center.

TABLE 1
Summary of the Findings

Assessed	% Rated Above Average in Job Performance in First Level Management	% Rated as Having High Management Potential	% Promoted
Acceptable	68	50	11
Questionable	65	40	5
Non-Acceptable	46	31	0

By far the most impressive AT&T study followed up 5,943 assessees as they advanced in management.[8] The criterion was advancement above first-level management, the level at which the assessment results were used and thus felt to be relatively clear of bias. Individuals assessed "more than acceptable" were twice as likely to be promoted two or more times than individuals assessed as "acceptable" and almost 10 times more likely than those rated "not acceptable." In addition it was found that the correlation of .461 was raised only minutely with the use of a mental ability test (r of .463).

Standard Oil (Ohio) validity studies include a managerial progress criterion and additionally includes 12 job performance ratings and a potential rating. The findings confirm the earlier AT&T findings of the moderate validity of a center in predicting managerial performance but its high validity coefficients substantially exceed those for performance ratings based upon the interview and projective tests.[9]

IBM Studies

IBM has conducted 11 studies of its assessment center programs. All show a positive relationship between center findings and various criteria of success with more than half of the 22 correlations being statistically significant.[10] One study [11] involved 94 lower and middle level managers. From job analyses of positions held, a criterion measure of progress (increase in management responsibility) was constructed and correlations of .37 were found between the progress criterion and the global assessment rating from the center. But interestingly it was found that if statistical methods were used in combining the judgments relative to the rating dimension, the correlation climbed to .62.

Another interesting study which was almost assuredly not contaminated involved sales managers demoted after becoming first-line managers.[12] Of 46 individuals assessed as having potential for higher management and subsequently promoted, 4 percent were demoted because of job failure. Of 71 individuals promoted in spite of the assessment center finding of low potential, 20 percent failed.

Extremely thorough and comprehensive research has been conducted by Sears Roebuck into the validity of its assessment centers. Both their center used for the initial selection of management trainees and their centers to assess management potential have been subjected to rigorous study which has shown most components of the center to be statistically related to various criteria of job success.[13]

Negative Studies

These are the principal studies established in the validity of the assessment centers. Other studies have either used such small samples or questionable methodology as not to warrant discussion.[14] The two studies which might be considered negative to assessment centers also suffer from a number of methodological problems. The first is not really a validity study as assessment centers were used as the criterion rather than job performance. This study[15] seems to indicate that a thorough study of a participant's personnel file and an interview will provide information comparable to the results of an assessment center. If true, such a finding would be a wonderful cost saving to organizations. Methodological and other factors relative to the study make generalizations difficult.

The only study indicating that assessment centers are less valid than normal assessment procedures was based on 37 participants in an assessment center conducted by the Caterpillar Tractor Company.[16] Two groups of recently promoted first-line supervisors were studied, including 37 subjects assessed in an assessment center program and 27 subjects assessed by traditional methods, which included a review of personnel files and personnel interviews with each candidate and his first-line supervisor. Using supervisor rating as a criterion, the study found that the assessed group was rated above average in performance slightly more often than the non-assessed group. But both were highly accurate.

A detailed analysis of all known validity studies relative to assessment centers can be found in "Validity of Assessment Centers" by Cohen, Moses and Byham (in press). With the exception of the two "pure" AT&T research projects, all the studies mentioned above are subject to various biases, statistical restrictions in range, etc., which are typical of practical operational programs. Yet, putting them all together, the impact seems clear. The assessment center is a superior method of predicting management potential—compared with methods such as supervisor appraisals and tests.

Differential Validity

An important consideration is whether, like some paper and pencil tests, assessment centers are biased against minority groups and women. There is no published research on this question, but unpublished studies indicate that the final judgment of a center is equally valid for whites and blacks. Performance on individual exercises is different, but this seems to be somehow taken into consideration by the assessors. The area is definitely in need of research. In the meantime, a number of organizations have adopted a policy that two or more blacks must be in a center or none at all. They feel that being the only black out of 12 participants might put the black at a disadvantage.

Even less information is available about possible discriminatory effects on women, apparently because center administrators have observed no problems in this area. Some organizations with large work forces of women have segregated centers by sex, but most have mixed the sexes with apparently no problem. Again this is an area much in need of research.

Problems in Assessment Centers

Two potential problems in using the assessment center method involve the employee who does not get nominated to the assessment center and the employee who attends and does poorly.

A philosophical weakness of most assessment center programs is the reliance on the supervisor to nominate employees for participation. Some high potential employees may never be nominated because qualities of aggressiveness, curiosity and intelligence that might make a person successful at higher levels of management are not always appreciated by lower-level supervision. To get around this problem, some companies use self-nomination or put everyone at a particular level of management through a program. Other organizations have experimented with nominations based on personnel department records indicating interest in advancement such as application for educational aid, etc., while IBM has investigated the use of tests to select people for attendance.[17]

Perhaps more of a concern to many managers is the attitudinal impact on those not nominated. Again no research evidence is available, but the feeling of "not getting to show what I can do" must be present in many individuals. Such feelings are not unique to assessment centers. The same feeling can be generated in those who are not tapped to attend any kind of managerial development program. Obviously anxiety is highest where the developmental program or assessment center is *the* stepping stone up in management. Self-nomination and other methods around the supervisor roadblock seem to be the only answer, but they can be expensive.

Typically the greatest concern of management is the individual who attends an assessment center and does poorly. As noted above, he usually recognizes his poor performance whether or not he receives a formal feedback. Will he look for another job where his chances are untainted by his poor assessment center performance? Research at three companies says no, while research at one says definitely yes—but maybe it is a way of clearing out the deadwood. It appears that organizations that have made a deliberate effort to avoid problems through expert handling of the feedback process and providing alternate methods of advancement (e.g., technical ladders) experience no problem. Most organizations go to great lengths to stress that the assessment center is only one portion of the assessment process—a supplement to regular appraisal and other information. They stress that the participant has an opportunity on the job to disprove any negative insights gained from assessment. If precautions are not taken, some increase in turnover of lower-rated participants can occur. Turnover may not actually be increased—just speeded. The assessment center process speeds the realization that promotion is questionable.

Anxiety

Anxiety at an assessment center can also be a problem. There is no doubt that the assessment process is stress-provoking and that the performance of a few participants is affected by the stress. The fact that the individual's performance may have been affected by stress is usually recognized by the assessors and taken into consideration in the final assessment judgment. Stress does not seem to be an important problem.

"Crown Princesses" or "Golden Boys" can emerge from an assessment center if the organization allows special treatment of successful participants in the program. This can be good or bad. It is natural for the outstanding participants in centers to get prime developmental experiences to prepare them for positions management sees in the future. This is not making a crown prince; it is just putting the company's money where it will reap the greatest dividends. But special treatment is wrong if the individual is given special consideration on his present job. A negative effect on the morale of other members in the unit can result if the individual is seen as being allowed to do less work because he is the "number one boy."

A frequently raised fear is that assessment centers will turn out more and more stereotyped versions of the particular organization's "organization man." The only data on this comes from IBM which found that far from being organization men, successful participants in assessment centers were less conforming and more independent. Because the assessment center method brings out a much broader range of data about the individual than is typical from interviews and other conventional means, decision-making is not restricted to the superficial characteristics often associated with an "organization man."

Costs

Costs vary dramatically among centers depending on the objectives of the center, number of participants and assessors, length, location and most of all what is figured in costs. Organizations have come up with cost figures for their programs ranging from $5.00 a head to $500. The figure, however, cannot be compared and may be vastly misleading because they include quite different elements. The cost of assessors' time (including training), participants' time, and administrators' time (including preparing for the center and writing reports) depends on the length of the center and the amount of training given assessors. Assessor and administrator commitment can be cut markedly if training is conducted separately from assessment or when the company reaches the situation that assessors are being repeated, thus requiring no additional training.

Costs of meals and facilities can be figured based on the organization's experience conducting training programs. Programs on company premises can cost as little as $50, while program at a resort can cost as much as $3,000 for 12 participants, six observers and one administrator.

Exercise costs depend on the length of the program and the nature of the exercises. They generally are between $100 and $200 for six participants. There is usually a one-time investment in reusable supplies which will run about $100. These costs assume all exercises are purchased commercially. In actual fact, many organizations develop at least one unique exercise for their center and some organizations prefer to have all unique exercises.

The remaining cost considerations are start-up costs. These costs depend upon the organization's needs for consulting help. Many organizations take information from articles such as this one, order exercises and start the assessment center. Other organizations send their potential assessment center administrators to workshops on assessor training. Many others use consultants to aid in planning, assessor training, administration of several pilot programs, the initial writing of assessment center reports and the planning of feedback interviews. Consultants can make their greatest contribution in planning a center and in assessor training.

Aid in Reaching a Decision

Attendance at an assessment center is the best way to get a real feel for the concept. Many organizations have arranged to have key managers attend a center run by another company as a way of selling the technique. Some organizations are happy to have guests, especially during the assessor discussion portion of the program. If this is not possible, showing videotape recordings of assessment centers in operation can accomplish nearly the same result. These are available from the author. Another effective means of acquainting managers with the methods is to put them through a representative exercise or two. Managers quickly see the potential value of the kinds of behaviors that are brought out.

Conclusions

Assessment centers are relatively new as aids in identifying and developing sales and management potential, but the method shows great promise. Many previous management development techniques and instruments have had great popular success but have waned when the spotlight of empirical research was trained on them. Their effectiveness could not be proved. Assessment centers, on the other hand, came out of a basic research study, AT&T's "Management Progress Study"; and research has continued on the method in almost every organization where it has been applied. Much more research is needed both on general validity and on specific exercises and procedures used; but based on the findings to-date, one must conclude that the method works. It also has the advantage of great acceptability to management. But it does not work equally well in all circumstances and should be used selectively. Nevertheless the method should be added to the repertory of tools available to the management development practitioner.

STEPS IN STARTING AN ASSESSMENT CENTER

The following outline represents the principal steps in establishing an assessment center:

1. Determine objectives of program
2. Define dimensions to be assessed
3. Select exercises that will bring out the dimensions
4. Design assessor training and assessment center program
5. Announce program, inform participants and assessors, handle administrative detail
6. Train assessors
7. Conduct center
8. Write summary reports on participants
9. Feedback to participants a summary of performance at center and development actions
10. Evaluate center
11. Set up procedures to validate center against a criterion of job success

While the task of starting a center may appear large and extremely time-consuming, it need not be. Numerous organizations have started operating centers less than one month after management gave the go ahead. Like most techniques that have considerable rational appeal to management, there usually is great pressure to get the program going after it is approved.

Notes

1. Carleton, F. O., *Relationships Between Follow-up Evaluations and Information Developed in a Management Assessment Center,* Paper presented at the meetings of the American Psychological Assn. Convention, Miami Beach, Fla. 1970.

Finley, R. M., Jr., *An Evaluation of Behavior Predictions from Projective Tests Given in a Management Assessment Assessment Center,* Paper presented at the meetings of the American Psychological Assn. Convention, Miami Beach, Fla. 1970.

2. Bray, D. W., and Grant, D. L., "The Assessment Center in the Measurement of Potential for Business Management, *Psychological Monographs,* 1966, 80 (17, Whole No. 625).

3. Bray andGrant, ibid.

4. Bray, D. W., and Campbell, R.J., "Selection of Salesmen by Means of an Assessment Center," *Journal of Applied Psychology,* 1968, 52, 36-41.

5. Bray, D. W., "The Management Progress Study," *American Psychologist,* 1964, 19, pp. 419-420.

6. Campbell, R. J., and Bray, D. W., "Assessment Centers: An Aid in Management Selection," *Personnel Administration,* Mar.-Apr. 1967.

7. Campbell and Bray, ibid.

8. Moses, J. L., *Assessment Center Performance and Management Progress* (ATT), Paper presented as part of the symposium, "Validity of Assessment Centers," at the 79th Annual Convention of the American Psychological Assn., 1971.

9. Carleton, op. cit; Finley, op. cit.

10. Dodd, W. E., Summary of IBM Assessment Validations," Paper presented as part of the symposium, "Validity of Assessment Centers," at the 79th Annual Convention of the American Psychological Assn., 1971.

11. Wollowick, H. B., and McNamara, W. J., "Relationship of the Components of an Assessment Center to Management Success," *Journal of Applied Psychology,* 1969, 53, pp. 348-352.

12. Dodd, op. cit.

13. Bentz, V. Jon, *Validity of Sears Assessment Center Procedures,* Paper presented as part of the symposium, "Validity of Assessment Centers," at the 79th Annual Convention of the American Psychological Assn., 1971.

14. Bender, J. M., Calvert, O. L., and Jaffee, C. L., *Report on Supervision Selection Program,* Oak Ridge Gaseous Diffusion Plant, Union Carbide Corporation, Nuclear Div., Apr. 17, 1970 (K1789).

Schaffer, A. J., *Information about Assessment Center for ES&D Program Finalists,* Memorandum from Director, Personnel Div., National Office, Internal Revenue Service, Sept. 16, 1970.

Tennessee Valley Authority, *TVA's Experiment in the Assessment of Managerial Potential,* undated.

15. Hinrichs, J. R., "Comparison of 'Real life' Assessments of Management Potential with Situational Exercises, Paper-and-Pencil Ability Tests, and Personality Inventories," *Journal of Applied Psychology,* 1969, 53, pp. 425-433.

16. Bullard, J. F., *An Evaluation of the Assessment Center Approach to Selecting Supervisors,* mimeo report, Caterpillar Tractor Co., May 1969.

17. Dodd, W. E., and Kraut, A. I., *The Prediction of Management Assessment Center Performance from Earlier Measures of Personality and Sales Training Performance,* a preliminary report, 1970 (internal company report).

Appendix A

A Typical Two-Day Assessment Center

DAY 1

Orientation Meeting

Management Game—"Conglomerate." Forming different types of conglomerates is the goal with four-man teams of participants bartering companies to achieve their planned result. Teams set their own acquisition objectives and must plan and organize to meet them.

Background Interview—A 1½ hour interview conducted by an assessor.

Group Discussion—"Management Problems." Four short cases calling for various forms of management judgment are presented to groups of four participants. In one hour the group, acting as consultants, must resolve the cases and submit its recommendation in writing.

Individual Fact-Finding and Decision-Making Exercise—"The Research Budget." The participant is told that he has just taken over as division manager. He is given a brief description of an incident in which his predecessor has recently turned down a request for funds to continue a research project. The research director is appealing for a reversal of the decision. The participant is given 15 minutes to ask questions to dig out the facts in the case. Following this fact-finding period, he must present his decision orally with supporting reasoning and defend it under challenge.

DAY 2

In-Basket Exercise—"Section Manager's In-Basket." The contents of a section manager's in-basket are simulated. The participant is instructed to go through the contents, solving problems, answering questions, delegating, organizing, scheduling and planning, just as he might do if he were promoted suddenly to the position. An assessor reviews the contents of the completed in-basket and conducts a one-hour interview with the participant to gain further information.

Assigned Role Leaderless Group Discussion—"Compensation Committee." The Compensation Committee is meeting to allocate $8,000 in discretionary salary increases among six supervisory and managerial employees. Each member of the committee (participants) represents a department of the company and is instructed to "do the best he can" for the employee from his department.

Analysis, Presentation and Group Discussion: "The Pretzel Factory." This financial analysis problem has the participant role-play a consultant called in to advise Carl Flowers of the C. F. Pretzel Company on two problems: what to do about a division of the company that has continually lost money, and whether the corporation should expand. Participants are given data on the company and are asked to recommend appropriate courses of action. They make their recommendation in a seven-minute presentation after which they are formed into a group to come up with a single set of recommendations.

Final Announcements

DAYS 3 and 4

Assessors meet to share their observations on each participant and to arrive at summary evaluations relative to each dimension sought and overall potential and training needs.

A Hard Look at Management Assessment Centers and Their Future

ALLEN I. KRAUT

The assessment center technique was pioneered by Dr. Douglas Bray and his associates at American Telephone and Telegraph Company in the mid 1950s. In the last decade, it has spread in usage to many other companies, large and small. The heart of the technique is a series of situational exercises in which a dozen candidates for management take part while being observed systematically by several raters who are usually managers themselves. The exercises are simulated management tasks and include individual exercises such as an in-basket and group exercises such as a leaderless group discussion. In some assessment centers, personal interviews and psychological tests are also used.

One of the most common questions asked is whether the method is valid. The earliest and strongest evidence comes from the work done by Bray and Grant (1966) with several hundred new hires into AT & T who were assessed and then followed-up several years later, without the data being allowed to influence their careers in any way. The raters' predictions about who would move into middle management ranks were accurate at significantly above the chance level. Similar data have been reported by Wollowick and McNamara (1969) on some 94 men from service and administrative occupations who were assessed and showed subsequent success. In this case also, the higher-rated men moved significantly further.

A study Kraut and Scott (1972) recently completed of 437 salesmen who had gone through an assessment center from 1965 to 1970 followed up on the number who had been promoted by the end of 1970. The data had been used to promote these men to first-line management, but subsequent promotions seemed unlikely to be influenced by the assessment ratings and anecdotal evidence supports this assumption. As shown in table 1, among the men who went on to first-line management after assessment, those who were higher rated were more likely to move on to second promotions.

Even more dramatic evidence on the program's validity comes from the number of management demotions. We see that salesman who are poorly rated in the assessment center were more likely to fail as managers. Again, anecdotal evidence supports the belief that demotions were uninfluenced by assessment ratings. We must also remember that the low-rated salesmen were promoted after the assessment program and *despite* their low rating. If anything, this additional screening helped to select the best of the low-rated group.

These studies and many others lead one to conclude that assessment programs have validity in predicting those who will move ahead in an organization. Many of the studies have flaws, but there is a consistent pattern of apparent validity.

Acceptability

The apparent validity also exists at another level, that of face validity. In table 2

Reprinted by permission of the author and the publisher from *Personnel Journal*, vol. 51 (May 1972), no. 5, pp. 317-26.

we can see the distribution of over-all rating awarded to the salesmen in our study. A very substantial proportion are poorly rated even though all of these men were rated promotable as a condition of nomination to attend. Discriminations of those who are judged to have more or less management potential are certainly being made. We know from the work of Greenwood and McNamara (1967) that they are also made with satisfactory reliability (r's mostly in the .70s and .80s). Interviews reveal that management observers generally feel the program is valid, the exercises seem reasonable and they can make discriminations which are meaningful to them.

TABLE 1
MOBILITY OF ASSESSMENT CANDIDATES AFTER BECOMING
FIRST-LINE SALES MANAGERS

Original Assessment Rating (of Ultimate Potential)	No. Promoted to First-Line Manager	A % Promoted to Higher Levels	B % Demoted from First-Line Manager	
Executive Management	12	42	0	
				— 4
Higher Management	34	50	6	
Second-Line Management	50	30	14	14
First-Line Management	40	15	20	
				—20
Remain Non-Management	31	13	19	
Over-all	167	28	14	14
		$X^2 = 16.18$	$X^2 = 5.82$	$X^2 = 5.57$
		$p < .01$	$p < .22$	$p < .07$

(From Kraut & Scott, 1972)

Face validity seems to extend to the participants themselves. This conclusion comes from data collected by the writer and several colleagues on similar assessment programs in several countries. Although the numbers of people in these studies are relatively small and the questions are not always worded identically, the major thrust of the evidence is clear. As shown in table 3, the assessees see the technique as really getting at the abilities important to being a manager.

This face validity on the part of most assessees goes even further. As shown in table 4, most of them also feel that this data would be useful in making promotional decisions in the selection of first-line managers.

Morality

Doubts about assessment centers have been thought of, but less often expressed, at another level—that of morality. Some people wonder whether assessment centers are morally proper. To judge the morality we must examine the consequences of the process and not merely the process itself. The consequences have to be compared against the effect of existing promotional systems. This comparison shows that assessment programs are more likely to encourage decision making about promotions to be made openly and objectively, with agreed upon standards, and based on relevant, systemically gathered data. Further, the explicitness of this method, contrasted with the relative invisibility of existing promotional systems, helps us to evaluate its appropriateness.

Doubts about the morality of assessment programs rest largely on a failure to critically examine current systems of promotional decision making. We must recognize that promotional decisions are continually being made, even in the absence of assessment centers, and usually on an inadequate basis. From what we know so far, the management assessment technique seems to be a morally superior technique.

TABLE 2
PROMOTION AND SEPARATION RATES OF SALES NON-MANAGEMENT CANDIDATES ASSESSED FROM 1965 TO 1970

Original Assessment Rating (of Ultimate Potential)	A Distribution of Ratings No.	%	B % Promoted to First-Line Manager	C % Later Separated From Company
Executive Management	14	3	86	0
Higher Management	57	13	60	5
Second-Line Management	114	26	44	5
First-Line Management	123	28	33	5
Remain Non-Management	129	30	24	3
Over-all	437	100	35 $X^2=38.69$ $p<.001$	4 N.S.

(From Kraut & Scott, 1972)

The advantages of a formal assessment approach are also apparent if we compare it to typical promotional systems in most companies on a psychometric basis. The typical system, with heavy reliance on the immediate manager, is overshadowed on several counts. The assessment center technique offers evaluations from multiple raters, who tend to be objective and trained to make judgments of management skills, based on attentive observation of relevant standardized tasks, with all candidates being compared on a common yardstick.

Value Added

At another level of validity, one must ask how much an assessment program adds to existing promotional systems. After all, current systems operate fairly well, according to many executives. Again, some of the early AT & T studies present some of the best evidence.

Campbell and Bray (1967) compared 40 first-line managers promoted before an assessment program was installed to 40 managers assessed and then promoted. Nearly twice as many among the assessed group were rated higher on both management job performance and future potential. In this case, the assessment program seems to have had a strong positive effect.

In a later and larger AT & T study (also reported by Campbell and Bray, 1967), high rated managers were judged higher on job performance only slightly more often than men not assessed, or rated as not acceptable, as shown in table 5. However, considerably more were rated as having higher future potential. It may be that the performance of first-line managers in this company is heavily dependent on technical skills which the men carry into that level of management and that the power of the assessment center shows up primarily when they are considered for higher levels of management.

TABLE 3
Assessors' Opinions: Face Validity

"To what extent do you believe the assessment program measures important qualitities required of (your company's) managers?"

		To a Very Great Extent	A Great Extent	To A Sufficient Extent	A Moderate Extent	Not Very Much	Not At All
United Kingdom	(11)	36%	55	N/A	9	0	0
Japan	(36)	47%	34	N/A	19	0	0
Germany I	(36)	11%	31	50	3	3	0

"Does It Appear To You That the Assessment Program Measures Many of the Important Qualities Required of Effective Managers?"

		Yes	No	No Opinion
U.S.A.	(138)	74%	18	8

TABLE 4
Assessees' Opinion: Use for Selection

"To what extent do you believe assessment information could be used to help in the selection of employees for promotion to first-line management?"

		Very Good for This Purpose	Good	Fair	Poor	Very Poor
United Kingdom	(11)	73%	27	0	0	0
Japan	(36)	14%	69	14	3	0
Germany I	(36)	8%	53	30	6	3

"Do you believe the assessment program can give valid predictions about a person's ability and future success as a manager?"

		Yes, Very Good Statement	Yes, Useful Statement	Only Partly Useful	No, Only Partly Relevant	No, Nothing
Germany I	(60)	22%	51	25	2	0
Germany II	(70)	30%	62	7	1 (Undecided)	0

"Do you believe that assessment program information should be used to help in the selection and promotion of men to first-line management?"

		Yes	No	No Opinion
U.S.A.	(135)	47%	47	7

A study done by John Hinrichs (1969) in a large technology-based company suggests where the advantage of the assessment program may lie. He compared the assessment ratings on 47 men to the ratings independently given by two executives after a review of the men's personnel jackets. The two sets of ratings overlapped considerably (r= .47) but, as shown in table 6, the assessment ratings correlated significantly with an outside criterion of relative salary standing (r= .37) whereas the executive ratings were insignificantly correlated with the criterion (r= .10). The two sets of ratings also overlap considerably on the three major factors tapped by the assessment program except for one. This factor, based on observed interpersonal activity, is exactly what contributed the greatest amount of unique variance to the criterion, as well as to the over-all assessment itself. Incidentally, the interrater reliability of the two executives was only .56 compared to considerably higher reliabilities typically reported for the assessment program.

Impact on the Organization

When an organization sees this method as having value and installs it, what is the impact on the selection system? One fear is that it may undermine the first-line

TABLE 5
PERCENTAGE OF MEN DESIGNATED AS (A) ABOVE AVERAGE PERFORMERS AND (B) HIGH POTENTIAL FOR ADVANCEMENT

	Total	High Performance	High Potential
Assessed Men			
Acceptable	136	68	50
Questionable	61	65	40
Not Acceptable	26	46	31
Men Not Assessed			
Promoted Since Pgm.	132	63	19
Promoted Before Pgm.	151	55	20

(From Campbell & Bray, 1967)

manager's position. But generally, a manager nominating a subordinate to an assessment center is in exactly the same position as before, namely, recommending his man to a higher level manager who is asked to choose between several eligible candidates. In most organizations without assessment programs, the manager's nominees are not automatically promoted. Thus, assessment data becomes an additional input for the higher level decision maker to use.

From another side, different critics may respond, "Doesn't this method serve merely to perpetuate the existing management system, breed conformity and fail to select the different kinds of talent needed for the future?" There may be some truth in this question. According to some research by Dodd and Kraut (1970), men nominated to attend assessment centers were more likely to be lower in independence and higher on conformity, as measured by the Gordon Survey of Interpersonal Values, than their peers who were not nominated. But these characteristics were unrelated to success in the assessment centers. Still, managers may have valid reasons for not nominating these particular non-conformists. Perhaps we should treat the manager's judgment as a moderator variable along with other measures which are useful predictors.

What techniques can be used to overcome blocks to the nomination of deserving candidates? The most obvious is to invite candidates to nominate themselves to attend the assessment centers. The self-nominations have been used by some companies with great success. We should also consider the use of nomination by peers, or promising test scores, or other unorthodox techniques which might foster greater opportunities to talented individuals.

TABLE 6

CORRELATION OF TWO PARALLEL EVALUATIONS OF MANAGEMENT POTENTIAL TO OTHER CRITERION (N=47)

Criterion	A Over-all Assessment Rating	B Personnel Jacket Evaluation	Contribution Made to Criterion Controlling for Existing Data (Partial R_1 A • B)
Relative Salary Standing	.37[1]	.10	.37[1]
Assessment Factors:			
1. Activity	.78[1]	.49[1]	.72[1]
2. Administrative	.50[1]	.48[1]	.36[1]
3. Stress Resistance	.25	.26	.15

[1] $p<.05$
(From Hinricks, 1969)

How to select men who will be suitable for the demands of the future is a difficult challenge, although a surmountable one, if we have an idea of what kind of characteristics, behaviors and skills are required. Appropriate exercises could be developed. But there is not yet a clear consensus as to what the future demands will be or how soon they will be demanded. We can get some clues by looking at the trends within our own organizations and looking at trends in organizations generally, and making educated guesses about a few years from now. In the meantime, it seems sensible to select people who can function well in today's organization. It's also realistic to expect that these people are the most likely to be adaptable to the demands of tomorrow's organization.

Characteristics Measured

Having gotten the right people into the assessment center, we might ask if we are really measuring relevant characteristics. It seems likely that we are doing so only in part. Most assessment programs are not based on an empirical study of the manager's role, as might be done through careful job analysis or a critical incident study. At best, they are based largely on a review of the research literature and the judgment of executives in the organization as to what makes for an effective manager. At worst, they tend to be copies of programs in other companies. As a result, various programs differ widely in the characteristics they measure, although there is a good deal of overlap.

Assessment programs generally measure administrative skills and to a much greater degree they measure emergent leadership skills. By contrast, there are some important characteristics rarely captured by current programs. Perhaps it is too much to expect relatively short programs to tap the skills related to building trust, confidence and team work, but at least we must recognize this limitation. Also, we should recognize that many people may act like capable managers if placed in such a role, although they may not have the ascendancy to wrench such a position from other candidates. People generally may act somewhat differently when placed in situations where they are more familiar and confident of the existing conditions and also expect to live with the consequences of their actions. Fortunately, it seems that most assessment center observers are astute enough to make some necessary allowances. Still, if we think about measuring relevant skills via management assessment programs, we must admit there is a great deal of room for improvement.

A related question about measurement is whether people behave naturally in assessment situations. On the one hand, we are told that some people show up poorly in such situations either because they choke up or because the situation is merely artificial. On the other hand, we are also told that some people distort their real selves to look good. But these adept games players may not be equally good in real life. Again, the evidence on this issue is sparse. Of course, we can assume that most people put into an assessment situation will try to look as good as they can. It may be that the ability to discern and operate on the relevant dimensions of the assessee's role is the major clue as to how one will discern and operate on relevant dimensions if put into a managerial role.

To the extent that the assessment center exercises are properly built, they will be work samples of the managerial role. As such, we would expect that they predict fairly well the performance in the actual managerial role. Research done by Carleton (1970) on Sohio's assessment experience supports such an assumption. On a sample of 122 men, he compared assessment center ratings on thirteen behavioral characteristics to supervisory ratings of the same behaviors several years later, after the men were promoted to managerial jobs. He found moderately high levels of consistency (.30's and .40's). Apparently, behaviors in assessment centers are somewhat comparable to behavior in actual managerial situations. Obviously, more research on this point would be very desirable.

Impact on Careers

Critics sometimes ask if two days' observation is enough to decide a man's entire career. The question is a red herring in two ways. First, we must recognize and admit that many promotional decisions are currently made on much less than two days' observation. The results of a twenty-minute speech, a lunch time conversation or a brief field visit may be the basis for an executive's decision to promote one man over another. The assessment center may represent two days' more of observation than existed before.

Secondly, the results are not intended to cast a final die on any man's entire career. Certainly, they impact his next promotional move, but even here the effect of a low rating is not quite a "kiss of death." The promotion rates associated with various assessment rating in our salesmen's study are shown in table 1. Admittedly, a poor rating slows one down, but the promotion rates for the lowest rated group is still two-thirds of the average of the total group.

This table also answers the fears that such a program must create "crown princes." Overall, only a third of all those assessed had been promoted by the end of 1970. Certainly this is not enough for program attendance alone to be a sign of being a "crown prince." The table also dampens our fears that a high rating in the program will have a "golden boy" effect. A high rating in the program increases one's chances of moving ahead, but does not seem to guarantee it. Promotions seem to be influenced by other things as well and not necessarily assured by a high assessment rating.

Incidentally, the fear of overly impacting a man's career with the assessment judgment would be minimized, if the over-all assessment rating does not express a person's *ultimate* career potential. It should express simply how well qualified he is at the present time to move to the next level job. This judgment is likely to be more accurate, more acceptable and less abused. The data should also be discarded for any decision making purpose after two years or so.

Another negative effect of assessment programs is a possible demoralization of those who perform poorly. If this might lead to the loss of trained, competent people, it would be very undesirable. Table 2 shows the separation rates of salesmen who got different assessment ratings. The proportion of the bottom rated people does not differ significantly from the top rated people. If we judge by attrition rates, the program does not seem to demoralize.

Impact of Stress

Perhaps this criterion of negative impact is too long term. Some critics have raised the issue of short-term negative impacts. In particular, they ask if the programs are not too stressful. Certainly the exercises involve a fair amount of stress, although nothing like that associated with sensitivity training. And attempts are made in many programs to keep stress to an acceptable level. This is done variously by adjusting the difficulty level of exercises, thoroughly informing participants about the program in advance, inviting only those judged to be promotable, making it easier to decline a program invitation, and being sensitive and supportive with persons manifesting signs of anxiety.

More research needs to be done on the degree and effects of stress. In the meantime, we must recognize that stress is often a fundamental part of the manager's job. Reactions to reasonable amounts of stress are important data in evaluating suitability for management and are rated in most assessment programs.

Developmental Segments

Some recent innovations in assessment programs may sharply influence the participants' reactions to stress as well as to poor performance. Many such programs have added significant development portions to the assessment procedures. A typical development session will add two or three days' activities to an assessment program with a specific purpose of integrating the two segments. Like other development programs, it may utilize films, discussions and outside speakers. Unlike most other programs, it will typically include videotape playbacks of the assessment exercises and a personal interview providing feedback on one's assessment performance, during which time specific development plans will be sketched out.

Such programs capitalize on the unusually high motivation of the assessees to learn more about the management skills just tested. The assessees want very much to develop their communications and leadership skills, to understand group dynamics and so on. The developmental portion also permits individuals to decompress from the intensive climate of the preceding days in a supportive climate. Judging by observations made during this period, the result is for participants to have a more realistic and positive self-image before leaving. The extra days of training have the effect of visibly affirming the company's interest in them and its sincerity in regarding them as its most promising people. Since most of these people have, in fact, been judged promotable by their nominating managers and many of them will be promoted, the extra developmental session can also be seen as an especially meaningful course in premanagement training.

TABLE 7
Assessees' Opinions: Self-Development

"How rate the program . . . for your self-development?"

A

United Kingdom (11) . . . "Value in giving you additional information?"

Very Great Value	Great Value	Some Value	Not Very Valuable	Not At All
18%	46	36	0	0

Japan (36) . . . "Effectiveness to promote self-development?"

Very Effective	Effective	Moderate	Ineffective	Very Ineffective
44%	50	6	0	0

Germany . . . "How do you feel about its usefulness for self-development?"

		Very Positive	Positive	Neither/ Nor	Bit Negative	Very Negative
Germany	(60)	36%	58	2	4	0
Germany II	(70)	37%	57	5	1	0

Some participants' reactions to these development programs are shown in table 7. Participants are quite favorable when asked about the effectiveness of programs in helping their self-development.

Another question, perhaps the most telling of all, asks if the participants would recommend a friend to attend the program. As shown in table 8, the number who say they would is rather impressive.

Development of Observers

The potential of the assessment center for furthering the development of participants is just starting to be fully appreciated and exploited. Even more promising is the potential in the assessment center for the development of the observers. These managers often gain greatly from their role in the center. In the future we may expect to see managers being sent to assessment centers as observers in lieu of other management development courses, specifically to become more astute in behavioral observation, group dynamics and problem solving. Even their observer training will be more explicitly geared to helping them develop as managers.

The research and experiences we have just reviewed answer only some of the questions we might ask. Yet the evidence seems persuasive that assessment centers are, indeed, a good solution to the difficult problem of management selection. Even though the technique might be abused and requires some improvements, there is enough value in the method to assure that it will be with us for some time. No doubt it will change. There will be changes in its form, its uses and its relationship to other organizational processes such as manpower planning and development. We can also expect to see it extended to new areas. We are already witnessing its use for the selection of salesmen, retail store management trainees, and the upgrading of women in industry.

TABLE 8
Assessees' Opinions: Participation

"Would you recommend to a good friend at about your level in the company that he volunteer to participate in an assessment programs?"

		Certainly	Probably	Undecided	Probably Not	Certainly Not
United Kingdom	(11)	82%	18	0	0	0
Germany I	(60)	53%	40	7	0	0
Germany II	(70)	59%	37	4	0	0

		To All Friends	To Some Friends	Not Strongly	Not At All
Japan	(36)	67%	27	6	0

Future Needs

Where do we go from here? We must keep asking questions about the assessment center technique and its impacts. For our answers, we should look to meaningful research to provide hard data. In the future we should look beyond simple-minded questions of validity to examine the broader effects of assessment programs. For example, our criteria of success should be expanded to include peer judgments and the ratings of subordinates about the assessees' managerial practices. We should look at the impact on participants' behavior, self-concepts and careers. We should look at the program's effectiveness for training observers to be better managers.

Also, our conduct of research should reflect the real world in which these techniques are being applied. From asking "is the technique good?" we should shift to asking "how much does this technique add to what we already have?" At the same time we must consider whether it isn't also time to apply our rigorous investigations and critical questions to other areas which may need them more urgently. For example, hasn't management development generally been taken on faith as being worthwhile, and isn't this an area of greater activity with large expenditures of time and money?

As for the assessment center technique itself, we can look forward to a continuation of critical questioning. This is healthy. We can also look forward to extensions and expansions of the method. If done right, this, too, is healthy. Any way you look at it, assessment centers are here to stay.

References

Bray, D. W., and Grant, D. L. The assessment center in the measurement of potential for business management. *Psychological Monographs*, 1966, 80 (17, Whole No. 625).

Campbell, R. J., and Bray, D. W. Assessment centers: an aid in management selection. *Personnel Administration,* 1967, 30, 6-13.

Carleton, F. O. Relationships between follow-up evaluations and information developed in a management assessment center. Paper presented at the American Psychological Association Convention, Miami Beach, Florida, 1970

Dodd, W. E., and Kraut, A. I. Will management assessment centers insure selection of the same old types? Paper presented at the American Psychological Association Convention, Miami Beach, Florida, 1970.

Greenwood, J. M., and McNamara, W. J. Interrater reliability in situational tests. *Journal of Applied Psychology,* 1967, 31, 101-106.

Hinrichs, J. R. Comparison of "real life" assessments of management potential with situational exercises, paper and pencil ability tests, and personality inventories. *Journal of Applied Psychology,* 1969, 53, 425-433.

Kraut, A. I., and Scott, G. The validity of an operational management assessment program. *Journal of Applied Psychology,* 1972.

Wollowick, H. B., and McNamara, W. J. Relationship of the components of an assessment center to management success. *Journal of Applied Psychology,* 1969, 53, 348-352.

Section E
Work Sampling as a Selection Technique

Signs, Samples, and Criteria

PAUL F. WERNIMONT
JOHN P. CAMPBELL

Many writers (e.g., Dunnette, 1963; Ghiselli & Haire, 1960; Guion, 1965; Wallace, 1965) have expressed concern about the difficulties encountered in trying to predict job performance, and in establishing the validity of tests for this purpose. In general, their misgivings center around the low validities obtained and misapplications of the so-called "classic validity model." To help ameliorate these difficulties it is proposed here that the concept of validity be altered as it is now applied to predictive and concurrent situations and introduce the notion of "behavioral consistency." By consistency of behavior is meant little more than that familiar bit of conventional wisdom, "The best indicator of future performance is past performance." Surprisingly few data seem to exist to either support or refute this generalization. It deserves considerably more attention.

Some History

It is perhaps not too difficult to trace the steps by which applied psychologists arrived at their present situation. During both World War I and World War II general intelligence and aptitude tests were effectively applied to military personnel problems. Largely as the result of these successes, the techniques developed in the armed services were transported to the industrial situation and applied to the personnel problems of the business organization. From a concentration on global measures of mental ability, validation efforts branched out to include measures of specific aptitudes, interests, and personality dimensions. The process is perhaps most clearly illustrated by the efforts of the United States Employment Service to validate the General Aptitude Test Battery across a wide range of jobs and occupations. In general, testing seemed to be a quick, economical, and easy way of obtaining useful information which removed the necessity

Reprinted by permission of the authors and the publisher from the *Journal of Applied Psychology*, vol. 52 (1968), no. 5, pp. 372-76. Copyright 1968 by the American Psychological Association.

for putting an individual on the job and observing his performance over a trial period.

It was in the context of the above efforts that an unfortunate marriage occurred, namely, the union of the classic validity model with the use of tests as signs, or indicators, of predispositions to behave in certain ways (Cronbach, 1960, p. 457), rather than as samples of the characteristic behavior of individuals. An all too frequent procedure was to feed as many signs as possible into the classic validity framework in hopes that the model itself would somehow uncover something useful. The argument here is that it will be much more fruitful to focus on meaningful samples of behavior, rather than signs of predispositions, as predictors of later performance.

The Consistency Model

To further illustrate the point, consider a hypothetical prediction situation in which the following five measures are available:
1. Scores on a mental ability test;
2. School grade-point average (GPA);
3. Job-performance criterion at Time 1;
4. Job-performance criterion at Time 2;
5. Job-performance criterion at Time 3.

Obviously, a number of prediction opportunities are possible. Test scores could be correlated with GPA; school achievement could be correlated with first-year job success; or the test scores and GPA could be combined in some fashion and the composite used to predict first-, second-, or third-year job performance. All of these correlations would be labeled validity coefficients and all would conform to the classic validity model. It is less clear what label should be attached to the correlation between two different measures of job performance. Few would call it validity; many would probably refer to it as reliability. There seems to be a tendency among applied psychologists to withhold the term validity from correlations between measures of essentially the same behavior, even if they were obtained at two different points in time. That is, the subtleties of the concept of reliability and the ingredients of the classic validity model seem to have ingrained the notion that validity is a correlation between a predictor and a criterion and the two should somehow be dissimilar.

However, each of the 10 correlations that one could compute from the above situation represents the degree of common variation between the two variables, given the appropriateness of the linear correlation model. After all, that is what correlation is all about. In this sense there is no logical reason for saying that some of the coefficients represent validity and others reliability, although there certainly may be in other contexts. An implicit or explicit insistence on the predictor being "different" seems self-defeating. Rather one should really be trying to obtain measures that are as similar to the criterion or criteria as possible. This notion appears to be at least implicit in much of the work on prediction with biographical data where many of the items represent an attempt to assess previous achievement on similar types of activities. Behavior sampling is also the basis on which simulation exercises are built for use in managerial assessment programs.

At this point it should be emphasized that for the consistency notion to be consistent, the measures to be predicted must also be measures of behavior. For example, it would be something less than consistent to use a behavior sample to predict such criteria as salary progression, organizational level achieved, or subunit production. The individual does not always have substantial control over such variables, and, even with the more obvious biasing influences accounted for, they place a ceiling on the maximum predictive efficiency to be expected. Furthermore, they are several steps removed from actual job behavior. In this respect, the authors are very much in accord with Dunnette (1966) who argues strongly for the measurement of observable job behavior in terms of its effect on meaningful dimensions of performance effectiveness. A . . . method for accomplishing this aim is the behavior retranslation technique of Smith and Kendall (1964). The applied psychologist should reaffirm his mandate and return to the measurement of behavior. Only then will one learn by what means, and to what extent, an individual has influenced his rate of promotion, salary increases, or work group's production.

In general terms, what might the selection or prediction procedure look like if one tried to apply a consistency model? First, a comprehensive study of the job would be made. The results of this effort would be in the form of dimensions of job performance well defined by a broad range of specific behavior incidents which in turn have been scaled with respect to their "criticalness" for effective or ineffective performance.

Next, a thorough search of each applicant's previous work experience and educational history would be carried out to determine if any of the relevant behaviors or outcomes have been required of him or have been exhibited in the past. Items and rating methods would be developed to facilitate judging the frequency of such behaviors, the intensity with which they were manifested, the similarity of their context to the job situation, and the likelihood that they will show up again. These judgments can then be related to similar judgments concerning significant and consistent aspects of an individual's job behavior.

Such a procedure places considerable emphasis on background data and is similar in form to the "selection by objectives" concept of Odiorne and Miller (1966). However, the aim is to be considerably more systematic and to focus on job behavior and not summary "objectives."

After the analysis of background data it might be found that the required job behaviors have not been a part of the applicant's past repertoire and it would be necessary to look for the likelihood of that job behavior in a variety of work-sample or simulation exercises. A number of such behavior measures are already being used in various management assessment programs.

Finally, individual performance measures of psychological variables would be given wider use where appropriate. For example, the Wechsler Adult Intelligence Scale (Wechsler, 1955) might be used to assess certain cognitive functions. Notice that such a measure is a step closer to actual performance sampling than are the usual kinds of group intelligence tests.

How does the above procedure compare to conventional practice? The authors hope they are not beating at a straw man if the usual selection procedure is described as follows. First, a thorough job analysis is made to discover the types of skills and abilities necessary for effective performance. This is similar to the consistency approach except that the objective seems to be to jump very quickly to a generalized statement of skills and abilities rather than remaining on the behavioral level. The conventional approach next entails a search for possible predictors to try out against possible criteria. Based on knowledge of the personnel selection and individual differences literature, personal experience, and "best guesses," some decisions are made concerning what predictors to include in the initial battery. It is the authors' contention that the classic validity model has forced an undue amount of attention on test and inventory measures at this stage. Witness the large amount of space devoted to a discussion of "test validation" in most books dealing with the selection problem. Again, signs seem to take precedence over samples. Lastly, one or more criterion measures are chosen. Too often the choice seems to be made with little reference to the previous job analysis and is based on a consideration of "objectivity" and relevance to the "ultimate" criterion. Unfortunately, even a slight misuse of these considerations can lead to criteria which are poorly understood. In contrast, working within the framework of a consistency model requires consideration of dimensions of actual job behavior.

It might be added that the above characterization of the conventional approach is meant to be somewhat idealized. Certain departures from the ideal might reinforce the use of signs to an even greater extent. For example, there is always the clear and present danger that the skill requirements will be stated in terms of "traits" (e.g., loyalty, resourcefulness, initiative) and thus lead even more directly to criteria and predictors which are oriented toward underlying predispositions.

Relationship to Other Issues

The consistency notion has direct relevance for a number of research issues that appear frequently in the selection and prediction literature. One important implication is that selection research should focus on individuals to a much greater extent than it has. That is, there should be more emphasis on intraindividual consistency of behavior. In their insightful discussion of the criterion problem, Ghiselli and Haire (1960) point out that intraindividual criterion performance sometimes varied appreciably over time, that is, is "dynamic." They give two examples of this phenomenon. However, after an exhaustive review of the literature, Ronan and Prien (1966) concluded that a general answer to the question, "Is job performance reliable?" is not really possible with present data. They go on to say that previous research has not adequately considered the relevant dimensions that contribute to job performance and very few studies have actually used the same criterion measure to assess performance at two or more points in time. In the absence of much knowledge concerning the stability of relevant job behaviors it seems a bit dangerous to apply the classic validation model and attempt to generalize from a one-time criterion measure to an appreciable time span of job behavior. Utilizing the consistency notion confronts the problem directly and forces a consideration of what job behaviors are recurring contributors to effective performance (and therefore predictable) and which are not.

In addition, the adoption of signs as predictors in the context of the classic model has undoubtedly been a major factor contributing to the lack of longitudinal research. It makes it far too easy to rely on concurrent studies, and an enormous amount of effort has been expended in that direction. Emphasis on behavior samples and behavior consistency requires that a good deal more attention be devoted to the former, along with very explicit consideration of the crucial parameters of a longitudinal study.

The moderator or subgrouping concept also seems an integral part of the consistency approach. The basic research aim is to find subgroups of people in a particular job family for whom behavior on a particular performance dimension is consistent. Subgrouping may be by individual or situational characteristics but the necessity is clear and inescapable. Only within such subgroups is longitudinal prediction possible.

Lastly, the process the authors are advocating demands a great deal in terms of being able to specify the contextual or situational factors that influence performance. It is extremely important to have some knowledge of the stimulus conditions under which the job behavior is emitted such that a more precise comparison to the predictor behavior sample can be made. Because of present difficulties in specifying the stimulus conditions in an organization (e.g., Sells, 1964), this may be the weakest link in the entire procedure. However, it is also a severe problem for any other prediction scheme, but is usually not made explicit.

It is important to note that the authors' notion of a consistency model does not rest on a simple deterministic philosophy and is not meant to preclude taking account of so-called "emergent" behaviors. Relative to "creativity," for example, the question becomes whether or not the individual has ever exhibited in similar contexts the particular kind of creative behavior under consideration. If a similar context never existed, the research must investigate creative performance and outputs obtained in a test situation which simulates the contextual limitations and requirements in the job situation.

An additional advantage of the consistency approach is that a number of old or persistent problems fortunately appear to dissipate, or at least become significantly diminished. Consider the following:

1. Faking and response sets—Since the emphasis would be on behavior samples and not on self-reports of attitudes, beliefs, and interests, these kinds of response bias would seem to be less of a problem.

2. Discrimination in testing—According to Doppelt and Bennett (1967) two general charges are often leveled at tests as being discriminatory devices:

(*a*) Lack of relevance—It is charged that test items are often not related to the work required on the job for which the applicant is being considered, and that even where relationships can be shown between test scores and job success there is no need to eliminate low-scoring disadvantaged people since they can be taught the necessary skills and knowledge in a training period after hiring.

(*b*) Unfairness of content—It is further maintained that most existing tests, especially verbal measures, emphasize middle-class concepts and information and are, therefore, unfair to those who have not been exposed to middle-class cultural and educational influences. Consequently, the low test scores which are earned are not indicative of the "true" abilities of the disadvantaged. Predictions of job success made from such scores are therefore held to be inaccurate.

The examination of past behaviors similar in nature to desired future behavior, along with their contextual ramifications, plus the added techniques of work samples and simulation devices encompassing desired future behavior, should markedly reduce both the real and imagined severity of problems of unfairness in prediction.

3. Invasion of privacy—The very nature of the consistency approach would seem to almost entirely eliminate this problem. The link between the preemployment or prepromotion behavior and job behavior is direct and obvious for all to see.

Concluding Comments

The preceding discussion is meant to be critical of the concepts of predictive and concurrent validity. Nothing that has been said here should be construed as an attack on construct validity, although Campbell (1960) has pointed out that reliability and validity are also frequently confused within this concept. Neither do the authors mean to give the impression that a full-scale application of the consistency model would be without difficulty. Using available criteria and signs of assumed underlying determinants within the framework of the classic model is certainly easier; however, for long-term gains and the eventual understanding of job performance, focusing on the measurement of *behavior* would almost certainly pay a higher return on investment.

Some time ago, Goodenough (1949) dichotomized this distinction by referring to signs versus samples as indicators of future behavior. Between Hull's (1928) early statement of test validities and Ghiselli's (1966) more recent review, almost all research and development efforts have been directed at signs. Relatively small benefits seem to have resulted. In contrast, some recent research efforts directed at samples seem to hold out more promise. The AT&T studies, which used ratings of behavior in simulated exercises (Bray & Grant, 1966), and the In-basket studies reported by Lopez (1965) are successful examples of employing behavior samples with management and administrative personnel. Frederiksen (1966) has reported considerable data contributing to the construct validity of the In-basket. In addition, Ghiselli (1966) has demonstrated that an interview rating based on discussion of specific aspects of an individual's previous work and educational history had reasonably high validity, even under very unfavorable circumstances. In a nonbusiness setting, Gordon (1967) found that a work sample yielded relatively high validities for predicting final selection into the Peace Corps and seemed to be largely independent of the tests that were also included as predictors.

Hopefully, these first few attempts are the beginning of a whole new technology of behavior sampling and measurement, in both real and simulated situations. If this technology can be realized and the consistencies of various relevant behavior dimensions mapped out, the selection literature can cease being apologetic and the prediction of performance will have begun to be understood.

References

Bray, D. W., & Grant, D. L. The assessment center in the measurement of potential for business management. *Psychological Monographs*, 1966, 80 (17, Whole No. 625).

Campbell, D. T. Recommendations for APA test standards regarding construct, trait, and discriminant validity. *American Psychologist*, 1960, 15, 546-553.

Cronbach, L. J. *Essentials of psychological testing* (2nd ed.) New York: Harper & Row, 1960.

Doppelt, J. P., & Bennett, G. K. Testing job applicants from disadvantaged groups. *Test Service Bulletin* (No. 57). New York: Psychological Corporation, 1967. Pp 1-5.

Dunnette, M. D. A modified model for test validation and research. *Journal of Applied Psychology*, 1963, 47, 317-323.

Dunnette, M. D. *Personnel selection and placement*. Belmont, Calif.: Wadsworth, 1966.

Frederiksen, N. Validation of a simulation technique. *Organizational Behavior and Human Performance*, 1966, 1, 87-109.

Ghiselli. E. E. *The validity of occupational aptitude tests*. New York: Wiley, 1966.

Ghiselli, E. E., & Haire, M. The validation of selection tests in the light of the dynamic character of criteria. *Personnel Psychology*, 1960, 13, 227-231.

Goodenough, F. *Mental testing: Its history, principles, and applications*. New York: Holt, Rinehart & Winston, 1949.

Gordon, L. V. Clinical, psychometric, and work sample approaches in the prediction of success in Peace Corps training. *Journal of Applied Psychology*, 1967, 51, 111-119.

Guion, R. M. Synthetic validity in a small company: A demonstration. *Personnel Psychology*, 1965, 18, 49-65.

Hull, C. L. *Aptitude testing*. New York: Harcourt, Brace & World, 1928.

Lopez, F. M., Jr. *Evaluating executive decision making: The In-basket technique*. New York: American Management Association, 1965.

Odiorne, G. S., & Miller, E. L. Selection by objectives: A new approach to managerial selection. *Management of Personnel Quarterly*, 1966, 3 (3), 2-10.

Ronan. W. W., & Prien, E. P. *Toward a criterion theory: A review and analysis of research and opinion*. Greensboro, N. C.: Richardson Foundation, 1966.

Sells, S. B. Toward a taxonomy of organizations. In W. W. Cooper, H. J. Leavitt, & W. W. Shelly, II (Eds.), *New perspectives in organization research,* New York: Wiley, 1964.

Smith, P. C., & Kendall, L. M. Retranslation of expectations: An approach to the construction of unambiguous anchors rating scales, *Journal of Applied Psychology,* 1963, 47, 149-155.

Wallace, S. R. Criteria for what? *American Psychologist,* 1965, 20, 411-417.

Weschler, D. *Manual for the Weschler Adult Intelligence Scale.* New York: Psychological Corporation, 1955.

Work Sampling for Personnel Selection

JAMES E. CAMPION

In a recent article Wernimont and Campbell (1968) proposed a new strategy for personnel selection. They argue that it would be beneficial in test validation to adopt a model that emphasizes samples of work behavior as predictors of future work behavior. Wernimont and Campbell prefer this behavioral consistency model to the classical model which focuses on the use of tests as signs of predispositions to behave in certain ways on the job. They assert that pursuing the behavioral consistency approach and making test content more relevant to work would have several immediate advantages, such as diminishing the problem of faking or response sets and reducing charges of discrimination and invasion of privacy in testing.

Initial applications in field settings have shown promise. For example, assessment center research (Bray & Campbell, 1968; Bray & Grant, 1966; Hinrichs, 1969) with simulation exercises has been successful in demonstrating the advantages of the consistency approach in selecting managers. Furthermore, Hinrichs (1970), in a controlled laboratory setting, found that the most precise predictors of proficiency in a rotary pursuit task were apparatus tests which closely resembled this psychomotor task.

These initial findings seem promising and suggest that the concept of behavioral consistency may have considerable applied value. However, before this concept can be translated into a useful strategy for the practitioner, additional work is needed to develop guidelines for constructing work sample measures. In particular, the lack of guidelines for behavioral sampling seems to be a major obstacle to wider use of the consistency approach. The present research was designed to examine the effectiveness of one sampling strategy. Specifically, a modified version of Smith and Kendall's (1963) retranslation method was used to provide a framework for behavioral sampling, and concurrent test validation data were used to determine the utility of this methodology.

Method

Sample Characteristics

The sample consisted of 34 males (32 Caucasian, 1 Negro, 1 Latin) maintenance

Reprinted by permission of the author and the publisher from the *Journal of Applied Psychology,* vol. 56 (1972), no. 1, pp. 40-44. Copyright 1972 by the American Psychological Association.

mechanics (Dictionary of Occupational Titles, Job Code 638.28) employed by a food processing company located in a large Southwestern city. Their ages varied between 23 and 47 yr., with an average age of 35.8 yr. Educational attainment varied between 10 and 16 yr., with an average level of 12.4 yr. Their job tenure varied between 9 and 139 mo. with an average of 32.3 mo.

Development of Work Sample

The development of the work sample measure required a thorough examination of the job. This information was obtained from several technical conferences with a group of job experts. These job experts were an industrial engineer, who was an assistant to the plant maintenance superintendent, and three foremen, who were responsible for supervising the work of the maintenance mechanics. These conferences progressed through several stages, each of which was designed to achieve a specific objective.

Stage 1. In the first stage the experts were requested to list all possible tasks that maintenance mechanics were required to perform in the company; and for each task they were asked to indicate frequency of performance and to evaluate its relative importance to the job.

Stage 2. In the second stage these experts, plus a member of the personnel department, were requested to provide another task listing based upon the previous work experiences of their maintenance mechanic applicants. All five members who participated in this conference were responsible for screening applicants for maintenance mechanic work.

Stage 3. In the third stage the objective was to delineate the crucial dimensions of work behavior for maintenance mechanics. A modified version of Smith and Kendall's (1963) retranslation technique was used. First, the group of experts listed the major dimensions of work behavior that they felt discriminated between effective and ineffective performance on the job. Second, each expert independently generated behavioral incidents to illustrate performance on each dimension. The procedures followed in this step adhere generally with the guidelines provided by Flanagan (1954) for use with his critical-incident technique. Following this, the experts pooled their information, discussed differences, and decided that there were two critical dimensions of work behavior for maintenance mechanics: use of tools, and accuracy of work. Speed of work also was suggested as a major factor of work behavior; however, the experts eliminated it due to a lack of agreement on choice of behavioral incidents to illustrate it.

Stage 4. In the next stage tasks were selected as possible work sample measures. It was important that the tasks selected were representative of the tasks performed by the maintenance mechanics in the plant, but they could not be unique to this plant. They also had to make them appropriate for the job applicants. These two requirements were satisfied by considering as possible job sample measures only those tasks which were common to the lists obtained in Stages 1 and 2. In addition, each job sample task had to meet two other requirements. Each task had to provide a situation where the opportunities were maximal for the examinee to exhibit behaviors relevant to use of tools and accuracy of work. Also, the behaviors elicited by the job sample tasks had to be the kind that a test administrator could reliably record.[1]

Based on the above criteria, four tasks were selected: installing pulleys and belts, disassembling and repairing a gearbox, installing and aligning a motor, and pressing a bushing into a sprocket and reaming it to fit a shaft.

Stage 5. In the final stage these four tasks were broken down into the steps logically required to complete them. Each step was then analyzed in detail, in order to determine the various approaches a job applicant might follow. The recordable behaviors associated with these approaches were specified and weights assigned to them based on their correctness as judged by the job experts. This resulted in a list of possible behaviors associated with each step in task performance, with every behavior assigned a weight for scoring purposes. Thus, the recording form was in a checklist format which required that the test administrator simply describe rather than evaluate the job applicant's behavior. The applicant's responses were later evaluated by adding the weights associated with the behaviors marked on the checklist.

Test instructions were written for the examiner to read. A set of tools and materials were selected that maximized the opportunity for the unqualified examinee to respond inappropriately. The tools and materials, the manner in which they were displayed, and the time given examinees to study them were standardized. All testing was done in the same test administration room, with only the examiner and examinee present. Four hours were allotted for test administration.

Example items and their corresponding weights are as follows:

Installing Pulleys and Belts

Scoring weights

1. Checks key before installing against:
   - ____shaft — 2
   - ____pulley — 2
   - ____neither — 0

Disassembling and Repairing a Gear Box

10. Removes old bearing with:
    - ____press and driver — 3
    - ____bearing puller — 2
    - ____gear puller — 1
    - ____other — 0

Installing and Aligning A Motor

1. Measures radial misalignment with:
   - ____dial indicator — 10
   - ____straight edge — 3
   - ____feel — 1
   - ____visual or other — 0

Pressing a Bushing Into Sprocket and Reaming to Fit a Shaft

4. Checks internal diameter of bushing against shaft diameter:
   - ____visually — 1
   - ____hole gauge and micrometers — 3
   - ____Vernier calipers — 2
   - ____scale — 1
   - ____does not check — 0

Paper-and-Pencil Measures

Scores on a battery of paper-and-pencil tests were also available for all members of the validation sample. These tests were: the Test of Mechanical Comprehension, Form AA (published by the Psychological Corporation); the Wonderlic Personnel Test, Form D (published by E. F. Wonderlic); and the Short Employment Tests (published by the Psychological Corporation).

TABLE 1
MEANS, STANDARD DEVIATIONS, AND INTERCORRELATIONS FOR CRITERIA MEASURES

| | | | Intercorrelations ||
Measure	$\bar{X}$	SD	Accuracy of work	Overall mechanical ability
Use of tools	51.6	13.3	.72	.67
Accuracy of work	51.3	13.7		.87
Overall mechanical ability	50.2	14.1		

The standard deviation on the Test of Mechanical Comprehension was restricted. This was due to the mechanics having been preselected, based upon their performance on this test. The cutting score was 44. The other tests were required of all employees but were ignored in selecting craft personnel.

Criteria

The criteria were collected employing the paired comparison method. The three foremen who had participated in the technical conferences as experts were asked to evaluate their subordinates on each of the following factors: use of tools, accuracy of work, and overall mechanical ability. Each mechanic was evaluated by the foreman who was most familiar with his work performance.

Data Collection Procedure

Concurrent validation data were collected in three stages. First, criteria information was obtained from the foremen. Second, performance on the paper-and-pencil measures was collected from personnel records. Last, the work sample test was administered to the 34 maintenance mechanics. A test administrator was hired from an outside consulting firm, in order to prevent contamination between predictor and criterion measures. The means, standard deviations, and intercorrelations for the criteria, paper-and-pencil tests, and the work sample measures are presented in Tables 1, 2, and 3, respectively.

TABLE 2
MEANS, STANDARD DEVIATIONS, AND INTERCORRELATIONS FOR PAPER-AND-PENCIL MEASURES

| | | | Intercorrelations ||||
| | | | Wonderlic Personnel Test | Short Employment Tests |||
Measure	$\bar{X}$	SD		Verbal	Numerical	Clerical aptitude
Test of Mechanical Comprehension (Form AA)	50.9	4.0	.56	.24	.15	.26
Wonderlic Personnel Test (Form D)	23.8	5.9		.62	.37	.50
Short Employment Tests:						
Verbal	23.6	9.5			.10	.22
Numerical	46.6	17.2				.62
Clerical aptitude	33.3	11.0				

Results

Examination of Table 4 indicates that the mechanics' performance on the work sample measure was in all instances significantly and positively related to their foreman's evaluations of their work performance, whereas, none of the 15 validity coefficients computed for the paper-and-pencil tests reached acceptable levels of statistical significance. As noted above, the validity coefficients for the Test of Mechanical Comprehension are difficult to interpret due to its being employed in selecting the mechanics in the validation sample. Normative data describing the standard deviation for a similar group of mechanics who had not been pre-selected on this test variable were not available. Consequently, the validity coefficients could not be corrected for restriction of range on the predictor.

Discussion

The approach developed here evolved from a need to solve a specific selection problem. The personnel decision was either to hire or reject. The applicants were being considered for only one position, and whether or not they were hired depended upon whether or not they possessed the appropriate work skills. It was assumed that the applicant population included persons with previous work experience that qualified them for the present job opening. A possible shortcoming of these findings is that the concurrent validities found for the experienced, employed mechanics may or may not accurately reflect predictive validity for less experienced applicants for mechanic work. This question can only be definitely answered with data obtained from predictive validation studies. However, as noted in Table 4, performance on the work sample measure and mechanic work experience were insignificantly correlated (—.27) for this sample.

TABLE 3
MEANS, STANDARD DEVIATIONS, AND INTERCORRELATIONS
FOR WORK SAMPLE MEASURES

Part	$\bar{X}$	SD	B	C	D	Total
A. Installing pulleys and belts	60.3	15.8	.25	.01	.16	.63
B. Disassembling and repairing a gearbox	62.9	12.9		.11	.27	.64
C. Installing and repairing a motor	71.1	11.2			.07	.42
D. Pressing a bushing into sprocket and reaming to fit a shaft	51.5	19.0				.70
Total	246.2	36.5				

The significant validity coefficients for the work sample measure support the Wernimont and Campbell (1968) assertions regarding the utility of the behavioral consistency approach. Furthermore, these positive findings suggest that the work sampling methodology developed here may provide useful guidelines for constructing work samples in other areas of personnel decision making.

For example, consider the situation where job applicants cannot be presumed to possess any of the prerequisite work skills for the job and, therefore, are first placed in training programs. Here, selection into training is usually based on general ability measures. This seems to be the correct strategy, for these instruments have been shown to work best for predicting training criteria in industrial settings (Brown & Ghiselli, 1952; Ghiselli, 1966). However, future decisions in the sequence concerning who should continue training or who should graduate from training may be more appropriately attacked within the behavioral consistency model. Fleishman's (1957, 1967) research on individual differences in learning is relevant here. This research has shown that ability requirements for task performance change over the training period. Particularly relevant is his finding that general ability measures predict performance during early stages of training, whereas, performance variance in the later stages is increasingly a function of habits and skills required in the task itself.

Consequently, the behavioral consistency approach has implications for sequential strategies of personnel decision making as well. Work sample measures for these decisions would be embedded in the training program. Whether the training is on the job or in the classroom, the goal would be to incorporate, early in training, exercises that maximize the opportunity for the trainees to exhibit behavior judged important for later job success. Thus, candidates with low probabilities of later success could be eliminated or rerouted to other training programs.

TABLE 4
CRITERION BETWEEN PREDICTOR AND CRITERION VARIABLES

Variable	Use of tools	Accuracy of work	Overall mechanical ability
Work sample[1]	.66[3]	.42[2]	.46[3]
Test of Mechanical Comprehension (Form AA)	.08	−.04	−.21
Wonderlic Personnel Test (Form D)	−.23	−.19	−.32
Short Employment Tests:			
Verbal	−.24	−.02	−.04
Numerical	.07	−.13	−.10
Clerical aptitude	−.03	−.19	−.09

[1] Performance on the work sample measure and mechanic work experience at this company were insignificantly correlated at −.27.
[2] $p<.05$.
[3] $p<.01$.

In summary, it seems that several aspects of personnel decision making could be affected by a strategy that used a behavioral consistency approach to determine a candidate's qualifications and/or deficiencies in hiring or promoting him.

REFERENCES

Bray, D. W., & Campbell, R. J. Selection of salesmen by means of an assessment center. *Journal of Applied Psychology*, 1968, 52, 36-41.

Bray, D. W., & Grant, D. L. The assessment center in the measurement of potential for business management. *Psychological Monographs*, 1966, 80 (17, Whole No. 625).

Brown, C. W., & Ghiselli, E. E. The relationship between the predictive power of aptitude tests for trainability and for job proficiency. *Journal of Applied Psychology*, 1952, 36, 370-377.

Flanagan, J. C. The critical incident technique. *Psychological Bulletin*, 1954, 51, 327-358.

Fleishman, E. A. A comparative study of aptitude patterns in unskilled and skilled psychomotor performance. *Journal of Applied Psychology*, 1957, 41, 263-272.

Fleishman, E. A. Individual differences and motor learning. In R. M. Gagne (Ed.), *Learning and individual differences*. Columbus, Ohio: Merrill, 1967.

Ghiselli, E. E. *The validity of aptitude tests*. New York: Wiley, 1966.

Hinrichs, J. R. Comparison of "real life" assessments of management potential with situational exercises, paper-and-pencil ability tests, and personality inventories. *Journal of Applied Psychology*, 1969, 53, 425-432.

Hinrichs, J. R. Ability correlates in learning a psycho-motor task. *Journal of Applied Psychology*, 1970, 54, 56-64.

Smith, P., & Kendall, L. N. Retranslation of expectations: An approach to the construction of unambiguous anchors for rating scales. *Journal of Applied Psychology*, 1963, 47, 149-155.

Wernimont, P. F., & Campbell, J. Signs, samples, and criteria. *Journal of Applied Psychology*, 1968, 52, 372-376.

Note

1. Of course, reliability is essentially an empirical matter. Unfortunately, the author was not able to convince company officials that it would be worth the added expenses of retesting or of using two test administrators.

Job-Sample vs. Paper-and-Pencil Trades and Technical Tests:
Adverse Impact and Examinee Attitudes

FRANK L. SCHMIDT
ALAN L. GREENTHAL
JOHN E. HUNTER
JOHN G. BERNER
FELECIA W. SEATON

This study was part of a larger project aimed primarily at the development and evaluation of a number of techniques designed to increase the economic and practical feasibility of performance testing.[1] Other objectives were to determine (1) whether performance tests might be expected to show smaller majority-minority score differences than paper-and-pencil job knowledge tests and (2) whether examinee attitudes toward, and evaluations of, the two kinds of tests differed.

Reprinted from *Personnel Psychology*, vol. 30 (Summer) 1977, with permission.

It is common knowledge that blacks and other disadvantaged groups average significantly below national means on most paper-and-pencil tests (e.g., see Dreger and Miller [1968] for a review of this research). While such tests are frequently valid in that they correlate with measures of job success, they may be tapping precisely those determiners of job success on which racial differences are largest; conversely, they may fail to tap important determinants of job success on which such differences are smaller or perhaps nonexistent. Well-constructed job-sample tests may have the potential for assessing samples of job success determinants that are more representative in terms of their subgroup differences. That is, such tests may be able to tap job success determinants on which racial differences are small or nonexistent as well as those on which differences are large.

In the well-known *Griggs* v. *Duke Power Case* (1971), the Supreme Court ruled that selection, promotion, or other personnel devices which have an "adverse impact" on protected minority groups are illegal under the 1964 Civil Rights Act unless shown to be job-related. Equal Employment Opportunity Commission guidelines[2] and Office of Federal Contract Compliance[3] guidelines call for separate validation studies, where feasible, on majority and minority employee groups, as does the most recent draft of proposed uniform federal employee selection guidelines.[4] This requirement is based, for the most part, on the assumption that the relation of test scores to performance—that is, the correlational validity—may be different for different ethnic groups. But a recent research study (Schmidt, Berner, and Hunter, 1973) based on 410 pairs of black-white employment test validities taken from a thorough review of research, has shown that single group validity does not occur any more frequently than would be expected on the basis of chance alone (cf. also O'Connor, Wexley, and Alexander, 1975). Tests that correlate with job performance for majority group members will apparently also correlate for blacks. Circumstances in which they do not are apparently due only to random sampling and measurement error—unavoidable in any selection device or study. Other recent studies (Schmidt and Hunter 1974; Linn, 1973), however, have shown that tests with essentially equal correlational validities for black and whites typically show greater racial differences in mean score than are found in actual criterion performance. Such tests are usually unbiased according to the EEOC-endorsed Cleary (1968) or regression definition of test fairness—the most widely accepted concept of test fairness—but not by Thorndike's (1971) definition, which requires equal subgroup differences on test and criterion.[5] Thus even in the case of validated and legal tests, blacks are often at a greater disadvantage on the test than they would be on actual job performance. In light of this situation, the potential advantage of job-sample or performance tests is the fact that, because content is essentially identical to job content, they should show racial differences no greater than actual job-performances differences. An additional advantage is that, because of the nature of its content and the methods used to determine content, well-constructed job sample tests are, *ipso facto,* content-valid and thus meet EEOC and OFCC content validity requirements.[6]

None of the 20 studies of performance testing found in the review of the literature had examined the relative "adverse impact" of job-sample and written job-knowledge tests. Two, however, have reported on examinee attitudes. Steel, Balinsky, and Lang (1945) reported that the majority of their (presumably nonminority) subjects preferred a job-sample test to a psychomotor dexterity test, despite their feeling that the job sample test was more difficult. Another group of researchers[7] reported highly positive attitudes toward their job-sample tests—designed as counseling and placement aids for unskilled workers—on the part of their disadvantaged (mostly black) subjects. This report, however, was based on casual observation. In addition, neither study assessed examinee attitudes toward the relative fairness of job-sample and written tests.

Since Oriel [8] had recently carried out an exhaustive task analysis of the work and skills domain of metals trades apprentices finishing their first year of training, it was decided, in the interests of economy of time and money, to conduct the study in this work area. Although apprentices completing the first year of training do not constitute an occupational group per se, the process of delineating and sampling from this domain is the same as in the case of a bona fide occupational domain, and there appeared to be no reason to believe that results bearing on adverse impact and examinee attitudes would be in any way affected.

Procedure

Test Construction

Using methods outlined by Miller (1963) and Folley,[9] Oriel (n. 8) delineated and thoroughly described the domain of tasks performed by journeymen in the various metals trades. Journeymen and their supervisors then indicated which of these tasks apprentices would be expected to master by the end of their first year of training. These tasks were used to determine 22 shop activity modules—independent performances, each carried out on one of the major machines, each requiring the actual cutting of metal, and each incorporating a number of the tasks identified above.[10] These modules are listed in table 1 by the machine on which they are performed. A group of 21 experienced journeymen machinists ranked the modules (within machines) on difficulty, importance and frequency of occurrence for apprentices and journeymen. Interjudge reliabilities, corrected by the Spearman-Brown formula, ranged from .85 to .97. (Corrected for unreliability,

TABLE 1
SHOP MODULES LISTED BY MACHINE
(From Oriel, 1974)

Horizontal Milling Machine
1. Plain (slab) milling
2. Side milling a slot
3. Form milling a radius
4. Sawing a slot

Vertical Milling Machine
5. Face milling
6. End milling a closed end slot
7. End milling a pocket

Lathe
8. Facing
9. Turning
10. Taper turning with the compound
11. Parting and grooving
12. Chamfering
13. Drilling and center-drilling
14. Boring
15. Reaming
16. Filing and polishing
17. Knurling
18. Taper turning with attachment
19. Cutting threads

Drilling Machine
20. Drilling, counterboring, and countersinking
21. Machine tapping

Surface Grinder
22. Truing and squaring

scores on each of the three scales correlated 1.00 across the journeyman-apprentice distinction, indicating apparently identical patterns of difficulty, importance, and frequency for apprentices and journeymen.) Time requirements for each task were estimated after execution in the shop by a machinist consultant. The number of tolerance and finish measures that could be taken on the end product of each module was then determined. Based on this information, a module was chosen to represent each of the five major metal-cutting machines. (Thus the test was designed to be content-valid for metals trades apprenticeship programs in general; it was not tailored to the specific apprenticeship programs from which the subjects were drawn.) A fuller description of this process can be found in Schmidt, et al. (n. 1).

Subjects

Subjects were 87 metals trades apprentices from three large midwestern manufacturing concerns. All were chosen so as to insure the equivalent of one year's machinist training, as evenly spread out as possible over the five machines. Twenty-nine (or 33.3 percent) were minority group members (27 black and 2 Spanish-speaking) and the rest majority. All had been selected into the apprenticeship program on the basis of aptitude test scores, among other variables. For administrative and practical reasons, complete data could not be obtained on all subjects. The numbers on which data were available ranged from 70 to 77 for the various analyses.

Test Administration

After brief introductory remarks, each apprentice was given a piece of steel stock, a blueprint, and a set of stickers with his identifying number, and assigned to a machine. The task station at the machine contained a tape recorder with instructions and all necessary tools, plus tools designed to serve as misleads or foils. Instructions emphasized speed and accuracy equally. When finished, the examinee put his sticker on the workpiece and placed it in a bin provided. (These procedures were among those designed to reduce performance testing costs by effecting a shift from individual to group administration.) The examinee then completed a questionnaire utilizing Likert-type items to measure his perceptions of the difficulty, fairness, quality, and clarity of the performance test (see Schmidt et al., n. 1, appendix G). No problems were encountered in moving the test from one organization to another.

Scoring

For cost reductions and other reasons (Schmidt, et al., n.1, p. 12), performance test scores were derived from end-product evaluation. Behaviors and processes were not scored or recorded. Each workpiece was scored on a number of tolerance and finish dimensions.

Modern precision instruments (dial-read micrometers and calipers) were used in tolerance measurements. Two points were assigned if the piece was within the stated tolerance, one point if within a second, less stringent tolerance, and zero otherwise. Total tolerance score was the sum of these points across the 28 tolerances. Finish evaluation was based on a "benchmark" procedure requiring relative rather than absolute judgments. "Benchmarks" were workpieces chosen in advance from examinee end products to correspond to specific quality levels of finish. End-product evaluators compared each workpiece to each benchmark and then decided which it was closest to. There were a total of 10 finish dimensions across the five workpieces; scores on each dimension ranged from one to three or one to four. Total time taken on each machine was recorded during test administration and reflected to provide a work-speed score. This scoring procedure produced a total tolerance score, a total finish score, and a total work-speed score. In combining these into a total score, the three subscores were weighted equally, i.e., transformed to standard scores and added.

Reliability of the Performance Test

Reliability becomes an especially important consideration when between-test comparisons are made to adverse impact, since greater unreliability alone can cause one test to appear less disadvantageous to minority groups than another. Accurate estimates of reliability are necessary to determine whether such between-test differences are due only to reliability differences or reflect real differences in the adverse impact of the constructs measured. Therefore, all performance test dimensions were scored by at least two judges. Interjudge reliability (corrected to two judges) of total tolerance score was .95; for total finish score, it was .89. Coefficient Alpha was computed across machines for the tolerance, finish, and work speed subscores and for total score; these coefficients are reported in the Results section, below.

Written Job Knowledge Test

Based on a careful examination of Baldwin's research procedures[11] and reviews of other reports, the Baldwin Machinist Achievement Test, developed for the Department of Health, Education, and Welfare under contract to the University of Illinois, appeared to be the most competently developed, content-valid, and reliable written achievement test extant for this trade. However, HEW officials, much to their chagrin, were unable to locate a copy of this test, even after a protracted search. In addition, neither the University of Illinois nor Baldwin himself could produce a copy of the test. Instead, the Machine Trades Achievement Test of the Ohio Trade and Industrial Education Achievement Tests series,[12] the best available alternative, was employed. This test was carefully constructed using content-validation procedures and was judged content-valid by the project's expert machinist consultant and by the apprenticeship program coordinator at one of the participating organizations. The series of tests of which it is a part was developed by Ohio State University for the Ohio State Department of Education for use in connection with the State's vocational and technical education programs. The test as used consisted of five subtests covering knowledge of each of the five major machines, plus a subtest covering general trades information. K-R 20 reliability of subscores and total score was determined on the total group of subjects. The written test was administered some weeks after the job-sample test. Upon completing the examination, subjects filled out an evaluative questionnaire similar to that for the performance test.

Results

Adverse Impact

The hypothesis of differential adverse impact was supported. In table 2 it can be seen that the written Machine Trades Achievement Test and each of its component subtests show large and significant minority-majority differences, while two of the three job sample subscores—"Tolerance" and "Finish"—show no significant subgroup differences. The third, "Work Speed," does, however, manifest a large difference,[13] and this produces a moderate subgroup difference on total score. Assuming normal distributions,[14] 24 percent and 9 percent of the minority group is above the majority mean on performance test total score and written test total score, respectively (21 percent and 8 percent, corrected for unreliability). Thus the adverse impact of the job sample test, at this cutting score, is less than one-half that of the written test.

TABLE 2
MINORITY-MAJORITY DIFFERENCES ON JOB-SAMPLE
VS. WRITTEN TRADES TEST

Test	N	r_{tt} [a]	r_{pp} [b]	Difference in SD Units [c] Raw Score	True Score [d]
Job Sample Total	76	.75	.30**	.70	.81
Tolerance score	76	.50	.14	—	—
Finish score	76	.59	−.05	—	—
Work speed	76	.61	.42***	.89	1.26
Written Trades Test total	70	.84	.56***	1.32	1.44
General Trades info.	77	.55	.49***	.43	.58
Lathe subtest	77	.74	.43***	.99	1.15
Milling subtest	77	.53	.40***	.84	1.15
Grinding subtest	72	.63	.38***	.73	.92
Drilling subtest	75	.45	.31***	.63	.94

a. Internal consistency reliability
b. Point biserial *r* with group membership.
c. Minority group SDs.
d. Difference corrected for unreliability in the test.
**$p<.01$
***$p<.001$

The difference between these two differences is significant ($p < .05$). (The reader is invited to compute relative adverse impact figures for other cutting scores he may be interested in.) In addition, the adverse impact of the performance test depends much more on the weights applied to its subscores than is the case with the written test. As the weight assigned to work speed becomes smaller, adverse impact decreases. Although a weight of zero will usually not be appropriate, in many situations work speed is relatively unimportant in relation to quality of end product, justifying a small weight for this subscore. Minority-majority differences would thus be considerably less than those in table 2 based on equal weighting of subscores.[15] In the case of the written test, however, virtually all sets of subscore weights will result in substantial adverse impact, since all subscores show large and significant subgroup differences.

Examinee Attitudes

Both the minority (93 percent) and the majority (74 percent) regarded the performance test as "about right" in difficulty. Comparable figures for the written test were 58 percent and 72 percent. Both groups judged the written test significantly more difficult than the performance test ($p < .01$ for minority; $p. < .001$ for majority), and both groups regarded the written test but not the performance test as deviating significantly from optimal difficulty ($p < .10$ for minority; $p < .01$ for majority). Differences between the two groups in perceptions of difficulty were not significant. Table 3 provides additional data on examinee attitudes. Both groups see the performance test as significantly fairer, and these differences are quite large. Both groups see the performance test as of higher quality (analysis II), but this difference reached significance only for the majority group. And finally, both groups see the performance test as superior in clarity to the written test. Analysis III compares clarity of the taped job-sample instructions and written test questions, and analysis IV compares job sample "blueprints" (work drawings) to questions on the written test. Both the minority and majority groups felt the performance test was clearer in both comparisons. These differences, expressed in standard deviation units, are quite large. There were no significant differences between the attitudes of minority and majority groups.

TABLE 3
EXAMINEE ATTITUDES TOWARD THE JOB-SAMPLE AND WRITTEN TRADES TEST

I. Overall, how fair do you think this test is?

	Job Sample $\overline{X}$	SD	N	Written $\overline{X}$	SD	N	Diff. in SD Units[a]
Minority	1.63	.62	27	2.09	.58	23	.76*
Majority	1.36	.48	53	1.84	.65	49	.85***
Diff. in SD Units[b]	.49			.40			

II. Overall, how good do you think this test is in evaluating your machinist skills?

	Job Sample $\overline{X}$	SD	N	Written $\overline{X}$	SD	N	Diff. in SD Units[a]
Minority	2.23	.71	28	2.57	.58	23	.39
Majority	2.04	.82	53	2.61	.85	49	.68**
Diff. in SD Units[b]	.36			.06			

III. How clear do you think this test was?

	Job Sample $\overline{X}$	SD	N	Written $\overline{X}$	SD	N	Diff. in SD Units[a]
Minority	1.38	.76	29	2.09	.72	23	.97***
Majority	1.11	.41	55	1.84	.71	49	1.30***
Diff. in SD Units[b]	.46			.35			

IV. How clear do you think this test was?

	Job Sample ("Blueprints") $\overline{X}$	SD	N	Written (Questions) $\overline{X}$	SD	N	Diff. in SD Units[a]
Minority	1.17	.38	29	2.09	.72	23	1.67***
Majority	1.11	.36	57	1.84	.71	49	1.36***
Diff. in SD Units[b]	.16			.35			

Note: Higher values indicate lower perceived fairness, quality, or clarity.
    a. SD used is average across the two tests.
    b. SD used is average across minority and majority groups.
  *p<.05
 **p<.01
***p<.001

Nothing in these findings implies that the written Machine Trades Achievement Test is invalid or fails to meet legal requirements. In addition to substantial evidence of content validity (n. 12), the test is supported in the present study by a significant ($p < .01$) correlation of .40 (corrected for unreliability) with the work speed subscore of the performance test.[16] The point is that, compared to the performance test, this test emphasizes heavily those performance-determining factors (and perhaps some nonvalid factors) on which minority-majority differences are apparently large. By contrast, two of the three dimensions tapped by the performance test appear to be among those which do not show subgroup differences.

Although not emphasized in this paper, the techniques used in this study to decrease cost and increase efficiency of performance testing (taped instructions, end-product evaluation, group administration, etc.) worked quite well. Taken together with the lesser adverse impact of the performance test and the fact that both the minority and majority groups perceived the performance test as fairer, clearer, and of more appropriate difficulty level, the indication is strong that industrial psychologists should explore more fully the potential of performance testing.

Notes

1. Schmidt, F. L., Greenthal, A. L., Berner, J. G., Hunter J.E., and Williams, F. M. *A performance measurement feasibility study: Implications for manpower policy.* Final Report to Manpower Administration, U. S. Department of Labor. This research was supported by the U. S. Department of Labor, Manpower Administration, Contract No. 82-17-71-48, and Development Systems Corporation, Chicago, Ill. Copies of the final report can be obtained from NTIS (Report No. PB240809/AS) for $7.50. The views expressed here are solely those of the authors and do not necessarily reflect Manpower Administration positions. Portions of this paper were presented at the 83rd annual convention of the American Psychological Association, Chicago, Illinois, August 31, 1975.

2. Equal Employment Opportunity Commission. *Guidelines on employment selection procedures:* Washington, D. C., 1970.

3. U. S. Department of Labor, Office of Federal Contract Compliance. *Regulations on employee testing and other selection procedures.* Washington, D.C. 1971.

4. Equal Employment Opportunity Coordinating Council. *Uniform guidelines on employee selection procedures.* Staff Committee Draft (Mimeograph). Washington, D. C. Sept. 24, 1975.

5. Such tests are unfair also when evaluated against Cole's (1973) concept of selection fairness. Cole's definition of test fairness is, under most circumstances, equivalent to Darlington's (1971) Definition 3 (Hunter and Schmidt, in press).

6. However, it should be noted that some court decisions have held that reliance on content validity is not permissible unless the employer can first demonstrate that criterion-related validity studies are not technically feasible. Obviously, such a position is extremely questionable scientifically. In addition, it has recently become apparent that such studies are technically feasible much less frequently than has traditionally been assumed (Schmidt, Hunter, and Urry, 1976, in press).

7. Jewish Employment and Vocational Service. *Work Samples: Signposts on the road to occupational choice.* Interim report to Manpower Administration, U. S. Department of Labor. Experimental Demonstration Project Contract No. 82-40-67-40, Sept. 30, 1968.

8. Oriel, A. E. *A performance-based individualized training system for technical and apprentice training: a pilot study.* Final report to Manpower Administration, U. S. Department of Labor. Contract No. 82-17-71-48, 1974.

9. Folley, J. D. Jr. *Development of an improved method of task analysis and beginnings of a theory of training,* Port Washington, N. Y., USNTDC, 1964, and *Guidelines for task analysis,* Port Washington, N. Y., USNTDC, 1964.

10. Eighteen "related-instruction" modules were also developed. Related instruction refers to cognitive and other skills necessary to actually perform the shop modules (e.g., fractions, blueprint reading, small tools). Formal training in these skills usually takes place off the shop floor in a classroom setting. Related-instruction modules were not employed in construction of the performance test for two reasons: (1) the shop module tasks assess these skills indirectly, since they are required in executing the shop tasks, and (2) measurement of related-instruction modules is typically by means of written test and scores are thus probably mediated by the same verbal factor found in written job knowledge tests—a factor which may not be required in actual on-the-job performance.

11. Baldwin, T.S. *The development of achievement measures for trade and technical education.* Final Report, Grant No. OEG-0-051319-3626-085, U. S. Office of Education, Washington, D. C., Sept. 1970.

12. Ohio Department of Education. *Ohio trade and industrial education achievement tests.* Division of Vocational Education, Columbus, Ohio, 1960.

13. The reason for this difference is not obvious. Training records available on 68 of the apprentices showed no significant subgroup differences in hours of training on the five machines used in this study. Project staff reported that the attitudes of the minority apprentices toward the performance tasks and toward the time requirements of the test were indistinguishable from those of the majority subjects. It is possible that the kinds of knowledges assessed by the written Trades test express themselves primarily in time requirements rather than in work quality. The finding of a significant ($p<.01$) correlation ($r=.40$, corrected for unreliability) between the work speed score and total score on the written test supports this hypothesis.

14. Figures based on an assumed normal distribution are likely to be more accurate in future settings than figures determined on unstable small sample empirical distributions.

15. This is not to suggest that subscore weights be chosen to minimize adverse impact. Weights should be determined on the basis of prior analysis of job demands. Obviously, in some cases, such an analysis will lead to a large weight for the work speed subscore and thus to greater adverse impact. The point, however, is that the opposite result may also obtain.

16. Correlations between the written test and the tolerance and finish subscores of the performance test did not reach significance in the total group of apprentices or in the majority group. In the minority group, however, the written test correlated significantly with the finish subscore ($r = .65$, $p < .01$, corrected for unreliability).

References

Cleary, T. A. Test bias: Prediction of grades of Negro and white students in integrated colleges. *Journal of Educational Measurement,* 1968, 5, 115-24.

Cole, N. S. Bias in selection. *Journal of educational measurement* 1973, 10, 237-55.

Darlington, R. B. Another look at "cultural fairness." *Journal of educational measurement,* 1971, 8, 71-82.

Dreger, R. M., and Miller, K. S. Comparative psychological studies of whites and Negroes in the United States: 1959-65. *Psychological Bulletin Monograph Supplement,* part 2, Sept. 1968, pp. 1-58.

Hunter, J. E., and Schmidt, F. L. A critical analysis of the statistical and ethical implications of various definitions of "test bias." *Psychological Bulletin,* in press.

Linn, R. L. Fair test use in selection. *Review of Educational Research,* 1973, 43, 139-61.

Miller, R. B. Task description and analysis. In R. M. Gogne (ed.), *Psychological principles in system development.* New York: Holt, Rinehart & Winston, 1963.

O'Connor, E. J., Wexley, K. N., and Alexander, R. A. Single-group validity: Fact or fallacy? *Journal of Applied Psychology,* 1975, 60, 352-55.

Schmidt, F. L., Berner, J. E., and Hunter, J. E. Racial differences in validity of employment tests: reality or illusion? *Journal of Applied Psychology,* 1973, 58, 5-9.

Schmidt, F. L., and Hunter, J. E. Racial and ethnic bias in psychological tests: divergent implications of two definitions of test bias. *American Psychologist,* 1974, 29, 1-8.

Schmidt, F. L., Hunter, J. E., and Urry, V. Statistical power in criterion-related validation studies. *Journal of Applied Psychology,* 1976, in press.

Steel, M., Balinsky, B., and Lang, H. A study on the use of a work sample. *Journal of Applied Psychology,* 1945, 29, 14-21.

Supreme Court of the United States. *Griggs* v. *Duke Power Company Decision,* Washington, D.C.

Thorndike, R. L. Concepts of culture fairness. *Journal of Educational Measurement,* 1971, 8, 63-70.

CHAPTER **3**

Personnel Decisions: Legal Constraints

Many federal laws impose demands on personnel managers and constrain their actions (Dunn and Stephens, 1972). One law stands out from the others, however, in its impact on personnel operations today. Title VII of The Civil Rights Act of 1964 (as amended in 1972) forbids discrimination on the basis of race, sex, religion or national origin in personnel decisions. It has engendered more changes in personnel practices, more discussion, more controversy, and more court suits than any other federal law bearing on personnel decisions. This law and its societal effects are so significant in the 1970s that it merits a chapter to itself.

During the 1970s, the emphasis placed on the prohibition in Title VII against discrimination on the basis of sex has increased dramatically. Many court decisions on sex discrimination have been handed down, and a significant body of precedent has built up. As Meacham makes clear in her article reviewing these decisions, the courts have generally taken a tough stance against the use of gender as the basis for any kind of personnel decision. Unless the courts change direction in the future, we will almost certainly see major changes in personnel practices in the late 1970s—changes designed to meet legal requirements for fairness to women.

Government antidiscrimination efforts—specifically those of the U.S. Equal Employment Opportunity Commission—are the topic of former EEOC Chairman Brown's paper. The 1972 Equal Employment Opportunity Act provides the EEOC with the power to take companies to court. This important new power, along with precedents set by recent court decisions and out-of-court settlements, has greatly increased the impact of EEOC activities on corporate and governmental personnel practices.

Most laws passed by Congress are open to a number of interpretations. In interpreting the laws, federal judges attempt to divine the "intent of Congress" in enacting the law. But in the case of any law, the Supreme Court of the United States has the final word as to what Congress in fact had in mind when it voted the bill into law. The Supreme Court has now handed down three Title VII decisions focusing directly on personnel selection and testing and three others that are indirectly relevant. Taken together, these decisions define what the law is today in the area of personnel selection and minority rights. Thaddeus Holt, one of the foremost attorneys in selection and testing law today, examines these cases in detail and concludes that the Supreme Court seems to be having difficulty in determining just what the law does mean.

Federal agencies, as well as Supreme Court Justices, sometimes find it hard to agree on what Title VII means. Taking note of the fact that different agencies of the Federal government had different interpretations of the requirements of Title VII in the area of personnel selection, Congress wrote a requirement into the 1972 Equal Employment

Opportunity Act that federal agencies get together and agree on interpretations and policies in the area of equal employment opportunity. The first order of business was a set of uniform guidelines on employee selection procedures. These guidelines would allow the federal government to "speak with one voice," that is, to have a single interpretation of what the law requires and a single standard against which to evaluate employer personnel practices. The federal agencies involved were: (1) the Equal Opportunity Employment Commission (EEOC), which has responsibility for enforcing Title VII among private employers; (2) the Labor Department, which has responsibility for antibias enforcement among federal contractors; (3) the Justice Department, which must handle many of the discrimination cases that wind up in court, and (4) the Civil Service Commission, which is responsible for both personnel procedures and antidiscrimination enforcement under Title VII in the federal government.

Among these four agencies, only the Civil Service Commission is an employer as well as an enforcer of the antidiscrimination legislation. This agency thus represented the viewpoints of both employers and enforcement agencies. In particular, the Civil Service Commission is required by law to base personnel decisions on "merit" (i.e., qualifications), rather than race, sex, or other such factors. Thus the new guidelines had to be consistent with a merit system of employment; they could not encourage or endorse quota hiring by race or sex.

For almost four years these agencies attempted to reach agreement while personnel managers and selection psychologists in both the private and public sectors watched anxiously, wondering why the process was taking so long and what the final set of requirements that would govern their activities for years to come would be like. William A. Gorham, a psychologist and director of the Personnel Research and Development Center of the Civil Service Commission, was an inside party to this highly political process almost from the beginning. His detailed account of how EEOC, the Labor and Justice departments, and the Civil Service Commission dealt with the problem of developing uniform guidelines is probably unique in the insights it affords into the politics of Equal Employment Opportunity. (The views expressed by Mr. Gorham in his article are his own, and not necessarily those of the U.S. Civil Service Commission.)

Ironically, when the uniform guidelines finally emerged, they were not uniform at all: EEOC had backed out. Thus the word "uniform" was dropped, and the new guidelines were adopted as the "Federal Executive Agency Guidelines on Employee Selection Procedures." EEOC elected to retain its much-criticized 1970 guidelines. The full text of the new Federal Executive Agency Guidelines is given in the Appendix to this book.

Reference

Dunn, J. D., and Stephens, E. C. Federal laws affecting personnel management. In *Management of Personnel: Manpower Management and Organizational Behavior*. New York, McGraw-Hill, 1972.

Sex Discrimination in Employment—The Law: Where It Is and Where It's Going

COLQUITT L. MEACHAM

The right to work for a living in the common occupations of the community is of the very essence of the personal freedom and opportunity that it was the purpose of the [Fourteenth] Amendment to secure.—*Truax* v. *Raich*, 239 U.S. 33, 41 (1915)

... When the Civil Rights Act of 1964 was being hotly debated in Congress, very little attention was given to the issue of sex discrimination. Indeed concern was so minor that coverage for women under the act was not originally planned or contemplated by its proponents. At the last minute—the day before the House of Representatives voted on the act—Representative Howard Smith added sex as a protected category to Title VII of the statute. It is generally believed that Smith's action was not motivated by concern for women workers, but rather was designed to torpedo the entire statute. The assumption was that legislators willing to give protection to racial minorities would balk at the absurd proposition of extending such equality of treatment to women and that passage of the act would be defeated. Smith's plan backfired, and the bill passed the House and Senate with the sex provision of Title VII, the only title to mention sex, receiving very little attention.

The year before passage of the Civil Rights Act, the Fair Labor Standards Act of 1938 was amended by the Equal Pay Act,[1] which guaranteed to women equal pay for work equal to that of male employees. Unlike the Civil Rights Act, the Equal Pay Act was passed by Congress after hearings establishing the fact that wage discrimination on the basis of sex was widespread. Representative Donahue, commenting on why the legislation was necessary, said, "This measure represents the correction of basic injustice being visited upon women in many fields of endeavor . . . extending simple wage justice to the increasing corps of America's working women."[2] In addition to these federal statutes more than half the states have by now legislated bans on sex discrimination in employment.[3]

Legislative Action

The passage of Title VII and the Equal Pay Act, coupled with the growing consciousness of women in our society, has resulted in progress toward equality for working women that few would have predicted. Complaints filed under the Equal Pay Act have resulted so far in businesses paying out $43 million to 104,000 employees over a ten-year period.[4] Most of these complaints have been settled without litigation, and of the approximately 400 lawsuits filed, most have been decided in favor of the female complainant.[5]

The Equal Employment Opportunity Commission (hereafter referred to as the EEOC) has responsibility for enforcing Title VII of the Civil Rights Act, and reports that approximately one-third of its complaints involve sex discrimination. Many of these

From *Bringing Women Into Management* by Gordon and Strober. Copyright © 1975 by McGraw-Hill Inc. Used with permission of McGraw-Hill Book Co.

complaints have resulted in litigation, and the first Title VII case to reach the United States Supreme Court involved sex discrimination.[6]

The judicial decisions under Title VII have generally been very favorable to the women plaintiffs. The procedural aspects of the statute have been construed broadly, in favor of the plaintiffs,[7] and the exceptions have been construed narrowly so as to defeat defendant employers' defenses.[8]

Recent Amendments

In 1972 important amendments were made to both Title VII and the Equal Pay Act. Coverage under the Equal Pay Act has now been extended to executive, administrative, professional, and outside sales employees.[9] This means that women working in such jobs must receive salaries equal to men performing the same duties. All employers are to review the salaries of women working in these categories, women in supervisory and administrative jobs high in the corporate structure, to make sure that pay is commensurate with that of male employees. The jobs of the women and men need not be identical, but only substantially equal as to skill, effort, responsibility, and working conditions. Attempts to disguise the similarity of two jobs by giving them different titles, or by assigning the men insignificant additional tasks, will not be allowed.[10]

For example, the female employees of a bank sued under the Equal Pay Act alleging that they were being paid substantially lower wages than male employees doing the same work. The bank responded by explaining that the men were in a training program that qualified the higher pay. The court found, from evidence presented, that the training program was little more than a hastily devised justification for the unequal pay. The program, if it in fact existed, was informal, sporadic, and unwritten. The training was essentially the acquiring of skills and knowledge of the business through performance of regular tasks also performed by women and was not a valid basis for the wage difference.[11]

The Equal Employment Opportunity Commission

The most important and controversial aspect of the amendments was granting to the EEOC the power to initiate court action against an employer.[12] Formerly the EEOC had no enforcement power and could merely seek voluntary compliance from employers through conciliation. Under the old law only the complainant could file suit in federal court to litigate the question of discrimination. Lack of enforcement power crippled the EEOC in the past and made it relatively ineffective. Now, with its new enforcement powers and a staff of attorneys at litigation offices throughout the country, the EEOC has begun to take a strong role in prosecuting evasive employers.

In the past, employers could engage in various dilatory tactics when dealing with a Title VII action, hoping the complainant would get discouraged at the prospect of finding a lawyer and filing suit and would eventually give up. Employers failed to take the EEOC conciliation procedure seriously because they knew the EEOC could do nothing if they failed to cooperate. This attitude has undoubtedly begun to change now, and employers are well advised to settle a complaint at the conciliation stage if possible, for a lawsuit against the EEOC could be costly.

An example of what the EEOC can now achieve is the settlement it made with AT&T in January 1973. AT&T agreed to pay approximately $15 million to 13,000 women and 2,000 minority men who had been denied pay and promotion opportunities. New policies agreed on by the company and EEOC should result in increased wages of $23 million a year.

The consent decree entered in the AT&T case includes a detailed affirmative action plan that requires the company to evaluate women in its management training program for promotion. The criteria employed in making the evaluations must be approved by the EEOC and women found satisfactory are to become candidates for promotion as vacancies occur. Additionally, those found satisfactory are to receive a salary increase of $100 a month as of the assessment date.[13]

Administrative and Judicial Decisions

Job Requirements

The second Title VII case to be decided by the United States Supreme Court, *Griggs v. Duke Power Co.*,[14] involved racial discrimination, but the principles articulated by the Court are equally applicable to cases involving sex discrimination.

The plaintiffs in the *Griggs* case were challenging Duke Power Company's practice of requiring an employee or job applicant to be a high school graduate or pass an intelligence test as a condition of employment or promotion. The requirement, though applied equally to whites and blacks, excluded a disproportionate number of blacks from eligibility.

The Court found that the intelligence tests and high school education did not bear a demonstrable relationship to the successful performance of the jobs for which they were used and were therefore not necessary for the employer's business. Because of their discriminatory impact on blacks, the tests were therefore in violation of Title VII.

In its opinion the Court said, "Good intent or absence of discriminatory intent does not redeem employment procedures or testing mechanisms that operate as 'built in headwinds' for minority groups and are unrelated to measuring job capability."[15]

The decision requires employers to take a close look at job descriptions and qualifications. If they contain irrelevant requirements that disproportionately exclude women, they are illegal, and should be revised to include only qualifications essential to performance of the job.

The "Bona Fide Occupational Qualification" Exception

Under Title VII, valid business necessity can excuse practices that are discriminatory in instances where religion, sex, or national origin is "a bona fide occupational qualification reasonably necessary to the normal operation of that particular business or enterprise. . . ."[16]

This is the famous "b.f.o.q." exception that employers seized upon after the passage of Title VII to justify their discriminatory practices. These attempts, however, have been thwarted by a narrow interpretation of the b.f.o.q. by EEOC and the courts.

In its *Guidelines on Sex Discrimination*,[17] the EEOC has stated that the following situations do not warrant application of the b.f.o.q. exception: (1) the refusal to hire a woman because of her sex based on assumptions about the comparative employment characteristics of women in general; (2) the refusal to hire an individual based on stereotyped characterization of the sexes; (3) the refusal to hire an individual because of the preferences of coworkers, the employer, clients, or customers. In fact, the EEOC has limited the b.f.o.q. for use only "where it is necessary for the purpose of authenticity or genuineness, . . . e.g., an actor or actress."[18] The EEOC *Guidelines* do not have the effect of law, but the courts have conceded to them great deference as a valid interpretation of the will of Congress.[19]

In most cases where defendants attempted to use the b.f.o.q. defense, the courts have followed the example of the EEOC and given the exception a narrow interpretation. Probably the most famous of these cases is *Diaz* v. *Pan American World Airways,*[20] in which the male plaintiffs challenged Pan Am's policy of hiring only females as flight cabin attendants.

Pan Am attempted to justify this policy by proof that sex was a "bona fide occupational qualification" for the position of stewardess. The court observed:

> Reviewing its own experience with the thousands of male and female cabin attendants it had hired over the preceding years, Pan Am determined in 1959 that the overall level of service provided by the females it had hired was superior to that provided by the males it had hired. While the males were found capable of satisfactorily performing what Pan Am describes as the "mechanical" functions of the flight attendant's job, such as the storage of coats and the preparation and service of meals and beverages, the male stewards were found, as a group, not to be the equal of the females in the "nonmechanical" functions which had now become more important—providing reassurance to anxious passengers, giving courteous personalized service, and in general, making flights as pleasurable as possible within the limitations imposed by aircraft operation.[21]

Evidence that their passengers overwhelmingly preferred service by females included an Opinion Research Corporation survey commissioned by the airline which showed that 79 percent of the passengers questioned preferred female stewardesses. The noted psychiatrist Dr. Eric Berne testified in psychological terms as to why passengers of both sexes prefer female stewardesses. The District Court was convinced by Pan Am's evidence and ruled that sex was a b.f.o.q. for position of flight attendant and denied the males relief.[22]

The Court of Appeals for the Fifth Circuit, however, reversed the District Court and held that sex was not a b.f.o.q. for the cabin attendant position. In its opinion the court adopted the EEOC *Guidelines* that require a narrow interpretation of the b.f.o.q. exception. In ruling that men as well as women must be considered for the jobs, the court said, "The primary function of an airline is to transport passengers safely from one point to another. While a pleasant environment, enhanced by the obvious cosmetic effect that female stewardesses provide as well as . . . their apparent ability to perform the nonmechanical functions of the job in a more effective manner than most men, may all be important, they are tangential to the essence of the business involved."[23]

Employers have frequently tried to justify their reluctance to promote women to management positions with arguments centered on customer or coworker preference. The assertion that clients do not want to have a female working on their account or that male employees do not want a female supervisor is not a legitimate defense for the employer. The Pan American case seems to have settled that question once and for all.

Fringe Benefits

Another area of sex discrimination, less widely discussed at first than the b.f.o.q. exemption, is the question of fringe benefits. Until recently employers felt justified in giving females lower fringe benefits on the assumption that most women work for a second family income or as a hobby, and are covered by their husbands' benefits.

In its *Guidelines,* the EEOC has defined as fringe benefits medical, hospital, accident, life insurance, and retirement benefits; profit-sharing and bonus plans; leave; and other terms, conditions, and privileges of employment.[24] According to the EEOC, it is an unlawful practice for an employer to discriminate between men and women with regard to fringe benefits by such distinctions as conditioning benefits on whether the employee is the "head of the household," or "principal wage earner;" giving benefits to the families of male employees but not to families of female employees; or having a pension or retirement plan that establishes different optional or compulsory retirement ages or benefits for men and women.[25]

As yet there has been very little litigation in this area, perhaps because most unions bargain for benefits plans that treat men and women equally. Employers should review their fringe benefit plans carefully to be sure men and women are receiving equal benefits. They are advised to revise discriminatory policies even if it means reopening a union contract. If the union refuses to cooperate, the employer can make the union a codefendant should a complaint or lawsuit be filed.

One case that reached the Court of Appeals for the Seventh Circuit[26] involved a retirement plan adopted pursuant to a collective bargaining agreement, in which it was agreed that women were to retire at sixty-two, men at sixty-five. The court found that the plan violated Title VII because it forced women to give up three years of work and wages, based on a sexual classification contrary to the intent of Title VII.

Because insurance companies who set up benefit programs rely on actuarial tables, they write plans that give men a larger annuity than women because women as a group live longer than men. The controversy over the use of actuarial tables will undoubtedly not be easily settled, but some questions must be asked about the accuracy of actuarial figures. Do working women as a group outlive working men? Many of the tables were compiled when fewer women were working. Are there regional variations in life expectancy? Why use sex when smoking or weight is far more relevant to life expectancy? This application of a stereotyped characteristic to individual workers is in direct contradiction to Title VII's directive that individuals be treated as such, and not as members of a sexual group.

Another recent case appears, at least implicitly, to reject actuarial figures as a legitimate basis for discriminating against men or women as a group under retirement plans. In *Rosen* v. *Public Service Electric Co.*[27] the court ruled that retirement benefits must be equal for men and women of like ages possessing comparable work experience. Where there were disparities, the company was required to raise the benefits of the group discriminated against.

Maternity Benefits

Probably the most troublesome problem for a woman who has decided she wants children and a career is how to arrange her pregnancies and child rearing to accommodate her job responsibilities. A satisfactory solution to these problems is critical if women are to enter and remain in managerial positions. These are the alternatives:

> If her employment is terminated or suspended with a loss of accumulated benefits [during pregnancy], her incentive to return to work is correspondingly reduced. If the woman who worked prior to motherhood waits until after her children are grown to re-enter the labor force, she becomes the victim of discrimination on the basis of her age as well as her sex. But if she can be reinstated after absence required by childbirth with no loss of benefits, she is more likely to view employment as a career in which she has a vested interest, rather than as a mere temporary source of income, and will arrange her pregnancies so as to disrupt her employment activity as little as possible.[28]

How employers treat pregnancy and what types of benefits are provided for female employees will profoundly affect many women's careers, especially their ability to progress to management positions.

Maternity benefits include job security, maintenance of accrued seniority and continuation of its accrual during pregnancy leave, eligibility for temporary disability compensation, continued membership in health and life insurance plans, and adequate maternity leave. Maternity leave should be distinguished from child-care leave. Only women employees require maternity leave for childbirth, generally not more than six weeks. Leave to take care of the child, however, should be treated differently from maternity leave and should be available to both male and female employees.

Concern for the health of the pregnant woman and her unborn child is often cited as the reason for extended maternity leave. This fails to recognize that many pregnant women care for small children and perform strenuous housekeeping duties up to the date of birth. Another common argument is that pregnant women do not work efficiently. While some pregnant women may have difficulties, this does not mean that all or even most women will be unfit to perform their jobs. Annual Public Health Service surveys show that men lose about the same amount of time from work because of disabilities as women, even including childbirth and the complications of pregnancy.[29]

The United States Supreme Court has recently spoken for the first time on the question of mandatory maternity leave. At the time the lawsuits were filed, local governments were not covered by Title VII, and so plaintiffs alleged violations of their constitutional rights under the Fourteenth Amendment. The two cases involved maternity regulations of the Cleveland, Ohio, Board.[30] The Cleveland regulation required pregnant teachers to stop work five months before the expected date of birth and remain out without pay until the first semester after the baby reaches three months of age. The Chesterfield regulation required the teacher to take leave without pay four months before the expected birth, but she could return when her doctor certified she was able to work.

The Supreme Court struck down both regulations, stating, "The rules contain an irrebuttable presumption of physical incompetency, and that presumption applies even when the medical evidence as to an individual woman's physical status might be wholly to the contrary. [Such] . . . permanent irrebuttable presumptions have long been disfavored under the Due Process Clauses of the Fifth and Fourteenth Amendments."[31] The Court stressed that "freedom of personal choice in matters of marriage and family life is one of the liberties protected by the Due Process Clause of the Fourteenth Amendment. By acting to penalize the pregnant teacher for deciding to bear a child, overly restrictive maternity leave regulations can constitute a heavy burden on the exercise of these protected freedoms."[32]

In a footnote, the Court conceded that the alternative of an individualized determination could be an administrative burden to the employer, and indicated that a more narrowly drawn regulation, requiring maternity leave during the last few weeks of pregnancy, might be permissible. In its most narrow interpretation, this decision says that mandatory maternity leaves may not be arbitrary and capricious and based on irrebuttable presumptions that have no basis in fact.

Another aspect of maternity provisions was considered when in June 1974 the United States Supreme Court ruled in *Geduldig* v. *Aiello*[33] that California's exclusion of normal pregnancy and childbirth from coverage under its statewide disability insurance program does not constitute "invidious" discrimination and therefore is constitutional under the Equal Protection Clause of the Fourteenth Amendment. The Court said the state had a legitimate interest in keeping the program self-supporting, in minimizing the employee contribution rate, and in keeping benefits for covered disabilities at an adequate level.

It is important to note that *Geduldig* v. *Aiello* involved the actions of legislators, not employers, and was decided pursuant to the Fourteenth Amendment, not Title VII of the Civil Rights Act. The EEOC has stated in its *Guidelines* that Title VII requires pregnant employees to be treated on the same basis as any other employee with a temporary disability under a health or sick leave plan available to employees.[34] (*Ed. note:* In December 1976, the Supreme Court ruled that employers are not required under the 1964 Civil Rights Act to provide disability pay to women during absence due to pregnancy and childbirth. This opinion overturned both lower court rulings on this question and EEOC Guidelines.)

In its "Friend of the Court" brief filed in the *Geduldig* case the EEOC stated that

> The Commission carefully scrutinized both the employer practices and their crucial impact on women for a substantial period of time and then issued its Guidelines after it became increasingly apparent that symptomatic or pervasive discrimination against women was frequently found in employers' denial of employment opportunity and benefits to women on the basis of the childbearing role, performed solely by women.[35]

Several lower federal courts have considered the "pregnancy as temporary disability" issue in cases filed under Title VII, and have ruled that discriminatory treatment of pregnant employees under health insurance plans violates the act.[36]

In light of the administrative and judicial rulings, what type of maternity leave program should an employer adopt? For the women who want to work as long as possible and take as little time off for childbirth as is physically necessary, short-term disability insurance should be available. If benefits and seniority accrue during leave for other disabilities, they should accrue during such maternity leave. If accumulated sick pay must be exhausted before disability benefits are paid, then pregnant women could so use their sick pay. A woman who wants to leave work in the early months of her pregnancy, although she is physically capable of continuing her job, clearly should not be entitled to disability compensation, but such voluntary leave might be treated in the same manner as educational leave so that these women retain seniority and receive preference in hiring when they are ready to return.[37]

In a society where many families have both parents working but child care is woefully inadequate, it is essential for both parents to have the flexibility to take voluntary leaves for child care. Voluntary leave to care for children should be available to fathers as well as mothers. Such leaves would provide no benefits, but would freeze the employees' seniority and assure them a job, though possibly not the same job, when they return to work. . . .

The momentum has been generated and some laws have been passed, but complete equality for women is yet to be realized. While many of the blatant discriminatory practices have disappeared, subtle barriers still remain. We have laws, but most women still work in low-paying, low-status jobs, and only a few find their way to the more prestigious positions. The successful woman is still a news item—something unusual—and the stereotypes about women persist. Only when women represent significant percentages of executives, professionals, and high government officials will we have achieved real equality.

Notes

1. 29 U.S.C. 206(d).
2. 109 Cong. Rec. 9212.
3. All laws and regulations dealing with sex discrimination in employment can be found in the *Employment Practices Guide*, published by the Commerce Clearing House, Inc., or *Fair Employment Manual*, published by the Bureau of National Affairs.
4. Burns, *Analysis of the Equal Pay Act*, 24 Lab. L. J. 92 (1973).
5. *Business Week*, Nov. 25, 1972.
6. *Phillips* v. *Martin Marietta Corp.*, 400 U.S. 542 (1971).
7. *Bowe* v. *Colgate-Palmolive Co.*, 416 F. 2d 711, 718 (7th Cir. 1969).
8. *Diaz* v. *Pan American World Airways*, 442 F. 2d 385 (5th Cir. 1971), *Sprogis* v. *United Air Lines Inc.*, 442 F.2d 1194 (7th Cir. 1971), cert. denied 404 U.S. 991.
9. Pub. L. 92-318, Title IX §906(b)(1), 86 Stat. 375 (June 23, 1972).
10. *Shultz* v. *Wheaton Glass Co.*, 421 F. 2d 259 (3d Cir. 1970, cert. denied 398 U.S. 905.
11. *Hodgson* v. *American Bank of Commerce*, 447 F. 2d 416 (5th Cir. 1971).
12. Pub. L. 92-261.
13. FEP 431:73.
14. 401 U.S. 424 (1971).
15. Id. at 432.
16. 42 U.S.C. §2000e-2(e).
17. 29 C.F.R. §1604.1-1604.31.
18. Id. §1604.2 (a)(z).
19. *Griggs* v. *Duke Power Co.*, 401 U.S. 424, 434 (1971).
20. 443 F. 2d 385 (5th Cir. 1971).
21. *Diaz* v. *Pan American World Airways*, 311 F. Supp. 559, 563 (1970).
22. Id.
23. *Diaz*, op. cit. supra note 21, at 388.
24. 29 C.F.R. 1604.9(a).
25. Id.
26. *Bartmess* v. *Drewrys U.S.A. Inc.*, 444 F. 2d 1186 (7th Cir.), cert. denied, 404 U.S. 939 (1971).
27. 477 F. 2d 90 (3d Cir. 1973).
28. *Love's Labors Lost: New Conceptions of Maternity Leaves*, 7 Harv. Civ. Rights-Civ. Lib. L. Rev. 260, 261 (1972).
29. U.S. Public Health Service, Dept. of Health, Education and Welfare, Pub. 1000, Ser. 10, No. 52, *Vital and Health Statistics, Current Estimates from the Health Interview Survey*, U.S., 1967.
30. *Cleveland Board of Education* v. *La Fleur*, 94 S. Ct. 791 (1974); *Cohen* v. *Chesterfield County School Board*, 94 S. Ct. 791 (1974).
31. Id. at 798.
32. Id. at 796.
33. 94 S. Ct. 2485 (1974).
34. 29 C.F.R. §1604.10(b).
35. *Geduldig* v. *Aiello*, 94 S. Ct. 2485, 2494 (1974).
36. *Wetzel* v. *Liberty Mutual Ins. Co.*, 372 F. Supp. 1146 (W.D. Pa. 1974).
37. *Love's Labors Lost*, supra, note 28, at 291.

The Equal Employment Opportunity Act of 1972

WILLIAM BROWN III

On March 24, 1972, President Nixon signed into law "The Equal Employment Opportunity Act of 1972" (P.L. 92-261), thereby concluding the long drought of a lack of effective Federal enforcement of equal employment opportunity. The 1972 Act, which in effect is a series of major amendments to Title VII of the Civil Rights Act of 1964 (42 U.S.C. § 2000e *et seq*), establishes for the first time in the Federal Government an independent agency which has the power to effectively prohibit all forms of employment discrimination based on race, religion, color, sex or national origin. This agency, the Equal Employment Opportunity Commission (EEOC), has, pursuant to the new law, been given the power to institute civil actions to eliminate violations of the nondiscrimination in employment requirements of Title VII. The adoption of the 1972 law concludes almost seven years of efforts by the EEOC and civil rights groups to enact such enforcement powers for the agency, and promises to usher in a new era of activism in the enforcement of equal employment opportunity in both private and public employment. The effect that this new law will have upon the personnel policies of the Nation's employers is self-evident, and should not be underestimated. The EEOC has been laboring with the handicap of lack of enforcement powers since its inception in 1965, and it is only fair to say that now having been granted that which it has sought for so long, it intends to use it.

The main purpose of the 1972 Act is to amend the existing provisions of Title VII to correct certain deficiencies which were allowed into the original version of Title VII. Of these, the lack of enforcement powers for the EEOC was the most serious.[1] The 1972 Act corrects this deficiency by empowering the EEOC to bring civil actions directly in the Federal courts to enforce violations of Title VII. The new law also expands the coverage of Title VII to encompass employees of state and local governments or governmental organizations, employees of educational institutions, and employers or labor organizations with 15 or more employees or members (the previous coverage had only included employers or labor organizations with 25 or more employees or members). The new law also provides additional protection for Federal employees as regards equal employment opportunity and clarifies certain procedures relating to the Office of Federal Contract Compliance (OFCC) in the Department of Labor.

Enforcement Provision

It was the opinion of both the House Education and Labor Committee and the Senate Committee on Labor and Public Welfare that the major shortcoming of the existing Title VII was its failure to provide the EEOC with direct enforcement powers.[2] As stated by the Committee, the earlier belief that complaints of employment discrimination could be resolved through the voluntary methods of negotiation, persuasion, and conciliation had been shown wrong, and that viable enforcement procedures would be

From *Personnel Administration*, May-June 1972. Reprinted by permission of the International Personnel Management Association.

required in order to insure that the provisions in Title VII were obeyed. Accordingly, both the House and Senate Committees recommended the adoption of proposed legislation which would grant the EEOC the ability to go beyond its voluntary compliance procedure to insure that employers whose employment practices were violating the prohibitions of Title VII would be required to change their practices in accordance with the law.[3] Both House and Senate agreed with the recommendations of the Committees and adopted enforcement procedures allowing the EEOC to bring civil actions directly in the Federal courts.[4]

The impact of this provision is obvious. Where before, employers against whom charges of employment discrimination had been filed could only be required by the EEOC to voluntarily resolve the allegations raised in a charge, with the adoption of the new law, the EEOC may now bring a civil suit against any employer covered by the Act if such voluntary resolution should fail.[5] While under the old law employers could choose to ignore Commission opinions and take a chance that individuals who had been aggrieved would not take the time, or could not afford, to take a case to court, the current provisions allow the EEOC to sue on its own initiative in such situations.

The basic procedures with respect to the enforcement provisions of the new law provide:

1. Existing procedures for filing a charge with the Commission shall remain. However, where before a charge of unlawful employment discrimination had to be filed with the Commission within 90 days after an alleged unlawful employment practice had occurred, that time limit has now been expanded to 180 days.[6] However, in cases where the unlawful employment practice is of a continuing nature, then the last day of the violation and not its inception determines the running of the 180 days;

2. Existing procedures have also been retained as regards deferral to State fair employment practice agencies.[7] In those cases where a charge arises in a jurisdiction to which the Commission normally defers, the time periods for filing a charge with the EEOC have been extended to 300 days after the alleged unlawful employment practice occurred or to 30 days after the State or local agency has terminated its proceedings.[8]

3. A new provision has been added which allows charges to be filed "by or on behalf of" an aggrieved individual.[9]

4. The provisions of the prior law with respect to the Commission's procedures for informal methods of settlement (i.e. conference, conciliation and settlement) have been retained. However, should such procedures fail, the Commission is then authorized to proceed with a lawsuit against the respondent;

5. The Commission may bring a lawsuit at any time after 30 days from the filing of the charge with the Commission.[10] The Commission may also request the court at any time for temporary or preliminary relief, before the final disposition of a charge.[11]

6. The individual complainant may also bring a case to court without recourse to the Commission or, if a charge is dismissed by the Commission or if within 180 days after a charge has been filed with the Commission it has not filed a civil action, the individual may take the case directly to court.[12]

Changes in Jurisdiction

The 1972 law also made some changes in the coverage of the Act. It eliminated the previous exemption for employees of State and local governments and employees of educational institutions.[13] It also expanded the coverage of the law, one year after enactment (i.e. March 24, 1973), to apply to all employers and labor unions with 15 or more full-time employees or members.[14] A specific exception was made with respect to elected officials of State or local governments and their immediate personal staff who would not be covered by the provisions of the Act. This exception, however, has been construed very narrowly in the legislative history and should not provide any major exemptions in this area.

The jurisdiction of Title VII as regards religious institutions was also modified. Where before, religious institutions could grant preference in employment to members of their particular religion only as regards religious activities within such institutions, this exemption has now been expanded to include all functions, giving such institutions the right to grant religious preference in hiring, but still prohibiting them from discriminating in any other of the prohibited categories under Title VII.[15]

State and Local Governments

The role of the Commission in enforcing, by civil action, the provisions has been specifically delimited to exclude the filing of suits against State and local governments or their political subdivision.[16] The role of enforcing violations of Title VII where the respondent is a State or local government has been specifically assigned to the U.S. Department of Justice. Complaints alleging employment discrimination by State or local governments would still be filed with the EEOC in the same manner as by employees of private businesses. The Commission would then investigate the charge and pursue resolution of the complaint through its informal negotiations and conciliation procedures. However, if the Commission is unable to achieve a satisfactory conciliation of the charge, it will then refer the case to the Justice Department which may then bring the case to court. While procedures between the Justice Department and the Commission have not yet been fully worked out at the time of the writing of this article, it is expected that these procedures will provide for close cooperation between the two agencies and a smooth transition from the EEOC to the Justice Department will be assured so that individuals who have charges of discrimination against State and local agencies will be fully protected.

Federal Employees Protection

The 1972 law also contains a new section which deals with the equal employment policies of the Federal Government.[17] This section gives the U.S. Civil Service Commission additional responsibility and greater authority to enforce the equal employment programs within the Federal competitive service. Particularly, it authorizes the Civil Service Commission to grant appropriate remedies for violations of equal employment opportunity including back pay for aggrieved individuals.[18]

The other major change effected by this section is the clear authorization for Federal employees to bring civil actions in the Federal courts for violations of equal employment opportunity. Under the provisions of this section, aggrieved employees are permitted to file a civil action within 30 days of a notice of a final action by an agency or by the Civil Service Commission or an appeal from an agency decision, or after 180 days from the filing of an initial charge with an agency or the Civil Service Commission.[19] This provision lays to rest much of the controversy in recent years regarding the rights of a Federal employee to sue the government for its employment policies.

Effect on Employers

The adoption of the 1972 Act places a greater responsibility than before upon all employers to insure that their employment and personnel policies are fully in accord with the principles of Title VII. The new amendments to Title VII are just that —amendments to the existing law. Most of the new provisions are procedural and do not change existing Title VII principles as developed by the Commission, the Department of Justice and the Courts since the 1964 enactment of the Civil Rights Act. The clear intention of the drafters of the new law was to retain the provisions of the previous law unless inconsistent with the new provisions. As stated by Senator Williams, the Senate sponsor of the legislation:

> In any area where the new law does not address itself, or in any areas where a specific contrary intention is not indicated, it was assumed that the present case law as developed by the courts would continue to govern the applicability and construction of Title VII.[20]

While retaining present interpretations, by the enactment of the new law, Congress strengthened some other areas and clarified some that might have been in question before.

The concept of employment discrimination has come a long way from the naive and simplistic concepts held in 1964 with the adoption of the 1964 Act. At that time, discrimination was thought to be comprised of individual acts of bad faith or distinguishable events, for the most part due to ill-will on the part of some identifiable individual or organization. It was essentially thought to be a "human" problem which could readily be eliminated by conciliatory processes. We now know that employment discrimination is much more than that. More often than not, it is the result of institutional "systems" and "effects" rather than isolated events, and the causes of employment discrimination are usually associated with such personnel systems as seniority, lines of progression, transfer provisions, perpetuation of past practices through present requirements, and testing requirements. All of these areas directly affect any management system in any business, and business administration in all its forms must meet all of these problems. While it is impossible, within the space of this article to explain all of the areas of employment discrimination which bear directly upon personnel administration, there are certain problems which can be pointed out in the space of a few lines.

Perhaps the most fundamental concept which bears directly upon employment practices and policies is that proof of intent to discriminate is not a prerequisite to a finding of an unlawful employment practice. Intent is inferred from the totality of the conduct and a party charged with a violation of the Act may not even be aware of his discriminatory acts. The relevant test for employment discrimination is whether the *effect* of a particular practice serves to exclude a disproportionate number of persons in a protected class.[21] Similarly, an employment practice based in part on unlawful considerations is not saved by the fact that other, non-discriminatory considerations may also have been present.[22]

The importance of careful analysis of personnel systems to determine possible violations of Title VII becomes even more important when read in light of the existing principle that most instances of unlawful discrimination under Title VII are by nature violations affecting an entire *class* and not just the single individual who may have actually brought the charge with the Commission.[23] This factor has led to the acceptance by the courts of the use of statistics to demonstrate existing systems of discrimination.

Statistics showing an underrepresentation of a particular class have been held to establish a *prima facie* case of unlawful exclusion and to infer the existence of discrimination.[24] Based on the foregoing principles, the following kinds of employment practices must be considered as potentially in violation of Title VII unless shown as required by business necessity:

1. All tests, either paper-and-pencil variety or other performance projection type which are used as a measure for employment decisions;
2. Minimum educational requirements (e.g., requirement of a high school diploma);
3. Arrest records as a means of disqualifying applicants for employment;
4. Word-of-mouth referral systems; and
5. Use of a rule permitting discharge when an employee's wages have been garnished.

This is by no means a complete list, but does serve to point out some of the common practices used by employers which have been held to violate Title VII. With the enactment of the new amendments to Title VII, all of these principles have been reaffirmed, and the Commission has been given the authority to pursue eradication of any such unlawful employment practices wherever they may be found.

With the new coverage of Title VII, virtually the entire Nation's labor force has now been placed under the protection of Title VII. This means that almost every business administrator in the country now has responsibility to insure that his company's personnel practices do not violate the principles of Title VII. It is incumbent upon business to familiarize itself with the requirements of Title VII and to establish positive programs to bring minorities and women into the mainstream of employment by establishing programs which will not only eliminate discrimination in the future, but will also correct any discrimination of the past. The Commission's role is clear. By granting it enforcement powers, the Congress has recognized the failure that lack of an overall enforcement of equal employment opportunity has generated. Discrimination in employment continues. The task assigned to this agency is to see that it does not continue and it will do its best to see that the job begun in 1964 with the adoption of the original Civil Rights Act is not left unfinished.

Notes

1. As originally proposed, Title VII did provide the EEOC with enforcement powers but this was deleted from the Act as part of a compromise in order to assure passage of other provisions of the 1964 Act. EEOC, Legislative History of Titles VII and XI of the Civil Rights Act of 1964 (G.P.O. 1967) pp. 3003-08, 3017-21.

2. For the views of the two congressional committees on this issue see the Committee Report issued by each Committee respectively to accompany the recommended adoption of the proposed legislation. H.R. Rep. No. 92nd Cong. 1st Sess. (1971) and S. Rep. No. 92nd Cong. 1st Sess. (1971).

3. The only disagreement in the two Committees as regards the enforcement power issue was which of two types of enforcement to adopt, i.e. the right of the EEOC to issue its own administrative cease-and-desist orders (this was the scheme which had been proposed by H.R. 1746, introduced by Congressman Augustus F. Hawkins (D-Calif.) and S. 2515, introduced by Senator Harrison A. Williams Jr. (D-N.J.)) or whether to allow the EEOC to bring civil actions directly in the Federal courts (this was the scheme proposed in H.R. 6760, introduced by Congressman John N. Erlenborn (R.-Ill.) and as an amendment to S. 2515 by Senator Peter H. Dominick (R.-Colo.). While both Committees recommended the cease-and-desist approach, both House and Senate adopted the direct court enforcement approach.

4. The House passed the legislation on September 16, 1971; the Senate passed its version of

the legislation on February 22, 1972; both Houses adopted the Conference Report resolving the differences between the two bills and establishing the final version of the legislation on March 8, and March 6, respectively.

5. P.L. 92-261, Sec. 4(a); VII, as amended, § 706(f) (1).

6. *Id.* § 706(e).

7. Under the new and the old law, pursuant to Section 706(c), the EEOC will defer charges to a State fair employment agency for 60 days. During this time, the EEOC will not act on the charge and will allow the appropriate State agency a first opportunity to resolve the charge. However, pursuant to a recent decision by the U.S. Supreme Court, a charge may be filed with the Commission before it is filed with a State agency; the EEOC may receive and then defer the charge on behalf of a complainant, *Love v. Pullman Co.*

8. *Op. cit.* § 706(e).

9. *Id.* § 706(b).

10. *Id.* § 706(f) (1).

11. *Id.* § 706(f) (2).

12. *Id.* § 706(f) (1).

13. P.L. 92-261, Sec. 2(1) & 2(2); Title VII, as amended, § 701.

14. *Id.*

15. *Id.* § 702.

16. See generally *id.* § 706(f) (1).

17. Title VII, as amended, § 717(a)-(e).

18. The intention of this particular provision of the new law indicates Congressional affirmation of the recent decision by the U.S. Court of Claims awarding back pay in a situation of employment discrimination in the Federal Government. *Chambers* v. *U.S.*, 451 F. 2d 1045 (U.S. Ct. Ct. 1971).

19. *See,* Section-by-section analysis of Sen. Williams, 118 Cong Rec. § 3463 (daily ed. March 6, 1972).

20. *Id.* at § 3460.

21. *Griggs* v. *Duke Power Co.*, 401 U.S. 424 (1971).

22. *King* v. *Laborers, Local 818.* (6th Cir., 1971).

23. *Jenkins* v. *United Gas Corp.*, 400 F. 2d 28 (5th Cir. 1968); *Sprogis* v. *United Air Lines*, 444 F. 2d 1194 (7th Cir. 1971) *cert. den.,*—U.S.—Dec. 14, 1971); *Bowie* v. *Colgate Palmolive Co.*, 416 F. 2d 711 (7th Cir. 1969).

24. *Marquez* v. *Omaha District Sales Office*, 440 F. 2d 1157 (8th Cir. 1971); *Jones* v. *Lee Way Motor Freight*, 431 F. 2d 245 (10th Cir. 1970); *Parham* v. *Southwestern Bell Tel. Co.*, 433 F. 2d 42 (8th Cir. 1970).

Personnel Selection and the Supreme Court

THADDEUS HOLT

Personnel selection has long been affected by legal restrictions of one sort or another. Veterans have had certain special rights for years. Collective bargaining agreements have had legal sanction in most of U.S. industry since the mid-1930s, and in some special

This article was prepared especially for this book.

segments, such as the railroad industry, for an even longer period. For a generation or more, some states have had laws against racial discrimination in personnel selection on their books. It is, however, only since the effective date of Title VII of the Civil Rights Act of 1964 that there has come to be a comprehensive involvement of federal law in the employment selection process.

This article deals with a small group of the most significant milestones in the development of that law: six decisions in which, beginning in 1971, the Supreme Court has ruled upon fundamental questions in the interpretation and administration of Title VII and related statutes.

The law is, of course, not a static entity. Any description of the state of the law as of any particular time may well be outmoded by the time it reaches print, especially in such an active and dynamic field as the one under present discussion. Nevertheless, a review of the key Supreme Court decisions of 1971-76 may be of value both as a snapshot of this process at one particular time and—perhaps more usefully—as an introduction to the decisional process in the evolution of the law.

The Federal Judicial System

First, a brief review of the position of the Supreme Court in the federal judicial structure may be appropriate. The federal judicial system is divided into three tiers. At the lowest level, the courts of general original jurisdiction are the district courts. The United States is divided into nearly 100 judicial districts, each comprising a state or a portion of a state, and for each of which there is a United States District Court. It is in these courts that cases originate and trials are held. A party who contends that such a court has committed an error of law may appeal to the appropriate court of appeals. There are 11 of these, each having jurisdiction over the district courts in its "circuit," or regional group of states (except that the District of Columbia is a separate circuit unto itself). Finally, above the courts of appeals, at the top of the hierarchy, is the Supreme Court.

A party who contends that a district court has committed an error of law in his case has an appeal from the district court to the court of appeals "as of right"—that is, the court of appeals has no choice but to hear and decide the appeal. He has no appeal as of right, however, from the court of appeals to the Supreme Court in the great bulk of cases (there are certain exceptions). Cases usually go from the courts of appeals to the Supreme Court not, technically, by "appeal" but by "certiorari." This means in effect that the Supreme Court hears only those cases from the courts of appeals that it want to hear. A party dissatisfied with the result in the court of appeals "petitions for certiorari." Certiorari, or "cert" in everyday legal parlance, may be granted or denied. If denied, that is the end of the matter. If granted, both parties file written briefs and present oral arguments, and the case is decided by the Court with a written opinion or opinions.

It takes the affirmative votes of four of the nine justices for certiorari to be granted. Except in extraordinary instances, these votes are not made public, and no reasons of grant or denial of certiorari are given. Denial of certiorari does *not* indicate that the Court approves of the decision by the court below. It indicates simply that there were not four justices who wanted to hear the case. A justice may vote against grant because he does not think the question presented is of sufficient general importance by comparison with other questions which are competing for the Court's limited time; or because he does not think the case presents the question in just the right way; or because he thinks it prudent to let the law on the question be developed further by the various courts of appeals before the

Supreme Court speaks on the matter; or, it might be, because he thinks the Court might decide the question adversely to his own view, and a Supreme Court with a different membership might come to a different conclusion in some future case presenting the same question; or for any other reason. The best single reason for grant of certiorari is to settle a conflict between the rulings on a point made by two different circuit courts of appeals. For the courts of appeals are not bound by each other's decisions. They can, and sometimes do, disagree with each other. Most petitions for certiorari—over 90 percent—are denied.

One point of nomenclature that often confuses laymen is worthy of explanation. When a case is initially filed in the district court, it is called by the name of the plaintiff, or party bringing the action, versus (abbreviated "v." and properly pronounced "and," believe it or not) the defendant, or the party against whom the claim is made. On appeal, the name of the party appealing (called the "appellant") comes first. Thus, if the original defendant loses in the district court and takes an appeal, the original name of the case will be reversed in the court of appeals. In the Supreme Court the name of the party who is asking the Supreme Court to reverse the decision of the court of appeals (the "petitioner") will once more come first, and the names may thus be reversed again.

The Supreme Court decides cases by majority vote of the justices participating. The normal pattern is for one of the justices to write a "majority opinion," a statement of the decision and the reasons for arriving at it, on behalf of all the justices who agree with the majority result. Dissenters may or may not file opinions of their own stating why they disagree with the majority. Sometimes one or more justices will agree with the majority result, but not necessarily with the reasoning of the majority opinion, or with everything that is said in it. Such a justice may write a "concurring opinion."

Since the Supreme Court is the court of last resort, there is an irresistible tendency for lawyers and lower courts to squeeze every drop of interpretation out of each phrase and clause of a Supreme Court opinion. This is unfortunate, for opinions can rarely stand such treatment. Each phrase or clause is simply not necessarily the product of close attention by the majority. Majority opinions are in effect committee products. They sometimes have the proverbial cameloid properties of such products. Also, judges are human. They do make mistakes. Sometimes they get carried away with the sounds of their own opinions, and say things in them that are not necessary to the decision. And sometimes they may find it irresistible to hold forth at length on subjects in which they have no sophisticated background.

Judges are busy people. In the 1975-76 term, the latest for which careful statistics are available as of this writing, the Supreme Court disposed of nearly 4,000 appeals and certiorari petitions.

With this background, we turn to our cases.

Griggs v. Duke Power Co.

Title VII of the Civil Rights Act of 1964 came into effect on July 2, 1965. It made it unlawful, among many other things, for an employer "to fail or refuse to hire, or to discharge, any individual, or otherwise to discriminate against any individual with respect to his compensation, terms, conditions, or privileges of employment, because of such individual's race, color, religion, sex, or national origin." The basic approach of the Act, as originally adopted, was to establish an administrative body, the Equal Employment Opportunity Commission, to act as a conciliation agency. An individual wishing to complain against an employer could file a charge with the EEOC. The EEOC would investigate the charge (deferring to any appropriate state agency) and, if it found a probable violation of the statute, could seek to work out a conciliation agreement between the parties. If conciliation failed, or if the EEOC found no probable cause to believe the law had been violated, the individual could sue the employer in the federal district court. The court, if it found a willful violation, was empowered to order such relief as was appropriate, with or without back pay. The EEOC was strictly a conciliation agency; it had no power to make rules and regulations (except procedural ones), and no enforcement powers. Enforcement was left to individuals for individual complaints, and to the Department of Justice with respect to group complaints—so-called "patterns or practice" cases, in which an employer is charged with systematically discriminating against members of a particular protected group.

It was not until nearly seven years after passage of the Act, and nearly six years after its effective date, that the Supreme Court spoke for the first time in a case interpreting the Act's substantive provisions. During those years, a considerable body of law was developed by the lower courts. They considered such questions as whether the provisions of the Act vesting standing to bring "pattern or practice" cases in the Justice Department could be circumvented by the use of so-called "class" actions, under which one individual who had complied with the statutory procedures before the EEOC could sue on behalf of himself and the class of "all others similarly situated," even though those others had not so complied; whether the law required accelerated promotional opportunities for employees who had been the subject of discrimination prior to the adoption of the Act; and numerous other issues. Although losing parties in these cases often petitioned the Supreme Court for certiorari, the Court, for whatever reason—most probably, in order to give the lower courts the maximum opportunity to erect a basic framework in this new and controversial area before stepping in—did not grant such a petition until 1970. It did so, finally, in order to settle perhaps the most fundamental question of all: whether or not an employer had to *intend* to discriminate in order to violate the law. In the landmark case of *Griggs* v. *Duke Power Co.*, the court held that such an intent is unnecessary.

In the *Griggs* case, prior to the effective date of Title VII, the employer had hired blacks only as common laborers. As of that effective date, it instituted the Wonderlic and Bennett Mechanical Aptitude tests as a prerequisite for employment except in common labor jobs. It performed no validation of these tests, and adopted cutoff scores based on the approximate national median scores of high school graduates, with no attempt to establish any local norms. Moreover, the company had for some time required a high school diploma for employment otherwise than as common labor. Both these requirements were shown to screen out proportionately more black employees than white employees. However, the district court found that these requirements were not adopted with any discriminatory intent. The question squarely presented, therefore, was whether, in view of the fact that Title VII affords in a court remedy only if the employer has "intentionally engaged in . . . an unlawful employment practice," the fact that the employer had not intended to discriminate was a defense.

The Court of Appeals for the Fourth Circuit ruled on appeal in the *Griggs* case that lack of discriminatory intent *was* a defense. Other circuit courts had ruled that it was not. The Supreme Court sided with the latter. Speaking through Chief Justice Burger in a unanimous opinion, the Court held that no invidious intent is necessary to constitute a violation of the Act. "Under the Act," it said, "practices, procedures, or tests neutral on their face, and even neutral in terms of intent, cannot be maintained if they operate to 'freeze' the status quo of prior discriminatory employment practices." "The Act proscribes not only overt discrimination but also practices that are fair in form, but discriminatory in operation. The touchstone is business necessity. If an employment practice which operates to exclude Negroes cannot be shown to be related to proper performance, the practice is prohibited." "Good intent or absence of discriminatory intent does not redeem employment procedures or testing mechanisms that operate as built-in headwinds for minority groups and are unrelated to measuring job capability." "Congress directed the thrust of the Act to the consequences of employment practices, not simply the motivation. More than that, Congress has placed on the employer the burden of showing that any given requirement [has] a manifest relation to the employment in question."

Stated succinctly, the *Griggs* case established the proposition, fundamental to federal equal employment law, that once a plaintiff shows that a defendant's employment practice has an adverse effect on persons of the plaintiff's race, sex, religion, or national origin, the plaintiff has, in lawyer's terms, made out a *prima facie* case: that is, the defendant must present evidence that the employment practice is job-related, and if he does not do so the plaintiff wins. How much evidence the defendant must present, and what in fact constitutes "job-relatedness," were questions left unanswered in the *Griggs* opinion. For in the *Griggs* case the employer had presented no evidence of job-relatedness at all.

A corollary of the *Griggs* decision was the Court's first interpretation of the so-called "Tower Amendment" to Title VII, which provides that it is not an unlawful employment practice to utilize "any professionally developed ability test provided that such test, its administration or action upon the results is not designed, intended or used to discriminate because of race, color, religion, sex, or national origin." This provision was inserted into Title VII in the Senate in reaction to a decision by an inferior official of the Illinois Fair Employment Practices Commission, ordering the Motorola Company to cease giving prospective employees a particular aptitude test on the ground, in part, that it was culture-biased. Opposition to this decision in the Senate was unanimous. The sponsors of the bill maintained that such a result could not happen under the proposed Title VII; that it would not require the abandonment of "bona fide qualification test where, because of differences in background and education, members of some groups are able to perform better on these tests than members of other groups. An employer may set his qualifications as high as he likes. He may test to determine which applicants have these qualifications, and he may hire, assign, and promote on the basis of test performance." Notwithstanding these assurances, the Senate adopted the Tower Amendment. In light of this background, most observers assumed that the Tower Amendment was intended to permit employers to use general intelligence and ability tests without requiring specific validation or proof of job-relatedness. Under this interpretation, the Tower Amendment would have carved out for "professionally developed ability tests" an exception to the general rule proclaimed in *Griggs,* that an employment requirement with an adverse effect on a protected group must be job-related. The *Griggs* opinion, however, declined to adopt that construction, and held that aptitude tests, like other employment requirements, must be "job-related."

McDonnell Douglas Corp. v. Green

Two years passed before the Court again gave full-dress consideration to a Title VII case. Then, in 1973, in *McDonnell Douglas Corp.* v. *Green,* it addressed one of the questions left open in the *Griggs* case. Under the *Griggs* case, once the plaintiff makes out a *prima facie* case—as, for example, by showing that the defendant is using a selection device with an adverse effect on the plaintiff's group (as in *Griggs*)—the burden of proof shifts to the employer. But there are two kinds of burden of proof. One is what lawyers call "the burden of coming forward with evidence." If this was the employer's burden, it would mean that the employer would simply have to show some evidence that its action had some legitimate, nondiscriminatory reason, and the plaintiff's case would be neutralized. But if the employer had what lawyers call the "burden of persuasion," he would have to come forward not merely with *some* evidence, but with some strong evidence that the preponderance of the evidence was on his side. Obviously, plaintiffs would prefer the second interpretation, and defendants the first. For under the first, if the defendant comes forth with any evidence at all, the plaintiff's *prima facie* case is neutralized, and if the plaintiff does not adduce further evidence, the defendant wins. The *Green* case appears to hold that the defendant's burden is merely one of coming forward with evidence.

In that case, the plaintiff, a black employee, had been laid off in the course of a general reduction in force. The plaintiff, a long-time activist in the civil rights movement, protested that his discharge and the general hiring practices of the employer were racially motivated. He and fellow members of an activist organization organized a "stall-in" against the company in which they illegally stalled their cars on the main roads leading to the employer's plant so as to block access to it at the time of the morning shift change. Later, the plaintiff applied for a new job with the employer in response to a newspaper advertisement seeking craftsmen in the trade in which he was skilled. He was turned down. The reason given was his participation in this "stall-in." He sued, claiming discrimination.

The Court held that the plaintiff had made out a *prima facie* case by showing that he was black, was qualified, and was rejected, while thereafter the defendant continued to try to fill the vacancy. It held further that proof by the defendant of plaintiff's "participation in unlawful conduct against [the employer]... suffices to discharge [the defendant's] burden of proof at this stage and to meet [the plaintiff's] prima facie case of discrimination." Hence, the Court said, the employer's "reason for rejection thus suffices to meet the prima facie case...." However, the Court held further that the plaintiff must then be afforded an opportunity to show that the employer's stated reason for rejecting the plaintiff was in fact "a pretext for the sort of discrimination" prohibited by Title VII.

The *Green* case is profoundly important. Portions of it are somewhat obscure, reflecting, perhaps, some difficulty in securing a consensus among the Justices. It has received less attention than it deserves; partly, perhaps, because it is an unsatisfactory decision from the plaintiff's viewpoint.

Combining the principle of the *Griggs* case, dealing with selection practices, with that of the *Green* case, dealing with the shifting of the burden of proof, leads to the proposition that, while a plaintiff has made out a *prima facie* case if he shows that a selection device has an adverse effect on his class, proof by the defendant that the selection practice is "job-related" will cancel out this *prima facie* case; and then in order to prevail the plaintiff must show that the selection device is merely a pretext for discrimination. But what constitutes a sufficient showing of "job-relatedness" of a selection practice? In the *Green* case, the Court took the reasonable view that engaging in illegal activity designed to harass and intimidate an employer was sufficiently related to an employer's interest in a loyal and efficient workforce to be a legitimate employment criterion. But what about a selection criterion that is less obviously and commonsensically related to the job? In particular, what about sophisticated aptitude testing, which may have no such obvious relationship at all? This question was addressed in 1975 in the next case in which certiorari was granted, *Albemarle Paper Co.* v. *Moody.*

Albemarle Paper Co. v. Moody

In the Supreme Court, the *Albemarle* case presented two totally unrelated issues. One was the question of the extent to which a district court may be required to award a money judgment for back pay against an employer once a violation has been found, even though, under the *Griggs* principle, the violation may have been a totally innocent and unintentional one. The other was the question of what constitutes a sufficient showing of job-relatedness with respect to an aptitude test.

The Court's holding on the back pay issue is not relevant to our present inquiry; we may simply note in passing that the Court held that back pay "should be denied only for reasons which, if applied generally, would not frustrate the statutory purposes of eradicating discrimination throughout the economy and making persons whole for injury suffered through past discrimination." This ruling puts sharp teeth into the statute, for under it an employer whose personnel practices are found to violate the statute will have to pay money, however innocent he may be, and in whatever good faith he may have acted.

It is not impossible that the justices participating in the *Albemarle* case were focused more closely on the back pay issue, which presented questions of a familiar legal type, than on the question of how job-relatedness should be proved in the alien context of technical test validation. Thus, for example, Mr. Justice Rehnquist addressed only the back pay issue in his concurring opinion. A second special factor with respect to the *Albemarle* decision was that only eight Justices participated in the case. Mr. Justice Powell, the author of the *Green* opinion, excused himself from participation because his old law firm represented the employer. For whatever reason, the *Albemarle* majority opinion with respect to aptitude testing offers a classic example of the Court's getting far over its head in technicalities which were not fully explored on the record and the implications of which they could not possibly have fully understood.

It will be recalled that in the *Griggs* case there was *no evidence at all* to show *any* job-relatedness of the tests and educational requirements; and the Court declined to find that they were job-related on their face. The employer in *Albemarle* was utilizing several standard tests with cutoff scores which had apparently been established on the basis of published national norms. He had performed no validation studies whatever; but there was no evidence that he was intentionally discriminating. The case arose in one of the districts in the Fourth Circuit where, until the Supreme Court decision in the *Griggs* case, the law was that an employer was liable only for intentional discrimination. The *Griggs* case was decided on the eve of the decision of the *Albemarle* case, which first made it evident that proof of job-relatedness would be required. Faced with this last-minute requirement, the employer hastily conducted a "quick and dirty" validation study; it had many shortcomings that would be obvious to any qualified expert in the testing field, but was the best that could be done under the circumstances. It produced some positive correlations, and it therefore constituted some evidence at least that the tests were job-related. But the Court held that merely *some* evidence of job-relatedness was not enough. It held in effect that the employer must show that selection devices are job-related by a preponderance of the evidence. And the Court appeared to hold that the only way of making such a showing was by proving compliance with the Guidelines on Testing and Selection that had been promulgated by the EEOC in 1970. (See the Gorham article in this chapter.)

For present purposes, it is enough to note that these Guidelines have not been the objects of uniform admiration. Many (if not most) industrial psychologists believe that some principles embodied in them—such as the rejection of validation strategies other than criterion-related validation unless criterion-related validation were shown not to be feasible; the wholesale adoption of hypotheses concerning differential validity; and the inclusion of a requirement called "practical significance"—placed these Guidelines outside the general professional consensus as to good practice. It has been widely contended, indeed, that strict compliance with the 1970 EEOC Guidelines is literally impossible. More serious, from the purely legal point of view, was the avenue which these Guidelines opened for those who wished to take advantage of the refusal of Congress to give the EEOC power to make substantive rules and regulations; for, faced with disputes concerning such a highly technical subject as test validation, judges with no specialized background would inevitably reach for the Guidelines as the only apparent certainty in an incomprehensible field. Every instinct of their professional training and experience would lead them to do so; and the net effect would be to give the Guidelines the force of law.

And that was what the majority opinion in the *Albemarle* case seemed to be doing. Although it paid lip service to the proposition that the guidelines are "not administrative 'regulations' promulgated pursuant to formal procedures established by the Congress," they were nevertheless entitled to "great deference"—so much deference, indeed, that an employer's showing must be measured point-by-point against them. Semantics aside, this amounts as a practical matter to giving the Guidelines the force of law. And, having so held, the majority opinion then expounded in some detail on several specific technical elements of the Guidelines, and how the employer's showing in the case before them failed to meet their requirements.

With all due respect to the Supreme Court, it is composed of nine human beings who are no less subject to human failings than all the rest of us. Like the rest of us, they sometimes find the temptation irresistible to expound in a learned fashion on some arcane topic. It is hard not to think that this happened to some extent in the *Albemarle* opinion.

Chief Justice Burger and Justice Blackmun dissented forcefully from what the Chief Justice called the "wodden application of EEOC guidelines." He pointed out the very considerable distinction between his use of those Guidelines in the *Griggs* case, as simply showing that the EEOC confirmed the Court's view on the question whether tests had to be shown to be job-related *at all,* by contrast with the majority's use of the Guidelines in the *Albemarle* case as defining the *method* of proving job-relatedness in fact. Pointing out that the Guidelines had never been submitted to public comment and scrutiny, as all true administrative regulations are by law required to be, and that their technical provisions were not universally accepted by qualified professionals, they concluded that "slavish adherence" to the Guidelines as the touchstone of acceptable test validation should not be required.

Washington v. Davis

The *Albemarle* opinion was issued in the spring of 1975. A few months thereafter, the Court granted certiorari in the case of *Washington* v. *Davis.* That was a case in which black plaintiffs had charged that an aptitude test used by the District of Columbia in the selection of policemen screened out blacks disproportionately, and was therefore discriminatory unless shown to be job-related under the *Griggs* principle. In response, the employer (the District of Columbia) accepted the *Griggs* principle, but contended that the test *was* job-related, offering evidence tending to show that success on the test was correlated with success on the District's police training program. It offered no evidence, however, as to whether success on the training program was correlated with success on the job. In addition, it offered evidence showing that, notwithstanding the fact that more blacks than whites failed the test, overall the District was not hiring white applicants disproportionately. It argued that "adverse effect," triggering the *Griggs* principle, should be measured by the bottom-line result, and not by one element of the selection process standing alone.

The district judge held for the employer, saying in effect that, on its face, the test in question obviously tested general literacy and intelligence, and that these in turn were manifestly related to a policeman's job.

The court of appeals reversed. It held that the disproportionate impact of the test on blacks, standing alone, was sufficient to establish a *prima facie* case, which could only be rebutted by proof that the test was an adequate measure of job performance itself, and not merely a measure of performance on the training program.

In a confusing and unsatisfactory opinion, the Supreme Court reversed the court of appeals. In so doing, it appears to have corrected the most questionable elements of the *Albemarle* opinion, less than a year after it had been issued.

In an opinion by Mr. Justice White, the Court ruled at the outset that the case was before it, not under the substantive provisions of Title VII or any other statute, but under the Constitution itself. This requires a word of explanation. Public employers, as contrasted with private employers, are subject to the constitutional requirement that the state and federal governments afford all persons the equal protection of the laws. And this "equal protection" clause has been interpreted to include a requirement that such agencies afford equal employment opportunitites, wholly independently of Title VII or any other statute. Although the plaintiffs had claimed both under the Constitution and under statutes applicable to public employment in the District of Columbia which are comparable to Title VII, for procedural reasons only the constitutional claims were before the Court of Appeals and the Supreme Court. The Court of Appeals had held that Title VII principles—and, in particular, the *Griggs* principle under which the employer's intent is irrelevant—governed claims under the equal protection clause of the Constitution. The Supreme Court reversed on this point. Citing prior decisions by it in such fields as jury selection, legislative appointment, school segregation and other areas, the Court held that an adverse effect on a minority group, standing alone, is *not* enough to make out a *prima facie* case of discrimination under the equal protection clause: under the constitutional provision, there must also be some proof of an *intent* to discriminate.

The vital portion of the Court's opinion is a passage in which it contrasted the situation under Title VII. Under the statute, as interpreted in *Griggs,* it said, once adverse effect on the plaintiffs is shown, discriminatory purpose need not be proved; and, it noted further, the mere demonstration by the employer that the challenged practice has some rational basis is insufficient to legitimate it; rather, "it is necessary that the challenged practice be 'validated' in terms of job performance in any one of several ways." In a footnote, the Court observed significantly that "it appears beyond doubt by now that there is no single method for appropriately validating employment tests for their relationship to job performance." Referring to the APA's 1966 Standards for Educational and Psychological Tests and Manuals, it cited the three basic methods of validation (by criterion, content, and construct), and observed that the APA Standards had been relied upon by the EEOC in fashioning its Guidelines and had been judicially noted in some other law cases. (The Court was evidently unaware of the fact that the APA Standards had been revised and updated in 1974.) This constituted a patent rejection of the Guidelines, which insist on the primacy of criterion validation.

This portion of the *Washington* opinion is both obscure and vital. It appears beyond question to mark a quiet retreat from the overwhelming emphasis which the *Albemarle* opinion placed on the Guidelines as the exclusive measure of whether an employer has shown that his tests are job-related. This is particularly true in view of the fact that Mr. Justice Stewart, who wrote the *Albemarle* opinion, concurred in this part of the *Washington* opinion; and certainly the two dissenting justices, whose views are discussed below, saw it that way.

Although, as we have noted, the Court held that the *Washington* case was before it only on constitutional grounds, for procedural reasons the Court felt that it should address the case in Title VII terms as well. Under Title VII principles it concluded—apparently—that the district judge was warranted in concluding that training program validation was sufficient. It said that "it is also apparent to us, as it was to the district judge, that some minimum verbal and communicative skill would be very useful, if not essential, to satisfactory progress in the training regimen." Mr. Justice Stewart did *not* concur in this portion of the opinion, and, as noted below, Mr. Justice Stevens was carefully guarded as to his concurrence with this portion.

Mr. Justice Brennan and Mr. Justice Marshall dissented, with an opinion by Mr. Justice Brennan. Incomprehensibly, in light of the very clear and unchallengeable fact that the EEOC has *always* been denied authority to issue substantive regulations, the dissent repeatedly referred to the Guidelines as "regulations," which were allegedly "issued pursuant to explicit authorization in Title VII." Working through the Guidelines point by point in the style of the *Albemarle* opinion, the dissent noted a succession of respects in which the employer's showing in the *Washington* case did not comply with the Guidelines. And the dissent pointed out, quite correctly, that the majority's conclusion was inconsistent with the *Albemarle* case. It pointed specifically to the requirement of *Griggs* and *Albemarle* that job-relatedness must be shown, and contended, correctly, that a showing that success on a test is correlated with successful *training* for a job is not necessarily a showing of *job*-relatedness and is not an adequate showing under the Guidelines.

One possible synthesis of the *Albemarle* and *Washington* decisions would be as follows: Under *Griggs*, if the plaintiff proves that a test has an adverse effect on his class, he has proved a *prima facie* case. Under *Green*, the defendant can rebut this *prima facie* case by offering evidence that the test is job-related. Under *Washington*, if the test appears to be job-related on its face, that is sufficient. If, however, the test is not job-related on its face, under *Albemarle* it must be proven to be job-related by recourse to the EEOC Guidleines. This synthesis, though, raises as many questions as it answers. If it means an acceptance of "face validity," it is contrary not only to generally recognized professional standards in the field of industrial psychology, but also to the Guidelines themselves. It certainly does not seem to reflect the conclusion that the dissenters drew from the majority opinion in *Washington;* nor, for that matter, does it seem to be what the majority themselves had in mind.

The *Washington* majority opinion is confused and unsatisfactory. One possible reason for this is that it reflects the problem of securing a majority vote for recognizing that some elements of the *Albemarle* decision were not fully considered in their implications, combined with deference to the strength with which the dissenters held their views. About all that can be said with confidence at the time of this writing is that it seems reasonably clear that the Court had receded from the *Albemarle* opinion's "wooden reliance" on the EEOC's Guidelines.

Johnson v. Railway Express Agency

So far, we have talked almost entirely about Title VII of the Civil Rights Act of 1964. But there is another statute which is nearly a century older than Title VII, and which has now been authoritatively construed to cover even more ground, at least in the racial field—and to do so directly, without the intervention of any administrative proceedings before state agencies or the EEOC. This is the Civil Rights Act of 1866, now codified in relevant part as Section 1981 of Title 42 of the United States Code (42 U.S.C. § 1981).

Students of U.S. history will recall that in the pre-Civil War era, many states had laws which sharply limited the legal status of blacks. Indeed, more than one state in the north and west forbade any Negro even to enter the state. Such laws commonly limited or prohibited the holding of property by blacks; limited their capacity to make contracts which were legally enforceable; forbade black plaintiffs to sue white defendants; forbade the testimony of a black person in a lawsuit, except perhaps in a lawsuit between two blacks; and otherwise limited the legal capacity of such persons. After slavery was abolished by the Thirteenth Amendment in 1865, many of the former slave states adopted extensive legislation of this nature. Dubbed "Black Codes" after the legislation which had regulated slavery in the French colonies, these statutes became an early target of Reconstruction forces. In 1866, Congress, acting pursuant to the provision of the Thirteenth Amendment which gave it the authority to enforce the abolition of slavery by appropriate legislation, overrode the Black Codes by the Civil Rights Act of 1866. This statute provided, in part, that "all persons in any state or territory shall have the same right to make and enforce contracts, to sue, be parties, give evidence, and to the full and equal benefit of all laws and proceedings for the security of persons and property as is enjoyed by white citizens"; that all such persons should have the same right to hold property as is enjoyed by white citizens; and other similar provisions.

For more than a century it was taken for granted that the purpose of this legislation was to effectuate the abolition of slavery by placing black persons on the same footing as white persons as far as legal *capacity* was concerned; that is, a state could not pass a law which prevented a black person from owning land, or which said that a black person's contract was not equally as binding as a similar contract made by a white person. But to nearly universal astonishment, in the case of *Jones* v. *Alfred H. Mayer Co.*, the Supreme Court held in 1968 that the Civil Rights Act of 1866 in fact went much further than this; that it did not simply insure that black people had the *legal capacity to own* real estate, but actually *forbade discrimination by private persons in the sale of real estate*. An almost immediate corollary of this decision was that the statute forbade any kind of discrimination in the making of any contractual relationship; and the courts of appeals began to rule shortly thereafter that the specific contractual relationship of employment was covered by this statute, and that accordingly a private right of action at law for employment discrimination had been on the books, invisible to all, for more than a century.

In the spring of 1975, the Supreme Court upheld this view in *Johnson* v. *Railway Express Agency*. It held, furthermore, that this newly discovered right of action had not been affected in any way by the elaborate legislative and administrative structure which Congress had hammered out through the political process and embodied in the Civil Rights Act of 1964.

It would, no doubt, have come as the greatest of surprises to the Freedom Riders and Freedom Marchers, the sit-in demonstraters and boycott organizers, whose unremitting efforts over a decade brought about the civil rights revolution of the twentieth century— and to their opponents as well—to discover that all their labor, struggles, and suffering had been pointless and unnecessary, because the laws they fought for had already been on the books for a hundred years. Nor has this remarkable discovery gone unquestioned by members of the Supreme Court itself. In the most recent case on the subject at the time of this writing, *Runyon v. McCrary,* holding that the 1866 Act forbids a private, nonsectarian, commercially-operated school from discriminating in admissions on grounds of race, Mr. Justice White and Mr. Justice Rehnquist dissented with a long and scholarly opinion filled with historical analysis supporting the proposition that the Act of 1866 was limited solely to the question of legal capacity. Mr. Justice Powell said that "if the slate were clean I might well be inclined to agree with Mr. Justice White that § 1981 was not intended to restrict private contractual choices," but concluded, in view of the Court's previous decisions, that it was now too late to correct matters; and Mr. Justice Stevens said that "there is no doubt in my mind that [this] construction of the statute would have amazed the legislators who voted for it," and that he was willing "to follow a line of authority which I firmly believe to have been incorrectly decided" only because for the Court now to overrule the *Jones* case "would be a significant step backwards, with effects that would not have arisen from a correct decision in the first instance."

The law sometimes moves in mysterious ways.

McDonald v. Santa Fe Trail Transportation Co.

On the same day in June of 1976 as the Court handed down its decision reconfirming the new interpretation of the Civil Rights Act of 1866, it handed down another decision that makes an appropriate coda to this brief survey of cases involving equal employment opportunity. In *McDonald* v. *Santa Fe Trail Transportation Co.,* a case that the popular press immediately dubbed the "reverse discrimination" case—as if discrimination were a one-way concept—the Court reconfirmed that the protections of Title VII and Section 1981 apply to whites as well as to blacks. That was a case brought by two white employees who had been accused of stealing their employer's property. They charged that although they had been fired, a black employee similarly accused had not been fired.

The Court had no trouble in holding that the protections of Title VII against racial discrimination extend to whites just as much as to blacks. This much should have been obvious. Less obvious was the question whether Section 1981, which as we have seen had its historic origins in an effort to protect the legal status of the black freedman in the Reconstruction era, and which gives to "all persons . . . the same right . . . to make and enforce contracts . . . as is enjoyed by white citizens," was nevertheless applicable to a situation in which a white person had been the victim of discrimination. Basing its opinion largely on the language used by various members of Congress during the debates on the bill in 1866, the Court concluded that the effect of the statute is "to proscribe discrimination in the making or enforcement of contracts against, or in favor of, any race."

It was not a surprising decision, perhaps; but it came as a salutary reminder of the bedrock truth, too often lost sight of, perhaps, in the turmoil of the preceding 20 years, that every man, be he a member of a "majority" or a "minority," is equal in the sight of the law.

References

(All references are to the United States Reports, which are customarily cited by volume number, the abbreviation "U.S.," the page, and the year of the decision.)

Jones v. *Alfred H. Mayer Co.*, 392 U.S. 409 (1968)
Griggs v. *Duke Power Co.*, 401 U.S. 424 (1971)
McDonnell Douglas Corp. v. *Green*, 411 U.S. 792 (1973)
Johnson v. *Railway Express Agency*, 421 U.S. 454 (1975)
Albemarle Paper Co. v. *Moody*, 422 U.S. 405 (1975)
Washington v. *Davis*, 426 U.S. (1976)
Runyon v. *McCrary*, 426 U.S. (1976)
McDonald v. *Santa Fe Trail Transportation Co.*, 427 U.S. (1976)

Political, Ethical, and Emotional Aspects of Federal Guidelines on Employee Selection Procedures

WILLIAM A. GORHAM

There are probably many ways that professional mystery writers go about constructing a story. One of the ways must be to start with an intriguing solution and then, in planning the story, work back through the events that could have led to it. Another might be to outline the plot in detail from beginning to end, keeping in mind the eventual outcome. It does not seem likely that many writers start out just writing, without knowing where they intend to lead the reader, and without planning the ending. Mystery plots are typically so intricate that their writers could not work themselves out of the contrived complex of their self-induced difficulties without having a plausible solution in mind.

The writers of the real story that I will recount here began much as our good mystery plotters do—by projecting the ending. All knew where we would come out. There would be a single set of federal guidelines—uniform guidelines—on employee selection procedures. But some funny things happened on the way to the uniform guidelines. There were some unexpected plot developments—some contrived by our writers, others inserted by outside forces. As a result, and because publishers cannot wait indefinitely, this is a story with considerable plot, but without an ending. My purpose, therefore, is not to recount how those of us who engaged in this plotting successfully overcame many obstacles to emerge with new Uniform Federal Guidelines on Testing. Rather it is to *sample* selected moments in a complex process, and to give readers glimpses of reality showing that psychometric life at the policy level is neither simple nor bland. The process I have chosen to sample is the attempt to create a set of Guidelines on employee selection procedures to represent the unified position of the executive branch of the federal government in interpreting Title VII of the Civil Rights Act of 1964, as amended in 1972.

This article was prepared especially for this book.

The Law and Personnel Psychology—1964-70

Section 703(h) of Title VII of the Civil Rights Act of 1964 provided:

> ... nor shall it be an unlawful employment practice for an employer to give and to act upon the results of any professionally developed ability test provided that such test, its administration or action upon the results is not designed, intended, or used to discriminate because of race, color, religion, sex or national origin.

The first federal interpretation of "professionally developed ability test" under this law was published on August 24, 1966, by the Equal Employment Opportunity Commission (EEOC). It consisted of very general principles and a four-page report from a group consisting of a three-man "panel of outstanding psychologists, all of whom have broad practical experience in the testing field" (EEOC, 1966),[1] and an attorney. In the report EEOC advocated a total personnel assessment system; recommended adopting the *Standards for Educational and Psychological Tests and Manuals* (issued jointly by the American Psychological Association, the American Educational Research Association, and the National Council on Measurement in Education, 1966); stressed the importance of job analysis; set forth some cautions relating to criterion-related validity; and dealt with norms and the training of professionals.

This paper tracks through one issue in the development of federal guidelines on testing; the question of what is known in 1976 as "differential prediction." Here is the position of the 1966 panel on this issue:

> ... the test user should, therefore, select instruments, when possible, which minimize cultural differences ... where there is a strong indication that a cultural deficit is seriously affecting test reliability and validity, other methods of assessment such as job performance should be used. It would seem desirable, however, that the Commission (EEOC) encourage that as rapidly as possible, validation studies be conducted with minority groups using measures of cultural background as moderator variables (EEOC, 1966 pp. 6-7).

Let's examine the above statement from the perspective of a decade later. The hypothesis that cultural deficit can affect reliability and validity was and still is a respectable one. A strict reading of the recommendation seems to imply that minorities in a validation sample must be sorted out on cultural variables and that validity studies must then compare these different minority subgroups. If the panel meant to recommend majority-minority comparisons on the basis of cultural variable sorts, from the viewpoint of the law that approach was and still is irrelevant. The law did not prohibit different treatment of those with different cultural advantages or disadvantages; it prohibited discrimination on the basis of race, color, religion, sex or national origin. The 1966 Guidelines themselves were fuzzy on the issue:

> Tests should be validated for minorities. The sample population (norms) used in validating the tests should include representative members of the minority groups to which the tests will be applied. Only a test which has been validated for minorities can be assumed to be free of inadvertent bias (EEOC, 1966, p. 3).

At best this section seems to have mixed the concepts of including minorities in a validation study and performing separate validity studies for minorities. A literal reading seems to lead to the first interpretation, that is, that minorities be included in a validation sample. It is interesting that nowhere is the real issue frontally addressed: the oft-noted differences in test scores between minorities and others.

Test Score Differences

In 1953, Mary Agnes Gordon was the first (as far as I am able to determine) to describe research on the observed differences between aptitude test scores of whites and Negroes as they related to some job performance measure (Gordon, 1953). Using final technical school grades as criteria, she concluded that the same minimum aptitude indexes should be used for Negro and white Air Force males, but that lower minimums should be used for Air Force females. Gordon was later to study these differences by geographic region and by background factors, but the early results did not indicate that tests operated differently for Negro and white males, and the problem seems to have been set aside. It was resurrected in the mid-1960s (Guion, 1965) and erupted with full vigor in the late 1960s, as a result of what are now recognized as rather inconclusive studies. (Culture-free and culture-fair test searches had by this time lost their empirical and philosophical popularity.) The technical spokesperson for EEOC early, and in congressional testimony, described studies of the "new" concept, "differential validity," as "truly amazing" with implications that could be "enormous" (Enneis, 1967). In 1969 he cited three studies (one more than he cited in 1967) to support the conclusion that ". . . much evidence has been accumulated that minorities' test scores may underestimate their job performance . . ." (Enneis, 1969). The concept of differential validity held that an employment test might be valid for one group (usually the majority) on whom it was validated, but not for (minorities) who were not included in the validation sample. Differential prediction, however, connotes over- or underestimation of predicted job performance, and could occur with or without differential validity. Test fairness in criterion-related validity studies was the issue.

Research on Test Fairness

In the meantime, other researchers began some serious study of the issue. In 1966 the Educational Testing Service (ETS) and the U.S. Civil Service Commission (CSC) began a cooperative research effort to study the fairness to blacks and Chicanos of a variety of employment tests for different kinds of occupations. The study was to take six years. On May 8, 1967, a briefing was held at the Civil Service Commission in Washington, D.C., for representatives of certain federal agencies and equal employment opportunity groups to discuss specific plans for the research. It was at this session that the Civil Service Commission first learned of the plans of other federal agencies to create new testing guidelines or a testing Order. The Civil Service Commission was also told by two federal agencies that (although the guidelines/Order had not been completed) the federal government's testing and examining practices would probably not meet the Standards. Neither of these representatives had made any study of the federal government's testing and examining practices. The position was a parroting of that taken by Phyllis Wallace et al. in 1966, based on no empirical data (Wallace, 1966). When the Civil Service Commission subsequently and promptly attempted to participate in the effort to create a new testing

Order, however, it was told, "Don't call us, we'll call you." The call never came. On September 24, 1968, the Secretary of Labor issued an Office of Federal Contract Compliance Testing Order (OFCC, 1968).

The "Coup"—The 1970 EEOC Guidelines

Subsequently the Office of Federal Contract Compliance created an Advisory Committee on Selection and Testing, apparently to work on what was intended to be another order on testing pertaining to federal contractors. The Advisory Committee, composed mainly of eminent psychologists from industry and academia, held its first meeting on January 13-14, 1969. An EEOC psychologist also met with the Advisory Committee. While the Committee clearly thought it was working on another testing Order, a 1976 EEOC version of the meeting has indicated that the Committee *"generated substantial input* for a revised version of the OFCC Testing Order and for a revised version of the EEOC Guidelines" (Robertson, 1976; emphasis added). This "substantial input" was removed from the Committee's oversight sometime in 1969 by the EEOC, which stated that "... members of that Committee are not responsible for the ultimate document..." (Robertson, 1976). As a Committee member has told the author, the material which it had been drafting and which was removed from its oversight was reported as "being worked on" by EEOC legal staff.

In what was clearly a surprise move, the EEOC Guidelines were published in the *Federal Register* on August 1, 1970 (EEOC, 1970). The Chairman of EEOC promptly held a press conference in which he announced that the Department of Labor (Office of Federal Contract Compliance) would follow with a substantially similar Order. Officials at Labor smarted, but felt boxed in. If they came out with a different position, they would risk an interexecutive agency squabble and would erode the "government speaking with one voice" concept. According to a 1974 report, the Advisory Committee did not have prior notice of the publication. The report states "these published Guidelines contained material which had never been seen in any form by members of the Advisory Committee and with which most members took great exception as being either untenable or unworkable" (Activities of an ad hoc industry group, 1974). The Committee held a crisis-generated meeting, but by that time was impotent to effect any substantive changes in the eventual OFCC Order (OFCC, 1971).

As an example of what can happen, we again have the issue of differential validity—required as part of the 1970 Guidelines, and the 1971 OFCC Order. In effect, test users were put on notice, *clearly without minimal scientific support,* that it would be dangerous to a test user's health to use a test without a study of differential validity. Before warning the public about the hazards of cigarette smoking, the Surgeon General developed comprehensive and reasonably convincing scientific evidence on which to base the conclusion. But there was no such evidence available to the government regarding differential validity in 1970. Based upon an untested hypothesis, tests were presumed guilty of being anti-equal employment opportunity until proven innocent.

We have never been told what went on when the Guidelines were being "worked on" within the confines of EEOC. Therefore, when courts accord these Guidelines "great deference," that deference is to an unknown and possibly faulty process. We do know that EEOC had only one professional psychologist on its staff at that time. At least one lawyer was involved. Were there more? Did the Congress intend that its will be interpreted by only a few people (perhaps as few as two)? The gap in our information, the lack of opportunity for public comment and discussion, and the subsequent professional denunciation of the EEOC Guidelines clearly casts a shadow on them. The courts' subsequent "deference" to the Guidelines has been in good faith, but based upon originally suspect administrative processes of which they have never been made aware. One does not have to search far in our recent national history to conclude that covert government is neither tolerable nor desirable. Why, then, has there never been a direct legal challenge to these Guidelines? We can speculate that there may be at least two reasons: (1) a challenge to the Guidelines would not be a popular thing to do—there would be an aura of anti-civil rightsism about it at a time when equal employment opportunity is a national objective; (2) the most affected group has been U.S. private industry. A challenge by a business organization could risk federal retaliation.

Litigation Enters the Scene

Despite the May 8, 1967, meeting in which the Civil Service Commission's examining practices were attacked, there was little perceptible interagency tension up to 1971. Two court cases, however, had a profound effect in creating sharp differences between the EEOC and the Civil Service Commission. In *Davis* v. *Washington* (1970), the employment testing practices for patrolmen in the District of Columbia were challenged[2] on the grounds of racial discrimination.[3] Shortly thereafter a suit was filed challenging the written test used in the Federal Service Entrance Examination (FSEE) on the same grounds, *Douglas* v. *Hampton* (1971). In the latter case the EEOC psychologist helped plaintiffs collect data from the Civil Service Commission to support their cause, and EEOC attorneys appeared in court with plaintiffs' attorneys filing an *amicus curiae* brief for the plaintiffs. Thus one executive branch agency was clearly pitted against another. In the middle was the Department of Justice which defends federal agencies in litigation, and, of course, prosecutes violators of federal law, including the civil rights laws. The Department of Housing and Urban Development (HUD) was also a defendant in the latter case. In fact, in an affidavit filed in the case, the HUD Assistant Regional Administrator for Equal Opportunity (Chicago) stated that he suggested "to the plaintiffs herein, and to each of them, that they pursue such legal remedies as might then have been available to remove the major obstruction to their pursuit of an opportunity for employment within the Federal Service." Thus a senior management official of HUD, apparently by his own admission, helped instigate a suit against the agency for which he worked. The *Davis* and *Douglas* cases were to affect movement toward a unified federal position on testing for years to come.

Plaintiffs' initial legal filing in *Douglas* v. *Hampton* was a request for a preliminary injunction to stop further use of the written test and hiring from the FSEE. The Judge in the U.S. District Court, instead of holding a trial, granted the Civil Service Commission time to develop a regulation in order that the case could be remanded to the Commission for an administrative hearing. The regulation was published on August 13, 1971. On February 14, 1972, the District Court found the test lacking in adverse impact and valid, denied the request for a preliminary injunction and remanded the case to the Civil Service Commission for a full administrative hearing. This finding was appealed by the plaintiffs. In the meantime the Civil Service Commission, under the new regulation, developed its own guidance material on testing for competitive examining. While it was not required to do so, the Commission published these documents in the *Federal Register* for a comment period on June 30, 1972. Some commenters (including Brown, the Chairman of EEOC) faulted the guidance and urged that the Commission adopt the EEOC Guidelines. Over a year earlier (March 8, 1971), the case of *Griggs* v. *Duke Power Co.* (401 U.S. 424) had been decided, in which the EEOC Guidelines were given "great deference" by the Supreme Court; (Griggs, 1971) and the Civil Rights Act of 1972 had been passed, extending coverage of the 1964 Act to state, local, and federal governments. Brown, then Chairman of EEOC, in criticizing the Commission's new regulations pointed out to the Chairman of the Civil Service Commission that the latter event "dispels all doubts as to the applicability of the principles enunciated in *Griggs* v. *Duke Power Co.* . . . to the Federal Civil Service system." The Commission, taking this view into account as well as the many thoughtful and supportive comments about its new proposed regulations and guidance material, concluded that the EEOC Guidelines had not been developed with public employment in mind[4] and were simply unworkable; and published the final version of its own testing guidance (USCSC, 1972). As an example of the differences between the two documents, the EEOC Guidelines, as indicated above, required differential validity studies. The CSC guidance was silent on this matter—for a very important reason. The results of new research, especially the six-year ETS-CSC study, now completed (Crooks, 1972; Campbell et al., 1973), had not only cast serious doubt on this concept, but had caused major thinkers in the field to renounce their former views on its viability. For example,

Guion:

> In light of my previously published views (Guion 1966), the findings of these studies are not personally very satisfying. There is some, but certainly not much, support for a general phenomenon of differential validity . . . I would summarize the information here, and that emerging in the general literature as well, by suggesting that, as a general rule, the validity of a test against a specified criterion is likely to be about the same for all comers (Crooks, 1972, p. 133).

and Wallace:

> It appears to me to be about time for us to accept the proposition that written aptitude tests, administered correctly and evaluated against reasonably reliable, unbiased, and relevant criteria, do about the same job in one ethnic group as in another. It seems clear that people like me who expected race to act as a moderator variable for validity relationships were wrong. It seems also clear that people who assumed that all written tests were inappropriate and unfair instruments if applied outside of the WASP culture were equally wrong (Crooks, 1972, p. 137).

The Equal Employment Opportunity Coordinating Council (EEOCC)

The EEOCC, which is composed of the Department of Justice, the Department of Labor, the Equal Employment Opportunity Commission, the Civil Rights Commission, and the Civil Service Commission, was created by the 1972 amendment to the Civil Rights Act. The Council was established to

> have the responsibility for developing and implementing agreements, policies and

practices designed to maximize effort, promote efficiency, and eliminate conflict, competition, duplication and inconsistency among the operations, functions and jurisdictions of the various departments, agencies and branches of the Federal Government responsible for the implementation and enforcement of equal employment opportunity legislation, orders, and policies (P.L. 92-261, p. 9).

The first meeting of the Council was held on November 9, 1972.[5]

Toward Uniform Federal Testing Guidelines

In view of the above events, it is easy to see why the Council directed its attention to the testing issue, and to the desirability of a common federal position on testing guidelines.[6] Specifically, the Council at its first meeting on November 9, 1972, directed that staff from the various agencies get together and set out their differences on testing.

This staff group, hereinafter referred to as T-2 (for some obscure reason which I am unable to trace, it is usually referred to in this way) consisted of psychologists, lawyers, administrators, and EEO specialists from Labor, EEOC, and the Civil Service Commission. Justice had one attorney, and the Civil Rights Commission usually had a single observer. T-2 met several times in November and December 1972 and in January 1973. On January 31, 1973, a document on differences was produced (EEOCC, 1973). Since the group was directed to come up with a paper, and was determined to do so, positions were not stated as they might have been had any one of the parties written the paper. That is to say, 16 people had a difficult time agreeing on statements of their disagreements. What resulted from the decision to set out differences on testing was a number of highly interactive meetings which provided as much ventilation as productivity, and a rather superficial 17-page double-spaced paper which addressed some interagency differences.

In retrospect, therefore, it can easily be understood why the Council principals in reading the report might have concluded that the differences were capable of resolution. On February 8, 1973, the principals directed the T-2 group to reassemble, iron out the differences, and, within a month, produce uniform testing guidelines. By the February 8, 1973, meeting, thinking on the problem had become sharper. If uniformity could not be achieved, there would be clear conflicts in relation to state and local governments since, as a result of the Intergovernmental Personnel Act, the 1972 amendment to the Civil Rights Act, and Executive Orders, Labor, Justice, EEOC and the Civil Service Commission all had important legal responsibilities to public employment. The Council therefore directed the staff to draft one set of testing guidelines for state and local government agencies. Agreeing to work with the EEOC guidelines as a starting point, the Council directed that the effort be completed by March.

At this point there was no formal interagency talk of a set of testing guidelines which would apply to *all* employers. The focus was on a consistent approach to state and local governments. However, the Civil Service Commission representatives had agreed among themselves that it would be desirable to work toward guidelines which could also be adopted by the federal government, and EEOC was clearly thinking along the lines of one set of guidelines which could be used in its enforcement role for all employers. It simply did not make sense to ask state and local governments to adhere to one set of standards, industry to another, and the federal government to a third.

Uniform Guidelines—Draft 1

When T-2 actually began work, 13 principles were agreed upon by the chief staff representatives which, it seemed, would make the drafting process somewhat easier than the task of setting forth differences had been. Some of the principles were intended to hasten the writing process. Among these were: there would not be a preference among the three validity strategies; the choice would depend on the situation; differential prediction would be included in the Guidelines. The first (all methods of validation acceptable) was obviously hard for EEOC to swallow. Its position in *Douglas* v. *Hampton,* still in the appeals process, would thereby be undermined;[7] as well as its posture in regard to all employers that criterion-related validity is the preferred method, so that to resort to any other method required prior proof that criterion-related validity was infeasible. In a memorandum to David Rose, Chief of Employment Section of the Civil Rights Division, Department of Justice, and chief staff representative from Justice to T-2, attorneys from EEOC stated in relation to criterion-related validity, "the policy which the Commission [EEOC] has followed is that an employer acts at his own peril when he uses some other validation approach." The paper setting forth the principles for Uniform Guidelines was dated February 26, 1973; the EEOC memo containing the above quote was dated March 27, 1973. Already cracks of inconsistency regarding a key principle were appearing. The Civil Service Commission found it equally as difficult to swallow the principle of including differential prediction, since it was now convinced by research evidence that this concept was a nonphenomenon, a function of chance and ill-designed studies. Nevertheless, the principles held up fairly well through the final draft in 1976. Only a principle called "practical usefulness" as a requirement for a validity study of an employment practice was eventually dropped from the Guidelines.

The March deadline was not met. The Council principals advised the staff that if they could not finish the guidelines the Council itself would solve all unresolved issues, which now exceeded those outlined in the original paper. But, since many of these differences were technical in nature, the principals could only urge that solutions be found. The T-2 group continued working with pressure from the Council until in August, 1973, a draft was produced to which all parties agreed. A wide national distribution invited comments and a large number was received. T-2 held meetings with public interest groups on October 26, 1973, and there was an open public forum for others on November 15, 1973. The clear message from all commenters was that the draft was far from satisfactory. A rewrite was necessary.

Uniform Guidelines—Draft 2

My 1974 appointments calendar shows that I attended 31 meetings of T-2 between January and June. There were probably some I did not attend. Readers should be aware that those of us working on this interagency effort had other highly responsible full-time jobs. During the course of the effort some changed jobs, were sick, retired, died, were replaced, promoted, and all dealt with the daily requirements and crises of their own work. Progress seemed slow. We were also looking for the final publication of new APA Standards (APA, 1974), hoping that resolution to some of our problems would be found there. New competing definitions of test fairness were emerging which polarized the views of the different agency members and confounded the issue of differential prediction. The differences among some of the staff at T-2 were also increased by the first round of comments on the draft Guidelines. Other staff were stimulated by the comments to try to find thoughtful new language. New issues were introduced by the staff, many of which were controversial. Sometimes redrafting a paragraph was the total accomplishment of a three- or four-hour session, and that became a "tentative agreement." Many drafts of the same sentence or paragraph in one or more sessions were common. In order to keep these drafts straight, the typist put a time as well as a date on them. Finally another draft document was completed and circulated in August, 1974. The comments of the public were less critical than those on the first draft, but still reflected great disappointment.

In the meantime, three of the Council principals had changed. The new Council, faced with a document that satisfied few, held a public hearing on October 23, 1974. Representatives of the American Psychological Association, public interest groups, industry, and others made personal presentations. There was, at best, restrained enthusiasm about the document. Its workability was still under serious question. However, people had begun to organize themselves into groups in showing concern and in recommending constructive alternatives. As a result, the Council met on November 13, 1974, and told the T-2 staff to continue work, but to rewrite the guidelines completely.

> The new draft should be simpler and shorter, and comprehensible. The draft should be tested against the proposal of the business employers and the public interest groups made at the October 23rd meeting.

Uniform Guidelines—Draft 3

The staff began again. But in January, 1975, *Davis* v. *Washington* and *Douglas* v. *Hampton*, which had been won by defendants in the District Court, were both reversed by the Court of Appeals. Going further, the court ordered that the *Douglas* case be heard using the EEOC Guidelines' principle that criterion-related validity must be shown to be infeasible before another strategy may be used. EEOC negotiators reported that there was no use in going on with the Uniform Guidelines writing since the Appeals court had endorsed the EEOC Guidelines, this time bringing the federal government to its knees. Petition for certiorari (review by the Supreme Court) was, however, being considered by the Solicitor General in both cases.[8] He finally decided against this move, but wrote that although he disagreed with the Court of Appeals in *Douglas* on the criterion-related validity issue, because of the posture of the case (request for preliminary injunction) it was not ripe for appeal to the Supreme Court. He indicated that he would be prepared to take the case to the Supreme Court on this issue after trial on the merits of the case if the results were still unsatisfactory.

The District of Columbia, however, petitioned the Supreme Court in *Davis* v. *Washington,* and the Court accepted the case for hearing in the 1976 term. In the wake of the *Douglas* and *Davis* Appeals Court decisions and with another round of drafting in view, in April, 1975, the EEOC staff representatives recommended to their management that "negotiations be ended on the grounds that agreement on a set of principles consistent with EEOC principles was impossible." EEOC sent in a new negotiating team, "to continue negotiations, to obtain agreement if possible, and to bring that agreement back so the Commission could make judgment on whether the compromises necessary to achieve the agreement were too great." The rest of the T-2 staff was unaware at that time, however, that EEOC's new negotiators had no final authority. On the issue of differential prediction, EEOC's new technical negotiator had come to the conclusion that the use of results from studies concerning this issue would not be in the interests of the groups EEOC was interested in. This was further confirmation of the research findings which were continuing to build the case against differential prediction. In the meantime, the Supreme Court in *Albemarle* v. *Moody* supported the EEOC Guidelines for the second time (*Albemarle* v. *Moody,* 1975). Steady and productive meetings nevertheless continued through the summer, resulting in a new draft in September, 1975. There is no doubt that this period of redrafting produced the most remarkable changes in the proposed Uniform Guidelines in the direction of both consensus and professionalization. A true effort was made to test the draft against public comment.

In September, 1975, T-2 recommended to the Council that this draft be circulated for internal agency review concurrent with prepublication review by state and local governments, followed by publication in the *Federal Register* for general public review. EEOC (now without a chairman) disagreed with its negotiators, however, rejected the draft, opposed distribution for comments, and indicated that it would prepare its own draft for Council consideration. The Council, over EEOC's dissent, circulated the draft to state and local governments and to others for comment.

In June, 1976, the Supreme Court reversed the Court of Appeals in *Washington* v. *Davis,* hinting strongly also that it did not agree with the *Douglas* appeals court decision which reversed the original District Court finding for defendants (*Washington* v. *Davis,* 1976). One finding from that case is of particular importance. Footnote 13 from the majority opinion seems to endorse the notion of the equity of the three validity strategies. In February, EEOC negotiators presented a draft of its "new" guidelines to T-2. Labor, Justice, and the Civil Service Commission felt that meetings on this document would be tantamount to starting anew with the 1970 Guidelines. The document was regressive in tone and substance, and had not been endorsed as a starting point by EEOC itself. Instead, T-2 staff proceeded to make adjustments in the September, 1975, draft to be responsive to public comments. There was a major difference however: EEOC staff on T-2 were instructed to observe only. While there were important unified comments from groups favoring the new Uniform Guidelines, there were also important opposition groups which challenged the legal basis for change. David Rose, T-2's representative from the Justice Department, prepared a detailed legal rebuttal of one major opposition group, and in a letter to the Chairman of the EEOC, defended the new Guidelines vigorously and in detail and stated, "I do not agree that the Proposed Guidelines are in conflict with or inconsistent with principles adopted by the Supreme Court, or the appellate courts, or that they constitute a 'retreat' from the present guidelines."

During this period, Tyler, the Deputy U.S. Attorney General, asked for and received from Rose an analysis of the major difference between the new Guidelines and the 1970 EEOC Guidelines. For the first time, the Justice Department openly criticized the EEOC Guidelines (the complete Rose memorandum was later to appear in the *Congressional Record*) (*Congressional Record,* 1976). After detailing the differences Rose said:

> An unstated or covertly stated reason may underlie the apparent EEOC refusal to modify its present guidelines. Under the present EEOC Guidelines, few employers are able to show the validity of *any* of their selection procedures, and the risk of their being held unlawful is high. Since not only tests, but all other procedures must be validated, the thrust of the present guidelines is to place almost all test users in a posture of non-compliance; to give great discretion to enforcement personnel to determine who should be prosecuted; and to set aside objective selection procedures

in favor of numerical hiring . . . The Uniform Guidelines, while adhering to Federal law as developed by the Supreme Court and other appellate courts and the standards of the psychological profession, provide some definitive standards which enable those employers and other users who wish to do so to bring themselves into compliance with Federal law.

Tyler communicated the situation to Philip Buchen, Counsel to the President, and then, sounding exasperated, wrote to him as follows:

> . . . the posture now is as it has been virtually for three and one-half years—mainly, that of agreement by all concerned except the Equal Employment Opportunity Commission. Excepting the latter agency, all other agencies and departments have made many efforts to change their positions in order to reach a unanimous position. Regrettably, that has never been achieved . . . my efforts have been unavailing . . .

According to an EEOC official, Buchen subsequently approached EEOC with an offer to use his offices to "settle the dispute between EEOC and the rest of the Federal Government." On July 14, 1976, the three concurring federal agencies entered the proposed Uniform Guidelines in the *Federal Register* for a 45-day comment period. EEOC opposed this action. In a letter to the General Accounting Office dated August, 29, 1976, it had hardened its position still more:

> . . . EEOC believes that the technical perception of employment discrimination contained in its 1970 Guidelines has been approved, ratified and reratified by the Congress and the Supreme Court and that it is inappropriate to change it unless there is a specific binding, unambiguous and final decision of the U.S. Supreme Court making it clear that the technical perception adopted by EEOC is not shared by that Court. EEOC will probably not consider major substantive changes absent that kind of court mandate. . . .

By early September, over 150 comments on the draft had been received. The world had obviously become well organized to deal with another draft; some of the comments represented the unified position of large groups. The general thrust of these final comments can be summarized as follows:

Most employers, business, industry, and governmental, found the new guidelines to be far better than the current EEOC guidelines, more workable, more professionally sound. They still wanted changes (e.g., elimination of differential prediction), but even if none were made, found the new document far better than the 1970 EEOC Guidelines.

Those from civil rights-oriented organizations found the new Guidelines to be a "retreat" from the 1970 EEOC Guidelines. This draft drew the first formal comments from the American Psychological Association. A special subcommittee found the document to be professionally sound and flexible.

Final Draft

On September 14 and 16, 1976, T-2, now down to four working persons, met to consider all of the comments. Final adjustments in language were made. EEOC did not participate actively in these adjustments. The Civil Rights Commission joined EEOC in demanding that the word "Uniform" be removed from the title, and that the text be stripped of all reference to the final product's being devised under the "auspices" of the EEOCC.

What Are the Issues?

This four-year story began with a set of rather simple principles upon which new federal Guidelines on testing would be built. The issues were not confined to those principles, because as the principles were explored, they were discovered to be not quite so simple as first thought. The objectives of different agencies were clearly not of the same priority. The participants' views vis-à-vis employers ranged from sympathetic assistance to tough enforcement. Professional standards were not always clear. New professional knowledge was emerging which impacted on the Guidelines, and controversy arose. Case law developed. It became necessary to examine what was and was not the government's proper role. The cast of participants and principals changed, and with changes viewpoints were sometimes stronger, sharper, more or less conciliatory. All of these factors contributed to a negotiating process which resembled trying to hit a target which was moving unpredictably.

The whole process of guidelines development has not been detailed here, but there are two observations I want to make. First, there were never any tradeoffs. At no time did someone give something to get something. Had that occurred, agreement could have been reached much sooner, but such an agreement would have been fragile. Solutions were sought which would serve the objectives. Second, the process involved extensive public involvement. Thus opportunities to share in the direction which federal guidance should take were fully available to all interested parties.

Federal Priorities

Equal employment opportunity is a national objective, and various federal bureaucratic structures have been created to effect this objective. For employers, private and public, efficiency is also a respectable if not vital objective both for the organization and for our total national economic well-being. These objectives are not necessarily compatible. Technically, validation provides a defense against imbalances (known also as *adverse impact*) caused by an employment practice. For many public employers validity is a requirement. But there is also another view:

> ... EEOC believes that test validation can serve a useful purpose but that it is not the only goal. EEOC believes that employers can validate tests and still discriminate ... (Robertson, 1976, p. 32).

The federal government is an enforcer of the civil rights laws, but also an important employer. As such it uses and validates almost the full range of selection procedures. As a merit system employer it is required by law to select from among the best qualified. Given options, it would use those devices with the least adverse impact to support the national objective of equal opportunity. But given no options the enhancement of validity has economic standing.

Professional Priorities

There is, at present, no systematic body of knowledge on adverse impact on which to base options as there is on validity. Given the Supreme Court decision in *Albemarle* v. *Moody*, an employer seems to have been relieved of the burden of searching for alternatives if its employment procedures pass muster by meeting validity requirements. But the seminal case has not been heard in this area—that of an employment test which by any standard is valid but which has a severe, perhaps exclusionary, adverse impact. Professional wisdom then calls for a balance between validation and accumulating information on the adverse impact of alternative selection procedures.

Validity Strategies

Criterion-related validity has become the moribund victim of its own elegance. Schmidt, Hunter, and Urry's article (Schmidt, 1976) and the final draft of the Guidelines call for caution—and a large sample—before committing the resources necessary to do a meaningful study.[9] If the technical conditions are not present to do a study, and such a study is clearly the appropriate strategy for the situation, what does one do? Borrow a selection procedure, or go to another strategy. More personnel decisions are made on the basis of content validity than any other strategy. Yet employment psychology in the content and construct strategies is just coming of age. How far can content validity be extended? What well-developed constructs are relevant to selection for employment? Must the user be concerned with nomological networks? Many of these problems are with us now and beg for thoughtful work.

Guidelines and Equal Employment Opportunity

The real question remains: Will testing guidelines promote equal employment opportunity? Unfortunately, we have no scientifically acceptable evidence that they have or will, as contrasted with our knowledge of how validity promotes organizational effectiveness. The major concern in guideline construction has been to assure that some minimum level of professionalism and validity was present in employment procedures. To assume, however, that validity would assure equal employment opportunity goes beyond what psychometricians have so far promised or been able to deliver.

Epilog

The text of the foregoing story was submitted to the publisher in order to meet an agreed-upon deadline. The last sentence had been, "The denouement of our story must wait for a later chapter." But then another significant chapter in this national event occurred, and thus this epilog.

At a meeting of the Equal Employment Opportunity Coordinating Council on October 13, 1976, the EEOC predictably opposed the adoption of the proposed new Guidelines. In the ensuing weeks, Justice, Labor, and the Civil Service Commission continued to deliberate what should be done. The Guidelines were the result of many years of thoughtful effort, involving government agencies, professional, business, and public groups; and momentum for change and advancement was strong. The final publication of the Federal Executive Agency Guidelines on Employee Selection in the *Federal Register* on November 23, 1976, by the three concurring agencies was preceded by a press release which said, in part:

> The Departments of Justice and Labor and the CSC decided to adopt the new guidelines because:
> (1) they are in accord with professionally accepted standards of test validation;
> (2) federal guidelines now in use are more than five years old and, therefore, do not take into account subsequent psychological and legal developments;
> (3) the new guidelines are applicable to the federal government itself, as well as to federal contractors and subcontractors;
> (4) the new guidelines are more practical and realistic than existing guidelines and provide more guidance to users seeking to comply with federal laws;
> (5) the new guidelines bring consistency to at least three federal agencies and thus are a step toward achieving a uniform federal position on employee testing and selection procedures.

Clearly what is envisioned is that workable federal Guidelines will encourage employers both to validate their employment procedures, and to work more affirmatively to achieve results in the national objective of equal employment opportunity.

Notes

1. The usual training and experience which is relied on in these cases is that of industrial psychology. One psychologist was a fellow of Division 14, the Division of Industrial-Organizational Psychology, American Psychological Association; the second was a diplomate in Clinical Psychology of the American Psychological Association; the third was apparently not a member of APA since his name was not in the Directory.

2. The U.S. Civil Service Commission was and is responsible for developing the written test used to select candidates for training in the police academy for the District of Columbia. District of Columbia and U.S. Civil Service Commission were both defendants.

3. Defendants won in District Court. The case was appealed.

4. In a May 21, 1973, meeting of the OFCC Advisory Committee, one of its last, some of the problems and differences between private and public employment were recognized and discussed without either resolution or agreement that the same principles could be applied in both settings. The Committee shied away from the issue on the grounds of lack of expertise. The EEOC representative was, however, particularly cognizant of the effects of certain aspects of public employment limiting the ability of public employers to meet technical feasibility requirements for criterion-related validity. It is the author's view that the OFCC Committee was unwilling to endorse blind, unconsidered application of the extant order (and hence the 1970 EEOC Guidelines) to public employment.

5. The Council's representatives are: Deputy Attorney General, Justice (Chair); Secretary of Labor; Chairman, EEOC; Chairman, Civil Rights Commission; and Chairman, Civil Service Commission. For brevity's sake, these will be referred to as the Council's "Principals."

6. The Council's agenda item was: "Establishment and adoption of uniform federal standards in the enforcement of employment discrimination laws and orders as they affect the uses of tests and similar personnel selection devices."

7. In *Douglas* v. *Hampton,* the test was being defended on the basis of construct validity.

8. The Solicitor General is the federal government's "lawyer" in these and other matters.

9. Schmidt's article contributed to the decision to leave differential prediction in the Guidelines despite the overwhelming evidence against its likelihood. Under the Guidelines studies of differential prediction need only be carried out when technically feasible. This means a large N in a job class, criteria with known reliability, and the other requirements listed by Schmidt. If an employer can meet these conditions—and few will—that employer is also likely to have the resources to do the additional work required for such a study.

References

Activities of an ad hoc industry group: *Uniform Guidelines on employee selection*. Washington, D.C.: Ad Hoc Industry Group, October 1974.

Albemarle Paper Co. et al. v. *Moody et al.*, 422 US 405 (1975).

American Psychological Association, American Educational Research Association, and National Council on Measurement in Education. *Standards for educational and psychological tests and manuals*. Washington, D.C.: APA, 1966.

American Psychological Association, American Educational Research Association, and National Council on Measurement in Education. *Standards for educational and psychological tests*. Washington, D.C.: APA, 1974.

Campbell, J. T., Crooks, L. A., Mahoney, M. H., and Rock, D. A. *An investigation of sources of bias in the prediction of job performance: a six-year study*. Final project report. Princeton, N.J.: Educational Testing Service, 1973.

Crooks, L. A. (ed.) *An investigation of sources of bias in the prediction of job performance: a six-year study*. Proceedings of an invitational conference held June 22, 1972, The Barclay Hotel, New York, New York. Princeton, N.J.: Educational Testing Service, 1972.

Davis, Alfred E. et al. v. *Washington, Walter E. et al.*, 512 Fed. 2nd.956 (1975).

Douglas, Jesse et al. v. *Hampton, Robert et al.*, 512 Fed. 2nd.976 (1971).

Enneis, W. H. Measures of tests. Paper presented August 31, 1969 as part of a symposium, "Testing as a Social Problem; Issues and Responsibilities," 77th annual convention, American Psychological Association. In Anderson, B. R. and Rogers, M. P. (Eds.) *Personnel testing and equal employment opportunity*. Washington, D.C.: Equal Employment Opportunity Commission, 1970.

Enneis, W. H. Statement before the House Post Office and Civil Service Subcommittee. In Anderson, B. R. and Rogers, M. P. (eds.) *Personnel testing and equal employment opportunity*. Washington, D.C.: Equal Employment Opportunity Commission, 1970.

Equal Employment Opportunity Commission. *Guidelines on employment testing procedures*. Washington, D.C.: EEOC, 1966.

Equal Employment Opportunity Commission. Guidelines on employee selection procedures. *Federal Register*, 35, No. 149, August 1, 1970, 12333-12336.

Equal Employment Opportunity Coordinating Council. *Testing: a summary of differences in approach*. Washington, D.C.: Author, January 31, 1973.

Gordon, M. A. *A study in the applicability of the same minimum qualifying scores for technical schools to white males, WAF, and negro males*. Technical Report 53-34. Lackland Air Force Base, Texas: Personnel Research Laboratory, 1953.

Griggs v. *Duke Power Company*, 401 US 424 (1971).

Guion, R. M. *Personnel testing*. New York: McGraw-Hill, 1965.

Guion, R. M. Employment testing and discriminatory hiring. *Industrial Relations*, 1966, 5, 20-37.

Office of Federal Contract Compliance. Employee testing and other selection procedures. *Federal Register*, 36, No. 192, October 2, 1971, 19307-19310.

Office of Federal Contract Compliance. Validation of tests by contractors and subcontractors subject to the provisions of Executive Order 11246. *Federal Register*, 33, No. 186, September 24, 1968, 14392-14394.

Robertson, P. *Background paper dealing with history of Guidelines*. Washington, D.C.: Equal Employment Opportunity Commission, 1976.

Schmidt, F. L., Hunter, J. E., and Urry, V. W. Statistical power in criterion-related validity studies. *Journal of Applied Psychology,* 1976, 56.

United States Civil Service Commission. *Federal Personnel Manual Supplement 271-2.* Tests and other applicant appraisal procedures. Washington, D.C.: November 1972.

United States Congress. *An act to further provide equal employment opportunity for American workers.* Public law 92-961, 92nd Congress, 2nd Session. H.R. 1746, March 24, 1972.

United States Congress, Senate. Remarks of Senator Helms, Bureaucratic absurdities and citizen harassment. 94th Congress, 2nd Session, July 19, 1976. *Congressional Record,* 11782-11784.

Wallace, P., Kissinger, B., and Reynolds, B. Testing of minority group applicants for employment, March 1966. In Anderson, B. R. and Rogers, M. P. (eds.) *Personnel testing and equal employment opportunity.* Washington, D.C.: Equal Employment Opportunity Commission, 1970.

Washington et al. v. *Davis et al.* 426 US 229 (1976).

CHAPTER **4**

The Impact of Training on Future Performance

Once the personnel manager has selected his employees (see chap. 2), he must then choose training objectives and techniques which accurately match individual and organizational needs. A well-chosen training program can increase individual productivity and job satisfaction for the individual and the overall effectiveness of the organization.

Yukl and Wexley (1971) have outlined several reasons for the popularity of formal training programs in most organizations today. First, personnel selection and placement programs do not usually provide organizations with new employees skillful enough to meet the demands of their job as soon as they are hired. Second, experienced employees must be continually retrained because of changes in job content due to promotions, refinements in technology, and transfers. Third, management is aware that effective training programs result in increased productivity, decreased absenteeism, reduced turnver, and greater work satisfaction. (We will have more to say about these topics in chaps. 7 and 8.)

A wide range of training techniques is available to the personnel manager. The first reading in this chapter, the article by Campbell, Dunnette, Lawler, and Weick, compares the advantages and disadvantages of various formal training methods, including the lecture method, conference method, sensitivity training, laboratory education, and simulated methods of training. This article also includes a discussion of the advantages and disadvantages of using an on-the-job training program instead of a formal program.

In order to choose the most effective training method, one must have accurate information as to the relative effectiveness of different available training techniques for the learning problem at hand. In the second article in this chapter, Carroll, Paine, and Ivancevich compare training directors' evaluations of training methods with the results of research and find that the training directors are sometimes off-base. For example, the training directors felt that the lecture method was ineffective for acquisition of knowledge and in obtaining participant acceptance, but research results contradict their beliefs. On the other hand, they overestimated the effectiveness of programmed instruction. Could it be that training directors are too much influenced by fads in training methods—fads that are almost never research-based?

Reference

1. Yukl, G., and Wexley, K., *Readings in Industrial and Organizational Psychology,* Oxford Press, New York, 1974.

Training and Development: Methods and Techniques

JOHN P. CAMPBELL
MARVIN D. DUNNETTE
E. E. LAWLER
K. E. WEICK

The terms "training" and "development" are often given somewhat different meanings. They may be distinguished on the basis of either the subject matter involved or the level in the organization from which the participants are drawn. In the former instance training usually refers to rather specific, factual, and narrow-range content, while development implies a focus on general decision making and human relations skills. Relative to the latter distinction, development usually refers to activities provided for middle and upper management.

However, the two terms are used synonymously [here] and are meant to entail the following general properties and characteristics:
1. Management training and development is, first of all, a learning experience.
2. It is planned by the organization.
3. It occurs after the individual has joined the organization.
4. It is intended to further the organization's goals.

The first item implies that a relatively permanent change in the individual must be intended, whether it be an increased body of knowledge, new methods for solving problems, or more effective interactions with other people. Programs that are meant only to stimulate momentary feelings of goodwill, company zeal, or other marked but temporary behavior changes are not training programs. It is obvious that a considerable amount of learning relative to the managerial job is not consciously planned by the organization and that an individual learns a great deal, both good and bad, about managing before he joins the organization. However, these kinds of learning are excluded from our definition of management development for the following reason: Some of the areas most in need of research involve the *interaction* of the organization's training efforts both with the skills, knowledge, and attitudes that the individual brings to the job and with the unplanned kind of training that goes on between superior and subordinate and among coworkers. To include all these learning experiences under the rubric "management development" might obscure some of these very important joint influences.

Management development is thus a teaching activity planned and initiated by the organization. The word "planned" is not meant to imply negativistic things about manipulation or efforts toward eliciting conformity behavior, nor does it necessarily mean the planning must be done by the management hierarchy—in fact, it is usually delegated. Its aim is to further the goals of the organization by enhancing the managerial inputs which are in the form of abilities, skills, motives, and attitudes of individuals. However, participants in programs that fall within our definition of management de-

From *Managerial Behavior, Performance, and Effectiveness* by John P. Campbell et al. Copyright 1970 by McGraw-Hill. Used with permission of McGraw-Hill Book Co.

velopment need not be managers. In fact, such training programs tend to break down into two general classes: those which are directed toward *preparing* nonmanagement people for future management responsibilities and those which are intended to improve the performance of individuals who are already functioning as managers (Miner, 1966). Although the development effort must have something to do with the organizational goals, the particular goals under consideration need not be restricted to narrow economic aims. Personal development for personal development's sake may indeed be a conscious objective of the organization.

Given the obvious and overwhelming importance of the managerial inputs to an organization and the tremendous amount of time and money that is spent on trying to enhance these inputs through training, it is little wonder that a considerable body of written literature has accumulated on the topic of management training and development. It is the purpose of [this paper] to examine and summarize, in some coherent fashion, [some of] this body of knowledge. Special attention will be paid to reports of research that try to evaluate whether or not the managerial inputs to the organization are indeed being enhanced by means of the various training and development efforts. On the basis of this look at "what is known" in the training area, some suggestions will be made as to what kinds of research and investigation must be carried out in the future to make management development as meaningful and fruitful as possible.

The professional literature seems to organize itself under four general headings:

1. Descriptions of the various programs and techniques

2. Discussions of the application of principles of learning and motivation to problems of training

3. Methodological articles on how the effects of training should be evaluated, including discussion of the necessity of various aspects of evaluation

4. Empirical or quasi-empirical studies of the effects of training on the attitudes, opinions, and job performance of managers. . . .

Training Techniques, or "How to Teach"

Management development and training methods seem to fall roughly into three different categories, which we shall label *information presentation techniques, simulation methods,* and *on-the-job practice.* Specific training methods will be discussed under each of these categories.

Information Presentation Techniques

These are devices which have as their aim the teaching of facts, concepts, attitudes, or skills without requiring simulated or actual practice on the job itself.

The lecture. This most traditional of teaching methods has taken its share of lumps from educators and industrial training personnel. McGehee and Thayer (1961) conclude that as usually employed, the lecture is of little value in industrial training. Its principal difficulties seem to be that no provision is made for individual differences on the part of the learners, the lecturer must be an outstanding teacher, it is very difficult for the learners to obtain feedback regarding how they are doing, and there is little opportunity for the learner to participate in the process. The lecture method is not without its friends, however. D. S. Brown (1960) argues that this technique is valuable because of its sheer information-giving ability, its wide acceptance, the fact that it is economical, and the opportunity it affords a master teacher to provide an inspirational model of scholarship for his students. Bennett (1956) makes the point that managers are an intelligent lot and lectures by recognized authorities are in keeping with the status and complexity of the managerial job. Both these writers agree, however, that the lecture must be used sparingly and with due regard for its shortcomings. Tiffen and McCormick (1965) also point out that the lecture might profitably be considered for the presentation of new material or when summarizing material developed by another instruction method.

The conference method. This technique is really the management development analog to the graduate school seminar. The emphasis is on small group discussion, and the leader provides guidance and feedback rather than instruction. Its usual objectives are to develop problem-solving and decision-making capabilities, present new and complex material, and modify attitudes. The keystone is active participation of the learner, primarily by means of verbal discussion with the other group members. The conference is almost always oriented toward discussion of specific problems or new areas of knowledge. The topics for discussion may be chosen by the leader or by the participants themselves (Buchanan & Ferguson, 1953). Each of the participants may also be given practice in leading conference sessions (Zelko, 1952). Along with the participative aspect, feedback to the participant regarding his performance and attitude is an extremely important part of the conference method. It may be provided by the leader, the other participants, or a trained observer. The conference technique was really one of the first products of the reaction against the lecture method and has served as the backbone of the "human relations" type of training. It is most often used to teach such things as effective communication, supervisory techniques, and general approaches to problem solving and decision making. The conference method is perhaps the most widely used managerial training technique (Yoder, 1962).

A serious constraint on this method is its restriction to small groups. However, a large group may be broken down into smaller groups called "buzz" groups (H. A. Boyd, 1952), which then operate as problem-solving or discussion groups and report back to the main body. This technique may be used to illustrate approaches to the same problem, or each group may be assigned a portion of the main topic.

Criticisms of the conference method as a training technique center around its inability to cover much substantive content in a reasonable length of time, the frequent lack of organization, and an emphasis on demonstrating verbosity rather than learning (Jennings, 1956).

Yet another embellishment of the buzz-group technique is the method of forced leadership training described by Jennings (1953a). In most buzz groups a natural leader usually emerges to guide the discussion and keep the conversation going. This individual is identified, and in the second training session the leaders from the first buzz groups are all placed together and new buzz-groups are formed, using individuals who did not act as leaders during the first session. Thus in the second buzz-group session an individual who has not previously acted as leader is almost forced to assume this role. The cycle of regrouping nonleaders into new buzz groups is repeated until as many as possible have been given practice in leading the group.

T (training) groups or sensitivity training. This is a difficult technique to describe in a few words or paragraphs, chiefly because there are now so many different variations with different characteristics and different goals. In general, the method is a direct descendant of the conference technique, with its emphasis on small groups and individual participation. However, in the *T* group as it orginally evolved, the subject matter for discussion is the actual behavior of the individuals in the group, or the "here and now." That is, the group members discuss why they said particular things, why they reacted in certain ways to what others said, and what they thought was actually going on in the group. They examine one another's ability to communicate, the defenses an individual throws up to protect his self-image, why some people seem to attack or reinforce others, why cliques or subgroups seem to form within the main group, and so on. This is accomplished by having the group members honestly and openly communicate as best they can what they are thinking and feeling relative to what they or someone else is saying or doing. For example, one individual may inform another that even though he is verbally expressing approval, his facial expression says the opposite. The other individual may then try to communicate what he was actually thinking and feeling as he was talking.

Perhaps the most succinct characterization of a *T* group is given by Shepard (1964, p. 379), who defines a *T* group in terms of a norm that must be shared by the members. It consists of a "joint commitment among interdependent persons to process 'analysis,' that is, to shared examination of their relationships in all aspects relevant to their independence."

Descriptive accounts of some specific *T* groups have been given by Schein and Bennis (1965); Klaw (1962); Kuriloff and Atkins (1967); Bradford, Gibb, and Benn (1964); and Tannenbaum, Weschler, and Massarik (1961). A basic ingredient of this technique seems to be a certain amount of frustration and conflict (Argyris, 1963), which occurs when an individual attempts to use his previous modes of operation in the *T* group and is brought up short by the other group members, who wonder aloud why he tries to project his particular self-image, why he gets defensive when questioned about certain things, or why he tries verbally to punish other participants.

Many of the variations in the *T* group method revolve around the role of the trainer. In most *T* groups the trainer acts as a resource person and as a behavior model for the other group members; that is, he expresses his own feelings openly and honestly, does not become defensive and withdrawn when criticed, and exhibits an acceptance of the behavior of others. Beyond this, however, some trainers may try to be as nondirective as possible and let the group move along as it sees fit. Others may exhibit considerably more guidance and periodically attempt to point out to the group what is happening and offer an interpretation of what people are really saying to one another. Another kind of *T* group, referred to as the "instrumented group" (Blake & Mouton, 1962), operates without any trainer at all. The participants are provided with a set of rating scales with which they can rate themselves, the other group members, and the group itself on such things as openness, willingness to express feelings, ability to listen to other people, defensive behavior, and the formation of cliques. The positive ends of the scales implicitly define desirable behavior on the part of the group members, and over a series of ratings made during the life of the group the members tell themselves how they are progressing.

Although sensitivity training originally dealt only with behavior expressed in the group, more recent variants of the technique have introduced a specific problem-solving element, and the group members may examine their interpersonal skills as they affect efforts to work out a solution to a problem. This is frequently the technique used when all the people in the group are from one organization (Morton & Bass, 1964).

The type of group composition is another dimension along which groups can vary. They may be "stranger" groups made up of people from different organizations or "family" groups comprised of people from the same organization. In the latter case participants might be from the same level within a firm, or they might represent a vertical slice that includes a number of levels of responsibility.

Other variations of this basic technique include systematically introducing additional conflict in the group (Reed, 1966), to give the group members more practice in handling severe interpersonal stress, or running the group continuously for twenty-four or forty-eight hours instead of a few hours each day. Supposedly a process which normally stretches over a period of one to three weeks can be compressed into one or two days in this fashion and have even greater impact.

Very distinct from the weekend *T* groups, but still aimed at a compression of time, are the so-called micro *T* groups. With this method sessions are compressed into ten- or fifteen-minute intervals with brief lectures and problem-solving sessions interspersed.

Lastly, a procedure described by Tannenbaum and Bugental (1963) involves breaking the parent *T* group into smaller groups of four to six people or even into pairs. The pairs and smaller groups are intended to allow more interaction per person and provide additional feelings and impressions that the entire group can discuss when it meets together.

The objectives of this kind of training have been stated by many (Argyris, 1964b; Bradford et al., 1964; Schein & Bennis, 1965; Shepard, 1964; Tannenbaum et al., 1961) and in summary they seem to amount to the following:

1. To give the trainee an understanding of how and why he acts toward other people as he does and of the way in which he affects them
2. To provide some insights into why other people act the way they do
3. To teach the participants how to "listen," that is, actually hear what other people are saying rather than concentrating on a reply
4. To provide insights concerning how groups operate and what sorts of processes groups go through under certain conditions
5. To foster an increased tolerance and understanding of the behavior of others
6. To provide a setting in which an individual can try out new ways of interacting with people and receive feedback as to how these new ways affect them

Which of these relative specific objectives is adopted by a particular training effort depends upon whether the general objective is to teach individual self-awareness and personal development or to enhance understanding of group processes for the sake of organizational effectiveness.

In addition, *T* groups that are made up of individuals from one organization usually have as their aim the release and subsequent understanding and acceptance of the repressed feelings on the part of superior and subordinate that often inhibit communication. They also usually strive for increased tolerance and understanding among the various levels of management and for the building of a cohesive "team" feeling. The implicit assumption in all this seems to be that if these objectives are met, the result will be improved managerial performance.

Laboratory education. Laboratory education is the label applied to a more complete program of training experiences in which some form of *T* group is the prime ingredient. The other ingredients may consist of short lectures, group exercises designed to illustrate problems in interpersonal or intergroup behavior, role-playing sessions, and the like. Specification of the content of the various elements, their duration, their participants, and their sequencing constitutes the training or laboratory "design." Designs may vary depending on the training needs and situational elements the planners feel to be crucial. The laboratory education practitioner responsible for guiding the program is often referred to in the literature as a "change agent."

The variations in the laboratory designs are numerous, and we shall attempt no summary.

Discussions may be found in Bradford et al. (1964), Schein and Bennis (1965), and almost any issue of the *Journal of Applied Behavioral Science*.

Systematic observation. A little-used technique, but one advocated by Crow (1953), involves having the individuals in the development program observe an experienced manager or management group in action by sitting in on management committee meetings or observing a manager's meeting with his staff. The learner is cast in a very passive role, but the material being presented is the "real thing" and is presumably relevant for the trainee. A potential drawback is that the relative importance of what is observed is left to the judgment of the trainee.

Closed-circuit television. Although this technique has found wide application in educational institutions, it has had very limited use in management training. A rather unique utilization of television in a large aircraft company was reported by Niven (1966). After a certain hour in the evening, the educational television station in the region scheduled no regular programs, and the company used this open time to present courses in supervision, industrial relations, etc., to its managers and supervisors. Achievement tests were given to all those who participated, which turned out to be several hundred people.

Programmed instruction. The programmed technique involves defining what is to be learned, breaking it down into its component elements, and deciding on the optimal sequence for the presentation and learning of these elements. The presentation may be by "teaching machine," programmed texbook, or some other device, but the essential ingredient in the procedure is that the learner must make an active response to each element (or "frame") such that his response reveals whether or not he has learned what he is supposed to have learned at that point. There is immediate feedback concerning whether the learner was right or wrong, and the entire procedure is automated, which allows each individual to proceed at his own rate. The sequencing of the elements and the proper feedback are provided by the machine or the programmed book.

There are two principal variants of the above procedure—the so-called linear technique, developed by Skinner (1954), and the branching technique, developed by Crowder (1960). With the linear method the objective is to lead the learner from the simple to the complex in such a way that he almost never makes an incorrect response. The branching technique adopts the notion that incorrect responses may be indicative of certain misconceptions, and subprograms are provided to explore and correct the reasons for an incorrect response. After completing a subprogram, the learner continues on with the main program.

The programmed technique has not been widely utilized in management training, although the situation may be changing. It has been used in one instance to teach motivational principles to managers in a photochemical firm (Lysaught, 1961). At the National Institute of Health a program (teaching machine) was used in an attempt to increase supervisory skill in scheduling appointments, conducting meetings, handling reports, and delegating responsibility (Prather, 1964). It would also seem to have possible merit for teaching factual material in such areas as accounting, finance, contract management, and the like.

The advantages that have been claimed for programmed instruction are that it recognizes individual differences by allowing each individual to set his own pace, requires that the learner be active, provides immediate knowledge of results, and forces the people doing the teaching to break down the topic into meaningful elements and then present these elements in a sequence conducive to optimal learning (Hilgard, 1961). Also, once a program is ready, it obviously has a great deal of operating flexibility.

Some disadvantages often pointed out are its high initial cost, the considerable amount of time required to develop and perfect a program, and the seductive nature of the hardware itself (teaching machines, computers, etc.). Pressey (1963) has forcefully warned that the glamour value of the technique may detract from the fundamental and very difficult task of defining what is to be learned, breaking the subject into its component elements, and sequencing their presentation in an optimal fashion.

Training by correspondence. This method was used in one company to teach principles of business administration and personnel management to supervisors located in over two thousand scattered offices around the country (Krist & Prange, 1957). An achievement test was given at the end of each section, and small study groups were encouraged at each office to discuss the individual lessons.

Motion pictures. A survey reported by Bobele, Maher, and Ferl (1964) showed that some firms do use films in management training, but primarily at the lower levels and usually for introducing new subject matter and stimulating discussion relative to human relations problems. One drawback of films, according to the survey, seems to be the entertainment stigma. A variant of the film presentation is the so-called interruption technique, in which a problem is presented or a situation partially portrayed and the participants are asked to respond to the problem or complete the situation.

Reading lists. Besides providing straight information, executive reading programs can be organized around regular discussion sessions (Hook, 1963), in which managers can exchange opinions and ideas about what they have been reading.

Simulation Methods

In this category are included the techniques in which the trainee is presented with a simulated or artificial representation of some aspect of an organization or industry and is required to react to it as if it were the real thing. In other words, these techniques require actual practice of the managerial role with varying degrees of realism, but the actions of the trainees have no effect on the operation of the organization.

The case method. With this technique certain aspects of the firm are simulated by describing the organizational conditions on paper. The trainees are then usually required to identify problems, offer solutions, and otherwise react to the paper organization which is presented. Cases vary a great deal in length and complexity, but the objective is to be as representative of the problems of the real organization as possible. Cases are usually presented to groups of trainees, and active participation in suggesting a solution is encouraged. This allows an individual to obtain feedback regarding his own suggestions and to learn from watching others approach the same problem. Critics of the case method point to its inability to teach general principles and the general lack of guided instruction concerning the inferences the trainees draw from discussion of the case. Advocates point out that self-discovery is more meaningful and that general principles generated by the trainees themselves are learned better and remembered longer. Of course, cases can also be used in conjunction with other training techniques for the purpose of illustrating and reinforcing general principles that have been previously presented in some more direct fashion.

A variant of the case method is the "demand" technique described by Potter and Strachan (1965). With this procedure the trainees are divided into small groups of three or four individuals, and each team is given an organizational problem to research and present to the entire group. The various solutions are then discussed and critiqued within the entire group.

The incident method. Closely related to the case method is the incident technique (Pigors & Pigors, 1955). With this procedure the trainees are given a sketchy outline of a particular incident which requires action on the part of the manager, and they have to ask questions of the trainer to get more information. When the trainees think they have enough information, they try to come up with a solution. At the conclusion of the session, the trainer reveals all the information that he has, and a solution based on complete information is compared with the solution based on the information the trainees obtained.

Role playing. Here the realism of the simulation is heightened by having trainees "act out" the roles of individuals who are described in the case. With this technique the focus is almost exclusively on the human relations aspect of management and supervision, and the trainee has the opportunity to work through the problem exactly as he would if he were on the job. The success of the method rests on the ability of the players actually to adopt the roles specified in the case problem and to react to the actions of the other players just as they would if they were in the work situation. If they are successful, the trainee can try out various solutions and judge their success. He can also receive feedback regarding his supervisory techniques, communication skills, and attitudes toward superiors and subordinates.

The method is time-consuming and expensive in that only a few people can play at a time. Some variants of the role-playing method designed to overcome this problem are described by Maier, Solem, and Maier (1957). One of these is the multiple role-playing procedure, in which a large group breaks down into smaller groups and the same problem is role-played within each group without a trainer. All the players then reassemble and discuss, with the trainer, what happened in their groups, what sort of solutions were suggested, what kinds of human relations problems emerged, and how they were handled. A less satisfactory solution is to have some members of the group role play the situation while the rest of the trainees act as observers and take part in the critique session later.

Another type of role-playing method is described by Speroff (1959). He calls it the "substitution method," and it consists of role playing a meeting between a superior and a subordinate or between a union and a management representative in such a way that one of the pair is kept constant but a number of different people take turns playing the other role. The relative successes and failures of each of the substitutes are then analyzed in a critique session.

Speroff (1954) has also described a technique that combines the notions of job rotation and role playing and allows every manager to continue in his job while attempting to learn about the operations and problems of other parts of the organization. For example, a production manager might be given a sales problem along with all the relevant information the sales organization possesses. He may then adopt the role of the sales manager and sit in on sales conferences, ask questions, and talk to various sales personnel. After a week or two, the production manager (still role playing the sales manager) meets with the appropriate sales people and role plays a problem-solving meeting, centered around the sales problem orignally given him. (At the end of each session all the participants join in a critique session.) The production manager may continue to role play the sales manager for a period of several months, and over the course of one to five years each manager role plays the jobs of managers from many different parts of the business.

Business games. The nature of the simulation in this method is considerably different from that in role playing or the case method. The business game attempts to represent the economic functioning of an industry, company, or organizational subunit. The game actually consists of a set of specified relationships or rules which are derived from economic theory and/or from detailed studies of the operations of relevant businesses and industries. These relationships describe how variation in the inputs to a firm (raw materials, capital, equipment, and people) coupled with variation in certain mediating factors (wage rates, price of finished product, advertising budget, amount spent on research and development, etc.) influences the firm's outputs (amount sold, profit, net worth, etc.). The trainees play the game by making decisions about what price to charge for products, how much to spend on advertising, how many people to hire, and so on. The quality of their decisions is reflected by the variation in the output variables. The objective may be to teach general decision-making skills or to convey information as to how a specific business or industry actually operates. In either case the trainee is also supposed to come away with a realization of the complex interrelationships between various parts of an organization and an appreciation for how the effects of a decision made in one department may be felt in another.

There are literally hundreds of business games in use today of varying shades of complexity and realism (Croft, Kibbee, & Nanus, 1961). Some require as many as several hundred operating decisions every period (K. J. Cohen, 1960) and incorporate a number of firms in competition with one another. Several players may make up a firm. With the larger games there must be a division of labor among the players, and this allows some of the supervisory and human relations aspects of management to come into play. One of the characteristics of the business game is that it may become extremely realistic for the players. The frequent use of a computer to calculate the effects of operating decisions on outputs adds to the status and glamour of this training method.

The business games in use tend to fall into two general categories: top management games and functional games. Top management games are those which attempt to simulate the major decision-making functions of the chief officers in an organization. Functional games are much narrower in scope and are intended to simulate the operations of specific functional areas in an organization such as production control, marketing, or finance.

Some of the criticisms that have been voiced are that games do not allow for the novel approach and may teach an overreliance on particular kinds of decisions unless they are a balanced representation of the real world. A great deal of reliance is placed on the validity of the simulations. For example, if the model used in the game incorporates an oversimplified relationship between research and development investment and profits, the participants may carry away the notion that a surefire way to increase profits is to divert more funds into developmental research. On the other hand, the game may be too realistic, and the trainees may play with such fervor that the training objectives fall by the wayside. The participants may also spend too much time trying to discover "gimmicks" in the model which can be exploited. Most of the users of business games recommend lengthy critique meetings at the end of each session to help avoid some of these pitfalls.

The task model. Keltner (1965) describes a technique which he claims combines the advantages of role playing and business games. Some complex but easily built physical object is constructed, and a group of trainees is assigned the task of duplicating the model, given the proper materials. Various communication arrangements are used, and only certain trainees are allowed to view the object. Difficulties in communication are discussed as they arise, and solutions are obtained through group discussion. The method may also be used to incorporate competition between teams of trainees, or a portion of the training group can be used as observers to train them to recognize emerging leadership patterns and the like.

The In-basket technique. As described by Frederiksen, Saunders, and Wand (1957) and Lopez (1965), this development method consists of presenting the trainee with a description of a managerial role he is to assume and an In-basket containing such things as customer complaints, correspondence, operating statements, requests for advice from subordinates, and the like. The In-basket materials are intended to resemble a realistic operating situation with a variety of problems of varying complexity. The trainee must work through the In-basket, making decisions and giving advice where called for. The heart of the training is in the follow-up discussions, which allow the trainer and trainees to evaluate and interpret what each man did.

As is the case with business games, the objective seems to be primarily the teaching of decision-making skills, with little or no attention paid to learning new facts, human relations attitudes, or interpersonal skills.

A variant of the In-basket technique which does tend to incorporate some of these other considerations is the Kepner-Tregoe approach (Kepner & Tregoe, 1960). Instead of one trainee working in isolation, four individuals operate together as members of one company. The training begins with each man seated at his desk faced with an In-basket of work. The four In-baskets are meant to simulate an interrelated set of organizational problems typical of those faced by any management group. The participants may call each other on the phone to obtain additional information relevant to their own problems, or they may meet together in a conference room. All these things take time, however, and in the evaluation of the session a premium is placed on obtaining the most relevant information as quickly as possible. Again, the heart of the training is in the critique session, and although a certain number of interactive elements are introduced, the main objective is still to teach problem-solving and decision-making skills.

To incorporate still more realism into the In-basket format, Gibson (1961) suggests using a movie along with the In-basket. The film shows a vice-president who periodically interrupts the trainee's work on the In-basket to suggest additional problems that must be handled immediately. Supposedly this builds a realistic amount of tension into the situation.

On-the-job Training

The methods within this category all incorporate the notion of practice—practice on the actual task to be performed, i.e., the managerial job itself.

Job rotation. This technique is by far the most long-term and expensive way to train management personnel, but many people argue that it is both a necessary and an effective development method (Koontz & O'Donnell, 1955). The main objective is to give the trainee factual knowledge about the operations of different parts of the organization and practice in the different management skills that are required. Learning is largely by trial and error, unless combined with some other technique, and this lack of guidance or structure is the focus of most of the criticism of the method. Wall (1963) suggests that for job rotation to be effective, managers must be given instruction in how to coach and give feedback to the trainer and that definite training goals should be set for each job assignment. The success of job rotation also depends on the job assignments' being actually different so that the trainee learns more than he would by spending all his time on the job for which he was actually selected.

As noted by Koontz and O'Donnell (1955), the general term "job rotation" obscures a number of variations in the method which may or may not be important for a particular organization. First of all, the trainee may be rotated through a series of *nonsupervisory* work situations so as to acquaint him with the range of activities actually undertaken by the firm. Although such a scheme allows the trainee to learn the "production" end of things, many of the training positions may not offer enough of a challenge to the management trainee and indeed may bear little relationship to the skills that will be eventually needed in the management position. It is not inconceivable that such a rotation plan would make the trainee a less effective manager than he would be otherwise. However, for certain types of managerial jobs this kind of training could be very valuable. Rotation among actual managerial positions is perhaps the most common variant and obviously entails something quite different from rotation among nonsupervisory jobs. This difference is illustrative of the argument over whether a potential manager should concentrate on learning administrative and supervisory skills or become proficient in the actual work he is going to manage. Koontz and O'Donnell also discuss rotation among "assistant to" or "acting" managerial positions. Such rotation plans obviously attempt to use actual job experience for training in administrative and supervisory skills, but with some of the risk removed. However, there is also a risk that some of the commitment and involvement of the trainee will be diminished and that much of the substance of the job to be learned will be withheld from him.

Committee assignments or junior executive boards. A more short-term and less comprehensive method involves having the trainees form committees, which then are given real organizational problems to tackle and solve (McCormack, 1938). Problems may be selected from a number of different functional areas, and the trainees may be required to do a considerable amount of information gathering before suggesting a solution. This method differs from the role-playing committee assignment in that the solutions given are the ones actually utilized by the organization.

On-the-job coaching. With this method the superior-subordinate relationship is also a teacher-learner relationship, and the superior acts very much like a tutor in an academic setting. Coaching may vary from being very systematic to being very unsystematic and informal. Regardless of the particular form it takes, most people would argue (e.g., Haire, 1965) that it is one of the prime responsibilities of a superior. However, others (e.g., Argyris, 1961) have pointed to the difficulty of the teacher-learner roles and to the fact that they require the learner to continually try new methods and the teacher to be tolerant of mistakes. These are activities which may not be rewarded by the organization, and the roles of the superior as a good manager and as a good coach may be in conflict.

Performance appraisal. One of the stated goals of performance appraisal usually found in most textbooks is to provide feedback to the subordinate concerning good and bad features of his performance. Presumably this will motivate the individual to improve his performance. As a development technique, appraisal provides an opportunity for the superior and subordinate to discuss means of improving the subordinate's performance. In this sense it is systematic coaching and is distinct from the use of appraisal to identify training needs which may then be approached using other training and development techniques.

Other specialized practice techniques. In addition to exposing trainees to operational and managerial problems in various parts of the organization, other on-the-job techniques seem aimed at more specific goals. For example, some firms (Wilson, 1965) provide opportunities for managers to serve as recruitment and selection interviewers of college graduates. The manager may operate by himself or with other managers on a selection committee. Another firm (P. B. Smith, 1964) has used its management trainees as interviewers to follow up on company-wide attitude surveys. The trainees are first given instruction and practice in nondirective interviewing techniques. Then after the survey results are complete, they conduct interviews with personnel in the departments which showed dissatisfaction in certain areas. The objectives are to find out whether the sources of the dissatisfaction are such that they can be remedied by the company and at the same time to train the prospective managers in this type of face-to-face interaction. The problems of establishing rapport and assuring the employees of his anonymity are obvious. Lastly, in order to train managers in public speaking and simultaneously serve the cause of company public relations, some organizations often set up speaking engagements for their managers and encourage them to give talks at professional meetings.

Training Content, or "What to Teach"

Up to this point we have been talking about techniques and methods in management training and development. When an organization decides to institute or alter a development program, the decision regarding which technique(s) to use is not the only decision that must be made. The decision about *what* to teach also looms large on the horizon and obviously should be made even before techniques are considered.

On their face at least, management training programs have been used to teach a bewildering variety of topics; however, for the sake of a meaningful organization, we have attempted to group them into five categories:

1. *Factual content.* Such a category would include everything from company rules and policies to courses in the humanities. Perhaps the most popular topics in this category are personnel management and business administration concepts. A somewhat novel body of knowledge is utilized by Miner (1965) in a carefully worked-out program to teach managers the causes of ineffective managerial performance and some means for overcoming them.

2. *Approaches and techniques for problem solving and decision making.* Examples of this sort of content are skill in adequately defining the problem of elements in the decision, an appreciation for the interrelatedness of decisions, the importance of planning or optimal sequencing of the steps in the decision-making process, and the realization that many problems do not have one best solution or any permanent solution. Attempts to teach creativity such as those by Parnes and his associates (Meadow & Parnes, 1959) and the means for effective group problem solving as discussed by Maier (1963) would also have to be included here. The creativity work tends to focus on the

individual's approach to obtaining solutions and stresses nonroutine, or "divergent," thinking. Maier's efforts, on the other hand, are aimed at teaching leaders and groups how to utilize more effectively the knowledge and contributions of the individual members to achieve a more effective combined solution.

3. *Attitudes.* Although extremely difficult to define, this sort of training content refers to such things as a positive regard for democratic leadership, consideration for the contributions of others, tolerance for other people's mistakes, and the like. It seems vital to many people that such attitudes go hand in glove with the teaching of human relations skills in order to avoid teaching a role that is only manipulative and not effective (Jennings, 1953b). Somewhat unique in this category is the training program developed and described by McClelland (1965), which attempts to instill in the trainees a high need for achievement. This program attempts to go somewhat beyond attitude change and actually tries to modify the individual's motivated structure.

4. *Interpersonal skills.* In this category fall such things as effective communication, how to listen to other individuals, and how to be an effective group member.

5. *Self-knowledge.* Knowledge concerning how one's behavior affects others and what other people think of one and a realistic perception of one's abilities and limitations should be included here. The state of one's physical health, as it may influence job effectiveness, is also relevant.

Modifiers

When one looks at the myriad training efforts described in the literature, the two dimensions of "*what* is taught" and "*how* it is taught" still do not satisfactorily describe all the variations in programs. There is an additional set of characteristics, which we shall label "modifiers," that various writers and investigators in the field sometimes view as important for training outcomes. Included here are such things as whether the training is on company time or individual time, the total time involved in the training (can the same learning be accomplished in less time?), and the locale of the training session, that is, whether the training is conducted inside or outside the plant. With regard to this latter modifier, the virtues of university versus company programs have often been argued (Anshen, 1954; Boudreaux & Megginson, 1964; Huneryager, 1961), and the prestige, teaching facilities, and isolation of the university setting are pointed to as either desirable or distracting elements. T-group advocates often speak of the "cultural island" as a necessary or unnecessary part of such training. Here the choice is between conducting the training sessions at a very isolated setting where little contact with the outside world is allowed and holding the program in-house. A great deal of discussion has also been centered around who does the training—the line, the staff, or some outside consultant. Here there are the obvious considerations of relative costs, trainer competence, and flexibility. However, the motivational considerations relative to both trainer and trainee are also often pointed out as having a direct bearing on deciding who trains. Many people argue that trainees respond much more favorably when the training is carried about by their own management and management has obviously assumed the responsibility (e.g., Blake & Mouton, 1966b).

In brief, these things we have called "modifiers" can be summed up in a few questions: Where should training take place? Who should train? How much time should be spent for training? Whose time?

Obviously, not all training and development programs utilize just one technique or are intended to teach one particular topic. The objectives and scope of a two-year job rotation program are not all comparable to those of a two-hour seminar on human relations employing role playing and the conference method. By arranging all these methods in an organized "list," we do not mean to imply that they are comparable in terms of the "domain of behavior" they seek to influence.

However, it is also true that many more than one combination of training method and modifier can be used for a particular training or development objective. For example, a programmed booklet may attempt to teach the same thing as a business game, or role playing may be used to reach the same objective as a T group. It is a truism to say that given a particular objective, different costs and different payoffs are associated with different combinations of techniques and modifying circumstances.

Perhaps it would be well for people interested in training and development to examine a number of possible combinations with a view toward systematically justifying, on the basis of theory and empirical findings, the pros and cons of each one. . . . Briggs (1966) suggests that there is an optimal combination of training method and "what is to be learned" and that it behooves educators, organizational training specialists, and learning theorists alike to get on with the job of finding out what these optimal combinations are.

Team Training

Up to now we have been talking about training and development efforts in the context of the individual trainee. Somewhat distinct from this orientation is the notion of team training (Blake, Mouton, & Blansfield, 1962; Boguslaw & Porter, 1962; Porter, 1964). Instead of developing individual managers, the emphasis is on training teams of managers. Blake et al. (1962) use the analogy of a baseball team to illustrate that individual training cannot do the whole job. The team must be trained as an interacting unit. Porter (1964) has pointed out that the skills, information, and attitudes obtained from team training revolve largely around problems of coordination and thus are not the same as what is learned in individual training. Viewed in this fashion, it would seem that for team training to be effective, a great deal of individual training must have gone before. That is, there must be individual skills and attitudes available for coordination in the team setting. On the other hand, it also seems reasonable that an individual must learn something about the various aspects of team performance before the crucial requirements for individual training become apparent. The two interact.

The literature regarding the use of team training for executive development is rather sparse. Not much has been said about possible training techniques, what is to be taught, or what the modifiers of such training are. However, some of the simulation methods seem especially appropriate for this kind of training. Porter (1964) describes the use of a simulated situation to train the entire work force in an air defense installation, including people with managerial responsibilities. The larger, more complex business games which allow a number of trainees to make up a firm and which require effective coordination among the trainees could be used for team training if the players making up a firm were a functioning management group in real life.

A very specialized method which, according to Blake, Mouton, Barnes, and Greiner (1964), does attempt to develop both individual and team or organizational skills is the Management Grid approach. The content is also quite specialized, and the initial objective is to teach a particular management style, referred to as the "9,9 style." Managerial style is conceived as having two dimensions—a concern for people and a concern for production—and Blake and Mouton (1964) have developed questionnaire-type measures to locate individual managers on these two dimensions (or grids). A 9,9 style describes a manager who has both a maximal concern for people and a maximal concern for production. The first steps in the training focus on the individual, and a modified *T*-group method is used to teach each participant how the other group members see his managerial style. Trainees are first familiarized with the grid language and theory. The group then proceeds to work through a series of exercises and case problems which allow each individual to exhibit his management style, and this behavior then becomes the object of *T*-group type of feedback. Participants supposedly develop skills which enable them accurately and candidly to reflect the management behavior of each individual. This process is intended to instill an appreciation for the human problems of production and move the trainees toward the 9,9 region of the grid.

After this initial phase, the trainees are supposed to go back to their functional groups and use what they have learned to move the entire team to 9,9 methods of operating. It is intended that the "openness" and "candor" learned in the first group carry over to the functional group, starting with the boss and his chief subordinates, and that they become a part of the daily work routine. Finally, attempts are made to extend the utility of the 9,9 approach beyond a particular work team by identifying actual sources of intergroup or interdepartment conflict and incorporating the 9,9 approach in intergroup problem-solving exercises. New attempts are also made to redefine problems and set goals for the organization as a whole. In order for these objectives to be realized, all the managers in an organization must take part in the training. Blake et al. (1964) thus conceive of their program as organizational development rather than management development. The same is true for certain advocates of laboratory education (Schein & Bennis, 1965).

It should be emphasized again that team training is meant to be something distinct, but not entirely independent, from individual training and that the success of the former depends to a degree on the success of the latter. The two obviously interact. As with the other training techniques, team training can potentially at least be directed at a number of content areas. For example, the "family" type of *T* group can be used to familiarize members of a management team with one another's methods of communication, self-images, etc. It is hoped that this will reduce some of the interpersonal barriers that dampen effective coordination. Notice that in such an instance the contribution of team training would be knowledge about the behavior of specific people, i.e., the people who work together in the job situation. The functional team must thus be trained intact. As another example, perhaps a business game could be used to teach team procedures for planning an organization's short-term and long-term goals. The team members could learn which individual functions best as a "critical evaluator," who is an "idea" man, etc., and then devise means for coordinating these specialized skills in future goal-setting tasks.

The interactions between the objectives of individual and team training are obviously complex, and not all aspects of these interactions are always relevant. However, the notion of team training as applied to the management development sphere deserves more attention than it has received.

References

Anshen, M. Executive development: In-company vs. university programs. *Harvard Business Review*, 1954, *32*, 83-91.

Argyris, C. Puzzle and perplexity in executive development. *Personnel Journal*, 1961, *39*, 463-465, 483.

Argyris, C. A brief description of laboratory education. *Training Directors Journal*, 1963, *17* (10), 4-8.

Argyris, C. T-groups for organizational effectiveness. *Harvard Business Review*, 1964, *42* (2), 60-74.

Bennett, W.E. The lecture as a management training technique. *Personnel*, 1956, *32*, 497-507.

Blake, R.R., & Mouton, J.S. The instrumental training laboratory. In I.R. Weschler & E.H. Schein (Eds.), *Issues in human relations training*. NTL Selected Readings Series, 1962, No. 5.

Blake, R.R., & Mouton, J.S. *The managerial grid*. Houston: Gulf, 1964.

Blake, R.R., & Mouton, J.S., & Blansfield, M.G. How executive team training can help you. *Journal of the American Society of Training Directors*, 1962, *16* (1), 3-11.

Bobele, H.K., Maher, C.R., & Ferl, R.A. Motion pictures in management development. *Training Directors Journal*, 1964, *18* (9), 34-38.

Boguslaw, R., & Porter, E.H. Team functions and training. In R.M. Gagne (ed.), *Psychological principles and systems development*. New York: Holt, 1962.

Boudreaux, E., & Megginson, L.C. A new concept in university sponsored executive development programs. *Training Directors Journal*, 1964, *18* (11), 31-41.

Boyd, H.A. The buzz technique in training. *Personnel*, 1952, *31*, 49-50.

Bradford, L.P., Gibb, J.R., & Benne, K.D. *T-group theory and laboratory method*. New York: Wiley, 1964.

Briggs, L.J. *A procedure for the design of multi-media instruction*. Palo Alto, Calif.: American Institutes for Research, 1966.

Brown, D.S. The lecture. *Journal of the American Society of Training Directors*, 1960, *14* (12), 17-22.

Buchanan, P.C., & Ferguson, C.K. Changing supervisory practices through training: A case study. *Personnel*, 1953, *30*, 218-230.

Cohen, K.J., et al. The Carnegie Tech management game. *Journal of Business*, 1960, *33*, 303-321.

Croft, C.J., Kibbee, J., & Nanus, B. *Management games*. New York: Reinhold, 1961.

Crow, R. Group training in higher management development. *Personnel*, 1953, *29*, 458-460.

Crowder, N.A. Automatic tutoring by intrinsic programming. In A.A. Lumdsdaine & P. Glaser (Eds.), *Teaching machines and programmed learning: A source book*. Washington: National Education Association, 1960.

Frederiksen, N., Saunders, D. R., & Wand, B. The in-basket test. *Psychological Monographs*, 1957, *71* (9, Whole No. 438).

Gibson, G.W. A new dimension for "in-basket" training. *Personnel*, 1961, *38*, 76-79.

Haire, M. The incentive character of pay. In R. Andrews (Ed.), *Managerial compensation*. Ann Arbor, Mich.: Foundation for Research in Human Behavior, 1965. Pg. 13-17.

Hilgard, E.R. What support from the psychology of learning? *NEA Journal*, November, 1961, *50*, 20-21.

Huneryager, S.G. Re-education for executives. *Personnel Administration*, 1961, *24* (1), 5-9.

Jennings, E.E. Advantages of forced leadership training. *Personnel*, 1953, *32*, 7-9. (a)

Jennings, E.E. Attitude training versus technique training. *Personnel*, 1953, *31*, 402-404. (b)

Jennings, E.E. Today's group training problems. *Personnel*, 1956, *35*, 94-97.

Keltner, J.W. The task-model as a training instrument. *Training Directors Journal*, 1965, *19* (9), 18-21.

Kepner, C.H., & Tregoe, B.B. Developing decision makers. *Harvard Business Review*, 1960, *38*, 115-124.

Klaw, S. Two weeks in a T-group. *Fortune*, 1961, *64* 114-117.

Koontz, H., & O'Donnell, C. *Principles of management.* New York: McGraw-Hill, 1955.

Krist, P.C., & Prange, C.J. Training supervisors by mail: The Railway Express program. *Personnel,* 1957, *34,* 32-37.

Kuriloff, A.H., & Atkins, S. T-group for a work team. *Journal of Applied Behavioral Science,* 1966, *2,* 63-94.

Lopez, F.M., Jr. Evaluating executive decision making: The In-basket technique. American Management Association Research Study No. 75, 1966.

Lysaught, J.P. *Programmed learning: Evolving principles and industrial applications.* Ann Arbor, Mich.: Foundation for Research on Human Behavior, 1961.

Maier, N.R.F. *Problem-solving discussions and conferences: Leadership methods and skills.* New York: McGraw-Hill, 1963.

Maier, N.R.F., Solem, A., & Maier, A. *Supervisory and executive development.* New York: Wiley, 1957.

McClelland, D. Achievement motivation can be developed. *Harvard Business Review,* 1965, *43,* 6-24, 178.

McCormack, C. *Multiple management.* New York: Harper, 1938.

McGehee, W., & Thayer, P.W. *Training in business and industry.* New York: Wiley, 1961.

Meadow, A., & Parnes, S.J. Effects of "brainstorming" instructions on creative problem solving by trained and untrained members. *Journal of Educational Psychology,* 1959. *50,* 171-176.

Miner, J.B. Relationships between management appraisal ratings and promotions. Mimeographed paper, personal communication, 1966.

Morton, R.B., & Bass, B.M. The organizational training laboratory. *Journal of the American Society of Training Directors,* 1964, *18* (10), 2-15.

Niven, J.R. Personal communication, 1966.

Pigors, P., & Pigors, F. *The incident process: Case studies in management development.* Washington: Bureau of National Affairs, 1955.

Porter, L.W. *Organizational patterns of managerial job attitudes.* New York: American Foundation for Management Research, 1964.

Potter, C.J., & Strachan, G.D. Project training groups: A "demand" technique for middle managers. *Training Directors Journal,* 1965, *19* (9), 34-41.

Prather, R.L. Introduction to management by teaching machine. *Personnel Administration,* 1964, *27* (3), 26-31.

Pressey, S.L. Teaching machine (and learning theory) crisis. *Journal of Applied Psychology,* 1963, *47,* 1-6.

Reed, J.H. Two weeks of managed conflict at Bethel. *Training Development Journal,* 1966, *20,* 6-16.

Schein, E.H., & Bennis, W.G. *Personal and organizational change through group methods: The laboratory approach.* New York: Wiley, 1965.

Shepard, H.A. Explorations in observant participation. In L.P. Bradford, J.R. Gibb, & K.D. Benne, *T-group theory and laboratory method,* New York: Wiley, 1964.

Skinner, B.F. The science of learning and the art of teaching. *Harvard Educational Review,* 1954, *24,* 99-113.

Smith, P.B. Attitude changes associated with training human relations. *British Journal of Social and Clinical Psychology,* 1964, *3,* 104-113.

Speroff, B.J. Rotational role playing used to develop managers. *Personnel,* 1954, *33,* 49-50.

Speroff, B.J. The substitution method in role playing grievance handling. *Personnel,* 1959, *38,* 9-12.

Tannenbaum, R., Weschler, I.R., & Massarik, F. *Leadership and organization: A behavioral science approach.* New York: McGraw-Hill, 1961.

Tiffin, J., & McCormick, E.J. *Industrial psychology.* Englewood Cliffs, N.J.: Prentice-Hall, 1965.

Wall, R.G. Untangling the snarls in a job rotation program. *Personnel,* 1963, *42,* 59-65.

Wilson, A.T.M. Personal communication, 1964.

Yoder, D. *Personnel management and industrial relations.* (5th ed.) Englewood Cliffs, N.J.: Prentice-Hall, 1962.

Zelko, H.P. Conference leadership training: A plan for practice projects. *Personnel*, 1952, *29* (1), 37-42.

The Relative Effectiveness of Training Methods—Expert Opinion and Research

STEPHEN J. CARROLL
FRANK T. PAINE
JOHN J. IVANCEVICH

Programmed instruction, sensitivity training, computer games, television, and role playing have been widely used in training only in recent years. These newer techniques when added to the older methods of the lecture, conference method, movie films, and case study method provide the fields of training and education with a number of alternatives to use in a particular situation. While availability of resources in the form of money, time, and personnel do play a significant part in the choice of one training method or another, another important criterion must be the relative effectiveness of the training method being considered for a particular training objective.

The obvious approach for identifying the relative effectiveness of various training methods for particular training objectives would be to analyze the research data on the subject. An attempt by the authors to do this, however, identified many limitations in the research studies that were carried out and great variability in the amount of research carried out on particular training methods.

With the difficulties experienced in examining the research on the subject, the authors decided to focus on expert opinion. Therefore, a survey was conducted of the 200 training directors who worked for the companies with the largest numbers of employees as indicated on *Fortune's* list of the top 500 corporations. It was felt that the number of employees in a firm would be a rough indicator of the amount of training the organization carries out. Since the research data on the effectiveness of various training methods was available, it was also decided to compare the limited research available with the judgments of the training directors. This might provide some indication of the extent to which research results on training method are known to training directors. In comparing ratings of effectiveness of the training directors with research, primary emphasis was placed on research studies carried out with adults in the employment situation since this would be the group most familiar to the training directors. Of course, this involves a minority of research studies done in this area. Most research studies on the effectiveness of alternative training methods have been carried out with college students.

Reprinted by permission of the authors and the publisher from *Personnel Psychology*, vol. 25 (1972), pp. 495-509.

Method

Questionnaire

A questionnaire was constructed which asked respondents to indicate the relative effectiveness of nine different training methods for achieving each of six training objectives. In the questionnaire, each training method was considered one at a time for the six different training objectives. In the effectiveness rating, five alternative degrees of effectiveness were used and these were scored as follows: highly effective (5), quite effective (4), moderately effective (3), limited effectiveness (2), and not effective (1).

Sample and Analysis

Two hundred questionnaires were mailed to the training directors of the two hundred firms with the largest number of employees. A follow-up letter was also used. There was a final usable return from 117 of these training directors for a return rate of 59 percent.

The average effectiveness ratings of the various training methods for each of the six training objectives were calculated and compared to each other by means of a "t" test.

Training Methods and Training Objectives

The training methods compared by the training directors were: programmed instruction, case study, lecture method (with questions), conference or discussion method, role playing, sensitivity training (t-group), TV-Lecture (lecture given to large audience over TV), Movie films, Business Gaming (using computer or hand calculator).

The training objectives used in the study were: acquire knowledge, change in attitudes, participant acceptance, retention of what is learned, development of interpersonal skills, development of problem solving skills.

Results

The results of the study are presented in table 1. This table indicates the relative ranking of the nine training methods for each of the training objectives, the average effectiveness rating given for each training method for each objective, and whether the differences in average ratings between any two training methods are large enough to be statistically significant.

Acquisition of Knowledge

Table 1 indicates that the training directors rated programmed instruction highest of all training methods on effectiveness in the acquisition of knowledge. The lecture is ranked as least effective of all training methods. The mean ratings indicate the average respondent believes that programmed instruction is "quite effective" for acquiring knowledge and the lecture method has only limited effectiveness for this objective.

Research on the subject seems to support the high relative rating given to programmed instruction by the training directors for knowledge acquisition. In 20 studies which compared programmed instruction to conventional lecture and discussion in an industrial situation, it was found that immediate learning was at least 10 percent higher under programmed instruction in seven comparisons, and there was not a practical difference between the conventional and programmed instruction in 13 comparisons (Nash, Muczyk, and Vettori, 1971). In 18 studies where programmed instruction and

TABLE 1
RATINGS OF TRAINING DIRECTORS ON EFFECTIVENESS OF ALTERNATIVE TRAINING METHODS FOR VARIOUS TRAINING OBJECTIVES

Training Method	Knowledge Acquisition Mean	Knowledge Acquisition Mean Rank	Changing Attitudes Mean	Changing Attitudes Mean Rank	Problem-Solving Skills Mean	Problem-Solving Skills Mean Rank	Interpersonal Skills Mean	Interpersonal Skills Mean Rank	Participant Acceptance Mean	Participant Acceptance Mean Rank	Knowledge Retention Mean	Knowledge Retention Mean Rank
Case Study	3.56[2]	2	3.43[4]	4	3.69[2]	1	3.02[4]	4	3.80[4]	2	3.48[5]	2
Conference (Discussion) Method	3.33[4]	3	3.54[4]	3	3.26[5]	4	3.21[4]	3	4.16[1]	1	3.32[6]	5
Lecture (with questions)	2.53	9	2.20	8	2.00	9	1.90	8	2.74	8	2.49	8
Business Games	3.00	6	2.73[6]	5	3.58[2]	2	2.50[5]	5	3.78[4]	3	3.26[6]	6
Movie Films	3.16[7]	4	2.50[6]	6	2.24[7]	7	2.19[7]	6	3.44[7]	5	2.67[8]	7
Programmed Instruction	4.03[1]	1	2.22[8]	7	2.56[6]	6	2.11[7]	7	3.28[7]	7	3.74[1]	1
Role Playing	2.93	7	3.56[4]	2	3.27[5]	3	3.68[2]	2	3.56[5]	4	3.37[6]	4
Sensitivity Training (t group)	2.77	8	3.96[1]	1	2.98[5]	5	3.95[2]	1	3.33[7]	6	3.44[6]	3
Television Lecture	3.10[7]	5	1.99	9	2.01	8	1.81	9	2.74	9	2.47	9

[1] More effective than methods ranked 2 to 9 for this objective at .01 level of significance.
[2] More effective than methods ranked 3 to 9 for this objective at .01 level of significance.
[3] More effective than methods ranked 4 to 9 for this objective at .01 level of significance.
[4] More effective than methods ranked 5 to 9 for this objective at .01 level of significance.
[5] More effective than methods ranked 6 to 9 for this objective at .01 level of significance.
[6] More effective than methods ranked 7 to 9 for this objective at .01 level of significance.
[7] More effective than methods ranked 8 to 9 for this objective at .01 level of significance.
[8] More effective than method ranked 9 for this objective at .01 level of significance.

conventional lecture and discussion methods used in an industrial situation were compared with respect to time required to reach a certain level of proficiency, programmed instruction was superior to conventional instruction in 14 comparisons and there were no practical differences in four studies (Nash, Muczyk, and Vettori, 1971). A very large number of studies conducted with students also support the findings that programmed instruction is probably more effective than conventional instruction on amount of time taken to learn the material or on amount of material learned (Nash, et al., 1971; Schramm, 1962a). Nash and his colleagues, however, have pointed out that most of the studies involving a comparison of programmed with conventional instruction have not used a well planned and well carried out conventional class as the basis for comparison (Nash, et al., 1971).

The very low rating given to the lecture method as compared to the discussion method by the training directors with respect to effectiveness for knowledge acquisition is not congruent with research results in a few studies carried out with adults and in many studies with students as subjects. For example, Richard Hill (1960), in a controlled study, compared three lecture classes of 233, 25, and 25 participants with twelve discussion classes made up of 22 to 28 members each and found no difference in amount learned. Andrew (1954) found a lecture approach superior to that of a discussion and a film for imparting mental health information. Four extensive reviews of the literature where the subjects were primarily college students all concluded that on the basis of research comparisons made, lecture and discussion methods are equally effective for the acquisition of knowledge (Buxton, 1956; Dietrick, 1960; Stovall, 1958; and Verner and Dickinson, 1967).

The training directors also rated the television lecture as more effective than the conventional lecture. No studies were found where adults in the employment situation were compared, but the training directors' ratings are not supported by research results with students as subjects which generally show no significant differences between television lecture courses and conventional lecture courses. For example, in 32 comparisons between television and conventionally taught college students there was no difference in 29 of the comparisons (Carpenter and Greenhill, 1958). In 28 comparisons between television and conventionally taught courses at Miami (Ohio) University, only four differences were significant at or beyond the .05 level and three of these favored the conventional (Klausmeier, 1961). Schramm (1962b) in summarizing 393 studies of the amount learned in television courses versus conventionally taught courses found that in 65 percent of the comparisons there were no differences, in 21 percent of the comparisons the television approach was more effective, and in 14 percent of the comparisons the participants in the television courses did worse.

The training directors indicated that movie films and the case method were superior to the lecture method for knowledge acquisition. In the Andrew study (1954) cited earlier, the lecture was superior to a film for imparting knowledge to adult subjects. In a well controlled study where a class taught by the case method was compared to a class taught by a lecture-discussion approach, the case study section scored significantly higher on achievement tests (Butler, 1967).

Changing Attitudes

Table 1 indicates that the training directors believe that, in a relative sense, sensitivity training is the most effective way to change attitudes. They also believe that role playing, the conference method, and the case study method are more effective in changing attitudes than management games, movie films, programmed instruction, lecture and TV. The scores given the various methods indicates that most of the training directors only consider the first four methods listed in the table as having any effectiveness in changing attitudes.

The training directors indicated that the discussion method was superior to the lecture method in changing attitudes. In two fairly well controlled studies where the lecture and discussion approaches were compared in situations involving attitude change among adults (prisoners and executives), the discussion approach was more effective (Butler, 1966 and Silber, 1962). In five controlled studies involving changes in behavior of adults, the discussion approach was more effective than the lecture method in changing behavior (Bond, 1956; Levine and Butler, 1952; Lewin, 1958). Some of these comparisons were not entirely fair to the lecture method, however, since in the discussion groups the participants were usually asked to commit themselves to future actions while the subjects in the lecture groups were not asked to do this. In spite of this, it does appear that the discussion approach is superior to the lecture in changing attitudes and behavior as the training directors indicated.

The training directors believe that role playing can be quite effective in changing attitudes. Several studies conducted among students do show that role playing can be effective in changing attitudes (Festinger and Carlsmith, 1959; Harvey and Beverly, 1961). Role playing seems especially effective if the subjects participating in the role playing situation are asked to take the point of view opposite to their own and to verbalize this opposite point of view to others (Culbertson, 1957; Janis and King, 1954; King and Janis, 1956; Janis and Mann, 1965).

The low rating on effectiveness given to movies and business games by the training directors may not be justified. A U.S. Army study among adults showed that attitudes could be changed by films and that at least half of the attitude changes found persisted for at least nine weeks (U.S. War Department, 1943). Another study found that participation in a business game by students significantly changed attitudes toward risk taking (Lewin and Weber, 1969). However, this is obviously a very specific type of attitude.

The training directors rated the case method as more effective than the lecture in changing attitudes. In the one study found which made such a comparison, attitudes did change significantly more in a section where the case study approach was used than in the section of the course taught by the lecture-discussion method (Butler, 1967).

Finally, the training directors believe that sensitivity training is fairly effective in changing attitudes. Four studies using control groups have been conducted with adults where an attempt was made to see if behavior was changed as a result of sensitivity training (Boyd and Ellis, 1968; Bunker, 1965; Miles, 1965; Underwood, 1965; and Valiquet, 1968). These studies did find behavioral changes as a result of sensitivity training. With respect to attitude rather than behavior change, two studies, using a "before-and-after" measure without controls and with student and adult participants, found attitude changes as a result of sensitivity training (Schutz and Allen, 1966; Smith, 1964). Although there were certain methodological deficiencies in these studies, on balance, the results do indicate that sensitivity training can result in at least short run behavioral and attitudinal change although such change may not be related to greater job effectiveness (Campbell and Dunnette, 1968).

Problem Solving

For purposes of developing effectiveness in problem solving skills, the training directors rated the case study method, business games, role playing, and the conference method as having some effectiveness. In addition, these methods were rated more effective than sensitivity training, programmed instruction, movie films, the TV lecture, and the conventional lecture. These results are listed in table 1.

The case study method was rated highest in effectiveness for this training objective by the training directors and certainly it is true that the case study is probably generally considered to be the primary means of developing problem solving skills. Unfortunately, the research on the effectiveness of the case study as a training approach is very limited. Only a few studies were found that involved more than an attempt to obtain testimonials from course participants. Fox (1963) found that about one third of the students exposed to case study analysis improved significantly in their ability to handle cases, about a third made moderate improvement and a third made no improvement. Solem (1960) found that both the case study method and role playing were effective in learning how to derive solutions to problems but felt role playing better taught participants about how to gain acceptance of solutions. There is more evidence on the effectiveness of role playing in developing problem solving skills. In addition to the study by Solem (1960), studies by (Maier, 1953), Maier and Maier (1957), Maier and Hoffman (1960a; 1960b) and Maier and Solem, 1952) indicate that problem solving skills can be improved for both students and managers with the use of role playing. Two studies (Parnes and Meadow, 1959; Cohen, Whitmyre, and Funk, 1960) found that training in brainstorming could improve problem solving ability. Brainstorming could be taught by means of role-playing.

The training directors also ranked business games as being an effective training method for developing problem solving skills. However, as with the case study method, there is little research or analysis. Dill and Doppelt (1963) conducted a student self-report study which indicated that the students did not seem to learn much about specific problem solving solutions or strategies that could be used in other situations. Raia (1966) found that experience with a business game did not improve the ability to handle cases. However, the comparison group used case material. McKenney (1962) found that students in sections with games plus lectures understood the interrelationship between organizational factors better than students in sections with cases plus lectures.

Interpersonal Skills

Table 1 indicates that the training directors see the sensitivity training and role playing as being the most effective of the training methods in developing Interpersonal skills and feel the conference or discussion method and the case study method also have some effectiveness for this objective. In general, business games, movies films, programmed instruction, and the conventional and TV lecture are not considered effective for the development of interpersonal skills.

Most of the research which has concerned itself with the effectiveness of training methods in developing interpersonal skills have been on sensitivity training. Six studies of sensitivity training indicate that participants in sensitivity training describe others in more interpersonal terms than people without such training (Campbell and Dunnette, 1968). However, research specifically measuring changes in perceptual accuracy of others as result of sensitivity training has been inconclusive.

Some research on the development of interpersonal skills has examined role playing. A study by Bolda and Lawshe (1962) showed that role playing can be effective in increasing sensitivity to employee motivations, if the participants were involved in the role play. Another study indicated role playing effective in improving interviewing skills (Van Schacck 1957). In addition, studies by Maier, 1953; Maier and Hoffman,

1960a; and Maier and Maier, 1957) indicate that role playing can be used to improve group leadership skills which are a form of interpersonal skills.

Participant Acceptance

As table 1 indicates, the training directors rated the conference or discussion method, the case study method, and the use of business games as being significantly more acceptable to training course participants than movie films, sensitivity training, programmed instruction, the conventional lecture method, and the television lecture. In absolute terms the training directors seem to believe that all the methods except for the conventional and TV lecture are effective for achieving the objective of participant acceptance.

Several studies on managerial acceptance of the lecture versus the discussion approach indicate a preference among managers for the lecture or more leader centered approach. (Anderson, 1959; Filley and Reighhard, 1965; House, 1962; Mann and Mann, 1959). Two other studies of managers and a study of adults found no difference in reactions or attitudes to the use of the lecture and discussion approaches (Hill, 1960; House, 1965).

The training directors also indicated that the television lecture rated low on participant acceptance. Reviews of research by Kumata (1956 and 1960; and Schramm, 1962a) indicate that television has fairly high acceptance among adults as a training method and with young children, and much lower acceptance among high school and college students.

The training directors rated business games as high on participant acceptance. Raia (1966) found that business students in sections of a course which used a business game did not differ in attitudes toward the course from students who had sections without the business game. Rowland, Gardner, and Nealey (1970) found only a few students participating in a business game felt the game was a valuable learning experience and attitudes toward the course were not improved as a result of the addition of the business game to it.

The training directors rated role playing as effective in participant acceptance. A series of studies in six organizations by Bolda and Lawshe (1962) indicated fair acceptance for role playing by managerial personnel. The training directors also rated the case study method as high on participant acceptance. A study by Fox, 1963; found that attitudes toward the case study method in the form of student testimonials were favorable. However, Castore (1951) found interest in cases dwindled after a period of exposure to them. The relatively higher rating given by the training directors to programmed instruction versus the lecture method is supported in a study conducted at IBM (Hughes and McNamara, 1961), and in a study by Neidt and Meredith (1966). It should be remembered, however, that several studies show that participant acceptance of a training approach is a function of their experience with it (Guetzkow, Kelly and McKeachie, 1954; Harris, 1960; and Hughes, 1963).

Retention of Knowledge

As table 1 indicates, the training directors rate programmed instruction, the case study method, sensitivity training, role playing, the conference method and business gaming as significantly more effective than movie films and conventional and television lectures. These latter three training methods are also rated in absolute terms as not being effective for retention of knowledge.

There has not been much research on this topic. The research that has been completed has been primarily with college students and shown no clear superiority for the lecture or discussion methods as compared with each other (Dietrick, 1960, Verner and Dickinson, 1967), for the movie film as compared with the lecture and discussion methods (Sodnovitch and Pophorn, 1961; VanderMeer, 1948; Verner and Dickinson, 1967), for the television lecture as compared to the conventional lecture or discussion approach (Kumata, 1960; Klausmeir, 1961), or for programmed instruction as compared to the conventional lecture or discussion methods (Nash, Muczyk, Vettori, 1971). The research reviews generally conclude that the amount of material retained is proportional to the amount learned (Dietrick, 1960; Verner and Dickinson, 1967).

Discussion

For most of the training objectives the training directors believed that about half of the training methods listed were effective and the other half not very effective for the training objective stated. Furthermore, the training methods considered effective for one objective were usually considered ineffective for another objective. This seems to indicate that the training directors are properly discriminating in their evaluations of the various alternative training methods. The training directors differ most from the research results in their ratings of effectiveness for the lecture method for various training objectives. In general the research shows that the lecture method has more effectiveness for acquiring knowledge, and for participant acceptance, than the training directors believe it has. It is not known why such a negative attitude toward the lecture method exists. Among reasons suggested for this bias against different forms of the lecture are: the current emphasis on "participation," the fact that nonspecialists can use the lecture method, but not other methods, the downgrading of the lecture method by advocates of other approaches, or unsatisfactory personal experiences with the lecture approach.

The training directors may err somewhat too much toward the positive side in the evaluations of programmed instruction. While it is an effective training method, it does not seem to be as superior as the training directors believe it is. (Nash, et al., 1971)

With respect to particular training objectives the training directors seem to be most different from the research on participant acceptance. The evidence to date certainly would indicate that the conference or discussion method, and the business games are not rated as high by participants as by the training directors. Also the lecture, conventional and TV lectures, and sensitivity training are rated higher than the training directors indicate.

The review of the literature reveals great gaps in knowledge about the effectiveness of various training methods. While a considerable amount of research has been conducted on sensitivity training, the conventional and TV lecture, and conference methods, little research has been conducted on the case study method, the business game and role playing. In addition, much more research needs to be focused on the personal and situational factors which moderate the effectiveness of alternative training methods.

In carrying out new research studies it is important that the alternative training methods being compared are subjected to a fair evaluation. As indicated previously, we and others, have noticed in several studies that although control groups were used and before and after measures were taken, fair comparisons were not always made between the alternative training methods studied.

References

Anderson, R. C. Learning in discussions: A resume of the authoritarian-democratic study. *Harvard Educational Review,* 1959, 29, 201-215.

Andrew, G. A study of the effectiveness of a workshop method for mental health education. *Mental Hygiene,* 1954, 38, 267-278.

Bolda, R. A. and Lawshe, C. H. Evaluation of role playing. *Personnel Administration,* 1962, 25, 40-42.

Bond, B. W. The group discussion-decision approach—An appraisal of its use in health education. *Dissertation Abstracts,* 1956, 16, 903.

Boyd, J. B. and Ellis, J. D. *Findings of research into senior management seminars.* Toronto: The Hydro-Electric Power Commission of Toronto, 1962. Cited by J. P. Campbell and M. D. Dunnette. Effectiveness of T-group experiences in managerial training and development. *Psychological Bulletin,* 1968, 70, 73-104.

Bunker, D. R. Individual applications of laboratory training. *Journal of Applied Behavioral Science,* 1965, 1, 131-148.

Butler, E. D. An experimental study of the case method in teaching the social foundations of education. *Dissertation Abstracts,* 1967, 27, 2912.

Butler, J. L. A study of the effectiveness of lecture versus conference teaching techniques in adult education. *Dissertation Abstracts,* 1966, 26, 3712.

Buxton, C. E. *College teaching: A psychologist's view.* New York: Harcourt-Brace, 1956.

Campbell, J. P. and Dunnette, M. D. Effectiveness of T-group experiences in managerial training and development. *Psychological Bulletin,* 1968, 70, 73-104.

Carpenter, C. R. and Greenhill, L. *An investigation of closed circuit television for teaching university courses.* Instructional Television Project Report #2, University Park, Pennsylvania. Penn. State University, 1958.

Castore, G. F. Attitudes of students toward the case method of instruction in a human relations course. *Journal of Educational Research,* 1951, 45, 201-213.

Cohen, D., Whitmyre, J. W., and Funk, W. H. Effect of group cohesiveness and training upon creative thinking. *Journal of Applied Psychology,* 1960, 44, 319-322.

Culbertson, F. Modification of an emotionally held attitude through role playing. *Journal of Abnormal and Social Psychology,* 1957, 54, 230-233.

Dietrick, D. C. Review of research, in R. J. Hill, *A comparative study of lecture and discussion methods.* Pasadena, California: The Fund for Adult Education, 1960, pp. 90-118.

Dill, W. R. and Doppelt, N. The acquisition of experience in a complex management game. *Management Science,* 1963, 10, 30-46.

Festinger, L. and Carlsmith, J. Cognitive consequences of forced compliance. *Journal of Abnormal and Social Psychology,* 1959, 58, 203-210.

Filley, A. C. and Reighard, F. H. *A preliminary survey of training attitudes and needs among actual and potential attendees at management institute programs.* Madison: University of Wisconsin, 1962, cited in R. J. House, Managerial reactions to two methods of management training. Personnel Psychology, 1965, 18, 311-319.

Fox, W. M. A measure of the effectiveness of the case method in teaching human relations. *Personnel Administration,* 1963, 26, 53-57.

Guetzkow, H., Kelly, E. L. and McKeachie, W. J. An experimental comparison of recitation, discussion, and tutorial methods in college teaching. *Journal of Educational Psychology,* 1954, 45, 193-207.

Harris, C. W. (Ed.) *Encyclopedia of educational research.* New York: Macmillan, 1960.

Harvey, O. and Beverly, G. Some personality correlates of concept change through role playing. *Journal of Abnormal and Social Psychology,* 1961, 63, 125-130.

Hill, R. A. *A comparative study of lecture and discussion methods.* Pasadena, Calif.: The Fund for Adult Education, 1960.

House, R. J. An experiment in the use of management training standards. *Journal of The Academy of Management,* 1962, 5, 76-81.

House, R. J. Managerial reactions to two methods of management training. *Personnel Psychology*, 1965, 18, 311-319.

Hughes, J. L. Effects of changes in programmed text format and reduction in classroom time on achievement and attitudes of industrial trainees. *Journal of Programmed Instruction*, 1963, 1, 143-55.

Hughes, J. L. and McNamara, W. J. A comparative study of programmed and conventional instruction in industry. *Journal of Applied Psychology*, 1961, 45, 225-231.

Janis, I. and King, B. The influence of role playing on opinion change. *Journal of Abnormal and Social Psychology*, 1954, 49, 211-218.

Janis, I. and Mann, L. Effectiveness of emotional role-playing in modifying smoking habits and attitudes. *Journal of Experimental Research in Personality*, 1965, 1, 84-90.

King, B. and Janis, I. Comparison of the effectiveness of improvised vs. non-improvised role playing in producing opinion changes. *Human Relations*, 1956, 9, 177-186.

Klausmeier, H. J. *Learning and human abilities*. New York: Harper and Bros., 1961.

Kumata, H. *An inventory of instructional television research*. Ann Arbor, Michigan: Educational Television and Radio Center, 1956.

Kumata, H. A decade of teaching by television. In W. Schramm, (Ed.), *The impact of educational television*. Urbana: University of Illinois Press, 1960, 176-192.

Levine, J. and Butler, J. Lecture vs. group decision in changing behavior. *Journal of Applied Psychology*, 1952, 36, 29-33.

Lewin, A. Y. and Weber, R. L. Management game teams in education and organization research: An experiment on risk taking. *Academy of Management Journal*, 1969, 12, 49-58.

Lewin, K. Group decision and social change. In E. E. Maccoby, T. M. Newcombe, E. L. Hartley, (Eds.), *Readings in social psychology*. New York: Henry Holt and Company, 1958, pp. 197-211.

McKenney, J. L. An evaluation of a business game in an MBA curriculum. *The Journal of Business*, 1962, 35, 278-286.

Maier, N. R. F. and Solem, A. R. The contribution of the discussion leader to the quality of group thinking. *Human Relations*, 1952, 3, 155-174.

Maier, N. R. F. An experimental test of the effect of training on discussion leadership. *Human Relations*, 1953, 6, 161-173.

Maier, N. R. F. and Maier, R. A. An experimental test of the effects of "developmental" vs. "free" discussions on the quality of group decisions. *Journal of Applied Psychology*, 1957, 41, 320-323.

Maier, N. R. F. and Hoffman, L. R. Quality of first and second solutions in group problem solving. *Journal of Applied Psychology*, 1960, 44, 278-283. (a)

Maier, N. R. F. and Hoffman, L. R. Using trained "developmental" discussion leaders to improve further the quality of group decisions. *Journal of Applied Psychology*, 1960, 44, 247-251. (b)

Mann, J. H. and Mann, C. H. The importance of group tasks in producing group-member personality and behavior change. *Human Relations*, 1959, 221, 75-80.

Margulies, S. and Eigen, L. D. *Applied programmed instruction*. New York: John Wiley and Sons, 1962.

Miles, M. B. Changes during and following laboratory training: A clinical-experimental study. *Journal of Applied Behavioral Science*, 1965, 1, 215-242.

Nash, A. N., Muczyk, J. P., and Vettori, F. L. The relative practical effectiveness of programmed instruction. Personnel Psychology, 1971, 397-418.

Neidt, C. O. and Meredith, T. Changes in attitudes of learners when programmed instruction is interpolated between two conventional instruction experiences. *Journal of Applied Psychology*, 1966, 50, 130-137.

Parnes, S. J. and Meadow, A. Effects of brainstorming instructions on creative problem solving by trained and untrained subjects. *Journal of Educational Psychology*, 1959, 50, 171-176.

Raia, A. P. A study of the educational value of management games. *The Journal of Business*, 966, 39, 339-352.

Rowland, K. M., Gardner, D. M., and Nealey, S. M. Business gaming in education and research, in *Proceedings of the 13th Annual Midwest Management Conference Academy of Management*, Midwest Division, East Lansing, Michigan, April, 1970.

Schramm, W. *The research on programmed instruction: An annotated bibliography*. Stanford, Calif.: Institute for Communication Research, 1962. (a)

Schramm, W. What we know about learning from instructional television, in *Educational Television–The Next Ten Years*, Stanford: Stanford University Press, 1962, 52-74. (b)

Schutz, W. C. and Allen, V. L. The effects of a T-group laboratory on interpersonal behavior. *Journal of Applied Behavioral Science*, 1966, 2, 265-286.

Silber, M. B. A comparative study of three methods of effecting attitude change. *Dissertation Abstracts*, 1962, 22, 2488.

Smith, P. N. Attitude changes associated with training in human relations. *British Journal of Social and Clinical Psychology*, 1964, 3, 104-113.

Sodnovitch, J. M. and Pophorn, W. J. *Retention value of filmed science courses*. Kansas State College of Pittsburg, 1961.

Solem, A. R. Human relations training: Comparisons of case study and role playing. *Personnel Administration*, 1960, 23, 29-37.

Stovall, T. F. Lecture vs. discussion. *Phi Delta Kappan*, 1958, 39, 255-258.

Underwood, W. J. Evaluation of laboratory method training. *Training Directors Journal*, 1965, 19, 34-40.

U. S. War Department. *What the soldier thinks: A monthly digest of war department studies on the attitudes of American troops*. Army Services Forces, Morales Services Division, I, 1943, 13.

Valiquet, I. M. Contribution to the evaluation of a management development program. Unpublished master's thesis. Massachusetts Institute of Technology, 1964. Cited by J. P. Campbell and M. D. Dunnette. Effectiveness of T-group experiences in managerial training and development. *Psychological Bulletin*, 1968, 70, 73-104.

VanderMeer, A. W. *Relative effectiveness of exclusive film instruction, films plus study guides, and typical instructional methods. Progress Report #10*. Instructional Film Program. State College, Pennsylvania: Pennsylvania State College, 1948.

Van Schacck, H. Jr. Naturalistic role playing: A method of interview training for student personnel administrators. *Dissertation Abstracts*, 1957, 17, 801.

Verner, C. and Dickinson, G. The lecture, an analysis and review of research. *Adult Education*, 1967, 17, 85-100.

CHAPTER 5

Development Problems: The Individual's Career

One of the new emphases of the personnel administrator of the 1970s (see the Johnson reading in chap. 1) is consideration of the needs and desires of the individual when making job assignments. Along these same lines, the personnel manager must be able to project his or her human resource needs on a long-range basis. By examining the organization's needs for future manpower assignments, the personnel department can better help the new employee plan his career—not just his first job assignment.

More and more organizations are currently employing career development specialists to help new and older employees alike plan their future with the organization. While a training program (as described in chap. 4) is designed to help the employee adjust to the organization at a specific point in time, career development is on ongoing program which is designed to help the employee best serve himself and the organization during his working life.

Hall and Morgan present a model of career development which they recommend to the personnel administrator as a method of increasing a manager's commitment and improving the organizational climate. In addition to presenting an important theory of career development, Hall and Morgan describe how people at various stages in their careers react to their jobs and to others in the organization. Thus we see that managers who are attempting to resolve conflict or increase motivation among employees would do well to be responsive to the various career stage needs of employees.

Career Development and Planning

DOUGLAS T. HALL
MARILYN A. MORGAN

Organizations can only be as flexible, adaptive, and creative as the people they employ. People bring organizations to life. If organizations are to be effective, their people must perform effectively. Therefore, to improve the functioning of an organization, it is necessary to maximize the development and utilization of its human resources. This essay will explore one avenue for the improved utilization of human resources: career development and planning.[1]

Why are careers important? Isn't the career the employee's own business—a private matter? Not really. For one thing, a person's career experiences and outcomes affect his or her performance, absenteeism, work quality, and turnover, all of which mean plus or minus dollars to the organization. For another, careers are a target for implementing equal employment opportunity. For many managers, in fact, career development and affirmative action are synonymous. For a third thing, one's work career is a major input to overall quality of life. People now have greater mobility and personal freedom than in the past, making it easier to achieve career fulfillment, which in turn puts more pressure on a person's employer to provide satisfying career opportunities. And, finally, given a sluggish, slow-growth economy, career opportunities have become more limited, making career planning more important if the person's career goals are to be met.

We will address three issues involved in career development. First we will present some basic concepts: What is a career and what constitutes development? Next, we will look at careers in the context of organizations. Finally, we will describe actions—both individual and organizational—which can facilitate career development.

Human Development Processes in Organizations

The Career Success Cycle
  Let's start at the beginning—with the individual. Our basic assumption is that people seek rewards and positive reinforcement from their work. These rewards can be extrinsic, such as a pay raise or a pat on the back, or intrinsic, such as a feeling of worthwhile accomplishment. We will further assume that work behavior which is rewarded will tend to be repeated.

  Our third assumption is that whenever possible people attempt to increase their sense of self-esteem and avoid lowering their self-esteem. One way people can enhance their self-esteem is through the development of their competence, which is the ability to act successfully on one's environment (White, 1959).

  Lewin (1936) and Argyris (1964) have described the conditions under which effective task performance will lead to increased self-esteem. For example (1), if a woman sets a challenging goal for herself, and (2) the woman determines her own means of attaining that goal, and (3) if the goal is central to her self-concept, then she will experience *psychological success* upon attainment of that goal. This sense of personal success will lead to an

This article was prepared especially for this book.

increase in self-esteem. Since increased self-esteem is a powerful reinforcer, it will in turn lead to increased involvement in the task. This increased involvement will then lead the person to set additional goals in the same task area and to set higher levels of aspiration (Lewin, Dembo, Festinger, and Sears, 1944; Porter and Lawler, 1968). This "success cycle" is illustrated in figure 1.

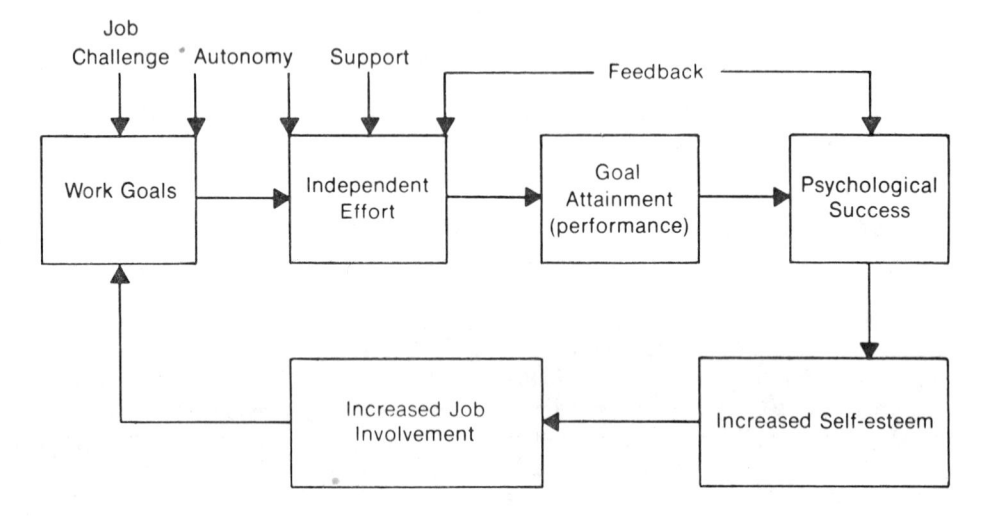

```
    Job
 Challenge   Autonomy   Support                  Feedback
     |          |          |            _____
     v          v          v           |                           |
  ┌──────────┐    ┌──────────────┐   ┌──────────────┐   ┌──────────────┐
  │          │    │              │   │     Goal     │   │              │
  │  Work    │───▶│ Independent  │──▶│  Attainment  │──▶│ Psychological│
  │  Goals   │    │    Effort    │   │ (performance)│   │   Success    │
  └──────────┘    └──────────────┘   └──────────────┘   └──────────────┘
       ▲                                                        │
       │                                                        ▼
  ┌──────────────┐                              ┌──────────────────────┐
  │ Increased Job│◀─────────────────────────────│ Increased Self-esteem│
  │ Involvement  │                              │                      │
  └──────────────┘                              └──────────────────────┘
```

Figure 1. The Career Success Cycle (Adapted from Hall, 1971.)

Simply put, this theory suggests that success breeds success. This cycle of events can be self-reinforcing and can be generalized beyond simple tasks to people's careers. When a man experiences a success cycle at work, he may develop great enthusiasm for the career area represented by the successful activity. He may talk about "really finding himself" or being "turned on" by his work.

Also shown in figure 1 are some conditions in the work environment which feed in to the career success cycle. A *challenging job* makes it possible for the person to set difficult work goals. *Autonomy* on the job enables the person to determine his or her own means of attaining work goals. *Support*, help, and coaching from the boss and peers can be helpful in solving problems and maintaining work motivation. *Feedback*—information about how close the person is to attaining his or her work goals—is important in two ways. First, it helps the person direct his or her effort more effectively to improve performance. Second, it helps the person evaluate or confirm the level of performance that has been achieved. Unfortunately, in many jobs, performance standards are unclear and ambiguous, so that the person may not always know just what level of success has been attained unless external feedback is provided.

Research conducted at the General Electric Company illustrates how the career success cycle operates. In work planning and review sessions, employees who were given the most difficult goals (as opposed to either impossible or easy ones) showed the greatest gains in performance in later months (Stedry and Kay, 1962). People who participated in work planning and review sessions showed more positive work attitudes than people who received traditional performance appraisal sessions (in which the focus was on evaluating the person's performance.) Key features of the work-planning sessions were self-appraisal, mutual goal setting, and collaborative problem solving on how to achieve future work goals (Kay and Hastman, 1966). Thus, in these GE studies, work performance and attitudes became more positive under two conditions necessary for psychological success: setting challenging self-relevant work goals, and independent effort in attaining work goals.

It appears that the success cycle is more likely to be operative when there is a certain level of support, feedback, and autonomy in the climate of the organization. In a study of Roman Catholic parish priests, Hall and Schneider (1973) found that for priests who had high levels of autonomy and support (professional specialists), work satisfaction was related to intrinsic work satisfaction, which was in turn related to self-esteem. For people with low autonomy, the cycle appeared to be "short-circuited," and the person's self-esteem was unrelated to job attitudes. Apparently, a person's psychological reaction to a low-autonomy job is not to become less involved, but to insulate his or her self-esteem from low job satisfaction. A study of students similarly found that the success cycle "works" better in an organization with high levels of support than in a lower-support organization (Hall and Hall, in press). Further evidence for the existence of the success cycle has been found among AT&T employees (Hall and Nougaim, 1968; Bray, Campbell, and Grant, 1974), students playing an executive simulation (Hall and Foster, 1977) and among operating employees in a government agency (Goodale, Hall, and Rabinowitz, 1976).

If a person insulates his or her self-esteem from the frustrations of an unchallenging job, what the the long-term effects of this adaptive and coping behavior? In the study of Roman Catholic priests referred to earlier, Hall and Schneider (1973) found that it was necessary for a man to spend 22 years as an assistant pastor (a job with extremely low autonomy and challenge) before becoming a pastor (a job with the opposite characteristics). Among pastors, work satisfaction was less related to work challenge and use of skills than it was for assistant pastors. It appears, then, that when people are deprived of opportunities for psychological success in an organization over many years, they may lose much of their desire to utilize conditions for psychological success when challenging work is finally made available. Thus, peoples' work abilities operate much like physical abilities: If you don't use them, you lose them.

Career Stages: Changing Needs and Values
What Are Stages? Stages in human development are rather predictable, often stressful and trying (for the individual as well as others), and marked by potential for failure if mishandled.

A stage is a period of time in a person's life characterized by distinctive developmental tasks, concerns, needs, values, and activities. A stage is generally separated from the previous and subsequent stages by a role transition or status passage, and successful mastery of the developmental tasks at one stage is a necessary prerequisite to moving on to the following stage.

We tend to associate stages of development more with childhood than with adulthood. There are plenty of everyday terms available to describe life stages of children: "infancy," "childhood," "pre-teen," "adolescence," "high-schooler," "college student," and so forth. One reason for this is that there are more distinct statuses and status passages in childhood than in adulthood (starting grade school, becoming a teen-ager, getting a driver's license, graduating from high school, attaining legal age). The child's development is aided by the pacing which these clear passages provide.

The important passages and changes in adult life are harder to identify (Mills, 1970). Marriage and parenthood (and perhaps divorce) are often the last institutionalized role transitions a person moves through until retirement. Thus, the person must pace his or her development as an adult in terms of more subtle changes.

One guide for the pacing of adult development is the family and the life cycle of one's children. Since the passages of children are so clear, they can also serve to mark the parents'. In fact, an adult's development and social behavior may have more to do with the family life cycle than with his or her own age. As Cain has observed, "To be the father of a teen-age daughter elicits certain behavior patterns, whether the father be 30 or 70 years of age" (Cain, 1964, p. 289).

A second guide for pacing stages in adult development is the work career, which again may or may not be tied to age. As Hall has argued, "A lawyer or manager who is in the first permanent job following professional training (law school or business school) will probably be concerned about advancement and establishing a reputation among colleagues, whether he or she is 25 or 45" (Hall, 1976, p. 48). Let us examine the major career stages in some detail. (For an elaboration of the stages in adult development, the reader is referred to Gail Sheehy's [1974] *Passages*.)

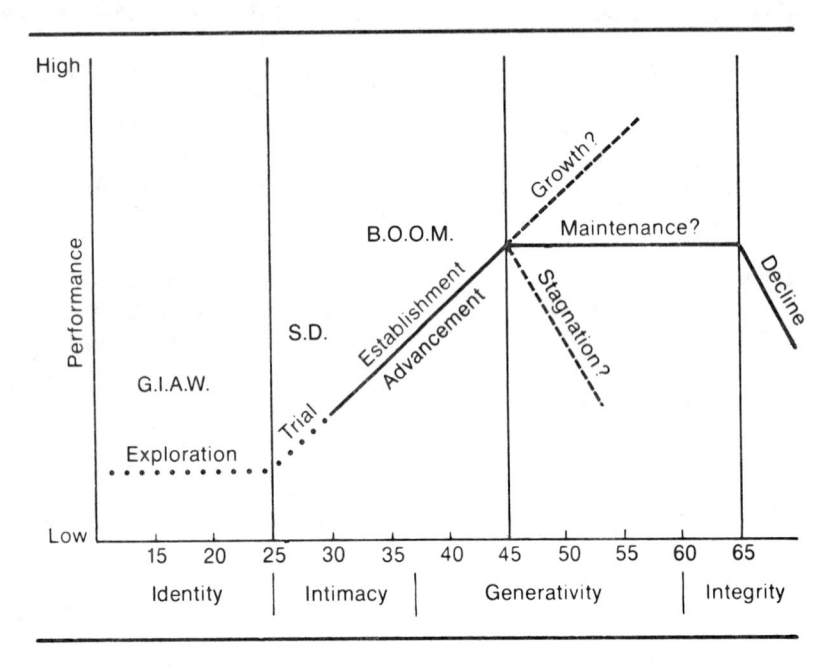

Figure 2. An Integrative Model of Career Stages (From Hall, 1976, p. 57.)

A Model of Career Stages

Because the passages which mark adult life stages are less clear-cut than those of children, there is less agreement about just what are the main adult stages. However, enough work in different areas points in similar directions so that a tentative composite model can be constructed (see fig. 2; this model draws from the work of Donald Super, Daniel Levinson and associates, Erik Erikson, and that of the first author).

Erik Erikson (1963) describes the adolescent exploratory period as a stage of identity formation. Through personal exploration at a time when the personal stakes are not too high, the person clarifies his or her self-concept and intentions for a future career. Levinson, Darrow, Klein, Levinson, and McKee (1974) refer to this period as "Getting Into the Adult World" (GIAW).

The most comprehensive statement of career stages comes from Donald Super (Super, 1957; Super and Bohn, 1970). Following a period of growth in childhood, the person goes through a period of *exploration,* in which self-examination, role tryouts, and occupational exploration take place. The final part of the exploration stage is a *trial* period, a time when a seemingly appropriate field has been selected, the person has found a beginning job, and is trying it out as a life work. This trial period may involve several job changes as the person attempts to find a good fit between his or her work interests, needs, and skills, on the one hand, and the demands and rewards of a particular job, on the other.

It is ironic that what is a trial period to the individual (a perfectly natural, necessary stage of human development) translates into high turnover for the organization. This high turnover occurs among new employees, and since turnover costs money (in testing, interviewing, training), organizations usually try to keep turnover as low as possible. To this extent, then, at this point in the employee's career, the goals of the organization and the developmental needs of the young employee are in conflict.

The next stage (between approximately ages 25 and 44) is termed *establishment* by Super:

> Having found an appropriate field, effort is put forth to make a permanent place in it. There may be some trial early in this stage, with consequent shifting, but establishment may begin without trial, especially in the professions (Super et al., 1957, pp. 40-41).

Once the person has settled into a particular job or field, establishment consists of achievement, performance, and advancement. Levinson et al. (1974) refer to the start of this establishment period as "Settling Down" (SD), and to the end of it, after one has severed ties with one's mentors, as "Becoming One's Own Man" (BOOM). In terms of general human development, Erikson calls this a stage of developing intimacy. By "intimacy," he means forming attachments and making commitments, to organizations and careers as well as to people (e.g., mates).

The forties mark the start of a *maintenance* stage, a mid-career plateau, according to Super: "Having made a place in the world of work, the concern is now to hold it. Little new ground is broken, but there is continuation along established lines" (Super et al., 1957, pp. 40-41). More recent writings, however, indicate that mid-career is not always the smooth plateau implied by Super. It can be a period of searching, reappraisal, depression, and redirection. Out of this mid-life "crisis" can come either continuing growth, or stagnation and early decline, depending on how successful the person is in confronting and overcoming the developmental tasks of this period. In a similar vein, Erikson describes mid-life as a time for generativity, a concern for producing something meaningful to be left for the next generation.

The passages into the trial and establishment periods are fairly easy to define. Trial often starts when the person leaves school and starts to work. Establishment begins after the person decides to stay in one career field or job. Mid-life is harder to pinpoint. (In fact, we don't even have a good descriptive term to use for it; we have to fall back on a chronological referent, "mid-life.")

Rather than one single transition point marking mid-life, it seems to be triggered by a complex set of factors (from Hall, 1976):

Awareness of advancing age and awareness of death (the "psychology of turning 40").

Awareness of physical aging.

Leveling off of career advancement; the person knows how many career goals have or will be attained.

Search for new life goals.

Marked change in family relationships (e.g., teenaged children, a divorce).

Change in work relationships (e.g., now *you* are the boss, the S.O.B.)

Growing sense of obsolescence (as Satchel Paige put it, "Never look back; someone may be gaining on you").

Reduction in perceived occupational mobility.

These changes occur gradually, in contrast to earlier abrupt transitions such as college graduation or becoming a parent. Therefore, the person may experience vague, generalized discomfort and restlessness which cannot be explained or tied down to one simple causal factor. In this sense, mid-life may be more difficult to deal with than other stages because of its ambiguity, which in turn can aggravate its frustrations. Especially lucid popular descriptions of mid-life experiences are found in Sheehy's (1974) *Passages,* Persig's (1974) *Zen and the Art of Motorcycle Maintenance,* and Heller's (1974) *Something Happened.*

The final stage is termed *decline* by Super. Reacting to the unattractiveness of this term, Super, who had just retired himself, commented, "You can call it what you want—the Golden Years, the Sunshine Years, whatever. But I'm there; take my word for it, it's decline!" (Super, 1973, personal communication).

Erikson refers to this final period with a more pleasant term, "integrity," which is the feeling that the person is satisfied with his life, choices, and actions; he sees his life as having been meaningful and is willing to leave it as is. In terms of an organizational work career, this final stage involves the transition from membership in the organization to retirement and a new set of activities.

Organizational Career Movement

Another way of anlayzing career development is by tracking people's movements through organizations. This is in contrast to the model of career stages shown in figure 2, which shows the career in terms of changes in the person.

Schein (1971) has developed a model of organizational career passages, based on the cone-like shape of an organization (shown in fig. 3). The three dimensions of the cone represent three types of moves the person may make in the organization:

Vertical—moving up or down represents changing one's rank or level in the organization.
Radial—moving more (or less) "inside" the system, becoming more (or less) central, part of the "inner circle," and acquiring more (or less) influence in the system.
Circumferential—transferring laterally to a different function, program, or product in the organization.

There are three types of boundaries which correspond to each type of movement.

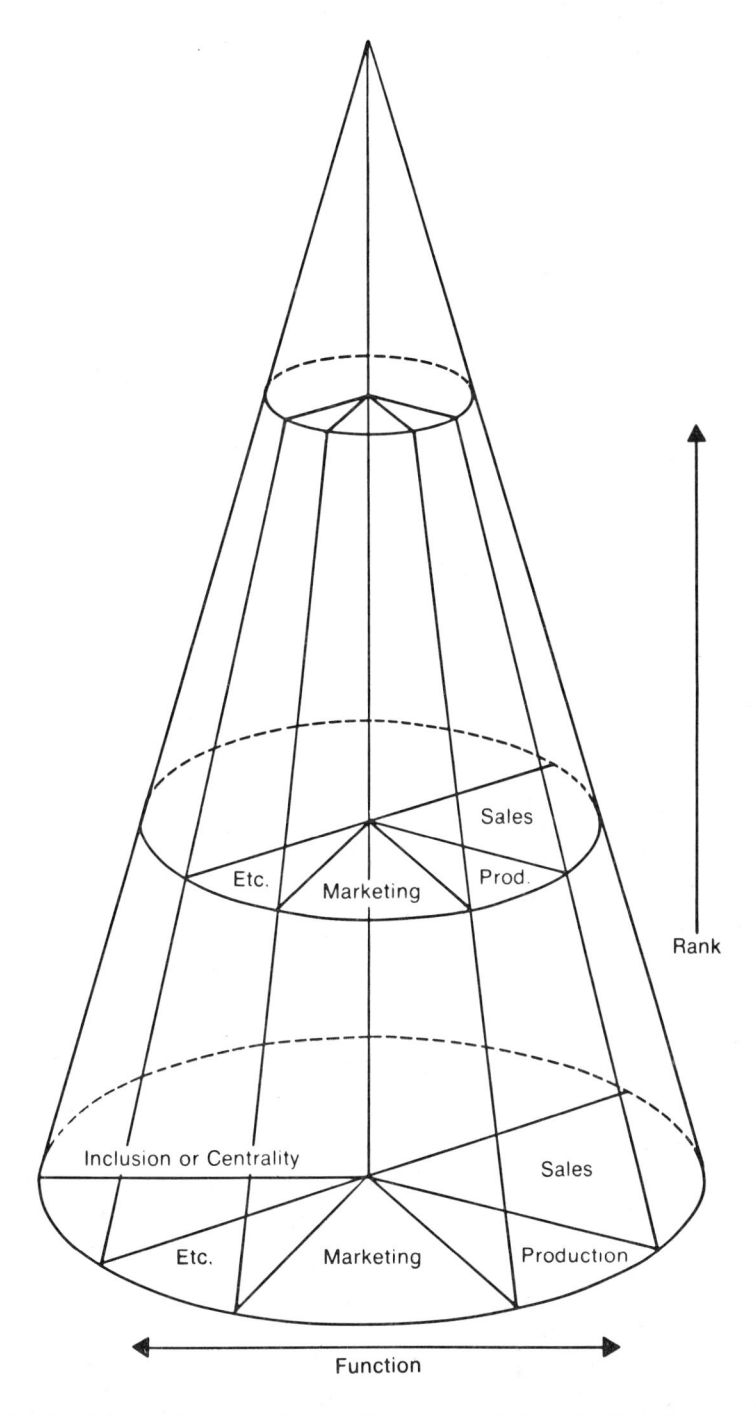

Figure 3. Schein's Model of an Organization (From Edgar H. Schein, "The Individual, the Organization, and the Career: A Conceptual Scheme," *Journal of Applied Behavioral Science*, 7 [1971].)

Hierarchical—these separate the hierarchical levels from each other.
Inclusion—these separate individuals or groups who differ in the degree of their centrality.
Functional or departmental—these separate departments, or different functional groupings from each other.

Individuals pass through different types of boundaries in different stages of their careers. In the exploration and trial periods, the person passes through several inclusion boundaries, moving in and out of several organizations, perhaps. Trial experiences may also contain many functional moves, as with trainees in a job-rotation development program. In the establishment/advancement stage, the person may have settled down into one function and is making hierarchical moves (e.g., promotions), as well as continuing to make inclusion moves (becoming more involved in and central to the organization). A mid-career plateau is just that, involving few changes or passages of any kind. And in decline, the main developmental task is to reverse the inclusion moves made earlier—that is, to move out of the organization.

These changes in organizational roles stimulate corresponding shifts in the identity and values of the job-holder and therefore are a strong means of organizational socialization:

> These changes which occur during the course of his career, as a result of adult socialization or acculturation, are changes in the nature and integration of [the person's] social selves. It is highly unlikely that he will change substantially in his basic character structure and his pattern of psychological defenses, but he may change drastically in his social selves in the sense of developing new attitudes and values, new competencies, new images of himself, and new ways of entering and conducting himself in social situations. As he faces new roles which bring new demands, it is from his repertory of attributes and skills that he constructs or reconstructs himself to meet these demands (Schein, 1971, pp. 308-9).

Now that we have an idea of what the person looks like over the course of a career, let's put the person in context—in the organization. How do organizational careers evolve?

People in Organizational Career Settings

For individuals, career planning means identifying major career goals and interim objectives so that one becomes more than a manager of his or her own career. Similarly, the organization needs to assume the responsibility for facilitating self-management of careers by assisting the individual in planning expected progress through the organization. It seems, then, that the implications of career development are best expressed in terms of the importance of the *management* of careers. Such a perspective allows us to view career planning or development as an ongoing process designed to help both the individual and the organization.

Two factors—*job characteristics* and *workforce composition*—are critical in career planning. First, the nature of the jobs through which the manager progresses is crucial. Since the elements in the model of psychological success are challenging goals, effort, performance, psychological success, self-esteem, and involvement, the job itself is an important "trigger" to a positive success cycle. Jobs should be designed and selected on the basis of the degree to which they provide the necessary factors to better assure psychological success.

Second, the nature of the current work force has an impact on career development. What happens when "nontraditional" workers occupy these enriched jobs in organizations? The current work force has been expanded in the last decade to include women and members of minority groups. With these new members selected, the organization must work to plan their advancement within organizational settings. Similarly, we are seeing increasing numbers of dual career couples. The problems and opportunities created by such situations are beginning to be explored by organizations.

The Nature of the Job

The Initial Job. The importance of the first assignment is often underestimated. Research in the area of early job challenge suggests that employees who receive especially challenging job assignments early in their careers do better in later jobs (e.g., Berlew and Hall, 1966; Bray, Campbell, and Grant, 1974).

Too often managers are afraid to give new employees any real responsibility until they have adjusted to the new work situation and have demonstrated their capabilities. Consequently, the initial job most often involves being assigned to a training program of some sort, working on a small or easy project, or serving as an "assistant." The problem with the "prove yourself before we give you any responsibility" philosophy is its self-fulfilling nature. How can an organization identify the capabilities and potential of a new employee if they begin by placing severe limits on the opportunities to perform? Most people can complete successfully a simple task or project. New employees can usually perform well as an assistant when they are told exactly what to do. It is difficult, however, to identify the limitations of individuals in such controlled assignments. Similarly, the individual is not provided the opportunity to "stretch" or use many of the skills developed in the years of schooling. He or she will often feel frustrated or bored by the routine nature of initial assignments. Thus, when organizations give low initial challenge and responsibility to new employees, they are actually "developing" low performance standards.

If initial career experiences have a continuing impact on the development of a person's career, then the entry-level job assignment is a crucial aspect of an employee's overall career planning effort. Organizations should analyze entry-level jobs in order to provide a meaningful, challenging experience for their new members. It is not easy to make these jobs more challenging, but such long-term payoffs as performance, commitment, and involvement make the effort worthwhile.

Some organizations believe in an initial period of job rotation. Rotation which sends an employee through a series of short-term, meaningless positions where he or she is nothing more than an observer of different parts of the organization will not provide the new hire with the necessary amounts of job challenge. However, it seems reasonable to expect that an entry-level assignment which relies heavily upon *planned job rotation* will be able to reconcile competing problems created by the dual needs of initial job challenge and training. Planned job rotations rely upon a series of meaningful job moves during the first 6 to 12 months of the employee's career. This set of jobs should be selected to encourage the development of skills essential to future job performance. Planned job rotations are an efficient means of providing the employee with a variety of meaningful experiences in a short time, as well as the opportunity to "self-test" working in different settings as part of a career development plan.

The Individual's Career Path

The sequence of jobs through which an employee moves during a career constitutes his or her individual *career path* or *job history*. Research on the initial job assignment demonstrates the effect the first job has on the employee's overall growth and development. Consider the combined impact of a sequence of jobs on overall success over a 30- to 40-year career. Consider, for example, the potential paths to the job of store manager in a large retailing organization. The individual who moves through a series of jobs which provide him with increasing amounts of various job dimensions (e.g., challenge, variety, and functional area) will be better prepared to handle the responsibilities of store management because of it.

The career path or job history of an employee has a potentially stronger effect on overall development than any other experience or set of experiences in his or her career. A challenging job provides opportunities for varied experiences and skill development. Such experiences contribute to successful performance in the new job situation and are readily transferable to future situations. After performing well on a job, the employee has a better chance of moving on to another job which will provide opportunity for additional growth and development. Since most jobs have different characteristics, a variety of them encourages the development and use of varied skills. Movement through a variety of jobs increases the chances of career success, since performing well on one job will improve the chance of being assigned to a more demanding one. This means that a carefully planned sequence of job moves should be undertaken in an effort to assure levels of career success.

If job moves are to be used for growth and developmental purposes, care must be taken to use the career-planning process effectively. The following steps are important:

Selection of a Target Job. The individual must consider his or her career aspirations within the organization. In some cases the target job is determined by the nature of the business. For example, in retailing, likely target jobs would be store manager and head buyer. Similarly, the target job is often determined by the nature of the profession. In the case of academia, for instance, the target job is most often full professor.

Identification of the Necessary Skills and Experiences. Although it is difficult to get accurate, objective information with which to identify the skills and experiences necessary to successfully perform the target job, job descriptions and analyses are probably the best sources of evaluative information. Individuals employed by organizations which have implemented the Hay System[2] have a definite advantage in this area since the characteristics of each job have been measured and can be used as an indication of skill requirements.

Identification of the Necessary Sequence of Jobs. The following guidelines are useful in considering the sequencing of planned job moves which will provide the required levels of experience and skill development:

1. Select jobs which provide changes which are large enough to "stretch" skills and capabilities, yet small enough to be manageable.
2. Consider lateral moves as well as promotions, since moves at the same level often provide opportunities for skill development (e.g., change in function).
3. Allow for enough time to master the job but not so long an assignment that the performance of the job becomes routine.

4. Consider jobs which complement or supplement, not those which duplicate previous experiences.

5. Provide alternative moves or sequences (i.e., a contingency plan), since it is unlikely that the normal demands of the organization will allow for all the scheduled moves exactly as planned.

The Nature of the Work Force: Nontraditional Employees
Women and Minorities. Five or so years ago a major organizational concern was to attract women and minorities into professional and managerial positions. The literature was full of cases describing the types of discriminatory practices common to most organizations. While there is still a concern for recruitment and selection, another issue is how best to assure the successful performance and advancement of women and minorities in organizational settings. The following comment from *Business Week* offers evidence of this problem.

> It took a decade of federal legislation, relentless agitation from the women's (and civil rights) movements, and seismic shifts in public opinion, but women (and minorities) are moving boldly into the mainstream of corporate management. The battle for equality in blue-collar and clerical jobs moved faster because bias was easier to prove. The far more complex struggle for equal status up the corporate ladder has taken longer and is far from over. But the big news is that women (and minorities) are making headway—slowly in the executive suite, faster at the lower rungs of middle management. (Nov. 24, 1975).

Career planning is recognized as an effective means of developing opportunities for minorities and women. Members of these groups need to plan their career moves very carefully in order to develop the necessary skills to assure successful performance in the more demanding jobs they will encounter as they move up the corporate ladder.

O'Leary (1974) identifies several factors which serve to inhibit the expression of upward occupational aspirations of women and could subsequently affect their overall career success: fear of failure, low self-esteem, sex role stereotypes, role conflicts, and the prevalence of the male managerial model. It is important that organizations consider these barriers to success in planning the career moves of women. Assignment to jobs which provide at least a minimal amount of support should be an important consideration. Support may take the form of good supervision, assignments which provide female peers or role models, and feedback on performance.

As with women's careers, careful career planning is important for the development of minorities. The challenge of integrating these employees into the workforce is an issue being addressed by most organizations. Hence, variables affecting the careers of women and minorities seem to be an important area for future research.

Dual Careers. Dual career couples are those in which both husband and wife pursue a full-time career. As more married women enter the work force, dual careers are becoming increasingly important factors for career management, because it is difficult to relocate one partner if the other is unable or unwilling to move. When both husband and wife have full-time careers, career flexibility decreases and planning becomes more crucial. The problem of dual-career families is becoming increasingly common among young employees and must be dealt with by organizations.

For example, a large manufacturing firm in the Midwest recently experienced the following effects of a dual-career situation. A very promising and also married young attorney had been working in its legal department for five years. Not only was he well respected in his own department but he had caught the attention of the company president and had been identified as one of several "high-potential" employees. During the couple's stay in the Midwest, the wife worked toward a Ph.D. in psychology. Upon receiving this degree she was offered an academic position in a prestigious university on the East Coast. Recognizing that such a position would be a very good way to start his wife's academic career, her husband requested a transfer to the eastern division of the firm. The head of the legal department and the president refused to consider the request. This attorney is now working for a competitor in the competitor's New York office and his wife is teaching at the Eastern university.

This example suggests that the biggest problem created by dual-career situations is job transfers. A transfer to another location means that the working spouse must relocate, too. If both husband and wife are employed by the same organization, both career moves are within the control of one organization. In the much more frequent situations where employment is by different organizations, there is the risk of either losing employees when one spouse is transferred or of being asked to arrange a transfer to the same location. An article in *Business Week* (Aug. 23, 1976) stated that working wives were the most critical factor in the unwillingness to move of male executives.

Similar dual-career issues are found in recruiting employees. It is sometimes difficult to attract a person to an organization if its location does not provide career opportunities for the spouse. Organizations are often required to recruit both husband and wife, or to help find a job for the spouse. The point is that the spouse's career opportunities increasingly affect the recruitment and advancement of today's employees. The issue, however, has not yet been realized by many organizations, but it seems destined to become a crucial organizational problem. Consideration of the spouse's career must be made in the career planning and development efforts or the organization runs the risk of losing many good employees.

Organizational Management of Careers

What, then, can organizations do to manage employees' careers more effectively? We will now examine this critical, practical issue.

Stage-specific training

Much training in organizations is done across the board with large groups of employees. It may be aimed at all people at a particular job level or to all people about to enter a given job. This is reasonable. It is also reasonable that people in a given career stage—or people about to enter a given stage—may also need training in how to deal with the developmental tasks of that stage. Unfortunately, this sort of stage-specific training is rarely done. What would such training entail?

Assessing Stages. First, it is necessary to have a way to identify who is at a given career stage. The time at which people move through various stages varies with the occupation and with the organization. In most organizations there is usually some commonly accepted age at which advancement starts to level off. This could be taken as the start of mid-career. The trial period is easier to identify—people at this point are usually new employees in their first year or two. Establishment/advancement would probably span the second or third year of employment through the start of mid-career. Decline could be defined in terms of when people in the organization begin thinking about and preparing for retirement, perhaps five years before.

Once the stages have been defined, training needs can be identified. These can be broken down into two areas: task needs (dealing with job activities) and emotional needs (covering the feelings associated with career changes.) These needs are summarized in table 1.

Trial Stage Needs. In the trial stage, the individual needs to be encouraged to spend some time in various job activities, but with enough time spent in each activity so that challenge and success can be experienced. Self-exploration, through career assessment and planning exercises, should also be encouraged. On the emotional side, the person should be pressed to begin making choices and settling in to an area of specialization. Even if the organization does not have a job-rotation training program, it would be a mistake to keep a young person in one function from the first day of employment without some opportunity to try some other areas.

Advancement Needs. In the establishment/advancement stage, job challenge is the critical need. The person needs to develop competence in some area of specialization. Technical training programs are especially important in this stage. A special effort should be made to develop creativity and innovation, since these qualities are usually at their peak in the early career years. After the person has developed specialized skills, the organization should avoid the temptation to keep the person in this area for too long. (Such a course is tempting because it would be a way of reaping a high return on the company's investments in the person's training, as, for example, when managers—especially sales managers—"capture" a good person and won't let that person advance.) After three to five years, the person should be moved into a new specialty, to prevent overspecialization and early absolescence. On the emotional side, the advancing person needs to deal with strong feelings of rivalry and competition with peers. There may also be concerns about failure and about career-family conflicts which will call for opportunities to discuss them and emotional support from someone in the organization. Autonomy will be necessary to permit feelings of individual achievement and psychological success. An occasional "rap group" dealing with the stresses and conflict of expending high energy on success can be a beneficial way of dealing with these feelings.

Mid-career Needs. In mid-career, an individual's skills may need some updating if the person has not been rotated through new specialties at three- to five-year intervals earlier in the career. At this career point the person is doing less technical work and more administrative work. Harry Levinson (1969) posits that individuals should shift from being "quarterbacks" to "coaches" at this stage, and this calls for advanced training in human relations, communication, and management skills. Continued job rotation is still important to keep the person fresh and always learning. This is also a time when the person begins to identify more with the organization and can see his or her own work better in relation to the total organization's purposes. Seminars on company history, policies, and goals may be, ironically, better received by mid-career employees than by new employees, who usually get such material in their initial orientation sessions.

The emotional side of mid-career calls for an opportunity to talk with others about the feelings of mid-life (anguish, re-examination of goals, limited time, restlessness, etc.). It

TABLE 1
Training Needs Within Career Stages

Stage	Task Needs	Emotional Needs
Trial	1. Varied job activities	1. Make preliminary job choices
	2. Self-exploration	2. Settling down
Establishment/ Advancement	1. Job challenge	1. Deal with rivalry and competition; face failures
	2. Develop competence in a specialty area	2. Deal with work-family conflicts
	3. Develop creativity and innovation	3. Support
	4. Rotate into new area after 3-5 years	4. Autonomy
Mid-career	1. Technical updating	1. Express feelings about mid-life
	2. Develop skills in training and coaching others (younger employees)	2. Reorganize thinking about self in relation to work, family, community
	3. Rotation into new job requiring new skills	3. Reduce self-indulgence and competitiveness
	4. Develop broader view of work and own role in organization	
Late career	1. Plan for retirement	1. Support and counseling to see one's work as a platform for others
	2. Shift from power role to one of consultation and guidance	2. Develop sense of identity in extraorganizational activities
	3. Identify and develop successors	
	4. Begin activities outside the organization	

(Adapted from Hall, 1976, p. 60.)

also helps to encourage or help employees to do some life planning and re-relate their work commitments to family, community, and other involvements. Since advancement is leveling off, there may be need to redirect competitive energies, perhaps into the vicarious success of aiding subordinates' careers.

Late Career Needs. In the decline stage, it is important to begin planning for retirement, since good planning leads to a good transition. This means, in a sense, starting the career cycle again, but now in the area of retirement activities (exploration, trial, establishment). After all, there is a *retirement career* to be planned for and managed, as well as the remaining work career. At the same time, the person must make arrangements to terminate the activities and responsibilities of the work career. This demands skills in identifying and developing successors, gradually involving successors in job activities and decisions. As the person plays a less active role in the organization, he or she can become more available as a source of consultation and organizational wisdom.

On the emotional side, there is a need to see how one's work has provided a foundation for the work of future generations of employees. There is a need to come to terms with one's overall work career and with the fact that it is ending. It is also important for the person to develop relationships and an identity outside the organization so that the end of employment is not seen as the end of his or her identity.

Why should an organization be concerned about the employee's planning for retirement? First, the late-career person can be a valuable resource in the development of younger employees *if* he has been well-treated by the organization and is thus motivated to be helpful. Furthermore, younger employees are more likely to make commitments of time, energy, and involvement to the organization if they see that the organization maintains its interest in the development of employees through their later career stages (i.e., "If the organization treats pre-retirement employees well now, they'll probably treat me well, too").

Changing the Work Environment

Some of the stage-specific training we have just discussed can be done off the job in training facilities. As mentioned earlier, however, there is much potential for career-development training inherent in the nature of the work environment. Let us quickly run down the different facets of the work environment (employee, job itself, boss, organization structure, and personnel policies) to see how it can be redesigned to foster employee career growth.[3]

Entry: Changing Employee Inputs. Young people just out of school and working on their first jobs often experience "reality shock"—that is, a job which falls far short of their expectations for experiences such as challenge, responsibility, autonomy, and feedback. There are two ways to reduce this expectation versus reality gap: either improve the experience, or modify the expectations. One way to do the latter is for organizations to use *realistic job previews* (RJPs) in recruiting (Wanous, 1975). An RJP gives the negative features of a job as well as its positive ones (e.g., a telephone operator's job has low variety and close supervision as well as good pay and security). Realistic job previews seem to result in subsequent lower turnover, and they do not appear to hurt recruiting success (Wanous, 1975).

Another way of providing more realistic job orientations is to give students more training in job-related skills in educational systems, such as business and professional schools. Better links between educators and employers (e.g., through job internships, field projects, executive-in-residence programs) will help on this score, too.

Finally, better selection methods can be used by employees to get a better fit between employee and job. This does not necessarily mean luring the brightest or best-educated candidates. One manufacturing firm in Connecticut sharply reduced its reject rate and employee turnover when it started hiring people in the second quartile—an ability level which fit the routine assembly jobs much better than hiring the highest-ability applicants.

Development Through the Job Itself. We have already heard about challenging initial jobs and career pathing as a way of building "stretching" experiences into the work environment. Employees should have several years to develop specialized competencies, but they should then be rotated into new activities every few years to prevent obsolescence. New job activities can force learning much more effectively than a whole string of university "up-date" courses.

Peer stimulation can be an excellent means of learning skills and positive work attitudes. Assigning the new employee to a work group or team of outstanding performers will pay dividends.

One of the largest areas of undeveloped potential for employee growth is feedback and performance appraisal. Feedback is essential in any kind of performance, and it is unfortunate that most of us "fly blind" on our jobs. We usually have to "read in" meaning to every subtle evaluative cue we receive from our bosses, and these inferences may be totally invalid. (That gruff "Hello!" this morning may have said more about his fight at home than about the report you turned in yesterday.) A simple, well-planned performance appraisal process (with a superior trained in how to do it) can be of the utmost value to the individual and the organization.

Finally, when you get good performance from an employee, don't let it pass unnoticed. As the work of many researchers shows, one of the simplest ways to increase the likelihood of occurrence of a behavior is to positively reinforce it. A word of recognition, a letter of congratulation, a pat on the back, a bonus—these are all ways to reward good performance and to encourage the performer to repeat it. Most of the time managers fail to respond to either good or poor performance—which in effect rewards poor performance and negatively reinforces good performance.

Changing the Superior's Role. To involve the boss in career development, give her or him the skills necessary to be a good career developer. Skills such as performance appraisal, feedback, counseling, job design, and career plotting are fairly easy to develop in two- or three-day training sessions. One of the big reasons managers don't do more about career development is that they lack the skills for it.

Another way to utilize the boss for employee development is to assign new employees to outstanding managers who will set high standards of expected performance. Research has shown that people tend to perform at whatever level is expected (Livingston, 1969), which casts the manager in the role of organizational Pygmalion. Often new employees are assigned to bosses on a random basis; more care in the job assignment process costs little and has a high payoff.

Changing Organization Structures. The design of the organization shows up in the "fingerprints" it puts on people. A functional organization produces (possibly narrow) functional specialists. A product organization trains people who are loyal to their product (perhaps at the expense of concern for the firm's other products). A matrix structure (in which people work on cross-functional product teams) can combine the best of both orientations. It also offers two directions for moving people—to a new product but in the same function, or vice versa—which makes a person branch out a bit while still staying to some extent in familiar territory.

One of the reasons more effort is not placed on employee development is that this activity is often not rewarded. And it is not rewarded because it is hard to measure. Human-resource accounting is a way of measuring an organization's investments in people and the resulting returns. Therefore, as more companies develop human-resource information systems, this change can make the payoff to a manager for employee development more tangible (Hall, Alexander, Goodale, and Livingstone, 1976).

A third area of activity for many organizations is career-planning services. These activities, designed specifically to stimulate career development, can range from very employee-oriented life planning (as at Continental Illinois Bank and The Travelers Insurance Companies, for example) through assessment center feedback (3M Company) to a combination of personal counseling, job design, and training bosses in career developing skills (AT&T). The range of these programs is wide, but though much activity is taking place, there is precious little evaluative research to help us separate the good from the godawful.

Changing Personnel Policies. The final aspect of the work environment which can be altered to stimulate career development is the area of personnel policies.[4] For example, a policy of rotating managers through "people departments," such as personnel or organization development, can do as much to heighten line managers' sensitivity to employee development needs as can years of information campaigns. A policy of life-long job rotation, as we have said before, can counteract obsolescence and maintain employee flexibility.

Another policy which can aid development is lateral and downward job transfers. Lateral interfunctional transfers can be a way of developing new skills without promoting the person. (If economic and organizational growth slows, promotion opportunities will diminish accordingly, and other movement possibilities must be explored.)

More controversial is the idea of downward transfers. The option of moving employees down (even if only temporarily) immensely increases an organization's degrees of freedom. Two conditions are important in reducing an outcry against demotions: (1) a guarantee that no one will take a pay cut; and (2) a guarantee that anyone who is moved down will never lose his or her job (a form of organizational tenure). One organization started a downward transfer policy by deliberately moving down two key and obviously successful vice presidents in order to counter the belief that demotion means failure. The two VPs were assigned temporarily to "hot spots" in the organization, where they promptly shaped up ailing operations. The change also had the side effect of improving communications up to the other vice presidents. The antidemotion norm is a tough one to buck, however, and in many organizations the benefits will not be worth the cost. However, it is worth thinking the "unthinkable" and at least considering the possibility of downward moves. Because of the ambiguity in the structure of most organizations, whether a particular move is a promotion or a demotion is often the subject of debate anyway.

One way to reduce the risks of promotions or crossfunctional lateral moves is through fallback positions. A fallback position is identified before the transfer is made, and the organization and the employee agree in advance that if the transfer or promotion does not work out, the person will move to the fallback position with no stigma. This represents an acceptance by the organization that the transfer or promotion entails some risk, and that the company is prepared to share in the risk and help resolve any resulting problems. Companies such as Heublein, Procter and Gamble, Continental Can, and Lehman Brothers have used fallback positions *(Business Week,* Sept. 28, 1974).

Another personnel innovation is organizational tenure. Using the university as a model, one Pennsylvania manufacturing company introduced a policy of evaluating new employees in two ways after their probationary periods. First, the standard retain-or-terminate decision was made. Then company management asked the question, "If we had to lay off 20 percent of our workforce because of economic setbacks, would this be a person we would let go (on the basis of performance)?" If the answer was yes, the person would still be offered the job, but feedback about being in the lowest 20 percent would be given. (Many of the low 20 percent employees stayed on, and the feedback improved performance for some, in which case the "contract" was revised.) The top 80 percent employees also received feedback and were given a form of tenure in the organization. The active ingredient in this system, of course, is the feedback, which is probably more important than the tenure itself.

A final important personnel policy area relates to the dual-career employee. As more women take up work careers (and assuming men continue to do so), and as long as men and women marry and/or live together, there will be increasing numbers of dual-career employees in organizations. If an organization sees it as the couple's responsibility to cope with the stresses of dual-career responsibilities, that organization runs the risk of losing—or failing to hire—talented, career-involved employees. A small interview survey conducted by Alison Martier, covering approximately 30 organizations in the Chicago area, identified the following policies for accommodating dual-career employees:

1. Recognition of the existence of problems in dual careers.
2. Help with relocation in the case of transfer of a spouse (or helping the spouse relocate if your employee is being transferred).
3. Flexible working hours (to facilitate child care).
4. Initiation of counseling for dual-career employees.
5. Family day-care centers.
6. Improved career planning and counseling.
7. A change in antinepotism rules (to make it easier for two members of the same family to work for the organization or perhaps the same unit in the organization.)

These are preliminary approaches because we are at a preliminary stage in the recognition

TABLE 2.
Organizational Actions for Facilitating Career Development
(Adapted from Hall, 1976, p. 177).

Entry: Changing Employee Inputs
   1. Better links between school and work.
   2. Training students in job-related skills.
   3. Realistic job previews in recruiting.
   4. Better selection for person-job fit.

Development Through the Job
   1. Challenging initial jobs.
   2. Periodic job rotation.
   3. Colleague stimulation.
   4. Frequent feedback and performance review.
   5. Rewarding good performance.

Changing the Boss's Role
   1. Make bosses career developers.
   2. Train managers in job design and career planning.
   3. Reward managers for employee development.

Changing Organizational Structures
   1. Matrix organization structures.
   2. Accounting for human resources.
   3. Career planning services.

Changing Personnel Policies
   1. Rotation of managers through "people departments."
   2. Life-long job rotation.
   3. Downward and lateral transfers.
   4. Tenure.
   5. Fallback positions for promoted employees.
   6. Support for dual-career employees.

of dual-career problems. As dual-career employees who are now relatively young and low in power in most organizations rise to higher levels, more pressure for solutions will be generated. For this reason, the dual-career issue has been called an "organizational time bomb" (Hall and Hall, 1976).

Planning for Your Own Career

A summary of the ideas presented in the preceding section is given in table 2. This section is based upon the work of Schein (1964), Hall (1976) and others. We'll be talking about *typical career experiences,* but of course each person's career is unique, so don't panic if you don't like what you read here. We want to discuss your expectations, the company's expectations, how its members may perceive you, what you may experience in your first job, and how you can help yourself.

Your Expectations
If you're typical, from your first job you'll probably want opportunities for advancement, responsibility, interesting, meaningful and challenging work, a chance to use your skills and educational training, security, and good pay. (In a Doonesbury cartoon, when Mark told his father that he was expecting these qualities in his first job, his father's response was, "In short, you have no intention of getting a job!")

What The Company Will Expect of You
The company will expect you to have *competence* to get a job done—to identify problems and see them through to solutions. It will also expect you to *accept "organizational realities,"* that is, the need for stability and survival, informal power relationships, recognition of group loyalties, office politics, and the like. You will be expected to *generate and sell ideas.* This involves a wide range of human relations skills, such as translating technical solutions into practical, understandable terms, patiently overcoming resistance to change, and the ability to influence others. *Loyalty and commitment* may be important, especially in organizations with strong promotion-from-within policies. This loyalty may involve some sacrifice of parts of your personal life. *Personal integrity and strength* will also be highly valued as shown by your ability to stick to your own point of view without being a rebel, yet knowing how to compromise when necessary. Finally, the organization will look for your *ability to grow,* to assume responsibility and learn from mistakes (mistakes are expected, but not repeated mistakes).

How The Company Will Perceive You
How you are perceived naturally depends a lot on both you and the organization. The company may see you as overambitious and unrealistic in your expectations. You may seem too theoretical, too idealistic, or too naive and immature. You will probably lack experience. It may see you as too security-conscious and unwilling to take risks. You may have underdeveloped interpersonal skills, and you may have trouble selling your ideas. Overall, your boss and the organization may see you as a potentially *useful* resource, who must be broken in first ("house broken" in the words of some managers).

What You Will Experience
The most common complaint of new graudates is *lack of challenge*—that is, under-

utilization of your skills and training. (But remember: You're being trained for managerial jobs 5 to 15 years off, not just for the first assignment). Turnover is extremely high in the first year of employment, often around 50 percent. Because the actual job is so different from what you expected, you may experience reality shock.

To compound these problems, you may threaten your boss. Your starting pay may be uncomfortably close to his or hers, yet you may be young enough to be your boss' daughter or son. And you'll be promoted above your present boss in a few years. And your boss may be a bit obsolete, threatened by your more recent skills and knowledge. And your boss may be going through a "mid-career crisis," and so forth.

You may get little or no feedback on your performance. You may have trouble creating your own challenges. And your company training may be inadequate (in many companies, training is just a sink-or-swim process).

What You Can Do

The organization you work for and chance events have a lot of control over your career, but that control is not absolute. *Develop some career goals* and *do some career planning*. Many universities have counseling centers which provide excellent career-planning services. A useful guide for self-management of careers is *What Color is Your Parachute?* by R. N. Bolles (1974).

Career maturity involves the following career competencies: self-appraisal, obtaining occupational information, problem-solving, planning, and choosing goals. Try to develop these skills.

Try to get realistic information about any organizations from whom you have offers. Research has shown that people with good information (positive and negative) about the company are more satisfied and are less likely to quit.

If you have a choice of offers, go for the most challenging job. One of the best predictors of career success is the amount of challenge in your first job. In choosing your first job, challenge and potential for career growth should be more important than shorter-term considerations such as salary or location. If you are stretched and pushed toward excellence in your first job, you will be more successful later, and will have plenty of later offers with good salaries and locations.

Develop your communications and human relations skills. The most critical part of your job will be working with people, even if you are doing technical work.

Don't become overspecialized. It may be flattering to become the world's greatest expert on inflation accounting, but what happens to you when prices stabilize? To force yourself to keep learning and growing, move into a new area every three to five years. The time to begin fighting career obsolescence is now, when that obsolescence could be starting.

Finally, reassess your career periodically. Ask where you're headed and where you want to be, because the only way to get there from here, is to know where "there" is.

Notes

1. For further discussion of the issues raised in this essay, see D. T. Hall, *Careers in Organizations* (Pacific Palisades, Calif.: Goodyear Publishing Co., 1976), and M. A. Morgan, "The Relative Impact of Job Histories on Career Outcome Variables," unpublished Ph.D. dissertation, Northwestern University, 1977.

The material in this essay was prepared under Grant No. 91-17-76-18 from the Manpower

Administration, U.S. Department of Labor, under the authority of Title III, Part B, of the Comprehensive Employment and Training Act of 1973. Points of view or opinions stated in this essay do not necessarily represent the official position or policy of the Department of Labor.

2. The Hay System is a method of evaluating jobs by relying on factors that are common to all jobs in varying degrees. The system provides useful information about certain characteristics of each job by considering factors such as accountability, problem-solving opportunities, and technical skill requirements, and compares jobs to determine which contain more of these factors than others.

3. This material is based on Hall (1976), pp. 151-65.

4. More detail on personnel policies to promote career development can be found in Hall and Hall (1976).

References

Argyris, C. *Integrating the Individual and the Organization.* New York: Wiley, 1964.

Berlew, D. E. and Hall, D. T. The socialization of managers: Effects of expectations on performance. *Administrative Science Quarterly,* 1966, *11,* 207-223.

Bolles, R. N. *What Color is Your Parachute? A Practical Manual for Job-Hunters and Career Changers.* Berkeley, Calif.: Ten Speed Press, 1974.

Bray, D. W., Campbell, R. J. and Grant, D. L. *Formative Years in Business: A Long Term AT&T Study of Managerial Lives.* New York: Wiley, 1974.

Cain, L. D., Jr. Life course and social structure. In R. Faris (ed.), *Handbook of Modern Sociology.* Chicago: Rand McNally, 1964.

Erikson, E. H. *Childhood and Society.* New York: Norton, 1963.

Goodale, J. G., Hall, D. T., and Rabinowitz, S. A test of an integrative model of job involvement. Working paper, York University, 1976.

Hall, D. T. A theoretical model of career subidentity development in organizational settings. *Organizational Behavior and Human Performance,* 1971, *6,* 50-76.

Hall, D. T. *Careers in Organizations.* Pacific Palisades, Calif.: Goodyear, 1976.

Hall, D. T. and Foster, L. W. Effects of goals, performance, and psychological success upon attitudes toward self, task, and career, *Academy of Management Journal,* 1977, in press.

Hall, D. T. and Hall, F. S. What's new in career management? *Organizational Dynamics,* 1976.

Hall, D. T. and Hall, F. S. The relationship between goals, performance, success, self-image, and involvement under different organization climates. *Journal of Vocational Behavior,* 1976, in press.

Hall, D. T., and Nougaim, K. E. An examination of Maslow's need hierarchy in an organizational setting. *Organizational Behavior and Human Performance.* 1968, *3,* 12-35.

Hall, D. T. and Schneider, B. *Organizational Climates and Careers: The Working Lives of Priests.* New York: Seminar (Academic) Press, 1973.

Hall, D. T., Alexander, M. O., Goodale, J. G., and Livingstone, J. L. How to make personnel decisions more productive. *Personnel,* 1976, *53,* 10-20.

Heller, J. *Something Happened.* New York: Ballantine Books, 1974.

Kay, E. and Hastman, R. *An Evaluation of Work Planning and Goal-Setting Discussions.* Crotonville, New York: Behavioral Research Service, General Electric Company, 1966.

Levinson, D. J., Darrow, C., Klein, E., Levinson, M., and McKee, B. The psychological development of men in early adulthood and the mid-life transition. In D. F. Hicks, A. Thomas, and M. Roff (eds.), *Life History Research in Psychopathology,* Vol. 3. Minneapolis: University of Minnesota Press, 1974.

Levinson, H. On being a middle-aged manager. *Harvard Business Review,* 1969, *47,* 51-60.

Lewin, K. The psychology of success and failure. *Occupations,* 1936, *14,* 926-930.

Lewin, K., Dembo, T., Festinger, L., and Sears, P. Level of aspiration. In J. Mc V. Hunt (ed.), *Personality and Behavior Disorders.* New York: Ronald Press, 1944.

Livingston, J. S. Pygmalion in management. *Harvard Business Review,* 1969, *47,* 81-89.

Managers move more but enjoy it less. *Business Week,* August 23, 1976, 19-20.

Mills, E. W. Career development in middle life. In W. Bartlett (ed.), *Evolving Religious Careers.* Washington, D. C.: Center for Applied Research in the Apostolate, 1970.

O'Leary, V. E. Some attitudinal barriers to occupational aspirations in women. *Psychological Bulletin,* 1974, *81,* 809-826.

Persig, R. M. *Zen and the Art of Motorcycle Maintenance: An Inquiry into Values.* New York: Bantam Books, 1974.

Porter, L. W. and Lawler, E. E., III. *Managerial Attitudes and Performance.* New York: Irwin-Dorsey 1968.

Schein, E. H. How to break in the college graduate. *Harvard Business Review,* 1964, *42,* 68-76.

Schein, E. H. The individual, the organization, and the career: A conceptual scheme. *Journal of Applied Behavioral Science,* 1971, *7,* 401-426.

Sheehy, G. *Passages: Predictable Crises of Adult Life.* New York: E. P. Dutton, 1974.

Stedry, A. and Kay, E. *The Effects of Goal Difficulty on Performance.* Lynn, Mass.: Behavioral Research Service, General Electric Company, 1962.

Super, D. E. *The Psychology of Careers.* New York: Harper & Row, 1957.

Super, D. E. and Bohn, M. J., Jr. *Occupational Psychology.* Belmont, California: Wadsworth, 1970.

Super, D. E., Crites, J., Hummel, R., Moser, H., Overstreet, P., and Warnath, C. *Vocational Development: A Framework for Research.* New York: Teachers College Press, 1957.

Up the ladder, finally. *Business Week,* November 24, 1975, 58-68.

Wanous, J. P. Realistic job previews for organizational recruitment. *Personnel,* 1975, *52,* 50-60.

White, R. W. Motivation reconsidered: The concept of competence. *Psychological Review,* 1959, *66,* 297-323.

CHAPTER **6**

Performance Evaluation and Human Resource Accounting

In the first five chapters of this book, two major points have repeatedly been made: First, the federal government requires that selection procedures must be demonstrated to be related to job performance. Generally, the criterion measure used to validate the selection procedure (chap. 2) has not been an objective measure of job performance, but rather a subjective evaluation in the form of performance ratings by superiors. An important question remains to be answered by industrial psychologists: Are performance appraisals accurate? In the first article in this chapter, Miner examines the relative advantages and disadvantages of appraisals made by superiors, peers, subordinates, and the employee himself. He then makes recommendations for improving the accuracy and consistency of managerial appraisals. In his article we have noted a number of points with which we are in disagreement with Miner, but these caveats should simply point out to the reader that much research is needed in this area. One of the things we recommend is that whenever feasible personnel managers continually compare the performance ratings of the employee to some objective measure of performance. Also, it is recommended that training in performance appraisal techniques be made a regular part of any supervisory development program. With an all-white sample, Scott and Hamner ("The Effects of Order and Variance in Performance on Supervisory Ratings of Workers," *Organizational Behavior and Human Performance,* 1975) found that supervisory ratings were accurate in the sense that as performance levels increased, the performance ratings of those subjects increased. However, Hamner et al. ("Race and Sex as Determinants of Supervisory Ratings in a Work Sampling Task," *Journal of Applied Psychology,* 1974) found that males versus female subjects and black versus white subjects were rated differently even when their average performance remained the same. In our second reading, Lazer examines how the federal legislation we discussed in chapter 3 will soon affect the area of performance appraisal.

The second point to be made is that the personnel function is concerned with human resource management. Attainment of any organization's goals requires that the performance of managers be measured, compared, and recorded. In our third reading in this chapter, Goodale presents a method by which the personnel manager can achieve both the objective of making subjective evaluations more valid and at the same time improve human resource management's goal of giving feedback to employees that is motivationally meaningful.

Management Appraisal:
A Review of Procedures and Practices

JOHN B. MINER

Does the supervisor appraise your performance? Is this appraisal written, formal, and permanent? Does it affect your performance? Are you a manager who must appraise subordinates and write up these appraisals? Has the company recently instituted a system of appraisal and development by objectives? The chances are that you answered "yes" to many or all of these questions, for approximately 80 percent of all U. S. companies have a formal management appraisal system (10). I stress management, for the shift is away from appraisal of the rank and file (42).

Many of these companies, and most of the managers being appraised, are unsatisfied with their formal appraisal system. This is a fair conclusion, for the whole concept is in a state of flux—new approaches, new plans, and new methods. With this constant change, where is a manager to turn for guidance?

For most of us, management appraisal is extraordinarily difficult. It is hard to pass judgment on a fellow man, especially if that judgment will become a permanent part of his company record, affecting his future. The procedure is further complicated by the absence of many needed facts and of widely accepted theories. Yet the attainment of any organization's goals requires that the performance of our managers be measured, compared, and recorded. Growth requires that potential be evaluated. These requirements can best be met by a thoughtfully adopted formal appraisal system, one that best conforms to current knowledge and theory.

The purposes of this article are to provide this knowledge and theory in capsule form, and to offer a handy reference to current work. I have done this by asking—and answering—questions, those most frequently asked about the evaluation of executives. . . .

What Are the Relative Merits of Appraisals Made by Superiors, Peers, Subordinates, and the Man Himself?

Appraisals made by superiors, peers, subordinates, or the man himself all have merit, but for different qualities.

About 98 percent of all evaluation forms are designed to be completed by the immediate superior. Furthermore, this approach appears to have widespread acceptance. Subordinates characteristically prefer to have their work evaluated in this manner (21).

There is ample evidence that ratings made by peers differ considerably from those made by superiors. The results of a study conducted at North American Aviation (39) indicate that two levels of supervision agree reasonably well; superiors and co-workers do not. Co-workers apparently consider somewhat different factors and additionally, on the average, give higher ratings.

Reprinted with the permission of author and publisher from *Managerial Motivation and Compensation* (MSU Business Series), 1972, Tosi, House, and Dunnette, eds. A condensed version of this article appeared in the October 1968 *Business Horizons,* copyright 1968 by the Foundation for the School of Business at Indiana University. Reprinted by permission.

Similar discrepancies occur when self-ratings are compared with those of superiors. While various levels of supervision tend to agree, superior and self-ratings rarely do (34). Self-ratings emphasize getting along with others as important for success, while superiors stress initiative and work knowledge (21). Furthermore, self-ratings are usually inflated: the self-ratings consistently run higher (32).

There is reason to believe that self-interest can exert considerable influence on peer, subordinate, and self-ratings to the point where the evaluations may lack organizational relevance. Where favorable results have been reported with these techniques, it has been almost exclusively in an artificial research setting. It seems likely that their use as the *primary* element of a regular on-going appraisal system would produce somewhat different results, and that mutual- and/or self-protection could well become a more important consideration in the ratings than the profitability of the company (2).

Although the above statements argue strongly for appraisal by superiors, certain additional facts limit this conclusion. For one, many companies use a management-by-objectives approach, which has a considerable participative component. Managers have a say in setting their own objectives and in determining whether their objectives have been met. This is actually self-rating. Experimental evidence from studies done at General Electric indicates that such participation in the appraisal situation can contribute to more effective performance (12). Thus, at least for purposes of management development, self-rating of a kind has some value.

Peer rating also has received significant support from recent research. A study utilizing middle-level managers at IBM indicates quite clearly that those men rated high by other managers at the same level were more likely to be promoted subsequently (36). It seems entirely possible that at the middle and upper levels of management, where organizational commitment is often high, objective peer evaluations that are relatively free of protective bias can be obtained. Such evaluations may well prove particularly valuable in the identification of leadership potential, just as self-evaluations appear to be most useful for developmental purposes. The Air Force currently is experimenting rather extensively with peer ratings, operating on the theory that they are particularly significant in the measurement of potential.

A recent proposal favors a combination appraisal process utilizing superior, peer, and self-ratings (19). The advantages are sizable. The knowledge that superior ratings also are being obtained reduces bias in the peer and self-ratings. At the same time, the latter two techniques capitalize on unique observational opportunities. The match, or correlation, between the different types of ratings provides a measure of integrated perception among different people in the company, and thus of the capacity to concentrate effort behind goals (29). To the extent that peer and self-ratings support superior ratings, acceptance is likely to be at a high level, and personnel actions, such as promotion and firing, can be carried out without resistance. To the extent they do not, resistance is likely to emerge. Furthermore, self-ratings and peer ratings are available for purposes of development and the identification of potential. Finally, special attention can be focused on those individuals whose ratings diverge sharply. An appraisal involving high superior and self-ratings combined with very low peer ratings is clearly not the same as one with high ratings from all three sources. Yet, if only superior evaluations are obtained, significant aspects of the situation may go undetected.

The major advantage of the tripartite approach is that it provides a wealth of information about the individual and the organization. This approach also pulls together a number of schools of thought on appraisals. All in all, it appears to be *the* approach to management appraisal of the future. Development of such complex programs and effective utilization of the information made available, however, will require expertise beyond that currently available in many companies.

Are There Advantages in Using More Than One Rater?

Research consistently shows that using more than one rater is advantageous. The best evidence comes from studies conducted by the U.S. Army (4), which indicate a clear superiority for the average of ratings made by several individuals over those made by only one person. The rationale behind averaging ratings from the same type of source—either superiors, peers, or subordinates—is that an average tends to reduce the impact of any single biased rating. The larger the number of raters, the more diluted the effects of individual bias. In one study, for example, managers who were found to be particularly considerate and kind to their subordinates also gave them very high ratings (17). When averaged with the evaluations of more production-oriented managers, such overly lenient ratings have less impact on the final appraisal. Alone, their impact is complete.

However, the availability of raters with access to a sufficiently large sample of work behaviors can set a limit on the number of raters that should be used. Increasing the size of the rating group by adding people who are not really qualified to evaluate and who, therefore, will give erroneous data defeats the value of the averaging process. One of the potential values of peer and subordinate appraisals is the availability of a large number of individuals who can qualify as raters because of their particularly good opportunities for observation.

What Is the Value of Rating Reviews by a Hierarchical Superior of the Rater?

Various provisions for reviews by the direct-line superior of a rater are a common feature of appraisal systems (21). In the U.S. Army procedure, there are in essence two reviews—one by the indorser, who also makes his own rating, and one by the reviewer, who merely indicates that a review has been made. Thus the original rater has his evaluations scrutinized twice, the indorser once (7). A review procedure may operate in a number of ways. One approach requires the rater to present his evaluations orally to a review board of superiors (37). In other cases, as with the military, only the written forms are reviewed at higher levels. A reviewer may have the authority to change evaluations directly without any consultation, to personally require the rater to make changes, to advise on changes, or merely to indicate disagreement on the rating form.

Under appropriate circumstances, such review does appear to contribute to evaluation quality (2). Ideally, adequate knowledge of a manager's performance exists at several hierarchical levels above him. Given this requirement, the best approach is to pass the appraisals upward so each manager can make his evaluation either independently, as in the case of the immediate superior, or with knowledge only of what those below him think. This chain of evaluation should stop when it reaches a level in the hierarchy where adequate knowledge of performance does not exist. There is little point in including at the top of the chain a reviewer who does not also evaluate. If such an individual does not have any basis for evaluating a man, then there is nothing gained by adding his signature to a form. If he does have such a basis, then his ratings should be averaged with the others.

This rater-indorser chain approach has the advantage that each manager, except the one at the top, knows that his evaluations will be scrutinized. The approach also provides for multiple ratings under conditions that protect against undue influence from a superior who may have the least adequate basis for appraisal. The information flow is upward from what can be presumed to be the most knowledgeable individual to the least, rather than the reverse. The use of such an approach assumes that a superior will not change or influence his subordinate's ratings in any way. Evidence indicates that, when actual changes at higher levels are permitted, they do nothing to improve the evaluation process. However, the superior can disagree in his own ratings and thus mitigate the effects of what he feels is an error.

Should Management Appraisals Be Made at the Same Time As Salary Recommendations?

The real problem is not whether management appraisals and salary recommendations should be done together, although traditionally this is the case, but rather, to find some method of avoiding the common tendency to decide on salary first and then adjust the performance ratings to fit. Because salary, in practice, is influenced by many factors other than merit, the ratings frequently are distorted. I cannot locate any research that bears directly on the question. Nonetheless, studies at General Electric clearly indicate that feeding back information on salary actions concomitantly with management appraisal data is not desirable insofar as motivational and developmental goals are concerned (24). Criticism tied directly to pay action produces so much defensiveness that there is little prospect of learning occurring. Energies focus primarily on self-protection rather than self-improvement (33).

Separating appraisals and salary actions in time is one way of reducing distortion. Yet many managers unquestionably do prefer to couple them, which well may lead to biased appraisals. An approach that would overcome bias and still permit a simultaneous dual decision clearly would be helpful. A means of changing perceptions—of both the salary administration and appraisal processes—seems called for. Although evidence is lacking, I believe this change could be achieved through a training program, provided the content of the program truly represented top-management philosophies. The training would consider various factors that inevitably influence salary actions, including the labor market, previous salary history, budgetary limitations, equity considerations, and rate ranges as well as merit. The training also would consider sources of bias in appraisal. With such an approach, pay and performance possibly could be separated in the manager's mind just as, or perhaps more, effectively as through the interposition of time.

What Are the Pros and Cons of Feedback from the Rater to the Man Being Rated?

Usually, the results of appraisals are given to the man who has been evaluated; this may be done in a number of different ways and with varying amounts of detail (21). The question is whether it should be done at all. An adequate answer requires two kinds of information stemming from two sub-questions: (1) how does the feedback requirement affect the ratings, and (2) how does the feedback requirement affect the man who has been rated?

Feedback and Ratings

A Lockheed Aircraft study (40) provides the best example of how the feedback requirement may influence ratings. The regular evaluations, which were not revealed to subordinates, were followed at a two-week interval by a second appraisal, which included discussions of the ratings with the men. The mean score for the 485 men involved rose dramatically, from an initial 60 to 84, out of a possible 100. Apparently, when faced with the prospect of making face-to-face negative comments, many managers avoided the problem by inflating their ratings. Thus almost everyone was placed toward the top of the scale.

This problem of inflation when the man rated has access to the results has plagued the armed forces for years (7). Although direct feedback by the superior is not required by law, the legal structure does indicate that an officer may inspect the evaluations in his file and that under certain conditions he may appeal. Anticipating that efficiency reports might be inspected, raters tend to make favorable statements. A variety of techniques, including forced choice, forced distribution, and critical incidents, have been introduced with little success over the years to deal with this inflation of ratings, which remains the major problem of the armed forces appraisal systems today.

Thus, where valid ratings are necessary for salary administration, promotion, transfer, discharge, and evaluation of selection procedures, feedback is not desirable. [Editor's note: This is a somewhat controversial opinion. See the article "Worker Motivation Programs," by W. Clay Hamner, in chap. 7.] It is particularly important to avoid optional feedback, in which a manager does as he pleases. Under such circumstances, managers who plan to discuss their evaluations with subordinates will inflate them; those who do not plan to do so will not inflate them. As a result, the two types of ratings actually will be on different scales. Assuming the existence of a single scale under these circumstances not only will result in injustice to the individual, but also will produce decisions detrimental to the organization as well.

Feedback and the Man Rated

The major source of information on the motivational or developmental effects of feedback is a series of studies conducted at General Electric (12, 16, 24). The findings of this research on the dynamics of the feedback interview are summarized as follows:

1). Criticism tends to have a negative impact on achievement of goals.

2). Praise has little effect, either positive or negative. [Editor's note: A recent study by Daniel Grady and W. Clay Hamner ("Positive Reinforcement at Michigan Bell," Michigan State University, 1974, working paper) has shown that praise, when administered appropriately, has a very positive effect on performance.]

3). Performance tends to improve when specific objectives are established.

4). Defensiveness as a consequence of criticism results in inferior performance.

5). Coaching is best done on a day-to-day basis and in direct association with specific acts, not once a year.

6). Mutual goal setting by superior and subordinate yields positive results.

7). Interviews intended primarily to improve performance should not deal with salary and promotion at the same time.

8). Participation by the subordinate in establishing his own performance goals yields favorable results.

9). Separate performance evaluations are required for different purposes.

On the whole, the results of the General Electric research seem to provide appropriate guides for action. Nonetheless, subsequent research has raised some doubts about the value of goal setting as it actually is done within the context of the management-by-objectives approach (22).

Feedback can be an effective motivational and developmental tool, but often it is not. Whether systematic appraisal interviews should be attempted depends on the approach taken and the skill of the interviewer. Feedback very clearly can do more harm than good.

Ideally, a feedback interview should be goal-oriented and should take a problem-solving approach to make a positive contribution, but this is not easy to do. Getting a manager to agree on a set of objectives and standards is one thing; getting him to recognize where and why he has fallen short in his performance is quite another (25). However, the requisite skill can be developed in many managers through training (23, 31).

Based on the evidence currently available, the appropriate conclusion seems to be that only those ratings made specifically for motivational or developmental purposes should ever be fed back, and then only by a fully trained and skilled interviewer. Feedback has tremendous potential for harm as well as good. It can be a major source of managerial turnover.

On What Types of Characteristics Should Managers Be Rated?

In selecting the types of characteristics on which to rate a manager, it is most important to include only those characteristics which manifest themselves in the work situation. The rating factors should be firmly anchored in behavior manifestations that characteristically occur on the job and that influence performance (10). There is a tendency to include a variety of traits that do not meet these requirements. Often rating scales deal with aspects of "good" and "bad" people that cannot be adequately judged from job contact alone, or that matter little, if at all, in effective performance. In this connection, it is well to note that it is not always the "good" people who do well. One study found that an intense sense of honesty and ethics almost guaranteed failure in a particular type of sales job (26).

Ratings also should deal with characteristics that can be described clearly so that all raters will have the same kinds of behavior in mind (2). Considerable evidence indicates that certain personality traits, such as character and aggressiveness, are viewed so nebulously that agreement on whether people possess them is almost impossible. Such traits should not be included unless qualified in considerable detail. Generally, the closer the factors are to job behavior and results, the more raters will agree in their evaluations of a person.

How Can Ratings Be Spread Out Along a Scale Most Successfully?

One approach to spreading ratings out is the forced distribution technique, which is a variant of ranking. However, rather than having as many categories as there are managers to be rated, the number of categories is predetermined, as is the percentage of the men to be placed in each category. In theory, the technique, like ranking, has considerable appeal. In practice, however, it presents so many difficulties that, at least for *management* appraisal, it cannot be recommended. One problem is that the percentages are meaningless unless the group to be rated by a single manager is large. Where spans of control are limited, this condition is not met. Furthermore, there is the difficulty of combining groups. Is the lower 10 percent of one group likely to be at the same performance level as the lower 10 percent of another? This same problem of combining groups occurs, of course, with ranking also. Furthermore, raters tend to resist the forced distribution (42). The result is a continuing conflict between those responsible for administering the appraisal system and the managers doing the rating. In the end, either the ratings are adjusted to fit the required percentage distribution, with great potential for error (17), or the forced distribution technique is abandoned entirely.

Given the conclusion that forced distribution techniques are not satisfactory for management appraisal, what other procedures are available to produce a meaningful spread of ratings along a scale? The armed services have faced this problem continually over the years. As indicated previously, since the man rated has ready access to the Armed Service Efficiency Reports, scores tend to pile up at the high end of the scales. In the late 1940s and early 1950s, two rather complex procedures were developed to deal with this problem. The forced choice approach was introduced by the Army and then adopted by the Air Force, which subsequently developed the critical incident technique to replace it. Neither approach proved successful (9). Forced choice failed because rating officers resisted a procedure that made it difficult, if not impossible, for them to determine how they actually had rated a man; in addition, leniency was not entirely overcome. The critical incident approach proved too complicated, too time-consuming, resulted in too much concern with the final score, and did not really solve the leniency problem. In both cases, resistance from rating officers in the field eventually was sufficient to terminate use of the technique. Research evidence indicates that graphic rating scales are actually just as valid as these more complex procedures (4).

All this does not mean that steps cannot be taken to produce a satisfactory spread of ratings. The following procedures used in business organizations have proved successful in extending this range:

1). Maintain security so evaluations are not available to the men rated or fed back to them (40).

2). Avoid ambiguous descriptions of the characteristics to be rated and of steps on the scale; the rater must have a clear understanding of exactly what job behavior he is to consider (3).

3). Carry out training aimed at providing an understanding of the desirability of a wide range of scores (20). Particular stress should be placed on getting overly considerate managers, who want more than anything else to help men, to spread their ratings out. These are the raters who typically have the smallest ranges (17).

If these three conditions are met, and an adequate number of steps or levels exist in the scale, the usual graphic rating scale should yield a satisfactory spread of scores and should prove the most generally useful (2).

Does Stress on Recent Events Bias Ratings?

Studies do indicate, as many have hypothesized, that specific instances of effective or ineffective behavior occurring shortly before evaluations unduly affect the ratings (10). Apparently, raters remember recent events more vividly and, therefore, weigh them more heavily. This situation suggests the need for relatively frequent ratings—at least every three to six months. Averaging such evaluations to yield a running appraisal score will minimize the effects of any specific recency bias. Another antidote involves keeping managers aware of the recency problem. Some managers might be induced to keep notes on performance throughout the rating period and then to review these at appraisal time. Even without this technique, however, sensitivity to the fact that recent events can have an excessive effect should make it easier to counteract the tendency. All of this, of course, represents another training area.

Is There a Method That Will Ensure Consistency of Application?

Evidence on the value of introducing an educational process as an integral part of a total appraisal system is consistently positive. Normally, this educational process is based on the spoken word, but, on occasion, it may utilize written materials as well. Some uses of these procedures already have been noted, but additional features of the communication problem should be mentioned. Studies indicate that training can serve to increase the agreement between different raters, reduce bias (40), increase accuracy generally, prevent inflation of scores (5), and spread out the rating distribution (20). The evidence in support of training in the skills required to conduct an effective feedback interview already has been noted. In general, training sessions should be conducted by a person qualified as an expert on management appraisal and familiar with the details of the particular system in use. There should be an opportunity for considerable discussion and some practice with the rating forms. Various sources of error and bias, as well as factors that will make the ratings most useful, need primary attention (41).

In spite of the consistently favorable evidence, a great many companies do not build training procedures into their appraisal systems. In fact, a lack of adequate training is the major problem of most programs (21). In addition, there is reason to believe that many programs that have succumbed to widespread managerial resistance could have survived had they been introduced with adequate training. Although group sessions usually are used, these may be supplemented with some individual assistance at the time the ratings are made. Manuals containing information similar to the training program also have proved useful (5).

What Can Be Done to Overcome the Resistance That Hampers Many Appraisal Systems?

Many people look on the whole process of evaluating performance quite negatively. This feeling appears related to fears of receiving low ratings if an appraisal system is instituted and survives, and to a strong belief in the seniority principle (30). Evidence shows that less effective managers tend to be the ones most opposed to performance appraisal (14). Furthermore, many managers, in addition to rank-and-file employees, strongly believe seniority is the best guide for making personnel decisions. As a result of these factors, and perhaps others, any management appraisal system will encounter some resistance. This resistance may block the initiation of a program entirely, but it is particularly likely to manifest itself once a program is instituted and there is something to shoot at. Resistance will vary, depending on the values predominant in the company, and it may relate rather specifically to certain kinds of approaches.

Obviously, the greater the resistance the more those instituting the program will have to concentrate on those who will do the rating, and the more the management group as a whole will have to be involved in developing the system. These approaches demonstrate the willingness of those who will be using the data to do part of the work to ensure a successful program. The alternative procedure involves inducing the raters to come to the users of the data. This procedure is entirely satisfactory where acceptance is high, but where it is not merely mailing out forms along with directives and follow-up memorandums will only increase negative feeling. In addition to going to the raters, having large numbers of managers participate in the construction of the system itself is another successful approach (2). This can be done extensively if managers are used both as a source for developing items and as judges of proposed items (38).

The need for special procedures to help overcome resistance will vary, depending on the nature of the program. Many managers tend to resist feeding back appraisal results, for instance. Thus, acceptance problems may be anticipated when this is required. Many managers strongly dislike peer and subordinate ratings (2). Thus the use of a tripartite system along the lines noted previously may require special attention. Forced choice and forced distribution procedures are known to be sources of resistance and, accordingly, require more than the usual efforts to develop favorable attitudes.

How Can Potential Be Evaluated and What Factors Are Predictive of Potential?

To determine a method for evaluating potential and the characteristics that are predictive of potential, research must show that some measure did in fact predict success in management over a considerable period of time after the original measurement. The following discussion is restricted entirely to studies of this kind. Predictions made by managers are considered first, then predictions by psychologists.

Managerial Prediction

In connection with managerial appraisal programs, ratings of potential for advancement frequently are obtained. The difficulty with using ratings of this kind for research is that they are available and known and quite obviously can influence a man's career entirely apart from his actual competence. Even with this bias included, results with these potential ratings by superiors are not impressive. Clearly a great many individuals identified in this manner as having high potential do not advance very far (11). In one study, departments within a single company varied considerably in the extent to which potential ratings were even predictive of the first promotion after appraisal (29). Results like these have led some writers to conclude that the evaluation of potential is beyond the scope of the usual management appraisal system and that the matter should be left to specialists in the field (35). Many ratings of potential are believed to be merely the inverse of the manager's age and thus convey little new information.

The armed forces have carried out most of the research on the predictive value of ratings by superiors, usually with relatively short intervals between the initial predictions and the subsequent measurement of success (18). The correlations obtained are not impressive. These findings contrast sharply with those for peer ratings; in the latter case much better predictions of potential are obtained. Why this difference between superior and peer predictions exists is a matter of conjecture at the present time.

Psychological Prediction

A considerable amount of predictive research has used psychological techniques. Some studies utilize separate measures, such as psychological tests or biographical inventories; other use the overall evaluations of psychologists derived from a combination of sources, including interviews, observation of behavior, and tests. In general, tests of intelligence and mental abilities do seem to be predictive of success. However, in many highly selected managerial groups, intelligence tests are not very helpful in identifying potential because all the managers score at such a high level. At the foreman level, intelligence tests are more effective as indicators of subsequent performance (18).

Consistently positive results have been obtained with the Miner Sentence Completion Scale in a series of predictive studies (27). This measure was designed specifically for predicting success in management. Although the test discriminates most effectively at the graduate level, it can identify individuals with managerial potential as early as the third year of college (28).

Psychological tests in the personality area have produced uneven results when used individually. In a number of cases, they have not proved very useful (18). Yet, enough exceptions suggest that some personality tests can yield good potential estimates. In general, measures of characteristics such as dominance, self-confidence, and persuasiveness are most useful (10). A considerable amount of research has used biographical inventories containing questions similar to those found in application blanks. This research has produced sufficiently positive results to recommend the approach (10, 18). However, companies tend to keep the specific results of these studies secret so managerial candidates do not learn the "right" answers. Thus studies aimed at establishing those factors that are predictive in a given company must be carried out individually. Nonetheless, published research does show that a prior pattern of success is likely to be predictive of subsequent success.

Results with comprehensive evaluations by psychologists using a variety of source data also are encouraging. Studies using this approach have predicted success over a period as long as seven years (1, 8). Yet there have been some significant failures also.

A related approach, even more comprehensive in that managers are studied over a period of days with a whole host of techniques, is the assessment center. AT&T has conducted much of the research with this technique under the title of The Management Progress Study. Staff assessments of potential for advancement derived from these assessment situations have consistently proved predictive of promotion and salary progress over periods up to eight years (6). Those assessments were not made available to those making promotion and compensation decisions. Research indicates that those who have moved up most rapidly are more intelligent, more active, control their feelings more, are more noncomforming, exhibit a greater work orientation (6), are more independent, desire more of a leadership role, and have stronger achievement motivation (13). Although this type of approach is extremely expensive relative to the usual psychological evaluation (15), it appears to yield even higher correlations with later success in management jobs.

There is reason to believe that any psychological approach is likely to be effective only to the extent it is attuned to the value and reward structures of the particular organization (29). Thus the development of psychological predictors to identify potential within a given company must involve a complex interaction between analysis of the individual and analysis of the organization. Such an interaction involving both individual assessment and social psychological research seems to provide the best guide for management appraisal systems of the future.

References

(1) Albrecht, P. A.; Glaser, E. M.; and Marks, J. 1964. Validation of a multiple-assessment procedure for managerial personnel. *Journal of Applied Psychology* 48:351-60.

(2) Barrett, R. S. 1966. *Performance rating*. Chicago: Science Research Associates.

(3) ——————— et al. 1958. Rating scale content, I: Scale information and supervisory ratings. *Personnel Psychology* II:333-46.

(4) Bayroff, A. G.; Haggerty, H. R.; and Rundquist, E. A. 1954. Validity of ratings as related to rating techniques and conditions. *Personnel Psychology* 7:93-113.

(5) Bittner, R. 1948. Developing an industrial merit rating procedure. *Personnel Psychology* 1:403-32.

(6) Bray, D. W., and Grant, D. L. 1966. The assessment center in the measurement of potential for business management. *Psychological Monographs* 80:1-27.

(7) Brooks, W. W. 1966. An analysis and evaluation of the officer performance appraisal system in the United States army. M. S. thesis, George Washington University.

(8) Dicken, C. F., and Black, J. D. 1965. Predictive validity of psychometric evaluations of supervisors. *Journal of Applied Psychology* 49:34-47.

(9) Druit, C. A. 1964. An analysis of military officer evaluation systems using principles presently advanced by authorities in this field. M. A. thesis, The Ohio State University.

(10) Dunnette, M. D. et al. 1966. Identification and enhancement of managerial effectiveness. Richardson Foundation Survey Report.

(11) Ferguson, L. L. 1966. Better management of managers' careers. *Harvard Business Review* 44:139-52.

(12) French, J. R. P.; Kay, E.; and Meyer, H. H. 1966. Participation and the appraisal system. *Human Relations* 19:3-20.

(13) ———————; Katkovsky, W.; and Bray, D. W. 1967. Contributions of projective techniques to assessment of managerial potential. *Journal of Applied Psychology* 51:226-32.

(14) Gruenfeld, L. W., and Weissenberg, P. 1966. Supervisory characteristics and attitudes toward performance appraisals. *Personnel Psychology* 19:143-51.

(15) Hardesty, D. L., and Jones, W. S. 1968. Characteristics of judged high-potential management personnel—The operations of an industrial assessment center. *Personnel Psychology* 21:85-98.

(16) Kay, E.; Meyer, H. H.; and French, J. R. P. 1965. Effects of threat in a performance appraisal interview. *Journal of Applied Psychology* 49:311-17.

(17) Klores, M. S. 1966. Rater bias in forced-distribution performance ratings. *Personnel Psychology* 19:411-21.

(18) Korman, A. K. 1968. The prediction of managerial performance: A review. *Personnel Psychology* 21:295-322.

(19) Lawler III, E. E. 1967. The multitrait-multirater approach to measuring managerial job performance. *Journal of Applied Psychology* 51:369-81.

(20) Levine, J., and Butler, J. 1952. Lecture vs. group decision in changing behavior. *Journal of Applied Psychology* 36:29-33.

(21) Lopez, F. M. In press. *Evaluating employee performance*. Chicago: Public Personnel Association.

(22) Mendleson, J. L. 1967. Manager goal setting: An exploration into its meaning and measurement. D. B. A. thesis, Michigan State University.

(23) Meyer, H. H., and Walker, W. B. 1961. A study of factors relating to the effectiveness of a performance appraisal program. *Personnel Psychology* 14:291-98.

(24) Meyer, H. H.; Kay, E.; and French, J. R. P. 1965. Split roles in performance appraisal. *Harvard Business Review* 43:123-29.

(25) Michael, J. M. 1965. Problem situations in performance counselling. *Personnel* 42:16-22.

(26) Miner, J. B. 1962. Personality and ability factors in sales performance. *Journal of Applied Psychology* 46:6-13.

(27) ———————. 1965. *Studies in management education*. New York: Springer.

(28) ———. 1968. The early identification of managerial talent. *The Personnel and Guidance Journal* 46:586-91.
(29) ———. 1968. Bridging the gulf in organizational performance. *Harvard Business Review* 46:102-10.
(30) ———. 1969. *Personnel and industrial relations—A managerial approach*. New York: Macmillan.
(31) Moon, C. G., and Hariton, T. 1958. Evaluating an appraisal and feedback training program. *Personnel* 35:36-41.
(32) Parker, J. W. et al. 1959. Rating scale content: III. Relationships between supervisory and self-ratings. *Personnel Psychology* 12:49-63.
(33) Patton, A. 1968. Executive motivation: How it is changing. *Management Review* 57:4-20.
(34) Prien, E. P., and Liske, R. E. 1962. Assessments of higher level personnel: III. Rating criteria: A comparative analysis of supervisor ratings and incumbent self-ratings of job performance. *Personnel Psychology* 15:187-94.
(35) Richards, K. E. 1959. A new concept of performance appraisal. *Journal of Business* 32:229-43.
(36) Roadman, H. E. 1964. An industrial use of peer ratings. *Journal of Applied Psychology* 48:211-14.
(37) Rowland, V. K. 1951. Management inventory and development. *Personnel* 28:12-22.
(38) Smith, P. C., and Kendall, L. M. 1963. Retranslation of expectations: An approach to the construction of unambiguous anchors for rating scales. *Journal of Applied Psychology* 47:149-55.
(39) Springer, D. 1953. Ratings of candidates for promotion by co-workers and supervisors. *Journal of Applied Psychology* 37:347-51.
(40) Stockford, L., and Bissell, H. W. 1949. Factors involved in establishing a merit-rating scale. *Personnel* 26:94-116.
(41) Tiffin, J., and McCormick, E. J. 1965. *Industrial Psychology*. 5th ed. Englewood Cliffs, N. J.: Prentice-Hall.
(42) Whisler, T. L., and Harper, S. F. 1962. *Performance appraisal*. New York: Holt, Rinehart and Winston.

The "Discrimination" Danger in Performance Appraisal

ROBERT I. LAZER

Any selection instrument which is used as a screening device for some future employment opportunity—such as a promotion—may be viewed as an "employee selection procedure." As a result, if it has an adverse impact on the employment opportunities of any protected group—minorities, women and the 40 to 65 age group—its use may need

Reprinted from *The Conference Board Record*, March 1976, with permission to be justified as a matter of business necessity following the EEOC's "Guidelines on Employee Selection Procedures," and/or the Office of Federal Contract Compliance's (OFCC) "Order on Employee Testing and Other Selection Procedures."[1] Indeed, issues concerning the nature and administration of appraisal programs have already been raised and decided in several court cases. Knowledgeable experts warn that, given the current thrust of these initial court decisions, many organizations may find it necessary to make major changes.

At the minimum, companies need to check the appraisal programs and their applications for disparate impact on any of the groups protected by law. They may also need to be able to establish that the appraisal systems they are using have been carefully developed, are even-handedly administered, and are valid measures of job performance. However, recent research suggests that most companies are not currently in a position to justify their performance appraisal system in these terms.

The basic requirement of the Guidelines is that any selection tool or test that has an adverse impact must be validated, i.e., demonstrably shown to be related to job performance. The test must have a significant relationship with a minimum of one relevant job performance criterion measure, so as to be useful in predicting successful (or unsuccessful) job performance on the specific job for which the individual is being evaluated.[2]

It is helpful to think of the Guidelines as establishing a schematic equation: on the one side are test scores ("tests" is a broad category which includes "all formal, scored, qualified, or standardized techniques of assessing job suitability"); on the other side are the criterion measures of performance (which "must represent major and critical work behaviors as revealed by careful job analyses"). In essence, test scores = criterion measures of job performance; only if these two sides form an equation is the test deemed "valid."

Currently, performance appraisals (e.g., supervisory ratings) are often used as the criterion measures against which tests are validated. But—and this has only recently been recognized—when performance appraisals are used as the basis for making selection decisions (e.g., promotions), they then move over to the other side of the equation. Now they may be regarded, and appropriately so, as "tests." Should an adverse effect be produced on the employment opportunities of any protected group, the appraisals in turn may need to be validated following the rigorous provisions of the Guidelines.[3]

Appraisals as Criterion Measures

Although performance appraisal was not necessarily the primary issue in the court cases which will be discussed, it was nonetheless tangential to the original complaint of discrimination.

The question of performance appraisals as criteria in test validation studies was addressed by the U.S. Supreme Court in *Albemarle Paper Company v. Moody*.[4] This case focused on two important issues: subjective supervisory rankings and lack of job analysis.

When Albemarle's test scores were compared with supervisory rankings in a validation study, the Court found that employees had been ranked against a vague standard, open to each supervisor's own interpretation. Additionally, employees were rated against one another, even though the person they were rated against may not have been performing the same job. Regarding Albemarle's rating procedure, the Court stated that "there is no way of knowing precisely what criteria of job performance the supervisors were considering, whether each supervisor was considering the same criteria—or whether, indeed, any of the supervisors actually applied a focused and stable body of criteria of any kind."

Furthermore, the Court stated, there was "no way to determine whether the criteria *actually* considered were sufficiently related to the company's legitimate interest in job-specific ability to justify a testing system with a racially discriminatory impact." In the process of validating their tests. Albemarle made no attempt to analyze the jobs to delineate the particular job skills they might require.[5]

Appraisals as Test Scores

If performance appraisals are used as a decision-making tool for personnel selection and result in an adverse impact on any protected group, then a company may well find it must justify its discriminatory action. In establishing minimum standards for such tests, the Guidelines state that "tests must be administered and scored under controlled and standardized conditions."

There are several reasons for this requirement. One is to "protect the security of the test scores and to insure that scores do not enter into any judgments of employee adequacy that are to be used as criterion measures." Another is to insure that the test conditions are the same for all individuals. For example, if on a half-hour timed test of mechanical ability one individual is given 25 minutes to finish while another has the full 30 minutes, the test situations are substantially different and violate the Guidelines' requirement of a controlled and standardized condition.

Thus the standardization requirement challenges the propriety of appraisals based on supervisory ratings. Such ratings, often being of a subjective and interpretative nature—especially if the definitions of the factors to be rated are left to the supervisor's discretion—may easily raise the question of "controlled and standardized conditions." Such was the case in *Wade v. Mississippi Cooperative Extension Service*.[6]

Here a U.S. district court held that the evaluation instrument used by the state extension service to appraise the job performance of county professional workers discriminated against black employees. It was found that: (1) evaluations were influenced in large part by subjective supervisory judgments; (2) appraisal scores were statistically different and had a significant racial impact; (3) the evaluation instrument was not based upon job analysis; and (4) no data were presented to demonstrate that the evaluation instrument was a valid predictor of employee job performance.

In finding the extension service in violation of the Equal Protection Clause of the Fourteenth Amendment, the court emphasized two criteria used by the extension service for determining promotion: "concept of the job applied for" and "objective appraisal of job performance." In rendering its decision against *Extension Service* the court stated:

> [The] concept of the job applied for . . . is a criterion quite incapable of uniform administration and readily susceptible to bias. Even more noteworthy, the so-called "objective appraisal of job performance" . . . is based upon scores received by subordinates rated by supervisors on an evaluation instrument according to a number of factors. For example, a substantial portion of the evaluation rating relates to such general characteristics as leadership, public acceptance, attitude toward people, appearance and grooming, personal conduct, outlook on life, ethical habits, resourcefulness, capacity for growth, mental alertness, and loyalty to organization. As

may be readily observed, these are traits which are susceptible to partiality and to the personal taste, whim, or fancy of the evaluator. We must thus view these factors as presently utilized to be patently subjective in form and obviously susceptible to completely subjective treatment.

Because the appraisal scores had a disparate impact on the plaintiffs, the defendants had the burden of demonstrating that the appraisal instrument was job related and served "legitimate employment needs of the extension service." To retain use of the current procedures, the inference of discrimination had to be negated "by clear and convincing evidence."

Similar cases have been finding their way to the courts. In *Rowe* v. *General Motors Corporation*, General Motors was found to have violated Title VII of the Civil Rights Act of 1964 by relying upon its foremen to recommend hourly employees for transfer and promotion to salaried positions, where such recommendations had had a discriminatory effect in the past.[7] (The foreman's recommendation was the single most important factor in the promotion process; the foreman was given no written instructions relating to the qualifications necessary for the higher level jobs; recommendations were based on vague and subjective standards.)

The Savannah Sugar Refining Corporation[8] was also found to be in violation of Title VII with its promotion procedures. As in *Rowe*, supervisors were "not furnished written instructions specifying qualifications necessary for promotion" and the work standards were "vague and subjective." These standards included desire for improvement and leadership potential.

In *Brito* v. *Zia Company*,[9] Zia Company was found in violation of Title VII when on the basis of low performance appraisal scores a disproportionate number of a protected group was laid off. In its finding the court commented that the performance appraisal used by Zia Company in determining lay-offs was, in fact, an employment test. It also upheld a lower court's decision that Zia did not validate the performance evaluation test because it failed, in accordance with the EEOC Guidelines, to:

> introduce evidence of validity . . . consisting of empirical data demonstrating that the test was significantly correlated with important elements of work behavior relevant to the jobs for which the appellants were being evaluated.

The court found that the "evaluations were based on the best judgments and opinions

TABLE 1
PREVALENCE OF MANAGEMENT PERFORMANCE APPRAISAL SYSTEMS
(Percent of companies)

Industry (No. of companies)	Lower	Management Level* Middle	Top
Manufacturing/processing(148)	73.0	73.0	57.4
Insurance (39)	66.0	64.1	46.2
Banks/financial service (65)	78.6	70.7	56.9
Wholesale/retail trade (41)	78.0	73.3	48.8
Total (293)	74.3	71.3	54.8

*For the purposes of this study lower management is defined as supervisors, foremen, crew chiefs, etc. Top management is defined as the CEO and/or president and the immediate reporting personnel.

... but not on any identifiable criteria based on quality or quantity of work or specific performance that were supported by some kind of record." Also, "the test was not administered and scored under controlled and standardized conditions."

Standardization, when performance appraisals are used as tests, is also mentioned in *Harper* v. *Mayor and City Council*.[10] Here the court concluded that even though the minority employees had not been rated lower on efficiency or performance ratings than the white employees, they had been graded *differently*. Thus the rating procedure denied equal protection under the law to the plaintiffs.

Though there have not been any court cases addressing the issue of the performance appraisal being presented as evidence contradicting a company's discriminatory action, personnel experts feel that this is an important area of consideration. For example, a company wishing to terminate its older employees (45 to 60 years old) as "deadwood" may find that all those "excellent" and "good" performance ratings (used to justify salary increases and promotions) may be turned against them. The terminated employees, especially in a complaint of age discrimination, could possibly present their past appraisal ratings as evidence that the company's "deadwood" argument was not the real reason for termination.

These cases would seem to indicate that the courts are viewing performance appraisal as an employment screening device. The issues of job relatedness and standardization appear to be playing critical roles here, just as they did in the early controversy on the validation of more traditional "tests."[11]

Little Has Been Done

The appraisal of an employee's job performance is an integral component of most personnel systems and, as we have seen, the resultant information is often critical to an individual's future employment status. Personnel decisions affecting compensation, training and development plans, promotions, and even continued employment (or termination) have their foundations in data obtained from the appraisal.

In a recent Conference Board survey,[12] over 70% of the 293 companies participating acknowledge having formal performance appraisal systems for managers (see table 1). Companies not reporting a formalized procedure indicate that appraisal takes the form of a general, subjective evaluation of individual subordinates by supervisors—usually when salary review occurs.

Of the 217 companies reporting formal appraisal programs, 66% use this information to assist in identifying candidates for promotional opportunities. Yet, out of 217 only one had initiated an empirical validation study, and that study was never completed. Most of the companies have done nothing about validating their systems, and several companies say they rely on management feedback and subjective review (including attitude surveys) as evidence of validity.

Furthermore, of the companies reporting appraisal systems, half indicate that they have not analyzed the jobs being appraised as part of the system's development. Less than 40% of the companies had analyzed all the jobs covered by their performance appraisal system. Yet, job analysis is a crucial element in the validation process. It is from an analysis of the job that performance criterion measures are developed, and "job relatedness" is established.

Additionally, 60% of the companies require their appraisers to rate or scale subordinates' personal traits or characteristics,[13] a task many appraisers are not trained to perform. But even if the appraisers are competent to accurately measure these traits, the relationship between the traits and work performance would still need to be determined.

In 77% of the companies the appraisers are also asked to estimate their subordinates' potential for development and promotability. In many instances, however, the appraiser does not have the necessary personal and organizational data to make accurate predictions on these factors. For example, some companies ask their appraisers to predict how far a subordinate may rise in the hierarchy, and in some cases, to specify the job. How many supervisors know their organizations well enough to determine what it takes to be successful three levels up (i.e., two levels beyond where they themselves currently are)?

The emphasis on ratings of personal characteristics and estimates of potential provides ample opportunity for rater subjectivity and bias. Even though 75% of the companies surveyed have some type of training for appraisers in the use and administration of performance appraisal, the trait-based approach makes it hard to avoid bias.

Through the Looking Glass

In view of these problems the findings of the Board's survey of the opinions of 15 personnel executives and management consultants are revealing. Questioned as to the response they believe business and industry would make if performance appraisal was defined as a test and had to be validated, their answers tended to be bipolar: "best thing that could happen" vs. "disaster." However, the consensus was that criterion-related validity would be very difficult to achieve, especially at the management level. It was felt that management judgment cannot, and should not, always be quantified.

A manpower planning specialist believes that a ruling mandating that appraisals be validated would "force [managers] to look at what we should be looking at anyway. It's an educational process, but the courts should be aware of the limitations. It would set up positive pressures which, in the long run, should improve the appraisal process. Companies should not wait for it to be demanded."

On the other hand, a director of manpower development feels that validation is a luxury; that the time and money spent proving that performance appraisal is valuable is not very cost effective. And two management consultants voiced similar opinions:

> "It would force companies away from formalized rating systems into unquantified, subjective judgments. It would be a return to the smoke-filled room."
>
> "The research needed to get anywhere near the ultimate criteria is so overwhelming in scope that most companies could not begin to do it. It's just inconceivable to me, it's not realistic, it's almost Alice-in-Wonderlandish. Where do you stop?"

Will the Courts Decide this One?

The future emphasis placed on performance appraisal systems, and the direction this emphasis will take, appears to be in the hands of the courts. The definition of appraisal as an employment test has already begun (as evidenced by *Brito*). It may only be a matter of time before the use of appraisal data in making employment decisions is unequivocally defined as the use of a "test" and brought under the constraints of the EEOC and OFCC selection Guidelines.

The feeling of many of the personnel executives interviewed is that appraisals relying on ratings of personal characteristics present a serious disadvantage, especially when compared with appraisal systems revolving around preset performance objectives. In the latter approach, validation criteria are an integral part of the process. The objectives to be accomplished are inherently important to the job and, as a result, job relatedness is automatic.

On the other hand, rating scales designed to measure subjective personal characteristics are seen as not being inherently job related. Moreover, as one personnel vice president points out, each trait or scale might have to be validated for its individual relationship to particular jobs. This type of appraisal system is also seen as violating many of the standards established by the selection guidelines.

Obviously, the impact on business and industry of a court ruling equating performance appraisals with employment selection tests could be tremendous. If companies find any adverse effect on protected groups, then many may be expected to drop their formal appraisal programs; others may attempt validation studies; or temporarily equalize the impact of the appraisal score on each group of employees (by converting these scores to percentiles for each group) until a definitive study can be conducted. And the remainder will undoubtedly continue present practices until forced into action by a complaint or finding of discrimination (and thereby risk any number of judgments against them, including class action back pay awards).

Notes

1. There are *no* similar guidelines under the Age Discrimination in Employment Act of 1967. However, experts point out that the courts have been applying the basic line of reasoning expressed in the Guidelines in all employment discrimination matters.

2. This requirement is central, for the Guidelines state that "evidence of a test's validity should consist of empirical data demonstrating that the test is predictive of or significantly correlated with important elements of work behavior which comprise or are relevant to the job or jobs for which candidates are being evaluated."

3. The Guidelines establish several requirements for the criterion measures used in validation studies: that criteria "must represent major or critical work behaviors as revealed by careful job analyses"; and that supervisory rating techniques be carefully developed and closely examined for evidence of bias "in view of the possibility of bias inherent in subjective evaluations."

4. *Albemarle Paper Company* v. *Moody*. U.S. Supreme Court, nos. 74-389 and 74-428. 10 FEP Cases 1181 (1975). Also, *Moody* v. *Albemarle Paper Company*, 474 F. 2d. 134 (1973).

5. This point is discussed further in the *Rogers* v. *International Paper* case. In discussing the potential for abuse (discriminatory practices) in the use of subjective appraisals as criterion measures in the test validation process the Court stated that "the [resulting] absence of proper and careful job analyses [therefore] is fatal to the validation study."

6. *Wade* v. *Mississippi Cooperative Extension Service*, 372 F. Supp. 126 (1974).

7. *Rowe* v. *General Motors Corporation*, 457 F. 2d. 348 (1972).

8. *Baxter* v. *Savannah Sugar Refining Corporation*, 350 F. Supp. 139 (1972).

9. *Brito* v. *Zia Company*, 478 F. 2d. 1200 (1973).

10. *Harper* v. *Mayor & City Council of Baltimore*, 359 F. Supp. 1187 (1973).

11. *Griggs* v. *Duke Power Company*, 401 U.S. 424 (1971) established the precedent for preemployment test validation.

12. The results of this survey [are published in] *Appraising Management Performance*, Robert I. Lazer (The Conference Board Inc.).

13. These typically include such factors as: influence, initiative, judgment, resourcefulness creativity, mental alertness intelligence, attitude/personality, commitment, tact, courtesy, openness to criticism, stability, self-control, loyalty, integrity, maturity.

Behaviorally-based Rating Scales: Toward an Integrated Approach to Performance Appraisal

JAMES G. GOODALE

Evaluating the performance of employees has presented a severe challenge to managers, personnel officers, and behavioral scientists alike. Condensing an employee's performance over the period of six months or a year into a relatively concise and meaningful appraisal is difficult. Measures of performance can be objective or judgmental. Of the two, judgmental procedures probably create greater problems for supervisors because of the subjectivity required in translating an employee's performance into a series of evaluations on a sheet of paper. Objective measures such as sales volume, scrap, errors, and words per minute ease the difficulty somewhat, although even this type of measure may not accurately represent an employee's level of performance. Simple measures of output may suffer from criterion deficiency in that they reflect only a small portion of the individual's total contribution to the organization. In addition, measures of results may be contaminated by influences outside the employee's control (e.g., machine malfunctions, variations in market conditions, influence of team members or other departments), and thus misrepresent his actual performance.

The purpose of this essay is to evaluate a number of judgmental techniques for performance appraisal on two criteria. The first criterion is the psychometric quality of the appraisal tool. Is it reliable? Is it valid? Is it highly subject to rating errors such as central tendency, leniency, and halo? The second criterion is the usefulness of the performance appraisal to the employee. Does it assist him in making changes in his performance?

Performance appraisal techniques typically concentrate on one of the three kinds of information about the employee shown in table 1: traits (what he is), behavior (what he does), and goals (what he achieves).

TABLE 1
ALTERNATIVE PERFORMANCE APPRAISAL SYSTEMS

Information Collected	Traits (what employee is)	Behavior (what employee does)	Goals (what employee achieves)
Appraisal Method	Trait-rating scales	Essay appraisals Behavioral checklists Behaviorally-based rating scales	Management by objectives Work planning and review

Trait-rating Scales

By far the most common judgmental evaluation tool is the rating scale (see Guion,

This article was prepared especially for this book.

1965, p. 96). Rating scales come in many sizes and shapes (e.g., Guion, 1965, p. 98), but they typically are headed by the characteristic being rated (e.g., initiative, maturity, personality). Along the continuum of the scale are numbers and usually phrases to identify different levels of the characteristic under scrutiny (e.g., excellent, average, consistently exceeds requirements). Although widely used, rating scales tend to be unreliable measures; that is, two persons rating the same employee with the same scale tend to disagree in their evaluations.

Two psychometric problems characterize trait-rating scales. One problem is that what is being rated is not clearly defined. Consequently, two supervisors using the same scale, but interpreting if differently, will be using different standards. Another problem with a typical rating scale is that the points along the scale are not clearly defined. What is "good" to one rater may be only "average" to another. These two sources of ambiguity may lead to wide discrepancies in ratings two supervisors make on the same employee. Ambiguous scales can also lead to common rating errors such as central tendency (rating most employees average), leniency (rating most employees above average), stringency (rating most employees below average), and halo (forming a general impression of an employee's worth and then rating him at a similar level on each trait to be judged).

Rating scales of traits give an employee feedback about what he is, rather than what he does. They force the rater to evaluate unobservable, inferred characteristics such as initiative, maturity and attitude. This places the supervisor in the position of judging the basic character of their employees ("playing God" in McGregor's [1957] terms). Both the giver and the receiver find this kind of feedback very disconcerting. Anyone who has tried to explain to an employee why he has been rated low (unclear) in initiative (undefined and unobserved) knows why difficulty in performance appraisal interviews can often be attributed to rating scales.

Argyris (1970) and Anderson (1970) have discussed the characteristics of useful feedback. In particular they emphasize that feedback should be specific and behavioral in nature. If feedback is given to employees in order to change their job performance, then the most useful feedback is in terms of *specific job performance*. It is clear that ratings of employee traits fail to meet this criterion of useful feedback. Telling a subordinate that he is average in initiative, low in attitude, and above average in maturity creates defensive feelings and gives him little help in how to change. Similarly, a rating of "barely meets acceptable standards" in quality of work is too unspecific to be very useful to an employee. In sum, trait-rating scales are extremely ambiguous and, as a result, lead to common rating errors. In addition, they provide feedback which is of little use to the employee who wants to change his job performance.

Goal-oriented Performance Appraisal

These fundamental flaws in rating scales may have contributed to a hurried dash away from judgmental evaluation tools and toward more objective systems, such as management by objectives (Odiorne, 1965) and work planning and review (Meyer, Kay and French, 1965). These systems focus on employee goals (what he achieves). Goals are set either by the supervisor alone or jointly by the supervisor and his employee. Some examples of relatively objective goals are an increase of 2 percent in sales, or a reduction of 5 percent in turnover. Employees are evaluated very simply in terms of whether or not they meet their goals.

These appraisal systems have the advantage of relative precision of standards. There can be little misinterpretation of a performance standard which is stated in terms of sales or turnover. A major problem, however, is that these objectives may not fairly reflect the individual employee's performance. Goals are frequently influenced by many factors outside the control of the employee, such as economic conditions, regional variation in sales potential, and performance of other employees. Hence, while being reliable, the goals may not be valid.

Another problem arises in the nature of the feedback generated by goal-setting appraisal techniques. Feedback is given to an employee as a basis for improvement in job performance. Feedback about what he has or has not achieved, however, says little to the employee about what he must *do* in order to improve. We may tell an employee that he missed his sales quota by 2 percent, but this information alone is not very useful. He needs feedback about his daily on-the-job performance which contributed to his failure to accomplish his goal. He needs feedback about how well he communicates product knowledge, how well he establishes and maintains good relationships with customers, how well he closes the sale, and so forth. While most goal-oriented appraisal systems are supplemented with coaching about specific job performance, an alternative is a performance appraisal system in which both goal achievement and job performance are systematically evaluated and fed back to the employee.

Behaviorally-based Performance Appraisal

The two approaches to performance evaluation so far discussed represent the extremes of the continuum shown in table 1. The third approach, the evaluation of behavior, will now be addressed. Appraisal techniques which focus on employee performance can take a variety of forms. Narratives or "essay appraisals" (Oberg, 1972) describe specifically what the employee does on the job, and are rich in behavioral detail. Writing the narratives can be extremely time-consuming, however, and another weakness is that narratives do not allow for comparisons among employees. Behavioral checklists and critical incident techniques are more quantitative in nature and may allow for ordering of employees. A more recently developed tool for evaluating employee behavior, which builds on the strengths of narratives and critical incident techniques, is the behaviorally-based rating scale.

Smith and Kendall (1963) introduced a unique procedure for developing behavioral expectation scales (which have also been called "behaviorally-based rating scales"). In this procedure, areas of performance to be evaluated are identified and defined by the people who will use the scales. The scales are anchored by descriptions of actual job behavior which supervisors agree represent specific levels of performance. The result is a set of rating scales in which both dimensions and anchors are very precisely defined. In addition, all dimensions of performance to be evaluated are based on observable behaviors and are relevant to the job being evaluated, since the instrument is tailor-made for the job. Finally, since potential raters are actively involved in the development process, they are committed to the product.

Although behaviorally-based rating scales were originally thought to be technically superior to other types of rating scales (Dunnette, 1966; Campbell, Dunnette, Arvey, and Hellervick, 1973; Zedeck and Baker, 1972), recent evidence has questioned their superiority (Schwab, Heneman, and DeCotiis, 1975; Bernardin, Alvares, and Cranny, 1976). Their greatest advantage, however, is their clarity to both the rater and the employee being rated.

Performance Aspect: Understanding, sensitivity, support, courtesy, tact, and cooperation in interaction with patients, customers, visitors, supervisors, and staff.

Always shows understanding, sensitivity, support, courtesy, tact, and cooperation in interaction with others.

7 — ...could be expected to explain to patient that the nurse is supposed to roll up the bed and to show patient how to call the nurse.

6 — ...could be expected to remain calm and polite when confronted by an abrupt visitor, offering assistance to help with the problem.

5 —

...could be expected to feel for "weaker" subordinates occasionally and trade her easy tasks for their more difficult ones.

4 —

Usually shows understanding, sensitivity, support, courtesy, tact, and cooperation in interaction with others.

3 —

...could be expected to become frustrated in some staff dealings.

...could be expected to resent assistance offered by co-worker or supervisor.

2 —

Seldom shows understanding, sensitivity, support, courtesy, tact, and cooperation in interaction with others.

...could be expected to be concerned with own problems and not to help others.

...could be expected to speak abruptly and discourteously when answering a customer's inquiry about an entire dish that was new to the regular menu.

1 —

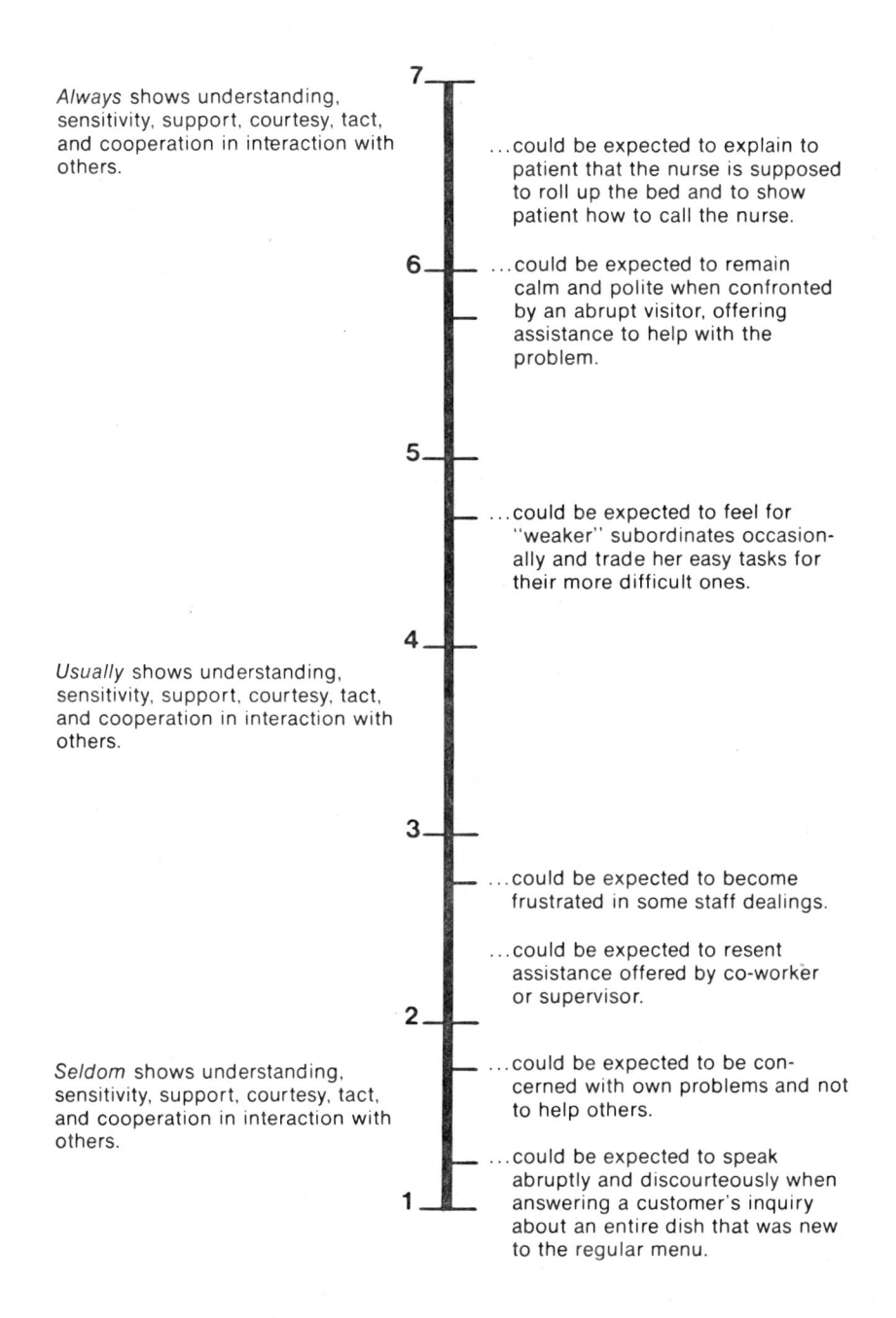

Figure 1. Forming and Maintaining Interpersonal Relationships

An example of a behaviorally-based rating scale is shown in figure 1. Compared to a trait-rating scale, it is more easily understood by both the person doing the evaluation and the employee receiving feedback. First, the aspect of performance being rated is defined. This definition acts as a common standard which will help raters interpret the scale in a consistent manner.

Second, the dimension to be rated, "forming and maintaining interpersonal relationships," can be directly observed. We can see how people relate to others, just as we can see them plan and organize, lead, and apply knowledge and skills on the job. Third, the anchors (words which give meaning to numbers on the scale) are examples of job performance, not ambiguous adjectives or phrases found in trait-rating scales. These descriptions of specific job-related behavior will be consistently interpreted by both supervisors and employees being evaluated.

Feedback given with behaviorally-based rating scales is specific and job-related. An employee who is rated "5" sees a specific performance incident which his supervisor feels is most comparable to that employee's level of performance of the aspect of his job under review. Behavioral incidents at "6" and "7" can be performance goals for the employee. In sum, behaviorally-based rating scales provide for the discussion of evaluations in specific, performance terms.

Developing Behaviorally-based Rating Scales

The procedure outlined below for developing behaviorally-based rating scales follows relatively closely that first introduced by Smith and Kendall (1963). More recently, however, variations in the original procedure have been discussed and tested by Bernardin, La Shells, Smith, and Alvares (1976), and may be of interest to the reader. Let's assume that a personnel officer is coordinating the program to develop a set of rating scales. Here are the steps to be followed:

Step 1. The number and kinds of jobs to which the rating scales will apply must be identified. Behaviorally-based rating scales may be developed for one job in organizations in which a large percentage of employees perform one job (e.g., nurses in hospitals), or the scales may be developed for all jobs in an entire organization (Goodale and Burke, 1974). The personnel officer, perhaps in collaboration with line management, must decide what jobs the scales will be used to evaluate (and, consequently, which supervisors will be involved).

Step 2: Orientation Meeting. Since the rating scales are developed by supervisors who will use them, it is important that the supervisors be given an overview of the entire procedure. In addition, an overview meeting provides an opportunity for the personnel officer to learn about performance appraisal issues which are important to the supervisors. He must also learn how strongly committed management is to a new set of rating scales. Between 10 and 30 supervisors should participate in the entire procedure of scale development. If in step 1 more than 30 supervisors are identified, a representative sample of 30 should be selected at this time.

Step 3: Definition of Areas of Performance. The supervisors next meet for up to a full day to identify the areas of performance they wish to evaluate, and to define those areas. The group is encouraged to propose any number of areas, subject to the following constraints: (1) the areas of performance should be observable; this eliminates traits such as initiative, maturity, and personality; (2) the performance areas should be attributable to individuals, rather than to groups; and (3) each area should be broad enough to be sufficiently important to be evaluated. Usually 40 or 50 potential areas are listed on the board in this brainstorming task. Then the list is reduced by combining similar areas, and eliminating those that really do not meet the three criteria. Typically between 5 and 15 areas of performance are selected.

Then the entire group struggles to define each area in terms of what it means in the context of their jobs and organization. This is a slow, difficult but very satisfying process. Incidentally, completing these first three steps would probably lead to an improvement over most existing rating systems.

Step 4: Generating Behavioral Examples of the Areas of Performance. The supervisors, working individually, are then asked to write behavioral items—actual, specific, observable behaviors they have seen or might see employees doing—which fall in each of the areas of performance. For each area of performance they are instructed to write some examples of a very high level of performance in that area, a moderate level, and a very low level. (An example of a very low level of forming and maintaining interpersonal relationships, for example, would be, "yells at customer not to bother him again and slams down the telephone receiver.")

The personnel manager would then read these items, eliminate duplicates, correct grammar and spelling, and omit those which are too general or unobservable. A group of 30 supervisors can easily generate 900 items.

Step 5: Assigning Examples to Performance Areas. The items are then listed in random order in a questionnaire. Working individually, supervisors read each item and assign it to the area of performance they think it represents best. They place an item in an "other" category if it doesn't seem to fit well anywhere.

The personnel officer then tallies a frequency distribution for each item. Items assigned to a given performance area by 80 percent or more of the supervisors are retained. Such a high level of agreement indicates that the example of performance is interpreted consistently by most of the supervisors. Items not meeting the 80 percent criterion are discarded.

Step 6: Assigning Scale Values to Items. The items surviving step 5 are then grouped by performance area and presented in questionnaire form. Again working individually, the supervisors read each item and assign it a value ranging from 1 (a low level of performance), through 4 (a moderate level), to 7 (a high level of performance). A good strategy to use in assigning scale values to items is to first decide which of the three levels of performance the item corresponds to (is it high, moderate, or low?) and then decide which number is most appropriate.

The personnel officer than computes means and standard deviations of the scale values assigned to each item. The mean represents the level of behavior illustrated by each item, and the standard deviation, a measure of dispersion or range, indicates how much the supervisors agree on the scale value. Because low standard deviations mean high agreement among supervisors, items with standard deviations of 1.50 or less should be retained. These retained items are the anchors which will define the points along the rating scale.

The time invested in the six steps ranges from two and one half to three days. The result is a set of rating scales which are very precisely defined and accepted by raters.

Using the Scales

There are two procedures which can be followed in evaluating a subordinate with behaviorally-based rating scales.

The first, and simplest, is to follow the procedure appropriate for any type of rating scale. The supervisor simply recalls what he can about a subordinate's performance in the area of, say, forming and maintaining interpersonal relationships, and assigns the performance a value from 1 to 7. With behaviorally-based scales the supervisor has two advantages. First, he knows what he means by forming and maintaining interpersonal relationships. Second, his standards of comparison are clearer. For example, he can compare his recollection of his subordinate's performance with each anchor on the scale and ask, "Is my subordinate's behavior similar to this standard, to this one, or to this one?" He then gives his subordinate the rating of the anchor which is most similar to what his subordinate typically does.

Keep a Diary

Of course this system depends heavily on the supervisor's recollection of his subordinate's performance. And we know that recent or extreme events stay in our minds and can bias our impressions of a person's typical performance over the period of six months or a year being evaluated. This deficiency is addressed in the second method of using behaviorally-based rating scales. The procedure requires the supervisor to observe and record his subordinates' performance systematically. In other words, the supervisor keeps a diary of a portion of the performance of his subordinates for, say, a year.

At evaluation time, the supervisor makes two judgments. First, he decides which of the main areas of performance (which rating scale) each diary anecdote falls under. Second, he compares each anecdote allocated to a given scale with the standard anchors on the scale and assigns it a scale value. The subordinate's rating in forming and maintaining interpersonal relationships would be the average of the scale values assigned to the anecdotes of his performance which fall into this category. This procedure obviously relieves the boss of the chore of remembering details about his subordinates' performance. Instead, he consults his anecdotal records and bases his evaluation on them. A more detailed description of this procedure may be found in Tate (1964) and in Burke and Goodale (1973).

Installing the System

The installation of any performance appraisal system represents a major organizational change. If it is viewed as such, then the change will probably be made most smoothly if the principles of organizational development are followed. Argyris (1970) had argued that organizational development has the greatest possibility of succeeding when employees (a) can generate valid information, (b) can develop internal commitment, and (c) have opportunity for free and informed choice. Another basic prerequisite for a successful program of organization development is a strong and widely felt need for change experienced by many employees in the client system.

In each of the four instances in which I have assisted an organization in developing a set of behaviorally-based rating scales, the need for a new system of performance appraisal has been voiced most strongly by relatively low-level employees. Their complaints against the existing rating forms eventually reached the personnel manager or a department/division head who was willing to make a change.

Typically, Ronald J. Burke, a colleague at York University, and I were then approached by the organization and invited to install a new performance appraisal system. We tried to follow consistently the basic steps of OD—entry, diagnosis, action, rediagnosis—and to involve members of the organization in each step. The procedure described below for installing a performance appraisal system follows from what Burke and I have learned from our experiences.

Entry. At entry, test the commitment for a new system at several levels of the organization. Commitment at the top is imperative since it is at that level that the decision must be made to develop a new performance appraisal system. The importance attached to performance appraisal is also set at the top. The commitment of the personnel department is critical to success of the system because they will administer and maintain it. Supervisors and managers must be committed because they will develop and implement the system. Finally, it is advisable to talk with or administer questionnaires to the employees who will be evaluated with the new system to determine what kind of evaluation and feedback they want.

Diagnosis. At this stage, the objectives of the performance appraisal system must be learned—how the ratings are to be used and for what purposes. This must be agreed upon internally before a system can be tailored to the organization's needs. At this stage the procedure for developing behaviorally-based rating scales is explained and the involvement of the supervisors is emphasized. The system will be only as good as the input from supervisors at the developmental stage.

Action. The action phase involves both the development of the set of rating scales (as described previously) and training in how to use the scales. In addition, extensive training is given in the techniques of performance appraisal interviewing, giving day-to-day feedback to employees, and goal setting.

Rediagnosis. Ideally, after the system has been operational for a year or longer, its psychometric characteristics should be assessed, and it should be examined in terms of the goals it was to meet. Revisions can then be made if necessary.

An Integrated System

In conclusion, a well-integrated performance appraisal system is one that includes measures of employee behavior and goals (columns 2 and 3 of table 1). My recommendation would be a set of behaviorally-based rating scales and a goal-setting approach such as management by objectives or work planning and review. Such a system evaluates the day-to-day job performance of an employee but also monitors more long-term goals and objectives. It provides feedback in terms of what the employee does and what he achieves. It combines the specificity and psychometric rigor of rating scales with the objectivity and future orientation of a results-based system.

Note

I would like to express my appreciation to Ronald J. Burke for his helpful comments on an earlier draft of this essay.

References

Anderson, J. Giving and receiving feedback. In Dalton, G. W., P. R. Lawrence, and L. Greiner (eds.). *Organization change and development.* Homewood, Illinois: Irwin, 1970.

Argyris, C. *Intervention theory and method: A behavioral science view.* Reading, Mass.: Addison-Wesley, 1970.

Bernardin, H. J., Alvares, K. M., and Cranny, C. S. A recomparison of behavioral expectation scales to summated scales. *Journal of Applied Psychology,* 1976, 61, 564-70.

Bernardin, H. J., La Shells, M. B., Smith, P. C., and Alvares, K. M. Behavioral expectation scales: Effects of developmental procedures and formats. *Journal of Applied Psychology,* 1976, 61, 75-79.

Burke, R. J., and Goodale, J. G. Developing behaviorally-anchored rating scales for evaluating nursing performance. *Hospital,* 1973 (Dec. 16), 62-68.

Campbell, J. P., Dunnette, M. D., Arvey, R. D., and Hellervik, L. W. The development and evaluation of behaviorally based rating scales. *Journal of Applied Psychology,* 1973, 57, 15-22.

Dunnette, M. D. *Personnel selection and placement.* Belmont: Wadsworth, 1966.

Goodale, J. G. and Burke, R. J. Behaviorally based rating scales need not be job specific. *Journal of Applied Psychology,* 1975, 60, 389-91.

Guion, R. M. *Personnel testing.* New York: McGraw Hill, 1965.

McGregor, D. An uneasy look at performance appraisal. *Harvard Business Review,* May-June, 1957, 35, 89-94.

Meyer, H. H., Kay, E., and French, J. P. R., Jr. Split roles in performance appraisal. *Harvard Business Review,* Jan.-Feb., 1965, 43, 123-29.

Oberg, W. Make performance appraisal relevant. *Harvard Business Review,* Jan.-Feb., 1972, 50, 61-67.

Odiorne, G. S. *Management by objectives: A system of managerial leadership.* New York: Pitman, 1965.

Schwab, D. P., Heneman, H. G. III, and DeCotiis, T. A. Behaviorally anchored rating scales: A review of the literature. *Personnel Psychology,* 1975, 28, 549-562.

Smith, P. C. and Kendall, L. M. Retranslation of expectations: An approach to the construction of unambiguous anchors for rating scales. *Journal of Applied Psychology,* 1963, 47, 149-155.

Tate, B. L. *A method for rating the proficiency of a hospital general staff nurse.* New York: National League of Nursing, 1964.

Zedeck, S. and Baker, H. T. Nursing performance as measured by behavioral expectation scales: A multitrait-multirater analysis. *Organizational Behavior and Human Performance,* 1972, 7, 457-66.

CHAPTER **7**

Motivating Performance in Organizational Settings

In the first reading in this section, Hamner compares and contrasts three proactive motivational programs which are currently being used by organizations. The *positive reinforcement* program, as used by Michigan Bell and Emery Air Freight, is based on the theory that behavior is determined by its consequences. The *task structure* (job enrichment) approach, as used by AT&T, assumes that making a task intrinsically rewarding will lead to increased output. The *climate* or organizational development (O.D.) approach, as used by General Motors and Saga Industries, is based on the premise that the work climate and attitudes of fellow employees can enhance or be detrimental to employee performance. (As noted by Beer and Huse, after the work group has been through a stage of unfreezing and trust building, recommendations made by the group for improving performance may include rearranging the task or changing the consequences of the task. O.D., then, is designed to change the attitudes of people as well as the task structure and reinforcement consequences, whereas a positive reinforcement approach is primarily interested in changing the feedback system, and a job enrichment approach is primarily interested in changing the task involvement. Therefore, the three programs reviewed in the Hamner article, while not independent approaches, work on different components of the job and involve different levels of intervention by the organization.)

As an elaboration on the three proactive programs discussed by Hamner, Hamner and Hamner review how positive reinforcement is being used by various firms today. Dowling traces the use of job enrichment in three major manufacturing firms in the U.S. and Europe, and Beer and Huse describe how a systems approach to O.D. was successfully applied in an ongoing setting.

In the last reading in section A of this chapter, Tosi and Carroll discuss how participation by subordinates in the goal-setting process can increase worker involvement, motivation, and planning behavior—which ultimately increases performance.

In section B, Hamner describes how pay can be used to motivate good performance. Following the premise of the positive reinforcement approach, Hamner's point is clear: If pay is not a motivator of performance, it isn't because the Law of Effect (Thorndike, *Individuality,* 1911) is wrong; it is because pay is not tied to performance. Hamner concludes his article by giving us several rules for improving merit programs found in organizations today.

Of course one of the problems of many merit programs is that they are based on individual performance, when in fact individuals do not, in most cases, perform independently. Many companies are now overcoming this problem by introducing a group incentive plan. Leisure and Puckett examine the leading group incentive plan, the Scanlon plan, as it is used in organizations today.

Section A
Applied Motivation Programs

Worker Motivation Programs: The Importance of Climate, Structure, and Performance Consequences

W. CLAY HAMNER

In the past few years, management, unions, and government agencies have joined workers in demanding that changes be made in the work environment in order to improve the quality of work life and to create an atmosphere which would lead to increased productivity. Levitan and Johnston (1973a) say that workers are able to demand more today because of a rise in income which has loosened the economic bond of the work place. Workers are now able to trade marginal boosts in income for more leisure.

In order to examine the current status of worker discontent, the Secretary of Labor commissioned the Survey Research Center at the University of Michigan to examine the attitudes of workers toward their jobs and the organizations for whom they worked. The results indicated that a significant number of American workers are dissatisfied with the quality of their working lives. Dull, repetitive, seemingly meaningless tasks, offering little challenge or autonomy, are causing discontent among workers at all occupational levels. This discontent has resulted in a restricting of output, poor quality work, and refusal of overtime. It has contributed to high absenteeism and turnover rates and to militant demands for higher wages, more fringe benefits, and greater participation in decision making *(Work in America,* 1973).

Long before this report was completed, management began to examine ways to improve the work environment in order to reverse the trends of higher absenteeism and turnover caused by worker discontent. Management's philosophy seems to be shifting away from the belief that an increase in the rights and benefits of workers leads to a decrease in the rights and benefits of management, and shifting toward a belief that an investment in a program which will benefit the worker will also benefit management. Stephen H. Fuller, Vice-president of Personnel and Organizational Development at General Motors said "We do not view this [worker motivation program] as an either/or situation. Our challenge is *not* people versus profit, it is people *and*

This article was prepared especially for this book.

profit" (Fuller, 1973). John F. Donnelly, President of Donnelly Mirrors, Inc., concurred, saying,

> We continued to invest heavily in consulting services and training in the behavioral sciences because these investments seemed to pay off more consistently than investments in equipment. In fact, we began to see that the more effectively we used behavioral science to engage our people, the more wisely we made our capital investments (Donnelly, 1971, p. 10).

In their attempt to improve the quality of the working experience, workers often find the union as much of an obstacle as management. When the auto workers in General Motors' Vega plant in Lordstown, Ohio, struck asking for an improvement in quality of their work life, the international leaders of the United Automobile Workers insisted on bargaining for more pay and shorter working hours to take the worker away from the job (Drucker, 1973). However, there are many indications that unions are now becoming interested in "people programs" which will improve the quality of the work environment and increase productivity. The new union attitude favoring increased productivity came about primarily as a result of the pressure of the energy crisis and foreign competition, rather than from demands of workers, management or governmental agencies. Unions, like management, appear to accept that an increase in productivity *and* an increase in the quality of the workers' involvement in the organization are compatible with each other and in the best interest of workers and unions as well as management. I. W. Abel, President of the United Steel Workers of America, summarized the changing attitude of unions toward productivity and quality of work life when he stated:

> I call upon every American to enlist in the crucial battle to improve our lagging productivity. Nothing less is at stake than our jobs, the price we pay, the very quality of our lives . . . . Things have been so good for so long that we've become wasteful and inefficient. So wasteful that, incredibly enough, many firms nowadays actually expect to scrap 20 percent of what they produce . . . . How can we improve? In these ways:
> *By stepping up the efficiency of each worker.* Does this mean work speedings, job eliminations? Hardly. It does mean cutting down on excessive absenteeism, tardiness, turnover, and overtime. It does mean improving the morale of workers, more effective work incentive—and really listening to the man at the work bench. . . .
> *By improving our technology and really using the technology we already possess* . . . . The steel industry and the United Steel Workers of America have established joint advisory committees on productivity at each plant. This cooperative venture is a recognition that workers and employers share a common problem. (Abel, 1973)

In response to pressure from these various groups to make the work more challenging and rewarding, many organizations have set up formal motivation programs. While there are many titles for these programs, most of the innovative programs currently being tried can be classified into one of three categories. The *positive reinforcement* program works on the premise that behavior is determined by its consequences. The *task structure* or job enrichment program assumes that a job which a worker finds intrinsically rewarding and challenging will motivate the worker to increase his level of performance. The *climate* or the organizational development program is based on the theory that the organizational climate and the attitudes of fellow employees can enhance or be detrimental to employee performance.

Each of these programs works on the premise that some form of change in the organization can lead to an improvement in employee performance. A climate approach is designed to change the task structure and reinforcing consequences as well as the attitudes of people, while a positive reinforcement approach is primarily interested in the feedback system and a task structure approach is primarily interested in changing the task involvement of the worker. While the three programs reviewed are not independent approaches, they work on different components of the job and involve different levels of intervention by the organization.

Each of these three kinds of worker motivation programs are "proactive" programs in the sense that they are programs which are designed not only to cure current "industrial ills," but are also designed to anticipate and prevent future problems with worker discontent. A fourth approach currently being used by some organizations is a program designed to give workers more time away from the work place and more variety in scheduling their hours of work. The *flexitime* and *four-day-work-week* programs are a reactive approach to the problem of worker alienation which are designed to allow the workers free time away from a negative work atmosphere, rather than designed to change one or more of the components of the work environment.

Each of these approaches will now be examined in relation to its theoretical assumptions and their effectiveness in organizational settings. Since each program has its own group of followers, it is only natural that criticisms for each program have also been generated. These criticism and disadvantages will also be presented along with recommendations for future use of motivation programs.

Positive Reinforcement Program

Theoretical Background

The principles of positive reinforcement are based on the premise that people perform in the way that they find most rewarding to them and that management can improve the worker's performance by providing the proper rewards. The theoretical underpinnings of this program are based on the learning principles described by Thorndike (1911) and Skinner (1953).[1] Thorndike's Law of Effect states simply that behavior which appears to lead to a positive consequence tends to be repeated, while behavior which appears to lead to a neutral or negative consequence tends not to be repeated. Skinner and his followers (see, e.g., Wiard, 1972; Whyte, 1972; Nord, 1969; Hamner, 1974) contend that when workers enter the work place they have developed a sense of right versus wrong and have been thoroughly conditioned by their parents and by society. Therefore, they argue that the only tool needed for worker motivation is the presence or absence of positive reinforcement. In other words, managers do not, as a general rule, need to use avoidance learning or punishment techniques in order to control behavior.

Whyte (1972) says "positive reinforcers generally are more effective than negative reinforcers in the production and maintenance of behavior" (p. 67). Wiard (1972) points out, "there may be cases where the use of punishment has resulted in improved performance, but they are few and far between" (p. 16). Drucker (1973) says "B. F. Skinner's rigorous research on learning theory leaves little room to doubt that rewards, or positive reinforcements, are the efficient way to learn" (p. 92). Skinner best summarizes the simplicity of a positive reinforcement program when he says:

> ... Supervision by positive reinforcement changes the whole atmosphere of the workspace and produces better results. A constantly critical position on the part of the supervisor encourages bad morale, absenteeism and job changing. ... With positive reinforcement you get at least the same amount of work, and the worker is more likely to show up every day and less likely to change jobs. In the long run, both the company and the worker are better off ("Conversations with B. F. Skinner," 1973, p. 35).

Sorcher and Goldstein (1972) agree with Skinner that one reason organizations fail to motivate workers is that they "turn them off" rather than "turn them on" with their reinforcement practices. They state that a good illustration of this maladaptive behavior is the manager who attempts to motivate an employee to improve his poor performance, but simply threatens him to the point where the employee becomes less effective and more hostile toward the manager.

A positive reinforcement philosophy of management differs from traditional motivational theories (see Hunt and Hill, 1970) in basically two ways. First, as noted above, a positive reinforcement program calls for the maximum use of positive reinforcement and the minimum use of punishment. Punishment tends to leave the individual feeling controlled and coerced and leads to immaturity in the individual, and therefore eventually in the organization itself (e.g., see Tannenbaum, 1962, and Argyris, 1964). Second, a positive reinforcement program avoids psychological probing into the worker's attitudes as a possible cause of behavior. Instead, the work situation itself is analyzed, focusing on the reward contingencies which cause a worker to act the way he does.

A positive reinforcement program, therefore, is results-oriented, rather than process-oriented. Geary A. Rummler, President of Praxis Corporation, a management consultant firm, claims that the motivational theories of behavioral scientists such as Herzberg and Maslow, which stress workers' psychological needs, are impractical. "They can't be made operative. While they help to classify the problem, a positive reinforcement program leads to solutions" *(International Management,* 1973, p. 35). Sorcher and Goldstein (1972) agree, stating that a positive reinforcement procedure is quite different from the traditional approach to behavior change in that it does not rely on an approach aimed at first changing attitudes, then hoping that behavior will fall in line with those attitudes. "Instead, this procedure is based on some of the fundamentals of social learning, i.e., imitation (behavioral rehearsal) and reinforcement, and is aimed directly at behavior change without relying on the diversionary tactics of attitude change" (p. 41).

Stages in Program Development

Positive reinforcement programs currently used in industry generally involve at least four stages. The *first step* according to E. J. Feeney, Vice-president of Emery Air Freight Corporation, is to define the *behavioral* aspects of performance and do a performance audit.[2] This step is potentially one of the most difficult, since some companies do not have a formal performance evaluation program, especially for the nonmanagerial employees, and those which do have a program are often rating the employee on nonbehavioral or nonjob-related measures (e.g., friendliness, overall attitude, etc.). But once these behavioral aspects of the job are defined, and managers see how poorly some of these are being performed, the task of convincing managers that improvement is needed and persuading them to cooperate with such a program is simplified. Feeney reports, "Most managers genuinely think that operations in their bailiwick are doing well; a performance audit that proves they're not comes as a real and unpleasant surprise" *(Organizational Dynamics,* 1973b, p. 42).

Not only does the performance audit help the manager accept the program, but it also helps the employees identify themselves as meaningful contributors to the objectives of the organization. Frost (1973) said:

> If the employees are helped to identify "what day it is"—the competitive bid made for the job, the cost of the materials, the cost of the machine, its coolants, and maintenance, the cost of set-up and down time, . . . the employees can perceive the relevance of their contribution and the rationale of management's administration. Everyone in the organization becomes important and an interdependent part. Everyone in the organization comes to play a small part or a big part, but an essential part. Everyone becomes a resource that is available and called upon to perform effectively to achieve the organization's objectives. The personal and professional goals for dignity, recognition and significance become compatible with the organization's need to be fiscally sound and competitive (p. 4).

Defined levels of performance which are specifically determined and clearly stated, therefore, help both the manager and the employee establish a base-line measure against which to measure their future performance (Wiard, 1972; Emery, 1973). Rummler *(International Management,* 1973) says that a person should get all the data that are available about his performance, not selective information. Ideally, it should come from the system, from a computer, so that it appears objective, neutral, and unemotional. In this manner, the employee and the manager are better able to accept the program as one that will mutually benefit them both.

The *second step* in developing a working positive reinforcement program is to develop and set specific and reasonable goals for each worker. Sorcher and Goldstein (1972) suggest that the failure to specify concrete behavioral goals is a major reason many programs do not work. They state, "Goals must be defined in measurable terms—they should be expressed in behavioral terms such as employee turnover or schedules met rather than only in terms of 'better identification with the company' or 'increased job satisfaction'" (p. 36). The goals set, therefore, should be in the same terms as those defined in the performance audit as being specifically related to the task at hand. The goals should be reasonable and set somewhere between "where you are" (as defined in the performance audit) and some ideal.

While goals can be set by the manager, it is important that they are accepted by the employee. An even better approach would be to allow the employees to work with management in the setting of the work goals. By using a participatory management technique to enlist the ideas of those performing the job, you gain not only the acceptance of goals, but also means and ways of obtaining new goals, according to J. C. Emery, President of Emery Air Freight Corporation (1973).

Luthans and White (1971) see the popular management system, management by objectives (MBO)[3] as providing an excellent system for meeting the first two stages of a positive reinforcement program. They state, "Manpower managers can utilize behavior modification[4] techniques to generate direction and self-control among all levels of personnel. . . . Management by objectives provides an opportunity for all personnel to contribute to job goals and encourages the setting of checkpoints to measure progress" (p. 45). However, both Luthans and White (1971) and Carroll and Tosi (1973) agree that MBO goal setting alone is ineffective without feedback and positive reinforcement.

The *third step* in a positive reinforcement program is to allow the employee to keep a record of his or her own work. This process of self-feedback maintains a continuous schedule of reinforcement (see Ferster and Skinner, 1957) for the worker and permits the worker to gain intrinsic reinforcement from the task itself. Where employees can total their own results, they can see if they are meeting their goals or not and whether they are improving over their previous level of performance (as measured in the performance audit stage). In other words, the worker has two chances of being successful—either by beating his previous record or by beating both his previous record and his established goal. E. D. Grady, Division Traffic Manager for Michigan Bell, says that the manager should set up the work environment in such a way that people have a chance to succeed. One way to do this he says is to "shorten the success interval." Grady says, "If you're looking for success, keep shortening the interval of measurement so you can get a greater chance of success which you can latch on to for positive reinforcements" *(International Management,* 1973, p. 34). For example, rather than set goals in monthly or quarterly terms, set them in weekly or daily terms. This doesn't reduce the level of the goal, but it may reduce the perceived difficulty of the goal.

The *fourth step* of providing positive reinforcement for good performance is the most important step in a positive reinforcement program and is one that separates it from all other motivation plans. The supervisor looks at the self-feedback report of the employee and/or other indications of performance (e.g., sales records) and then praises the positive aspects of the employee's performance (as determined by the performance audit and goals set). This extrinsic reinforcement should strengthen the desired performance, while the withholding of praise for the performance which falls below the goal should give the employee incentive to improve that level of performance. Since the worker already knows the areas of his or her deficiencies, there is no reason for the supervisor to criticize the employee. In other words, negative feedback is self-induced, whereas positive feedback comes from both internal and external sources.

As noted previously, this approach to giving feedback follows the teachings of B. F. Skinner, who believes that use of positive reinforcement leads to a greater feeling of self-control, while the avoidance of negative reinforcements keeps the individual from feeling controlled or coerced. Skinner says "You can get the same effect if the supervisor simply discovers things being done right and says something like 'good, I see you're doing it the way that works best'" *(Organization Dynamics,* 1973a). Sorcher and Goldstein (1972) say the reason punishment fails is because of the increased education level and social status of the employee. Drucker (1973) says, "the stick fails because fear is altogether incompatible with the reliable production of knowledge. It produces efforts and anxieties, but it generally inhibits learning" (p. 92). Rummler says that when a manager has to go into the negative aspect of a workers performance, he should do it in a positive manner—"What can I do to help?" If he accuses the employee, the worker will have a dozen excuses.

While the feedback initially used in step four of the positive reinforcement program is praise, it is important to note that other forms of reinforcements can have the same effect. M. W. Warren, the Director of Organization and Management Development at the Questor Corporation, says that the five "reinforcers" that Questor has found to be the most effective are (1) money, but only when it is a consequence of a specific performance, and the relation to the performance is known; (2) praise or recognition; (3) freedom to choose one's own activity; (4) opportunity to see one's self become better, more important, or more useful; and (5) power to influence both co-workers and management. Warren states, "By building these reinforcers into programs at various facilities, Questor is getting results" (1972, p 29). The need for using more than praise after the positive reinforcement program has proved effective is discussed by Skinner.

> It does not cost the company anything to use praise rather than blame, but if the company then makes a great deal more money that way, the worker may seem to be getting gypped. However, the welfare of the worker depends on the welfare of the company, and if the company is smart enough to distribute some of the fruits of positive reinforcement in the form of higher wages and better fringe benefits, everybody gains from the supervisor's use of positive reinforcements *(Organizational Dynamics,* 1973a, p. 35).

Results of Positive Reinforcement Programs

Companies which claim to be implementing and using positive reinforcement programs such as the one described above include Emery Air Freight, Michigan Bell Telephone, Questor Corporation, Cole National Bank in Cleveland, Ford Motor Company, American Can, Upjohn, United Air Lines, Warner-Lambert, Addressograph-Multigraph, Allis-Chalmers, Bethlehem Steel, Chase Manhattan Bank, IBM, IT&T, Proctor and Gamble, PPG Industries, Standard Oil of Ohio, Westinghouse and Wheeling-Pittsburgh Steel Corporation (see *Business Week,* December 18, 1971, and December 2, 1972). In addition, another 200 firms have contacted E. J. Feeney of Emery Air Freight since Emery's success with positive reinforcement was first reported *(Organizational Dynamics,* 1973b). Because the program is relatively new in industrial settings (most have begun since 1968), few statements of their relative effectiveness have been reported. In December, 1972 *Business Week* stated that "there's little objective evidence available, and what evidence there is abounds in caveats—the technique will work under the proper circumstances, the parameters of which are usually not easily apparent" (p. 49).

In the area of employee training, Northern Systems Company (Nord, 1969), General Electric Corporation (Sorcher and Goldstein, 1972) and Emery Air Freight *(Organizational Dynamics,* 1973b) claim that positive reinforcement has improved the speed and efficiency of their training program. In their programmed learning program, the Northern Systems Company says the trainee gains satisfaction only be demonstrated performance at the tool station. Through positive reinforcements, he quickly perceives that correct behaviors obtain for him the satisfaction of his needs, and that incorrect behaviors do not (Nord, 1969). Emery has designed a similar program for sales trainees. *Business Week* (December 18, 1971) reported the success of the program by saying:

> It is a carefully engineered, step-by-step program, with frequent feedback questions and answers to let the salesman know how he is doing. The course contrasts with movies and lectures in which, Feeney says, the salesman is unable to gauge what he has learned. The aim is to get the customer on each sales call to take some kind of action indicating that he will use Emery services. Significantly, in 1968, the first full year after the new course was launched, sales jumped from $62.4 million to $79.8 million, a gain of 27.8 percent compared with an 11.3 percent rise the year before.

Since 1969, Emery has instituted a positive reinforcement program for all of its employees and credits the program with direct savings to the company of over $3 million in the past three years *(Organizational Dynamics,* 1973b) and indirectly with pushing 1973 sales over the $160 million mark. While Emery Air Freight is by far the biggest success story for a positive reinforcement program to date, other companies are also claiming improvements as a result of initiating similar programs. At Michigan Bell's Detroit office, 2,000 employees are now under a positive reinforcement program. Michigan Bell credits the program with reducing absenteeism from 11 percent to 6.5 percent in one group, from 7½ percent to 4½ percent in another group, and from 3.3 percent to 2.6 percent for all employees. In addition, the program has resulted in reports being completed correctly and on time 90 percent of the time as compared to 20 percent of the time prior to the program's implementation *(Business Week,* Dec. 2, 1972; *International Management,* 1973). The Wheeling-Pittsburgh Steel Corporation credits its feedback program with saving $200,000 a month in scrap costs *(Business Week,* Dec. 2, 1972).

In an attempt to reduce the number of employees who constantly violated plant rules, General Motors implemented a plan in one plant that gave employees opportunities to improve or clear their records by going through varying periods of time without committing further shop violations. They credit this positive reinforcement plan with reducing the number of punitive actions for shop rule infractions by two-thirds from 1969 to 1972 and the number of production standard grievances by 70 percent during the same period of time (Schotters, 1973a).

Gamboa and Pedalino (1973) describe a company which used a lottery to solve the problem of employee absenteeism. The company adopted a plan suggested by Skinner when he said:

> . . . Let's take an example of how you could use a lottery to solve the problem of absenteeism. With today's high wages, missing a day's wages doesn't much matter. But suppose you have something like a door prize every day. When you come to work, you get a ticket, and at the end of the day there's a drawing. Then a man will think twice before staying away. If absenteeism is a real problem, a reasonable prize per day might solve it. *(Organizational Dynamics,* 1973a).

In this company, each day an employee came to work and was on time, he was allowed to choose a card from a deck of playing cards. At the end of the five-day week, he had five cards or a normal poker hand. The highest hand in each department won $20.00, and all full-time employees who worked 50 days straight had their names placed in a lottery from which two $50.00 prizes were drawn. Absenteeism dropped from 3.01 percent to 2.46 percent (18.3 percent decrease) until the program was discontinued, at which time the absenteeism jumped to 3.2 percent. Ford Motor Company tried a similar lottery in which all employees within one section of a plant with a perfect attendance record for a month were eligible for a drawing to determine the winner of a prize worth $150.00. After several months the program was dropped because no change in absenteeism took place.

Criticisms of the Program

While critics of Skinner's theory are abundant, critics of a positive reinforcement approach applied to industry are few. Whyte (1972) said while he agreed with the principles of a positive reinforcement approach to management, he criticized the application of the program to the work force on the basis that it is generally developed on an individual feedback basis while many work situations depend on group cooperation. A second major criticism by Whyte is that "at its simplest level, the problem of the prediction and control of behavior involves creating conditions in which the behavior that positively reinforces one person also positively reinforces the other person (in the same group or organization) . . ." (p. 98). Therefore, what one worker finds rewarding, another may not. The design of the rewards are crucial, according to Whyte.

Skinner *(Organizational Dynamics,* 1973) and Whyte (1972) both state that a feedback system alone may not be enough. Skinner recommends that the organization should design feedback and incentive systems in such a way that the dual objective of getting things done and making work enjoyable is met. He states:

> It is important to remember that an incentive system isn't the only factor to take into account. How pleasant work conditions are, how easy or awkward a job is, how good or bad tools are—many things of that sort make an enormous difference in what a worker will do for what he receives. One problem of the production-line worker is that he seldom sees any of the ultimate consequences of his work. He puts on left front wheels day in and day out and he may never see the finished car. . . . (p. 39).

Drucker (1973) worries that perhaps the use of positive reinforcers may be misused by management to the detriment of the economy. "The carrot of material rewards has not, like the stick of fear, lost its potency. On the contrary, it has become so potent that it threatens to destroy the earth's finite resources if it does not first destroy more economies through the inflation that reflects rising expectations" (p. 89). Skinner (1969; 1973) agrees that reinforcers can be misused. He says that what must be accomplished, and what he believes is currently lacking, is an effective training program for managers. "In the not too-distant future, however, a new breed of industrial manager may be able to apply the principles of operant conditioning effectively *(Organizational Dynamics,* 1973a, p. 40)."

Task Structure or Job Enrichment Program

Theoretical Background

Both research and practical experience have indicated that jobs should include opportunities for personal achievement, responsibility, recognition, growth, and achievement in order to provide high levels of employee performance. In other words, work should provide employees with positive satisfaction which is derived from using their individual talents and skills.

One method by which this objective is being achieved in organizations is through job enrichment. Job enrichment is a concerted attempt to stem and even reverse long-term trends among industrial engineering programs toward job simplification and specialization (Hulin and Blood, 1968). In simple terms, job enrichment involves the redefinition or restructuring of jobs so that employees have greater planning and control responsibilities in the execution of their overall assignment. Job enrichment should be distinguished from job enlargement, where workers are given more work to do without any greater planning and control responsibilities.

The theoretical principles on which job enrichment is based are not nearly as clear and straightforward as those of the positive reinforcement program already described. Skinner and his followers (known as *behaviorists*) see job enrichment as being a method of making the task intrinsically reinforcing and, therefore, they describe the enriched job as leading to higher levels of performance because it leads to a positive reward state and the absence of an enriched job leads to a negative or neutral reward state (see *Organizational Dynamics,* 1973a and Nord, 1969). According to Luthans (1973), job enrichment as it is currently practiced in industry is a direct outgrowth of Herzberg's two-factor theory of motivation (see Herzberg, 1968) and is therefore based on the assumption that in order to motivate personnel, the job itself must provide opportunities for achievement, recognition, responsibility, advancement, and growth. The program entails "enriching" the job so that these factors are included.

Scott (1966) offers a third theoretical explanation of why an enriched task design increases the motivation level of the worker. Scott's activation theory explanation is based on physiology. Briefly, this theory holds that cues received from the environment travel to the appropriate cortical projection region of the brain for information purposes and are also diffused over a wide area of the cortex in order to arouse or activate the organism. According to Scott, the more variety and stimulation in an enriched task, the higher is the state of arousal or activation and the more motivated is the worker. In short, with routine, repetitive tasks, after a period of time the "sameness" of the cue received leads to a decrease in arousal level and therefore a decrease in motivation and performance.

Lawler (1969) offers still a fourth theoretical explanation of why an increase in complexity of task design will lead to higher levels of performance. The theory of motivation that best describes "why" job enrichment increases commitment and involvement on the part of the employee is an "internal state" theory called "expectancy theory" (see Vroom, 1964). While the details of this theory are beyond the scope of this paper, this theory basically says that an enriched task is *perceived* by the worker as leading to an intrinsic reward. Lawler (1969) says:

> Thus, it appears that the answer to the *why* question can be found in the ability of job design factors to influence employee's perceptions of the probability that good performance will be intrinsically rewarding. Certain job designs apparently encourage the perception that it will, while others do not. Because of this, job design factors can determine how motivating a job will be (p. 429).

Regardless of their theoretical position, most behavioral scientists (e.g., see Argyris, 1957; Kornhauser, 1965; Likert, 1961; Whyte, 1972) regard extreme division of labor and the resulting job simplification and specialization as leading almost inevitably to monotony, job dissatisfaction, and decreased performance.

Even though there is disagreement as to *why* job enrichment works, the programs being put forth by the various "reformers" can be reduced to a few common elements (Levitan and Johnson, 1973a). The elements are: (1) Individuals should be given maximum freedom to control their work and develop their skills; (2) jobs should be designed to give each person a series of tasks which are varied, challenging, and meaningful in terms of the end product; and (3) the status differential which has separated supervisors and employees should be replaced by a team concept with an emphasis on shared goals.

Stages in Program Development

The leading advocate of job enrichment in the U. S. today is probably Robert Ford, Personnel Director—Work Organizations and Environmental Research at AT&T. From 1965 to 1968, AT&T conducted 19 formal field experiments in job enrichment and has expanded the program today to many other areas of the Bell system. Based on AT&T's

constant reaffirming of their job enrichment program, Ford (1973) sees the job enrichment strategy as involving three stages. The *first step* is designed to improve work through systematic changes in the modules of work. In this stage the worker is given a whole, natural unit of work and specific or specialized tasks are assigned to the individuals which enable them to become experts in this expanded work module. Ford says that in defining modules that give each employee a natural area of responsibility, AT&T tries to accumulate modules of work until one of these three entities has been created for the worker: (1) a customer outside the organization, (2) a client within the organization or (3) a task in the manufacturing end of the business where individuals can produce complete or large portions of the complete product.

AT&T has recently added a "nesting" of jobs together in this stage in order to improve morale and upgrade performance. This method goes beyond enriching *individual* jobs and puts together people whose work modules complement one another. Job nesting, therefore, is the opposite of job pooling (e.g., a secretarial pool) where workers who perform a similar task are located together.

The *second step* enriches the work through systematic changes in the control of the work module. In this stage, as an employee gains experience, the supervisor should continue to turn over responsibility until the employee is handling the work completely. The ultimate goal is to let the worker have complete control over his or her job. This increases the accountability and control of individuals over their own work and indeed makes each employee a manager of his task. Eugene Cafiero, Group Vice-president at Chrysler, sees this as a crucial stage in getting the most out of a job enrichment program. In a recent speech Cafiero discussed the results of Chrysler's recent experience at enriching workers' jobs. He said:

> A man doing a job all day long knows more about that job than anyone else; he knows how to improve it better than anyone else. We want to give our people a chance to speak up. We feel that this program is working through more satisfied employees. We at Chrysler Corporation are trying to avoid the impersonal feelings that are often associated with large corporations . . . *(Detroit Free Press,* July, 25, 1971).

The *third* and *final step* is perhaps the most important to the success of the job enrichment program. In this stage the job is enriched through systematic changes in the feedback that signals whether something has been accomplished. In this stage, periodic reports are made directly available to the worker himself rather than to the supervisor. Just as in the positive reinforcement program, this stage allows the worker to monitor the quality and quantity of his own work in order to make the corrections necessary. Ford (1973) says that "Definition of the module and control of it are futile unless the results of the employee's effort are discernible. Moreover, knowledge of the results should go directly to where it will nurture motivation—that is, to the employee. People have a great capacity for midflight correction when they know where they stand" (p. 99).

Unlike a positive reinforcement program, job enrichment requires a big change in managerial style. A positive reinforcement program, rather than trying to change managerial style, would be designed to increase the behavioral repertoire of a manager in his ability to give varied kinds of feedback as it relates to worker performance (Sorcher and Goldstein, 1972). Job enrichment calls for increasing modules, moving controls downward, and designing effective feedback systems. Therefore, the job enrichment program involves not only changing a worker's task involvement and the feedback he receives, but it also changes the traditional *relationship* of the supervisor with his subordinates.

Results of Job Enrichment Programs

There are literally scores of companies today involved to some extent in job-enrichment programs. These include Texas Instruments, Corning Glass Works, IBM, AT&T, Proctor and Gamble, Bankers Trust, Merrill, Lynch, Pierce, Fenner and Smith, Donnelly Corporation, Imperial Chemical Industry, Ltd., Maytag, Motorola, Gaines Food Company, and Buick.

Just as for positive reinforcement programs, evidence of the effectiveness of job enrichment programs is sketchy, lacks empirical rigor, probably is reported only by companies that have experienced success, and is often qualitative in nature (Hulin, 1971). As Levitan and Johnston (1973a) warn:

> These experiments with job redesign are all "success stories." Indeed, most of the literature on work reform is the product of advocates reporting positive results. But there are major gaps in the case for job reform. Companies which find authoritarian controls and unchanged job rewards to be successful as ever are not included in the surveys. Companies whose enrichment and participation plans turn sour rarely trumpet the news (p. 36).

Nevertheless, many companies are reporting success stories and, as a result other companies are eagerly spending millions of dollars each year trying to duplicate their success.

In 1966, Reif and Schoderbek found that 41 of 210 companies surveyed had used job enrichment. The most popular reasons for undertaking job enrichment were cost reduction, profit increase, and an increase in job satisfaction. As far back as 1950, Walker reported that a job enrichment program at IBM was a success. More recently, Ford (1969) reported that after job enrichment was installed in the Shareholder Relations Department at AT&T there was a 27 percent reduction in the termination rate and an estimated costs savings of $558,000 over a twelve-month period. In twelve districts of AT&T where the program was tried with service representatives, resignations and dismissals dropped by 14 percent, which could mean an annual savings of $10 million in operating costs (Janson, 1970). In the Imperial Chemical Industries, Ltd., salesmen productivity increased by 19 percent a year after job enrichment, whereas in a similar group without job enrichment, sales dropped by 5 percent a year (Janson, 1970).

Motorola found that bench (individual) assembly required 25 percent more workers in addition to increased training time in order to implement a job enrichment program. They report that the higher cost in wages was offset by greater productivity, less need for inspection, a higher quality product and lower work costs *(Business Week*, Sept. 4, 1971). The Maytag Company found that greater flexibility in terms of production scheduling was one of the major advantages of job enrichment over assembly-line production. They reported that they could add or subtract work stations or shifts without affecting production of other workers (Stewart, 1967).

Buick Motor Division has been involved in a substantial job enrichment program in its Product Engineering Area since 1971. Prior to this project, skilled hourly mechanics would work on cars in Buick's engineering fleet and perform assignments based on a work ticket that had been completed by engineering personnel. Now, however, mechanics not only complete the work tickets themselves, but also are encouraged to perform any repair they consider necessary and to inspect their work upon completion. They credit this program with increasing productivity by 13 percent, reducing petty grievances to near zero, and significantly reducing the number of rework cases (Schotters, 1973b).

Texas Instruments gave full responsibility for janitorial services to the worker involved. The men met to decide how the work would be divided and to set up schedules and establish standards. As a result of this job enrichment effort, manpower needs declined from 120 to 71, cleanliness improved, and turnover was reduced from 100 percent to 10 percent quarterly (Herrick, 1971). In 1971, Gaines Food Plant in Topeka, Kansas, attempted to enrich all jobs by organizing workers into teams where they are paid according to their skill level and not according to their position in the hierarchy (supervisor versus worker). Symbols such as assigned parking spaces and separate eating facilities have been eliminated and all decision-making, including goal-setting, has become a team process. They report the program has resulted in a 91 percent reduction in absenteeism over the industry average, 40 fewer employees than predicted necessary, and the best safety record in the General Food Corporation *(American Machinist,* 1973). As a result of the success of the Gaines Food project, similar efforts are being made by the Mead Corporation, Proctor and Gamble, and Scott Paper Company. Scott is building a small plant in Dover, Delaware, which it plans to operate under this new module approach in an attempt to combat production-line boredom *(Detroit Free Press,* October 29, 1973).

Bankers Trust and Merrill, Lynch, Pierce, Fenner and Smith adopted a job enrichment program where work modules were set up by customer or function. In both cases, significant money savings were realized in terms of increased productivity and reduced supervisory time (Rickleffs, 1972). A similar job enrichment program was initiated by Xerox for its technical representatives. Machine servicemen were given more authority to decide expenses, schedule work, order inventories, interview and train new personnel, and determine work loads. They credit this program with leading to increased performance level (Jacobs, 1972).

Other companies which have reported success with a job enrichment program include Monsanto, Weyerhauser, Exxon, Polaroid, and Ampex Tape in the United States; Volvo and Kockums Shipyards in Sweden; Daimler-Benz and Volkswagen in Germany, Renault in France; and Olivetti and Fiat in Italy *(American Machinist,* 1973). Regardless of the criticism leveled against job enrichment, it appears that job enrichment is seen as a success by many companies and cannot be dismissed as a passing fad. The president of Donnelly Mirror said, "If you need proof that involving people in their total job pays off, ask what you got in return for your last labor contract. If you are less than satisfied with the bargain, ask yourself how much it would be worth to get the support of your people in effecting just the cost reductions that your engineers already know about" (Donnelly, 1971, p. 12).

Criticisms of the Program

Criticisms of job enrichment programs have come from all groups, including academicians, managers, workers, union representatives, and industrial engineers. Academicians criticize the success studies as being incomplete and poorly designed and generally hold them to have little empirical validity. Hulin (1971) said, "It is unfortunate that most of these studies provide indirect evidence, at best. . . . Many of these studies have been poorly controlled, and most of the authors have attempted to generalize from severely limited data."

Many groups criticize the job enrichment advocates for pushing job enrichment as a social cure for worker discontent even when their organizations may lose profits as a result of such programs. Recognizing the cost involved in meaningful job reform, some reformers have argued that job enrichment should control the design of the production process, even if productivity is reduced. They suggest that "social efficiency" should be given priority over consideration of purely economic efficiency *(Work in America,* 1973). Many supporters of job enrichment criticize this stand as being impractical and unnecessary. Levitan and Johnston (1973a, p. 38) say, "If changes in technology and hardware to improve the quality of work are to be made, they must also promise higher profits." Drucker (1973, p. 92) agrees: "The manager who pretends that the personal needs of the worker—for affection, for example—come before the objective needs of the task is indeed a liar or poor manager. The rare worker who believes him is a fool."

Along these same lines, there are some jobs which cannot be enriched beyond a certain point. All the redesign in the world cannot make certain dull tasks exciting. According to Levitan and Johnson (1973a), "The basic limit to work redesign is that society requires that certain tasks be done. . . . The prospects for humanizing work are limited by the realities of the work to be done—realities which are beyond the power of planners to control" (p. 5).

Perhaps the most damaging criticism leveled by many critics is that many workers do not feel alienated from their jobs and do not desire more responsibility or involvement at their workplace. Levitan and Johnston (1973a) ask, "Is the quality of work life the main standard by which they judge the quality of their lives? It appears that for most workers the quality of work is less important than the standard of living" (p. 40). According to the Bureau of Labor Statistics, the predominant issue in collective bargaining is still wages. In 1971, three of every four days lost in strikes were the result of wages or benefit disputes.

Attempts to enrich jobs are often frustrated by union constraints in the form of restrictive job descriptions, tenure requirement, craft jurisdictions, and general mistrust (Myers, 1971). The labor unions tend to oppose job enrichment because they thrive on conflict with management (Gooding, 1970). Leonard Woodcock, President of the United Automobile Workers Union says, "Those who contend that boredom and monotony are the big problems among assembly workers, are writing a lot of nonsense" (Baxter, 1973).

Little and Warr (1971) say that workers on a piece rate oppose job enrichment as an attempt to cut the rate and lower their earnings. Conart and Kilbridge (1965) reported that in one company, about one-third of the workers who had an opportunity to move to enriched jobs expressed a preference for their present jobs because they felt that the existing incentive system maximized their earnings.

According to Reif and Luthans (1972) many groups of workers are not alienated, other groups of workers actually enjoy looking outside the organization for their intrinsic rewards, and still other groups of workers may have a high need for structure. Job enrichment may have a negative effect on each of these groups.

Mitchell Fein's research for the American Institute of Industrial Engineers, claims that a check into many of the job enrichment case histories and studies of workers done over the past 10 years indicates that job enrichment does not work—primarily because workers do not want it (Baxter, 1973).

Despite each of these criticisms, the evidence still shows that job enrichment works for some groups of people. The criticisms point out the necessity of considering individual differences of workers when deciding on a motivation program of job enrichment (Lawler, 1973a). Hulin and Blood (1968, p. 50) emphasize this point when they say:

Specifically, the argument for larger jobs as a means of motivating workers, decreasing boredom and dissatisfaction, and increasing attendance and productivity is valid only when applied to certain segments of the work force—white-collar and supervisory workers and non-alienated blue-collar workers.

Organizational Climate and Development Program

Theoretical Background

Many writers praise the positive reinforcement programs and the job enrichment or task structure programs as being a step in the right direction in the fight against worker discontent. Some of these same writers, however, claim that these programs are not enough. Neither of the previous programs does much to change the hierarchical structure of the organization and neither program examines the interpersonal and attitudinal problems of the worker with the people with whom he comes in contact. Lawler (1973b) suggests that what workers want most, as reflected in more than 100 studies in the past 20 years, is to become masters of their immediate environments and to feel that their work and they themselves are important. While advocates of both positive reinforcement and job enrichment programs would argue that this is one of the purposes of their respective programs, others would say that the worker cannot have high self-esteem unless the climate in which he works is a healthy one. "Climate," as used by these writers, can be defined as a set of properties of the work environment and is assumed to be a major force in influencing the behavior of the employees on the job (Gibson, Ivancevich and Donnelly, 1973). The properties include the size, structure, leadership patterns, interpersonal relationships, systems complexity, goal direction, and communication patterns of the organization (Forehand, 1968). Therefore, an improvement in the organizational climate would involve more than changing the task structure (job enrichment) or the reinforcing consequences (positive reinforcement), but also may involve a change in the organizational climate and structure and the interpersonal support of the employees.

Proponents of an improved climate approach contend that "the traditional hierarchical system of organizations breeds a climate of fear and mistrust, which reduces management effectiveness. Programs in team building, sensitivity training, encounter groups . . . are advocated to unfreeze the climate" *(American Machinist,* 1973, p. 80). Many times the task of building a climate which encourages achievement in an organization is one of changing the concern of management from power-compliance ("Here is what needs to be done, and here is how to do it") to one that offers warmth and support to each individual, communicating organizational goals and standards, but not attempting to control the means of reaching these goals (Kolb, Rubin and McIntyre, 1971, p. 71).

The climate that characterizes the work situation helps to determine the kinds of worker motivation actually aroused. Climates tend to mediate between the task requirements and the needs of the individual. "The capacity to influence the organizational climate is perhaps the most powerful leverage point in the entire management system. Because climates can affect the motivation of organizational members, changes in certain climate properties could have immediate and profound effects on the motivated performance of all employees" (Litwin and Stringer, 1973, p. 539).[5]

A healthy organizational climate, according to Schein (1970, p. 126) involves one that:

1. Takes in and communicates information reliably and validly.

2. Has internal flexibility and creativity to make the changes which are demanded by the information obtained.

3. Gains integration and commitment to the goals of the organization, from which comes the willingness to change.

4. Offers an internal climate of support and freedom from threat, since being threatened undermines good communication, reduces flexibility and stimulates self-protection rather than concern for the total system.

In recent years the term *organizational development,* or OD, has become the recognized classification for the motivation program used to help the organization reach the healthy climate described by Schein. Blake and Mouton (1967) says that "Organizational development deliberately shifts the emphasis away from the organization's structure, from technical skill, from wherewithal and results *per se,* as it diagnoses the organization's ills. Focusing on organization purposes, the human interaction process, and organization culture [climate], it accepts these as the areas in which problems are preventing the fullest possible integration within the organization" (p. 11). French (1969) adds, "Organization Development refers to a long range effort to improve an organization's problem solving capabilities and its ability to cope with changes in its external environment with the help of external or internal behavioral scientist consultants (change agents)" (p. 387).

A successful OD program requires skillful change agent intervention. The change agent's purpose is to affect planned change in the total personnel system both now and in the future (French, 1969). The term OD, therefore, implies a normative re-education strategy intended to affect systems of beliefs, values, and attitudes within the organization so that it can adapt better to the accelerated rate of change in technology in the industrial environment, and in society in general. Later stages in the OD process may include formal organizational restructuring which is frequently initiated, facilitated, and reinforced by the normative and behavioral changes (Winn, 1968).

Organizational development is based more on history and less on theory than the previous two programs discussed. The overall OD approach is an extension of the use of laboratory or sensitivity training methods. Sensitivity or laboratory (T-group) training evolved primarily from the field theory and group dynamics concepts of Lewin (1944, 1951, 1952).[6] In addition, Roger's (1942) client-centered therapy approach had a great impact on the change-agent's behavior in the sensitivity session. Rogers emphasizes the permissive, supportive, but nondirective role of the counselor. In Rogers' therapy, the counselor should not set the goals or the direction of the change but, instead, provide a method by which the client can set these for himself.

Based on the work of Lewin and Rogers, sensitivity training attempts to make the individual within the group more aware of himself and his impact on others. The objective of a sensitivity training session is to provide an environment which produces a learning experience for the group. The role of the trainer or change agent is to facilitate the learning process by encouraging the group to set their own directions and goals (Bradford, Gibb and Benne, 1964). Laboratory training as an organized method of bringing about attitude and behavioral change within groups began in 1947 at the National Training Laboratory in Bethel, Maine, under the direction of Lewin, Benne, Bradford, and Lippitt. Since the beginning at Bethel, sensitivity training has become *one* of the techniques widely used in a formal OD program.

In 1957, McGregor at Union Carbide and Shepard and Blake at Esso began to apply laboratory training systematically to the problems facing these organizations (Luthans, 1973). Based on McGregor's experience in ongoing organizations, he wrote his (1960) exposition of participatory theory "Y" to replace authoritarian theory "X" approaches to management. According to Leavitt (1965), McGregor's development of theory "Y" and Likert's (1961) development of interaction influence theory, which both call for "supportive relationships" by leaders in industry, has contributed a great deal to the usefulness of laboratory training in organizations. Other theorists who have contributed to the introduction of organizational development as we know it today include, among others, Argyris (1962), Bennis (1966), Beckhard (1969), Burke (1971), Blake and Mouton (1967) and Greiner (1967).

Stages in Program Development.

Because OD is an evolving field, it is difficult to describe a "typical" program (Strauss, 1973; Hampton, Summer, and Webber, 1973). Strauss says "as an evolving field, OD presents a moving target, making it difficult to define or criticize" (1973, p. 2). Hampton, et al. (1973) point out that while there are general similarities, "there are almost as many methods of organization development as there are consultants engaging in this kind of work" (p. 857). The general similarities in most approaches to OD has led Strauss (1973), Hampton, et al. (1973), and French (1969), to describe various stages in a "typical" OD program. The reader is reminded, however, that the actual OD program in any one organization may vary from the "typical" program described below.

The *first stage* of the OD program is a diagnostic stage of planned organizational change. This stage involves gathering data about the state of operations in the organization, and the state of interpersonal attitudes and behavior. In this stage, T-group type sessions may be held in order to develop problem solving skills, examine interpersonal relations, and examine basic attitudes. These sessions are generally designed to act as team-building or group problem-solving sessions. During this stage the change agent, who has usually interviewed each participant prior to the session, frequently provides *feedback* to the group in terms of the items or themes which have emerged (French, 1969). One of the purposes of this stage is to improve the way people work together. It involves changing basic attitudes of both supervisors and subordinates and opens up communication channels to allow all employees a larger voice in how they do their jobs.

Many advocates of OD recommend that the first team session should be held by the president of the firm and his staff, and then with groups throughout the organization. Without the support of top management, it is generally felt that the program is probably doomed to failure.[7] William Crockett, Vice-president of Saga Foods, recalls his fears about this first stage: "Do you really want him [the change agent] to dredge into the depths of all our feelings about one another and about you? Isn't it being disloyal for us to tell him our problems and our feelings? Does it serve any purpose for these problems to be brought in the open and exposed?" (Crockett, 1970, p. 295). The fears expressed by Crockett are not uncommon. Schein (1969) and others use the term "unfreezing" to describe this stage because people have a way of becoming "frozen" in their attitudes and relations with other people and often are unaware that they are seen as obstacles in the solving of operational problems.[8]

The *second stage* of the OD program is an *action* stage of planned organizational change. After group and intergroup relationships have been identified and a period of trust and communication has been established within the organization, these work groups begin to establish ways to deal with on-the-job structural and human relations programs. This stage represents the participatory stage of the other two programs discussed. The work team may suggest actual changes in structure and monitoring of the task, interdepartment communication procedures, or other changes they deem necessary to solve the problem they identified in the first stage. This stage may involve all of the steps involved in the positive reinforcement program and the job enrichment program, including team performance appraisal, goal-setting, task redesign, and self-monitoring. Of course the team, group, or department works within the boundaries set up by the organization and must be able to show that their suggested changes will lead to improvements for both the organization and the individuals involved.

The *third* and *final stage* is an extension of the first two stages in the sense that the team evaluates their progress and continues to search for *new problems* and to offer *new solutions*. The third stage is a *proactive* stage, where the purpose is to maintain the healthy climate established in the first two stages by a continual monitoring of the system and examining the team's working relationship to the system.

The OD program differs from the positive reinforcement program and the job enrichment program in that it examines attitudes as well as behavior, it is an organization-wide program as well as a department or team program, and it is a broad-based program which continues to examine the organization climate, the task structure, *and* the reinforcement consequences. Strauss (1973) notes that for OD to have a lasting effect, the participants must (1) move from confrontation to behavior, (2) move from training groups to work problems, (3) move from intent to implementation (including structural change), (4) move from sporadic action to routinization, and (5) widen and make permanent the entire OD effort. The essence of OD, therefore, is the concept of helping the organization to gain insight into its own processes, develop its own diagnostic and coping resources, and improve its own internal relationships with the help of an outside and/or inside consultant who acts as a catalyst (Schein, 1970).

Results of OD Program.

OD has become a big business. In 1969-70, one firm which specializes in OD consulting, Scientific Methods, Inc., numbered among its clients 45 of the top 100 U. S. corporations, conducted courses on every continent, and projected profits of $1.1 million (Strauss, 1973). Examples of companies using OD as a motivation plan include TRW systems, Polaroid, Union Carbide, Royal Dutch/Shell Group, J. Lyons and Company, Esso, Weyerhauser, U. S. Steel, Corning Glass, Clark Equipment Company, and General Motors.

Even though many companies are reportedly using an OD program, research on the effectiveness of OD efforts is as yet sparse, partly because of the great difficulty in defining criteria for organizational effectiveness (Schein, 1970). Strauss (1973) adds, "In the end, OD is likely to be evaluated in terms of gut reactions rather than dispassionate research. After all, OD deals with emotions [attitudes], and it engenders emotional reactions. For some, it is almost a religion" (Strauss, 1973, p. 42).

While most of the evidence is testimonial in nature, there is some evidence that OD has led to improvements in working satisfaction and increased company profits. Schein (1970) credits a team-building program in group dynamics and interpersonal relations for management trainees as resulting in the defeat of a union vote in a large oil refinery. Kaiser Steel Company credits a team effort by workers with increasing productivity by 32 percent and thereby keeping the plant open after it had a scheduled closing due to low productivity and a loss in profits.

Texas Instrument has initiated an OD program which they call a People and Asset Effectiveness Program. Mark Shepard, President of Texas Instruments, said, "We've found that if you get people involved, they'll set tougher goals for themselves than you would dare do, and have fun doing it" *(Business Week,* Sept. 29, 1973, p. 88). After a three-year period, Texas Instruments found that this program resulted in return on assets per person rising from 5.6 percent to 10.1 percent. When asked to what he credited the success of the program, Frederick Ochsner, Vice-president of Personnel at Texas Instruments, said,

> It is a whole bunch of things acting synergistically. It's the attitudes, team improvement programs, the campus involvement, the open-door management policy, the nonstructural pecking order. It's the unified goal-approach—with everybody looking at his own piece of that goal. . . . The key is flexibility. Two things people want in life. They want to achieve and they want to be loved. And if you provide an atmosphere where these things can occur with a minimum amount of structure in the work flow, you are going to get what you want *(Business Week,* Sept. 29, 1973, p. 88, 90).

Saga Administrative Corporation began an OD program in 1971 and today employs six full-time change agents. Saga stresses team building and has developed an overlapping team approach to management. (see Likert, 1961). In 1972, Saga held 225 team building sessions. Although the costs or benefits of Saga's OD program are not measurable, Board Chairman, W. P. Laughlin, claims that profitability is borne out by increased productivity. Saga claims its turnover rate among its 23,000 employees has been reduced to 19 percent annually—compared with 34 percent for the entire food industry—as a result of their OD program.

Donnelly Mirror Company has the longest history of success with an OD program. In the early 1950s Donnelly instituted democratic reforms which sought to humanize assembly-line production. Using the Scanlon plan, a type of OD program (Bennis, 1966; Frost, 1973) Donnelly has been able to show that their "humanistic" approach works. The president of Donnelly says, "We are not talking about a gimmick that someone can install by himself. The company has to change its relationship to its people. The company has to lead, it has to create the climate of trust. This is hard, demanding work that needs the leadership and support of the top people in the company" (Donnelly, 1971, p. 13). While the Scanlon plan is similar to most other OD programs in that it follows the three stages described in a "typical" program, it is unique in that the employees share directly in changes in profits in the form of a monthly bonus plan. All employees receive salaries, rather than hourly wages, and they collectively set the rates at which they would be paid. In return for this, the employees have the responsibility for implementing productivity increases to support pay raises.

As a result of their unique OD program, Donnelly's productivity gains have resulted in an average salary bonus of 12 percent of wages since the changes were instituted. Wages have risen steadily, while unit productivity costs have fallen, enabling the company to decrease prices, expand sales, and increase profits. Scrap losses dropped by 75 percent from their former level and goods returned due to poor workmanship dropped by 90 percent (Gooding, 1970).

While Donnelly Mirror has one of the longest histories with an OD program, the largest OD program is currently being conducted in the General Motors Corporation. Stephen H. Fuller, Vice-president of Personnel and Development, reports that formal OD functions are now operating in 20 major GM organizations. More than 125 OD change agents are working full-time in 55 GM plants in the United States, Canada, and overseas subsidiaries *(National Alliance of Businessmen,* 1973). The OD program used by GM is an eclectic approach where each plant program is designed differently according to the needs of that plant. F. J. Schotters, Director of Personnel Development, describes the OD program at GM as "a long range, planned program to improve the effectiveness of the *total* organization—whether it be a work group, department, plant, or staff. It can involve many types of activities, such as greater involvement and participation by employees with respect to their own jobs and in the particular areas in which they work, better communications, team building and changes in job content, supervisory relations and organizational structure" (Schotters, 1972a).

A survey conducted by the Institute for Social Research of the University of Michigan clearly demonstrated to GM that "the way employees see (and react to) the management climate and organizational structure has a direct, measurable effect on both employee behavior and work performance" (Schotters, 1972b). Landen and Carlson (in progress, 1973) said, "The survey findings clearly indicated sources of motivational potential needed improvement at each of the plant sites. The long-range program designed to bring about needed changes in the organization is now entering its third year [since 1969]. Results to date have been very encouraging."

One of the reasons that GM felt it had to institute some type of motivational program was a dramatic rising absenteeism and turnover rate. In 1972 Schotters reported that "Conservative estimates indicated that the current annual cost of absenteeism—considering only fringe benefits—is about $50 million. The cost of turnover involves another estimated $29 million. Thus, these are areas of major concern for every operation in GM—not only because of the costs involved but also because these trends indicate a serious deterioration of employee attitudes toward their work . . ." (Schotters, 1972c). To combat the high absenteeism rate, one Oldsmobile engine plant put several foremen and their hourly workers through group problem-solving (team-building) programs. As a result of these programs, several suggestions by the group for improving the absenteeism and turnover were accepted by the engine plant management. They credit this program with reducing total absenteeism in the plant during the first five months of 1971 by 6 percent, while absenteeism in the rest of Oldsmobile went up by 11 percent. Turnover in the engine plant was down by 38 percent in the engine plant, while the rest of Oldsmobile was down by 14 percent. Based on the success of this program, the project is now being extended throughout the Oldsmobile Division (Schotters, 1972c).

A full-fledged OD program was begun in 1971 in the Chassis Department of the General Motors Assembly Division (GMAD) at Arlington, Texas. With the help of two change agents, 104 hourly employees and four foremen were involved in a program designed to improve communications and attitudes. General Motors reports that this program resulted in a 50 percent decrease in grievances filed per month, housekeeping improved and foremen became more willing to make decisions on problems as they arose without relying on higher supervision. As a result of this program, similar projects are being inaugurated at GMAD (Schotters, 1972d).

Space does not allow us to give all the results of the OD progress in the 55 GM plants. Landen and Carlson (in progress, 1973) summarize the state of the OD programs in GM when they state "One vital point can be concluded from these and a variety of other programs now underway in the corporation: we are probably only beginning to touch the surface of a deep reservoir of untapped human potential among *all* GM employees. . . . Employee motivation is increasingly regarded as a core issue in the future of General Motors."

Criticisms of the Program

Of the motivational programs currently in use by industry, this is probably the most controversial. Strauss (1973) says:

For my taste, OD has been plagued by too much evangelical hucksterism. Though considerable thought has been given to professional ethics, there are as yet no generally accepted codes of behavior. OD techniques have been subject to some scientific research, but it is a bit premature to conclude that OD is truly a scientific method or the "science-based" approach. And it is downright misleading to suggest that OD's utility has been proven scientifically valid. . . . OD is a fad and American companies are suckers for gimmicks (p. 14).

The majority of the criticism leveled at the OD program centers around the "unfreezing" stage where attitudes and interpersonal relationships are examined. Whyte (1972) says, "Executives say, 'What we must do is change people's attitudes'; as politely as I can I tell them to forget attitudes. The problem is to change the conditions to which people are responding. If he does that, people will behave differently and he will find that attitudes—if they still interest him—will adjust themselves to the new situation" (p. 67). Sorcher and Goldstein (1972) report that "difficulties encountered by those who try to change behavior by first changing attitudes are well known. Moreover, there is no certainty that attitude change will lead to behavior change on the part of managers or supervisors, since other attitudes may intrude and prevent behavior change" (p. 36).

This criticism of the attitude change process centers around three issues. First, many psychologists believe that attitudes do not cause behavior, but rather behavioral experiences lead to attitude formations (see, e.g., Bem, 1964). Second, many critics feel that changing attitudes in a group setting may do more harm than good because the rewards of the organization will not reinforce the changed attitudes (e.g., see House, 1967). Third, many writers contend that there are many poorly trained change agents and consultants who may cause more harm than good in a team-building session (e.g., see Campbell and Dunnette, 1968; Bennis, 1969).

Maslow (1965) described his experiences with trying to apply theory Y management for Non-Linear Systems of Del Mar, California, and concluded that "The demands of theory Y were far higher than I had recognized and many involve 'inhumanity' to the weak, the vulnerable and the damaged who are unable to take on responsibility and self discipline" (quoted by Drucker, 1973, p. 87). Not only are some employees unable to cope with the OD process, but many managers as well are not willing to accept a different style of management. Andrew Kay, President of Non-Linear Systems, Inc., said that OD programs work fine during good times and periods of economic gains. In fact from 1960-65 production rose 30 percent and customer complaints dropped 70 percent under the OD program set up by Maslow. But when the aereospace industry fell apart in 1970, Kay said he had lost touch with his company and the company was not ready to respond to the changing environment. Vice-president Coombe agreed. "So much emphasis was put on the results of sensitivity sessions—and the long-run planning was not carried on in a businesslike manner" (*Business Week*, September 2, 1972, p. 68). By returning to a more autocratic leadership style, Kay claims to be back on solid financial grounds.

Hampton, et al. (1973) summarize the stage of development of OD by saying that until the advent of OD, nobody made participative management and structural job enlargement operational. They also warn:

But OD has its limitations; analysis, clarity, reality, openness, and facing up to the truth may be an alternative to closed-system stereotypical thinking, but there is no guarantee that it will work in all organizations. The viewpoint which the modern manager must take, therefore, is that this method of management has both powerful benefits and powerful limitations. The key is to try to understand when and under what circumstances such a technique will succeed (p. 870).

Flexitime—Escape or Motivation?

An alternative form of confronting the problem of worker discontent has recently been introduced in many firms throughout the world. This program is called *flexitime* and is designed to allow the employee more latitude and freedom in setting up his or her own schedule. This motivation plan originated in Germany in the late 1960s. The program allows the workers, either as individuals or team, to establish their own starting times, within limits set by the company (e.g., between 7:30-9:30 A.M.). The worker must complete 8 hours before closing. In some companies, if the employees like, they can build up time during the week by reducing their lunch hours and breaks and use the time to either leave early on Friday afternoon (e.g., at 3:00 P.M.) or else leave earlier in the day (e.g., at the end of 7½ *work* hours if the lunch hour were reduced by 30 minutes). The extent of flexibility is related to the degree of interdependence among jobs (Werther, 1973).

A similar program to the flexitime program is the four-day-week program. Under this program, each employee has to complete forty hours a week, but has a three-day weekend, rather than the traditional two-day weekend.

As noted earlier, the positive reinforcement, job enrichment, and organization development programs are *proactive* in nature because they seek to examine the causes of worker discontent and solve the problems in order to make the workplace a more stimulating and exciting place to work. The flexitime and four-day-week programs have been criticized by some as being *reactive* programs which tend to ignore the real problems of worker discontent. These critics claim that rather than facing up to the fact that high turnover and absenteeism is a symptom of either a poor feedback system, a boring task, or an unhealthy climate, they reward the workers' discontent by giving them more time away from the work place. Herzberg (1968) says, "This represents a marvelous way of motivating people to work—getting them off the job! We have reduced (formally and informally) the time spent on a job over the last 50 or 60 years until we are finally on the way to the '6½-day weekend' . . . The fact is that motivated people seek more hours of work, not fewer" (p. 67). Ford (1973), while not as critical as Herzberg, agrees; "The growing pressure for a four-day work week is not necessarily evidence that people do not care about their work: they may be rejecting their work in the form that it confronts them" (p. 96). Levitan and Johnson (1973b) say, "The easiest way to improve an unpleasant job is to reduce the working hours."

Counter-arguments against the critics could be made by saying that flexitime and the four-day-week programs are really considering the "total man" by allowing him the freedom to schedule, within reason, his work time to better meet his personal and family needs. Kahn (1973) says that allowing people freedom in choosing the hours they work and allowing them freedom to bid for the task they wish to perform are natural ways to recognize the individuality of man. Also, it should be noted that the programs, as currently designed, do not call for a reduction in hours, but only a rearranging of the hours. However, the critics feel that this may only be a first step by unions in a reduction of the number of hours and even number of years a worker would have to work before being allowed to escape the organization.

Regardless of these arguments, many companies are finding a flexitime program beneficial. Moles (1973) reported that 5,000 companies and 2.5 million workers worldwide are currently on the flexitime working hours plan. In the United States, 100,000 workers are currently on this plan in such companies as Sun Oil, National Bank, the city government of Baltimore, the city government of Washington, D.C., Hewlett-Packard, Samsonite, Nestlé's, and Scott Paper Company. Werther (1973) reviewed the success of these programs and reported that the companies found that worker tardiness decreased, absenteeism due to medical appointments or family commitments were reduced, and better use of parking facilities, cafeterias and locker rooms was possible. The disadvantages Werther noted were more time had to be spent on scheduling, and also that flexitime wouldn't work on shift-work and assembly-line operations because of the interdependency of the workers.[9] Sandoz-Wander of East Hanover, New Jersey, implemented a flexitime program for a six-month trial period. After the trial period, 88 percent of the supervisory personnel voted to adopt the system permanently, citing better worker morale and increased productivity as the reasons (Cray, 1973). While Hewlett-Packard of Palo Alto, California, did not find an increase in productivity, they did find that their flexitime program led to a significant reduction in absenteeism and turnover *(American Machinist,* 1973).

While the evidence for this program (as for all programs described in this paper) still lacks empirical validity, it appears that flexible working hours may become the way of the future for many workers. Before the program can claim to be a method of reducing worker discontent, however, much more objective research is needed.

Motivation Programs in the Future

The four programs described in this paper represent the most current programs designed to reduce worker discontent and increase productivity in operation today. Many writers believe we have only begun to "scratch the surface," however, and call for more innovative steps to be taken.

Porter (1973) sees the way of the future being through use of more effective positive reinforcement programs. He states:

> Whatever new systems are adopted by organizations, there is sure to be one prominent feature of the work environment in [the year] 2001: work and fun will be combined on the job. . . . The merger of work and enjoyment will not, however, occur at the expense of organizational performance; through the effective restructuring of the reward environment, high levels of organizational performance can become the means for direct, personal gratification. Employees of progressive organizations of the future will be eager to perform (p. 131).

The types of rewards Porter sees being used in the future to gain commitment to the organization and/or being made contingent on superior performance in addition to pay, include: (1) opportunity to schedule one's own working hours, (2) a redistribution of job duties, (3) opportunity to create new jobs, (4) opportunity to participate in bonus drawings, (5) opportunity to choose any area of the organization in which to work for a limited period of time, (6) on-the-job nonwork activities, (7) new organizational ventures, (8) accrual of time off for sabbatical or educational leave, and (9) intercompany exchange of employees (1973, p. 127).

Lawler (1973a) sees the programs being implemented in industry today as being a step in the right direction in the fight to humanize work. Lawler, however, fears that most programs will fail unless we consider the individuality of the worker in the design of our motivational programs. Lawler states:

> When I look at the psychological research on people, I see convincing evidence that individuals differ significantly in their needs, skills and abilities. This is not to say that individuals aren't similar in many ways, for they are; but to be human is to be unique. To be humanized, an organization must recognize the uniqueness and sovereignty of each human being. In practical terms, this means that organizations and jobs must be designed in ways that are responsive to the differences which exist among people. Approaches to organization design and management which recommend standardized jobs, authoritian management, and piece-rate incentive plans for all don't do this, and neither do approaches which recommend enriched jobs, democratic management and MBO plans for all. Therefore, neither of these approaches has produced or is likely to produce a humanized organization (1973, p. 2).

Lawler contends that the place to start in individualizing the work available to people is in the selection and placement process. During the job interview, the applicant should be given information about the situation which exists and the various jobs available for which he is qualified. The interview should include more of a counseling atmosphere in order to allow the applicant to make self-selection decisions. Weitz (1965) and Wanous (in press) both report evidence that when job applicants are given valid information about the job, they will make better choices. In building a selection model (see Korman, 1971), the personnel manager should consider such items as motivation, reactions to different leadership styles, and preferred organizational climate, and attempt therefore to place the employees in those departments and with those leaders where they will have the greatest chance of success (Lawler, 1973a, p. 6).

One company which is currently experimenting with placing people in the department and under the leadership style most appropriate to their personality makeup is Texas Instruments. Charles L. Hughes, Director of Personnel and Organization Development at Texas Instruments, says, Companies must develop existentially managed organizations that truly accept and respect people with differing values" *(Business Week,* Sept. 29, 1973). As a first step, Hughes has classified 600 employees into six work-personality categories according to the way they perceive the world. The six categories include: (1) tribalistic—workers who respond to strong leadership and who are happy and dedicated when shown genuine care and concern; (2) existential—employees willing to do a job only if it is meaningful; (3) egocentric—entreprenuerial workers; (4) conformists—traditional workers; (5) manipulative—achievement-oriented workers; and (6) sociocentric—socially-oriented employees. Hughes hopes this research will influence Texas Instruments' selection and placement procedures, producing a more flexible organization. In the future, for example, Hughes would like to see an existential worker given an existential supervisor.

In order to overcome the deficiencies of the current motivation program, and to make the work place more adaptive to individuality and thereby increase the productivity of the labor force, Jackson Grayson, Dean of the Graduate School of Business at Southern Methodist University recommends we create an American Productivity Institute. Grayson says:

> The current exploding attention to human factors in the work place is a relatively new Western phenomenon. I believe it will have as profound an impact on our

ways of performing and regarding work and increasing productivity as the phenomenon of capital investment did during the Industrial Revolution. So far, though, it has emerged more extensively abroad than in the U.S. It manifests itself in the groups called Quality Control Circles in Japan, and at Olivetti in Italy, Norsk-Hydro in Norway, ICI in Britain, and in the U.S. in companies such as AT&T, Proctor and Gamble, Corning Glass, and Texas Instruments (*Business Week*, July 14, 1973, p. 16).

By setting up this private institute, Grayson hopes that sociologists, psychologists, labor relations experts, industrial relations officers, union leaders, plant managers, and others could be brought together and share ideas on the ways to solve worker discontent and make the future of worker motivational programs more successful and rewarding for all.

It appears that the organization of the future will truly become a more enjoyable and exciting place to be. What is needed now is more sharing of information and ideas by advocates of various programs and by organizations themselves. In this way, methods of increasing productivity and decreasing worker discontent can be speeded up and we can move into the twenty-first century with a renewed pride in our jobs and the quality of our work life.

Notes

1. For a detailed explanation of the principles of learning theory, see W. Clay Hamner, "Reinforcement Theory and Contingency Management in Organization Settings," in H. Tosi and W. Clay Hamner (eds.) *Organizational Behavior and Management: A Contingency Approach*, St. Clair Press, 1974.

2. A performance audit is a procedure where management determines the behavioral and job-related aspects of a department or a work unit such as a 10 percent rate of absenteeism, a 15 percent scrap rate, a 90 percent of standard production rate, etc. This should be distinguished from a performance evaluation where a manager rates an individual on both behavioral and nonbehavioral aspects of his job over a specified period of time.

3. See S. J. Carroll and H. L. Tosi, *Management by Objectives: Application and Research*, Macmillan, 1973.

4. Reinforcement techniques. See A. Bandura, *Principles of Behavior Modification*, Holt, Rinehart and Winston, Inc., New York, 1969.

5. Schneider and Hall (1972) argue that organizational climate is a perceptual variable and therefore cannot be directly manipulated. Because it is an intervening variable, it is harder to influence than inputs (task) or outcome (reinforcement) variables.

6. According to Lewin (1944), to change an individual (or a group) you must change his "life space." The life space consists of the person and the psychological environments as it exists for him at that point in time. Lewin regarded the properties of the "field" of the life space at any given time as the only determinant of behavior. See M. E. Shaw and P. R. Costanzo. *Theories of Social Psychology*, McGraw-Hill, 1970, pp. 117-36.

7. M. Beer and E. F. Huse disagree with this common assumption. See "A Systems Approach to Organizational Development," *Journal of Applied Behavioral Science*, 8, 1972, pp. 79-101.

8. Beer and Huse (*op. cit.*) and others correctly point out that while O.D. evolved out of a T-group background, an O.D. program does not limit itself to climate changes and may not involve any T-group training.

9. It should also be noted that the need for car-pooling due to the energy crisis may be hurt by the flexitime schedule. However, the four-day-week program would lend itself to car-pooling and is proposed by some as a means of conserving energy.

References

Abel, I. W., Advertisement, *Sports Illustrated* 39, 17, October 22, 1973.

"How Industry is Dealing with People Problems on the Line," *American Machinist*, November 12 (1973), 79-91.

Arygris, Chris, *Integrating the individual and the organization*, Wiley, 1964.

Arygris, C. *Interpersonal Competence and Organizational Effectiveness*, Dorsey Press, 1962.

Argyris, C., *Personality and Organization*, Harper, 1957.

Baxter, J. D., "Whatever Happened to Job Enrichment?" *Iron Age*, November 8 (1973), 35-36.

Beckhand, R., *Organizational Development: Strategies and Models*, Addison-Wesley, 1969.

Bem, D. J., *An Experienced Analysis of Beliefs and Attitudes*, unpublished doctoral dissertation, University of Michigan, 1964.

Bennis, W. G., *Organizational Development: Its Nature, Origins, and Prospects*, Addison-Wesley, 1969.

Bennis, W. G., *Changing Organizations*, McGraw-Hill, 1966.

Blake, R. R. and J. S. Mouton, "Grid Organization Development." *Personnel Administration*, January-February, 1967.

Bradford, L. P., Gibb, J. R. and Benne, K. D., *T-group Theory and Laboratory Method*, Wiley, 1964.

Burke, W. W., "Management and Organizational Development: What Is the Target of the Change?" *Personnel Administration*, 34 (1971), 44-56.

"How to make Productivity Grow Faster," *Business Week*, July 14, 1973, 15-16.

"Motorola Creates a More Demanding Job," *Business Week*, September 4, 1971, 32.

"The Humanistic Way of Managing People," *Business Week*, July 22, 1972, 48-49.

"Where Being Nice to Workers Didn't Work," *Business Week*, September 2, 1972.

"How Texas Instruments Turns Its People On," *Business Week*, September 29, 1973, 88, 90.

"The 'Humanistic' Way of Managing People," *Business Week*, July 22, 1972, 48-49.

"New Tool: Reinforcement for Good Work," *Business Week*, December 18, 1971, 68-69.

"Where Skinner's Theories Work," *Business Week*, December 2, 1972, 64-65.

Carroll S. J. and Tosi, H. L. *Management by Objectives*, Macmillan, 1973.

Campbell, J. P. and Dunnette, M. D., "Effectiveness of T-group Exercises in Managerial Training and Development," *Psychological Bulletin*, 70 (1968), 73-104.

Conart, E. H. and Kilbridge, M., "An Interdisciplinary Analysis of Job Enrichment," *Industrial and Labor Relations Review*, April, 1965, 377-395.

Cray, D. W., "Coming to Work Whenever You Want," *The New York Times*, Sunday, Feb. 4, 1973.

Crockett, W. J., "Team Building—One Approach to Organizational Development," *Journal of Applied Behavioral Science*, 6 (1970), 291-306.

"Workers Get a Voice in Chrysler Operations," *Detroit Free Press*, July 25, 1971.

"A New way to Work," *Detroit Free Press*, October 29, 1973, sect. B, 10-11.

Donnelly, J. F., "Increasing Productivity by Involving People in Their Total Jobs," *Personnel Administration*, Sept.-Oct., 1971, 8-13.

Drucker, Peter F., "Beyond the Stick and Carrot: Hysteria over the Work Ethic," *Psychology Today*, Nov. 1973, 87, 89-93.

Emery, J. C., "How to Double your Sales and Profits Every 5 Years," speech before the *Sales Executive Club of New York*, 1973.

Ferster, C. B. and Skinner, B. F., *Schedules of Reinforcement*, Appleton-Century-Crofts, 1957.

Ford, Robert, "Job Enrichment Lessons at AT&T," *Harvard Business Review*, 1973, 96-106.

Ford, Robert, *"Motivation Through the Work Itself,"* American Management Association, 1969.

Forehand, G. A., "On the Interactions of Persons and Organizations," in R. Tagiuri and G. H. Litwin (eds.), *Organizational Climate*, Harvard University, Division of Research, 1968, 65-82.

French, W., "Organizational Development Objectives: Assumptions and Strategies," *California Management Review*, 12 (1969), 23-34.

Frost, Carl F., "A Change Agent's View of the Scanlon Plan," paper presented at the American Psychological Association, Montreal, August, 1973.

Fuller, Stephen H., "Employee Development," speech before the *National Alliance of Businessmen*, Detroit, Michigan, September 24, 1973.

Gamboa, V. U. and E. Pedalino, "Behavior Modification and Absenteeism: Intervention in One Industrial Setting," University of Michigan working paper, 1973.

Gibson, J. L., Ivancevich, J. M., and Donnelly, J. H., *Organizations: Structures, Processes, and Behavior*, Business Publications, Inc. 1973.

Greiner, L. E., "Patterns of Organization Change," *Harvard Business Review*. 45 (1967).

Gooding, Judson, "It pays to Wake up the Blue-collar Worker," *Fortune*, September, 1970.

Hamner, W. Clay, Reinforcement Theory and Contingency Management," in H. L. Tosi and W. Clay Hamner (eds.), *Organizational Behavior and Management: A Contingency Approach*, St. Clair Press, 1974.

Hampton, D. R., Summer, C. E., and Webber, R. A., *Organizational Behavior and the Practice of Management*, Scott, Foresmen and Company, 1973.

Herrick, N. Q., "The Other Side of the Coin," paper delivered at the 2oth Anniversary Invitational Seminar of the Profit Sharing Research Foundation, Evanston, Ill., Nov. 17, 1971.

Herzberg, F., "One More Time: How Do You Motivate Employees?" *Harvard Business Review*, 46, (1968), 53-62.

House, R. J., "T-group Education and Leadership Effectiveness: A Review of the Empirical Literature and a Critical Evaluation," *Personnel Psychology*, 20, 1967, 1-32.

Hulin, C. L., and Blood, M. R., "Job Enlargement, Individual Differences and Worker Responses," *Psychological Bulletin*, January, 1968, 41-55.

Hulin, C. L., "Individual Differences and Job Enrichment—The Case Against General Treatments," in J. Maher, *New Perspectives in Job Enrichment*, Van Nostrand Reinhold, 1971, 159-91.

Hunt, J. G. and Hill, J. W. "The New Look in Motivation Theory in Organizational Research," *Human Organizations*, Summer, 1969, 100-109.

"The Power of Praise," *International Management*, October, 1973, 32-35.

Jacobs, C. D., "Job Enrichment at Xerox Corporation," paper presented at the *International Conference on the Quality of Work Life*, Sept. 24-29, 1972, Arden House, New York.

Janson, R., Job enrichment: "Challenge of the 70's," *Training and Development Journal*, June, 1970, 7-9.

Kahn, R. L., "The Work Module—A Tonic for Lunchpail Lassitude," *Psychology Today*, 6, 1973, 35-39, 94-95.

Kolb, D. A., Rubin, I. M. and McIntyre, J. M., *Organizational Psychology: An Experimental Approach*, Prentice-Hall, 1971.

Korman, A. K., *Industrial and Organizational Psychology*, Prentice-Hall, 1971, 178-203.

Kornhauser, A. W., *Mental Health of the Industrial Worker: A Detroit Study*, Wiley, 1965.

Landen, D. L. and Carlson H. C. "Employee Motivation: A Vast Domain of Unrealized Human and Business Potential," chapter to be included in forthcoming book by A. J. Marrow, (Ed.) *American Management Association*, in preparation, 1973.

Lawler, E. E., "Job Design and Employee Motivation," *Personnel Psychology*, 22, 1969.

Lawler, E. E., "Individualizing Organizations: A Needed Emphasis in Organizational Psychology," paper presented at the *American Psychological Association Convention*, Montreal, August, 1973a.

Lawler, E. E., "What Do Employees *Really* Want?" paper presented at the *American Psychological Association Convention*, Montreal, August, 1973b.

Leavitt, H. J., "Applied Organizational change In Industry," in J. G. March (ed.), *Handbook of Organizations*, Rand McNally, 1965, 1144-1170.

Levitan, S. A. and Johnston, W. B., "Job Redesign Enrichment—Exploring the Limitations," *Monthly Labor Review*, July, 1973a, 35-41.

Levitan, S. A. and Johnston, W. B., "Changes in Work: More Evolution than Revolution," *Manpower*, September, 1973b, 3-7.

Levitan, S. A. and Johnston, W. B., *Work Is Here to Stay, Alas,* Olympus, 1973c.

Lewin, K., "Constructs in Psychology and Psychological Ecology," *University of Iowa Studies in Child Welfare,* 1944, 20, 1-29.

Lewin, K., "Group Decision and Social Change," in G. E. Swanson, T. M. Newcomb, and E. L. Hartley (eds.) *Readings in Social Psychology,* Holt, 1952, 459-473.

Lewin, Kurt, *Field Theory in Social Science,* Harper and Brothers, 1951.

Likert, R., *New Patterns of Management,* McGraw-Hill, 1961.

Little, A. and Warr, P., "Who's Afraid of Job Enrichment?" *Personnel Management,* Feb., 1971, 34-37.

Litwin, G. H. and Stringer, R. A., "Motivation and Organizational Climate, in D. R. Hampton, C. F. Summer, and R. A. Webber (eds.), *Organizational Behavior and the Practice of Management,* Scott-Foresman, 1973, 538-550.

Luthans, F., *Organizational Behavior,* McGraw-Hill, 1973.

Luthans, F. and White, D. O., "Behavior Modification: Application to Manpower Management," *Personnel Administrator,* July-August, 1971, 41-47.

McGregor, D., *The Human side of Enterprise,* McGraw-Hill, 1960.

Moles, L., "Workers Decide own Hours," *The State Journal,* Lansing, Mich., Sept. 23, 1973, 10.

Myers, M. S., "Overcoming Union Opposition to Job Enrichment," *Harvard Business Review,* May, 1971.

Nord, W. R., "Beyond the Teaching Machine: The Neglected Area of Operant Conditioning in the Theory and Practice of Management," *Organizational Behavior and Human Performance,* 1969, 375-401.

Conversation with B. F. Skinner, *Organization Dynamics,* 1973a, Winter, 31-40.

"At Emery Air Freight: Positive Reinforcement Boosts Performance," *Organizational Dynamics,* 1, 1973b, 41-50.

Poor, Riva, *4 Days, 40 Hours: Reporting a Revolution in Work and Leisure* (rev. ed.), Bursk and Poor Pub., 1973.

Porter, L. W., "Turning Work into Nonwork: The Rewarding Environment," in M. D. Dunnette (ed.), *Work and Nonwork in the year 2001,* Brooks/Cole, 1973, 113-133.

Reif, W. E. and Luthans, F., "Does Job Enrichment Really Pay Off?," *California Management Review,* Fall, 1972, 34-35.

Reif, W. E. and Schoderbek, P., "Job Enlargement: Antidote to Apathy," *Management of Personnel Quarterly,* Spring, 1966, 16-23.

Rickleffs, R., "The Quality of Work," *The Wall Street Journal,* August 21, 1972, 1.

Rogers, C. R., *Counseling and psychotheraphy,* Houghton Mifflin, 1942.

Schein, E. H., *Process Consultation: Its Role in Organizational Development,* Addison-Wesley, 1969.

Schein, E. H., *Organizational Psychology,* 2nd. edition, Prentice-Hall, 1970.

Schneider, B., and D. T. Hall, "Toward Specifying the Concept of Work Climate," *Journal of Applied Psychology,* 1972, 56, 447-455.

Schotters, F. J., "What Is 'Organizational Development'? Does It Work?," *G.M. Personnel Development Bulletin,* no. 9, August 17, 1972a.

Schotters, F. J., "New Tool to Measure Organizational Effectiveness," *G.M. Personnel Development Bulletin,* no. 5, May 1, 1972b.

Schotters, F. J., "Oldsmobile Action Program on Absenteeism and Turnover," *G.M. Personnel Development Bulletin,* no. 2, Feb. 3, 1972c.

Schotters, F. J., "Organizational Development at GMAD-Arlington," *G.M. Personnel Development Bulletin,* no. 6, May 17, 1972d.

Schotters, F. J., "GMAD Fremont's Absenteeism and Discipline Programs," *G.M. Personnel Development Bulletin,* no. 18, April 2, 1973a.

Schotters, F. J., "Job Enrichment at Buick Products Engineering," *G.M. Personnel Development Bulletin,* no. 22, June 4, 1973b.

Scott, W. E., "Activation Theory and Task Design," *Organizational Behavior and Human Performance,* 1, (1966), 3-30.

Skinner, B. F., *Science and Human Behavior,* Macmillan, 1953.
Skinner, B. F., *Contingencies of Reinforcement,* Appleton-Century-Crofts, 1971.
Sorcher, M. and Goldstein, A. P., "A Behavioral Modeling Approach in Training," *Personnel Administration,* Mar.-April, 1972, 35-41.
Stewart, P. A., *Job Enrichment: In the Shop, in the Management Function,* Center for Labor and Management, University of Iowa, 1967.
Strauss, G., "Organizational Development: Credits and Debits," *Organizational Dynamics,* 1 (1973), 2-18.
Tannenbaum, A. S., Control in Organizations: Individual Adjustment and Organizational Performance," *Administrative Science Quarterly,* 7 (1962), 236-257.
Thorndike, F. L., *Animal Intelligence,* Macmillan, 1911.
Warren, M. W., "Performance Management: A Substitute for Supervision," *Management Review,* October, 1972, 28-42.
Wanous, J. P., "Effect of a Realistic Job Preview on Job Acceptance, Job Survival, and Job Attitudes," *Jounral of Applied Psychology,* in press.
Wiard, H., "Why Manage Behavior? A Case for Positive Reinforcement," *Human Resource Management,* Summer, 1972, 15-20.
Winn, A., "The Laboratory Approach to Organizational Development," paper read at the Annual Conference, *British Psychological Society,* Oxford, September, 1968.
Weitz, J., "Job Expectancy and Survival," *Journal of Applied Psychology,* 1965, 245-247.
Werther, W. B., "The Good News and Bad News of Flexible Hours," *Administrative Management,* November, 1973, 78-79, 96.
Whyte, W. F., "Skinnerian Theory in Organizations," *Psychology Today,* April 1972, 67-68, 96 98. 100.
Work in America, report of a special Task Force to the Secretary of Health, Education and Welfare, Cambridge, Mass.: The MIT Press, 1973.
Vroom, V., *Work and Motivation,* Wiley, 1964.

Behavior Modification on the Bottom Line

W. CLAY HAMNER
ELLEN P. HAMNER

Setting up a Positive Reinforcement Program in Industry

Many organizations are setting up formal motivational programs in an attempt to use the principles of positive reinforcement to increase employee productivity.

A positive reinforcement approach to management differs from traditional motivational theories in two basic ways. First, . . . a positive reinforcement program calls for the maximum use of reinforcement and the minimum use of punishment. Punishment tends to

Reprinted by permission of the publisher from *Organizational Dynamics*, Spring 1976, © 1976 by AMACOM, a division of American Management Associations.

leave the individual feeling controlled and coerced. Second, a positive reinforcement program avoids psychological probing into the worker's attitudes as a possible cause of behavior. Instead, the work situation itself is analyzed, with the focus on the reward contingencies that cause a worker to act the way in which he does.

A positive reinforcement program, therefore, is results-oriented rather than process-oriented. Geary A. Rummler, president of Praxis Corporation, a management consultant firm, claims that the motivational theories of such behavioral scientists as Herzberg and Maslow, which stress workers' psychological needs, are impractical. "They can't be made operative. While they help classify a problem, a positive reinforcement program leads to solutions."

Stages in Program Development

Positive reinforcement programs currently used in industry generally involve at least four stages. The *first stage*, according to Edward J. Feeney, formerly vice-president, systems, of Emery Air Freight Corporation, is to define the behavioral aspects of performance and do a performance audit. This step is potentially one of the most difficult, since some companies do not have a formal performance evaluation program, especially for nonmanagerial employees, and those that do have a program often rate the employee's behavior on nonjob-related measures (such as friendliness, loyalty, cooperation, overall attitude, and so on). But once these behavioral aspects are defined, the task of convincing managers that improvement is needed and of persuading them to cooperate with such a program is simplified. Feeney asserts, "Most managers genuinely think that operations in their bailiwick are doing well; a performance audit that proves they're not comes as a real and unpleasant surprise."

The *second stage* in developing a working positive reinforcement program is to develop and set specific goals for each worker. Failure to specify concrete behavioral goals is a major reason many programs do not work. Goals should be expressed in such terms as "decreased employee turnover" or "schedules met," rather than only in terms of "better identification with the company" or "increased job satisfaction." The goals set, therefore, should be in the same terms as those defined in the performance audit, goals that specifically relate to the task at hand. Goals should be reasonable—that is, set somewhere between "where you are" (as spelled out in the performance audit) and some ideal.

While it is important for the manager to set goals, it is also important for the employee to accept them. An approach that tends to build in goal acceptance is to allow employees to work with management in setting work goals. According to John C. Emery, president of Emery Air Freight Corporation, the use of a participatory management technique to enlist the ideas of those performing the job not only results in their acceptance of goals, but also stimulates them to come up with goals.

The *third stage* in a positive reinforcement program is to allow the employee to keep a record of his or her own work. This process of self-feedback maintains a continuous schedule of reinforcement for the worker and helps him obtain intrinsic reinforcement from the task itself. Where employees can total their own results, they can see whether they are meeting their goals and whether they are improving over their previous performance level (as measured in the performance audit stage). In other words, the worker has two chances of being successful—either by beating his previous record or by beating both his previous record and his established goal. E. D. Grady, general manager-operator services for Michigan Bell, maintains that the manager should set up the work environment in such a way that people have a chance to succeed. One way to do this, he says, is to "shorten the success interval." Grady says, "If you're looking for success, keep shortening the interval of measurement so you can get a greater chance of success which you can latch on to for positive reinforcements." Instead of setting monthly or quarterly goals, for example, set weekly or daily goals.

The *fourth stage*—the most important step in a positive reinforcement program—is one that separates it from all other motivation plans. The supervisor looks at the self-feedback report of the employee and/or other indications of performance (sales records, for example) and then praises the positive aspects of the employee's performance (as determined by the performance audit and subsequent goal setting). This extrinsic reinforcement should strengthen the desired performance, while the withholding of praise for substandard performance should give the employee incentive to improve that performance level. Since the worker already knows the areas of his or her deficiencies, there is no reason for the supervisor to criticize the employee. In other words, negative feedback is self-induced, whereas positive feedback comes from both internal and external sources.

. . . This approach to feedback follows the teachings of B. F. Skinner, who believes that use of positive reinforcement leads to a greater feeling of self-control, while the avoidance of negative reinforcement keeps the individual from feeling controlled or coerced. Skinner says, "You can get the same effect if the supervisor simply discovers things being done right and says something like 'Good, I see you're doing it the way that works best.'"

While the feedback initially used in step four of the positive reinforcement program is praise, it is important to note that other forms of reinforcement can have the same effect. M. W. Warren, the director of organization and management development at the Questor Corporation, says that the five "reinforcers" he finds most effective are (1) money (but only when it is a consequence of a specific performance and when the relation to the performance is known); (2) praise or recognition; (3) freedom to choose one's own activity; (4) opportunity to see oneself become better, more important, or more useful; and (5) power to influence both co-workers and management. Warren states, "By building these reinforcers into programs at various facilities, Questor is getting results." The need for using more than praise after the positive reinforcement program has proved effective is discussed by Skinner.

> It does not cost the company anything to use praise rather than blame, but if the company then makes a great deal more money that way, the worker may seem to be getting gypped. However, the welfare of the worker depends on the welfare of the company, and if the company is smart enough to distribute some of the fruits of positive reinforcement in the form of higher wages and better fringe benefits, everybody gains from the supervisor's use of positive reinforcements (*Organizational Dynamics,* Winter, 1073, p. 35.).

Early Results of Positive Reinforcement Programs in Organizations, 1969-73

Companies that claimed to be implementing and using positive reinforcement programs such as the one described above include Emery Air Freight, Michigan Bell Telephone, Questor Corporation, Cole National Company in Cleveland, Ford Motor Company, American Can, Upjohn, United Air Lines, Warner-Lambert, Addressograph-Multigraph, Allis-Chalmers, Bethlehem Steel, Chase Manhattan Bank, IBM, IT&T, Proctor and Gamble, PPG Industries, Standard Oil of Ohio, Westinghouse, and Wheeling-Pittsburgh Steel Corporation (see *Business Week,* December 18, 1971, and December 2, 1972). Because such programs are relatively new in industrial settings (most have begun since 1968), few statements of their relative effectiveness have been reported. In the Winter 1973 issue of *Organizational Dynamics* (p. 49), it was stated that "there's little objective evidence available, and what evidence there is abounds in caveats—the technique will work under the proper circumstances, the parameters of which are usually not easily apparent."

In the area of employee training, Northern Systems Company, General Electric Corporation, and Emery Air Freight claim that positive reinforcement has improved the speed and efficiency of their training program. In their programmed learning program, the Northern Systems Company structures the feedback system in such a way that the trainee receives positive feedback only when he demonstrates correct performance at the tool station. The absence of feedback is experienced by the trainee when he fails to perform correctly. Therefore, through positive reinforcements, he quickly perceives that correct behaviors obtain for him the satisfaction of his needs, and that incorrect behaviors do not. Emery has designed a similar program for sales trainees. *Business Week* reported the success of the program by saying:

> It is a carefully engineered, step-by-step program, with frequent feedback questions and answers to let the salesman know how he is doing. The course contrasts with movies and lectures in which, Feeney says, the salesman is unable to gauge what he has learned. The aim is to get the customer on each sales call to take some kind of action indicating that he will use Emery services. Significantly, in 1968, the first full year after the new course was launched, sales jumped from $62.4 million to $79.8 million, a gain of 27.8 percent compared with an 11.3 percent rise the year before.

Since 1969, Emery has instituted a positive reinforcement program for all of its employees and credits the program with direct savings to the company of over $3 million in the first three years and indirectly with pushing 1973 sales over the $160 million mark. While Emery Air Freight is and remains the biggest success story for a positive reinforcement program to date, other companies also claim improvements as a result of initiating similar programs. At Michigan Bell's Detroit office, 2,000 employees in 1973 participated in a positive reinforcement program. Michigan Bell credits the program with reducing absenteeism from 11 percent to 6.5 percent in one group, from 7.5 percent to 4.5 percent in another group, and from 3.3 percent to 2.6 percent for all employees. In addition, the program has resulted in the correct completion of reports on time 90 percent of the time as compared with 20 percent of the time before the program's implementation. The Wheeling-Pittsburgh Steel Corporation credits its feedback program with saving $200,000 a month in scrap costs.

In an attempt to reduce the number of employees who constantly violated plant rules, General Motors implemented a plan in one plant that gave employees opportunities to improve or clear their records by going through varying periods of time without committing further shop violations. They credit this positive reinforcement plan with reducing the number of punitive actions for shop-rule infractions by two-thirds from 1969 to 1972 and the number of production-standard grievances by 70 percent during the same period.

While there was a great deal of interest in applying behavior modification in industrial settings after the successes of Emery Air Freight and others who followed suit were made known in 1971, the critics of this approach to worker motivation predicted that it would be short-lived. Any success would owe more to a "Hawthorne Effect" (the positive consequences of paying special attention to employees) than to any real long-term increase in productivity and/or worker satisfaction. The critics pointed out—quite legitimately, we might add—that most of the claims were testimonial in nature and that the length of experience between 1969-73 was too short to allow enough data to accumulate to determine the true successes of positive reinforcement in improving morale and productivity. With this in mind, we surveyed ten organizations, all of which currently use a behavior modification approach, to see if the "fad" created by Emery Air Freight had died or had persisted and extended its gains.

Specifically, we were interested in knowing (1) how many employees were covered; (2) the kinds of employees covered; (3) specific goals (stages 1 & 2); (4) frequency of self-feedback (stage 3); (5) the kinds of reinforcers used (stage 4); and (6) results of the program. A summary of companies surveyed and the information gained is shown in figure 1.

Current Results of Positive Reinforcement Programs in Organizations

The ten organizations surveyed included Emery Air Freight, Michigan Bell-Operator Services, Michigan Bell-Maintenance Services, Connecticut General Life Insurance Company, General Electric, Standard Oil of Ohio, Weyerhaeuser, City of Detroit, B. F. Goodrich Chemical Company, and ACDC Electronics. In our interviews with each of the managers, we tried to determine both the successes and the failures they attributed to the use of behavior modification or positive reinforcement techniques. We were also interested in whether the managers saw this as a fad or as a legitimate management technique for improving the productivity and quality of work life among employees.

Emery Air Freight
Figure 1 shows Emery Air Freight still using positive reinforcement as a motivational tool. John C. Emery commented: "Positive reinforcement, always linked to feedback systems, plays a central role in performance improvement at Emery Air Freight. *All* managers and supervisors are being trained via self-instructional, programmed instruction texts—one on reinforcement and one on feedback. No formal off-the-job training is needed. Once he has studied the texts, the supervisor is encouraged immediately to apply the learning to the performance area for which he is responsible."

Paul F. Hammond, Emery's manager of system performance and the person currently in charge of the positive reinforcement program, said that there are a considerable number of company areas in which quantifiable success has been attained over the last six or seven years. Apart from the well-publicized container savings illustration (results of which stood at $600,000 gross savings in 1970 and over $2,000,000 in 1975), several other recent success stories were noted by Emery & Hammond. They include:

- Standards for customer service on the telephone had been set up and service was running 60 to 70 percent of standard. A program very heavily involved with feedback and reinforcement was introduced a few years ago and increased performance to 90 percent of objectives within three months—a level that has been maintained ever since.
- Several offices have installed a program in which specified planned reinforcements are

Motivating Performance   289

FIGURE 1
Results of Positive Reinforcement and Similar Behavior Modification Programs in Organizations in 1976

Organization & Person Surveyed	Length of Program	Number of Employees Covered/ Total Employees	Type of Employees	Specific Goals	Frequency of Feedback	Reinforcers Used	Results
Emery Air Freight John C. Emery, Jr., President Paul F. Hammond, Manager–Systems Performance	1969–1976	500/2,800	Entire workforce	(a) Increase productivity (b) Improve quality of service	Immediate to monthly, depending on task	Previously only praise and recognition; others now being introduced	Cost savings can be directly attributed to the program
Michigan Bell– Operator Services E. D. Grady, General Manager– Operator Services	1972–1976	2,000/5,500	Employees at all levels in operator services	(a) Decrease turnover & absenteeism (b) Increase productivity (c) Improve union-management relations	(a) Lower level— weekly & daily (b) Higher level— monthly & quarterly	(a) Praise & recognition (b) Opportunity to see oneself become better	(a) Attendance performance has improved by 50% (b) Productivity and efficiency has continued to be above standard in areas where positive reinforcement (PR) is used
Michigan Bell– Maintenance Services Donald E. Burwell, Division Superintendent Maintenance & Services Dr. W. Clay Hamner, Consultant	1974–1976	220/5,500	Maintenance workers, mechanics, & first & second-level supervisors	Improve (a) productivity (b) quality (c) safety (d) customer-employee relations	Daily, weekly, and quarterly	(a) Self-feedback (b) Supervisory feedback	(a) Cost efficiency increase (b) Safety improved (c) Service improved (d) No change in absenteeism (e) Satisfaction with superior & co-workers improved (f) Satisfaction with pay decreased
Connecticut General Life Insurance Co. Donald D. Illig, Director of Personnel Administration	1941–1976	3,000/13,500	Clerical employees & first-line supervisors	(a) Decrease absenteeism (b) Decrease lateness	Immediate	(a) Self-feedback (b) System-feedback (c) Earned time off	(a) Chronic absenteeism & lateness has been drastically reduced (b) Some divisions refuse to use PR because it is "outdated"

(FIGURE 1 cont'd.)

Organization & Person Surveyed	Length of Program	Number of Employees Covered/ Total Employees	Type of Employees	Specific Goals	Frequency of Feedback	Reinforcers Used	Results
General Electric [1] Melvin Sorcher, Ph.D., formerly Director of Personnel Research Now Director of Management Development. Richardson-Merrell, Inc.	1973-1976	1,000	Employees at all levels	(a) Meet EEO objectives (b) Decrease absenteeism & turnover (c) Improve training (d) Increase productivity	Immediate—uses modeling & role playing as training tools to teach interpersonal exchanges & behavior requirements	Social reinforcers (praise, rewards, & constructive feedback)	(a) Cost savings can be directly attributed to the program (b) Productivity has increased (c) Worked extremely well in training minority groups and raising their self-esteem (d) Direct labor cost decreased
Standard Oil of Ohio T. E. Standings, Ph.D., Manager of Psychological Services	1974	28	Supervisors	Increase supervisor competence	Weekly over 5 weeks (25-hour) training period	Feedback	(a) Improved supervisory ability to give feedback judiciously (b) Discontinued because of lack of overall success
Weyerhaeuser Company Gary P. Latham, Ph.D., Manager of Human Resource Research	1974-1976	500/40,000	Clerical, production (tree planters) & middle-level management & scientists	(a) To teach managers to minimize criticism & to maximize praise (b) To teach managers to make rewards contingent on specified performance levels & (c) To use optimal schedule to increase productivity	Immediate—daily & quarterly	(a) Pay (b) Praise & recognition	(a) Using money, obtained 33% increase in productivity with one group of workers, an 18% increase with a second group, and an 8% decrease in a third group (b) Currently experimenting with goal setting & praise and/or money at various levels in organization (c) With a lottery-type bonus, the cultural & religious values of workers must be taken into account

City of Detroit Garbage Collectors[2]	1973-1975	1,122/1,930	Garbage collectors	(a) Reduction in paid man-hour per ton (b) Reduction on overtime (c) 90% of routes completed by standard (c) Effectiveness (quality)	Daily & quarterly based on formula negotiated by city & sanitation union	Bonus (profit sharing) & praise	(a) Citizen complaints declined significantly (b) City saved $1,654,000 first year after bonus paid (c) Worker bonus = $307,000 first year or $350 annually per man (d) Union somewhat dissatisfied with productivity measure and is pushing for more bonus to employee (e) 1975 results not yet available
B. F. Goodrich Chemical Co. Donald J. Barnicki, *Production Manager*	1972-1976	100/420	Manufacturing employees at all levels	(a) Better meeting of schedules (b) Increase productivity	Weekly	Praise & recognition; freedom to choose one's own activity	Production has increased over 300%
ACDC Electronics Division of Emerson Electronics Edward J. Feeney, *Consultant*	1974-1976	350/350	All levels	(a) 96% attendance (b) 90% engineering specifications met (c) Daily production objectives met 95% of time (d) Cost reduced by 10%	Daily & weekly feedback from foreman to company president	Positive feedback	(a) Profit up 25% over forecast (b) $550,000 cost reduction on $10M sales (c) Return of 1900% on investment including consultant fees (d) Turnaround time on repairs went from 30 to 10 days (e) Attendance is now 98.2% (from 93.5%)

1. Similar programs are now being implemented at Richardson-Merrell under the direction of Dr. Sorcher and at AT&T under the direction of Douglas W. Bray, Ph.D., director of management selection and development, along with several other smaller organizations (see A. P. Goldstein, Ph.D. & Melvin Sorcher, Ph.D., *Changing Supervisor Behavior*, Pergamon Press, 1974).
2. From *Improving Municipal Productivity: The Detroit Refuse Incentive Plan*, The National Commission on Productivity, April 1974.

provided when targeted levels of shipment volume are requested by Emery customers. All offices have increased revenue substantially; one office doubled the number of export shipments handled, and another averages an additional $60,000 of revenue per month.

A program of measuring dimensions of certain lightweight shipments to rate them by volume rather than weight uses reinforcement and feedback extensively. All measures have increased dramatically since its inception five years ago, not the least of which is an increase in revenue from $400,000 per year to well over $2,000,000 per year.

While this latest information indicates that positive reinforcement is more than a fad at Emery Air Freight, Emery pointed out that a major flaw in the program had to be overcome. He said, "Inasmuch as praise is the most readily available no-cost reinforcer, it tends to be the reinforcer used most frequently. However, the result has been to *dull* its effect as a reinforcer through its sheer repetition, even to risk making praise an *irritant* to the receiver." To counter this potential difficulty, Emery managers and supervisors have been taught and encouraged to expand their reinforcers beyond praise. Among the recommended reinforcers have been formal recognition such as a public letter or a letter home, being given a more enjoyable task after completing a less enjoyable one, invitations to business luncheons or meetings, delegating responsibility and decision making, and tying such requests as special time off or any other deviation from normal procedure to performance. Thus it seems that Skinner's prediction made in 1973 about the need for using more than praise after the reinforcement program has been around for a while has been vindicated at Emery Air Freight.

Michigan Bell-Operator Service

The operator services division is still actively using positive reinforcement feedback as a motivational tool. E. D. Grady, general manager for Operator Services said, "We have found through experience that when standards and feedback are not provided, workers generally feel their performance is at about the 95 percent level. When the performance is then compared with clearly-defined standards, it is usually found to meet only the 50th percentile in performance. It has been our experience, over the past ten years, that when standards are set and feedback provided in a positive manner, performance will reach very high levels—perhaps in the upper 90th percentile in a very short period of time.... We have also found that when positive reinforcement is discontinued, performance returns to levels that existed prior to the establishment of feedback." Grady said that while he was not able at this time to put a specific dollar appraisal on the cost savings from using a positive reinforcement program, the savings were continuing to increase and the program was being expanded.

In one recent experiment, Michigan Bell found that when goal setting and positive reinforcement were used in a low-productivity inner-city operator group, service promptness (time to answer call) went from 94 percent to 99 percent of standard, average work time per call (time taken to give information) decreased from 60 units of work time to 43 units of work time, the percentage of work time completed within ideal limits went from 50 percent to 93 percent of ideal time (standard was 80 percent of ideal), and the percentage of time operators made proper use of references went from 80 percent to 94 percent. This led to an overall productivity index score for these operators that was significantly higher than that found in the control group where positive reinforcement was not being used, even though the control group of operators had previously (six months earlier) been one of the highest producing units.

Michigan Bell-Maintenance Services

Donald E. Burwell, Division Superintendent of Maintenance and Services at Michigan Bell established a goal-setting and positive reinforcement program in early 1974. He said, "After assignment to my present area of responsibility in January, I found that my new department of 220 employees (maintenance, mechanics, and janitorial services), including managers, possessed generally good morale. However, I soon became aware that 1973 performances were generally lower than the 1973 objectives. In some cases objectives were either ambiguous or nonexistent."

With the help of a consultant, Burwell overcame the problem by establishing a four-step positive reinforcement program similar to the one described earlier in this article. As a result, the 1974 year-end results showed significant improvements over the 1973 base-year average in all areas, including safety (from 75.6 to 89.0), service (from 76.4 to 83.0), cost performance/hour (from 27.9 to 21.2, indexed), attendance (from 4.7 to 4.0) and worker satisfaction and cooperation (3.01 to 3.51 on a scale of 5), and worker satisfaction with the supervisors (2.88 to 3.70, also on a scale of 5); 1975 figures reflect continuing success.

While Burwell is extremely pleased with the results of this program to date, he adds a word of caution to other managers thinking of implementing such a program: "I would advise against accepting any one method, including positive reinforcement, as a panacea for all the negative performance trends that confront managers. On the other hand, positive reinforcement has aided substantially in performance improvement for marketing, production, and service operators. Nevertheless, the manager needs to know when the positive effects of the reinforcement program have begun to plateau and what steps he should consider taking to maintain his positive performance trends."

Connecticut General Life Insurance Company

The Director of Personnel Administration at Connecticut General Life Insurance Company, Donald D. Illig, stated that Connecticut General has been using positive reinforcement in the form of an attendance bonus system for 25 years with over 3,200 clerical employees. Employees receive one extra day off for each ten weeks of perfect attendance. The results have been outstanding. Chronic absenteeism and lateness have been drastically reduced, and the employees are very happy with the system. Illig noted, however, that, "Our property and casualty company, with less than half the number of clerical employees countrywide, has not had an attendance-bonus system . . . and wants no part of it. At the crux of the problem is an anti-Skinnerian feeling, which looks at positive reinforcement—and thus an attendance-bonus system—as being overly manipulative and old-fashioned in light of current theories of motivation."

General Electric

A unique program of behavior modification has been introduced quite successfully at General Electric as well as several other organizations by Melvin Sorcher, formerly director of personnel research at G.E. The behavior modification program used at G.E. involves using positive reinforcement and feedback in training employees. While the first program centered primarily on teaching male supervisors how to interact and communicate with minority and female employees and on teaching minority and female employees how to become successful by improving their self-images, subsequent programs focused on the relationship between supervisors and employees in general. By using a reinforcement technique known as behavior modeling, Sorcher goes beyond the traditional positive reinforcement ("PR") program. The employee is shown a videotape of a model (someone with his own characteristics—that is, male or female, black or white, subordinate or superior) who is performing in a correct or desired manner. Then, through the process of role playing, the employee is encouraged to act in the successful or desired manner shown on the film (that is, he is asked to model the behavior). Positive reinforcement is given when the goal of successful display of this behavior is made in the role-playing session.

Sorcher notes that this method has been successfully used with over 1,000 G.E. supervisors. As a result, productivity has increased, the self-esteem of hard-core employees has increased, and EEO objectives are being met. He says, "The positive results have been the gratifying changes or improvements that have occurred, especially improvements that increase over time as opposed to the usual erosion of effort after most training programs have passed their peak. . . . On the negative side, some people and organizations are calling their training 'behavior modeling' when it does not fit the criteria originally defined for such a program. For example, some programs not only neglect self-esteem as a component, but show little evidence of how to shape new behaviors. . . . Regarding the more general area of behavior modification and positive reinforcement, there is still a need for better research. There's not a lot taking place at present, which is unfortunate because on the surface these processes seem to have a lot of validity."

Standard Oil of Ohio

T. E. Standings, manager of psychological services at SOHIO, tried a training program similar to the one used by Sorcher at General Electric. After 28 supervisors had completed five weeks of training, Standings disbanded the program even though there were some short-term successes. He said, "My feelings at this point are that reinforcement cannot be taught at a conceptual level in a brief period of time. (Of course, the same comments can no doubt be made about Theory Y, MBO, and TA.) I see two alternatives: (1) Identify common problem situations, structure an appropriate reinforcement response for the supervisor, and teach the response through the behavioral model, or (2) alter reinforcement contingencies affecting defined behaviors through direct alternatives in procedural and/or informational systems without going through the supervisor directly."

Weyerhaeuser Company

Whereas Emery Air Freight has the longest history with applied reinforcement theory, Weyerhaeuser probably has the most experience with controlled experiments using goal setting and PR techniques. The Human Resource Research Center at Weyerhaeuser, under the direction of G. P. Latham, is actively seeking ways to improve the productivity of all levels of employees using the goal-setting, PR feedback technique.

According to Dr. Latham, "The purpose of our positive reinforcement program is threefold: (1) To teach managers to embrace the philosophy that 'the glass is half-full rather than half-empty.' In other words, our objective is to teach managers to minimize criticism (which is often self-defeating since it can fixate the employee's attention on ineffective job behavior and thus reinforce it) and to maximize praise and hence fixate both their and the employee's attention on effective job behavior. (2) To teach managers that praise by itself may increase job satisfaction, but that it will have little or no effect on productivity unless it is made contingent upon specified job behaviors. Telling an employee that he is doing a good job in no way conveys to him what he is doing correctly. Such blanket praise can inadvertently reinforce the very things that the employee is doing in a mediocre way. (3) To teach managers to determine the optimum schedule for administering a reinforcer—be it praise, a smile, or money in the employee's pocket."

Weyerhaeuser has found that by using money as a reinforcer (that is, as a bonus over and above the worker's hourly rate), they obtained a 33 percent increase in productivity with one group of workers, an 18 percent increase in productivity with a second group of workers, and an 8 percent decrease in productivity with a third group of workers. Latham says, "These findings point out the need to measure and document the effectiveness of any human resource program. The results obtained in one industrial setting cannot necessarily be expected in another setting."

Latham notes that because of its current success with PR, Weyerhaeuser is currently applying reinforcement principles with tree planters in the rural South as well as with engineers and scientists at their corporate headquarters. In the latter case, they are comparing different forms of goal setting (assigned, participative, and a generalized goal of "do your best") with three different forms of reinforcement (praise or private recognition from a supervisor, public recognition in terms of a citation for excellence, and a monetary reward). Latham adds, "The purpose of the program is to motivate scientists to attain excellence. Excellence is defined in terms of the frequency with which an individual displays specific behaviors that have been identified by the engineers/scientists themselves as making the difference between success and failure in fulfilling the requirements of their job."

City of Detroit, Garbage Collectors

In December, 1972, the City of Detroit instituted a unique productivity bonus system for sanitation workers engaged in refuse collection. The plan, which provides for sharing the savings for productivity improvements efforts, was designed to save money for the city while rewarding workers for increased efficiency. The city's Labor Relations Bureau negotiated the productivity contract with the two unions concerned with refuse collection: The American Federation of State, County and Municipal Employees (AFSCME), representing sanitation laborers (loaders), and the Teamsters Union, representing drivers. The two agreements took effect on July 1, 1973.

The bonus system was based on savings gained in productivity (reductions in paid man-hours per ton of refuse collected, reduction in the total hours of overtime, percentage of routes completed on schedule, and effectiveness or cleanliness). A bonus pool was established and the sanitation laborers share 50-50 in the pool with the city—each worker's portion being determined by the number of hours worked under the productivity bonus pool, exclusive of overtime.

By any measure, this program was a success. Citizen complaints decreased dramatically. During 1974, the city saved $1,654,000 after the bonus of $307,000 ($350 per man) was paid. The bonus system is still in effect, but the unions are currently disputing with the city the question of what constitutes a fair day's work. Both unions involved have expressed doubts about the accuracy of the data used to compute the productivity index or, to be more precise, how the data are gathered and the index and bonus computed. Given this expected prenegotiation tactic by the unions, the city and the customers both agree that the plan has worked.

B. F. Goodrich Chemical Company

In 1972, one of the production sections in the B. F. Goodrich Chemical plant in Avon Lake, Ohio, as measured by standard accounting procedures, was failing. At that time, Donald J. Barnicki, the production manager, introduced a positive reinforcement program that included goal setting and feedback about scheduling, targets, costs, and problem areas. This program gave the information directly to the foreman on a once-a-week basis. In addition, daily meetings were held to discuss problems and describe how each group was doing. For the first time the foreman and their employees were told about costs that were incurred by their group. Charts were published that showed area achievements in terms of sales, cost, and productivity as compared with targets. Films were made that showed top management what the employees were doing, and these films were shown to the workers so they would know what management was being told.

According to Barnicki, this program of positive reinforcement turned the plant around. "Our productivity has increased 300 percent over the past five years. Costs are down. We had our best startup time in 1976 and passed our daily production level from last year the second day after we returned from the holidays."

ACDC Electronics

Edward J. Feeney, of Emery Air Freight fame, now heads a consulting firm that works with such firms as General Electric, Xerox, Braniff Airways, and General Atomic in the area of positive reinforcement programs. One of Mr. Feeney's current clients is the ACDC Electronics Company (a division of Emerson Electronics). After establishing a program that incorporated the four-step approach outlined earlier in this article, the ACDC Company experienced a profit increase of 25 percent over the forecast; a $550,000 cost reduction on $10 million in sales; a return of 1,900 percent on investment, including consultant fees; a reduction in turnaround time on repairs from 30 to 10 days; and a significant increase in attendance.

According to Ken Kilpatrick, ACDC President, "The results were as dramatic as those that Feeney had described. We found our output increased 30-40 percent almost immediately and has stayed at that high level for well over a year." The results were not accomplished, however, without initial problems, according to Feeney. "With some managers there were problems of inertia, disbelief, lack of time to implement, interest, difficulty in defining output for hard-to-measure areas, setting standards, measuring past performance, estimating economic payoffs, and failure to apply all feedback or reinforcement principles." Nevertheless, after positive results began to surface and initial problems were overcome, the ACDC management became enthused about the program.

Conclusion

This article has attempted to explain how reinforcement theory can be applied in organizational settings. We have argued that the arrangement of the contingencies of reinforcement is crucial in influencing behavior. Different ways of arranging these contingencies were explained, followed by a recommendation that the use of positive reinforcement combined with oral explanations of incorrect behaviors, when applied correctly, is an underestimated and powerful tool of management. The correct application includes three conditions: *First,* reinforcers must be selected that are sufficiently powerful and durable to establish and strengthen behavior; *second,* the manager must design the contingencies in such a way that the reinforcing events are made contingent on the desired level of performance; *third,* the program must be designed in such a way that it is possible to establish a reliable training procedure for inducing the desired response patterns.

To meet these three conditions for effective contingency management, many firms have set up a formal positive reinforcement motivational program. These include firms such as Emery Air Freight, Michigan Bell, Standard Oil of Ohio, General Electric, and

B. F. Goodrich, among others. Typically, these firms employ a four-stage approach in designing their programs: (1) A performance audit is conducted in order to determine what performance patterns are desired and to measure the current levels of that performance; (2) specific and reasonable goals are set for each worker; (3) each employee is generally instructed to keep a record of his or her own work; and (4) positive aspects of the employee's performance are positively reinforced by the supervisor. Under this four-stage program, the employee has two chances of being successful—he can beat his previous level of performance or he can beat that plus his own goal. Also under this system, negative feedback routinely comes only from the employee (since he knows when he failed to meet the objective), whereas positive feedback comes from both the employee and his supervisor.

While we noted that many firms have credited this approach with improving morale and increasing profits, several points of concern and potential shortcomings of this approach should also be cited. Many people claim that you cannot teach reinforcement principles to lower-level managers very easily and unless you get managers to understand the principles, you certainly risk misusing these tools. Poorly designed reward systems can interfere with the development of spontaneity and creativity. Reinforcement systems that are deceptive and manipulative are an insult to employees.

One way in which a positive reinforcement program based solely on praise can be deceptive and manipulative occurs when productivity continues to increase month after month and year after year, and the company's profits increase as well, but employee salaries do not reflect their contributions. This seems obviously unethical and contradictory. It is unethical because the workers are being exploited and praise by itself will not have any long-term effect on performance. Emery Air Freight, for example, has begun to experience this backlash effect. It is contradictory because the manager is saying he believes in the principle of making intangible rewards contingent on performance but at the same time refuses to make the tangible monetary reward contingent on performance. Often the excuse given is that "our employees are unionized." Well, this is not always the case. Many firms that are without unions, such as Emery, refuse to pay on performance. Many other firms with unions have a contingent bonus plan. Skinner in 1969 warned managers that a poorly designed monetary reward system may actually reduce performance. The employee should be a willing party to the influence attempt, with both parties benefitting from the relationship.

Peter Drucker's concern is different. He worries that perhaps positive reinforcers may be misused by management to the detriment of the economy. He says, "The carrot of material rewards has not, like the stick of fear, lost its potency. On the contrary, it has become so potent that it threatens to destroy the earth's finite resources if it does not first destroy more economies through inflation that reflects rising expectations." In other words, positive reinforcement can be too effective as used by firms concerned solely with their own personal gains.

Skinner in an interview in *Organizational Dynamics* stated that a feedback system alone may not be enough. He recommended that the organization should design feedback and incentive systems in such a way that the dual objective of getting things done and making work enjoyable is met. He says what must be accomplished, and what he believes is currently lacking, is an effective training program for managers. "In the not-too-distant future, however, a new breed of industrial managers may be able to apply the principles of operant conditioning effectively."

We have evidence in at least a few organizational settings that Skinner's hopes are on the way to realization, that a new breed of industrial managers are indeed applying the principles of operant conditioning effectively.

Selected Bibliography

For an understandable view of Skinner's basic ideas in his own words, see B. F. Skinner's *Contingencies of Reinforcement* (Appleton-Century-Crofts, 1969) and Carl R. Rogers and B. F. Skinner's "Some Issues Concerning the Control of Human Behavior" (*Science*, 1965, Vol. 24, pp. 1057-1066). For Skinner's views on the applications of his ideas in industry see "An Interview with B. F. Skinner (*Organizational Dynamics*, Winter 1973, pp. 31-40).

For an account of Skinner's ideas in action, see the same issue of *Organizational Dynamics* (pp. 41-50. and "Where Skinner's Theories Work" (*Business Week*, December 2, 1972, pp. 64-69).

An article highly critical of the application of Skinner's ideas in industry is W. F. Whyte's "Pigeons, Persons, and Piece Rates" (*Psychology Today*, April 1972, pp. 67-68). For a more sympathetic and more systematic treatment see W. R. Nord's "Beyond the Teaching Machine: The Negative Area of Operant Conditioning" in *The Theory and Practice of Management, Organizational Behavior and Human Performance* (1969, No. 4, pp. 375-401).

For comments on behavior modification by the author, see W. Clay Hamner's "Reinforcement Theory and Contingency Management" in L. Tosi and W. Clay Hamner, eds., *Organizational Behavior and Management: A Contingency Approach* (St. Clair Press, 1974, pp. 188-204) and W. Clay Hamner's "Worker Motivation Programs: Importance of Climate Structure and Performance Consequences" in this chapter.

Last, the best discussion of the general subject of pay and performance is Edward E. Lawler III's *Pay and Organizational Effectiveness* (McGraw-Hill, 1971).

Job Redesign on the Assembly Line: Farewell to Blue-Collar Blues?

WILLIAM F. DOWLING

The authors of the much-quoted, much praised, and much-criticized HEW report *Work in America* wound up their study with a rhetorical bang: "Albert Camus wrote that 'without work life goes rotten. But when work is soulless, life stifles and dies.' Our analysis of work in America leads to much the same conclusion: Because work is central to the lives of so many Americans, either the absence of work or employment in meaningless work is creating an increasingly intolerable situation."

Most who argue that the rhetoric in the report is exaggerated and the thesis overstated would exempt the assembly line, particularly the auto assembly line, from their dissent. The auto assembly line epitomizes the conditions that contribute to employee dissatisfaction: fractionation of work into meaningless activities, with each activity repeated several hundred times each workday, and with the employees having little or no control over work pace or any other aspect of working conditions.

Two generations of social scientists have documented the discontent of auto workers with their jobs. Yet the basic production process hasn't changed since Ford's first Highland Park assembly plant in 1913. We read a lot about the accelerating pace of technology: Here's a technology that's stood still for 60 years despite the discontent.

The social explanations are easy. The automakers—when they thought about the problem at all—dismissed it. The economic advantages of the assembly line seemingly outweighed any possible social costs—including the high wages, part of which might properly be considered discontentment pay. In short, the cash register rang more clearly than the gripes.

Reprinted by permission of the publisher from *Organizational Dynamics*, Autumn 1973, © 1973 by AMACOM, a division of American Management Associations.

Recently, the situation has changed. The advent of an adversary youth culture in the United States, the rising educational levels, with a concomitant increase in employee expectations of the job, the expansion of job opportunities for all but the least skilled and the most disaffected, have raised the level of discontent. One of the big three automakers, for example, now has an annual turnover rate of close to 40 percent. G.M.'s famous Lordstown Vega plant, the latest triumph of production engineering—with the average time per job activity pared to 36 seconds and workers facing a new Vega component 800 times in each eight-hour shift—has been plagued with strikes, official and wildcat, slowdowns, and sabotage. At times, the line has shut down during the second half of the day to remedy the defects that emerged from the line during the first half.

Is Job Redesign the Answer?

Much has been written about the two automobile plants in Sweden, Volvo and Saab-Scania, that have practiced job redesign of the assembly line on a large scale. The results, variously reported, have appeared in the world press. Also receiving wide press coverage have been the efforts of Philips N.V. in The Netherlands to redesign jobs on the lines assembling black-and-white and color TV sets. So much for instant history!

We visited the three companies during a recent trip to Europe and shall attempt to evaluate and compare them. But first a caveat: We eschew chic terms, such as job enrichment, autonomy, job rotation, and employee participation, in favor of the drabber job redesign for several reasons. First, the other terms have taken on emotional connotations; they've become the rallying ground for true believers who view them as a partial answer or panacea to the problem of employee alienation in an industrial society. The term job redesign, by contrast, has no glamor and no followers. Second, most efforts at job redesign, certainly the three we're going to write about, include elements of job enrichment, autonomy, job rotation, and employee participation in varying degrees at different times, but none of the competing terms affords a sufficiently large umbrella to cover what's happened and what's planned in the three organizations. Last, true believers passionately define their faiths differently; using any of the other terms as central would involve us in tiresome and trivial questions of definition. Hence, our choice of job redesign. It's comprehensive, and noncontroversial.

"Job redesign—the answer to what?" might have been a more descriptive subhead than one implying that our sole concern would be the question of employee discontent and its converse, employee satisfaction. Ours is a wider net. We're going to ask and answer (the answers, of course, being partial and tentative) these questions:

1. What conditions on the assembly line are economically favorable to which forms of job redesign?
2. Do many employees resent and resist job redesign? Do they prefer monotonous, repetitious work?
3. Are the "best" results from job redesign obtained when it's at its most thorough (job rotation plus job enrichment plus autonomy plus employee participation)?
4. Is there any single element in job redesign that seems to account for the biggest increase in employee satisfaction?
5. What are the benefits of job redesign—both those we can measure and monetize and those that can only be described?
6. On balance, does management gain as much from job redesign as the employee whose job is redesigned?

7. Last, what's the impact of the overall culture and political system on job redesign? What's the evidence, pro or con, that the success of job redesign at Volvo, Saab-Scania, or Philips—or the lack of it—would be replicated on similar assembly lines in the United States?

A tall order, but remember that we promised only tentative and partial answers to the seven questions.

Job Redesign at Philips

First Generation, 1960-65

We start with Philips because, of our three companies, Philips is the pioneer; its experience with job redesign goes back to 1960. We use the term first generation, second generation, and so on to mark the stages of the Philips program because this is Philips' terminology—obviously appropriated from computer lingo.

In the first experiment, concern was more with the deficiencies of long assembly lines than it was with improving job satisfaction. Breaking up the existing line of 104 workers into five shorter assembly lines, installing buffer stocks of components between groups, and placing inspectors at the end of each group instead of the whole assembly line reduced waiting times by 55 percent, improved feedback, and improved the balance of the system—various short chains being stronger than one long chain because the line can never travel faster than the worker with the longest average time per operation.

Almost incidentally, morale also improved: Only 29 percent of the workers on the assembly line responded positively to the survey question "I like doing my job," versus a 51 percent positive response from the test line. Furthermore, when the test line was restructured with half the number of workers, so that each one performed twice the original cycle and workplaces alternated with empty seats, production flowed more smoothly and quality improved. Dr. H. G. Van Beek, a psychologist on the original study team, drew a dual lesson from the experiment: "From the point of view of production, the long line is very vulnerable; from the point of view of morale—in the sense of job satisfaction—downright bad."

Subsequent experiments in several plants involved rotating workers between different jobs on the assembly line, enriching jobs by having employees set their own pace within overall production standards, and enlarging them by making employees responsible for inspecting their own work. Most of the gains from the experiments Philips entered under the heading of "social profit." In other words, morale and job satisfaction improved but bread-and-butter items such as productivity and scrap showed little improvement.

Second Generation, 1965-68

The key feature of the second phase, a program that involved a few thousand employees scattered over 30 different locations, was the abolition of foremen. With supervisors' enlarged span of control, the men on the assembly line acquired autonomy and more control over their jobs. Even an authoritarian supervisor would find that he was spread too thin to exercise the same amount of control as the previous foreman had

Once again, the bulk of the profits were social. The bill for waste and repairs dropped slightly, and, of course, Philips pocketed the money that had been paid to the foremen. Otherwise, the gains to Philips were nonmonetary.

Third Phase, 1968

This phase, one that is ongoing, has focused on giving various groups of seven or eight employees total responsibility for assembling either black-and-white TV sets or color selectors for color TV sets, a task equivalent in complexity to assembling a black-and-white set from scratch.

We want to emphasize the word *total:* The group responsible for assembling the black-and-white sets, for example, not only performs the entire assembling task but also deals directly with staff groups such as procurement, quality, and stores, with no supervisor or foreman to act as intermediary or expediter. If something is needed from another department or something goes wrong that requires the services of another department, it's the group's responsibility to deal with the department.

"This third phase has had its problems," concedes Den Hertog, staff psychologist. "Typically, it's taken about six months for the groups to shake down—adjust to the increased pressures and responsibilities." Establishing effective relationships with unfamiliar higher-status employees in staff departments has proved the biggest single problem. On the other hand, anyone in an experimental group can opt out at any time—an option that has yet to be taken up. Of course, it may be the satisfaction of being a member of a select group, even physically separated from other work groups by a wall of green shrubbery, that accounts for no employee's having made a switch. Hertog, however, believes that the increase in intrinsic job satisfactions has more than compensated for any pains of adjustments and accounts for the lack of turnover.

What about results? What's the measurable impact of the program? There have been additional costs, such as increased training costs; more important, small, autonomous groups require new and smaller machines to perform traditional assembly line tasks. On the other hand, there have been measurable benefits. Overall, production costs in man-hours have dropped 10 percent, while waiting times have decreased and quality levels have increased by smaller but still significant amounts.

To restructure work and redesign jobs in ways that increase employee job satisfaction at no net cost to the company over the long run is all that Philips, as a matter of policy, requires of such programs. Short-term deficits caused by purchases of new equipment are something it's prepared to live with.

Where is Philips going from here? Obviously, the potential for effective job redesign is large. With 90,000 workers in 60 plants, Philips has barely scratched the surface. Part of the answer would seem to lie in the future strength of the movement for employee participation and power equalization that is particularly strong in Norway and Sweden and is gaining adherents in The Netherlands.

At Philips the primary response has been the establishment of worker consultation in some 20 different departments. Worker consultation is just what it sounds like: Employees meet with first- and second-level supervision to discuss problems of joint interest. Worker consultation exists at different levels in different departments, stresses Hertog, who attributes the difference to the level of maturity of the group itself: "In some groups we're still at the flower pot phase, talking about what should be done to improve meals in the cafeteria, while at other extremes we have departments where we have left the selection of a new supervisor for the group up to the workers."

It's significant that those groups who have considered the question of job redesign consistently have criticized Philips for not doing more of it. The expansion of job redesign, in part, would seem to depend on the expansion of work consultation and the pressures exerted by the workers themselves to get job redesign extended.

Job Redesign at Saab-Scania

To claim that Saab-Scania has abolished the auto assembly line would misrepresent the facts. Saab-Scania, or to speak more precisely, the Scania Division, has instituted small-group assembly of auto engines—not the whole car—in its new engine plant. Even so, this effort is limited to 50 employees in a plant with a workforce of approximately 300, most of whom monitor automatic transfer machines that perform various machining tasks. There's only one manual loading operation in the entire machining process.

More important, the humanization of the auto assembly line is the most dramatic single instance in a series starting in 1969 that Palle Berggen, the head of the industrial engineering department, characterized as "one phase in the development of enhanced industrial democracy."

We won't quarrel with his description, although we think he succumbed to the rhetoric of public relations. Scania, in its actions from 1969 on, has responded to some problems for which the best word is horrendous. Employee turnover was running around 45 percent annually, and in the auto assembly plant, 70 percent. Under such conditions, the maintenance of an even flow of production, something crucial in an integrated work system like Scania's, presented insuperable problems. Also, it was increasingly difficult to fill jobs on the shop floor at all. A survey taken in 1969 indicates what Scania was up against: Only four out of 100 students graduating from high school in Sweden indicated their willingness to take a rank-and-file factory job. In consequence, Scania became heavily dependent on foreign workers—58 percent of the current workforce are non-Swedes. This in turn created problems, both expected and otherwise—among the former problems of training and communications, among the latter, an epidemic of wildcat strikes, previously unknown in Sweden, that largely resulted from the manipulation by extreme left elements of foreign workers ignorant of the tradition among Swedish employees of almost total reliance upon the strong trade union organization to protect their interests.

Any reponse to these conditions *had* to have as its number one objective the maintenance of productivity. To assert anything else is window dressing—unconvincing as well as unnecessary. No one can fault an industrial organization for undertaking a program whose primary goal is the maintenance of productivity.

This is not to deny that one byproduct of the program has been "enhanced industrial democracy." What happened is that the pursuit of productivity led to an examination of the conditions that created job satisfactions; these, in turn, suggested the series of actions "that enhance industrial democracy"—a term subject to almost as many definitions as there are interpreters.

Production Groups and Development Groups

Employee representation is nothing new at Scania. Like every company in Sweden with more than 50 employees, it's had an employee-elected Works Council since 1949. However, these bodies have no decision-making function; their role is limited to receiving and responding to information from top management, and their effectiveness depends on the willingness of top management to seriously consider suggestions from the Works Council. David Jenkins, in his recent book *Job Power,* tells of asking a company president if he had ever been influenced by worker suggestions. His reply: "Well, yes. We were going to build a new plant and we showed the workers the plans at one of the meetings. They objected very much to the fact that the plant would have no windows. So we changed the plans and had some windows put in. It doesn't cost much more and, actually, the building looks better. And the workers feel better."

The production and development groups initiated in the truck chassis assembly plant in 1969, by contrast, have real decision-making power. Production groups of five to 12 workers with related job duties decide among themselves how they will do their jobs, within the quality and production standards defined by higher management; they can rotate job assignments—do a smaller or larger part of the overall task. At the same time, the jobs of all members of the production group were enlarged by making them jointly responsible for simple service and maintenance activities, housekeeping, and quality control in their work area, duties formerly performed by staff personnel.

Development groups, a parallel innovation, consist of foremen, industrial engineers, and two representatives of one or more production groups whose function is to consider ideas for improving work methods and working conditions. Representatives of the production groups are rotated in a way that guarantees that every member of a production group will serve each year on a development group.

Employee reception of the production group has been mixed but largely positive. The results appear to be favorable, although Scania has done little or nothing to measure them quantitatively. However, impressions have been sufficiently favorable so that within four years production and development groups have expanded to include 2,200 out of the 3,600 employees in the main plant at Södertälje, and within the year they will be extended throughout the company.

Work Design in the Engine Plant

The four machine lines for the components in the engine factory—the cylinder block, the cylinder head, the connecting rod, and the crankshaft—mainly consist of transfer machines manned or monitored by individual operations. Group assembly is restricted to the seven final assembly stations, each of which contains a team of fitters that assemble an entire engine.

Team members divide the work among themselves; they may decide to do one-third of the assembly on each engine—a ten-minute chore—or follow the engine around the bay and assemble the entire engine—a 30-minute undertaking. In fact, only a minority prefer to do the total assembly job. (Using traditional assembly line methods, each operation would have taken 1.8 minutes.) The team also decides its own work pace, and the number and duration of work breaks within the overall requirement of assembling 470 engines in each ten-day period, a specification that allows them a good deal of flexibility in their pacing. Incidentally, over half the employees in the engine plant are women, while the assembly teams are over 80 percent female. We personally saw four assembly teams with only a single man in the lot.

Benefits and Costs

Kaj Holmelius, who is responsible for planning and coordination of the production engineering staff, ticked off the principal credits and debits, along with a few gray areas in which it would be premature to estimate results. On the plus side, he cited the following:

1. Group assembly has increased the flexibility of the plant, making it easier to adjust to heavy absenteeism.

2. The group assembly concept is responsible for a lower balancing loss due to a longer station time.

3. Less money is invested in assembly tools. Even allowing for the fact that you have

to buy six or seven times as many tools, the simpler tools make for a smaller overall cost.

4. Quality has definitely improved, although by how much it's hard to estimate.

5. Productivity is higher than it would have been with the conventional assembly line—although once more, there is no proof. Lower production speed per engine, because it's not economical to use some very expensive automatic tools, is outweighed by higher quality and reduced turnover.

6. Employee attitudes have improved, although there have been no elaborate surveys taken. To Holmelius the best indication of job satisfaction is that it's impossible to fill all the requests to transfer from other parts of the plant to the assembly teams.

On the negative side, in addition to the reduced production speed, group assembly takes up considerably more space than the conventional assembly line.

In the neutral corner is the impact on absenteeism and turnover. Absenteeism is actually higher in the engine plant—18 percent versus 15 percent for overall plant operations at Södertälje. However, Holmelius attributes the difference to the fact that the engine plant employs a heavier percentage of women. As for turnover, with the plant in operation for a little more than a year, it's too early to tell. Because of an economic slowdown, turnover generally is down from the 45 percent crisis level of 1969 to 20 percent, and it's Holmelius' belief that turnover in the assembly teams will prove significantly lower than average.

What's the Future of Group Assembly?

It's easier to point out the directions in which Scania does *not* plan to extend group assembly. An experiment with having employees assemble an entire truck diesel engine—a six-hour undertaking involving 1,500 parts—was abandoned at the employees' request; they couldn't keep track of all the parts. Similarly, group assembly wouldn't work with the body of the trucks—truck bodies are too complex, and group assembly would require twice the space currently needed. The moot question at the moment is car assembly. So far, group assembly has been applied only to assembling doors. We suspect that in any decision, economic calculations will predominate, including, of course, the inherently fuzzy calculation about the economic value of job satisfaction.

Job Redesign at Volvo

Job redesign at Volvo began, almost accidentally, in the upholstery shop of the car assembly plant during the mid-1960s, but a companywide effort had to wait until 1969, when Volvo faced the same problems that plagued Scania—wildcat strikes, absenteeism, and turnover that were getting out of hand and an increasing dependence on foreign workers. Turnover was over 40 percent annually; absenteeism was running 20 to 25 percent, and close to 45 percent of the employees of the car assembly plant were non-Swedes. One other event in 1971 made a difference: Volvo acquired a young, hard-driving new managing director, Pehr Gyllenhammar, who developed a keen interest in the new methods of work organization.

Ingvar Barrby, head of the upholstery department, started job redesign by persuading production management to experiment with job rotation along the lines he had read about in Norway. The overwhelmingly female workforce complained frequently about the inequity of the various jobs involved in assembling car seats; some jobs were easier than others, while still others were more comfortable and less strenuous, and so on. To equalize the tasks, Barrby divided the job into 13 different operations and rotated the employees among tasks that were relatively arduous and those that were relatively comfortable. Jealousy and bickering among employees disappeared: First, jobs were no longer inequitable; second, employees perceived that they had exaggerated the differences between jobs anyway—the grass-is-greener syndrome. More important, turnover that had been running 35 percent quickly fell to 15 percent, a gain that has been maintained over the years.

Job Alternation and "Multiple Balances"

Volvo uses these phrases instead of the more commonly used job rotation and job enrichment, but the concepts are the same. In job alternation or job rotation, the employee changes jobs once or several times daily, depending on the nature of the work in his group. Take Line IV A, for example, whose function is to do the external and internal sealing and insulation of car bodies. Because internal sealing is such uncomfortable work—employees work in cramped positions inside the car body—the work is alternated every other hour. The remaining jobs are rotated daily.

"Multiple balances" is our old friend, job enrichment, under another name. One example involves the overhead line where the group follows the same body for seven or eight stations along the line for a total period of 20 minutes—seven or eight times the length of the average job cycle.

Not all employees have had their jobs rotated or enriched—only 1,500 out of 7,000 in the car assembly at Torslanda are affected by the program. Because participation is strictly voluntary, the figures at first glance seem to indicate a massive show of disinterest on the part of Volvo employees. Not so. True, some employees prefer their jobs the way they are. The bigger problem is that Volvo has, to date, lacked the technical resources to closely scrutinize many jobs to determine whether and how they can be enlarged or enriched, or it has scrutinized them and determined that it isn't economically feasible to enlarge or enrich them. A company spokesman gave the job of coating under the car body to prevent rust as an example of a thoroughly unpleasant job that so far has defied redesign.

Production Teams at Volvo Lundbyverken

In the truck assembly plant at Lundbyverken, Volvo has carried job redesign several steps further, with production teams who, in form and function, roughly duplicate the production groups previously described at Scania. The production team, a group of five to 12 men with a common work assignment, elects its own chargehand, schedules its own output within the standards set by higher management, distributes work among its members, and is responsible for its own quality control. In these teams, group piecework replaces individual piecework and everyone earns the same amount, with the exception of the chargehand. Currently, there are 23 production teams involving 100 out of the plant's 1,200 employees. Plans call for the gradual extension of the production team approach to cover most, if not all, of the factory workforce.

The Box Score at Volvo

Have the various forms of job redesign, job rotation, job enrichment, and production teams paid off for Volvo? If so, what forms have the payoff taken? Anything we can measure or monetize? Or are we reduced to subjective impressions and interesting although iffy conjectures about the relationship between factors such as increased job satisfaction and reduced turnover?

The two plants deserve separate consideration: Absenteeism and turnover traditionally have been lower at the truck assembly plant than at the car assembly plant. The jobs are inherently more complex and interesting—even before job enrichment, some individual jobs took up to half an hour. The workers, in turn, are more highly skilled and tend to regard themselves as apart from and above the rank-and-file auto worker. They see themselves more as junior engineers. Within this context, it's still true that the introduction of production teams has led to further improvement: less labor turnover, less absenteeism, an improvement in quality, and fewer final adjustments.

At the auto assembly plant the picture isn't clear. Turnover is down from 40 to 25 percent. However, an economic slowdown undoubtedly accounts for some of the decline, while other actions unrelated to job redesign may account for part of the remainder. When Volvo surveyed its employees to probe for the causes of turnover and absenteeism, most of the causes revealed were external—problems with housing, child care, long distances traveling to the plant, and so on. Volvo responded with a series of actions to alleviate these causes, such as extending the bus fleet, together with the community, to transport employees, loaning money to employees to purchase apartments at very favorable rates of interest, putting pressure on the community to expand day care centers, and so on. Such measures presumably contributed to the decline of turnover. Nevertheless, Gyllenhammar is convinced that "we can see a correlation between increased motivation, increased satisfaction on the job, and a decrease in the turnover of labor." Absenteeism is a sadly different picture: It's double what is was five years ago, a condition that Gyllenhammar attributes to legislation enabling workers to stay off the job at practically no cost to themselves.

As for output in that part of the auto assembly plant covered by job enrichment or job enlargement, there was no measurable improvement. Quality, on balance, has improved, and the feeling is that improved quality and decreased turnover had more than covered the costs of installing the program.

The Future of Job Redesign at Volvo

Despite the relatively ambiguous success of Volvo's job redesign efforts, whatever Volvo has done in the past is a pale prologue to its future plans. In about nine months, Volvo's new auto assembly plant at Kalmar will go on stream. And, for once, that overworked term "revolutionary" would seem justified.

Physically, the plant is remarkable. Gyllenhammar describes it as "shaped like a star and on each point of the star you have a work group finishing a big share of the whole automobile—for example, the electrical system or the safety system or the interior." Assembly work takes place along the outer walls, while component parts are stored in the center of the building. Architecturally, the building has been designed to preserve the atmosphere of a small workshop in a large factory, with each work team having its own entrance, dressing room, rest room, and so on. Each team is even physically shielded from a view of the other teams.

Each work team, of 15 to 25 men, will distribute the work among themselves and determine their own work rhythm, subject to the requirement of meeting production standards. If the team decides to drive hard in the morning and loaf in the afternoon, the decision is theirs to make. As with production teams in the truck assembly plant, the team will choose its own boss, and deselect him if he turns out poorly.

The new plant will cost about 10 percent more—some 10 million Swedish kroner—than a comparable conventional auto assembly plant. Time alone will tell whether the extra investment will be justified by the decreased turnover, improved quality, and even reduced absenteeism that its designers confidently expect at the new facility. In announcing the plan for the new factory, Gyllenhammar's economic objectives were modest enough, his social objectives more ambitious. "A way must be found to create a workplace that meets the needs of the modern working man for a sense of purpose and satisfaction in his daily work. A way must be found of attaining this goal without an adverse effect on productivity." With luck, he may achieve both.

What Does It Add up to?

On the basis of what we learned at Philips, Saab-Scania, and Volvo, what answers—tentative and partial—do we have to the seven questions that we raised earlier in the article? Or are the results of the programs so ambiguous and inconclusive that, as long as we restrict ourselves to the context of these three companies, we must beg off attempting to answer some of the questions at all? That none of the companies answered all of the questions, and that many of the answers rely on subjective impressions haphazardly assembled, rather than on quantitative data systematically collected, of necessity, limit our answers, but they don't prevent us from presenting them—with the appropriate caveats.

1. *What conditions on the assembly line are economically favorable to which forms of job redesign?*

The basic question here is under what conditions can a man-paced assembly line replace a machine-paced assembly line? Unless this is economically feasible, no form of job redesign is likely to be adopted. Even allowing for rhetoric, none of our three companies—and no other organization of which we are aware—has indicated a willingness to suffer economic losses in order to increase the satisfactions employees might feel if they switched over from machine-paced to man-paced assembly lines. Take the case of manufacturing a pair of man's pants in a garment factory. Give the job to one man and he will take half a day; divide the work among many people on a line with each one using advanced technical equipment, and it takes one man-hour to produce a pair of trousers. The future of job redesign is not bright in a pants factory.

The man-paced assembly line, however, has a couple of widely recognized advantages over the machine-paced line: First, it's much less sensitive to disruption; the whole line doesn't have to stop because of one breakdown—human or technical; second, extensive and costly rebalancing need not be undertaken every time production is increased or decreased. You simply add more people or groups. Of course, there are advantages to machine-paced production, the outstanding one being speed of production, which depends, in turn, on an even flow of production.

There's the rub—and there's the number one cause for job redesign, certainly at Volvo and Saab-Scania. Absenteeism and turnover had risen to the point where they canceled out the economic advantages of machine-paced production. At the same time, evidence had accumulated that job redesign organized around a man-paced assembly line might strike at the root causes of inordinate turnover and absenteeism.

... The design of the new engine plant at Scania ... incorporates Drucker's insight that "the worker is put to use to use a poorly designed one-purpose machine tool, but repetition and uniformity are two qualities in which human beings are weakest. In everything but the ability to judge and coordinate, machines can perform better than man." In the new engine plant, everything that can be automated economically has been—probably 90 percent of the total task—with the final assembly paced by teams on the assumption that the relatively slight increases in production time will be more than compensated for by better balancing and decreased disruption—improvements inherent in the technical change—and improvements in quality, turnover, and absenteeism, the anticipated byproducts of job satisfaction.

The results, as you have seen, are sketchy. However, we can affirm that none of the three organizations, by their own testimony, has lost economically by the changeover from a machine-paced to a man-paced assembly line. How much they have gained is decidedly a more iffy question.

2. *Do many employees resent and resist job redesign? Do they prefer monotonous, repetitious work?*

A flip answer might be "God only knows—and he isn't talking." Any answer, at best, is based largely on conjecture. Joseph E. Godfrey asserts that "workers may complain about monotony, but years spent in the factories lead me to believe that they like to do their jobs automatically. If you interject new things you spoil the rhythm of the job and work gets fouled up." As head of the General Motors Assembly Line Division he is qualified, but biased. But even Fred Herzberg, whose bias is obviously in the other direction, concedes that "individual reaction to job enrichment is as difficult to forecast in terms of attitudes as it is in terms of performance. Not all persons welcome having their job enriched." The Survey Research Center at The University of Michigan in a 1969 study concluded that factors such as having a "nutrient supervisor, receiving adequate help, having few labor standard problems all seem to relate at least as closely to job satisfaction as having a challenging job with 'enriching demands.'" One thing does seem clear: Assuming the job level is held constant, education is inversely related to satisfaction. And when Pehr Gyllenhammar foresaw a near future in which 90 percent of the Swedish population would at least have graduated from high school, he was realistically anticipating a situation in which Volvo would become almost entirely dependent on foreign employees unless it found ways of enriching the auto assembly jobs.

3. *Are the "best" results from job redesign obtained when it's at its most thorough (job rotation plus job enrichment plus autonomy plus employee participation)?*

Work in America flatly endorses the thesis that "it is imperative that employers be made aware of the fact that thorough efforts to redesign work, not simply 'job enrichment' or 'job rotation,' have resulted in increases of productivity from 5 to 40 percent. In no instance of which we have evidence has a major effort to increase employee participation resulted in a long-term decline in productivity." Obviously, in this context "best" results means increased productivity.

Before we can answer the question and respond to the claims asserted in *Work in America* a few definitions are necessary. Most descriptions of the elements that enter into a satisfying job concentrate on three: (1) variety, (2) responsibility, and (3) autonomy. Variety defines itself. Responsibility is more complex; it involves both working on a sufficiently large part of the total job to feel that it is a meaningful experience, and also having a sufficient amount of control over what you are doing to feel personally responsible.

Companies responding to this need for more responsibility may add set-up and inspection to the employee's duties or ask him to assemble one-third of an engine instead of a single component—both examples of horizontal job enrichment; and the employee may be permitted to control the pace at which he works—an example of vertical job enrichment. Everything that is subsumed under vertical job enrichment is included in autonomy but it also means something else and something more—giving to the employee himself some control over how his job should be enlarged or enriched—a clear demarcation point between almost all American approaches to job enrichment and some European.

We're describing a circular process; the worker in Sweden and The Netherlands places a higher value on autonomy than the worker in the United States. Therefore, job redesign that incorporates increased autonomy for the employee will be more appreciated and lead to more job satisfaction than comparable efforts would in the United States. Here, Huey Long's concept of a satisfying job, with allowances for the regional overtones, and the hyperbole, still makes sense: "There shall be a real job, not a little old sowbelly black-eyed pea job, but a real spending money beefsteak, and gray Chevrolet Ford in the garage, new suit, Thomas Jefferson, Jesus Christ, red, white, and blue job for every man." The employee did then and still does define, although to a progressively decreasing degree, a satisfying job in terms of how much it pays. For a measure of the difference, take the definition of a dissatisfying job by Malin Lofgren, a 12-year-old Swedish schoolboy: "A bad job is one where others make all the decisions, and you have to do what others say."

Now that the tedious, although necessary, business of definition is out of the way, how do we answer the question with reference to our three companies? Inconclusively. If we define "best" results in terms of gains in productivity, the only certifiable gain occurred with the Philips production groups that scored high on both horizontal and vertical job enrichment, and in which employees were consulted in advance about the ways in which their job should be enriched. In the body of the article, we didn't go into their institutional arrangements, but suffice it to say that both Saab-Scania and Volvo have comparable consultative institutions. Thus, the autonomy factor assumes less significance. The only significant differences would appear to be: (1) The increased status caused by making the production groups at Philips wholly responsible for liaison with other departments, (2) the Hawthorne, or, as the Philips personnel call it, the "Princess" effect—the groups having been visited and complimented by such dignitaries as Queen Juliana and Marshal Tito. On the other hand, the groups at Volvo that chose their own supervisors—certainly a measure of autonomy—have not increased their productivity. Quality, turnover, attendance had improved. But with productivity, there was no measurable impact.

4. *Is there any single element in job redesign that seems to account for the biggest increase in employee satisfaction?*

In a word—no. But that requires an explanation. Our failure to respond principally reflects lack of evidence; none of the organizations concerned asked themselves the question. None tried on any systematic basis to relate what they were doing in redesigning jobs to what they were accomplishing in increased job satisfaction. Word-of-mouth testimony and more cheerful figures—as in the case of Volvo and Saab-Scania with turnover—seemed sufficient to confirm the efficacy of past efforts and sanction future ones, on similar although expanded lines.

5. *What are the benefits of job redesign–both those we can measure and monetize and those that can only be described?*

We begin with a proposition shared by a generation of social scientists who have studied the problem and attempted to answer the question: Employee attitudes and job satisfaction are correlated much more clearly with factors such as absenteeism, turnover, and quality than they are with productivity.

The three companies reinforce this finding. Only one experiment at Philips establishes a positive correlation between job satisfaction and productivity, while several—Philips with productivity groups in Phase III, Saab-Scania in the engine plant and the truck assembly plant, and Volvo in its truck plant—all report improvements in quality, the problem in each case being the absence of quantifiable data. Turnover is another area in which the responses are positive, but suggestive rather than conclusive—"probably lower" in the Scania engine plant; lower in the truck assembly plant; down in both the truck assembly and auto assembly plant at Volvo—buth there are no firm figures at the Volvo truck assembly line, while the decrease in turnover at the auto assembly plant is partly attributed to causes unrelated to job redesign. Philips proffers no comparisons of absenteeism or turnover before and after job redesign. All we know is that so far no one in the production groups has decided to quit. In short, the evidence—what there is of it—is positive, but fragmented and based more on impressions than on data.

6. *On balance, does management gain as much from job redesign as the employee whose job is redesigned?*

A two-headed question that logically requires both extensive employee attitude surveys before and after job redesign, along with firm measurements that demonstrate the impact of job redesign on factors such as quality, output, absenteeism, and turnover. As we have seen, we have very little of either. The only attitude surveys were first, the one conducted at the Volvo auto assembly plant to determine the causes of excessive absenteeism and turnover—most of which had nothing to do with job satisfaction and where the subsequent substantial drop in turnover at best could only partially be ascribed to job redesign—and the survey at Philips, where the switchover from machine-paced to man-paced assembly line improved employees' satisfaction with their jobs.

On balance, as previously stated, management has achieved at least an economic draw from its efforts at job redesign, along with a measure of insurance against a fretful future in which employee expectations will become increasingly difficult to fulfill and the job redesign carried out or contemplated will, it is hoped, help to meet those expectations.

As for the satisfactions the employees have gained from the collective efforts at enlarging and enriching their jobs, we can only guess. We have a few pieces of anecdotal evidence, such as the flood of applications to work in the final assembly at Scania's engine plant, or the absence of turnover among the production groups at Philips. In short, we know too little to generalize.

7. *Last, what's the impact of the overall culture and political system on job redesign? What's the evidence, pro or con, that the success of job redesign at Volvo, Saab-Scania, or Philips—or lack of it—would be replicated in similar assembly lines in the United States?*

Technologically, there are no convincing reasons why assembly lines in new automobile factories or television plants in the United States couldn't be redesigned along lines similar to what has been done at Philips, Saab-Scania, and Volvo. It might prove prohibitively expensive in existing plants—after all, job redesign at Volvo's auto assembly plant was largely restricted, on economic grounds, to job rotation. However, new plants in the United States should present no more inherent problems of job redesign than new plants in Sweden. Yet auto executives in the United States have gone on record as feeling that the situation is hopeless. A 1970 report of the Ford Foundation found that none of the corporation executives interviewed "really believe that assembly line tasks can be significantly restructured," and "no one really believes that much can be done to make the assembly jobs more attractive."

Not that all the features of job redesign at Philips, Saab-Scania, and Volvo are equally exportable. The three companies exist in a different political and social ethos, one in which both management and the workers have gone much further in accepting the idea of employee participation in decision making than all but a handful of managers and a small minority of workers in the United States. A survey of Swedish managers in 1970, for example, showed that 75 percent favored more employee decision making in all departments. Even the idea of replacing the decision of the supervisor with collective employee decisions elicited a favorable response from 11 percent of the managers. Given this different ethos, it is not surprising that all three companies have experimented with what would be in the United States the radical step of either dispensing with first-level supervision or leaving it up to the employees to choose their own supervisor. It is a form of autonomy that few managements in the United States would consider for an instant, and one in which few employees would take much interest.

But why not consider it, as long as management continues to set overall standards of production and quality and to hold the group responsible for meeting them? The experiment of having employees choose their own bosses with the experimental groups in the truck assembly plant at Volvo works so well that it has been incorporated as one of the basic design features in the new auto assembly plant. Employees demonstrated that, given the opportunity, they would choose as leaders men who could organize the work and maintain order and discipline.

Let's indulge in speculation. The single quality that most clearly distinguishes between the efforts at job enrichment here and in the three companies we visited is the emphasis abroad on letting the employees have a part—and sometimes a decisive part—in deciding how their jobs should be enriched. By contrast, most exponents of job enrichment in the United States take the "papa-knows-best" approach. Fred Herzberg, the best-known work psychologist, asserts that when people took part in deciding how to change their own jobs, "the results were disappointing." We suspect that Herzberg's real objection is not to the results themselves, but to the difficulty of selling most managements on the idea that employee participation should be an integral part of any process of job enrichment. The experiences at Volvo, Saab-Scania, and Philips suggest that the objection to the employee's participating in how his own job should be enriched or redesigned has its roots in symbolism, rather than substance, in the irrational preoccupation with management prerogatives, rather than in any real or potential threat to productivity or profits.

What about the future? Technologically, there seem to be no compelling reasons why Ford, G.M., and Chrysler cannot take a leaf from Volvo and Saab-Scania. Whether they will is another question. The combination of inertia, custom, and commitment is a formidable one. So far the automakers have chosen to move in the opposite direction: shorter work cycles, smaller jobs, more rapidly moving lines. We would recall that it took a crisis—nothing less than the probability that most people would refuse to work at all or only for uneconomic periods on the jobs the organization had to offer them—to "break the cake of custom" at Volvo and Saab-Scania. Even today, it is clear that there are limits to which auto assembly jobs can be enriched, a limitation obvious in Gyllenhammar's bitter observation that " 'absenteeism with pay' is based on the very utopian hypothesis that people love to work, and no matter what happens they will strive to go to their job every morning." Still, the situation he is in is preferable to the situation he faced. And some of the difference is due to job redesign.

We suspect that it will take a crisis of similar magnitude, together with the belief that they have no choice, to unfreeze the attitudes of automakers in the United States and get them moving in the direction of man-paced assembly lines and the forms of job redesign they facilitate. That such a development, over the long run, is in the cards we strongly believe, but how long it will take for the cards to show up, we leave to the astrologers.

Selected Bibliography

On the general subject of job redesign we strongly recommend three books: The H.E.W. *Work in America*, MIT Press (Cambridge, 1971) is scarcely unbiased but it pulls together much material in the whole area of employee discontent. . . . David Jenkins' *Job Power: Blue and White Collar Democracy*, Doubleday (New York, 1973), is remarkable for the number of case studies of job redesign both here and in Europe. . . . Last, *Design of Jobs*, Penguin Books Ltd. (Harmondsworth, England, 1972). . . .

A Systems Approach to Organization Development

MICHAEL BEER
EDGAR F. HUSE

. . . This article is written to provide the reader with an understanding of the systems organizational model that guided our efforts as change agents; to describe the varied approaches used for organizational change; and to describe the results and what we have learned about the process of change and its prospects in large, complex organizations. Rather than consigning the conclusions to the end, we shall underscore our major findings as we proceed through the sections of the case study.

The organizational development program took place in a plant designing and manufacturing complex instruments for medical and laboratory use.

Through the efforts of the personnel supervisor, enough interest existed initially for our holding a series of seminars which contrasted traditional approaches with newer approaches based on behavioral research findings and theory. Although these seminars never succeeded in getting an explicit decision on the pattern of management that would prevail in the plant (indeed, as will be discussed later, there was considerable resistance to "theory"), they did start to unfreeze the managerial group (which was steeped in the tradition of the parent organization) sufficiently to commit themselves to "trying" some new approaches on a very limited basis. This constituted much less than commitment to a new pattern of management, but it did open the door to experimentation and examination.

Overworked Theories

A number of practitioners of OD stress the importance of top management commitment to OD if such a program is to be successful. As one author puts it, "Without such support, we have found no program of this kind can ever succeed. . . . First, we worked with top managers to help them fully understand. . . . This proved vital, not only in helping their understanding of the concepts but also in earning their commitment to the program" (Roche & MacKinnon, 1970). In the same vein, Beckhard (1969) and Blake and Mouton (1969) stress that OD must be planned and managed from the top down.

Reprinted by special permission from *The Journal of Applied Behavioral Science*, vol. 8 (1972), no. 1, pp. 79-100, copyright 1972 by NTL Institute for Applied Behavioral Science.

Certainly no one would dispute the proposition that top management commitment to OD is highly valuable and helpful. However, our experience in this study [*Finding 1*] indicates that *a clear-cut commitment at the top of the organizational unit to a particular OD approach is not necessary for a development program to succeed*. Indeed, an attempt to obtain too strong a commitment from top management in the early stages may be threatening enough to cause the withdrawal of any commitment to planned change, especially since the concept of OD and its technologies (e.g., Theory Y, job enrichment, sensitivity training, and the like) are foreign and threatening to the established beliefs of many managers.

Moreover, we found [*Finding 2*] that *total top management understanding of where the OD process will lead and the state of the organization at the end is not necessary for successful programs to take place*. Indeed, given the current state of the art, the OD practitioner himself may not have a clear view of the road ahead, except in very general terms.

What *is* necessary is that someone in a strategic position feel the need for change and improvement. In our plant, that person was the personnel supervisor. Although the plant manager was mildly interested in the initial stages, he was mainly submitting to pressures from the personnel man. Throughout his tenure in the plant, the plant manager's commitment and interest mildly increased, but he was never a strong proponent nor the most skilled manager in some of the new approaches. Futhermore, the plant manager's "boss" never fully knew what was going on in the plant nor did he ever commit himself in any way to the OD program. We now believe that it is possible to change a relatively autonomous unit of a larger organization without the total commitment or understanding of top management in that unit and, in larger and more complex organizations, even without their knowledge.

Initial Commitment to New Approaches

In addition to felt need, the second essential condition is that there be, somewhere in the organization, some initial commitment to experimentation, application, and evaluation of new approaches to present problems. A case study report by the second author (Huse, 1965) describes a successful OD program that took place because a middle manager in a large organization felt the need for change and requested help. He could not have cared less about specific OD principles. He simply wanted help in improving his organization. Davis (1967) points out, in his now classic case study, that top management was not really involved at the beginning and that a majority of the effort was expended in "on-the-job situations, working out real problems with the people who are involved with them."

Of course, it is obvious that top management support of both theory and practice makes it easier for the change agent; conversely, the lack of such support increases the risk involved for consultants and managers, and causes other systems problems, as we shall discuss later in this article. Furthermore, the conditions of a felt need, a strong and self-sufficient commitment to change, and relative unit autonomy are needed. What we *are* saying is that the commonly heard dicta that one must start at the top and that top management must be committed to a set of normative principles are overworked. *Change can and does begin at lower levels in an organization* [*Finding 3*].

A Conceptual Model

If the client system and its management in this case did not (need to) have specific OD concepts in mind, who did? The change agents did.

It is important that the change agent have in mind an organizational model and a flexible set of normative concepts about management with a systems orientation. The organizational model should be general and reflect the complex *interactive* nature of systems variables. The concepts must be updated and changed as new research findings become available and as more is learned about the functioning of the client system, the environment in which the client system operates, and the effects of changes made in the client system. This is, of course, an iterative procedure.

Figure 1 represents the model of organizational change which guided our efforts. This model has some basic characteristics which must be understood if we are to see how it can shape the planning of a change effort. It represents an organization as an open system engaged in a conversion process. Employee needs, expectations, and abilities are among the raw materials (inputs) with which a manager must work to achieve his objectives.

Inputs | **Organizational Processes** | **Outputs**

Needs and expectations Abilities →

Structural Variables
  Organizational Structure
  Job Structure
  Personnel Policies and Practices
    (pay scale, for example)
  Controls
  Selection and Training

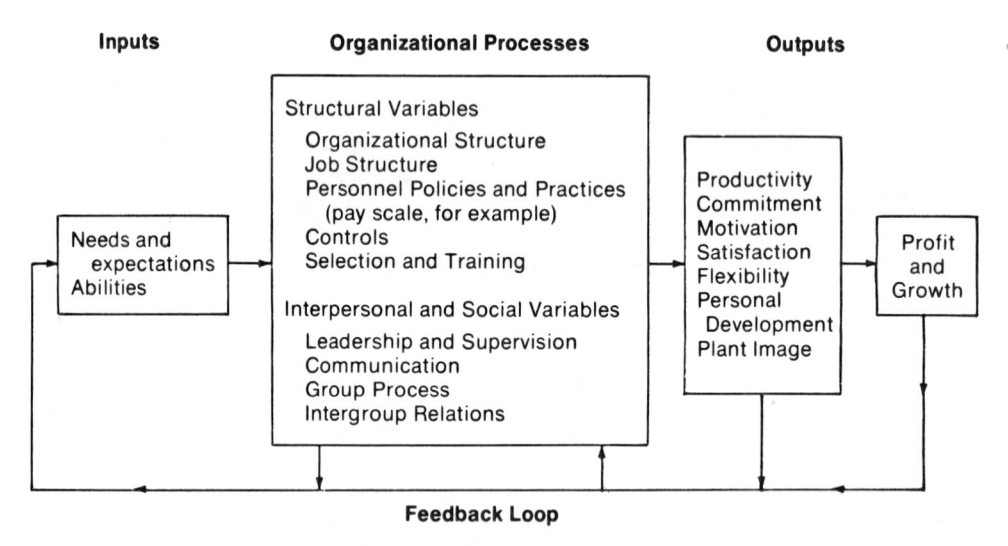

Interpersonal and Social Variables
  Leadership and Supervision
  Communication
  Group Process
  Intergroup Relations

→ Productivity
Commitment
Motivation
Satisfaction
Flexibility
Personal Development
Plant Image

→ Profit and Growth

Feedback Loop

Figure 1. Systems Model of an Organization

Organizations have many processes. Figure 1 includes only the more important ones in general terms, and these exist at both the structural and interpersonal levels. Leadership and communication, for example, are two of the interpersonal dimensions which serve to pull together, integrate, and shape the behavior of organizational members. They convert into effort and attitudes the potential brought to the organization in the form of needs and abilities of individuals. The structure or formalized dimensions of the organization obviously cannot exist independently of the interpersonal variables, but they are different from the interpersonal variables in terms of their susceptibility to managerial control, the means by which they might be changed, and the timing of their change. Previous literature on organizational change has emphasized interpersonal variables; more recent literature (Lawrence & Lorsch, 1969) has emphasized structural variables. It is our opinion, based upon experience, that both interpersonal and structural variables are crucial to effective organizational change. The effects of organizational design or managerial control systems on employees have been researched and documented but are still insufficiently understood. For example, we are convinced that an operant conditioning model can be used to understand the behavior of managers with respect to controls. "Beating" goals and looking good on standard measures are like food pellets to the manager.

In the output column, we have listed multiple outcomes. These are not completely independent, but they are conceptually distinctive enough in their relationship to the organizational process variables that it is useful to think of them individually. It is the optimization of the organizational outputs that leads to long-term profitability and growth for employees and the organization. Other final outcomes could be listed if we were discussing organizations with different objectives.

Inherent in this model are several basic notions: An organization is an open system which, from the human point of view, converts individual needs and expectations into outputs. Organizational outputs can be increased by improving the quality of the input. An example of this would be the selection of people with higher levels of ability and needs. However, because there are costs associated with selecting personnel of higher quality, we might say that efficiency has not increased. The organization may improve its performance, but this gain has been obtained only because the input, i.e., the quality of personnel has improved, not because there has been a change in the manner in which the organization *utilizes* its human resources.

Since organizations are open systems, organizational performance can also improve by unleashing more of the potential inherent in the human resources. If you will, outputs will increase because we have made the conversion process more efficient. This can be done, for example, by designing organizational processes which better fit the organization's environment or by changing organizational processes so that human resources can be fully unleashed and brought to bear on the task and objectives of the organization. The adjustment of organizational processes to reflect more accurately the needs of the environment and of the persons in it is one of the key objectives of our organizational development program.

Figure 1[1] does not cover some of the more traditional but vitally important concepts of an organization as a total system. For example, capital budgets, the R & D thrust of an organization, overhead or indirect budgets, and the marketing direction of an organization are extremely important aspects which need to be considered. Blake and Mouton (1969) have developed the Corporate Excellence Rubric as a means of assessing the health of the organization through a traditional functional framework. Furthermore, current research (Lawrence & Lorsch, 1969) points up the fact that the differentiation of functional units has a tremendous influence upon the effectiveness of an organization. However, for purposes of brevity, these aspects are not covered in this article.

Mechanisms of Change

We chose an eclectic approach to create change in the organizational processes listed in Figure 1, with the basic belief that a variety of approaches to change should be used with the plant in question. The primary mechanism was consulting, counseling, and feedback by a team of four. The primary change agents were the personnel man within the organization (there have been four different ones since the OD effort began); Beer as an external-to-the-plant agent but internal to the organization, and Huse as the outside change agent. The fourth member of the team was a research assistant whose responsibility it was to interview and gather data in the client system for diagnostic and feedback uses by the change agents.[2]

We began a basic strategy of establishing working relationships with individuals at all levels of the organization. We operated as resource persons who could be used to solve specific problems or initiate small experiments in management; we tried to encourage someone or some organizational component to start implementing the concepts inherent in our model of an organization. Managers gained familiarity with these ideas through consultation and, to a much lesser extent and without full understanding, from the initial few seminars that we held. The main ingredients were a problem or a desire to change and improve, combined with action recommendations from the change agents. Soon there were a few individuals throughout the organization who began, with our help, to apply some new approaches. Because most of these approaches were successful, the result was increased motivation to change. To a degree, nothing succeeds like success!

Models for Learning

There are at least two basic models for learning. The traditional method, that of the classroom and seminar, stresses theory and cognitive concepts before action. As Argyris (1967) points out, "The traditional educational models emphasize substance, rationality. . . ." However, a number of authors (Bartlett, 1967; Bradford, 1964; Schein & Bennis, 1965) make the point that behavior is another place to start. For example, Huse (1966) has shown that one's own facts are "much more powerful instruments of change than facts or principles generated and presented by an outside 'expert.' " The process of change in this OD effort started with behavioral recommendations, was followed by appropriate reinforcement and feedback, and then proceeded to attitudinal and cognitive changes.

Figure 2 summarizes the basic concept from our experience. *Effective and permanent adult learning [Finding 4] comes after the individual has experimented with new approaches and received appropriate feedback in the on-the-job situation.* This approach is analogous to, but somewhat different from, the here-and-now learning in the T Group.

In other words, a manager might have a problem. Without discussing theory, the change agent might make some recommendations relating to the specific situation at hand. If, in the here-and-now, the manager was successful in the attempt to solve the problem, this would lead to another try, as well as a change in his attitude toward OD. This approach capitalizes upon the powerful here-and-now influence which the job and the organizational climate can have upon the individual. Indeed, such changes can occur without *any* knowledge of theory.

Either model of learning can probably work to produce change in the individual. However, if one starts with cognitive facts and theory (as in seminars), this may be less effective and less authentic than starting with the individual's own here-and-now behavior in the ongoing job situation. In any case, the process is a cyclic one, involving behavior, attitudes, and cognition, each reinforcing the other. In our case, there was an early resistance to seminars and the presentation of "Theory." However, after behavior and attitude changes occurred, there began to be more and more requests for cognitive inputs through reading, seminars, and the like. It is at this later stage that seminars and "theory inputs" would seem to be of most value.

That learning starts with behavior and personal experience has been one of the most important things we have learned as we have worked to effect organizational change. The process is quite similar to what is intended to happen in laboratory training. What we have found *[Finding 5]* is that *the operating, ongoing organization may, indeed, be the best "laboratory" for learning.* This knowledge may save us from an overreliance upon sensitivity training described by Bennis (1968) when he states that "when you read the pages of this Journal, you cannot but think that we're a one-product outfit with a 100 per cent fool-proof patent medicine." This finding may also be the answer in dealing with Campbell and Dunnette's (1968) conclusions that "while T-Group training seems to produce observable changes in behavior, the utility of these changes for the performance of individuals in their organizational roles remains to be demonstrated."

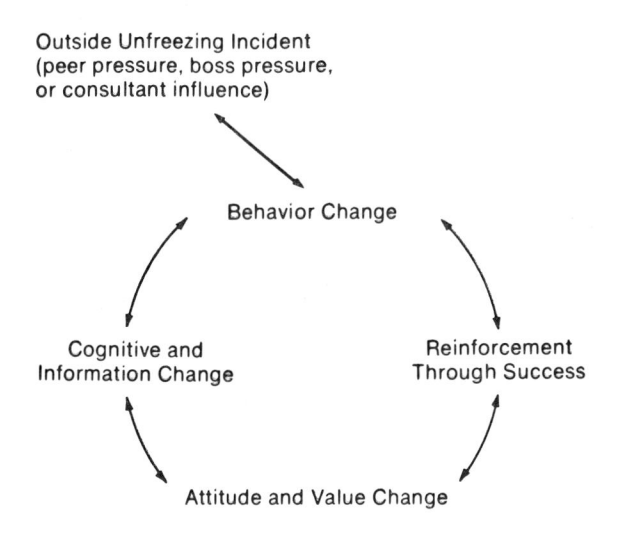

```
         Outside Unfreezing Incident
         (peer pressure, boss pressure,
         or consultant influence)
                    ↓
              Behavior Change
             ↗              ↘
   Cognitive and          Reinforcement
   Information Change     Through Success
             ↖              ↙
           Attitude and Value Change
```

Figure 2. The Learning Process

The unfreezing process. What triggers an individual to unfreeze and to allow the process to begin, if it is not "theory"? First, there are some individuals who are ready to change behavior as soon as the opportunity presents itself in the form of an outside change agent. These are people who seem to be aware of problems and have a desire to work on them. Sometimes all that they need are some suggestions or recommendations as to different approaches or methods they may try. If their experiences are successful, they become change leaders in their own right. *They then [Finding 6] are natural targets for the change agent, since they become opinion leaders that help shape a culture that influences others in the organization to begin to experiment and try out new behaviors.* As Davis (1967) points out, it is necessary to "provide a situation which could initiate the process of freeing up these potential multipliers from the organizational and personal constraints which . . . kept them from responding effectively to their awareness of the problems." Davis used "strangers" and "cousins" laboratories. In our case, the unfreezing process was done almost exclusively in the immediate job context.

An early example of the development of change leaders in our work with this company was the successful joint effort of an engineer and a supervisor to redesign a hotplate assembly operation, which would eliminate an assembly line and give each worker total responsibility for the assembly of a particular product. It resulted in a productivity increase of close to 50 per cent, a drop in rejects from 23 per cent, controllable rejects to close to 1 per cent, and a reduction in absenteeism from about 8 per cent to less than 1 per cent in a few months. Not all the early experiments were successful, but mistakes were treated as part of the experiential learning process.

As some in the organization changed and moved ahead by trying out new behaviors, others watched and waited but were eventually influenced by the culture. An example of late changers so influenced was the supervisor of Materials Control, who watched for two years what was going on in the plant but basically disagreed with the concepts of OD. Then he began to feel pressure to change because his peers were trying new things and he was not. He began by experimenting with enriching his secretary's job and found, in his own words, that "she was doing three times as much, enjoying it more, and giving me more time to manage." When he found that this experiment in managerial behavior had "paid off," he began to take a more active interest in OD. His next step was to completely reorganize his department to push decision making down the ladder, to utilize a team approach, and to enrich jobs. He supervised four sections: purchasing, inventory control, plant scheduling, and expediting. Reorganization of Materials Control was around product line teams. Each group had total project responsibility for their own product lines, including the four functions described above. We moved slowly and discussed with him alternative ways of going about the structural change. When he made the change, his subordinates were prepared and ready. The results were clear: In a three-month period of time (with the volume of business remaining steady), the parts shortage list was reduced from 14 I.B.M. pages to less than a page. In other words, although he was a late-changer in terms of the developing culture, his later actions were highly successful.

The influence of the developing culture was also documented through interviews with new employees coming into the plant. The perception by production employees that this was a "different" place to work occurred almost immediately, and changes in behavior of management personnel were clear by the second month.

In other words, while seminars and survey feedback techniques were used in our work with this plant, the initial and most crucial changes were achieved through a work-centered, consulting-counseling approach, e.g., through discussion with managers and others about work-related problems, following the model of adult learning described earlier.

So much for the manner in which the unfreezing process occurred and some of our learning about this process. What were some of the normative concepts applied and why? A brief overview of our approaches and findings follows.

A Normative Model

Communications

In this phase we attempted to open up communications at all levels. We started monthly meetings at every level of the organization, as well as a weekly meeting between the plant manager and a sample of production and clerical employees. The aim was to institutionalize the meetings to serve as a means for exchanging information and ideas about what had happened and what needed to happen. The meetings, especially between first-line supervisors and production workers, began primarily as one-way communications downward. Little by little, qualitative changes occurred and the meetings shifted to two-way communications about quality, schedules, and production problems. This effort to communicate (which was also extended through many other approaches) was an entire year in attaining success. It was an agonizingly slow process of change. In retrospect, this was a critical period during which trust was building and a culture conducive to further change was developing. Out of this, we concluded [*Finding 7*] that *organizational change occurs in stages: a stage of unfreezing and trust building, a take-off stage when observable change occurs, and a stabilization stage. Then the cycle iterates.* In addition to the communication type of meeting described above, confrontation meetings between departments were also held (Blake, Shepard, & Mouton, 1964). These, too, improved relationships between departments, over time.

Job Enrichment

A second area of change was in job structure, primarily through the use of job enrichment, or, as it has been called in the plant, "the total job concept." We have already discussed the importance of the job for psychological growth and development—our findings in this area parallel those of Ford (1969). Our first experience of tearing down a hotplate assembly line has already been discussed. This was followed by similar job enrichment efforts in other areas. In one department, girls individually assemble instruments containing thousands of parts and costing several thousand dollars. The change here allowed production workers to have greater responsibility for quality checks and calibration (instead of trained technicians). In another case, the changeover involved an instrument which had been produced for several years. Here, production was increased by 17 per cent with a corresponding increase in quality; absenteeism was reduced by more than 50 per cent.

The plant is presently engaged in completely removing quality control inspection from some departments, leaving final inspection to the workers themselves. In other departments, workers have been organized into autonomous workgroups with total responsibility for scheduling, assembly, training, and some quality control inspection. . . . Changes in these areas have evolved out of an attempt to utilize the positive forces of cohesive workgroups. However, like Ford (1969), we have found that not everyone in the assembly workforce responds positively to such changes, although a high majority do so over time.

Mutual goal setting has also been widely adopted. Instead of standards established by engineering (a direction in which the plant was heading when we started), goals for each department are derived from the plant goal, and individual goals for the week or month are developed in individual departments through discussions between the boss and subordinates. Our interview data clearly show that in this way workers understand how their individual goals fit into the plant goal structure and can work on their own without close supervision for long periods of time.

Changes toward a pay process more clearly based on merit (including appraisals for hourly and weekly salaried clerical and technical employees as well as for managerial and professional personnel) were made to reinforce and legitimate an escalating climate of work involvement. More and more employees are now involved in questions of production, quality, department layout, and methods. Assembly workers give department tours to visitors, including vice presidents. Organization-wide technical and product information sessions are held. Concerned more with strategy than with daily problems, the top team has for some time molded itself into a business team, meeting periodically to discuss future plans.

More recently, changes in organizational structure are taking place to move a functionally oriented organization to a matrix organization, using concepts derived directly from Lawrence and Lorsch (1969). This involves, among other approaches, the use of "integrators" at varying levels within the organization.

Systems Interaction

A systems approach requires that mutually consistent changes in *all* subsystems be made in affecting the organizational processes listed in our model. In other words, [*Finding 8*] *multiple changes in the subsystems are needed for the individual employee to change behavior and perceptions of his role.* For example, participative supervision should be accompanied by redesign of jobs to allow more responsibility, by a pay system that recognizes performance, by a communication system that is truly open, and by corresponding changes in other subsystems throughout the organization. Past attempts to change organizations through a nonsystems approach, e.g., through such single media as supervisory training or sensitivity training, have had limited success because other key leverage points have not been changed in the total system. Further, an attempt to change one subsystem too quickly or too drastically can have severely harmful results, as pointed out in the "Hovey and Beard Company" case (Lawrence, Bailey, Katz, Seiler, Orth, Clark, Barnes, & Turner, 1961). Whether structural *or* interpersonal changes should take precedence in a given period of time depends upon the readiness of the system to change and the key leverage points. The key concept [*Finding 9*] is that *structural and interpersonal systems changes must reinforce and legitimate each other.* Figure 3 presents this concept. The change can be in either direction in the model.

We also learned [*Finding 10*] that *systems changes set off additional interactive processes in which changes in organizational functioning increase not only outputs but also develop the latent abilities of people.* We have concluded that the real potential in organizational development lies in setting in motion such a positive snowball of change, growth, and development. For example, as assembly workers took on additional responsibility they became more and more concerned about the total organization and product. "Mini-gripes" turned into "mega-gripes," indicating a change in the maturity of the assembly workers (Huse & Price, 1970). At the same time, this freed up management personnel to be less concerned about daily assignments and more concerned about long-range planning.

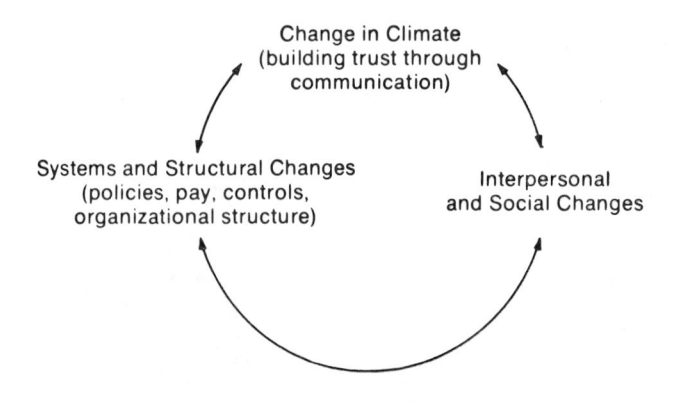

Figure 3. The Sequence of Organizational Change

To illustrate this, at the beginning of the OD effort, the organization had a plant manager, a production superintendent, and three first-line supervisors, or a total of five supervisory personnel in the direct manufacturing line. As the assembly line workers took on more responsibility, the five have been reduced to three (the plant manager and two first-line supervisors). The number of inspection and quality control personnel has also been reduced.

A Subsystem Within the Larger Organization

Up to this point in the case study we have been considering the plant as a system in its own right. However, changes set in motion here have also provided the first step in a larger plan for change and development to occur in the parent corporation (consisting of some 50 plants). As a subsystem within the larger system, this plant was to serve as a model for the rest of the corporation—as an example of how change should be planned and implemented. It was our hope that the systems approach to change would create such a clearly different culture in this plant that it would become visible to the rest of the corporation; that people from other segments of the larger organization would visit and become interested in trying similar models and mechanisms of change. Our hopes have been realized. Indeed, both authors are now applying OD concepts to other areas of the organization.

Influence is also exerted upward, with greater acceptance of these concepts by individuals at higher levels in the organization [Finding 11]. It is our perception that changes in organizational subsystems can have strong influences on the larger culture if the change is planned and publicized; if seed personnel are transferred to other parts of the system; if a network of change agents is clearly identified; and if careful planning goes into where and how change resources are to be used. Once again, top management commitment is not a necessary commitment for evolutionary change in a complex, multidivision, multilocation organization. *(Sometimes,* the tail begins to wag the dog.)

Subsystem Difficulties

However, this change process may cause some difficulties in the area of interface between the smaller subsystem and the larger system. For example, the increased responsibilities, commitment, and involvement represented by job enrichment for assembly workers are not adequately represented in the normal job evaluation program for factory workers and are difficult to handle adequately within the larger system. So pay and pay system changes must be modified to fit modern OD concepts. Figure 4 is a model which shows the effects of change in climate on individual model perceptions of equity in pay.

In addition to the larger system difficulties over wage plans, there still exists a great deal of controversy as to the importance of pay as a motivator (or dissatisfier). For example, Walton (1967) takes a basically pessimistic approach about participation through the informal approach, as opposed to the more formal approaches embodied in the Scanlon Plan (Lesieur, 1958), which "stress the economic rewards which can come from [formal] participation." On the other hand, Paul, Robertson, and Herzberg (1969) review a number of job enrichment projects and report: "In no instance did management face a demand of this kind [higher pay or better conditions] as a result of changes made in the studies." In a recent review of the Scanlon Plan (Lesieur & Puckett, 1969), the authors point out that Scanlon's first application did not involve the use of financial incentives but, rather, a common sharing between management and employees of problems, goals, and ideas. Indeed, Ford (1969) reports on the results of a series of job enrichment studies without ever mentioning the words "pay" or "salary." In the plant described in this case, no significant pressures for higher pay have been felt to date. However, there has been sufficient opportunity for promotion of hourly employees to higher level jobs as the plant has grown.

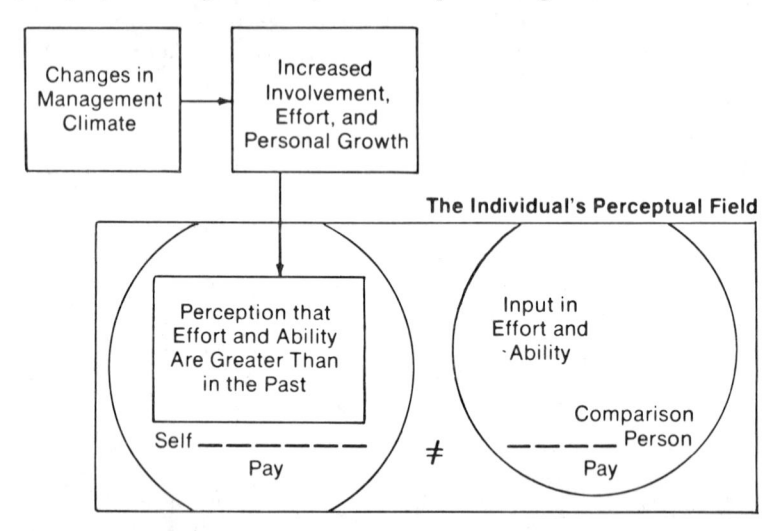

Figure 4. Equity Model

It is certainly not within the scope of this article to handle the controversy regarding the place of pay as a motivator. We do want to make the point that standard corporate job evaluation plans are only one instance of the difficulties of interface between the client plant as a subsystem and the larger system. In our experience, these and other areas have been minor rather than major problems, but they have been problems.

Changes in Consumption of Research Findings

An important by-product of our experience has been [*Finding 12*] that *the client system eventually becomes a sophisticated consumer of new research findings in the behavioral sciences.* As mentioned earlier, there was early resistance to "theory"; but as the program progressed, there was increasing desire for "theory." We also found that a flexible and adaptable organization is more likely to translate theory into new policies and actions. Perhaps this is where behavioral scientists may have gone wrong in the past. We may have saturated our client systems with sophisticated research studies before the culture was ready to absorb them. This would suggest that a more effective approach may be carefully planned stages of evolution from an action orientation to an action-research orientation to a research orientation. This implies a long-range plan for change that we often talk about but rarely execute with respect to the changes in organizations that we seek as behavioral scientists.

Results of The Organizational Development Program

To a great extent we have tried to share with you our results and findings throughout the article. In addition, we are retesting these concepts in several other plants. In retrospect, how much change really occurred at the client plant, and how effective have been the new approaches introduced? We have only partial answers since a control plant did not exist and since the plant was relatively new; no historical data existed against which to compare performance. However, considerable data do exist to support the thesis that change has occurred and that new managerial approaches have created an effective organization. (In addition, the second author is conducting ongoing research in another plant in the organization which has historical data. Before- and aftermeasures have already shown dramatic change: e.g., reduction in manufacturing costs for the plant of 40 to 45 percent.)

Extensive interviews by the researchers and detailed notes and observations by the change agents indicate considerable improvement after our work with this plant. Communication is open, workers feel informed, jobs are interesting and challenging, and goals are mutually set and accomplished.

In each of the output dimensions, positive changes have occurred which we think, but cannot always prove, would not have occurred without the OD effort. Turnover has been considerably reduced; specific changes in job structure, organizational change, or group process have resulted in measurable productivity changes of up to 50 percent. Recent changes in the Instrument Department have resulted in productivity and quality improvements. We have witnessed the significant changes in maturity and motivation which have taken place among the assembly workers. A change to a project team structure in the Materials Control Department led to a reduction of the weekly parts shortages. Following the findings of Lawrence and Lorsch (1969), the use of "integrators" and project teams has significantly reduced the time necessary for new product development, introduction, and manufacture. A fuller evaluation of the integrator role and the project organization as it affects intergroup relations and new product development is reported elsewhere (Beer, Pieters, Marcus, &, Hundert, 1971).

Several recent incidents in the plant are evidence of the effect of the changes and bear repeating. An order called for in seven days and requiring extraordinary cooperation on the part of a temporary team of production workers was completed in fewer than seven days. A threatened layoff was handled with candor and openness and resulted in volunteers among some of the secondary wage earners.

New employees and managers now transferred into the plant are immediately struck by the differences between the "climate" of this plant and other locations. They report more openness, greater involvement by employees, more communication, and more interesting jobs. Even visitors are struck immediately by the differences. For example, one of the authors has on several occasions taken graduate students on field trips to the plant. After the tour, the consensus is, "You've told us about it, but I had to see it for myself before I would believe it." Managers transferred or promoted out of the plant to other locations report "cultural shock."

Summary and Conclusions

The Medfield Project (as it can now be labeled) has been an experiment in a systems approach to organizational development at two systems levels. On the one hand, we have regarded the plant as a system in and of itself. On the other hand, we have regarded the plant as a subsystem within a larger organization. As such a subsystem, we wanted it to serve as a model for the rest of the organization. Indeed, as a result of this study, OD work is going forward elsewhere in the parent company and will be reported [elsewhere].

Although we have shared our findings with you throughout the article, it seems wise now to summarize them for your convenience, so that they may be generalized to other organizations and climates.

Findings

1. A clear-cut commitment to a particular OD approach is not necessary (although desirable) for a successful OD program to succeed.

2. Total top management understanding of where the OD process will lead and the state of the organization at the end is not necessary for organizational change to occur.

3. Change can and does begin at lower levels in the organization.

4. Effective and permanent adult learning comes after the individual has experimented with new approaches and received appropriate feedback in the on-the-job situation.

5. Rather than the T Group, the operating, ongoing organization may be the best "laboratory" for learning, with fewer problems in transfer of training.

6. Internal change leaders are natural targets for the change agent, since they become influence leaders and help to shape the culture.

7. Organizational change occurs in stages: a stage of unfreezing and trust building, a take-off stage when observable change occurs, and a stabilization stage. Then the cycle iterates.

8. Multiple changes in the subsystems are needed for the individual employee to change behavior and perceptions of his role.

9. Structural and interpersonal systems changes must reinforce and legitimate each other.

10. Systems changes set off additional interactive processes in which changes in organizational functioning not only increase outputs but also develop the latent abilities of people.

11. Influence is also exerted upward, with greater acceptance of these concepts by individuals at higher levels in the organization.

12. The client system eventually becomes a sophisticated consumer of new research findings in the behavioral sciences.

Perhaps the most important and far-reaching conclusion is that as organizational psychologists we have viewed our role too narrowly and with an insufficient historical and change perspective. Our research studies tend to be static rather than dynamic. We need to do a better job of developing a theory and technology of changing and to develop a flexible set of concepts which will change as we experiment with and socially engineer organizations. We are suggesting a stronger action orientation for our field and less of a natural science orientation. We must be less timid about helping organizations to change themselves. We must create a positive snowball of organizational change followed by changes in needs and expectations of organizational members, followed again by further organizational change. The objective of change agents should be to develop an evolving system that maintains reasonable internal consistency while staying relevant to and anticipating changes and adaptation to the outside environment. As behavioral scientists and change agents, we must help organizations begin to "become."

Notes

1. Cf. The traditional aspects included in the conceptual model developed by Huse (1969).
2. We should like to acknowledge the help and participation of Mrs. Gloria Gery and Miss Joan Doolittle in the data-gathering phase.

References

Argyris, C. On the future of laboratory training. *J. appl. Behav. Sci.*, 1967, *3* (2), 153-183.

Bartlett, A. C. Changing behavior as a means to increased efficiency. *J. appl. Behav. Sci.*, 1967, *3* (3), 381-403.

Beckhard, R. *Organization development: Strategies and models*. Reading, Mass.: Addison-Wesley, 1969.

Beer, M., Pieters, G. R., Marcus, S. H., & Hundert, A. T. Improving integration between functional groups: A case in organization change and implications for theory and practice. Symposium presented at American Psychological Association Convention, Washington, D.C., September 1971.

Bennis, W. G. The case study—I. Introduction. *J. appl. Behav. Sci.*, 1968, *4* (2), 227-231.

Blake, R. R., & Mouton, J. S. *Building a dynamic corporation through grid organization development*. Reading, Mass.: Addison-Wesley, 1969.

Blake, R. R., Shephard, H. A., & Mouton, J. S. *Managing Intergroup conflict in industry*. Houston, Tex.: Gulf, 1964.

Bradford, L. P. Membership and the learning process. In L. P. Bradford, J. R. Gibb, and K. D. Benne (Eds.), *T-Group theory and laboratory method: Innovation in re-education*. New York: Wiley, 1964.

Campbell, J. P., & Dunnette, M. D. Effectiveness of t-group experiences in managerial training and development. *Psycholog. Bull.*, August 1968, 70, (2), 73-104.

Davis, S. A. An organic problem-solving method of organizational change. *J. appl. Behav. Sci.*, 1967, *3* (1), 3-21.

Ford, R. N. *Motivation through the work itself*. New York: American Management Association, 1969.

Huse, E. F. The behavioral scientist in the shop. *Personnel*, May/June 1965, *42* (3), 50-57.

Huse, E. F. Putting in a management development program that works. *California Mgmt Rev.*, Winter 1966, 73-80.

Huse, E. F., & Price, P. S. The relationship between maturity and motivation in varied work groups. *Proceedings* of the Seventieth Annual Convention of the American Psychological Association, September 1970.

Lawrence, P. R., & Lorsch, J. W. *Organization and environment*. Homewood, Ill.: Richard D. Irwin, 1969.

Lawrence, P. R., Bailey, J. C., Katz, R. L., Seiler, J. A., Orth, C. D. III, Clark, J. V., Barnes, L. B., & Turner, A. N. *Organizational behavior and administration*. Homewood, Ill.: Irwin-Dorsey, 1961.

Lesieur, F. G. (Ed.) *The Scanlon plan: A frontier in labor-management cooperation*. Cambridge, Mass.: M.I.T. Press, 1958.

Lesieur, F. G., & Puckett, E. S. The Scanlon plan has proved itself. *Harvard Bus. Rev.,* Sept./Oct. 1969, *47,* 109-118.

Paul, W. J., Robertson, K. B., & Herzberg, F. Job enrichment pays off. *Harvard Bus. Rev.,* Mar./Apr. 1969, *47* (2) 61-78.

Roche, W. J., & MacKinnon, N. L. Motivating people with meaningful work. *Harvard Bus. Rev.,* May/June 1970, *48* (3), 97-110.

Schein, E. H., & Bennis, W. G. *Personal and organizational change through group methods: The laboratory approach.* New York: Wiley, 1965.

Walton, R. E. Contrasting designs for participative systems. *Personnel Admin.,* Nov./Dec. 1967, *30* (6), 35-41.

Management by Objectives

HENRY L. TOSI
STEPHEN CARROLL

Since Drucker (1954) and McGregor (1960) made favorable statements about management by objectives, organizations of all types have made increasing use of this method. While most of the early discussion of MBO emphasized its use as a tool for the development of more objective criteria for performance evaluation, it has become apparent that subordinate participation in goal setting has resulted in greater levels of ego involvement, increased motivation and increased planning behavior, all of which have an effect upon performance.

These advantages stemmed from the process of setting goals and using them, in place of personality traits and characteristics for evaluation of performance. Management by objectives has been described as a general process in which ". . . The superior and the subordinate manager of an organization jointly define its common goals, define each individual's major areas of responsibility in terms of the results expected of him and use these measures as guides for operating the unit and assessing the contribution of each of its members." (Odiorne, 1965).

The logic of MBO is, indeed, attractive. There is an intrinsic desirability to a method which motivates performance and enhances measurement while at the same time it increases the participation and involvement of subordinates.

The Elements of MBO

There are three basic aspects of MBO which will affect its success: goals and goal setting; participation and involvement of subordinates; and, feedback and performance evaluation.

Goals and Goal Setting.

A number of studies[1] have clearly demonstrated that when an individual or group

From *Personnel Administration*, vol. 33 (July-August 1970), pp. 44–49. Reprinted by permission of the International Personnel Management Association, 1313 East 60th Street, Chicago, Illinois 60637.

has a specific goal, there is higher performance than when the goals are general, or have not been set. Generally, high performance can be associated with higher individual or group goals. A number of studies[2] also suggest that performance improvement occurs when an individual is successful in achieving past goals. When there is previous goal success, the individual is more likely to set higher goals in future periods, and he is more likely to attain them.

Participation.

There have been a number of diverse findings about the relationship of participation in decision-making and productivity. These apparently contradictory findings have been resolved by concluding that if the subordinate perceives the participation to be legitimate, it will have positive effects on productivity. In addition, participation does seem to have an effect on the degree of acceptance of decisions reached mutually. There is also evidence[3] that involvement and participation are positively correlated with the level of job satisfaction.

Feedback.

Both laboratory and field research have demonstrated that relatively clear, unambiguous feedback increases problem solving capacities of groups and improves the performance of individuals.[4] Positive attitudes, increased confidence in decisions, and greater certainties of superior's expectations were found to be related to communications which clarified roles and role expectancies with more and better information.

Feedback, in the form of formal appraisal in a work setting, when based on relatively objective performance standards, tends to be related to a more positive orientation by subordinates of the amount of supervision their boss exercises. Positive actions are more likely to be taken by subordinates when feedback is viewed as supportive and is objectively based.

MBO and Employee Motivation

Studies of the MBO process in organizations strongly suggest that changes in performance and attitude, which seem positive and desirable, appear to be associated with how it is formally implemented. The implementation of MBO alters the expectations of organization members about performance appraisal and evaluation. These expectations, if not met, may affect the degree of acceptance of the MBO approach. (See Raia, 1965; and Tosi and Carroll, 1968.)

This problem may be resolved, to some degree, through proper setting of objectives and use of the MBO process. We believe certain minimal conditions must prevail if MBO is to have its motivational effect:

Goal Clarity and Relevance.

Few managers would quarrel with the notion that organizational goals should be made known to the members. Individual perceptions of the goal are important here. Tosi and Carroll (1968) have suggested some dimensions of goals which need to be communicated to members. First, goals should represent the unit's needs. The members must be aware of the importance of the goals. The development of relatively objective criteria increases the perception of goal clarity. If goals have these properties, they are more likely to have effects upon the individual working towards them.

Managerial Use and Support.

"Top management support" is important for the success of any program. The best evidence of support is the use of the technique by the manager himself. Formulating goals, discussing them with subordinates, and providing feedback based on these goals will have substantially greater effect on a subordinate than simply saying "this has the support of top management."

Many managers mistakenly feel the verbalization of support for a policy is adequate enough. They send a memo to subordinates stating that top management wishes a program to be implemented. This, obviously, does not insure compliance. "Do as I say, not as I do" will not work. Verbalized policy support must be reinforced by the individual's perception of the superior's action and behavior in using an objective approach. It is of little or no use to support MBO philosophy orally and not use it!

The Need for Feedback.

While a number of studies have concluded that goals have a greater impact on performance than just feedback alone we do not believe it to be an either/or situation. Feedback about well-developed goals seems a fundamental requirement for behavior change. It may be that the subordinate's perception of the specificity objectivity and frequency of feedback is interpreted as a measure of the superior's support of an objectives approach.

Some Other Cautions.

There are other significant points that cut across those made above: there are personal as well as organization constraints which must be taken into consideration in the development of goals. The organizational unit and the organization level affect the nature of the goals which can, and will, be set. Goals at lower levels may be more precise and probably more objectively measured. The goals of one functional area, engineering for instance, may be much more general than those of another, say the marketing department.

MBO and the Compensation Process

If, as McClelland (1961) suggests, individuals high in need achievement will expend more effort in reaching challenging goals irrespective of external rewards associated with goal accomplishment, MBO may supplement or complement standard compensations procedures. Tying MBO into the financial reward system could have a handsome pay-off. It is for this reason that we suggest how information obtained from MBO can be used in making improved compensation decisions.

Internal Wage Administration.

MBO can be of assistance in developing salary differentials within a particular job class. By assessing the level of difficulty and contribution of the goals for a particular job and comparing them with similar jobs, better determination of the appropriateness of basic compensation differentials may be made.

MBO may be useful in providing information about changes in job requirements which may necessitate re-evaluation and adjustment of compensation levels for different positions. By observing changes in objectives over time, changes in job requirements may be detected which could lead to revisions in compensation schedules.

The objectives approach can aid in determining supplementary compensation levels such as stock options, bonus plans, and administration of profit sharing plans. This type of compensation is usually given when performance exceeds the normal position requirements. A properly developed objectives approach will take into account both normal job duties as well as goals and activities which extend beyond them. The extent to which an incumbent is able to achieve these non-routine objectives should be one, but perhaps not the only, factor in ranking unit members in order of their additional contribution to group effectiveness. It will provide a sound basis for determining what the level of supplemental compensation should be. Needless to say, goals which extend beyond normal job requirements should contribute importantly to organizational success.

A possible problem needs to be noted here. When goals go substantially beyond the current job requirements it may be due to the individual's initiative and aggressiveness. If this happens, it may be more appropriate strategy to change the position of the individual, not to redefine his job and change his compensation levels. A method must be developed which takes this possibility into consideration, as well as the fact that different managers will have different goals. This does not seem to be the appropriate place to detail such a device. A weighing approach which considers the capability of the manager, the difficulty of the goal, and its importance to the unit might resolve this problem.

Performance-linked Rewards.

If goals are developed properly, their achievement may be more readily associated with an individual so that appropriate individual rewards may be given. The *goal statement* is the heart of the "objectives approach." It is a description of the boss's expectancies which will be used in the feedback and evaluation process. It is a communicative artifact which spells out, for both the boss and the subordinate, the objectives *and* the manner in which they will be obtained. It should *contain two elements,* the *desired goal level* and the *activities* required to achieve that level of performance. This permits not only a comparison of performance against some criterion, but also allows determination of whether or not events, which are presumed to lead to goal achievement, have taken place if appropriate criteria are not available.

This has important implications for the problems of assessment, evaluation, and compensation. Some goals may be neither measurable nor adequately verifiable. Yet, intuitively we know what must be done to achieve them. If this is the case, and we have distinguished between goals and activities, we can at least determine whether activities which are presumed to lead to desired ends have taken place.

It is important to recognize the distinction between measuring the achievement of a goal level and determining whether or not an event presumed to lead to goal achievement has taken place. If we are unable to quantify or specify a goal level in a meaningful way, then we must simply assume that the desired level will be achieved if a particular event, or set of activities, has taken place. For example, it is very difficult to find measurable criteria to assess a manager's capability in developing subordinates, yet we can determine if he has provided them with development opportunities. If they have participated in seminars, attending meetings or gone to school it may be *assumed* that the development activities are properly conducted.

Promises and Problems

By its very nature, MBO seems to be a promising vehicle for linking performance to the evaluation process and the reward system in order to encourage both job satisfaction and productivity. It appears that higher performance and motivation is most likely when there is a link between performance and the reward systems (Tosi and Carroll, 1968; Porter and Lawler, 1968). It may be that this link can be achieved through the process of feedback regarding goal achievement and the association of rewards and sanctions to achievement. Goal attainment should be organizationally reinforced, and the reinforcement should be different for individuals, as a function of their own attainment. The use of an "objectives" approach in conjunction with a compensation program may also result in less dissatisfaction with the allocation of compensation increases made. Certainly there is virtually universal agreement among managers that rewards should go for actual accomplishments rather than for irrelevant personal characteristics and political or social standing.

There may be problems arising from the use of MBO and its emphasis on goals and goal achievement. Many organizations have adopted the objectives approach because it seems to be a better appraisal device, and they have used it primarily in this manner. But, an appraisal system should furnish information needed to make other personnel decisions, such as promotion and transfer. Information furnished by the objectives approach may not be adequate for these purposes. Accomplishment of goals at a lower level job may be a good indicator of capability in the current job and/or level of motivation, but not of the individual's abilities to perform at higher levels of responsibility, especially if the requirements on the higher level job are much different from the current position.

Conversely, goals accomplished at a lower level may be indicative of promotability to a particular high level job if there is high goal congruence between the two positions. At any rate, there is certainly no reason to rely strictly upon the objectives approach for these decisions. It can be used along with other criteria, such as assessment of traits, when this is deemed an important dimension by the decision makers. Another potential difficulty should be pointed out. If the objectives approach becomes the basic vehicle for the determination of compensation increases, then managers may quickly learn to "beat the system." Unless higher level managers are skilled in the use of MBO, subordinates may set objectives which have high probabilities of achievement, refraining from setting high risk goals. When any system becomes too formalized, managers learn how to beat it, and those using it become more concerned with simply meeting the formal benefits for both the individual and the organization [and the results] are probably no different from earlier more traditional methods of appraisal.

The "objectives approach" seems to be a practical way of motivating organization members, but it is not an easy path to follow. It requires a considerable amount of time and energy of *all managers,* in addition to extensive organization support to make it work. MBO may lose some of its mystique, value, importance, and significance when it must be translated into a formal policy requirement. It is too easy to consider a formal MBO program as merely another thorn in the manager's side, with no positive gains for implementing it. To succeed, an MBO program must be relevant, applicable, helpful, and receive organization support and reinforcement. One way in which this can be done is to link it to other elements of the structural system which reinforce behavior, such as compensation and reward programs.

References

Drucker, Peter. *The Practice of Management.* New York: Harper and Brothers, 1954.

McClelland, D. C. *The Achieving Society*. Princeton: Van Nostrand, 1961.

McGregor, Douglas. *The Human Side of Enterprise*. New York: McGraw-Hill, 1960.

Odiorne, George. *Management by Objectives*. New York: Pitman, 1965.

Porter, Lyman and Lawler, Edward. *Managerial Attitudes and Performance*. Homewood, Illinois: R. D. Irwin, 1968.

Raia, Anthony. "Goal Setting and Self Control," *Journal of Management Studies*, II-I, February 1965, pp. 34-35.

Tosi, H. and Carroll, S. "Managerial Reactions to Management by Objectives," *Academy of Management Journal*. December 1968, pp. 415-426.

Notes

1. See for instance Bryan, J. F. and Locke, E. A. "Goal Setting as a Means of Increasing Motivation" *Journal of Applied Psychology*, 1967, Vol. 51, pp. 274-277; Locke, E. A. "Motivational Effects of Knowledge of Results: Knowledge of Results: Knowlege or Goal Setting?" *Journal of Applied Psychology*, 1967, Vol. 51, pp. 324-329.

2. See Lockette, R. R., *The Effect of Level of Aspiration Upon the Learning of Skills*. Unpublished doctoral dissertation, University of Illinois, 1956; Yacorzynski, G. K., "Degree of Effort III. Relationship to the Level of Aspiration" *Journal of Experimental Psychology*, 1941, 30 pp. 407-413; Horowitz, M, et. al., *Motivational Effects of Alternative Decision Making Processes in Groups*. Bureau of Education Research, University of Illinois, 1953.

3. Vroom, Victor. *Some Personality Determinants of the Effects of Participation*, Englewood Cliffs: Prentice Hall; Tosi, Henry, "A Reexamination of Some Personality Determinants of the Effects of Participation," *Personnel Psychology* (forthcoming).

4. See Wertz, J. A., Antoinetti, and Wallace, S. R. "The Effect of Home Office Contact on Sales Performance," *Personnel Psychology*, 1954, Vol. 7, pp. 381-384; Smith, E. E. "The Effects of Clear and Unclear Role Expectations on Group Productivity and Effectiveness," *Journal of Abnormal and Social Psychology*, 1957, Vol. 55, pp. 213-217; and, Leavitt; Hand Mueller, A., "Some Effects of Feedback on Communication," *Human Relations*, 1951, Vol. 4, pp. 401-410.

Section B
Compensation and Reward Systems

How to Ruin Motivation with Pay

W. CLAY HAMNER

Merit pay, or pay for performance, is so widely accepted by compensation managers and academic researchers that it seems foolhardy to criticize it. It is based on the "law of effect," which states simply that behavior that appears to lead to a positive consequence tends to be repeated. Most behavioral scientists believe in this principle, and it is followed by most large organizations that have a merit pay system for their management team.

Despite the soundness of the principle on which it is based, many academic researchers have criticized the merit system. They regard merit pay as detrimental to motivation rather than an enhancement, as it was designed to be.

One group of researchers contends that the merit system fails to increase motivation because managers mismanage merit programs and/or lack understanding of them. These critics therefore recommend that managers examine ways to improve the introduction of merit plans.

A second, though smaller, group criticizes the use of merit pay on grounds that it utilizes externally mediated rewards rather than focusing on a system in which individuals can be motivated by their jobs. They contend that employees who enjoy their jobs (that is, who are intrinsically motivated) will lose interest when a merit pay plan is introduced because they regard job satisfaction as their primary goal. These researchers, therefore, believe compensation managers should deemphasize merit pay and concentrate instead on improving other aspects of the job.

The research behind both of these positions deserves examination. And the review that follows concludes with recommendations designed to help managers utilize a "pay for performance" plan as a method of improving both quality and quantity of output.

Reprinted by permission of the publisher from *Compensation Review*, Third Quarter 1975, © 1975 by AMACOM, a division of American Management Associations.

Why Merit Pay Systems Fail

As indicated above, some researchers have concluded that when merit plans fail, it is not due to a weakness in the law of effect. Rather, they blame weakness in the implementation of merit pay systems by compensation managers and line managers involved. For example:

After reviewing pay research from General Electric and other companies, industrial psychologist Herbert H. Meyer concluded that despite the apparent soundness of the merit pay principle, experience tells us that it does not work with the elegance of its seeming simplicity. Instead, managers typically seem to be inclined to make relatively small discriminations in salary treatment among individuals in the same job regardless of perceived differences in performance. As a matter of fact, Meyer notes, when discriminations are made, they are likely to be based on factors other than performance, such as length of service, future potential, or perceived need for "catch up," where one employee's pay seems low in relation to others in the group.

Michael Beer, director of organizational development at Corning Glass, observes that pay systems evolve over time. And in the process, he says, administrative considerations and tradition often override the more important considerations of behavioral outcomes in determining the shape of the merit pay system and its administration.

If, as both of these analysts seem to believe, it is not the merit pay theory itself that is defective, it is important to look at the specific shortcomings that Meyer, Beer, and other researchers say cause low motivation to result from merit pay.

1. *Pay is not perceived as being related to job performance.* Edward E. Lawler III, a leading researcher on pay and performance, has noted that managers often are unhappy with their wage system because they do not perceive the relationship between how hard they work (productivity) and how much they earn.

In a survey of 600 middle- and lower-level managers, Lawler found virtually no relationship between their pay and their rated performance. Those who were most highly motivated to perform their jobs effectively were characterized by two attitudes: They said their pay was important to them, and they felt that good job performance would lead to higher pay for them.

Why don't managers perceive their pay as related to performance even when the company claims to have a merit pay plan? There are several reasons.

Many rewards (for example, stock options) are *deferred payments,* and the time horizon is so long that the employee loses sight of its relationship to performance.

The *goals* of the organization on which performance appraisals are based are unclear, unrealistic, or unrelated to pay. W. H. Mobley found that only 36 percent of the managers surveyed at a company using an MBO [management by objectives] program saw goal attainment as having considerable bearing on their merit increase; at the same time, 83 percent of their bosses claimed that they used the goal attainments to determine their pay-increase recommendations.

The *secrecy* that so often surrounds annual merit increases may lead managers to conclude that their recommended pay increase is not related in any direct way to their past year's performance.

R. L. Opsahl and M. D. Dunnette claimed that secrecy is due in part to a fear of salary administrators that they would have a difficult time mustering convincing arguments in favor of many of their practices.

Lawler summarized his extensive research on secrecy of pay by stating that managers did not have an accurate picture of what other managers were earning. He found a general tendency among managers to overstate the pay of managers at their own level (thereby reducing their own pay, relatively speaking) and at one level below them (again reducing their own pay, relatively speaking); they also tended to underestimate the pay of managers one level above them (thus reducing the value of future promotions).

2. *Performance ratings are seen as biased.* While many managers working under a merit program believe that the program is a good one, they are dissatisfied with the evaluation of their performance by their immediate superior. A merit plan is based on the assumption that managers can make objective (valid) distinctions between good and poor performance. Unfortunately, most evaluations of performance are subjective in nature and consist of a "summary score" from a general, and sometimes dated, performance-evaluation form.

The supervisor's key role in determining pay creates a problem in that it reminds the employee very clearly that he or she is dependent on the supervisor for rewards. Therefore, the merit plan should, whenever possible, be based on objective measures (such as group sales, cost reduction per unit, and goal attainment) rather than subjective measures (such as cooperation, attitude, and future potential).

Even if subjective performance appraisals are not biased, Lawler believes that the complaints of managers and employees about the subjective nature of their performance evaluation may be a sign of poor leadership. "Many plans seem to fail," says Lawler, "not because they are mechanically defective, but because they were ineffectively introduced, there is a lack of trust between superiors and subordinates, or the quality of the supervisor is too low. No plan can succeed in the face of low trust and poor supervision, no matter how valid it may be from the point of view of mechanics." L. W. Gruenfield and P. Weissenberg support this poor leadership theory in their findings that good managers are much more amenable to the idea of basing pay on performance than are poor managers.

3. *Rewards are not viewed as rewards.* Management often has difficulty communicating accurately to employees the message intended to be conveyed through the pay raise. A raise can tell the employee "you're loved a lot," but at the same time it can also suggest: "I'm only average," "I'm not appreciated around here," or "I'd better get busy." Management often believes it is communicating a positive message when in fact the employee receives a negative signal, an interpretation that can have a detrimental effect on the employee's future potential. Therefore, the relationship between performance and attainment of the pay incentive must be explicit.

Management and employees' interpretations of reward messages can differ for several reasons. For example, conflicting reward schedules may be operating, a problem of inequity among employees is perceived to exist, or the merit increase may appear as threatening to the self-esteem of the employee.

Each of these problems centers on the fact that pay increases are generally kept secret, causing employees to draw erroneous conclusions, or that there is little or no communication in the form of coaching or counseling by supervisors during the year or following the performance appraisal. Instead, the employee is "expected to know" what the supervisor thinks about his or her performance.

Research has shown that the more frequent the formal and informal reviews of performance and the more the individual is told about the reasons for an increase, the greater his preference for a merit increase system and the lower his preference for a seniority system.

Conflicting reward schedules result from defects in the merit plan itself. For example, individual rewards (such as giving the best manager a free trip to Hawaii) are often set up in such a way that cooperation with other managers is discouraged; a cost reduction program may be introduced at the expense of production; or one department (sales) suffers while another department (manufacturing) benefits in the short run.

Some compensation managers stress that pay plans must change constantly because of general business conditions, shifts in management philosophy, competitive pressures, participant feedback, and modification in the structure and objectives of the organization. These changes, however, should be designed in such a way that the negative side effect of reduced cooperation does not result. For this reason, many companies use a companywide merit plan (such as the Scanlon Plan) that offers a financial incentive to everyone in the organization based on the performance of the total organization.

The question of inequity in pay arises when the employee perceives the merit increase to be unfair relative to his own past year's performance. The employee may be dissatisfied with the performance evaluation, or he may view the performance evaluation as fair but believes his supervisor failed to reward him in a manner consistent with the rating.

A more common problem is one that occurs when an employee who is satisfied with the dollar amount of his pay perceives that others performing at levels below him are receiving increases equal to his; or else he believes those who are performing at his same level are receiving higher raises. For example, an employee who was rated as above average receives an 8 percent pay increase but perceives this to be low since he believes that the average increase was 9 percent when in fact it was only 6.5 percent.

To avoid this type of problem—which will contribute to dissatisfaction with pay and possible lower job performance—Lawler recommends that, as a minimum requirement, managers explain to their employees how the salary raises were derived (for example, 50 percent based on cost of living and 50 percent on merit) and tell them the range and mean of raises given in the organization for people at their job level. Says Lawler: "There is no reason why organizations cannot make salaries public information."

Employee self-esteem can be undermined by merit pay because employees so often rate themselves as above average in performance and are disappointed when the merit raise doesn't jibe with the self-evaluation. Meyer, for example, concluded on the basis of his research that 90 percent of the managers at General Electric rated themselves above average. According to Meyer:

> The fact that almost everyone thinks he is an above average performer probably causes most of our problems with merit pay plans. Since the salary increases most people get do not reflect superior performance (as determined by interpersonal comparisons, or as defined in the guide book for the pay plan), the effects of the actual pay increases on motivation are likely to be more negative than positive. The majority of the people feel discriminated against because, obviously, management does not recognize their true worth.

4. *Managers of merit increases are more concerned with satisfaction with pay than job performance.* Most studies of managers' satisfaction with their pay have shown high levels of dissatisfaction—the rate has run as high as 80 percent in some surveys. But Beer points out that too often dissatisfaction with pay is assumed to mean dissatisfaction with amount. Beer's research suggests, however, that a change to a merit system with no increase in amount paid out by the company will increase satisfaction if the reasons for the increases are explained.

In contrast to the volume of research on satisfaction with pay, data in the area of the relationship between pay and job performance is less solid than any other field. Because of this failure to deal with the role of pay, Lawler notes that many managers have come to the erroneous conclusion that the experts in "human relations" have shown that pay is a relatively unimportant incentive.

In fact, Cherrington, Reitz, and Scott found that the magnitude of the relationship between satisfaction and performance depends primarily upon the performance-reinforcer contingencies that have been arranged—that is, people who were appropriately reinforced were satisfied with their pay, while those who were dissatisfied with their pay were those who were inappropriately rewarded. Likewise, Hamner and Foster found that the best performers working under a contingent (piece-rate) pay plan were more satisfied than the poorer performers, but that there was no relationship between satisfaction and performance for those paid under a noncontingent (across-the-board) pay plan.

Managers need to be concerned with two questions: *Is the merit raise based on performance,* and *who is doing the complaining?*

Numerous studies show that pay is not closely related to performance in many organizations that claim to have merit ranges. Typically these studies show that pay is much more closely related to job level and seniority than performance. In fact, Belcher reports that low, zero, and even negative relationships between pay and supervisory ratings of performance occur even among managers where the relationship would be expected to be high.

Donald Finn, compensation manager at J. C. Penney, has said executives are often "hung up" as managers about the satisfaction of employees with pay recommendations. "So who is complaining and why?" asks Finn. "If low producers are low earners, the pay plan is working—but there will be complaints. If a company wants an incentive plan in which rewards are commensurate with risk, it must be willing to accept a relatively broad range of earnings and corresponding degrees of manager satisfaction."

5. *Trust and openness about merit increases is low.* A merit system will not be accepted and may not have the intended motivational effects if managers do not actively administer a performance appraisal system, practice good human relations, explain the reasons for the increases, and ensure that employees are not forgotten when eligibility dates come and go. The organization must provide an open climate with respect to pay and an environment where work and effort are valued.

The Xerox Corporation recognized the problem of trust and openness in a compensation planning model report that states this philosophy: "If pay and satisfaction are to be high, pay rates must vary according to job demands in such a way that each perceived increment in a job demand factor will lead to increased pay." The same document notes that organizations expect extremely high trust levels on the part of their employees, in that:

Only 72 percent of 184 employing organizations in the study had a written statement of the firm's basic compensation policy covering such matters as paying competitive salaries, timing of wage and salary increases, and how raises are determined.

Only 51 percent of these same organizations communicate their general compensation policies directly to all employees, while 21 percent communicate the policy only to managers.

Contrarily, 69 percent of the firms do not provide their employees with wage and salary schedules or progression plans that apply to their own categories, thus indicating a low trust level toward employees.

Over 50 percent of the firms do not tell their employees where this information is available.

In only 48 percent of the firms do managers have access to salary schedules applying to their own level in the organization, and in only 18 percent of the companies do managers have knowledge of the salaries of other managers at their own level or higher levels.

6. *Some organizations view money as the primary motivator, ignoring the importance of the job itself.* The shortcomings discussed above deal with the criticism of researchers that the failure of the merit plan is due to poor implementation and not due to a weakness in the theory of the "law of effect." The deficiency noted here centers on the criticism voiced by those who believe that employees who have interesting jobs will lose interest in the job when a merit pay plan is introduced.

An intrinsically motivating job can be defined as one that is so interesting and creative that certain pleasure or rewards are derived from completing the task itself. Until recently, most theories dealing with worker motivation have assumed that the effects of intrinsic and extrinsic reinforcement (such as merit pay) are additive—that is, a worker will be more motivated to complete a task that combines both kinds of rewards than a task where only one kind of reward is present.

E. L. Deci, among others, criticizes behavioral scientists who advocate a system of employee motivation that utilizes externally mediated rewards—such as money—administered by someone other than the employee himself. In so doing, according to Deci, management is attempting to control the employee's behavior so he will do what he is told. The limitation of this method of worker motivation, for Deci, is that it satisfies only man's "lower order" needs.

Deci recommends that we move away from a method of external control toward a system in which individuals can be motivated by the job itself. He believes that this approach will allow managers to focus on higher-order needs in activities for which the rewards are mediated by the person himself (intrinsically motivated).

To motivate employees intrinsically, Deci believes tasks should be designed to make them interesting and creative. He also says workers should have some say in decisions that concern them "so they will feel like causal agents in the activities in which they engage."

Deci has introduced research data that suggests that a person's intrinsic motivation to perform an activity decreases when he receives contingent monetary payment for performing an interesting task. From these findings he concludes that:

> ... it seems clear that the effects of intrinsic motivation and extrinsic motivation are not additive. While extrinsic rewards such as money can certainly motivate behavior, they appear to be doing so at the expense of intrinsic motivation. As a result, contingent payment systems do not appear to be compatible with participative management systems.

Deci brings out an important point: Managers should not use pay to offset a boring or negative task. However, like Herzberg before him, his results don't appear to completely support his conclusion about the effect of money as a motivator. Research by Hamner and Foster has shown that the effect of intrinsic and extrinsic monetary rewards are additive and that even Deci's results themselves on close examination support this more traditional argument. In addition, I am not sure that merit pay plans are incompatible with a participative management system.

On both of these last two arguments, B. F. Skinner recommends that the organization should design feedback and incentive systems in such a way that the dual objective of getting things done and making work enjoyable are met. He says:

> It is important to remember that an incentive system isn't the only factor to take into account. How pleasant work conditions are, how easy or awkward a job is, how good or bad tools are—many things of that sort make an enormous difference in what a worker will do for what he receives. One problem of the production-line worker is that he seldom sees any of the ultimate consequences of his work. He puts on left front wheels day in and day out and he may never see the finished car. . . .

Making a Merit Pay System Work

In my discussion of the shortcomings of merit pay plans, various suggestions for overcoming these deficiencies were implied. More detailed recommendations on how to improve the quality and quantity of performance under merit pay are given below.

1. *Openness and trust should be stressed by the compensation manager.* As a minimum, employers should know the formula for devising the merit increases and should be told the range and mean of the pay increases for people at their job level. This alone should reduce some of the feeling of low self-esteem and inequity present in many organizations today.

Unfortunately, however, most companies cannot specify the formula for giving merit increases because there is no formula. Performance appraisals don't distinguish managers from each other since most managers are rated above average or higher. Line managers in most companies aren't told what the formula is, and they distribute the merit pay based on their own individual rule, which varies department by department and manager by manager.

The point is that most firms may have a merit plan in principle but do not have a merit program in fact. As a test, ask yourself these questions:

Could I lay off managers based on their last merit increases—that is, if I had to reduce my managerial staff by 10 percent, could I identify these people by their last performance appraisal and merit increase?

Would my line managers trust their own performance appraisals enough to have no other say in the merit increase—that is, could the compensation manager apply your company's formula by using the performance appraisal data only with no other consultation with the supervisor? If not, I would venture that the reason lies in our failure to examine our merit plans to see why we do what we do and what impact it has on performance. Lack of knowledge about our own system is probably the main reason we don't have openness about our merit system.

2. *Supervisors should be trained in rating and feedback techniques.* Personnel managers should help design and carry out training programs that emphasize the necessity for consistency between performance ratings, other forms of feedback, and pay increases. In addition, managers should be trained to emphasize objective instead of subjective areas of job performance. Skinner in a recent interview in *Organizational Dynamics* states that poor training of managers is one of the greatest weakness in the motivation of workers through reinforcement principles. Stressing the need for effective training programs for managers, he predicted that "in the not too distant future, a new breed of industrial managers may be able to apply the principles of operant conditioning effectively."

3. *Components of the annual pay increase should be clearly and openly specified.* Organizations should allocate a certain percentage for both a cost-of-living increase (not to cover the total cost of living, however) and a percentage for merit. The percentage for merit should be an average and not a maximum, and the manager should be able to distribute this percentage in steps or degrees. In other words, it should not be an either-or-situation where the worker either gets the full amount of the merit increase or none at all.

Any pay increase due to an adjustment for past inequities and pay increases due to promotions should come out of the payroll increase first, but it should not be included in the stated average pay increase. For example, if the organization can afford a 10 percent increase in wages and benefits, it might take 2 percent of this amount to use for the adjustments mentioned above and then allocate an 8 percent average increase to cost of living (say, 4 percent) and merit (not including adjustments). Along these lines, I feel it is important to give the increases in percentages and not dollar amounts since managers have a tendency to "cheat" long-term good performers (high-pay managers) when a dollar amount is used.

While I oppose having an absolute upper limit placed on a job range, many companies have this type of system. Where they do, it is important that managers and staff people in this job classification system know about the upper limit so that they are not surprised when they reach it.

Along this same line, many companies, in an attempt to avoid reaching the upper limit, give managers merit increases every 29 or 36 months rather than once a year. This is too long a period between merit increases. I therefore suggest that less money be allocated to annual cost-of-living increments, with the larger remaining amount going into the merit fund, and the increases awarded at least every 18 months.

Another related issue should be noted: In departments with a large number of senior employees who are eligible for only the minimum raise (due to an upper limit classification system), the full 8 percent should not be allocated for the pay increases. If it is, the department manager is tempted to overcompensate the less senior department members in order to spend the money he is allocated.

4. *Each organization should custom tailor its pay plan to the needs of the organization and individuals therein—with participation a key factor in the merit pay plan design.* One of the reasons the Scanlon plan (a group incentive plan) has been so successful is that it combines participation with the company's ability to afford a merit increase. Workers understand how they get their increases and how the amounts are set. In addition, each company using a Scanlon approach has a unique pay plan designed especially for that organization by the members of the organization.

In an example of a creative merit system, the Bendix Corporation decided to distribute its 1974 Christmas bonus to middle and lower-middle managers based on merit. An average bonus of $1,500 per manager was distributed, but some managers received little or nothing whereas others received a healthy share. When combined with the regular merit increase, this feedback should have great informational value to the manager, especially in these economically depressed times when even managers themselves fear indefinite layoffs.

5. *Don't overlook other rewards.* Compensation managers should work with other staff people in the organization to improve the organizational climate, task design, and other forms of reward to ensure that an employee has as much chance of success as possible.

Ethical Implications

No discussion of effective uses of merit pay plans would be complete without a discussion of managers' ethical responsibilities in using pay as a motivator. There is no doubt that poorly designed reward structures can interfere with the development of spontaneity and creativity. Deceptive reinforcement systems and manipulation insult the integrity of man. The employee should be a willing party to the influence attempt, with both parties benefiting from the relationship.

The ethical responsibility of managers in the area of compensation is clear. The first step in the ethical use of monetary control in organizations is the understanding by managers of the determination of behavior. Since reinforcement is the single most important concept in the learning process, managers must learn how to design effective reinforcement programs that will encourage productive and creative employees.

The Scanlon Plan Has Proved Itself

FRED G. LESIEUR
ELBRIDGE S. PUCKETT

This is an excellent time to take a good look at the general principles of employee participation in management—and probably the best time in history to examine the Scanlon Plan in particular. Recent technological advances involving the computer, numerically controlled machine tools, and many other forms of automated processes have brought the activities of blue- and white-collar workers closer together than ever before. The ability of these employees to work together and with management has an enormous impact on a company's success in utilizing the new technologies. Moreover, a recent Supreme Court decision may have a profound effect on some kinds of incentive systems, particularly those of the individual and small group types.[1] In affirming a union's right to discipline an employee who exceeds his piecework norm, the Court has, in the opinion of many observers, undermined a long-established sector of the incentive system.

In contrast to other, more limited forms of incentive schemes, the Scanlon Plan offers a flexible vehicle through which company, union, and employees can meet changes in conditions, in technology, and in corporate structure in a manner that is mutually rewarding for all.

In the first section of this article we will briefly outline the basic philosophy and structure generally employed in a Scanlon-type plan.

Next we will analyze the experiences of three companies that have employed the

---

Reprinted by permission from *Harvard Business Review*, vol. 47 (1969), pp. 109–19; copyright © 1969 by the President and Fellows of Harvard College; all rights reserved.

Scanlon Plan and Scanlon's philosophy successfully for a long period of time. It should be noted at the outset that in each of the cases the company was economically healthy and successful prior to its adoption of the Scanlon Plan. This is a reflection of the fact that the work of Scanlon and his successors since World War II has been largely with "normal, healthy cases," as opposed to the Depression cases with which he worked in the prewar era.

In the third section we will draw some conclusions from these experiences and generalize as to their significance.

Operating Features

Although the Scanlon Plan is often thought of as comprising a structure of participation committees and a particular type of performance measurement, actually its most important feature is Scanlon's basic philosophy. Scanlon's first thoughts about employee participation in the workplace resulted from his experiences during the Depression, when citizens worked together in a common endeavor to solve the very austere problems facing the community. The first application of his philosophy, in a marginally profitable steel mill, contained no performance measurement or bonus provisions, but represented a successful attempt to harness the full efforts of management and the work force in order to save an organization that otherwise might very well have gone under.[2]

Scanlon deeply believed that the typical company organization did not elicit the full potential from employees, either as individuals or as a group. He did not feel that the commonly held concept that "the boss is the boss and a worker works" was a proper basis for stimulating the interest of employees in company problems; rather, he felt such a concept reinforced employees' belief that there was an "enemy" somewhere above them in the hierarchy and that a cautious suspicion should be maintained at all times. He felt that employee interest and contribution could best be stimulated by providing the employee with a maximum amount of information and data concerning company problems and successes, and by soliciting his contribution as to how he felt the problem might best be solved and the job best done.

Thus the Scanlon Plan is a common sharing between management and employees of problems, goals, and ideas. Scanlon felt that individual incentives worked against employee participation of this nature. He believed that individual incentives put the direct worker in business for himself, pitted him against the broader interests of the company, and produced inequities in the wage structure that in turn led to poor employee morale. His concept of a system of rewards that would stimulate employee interest and acceptance of technological change involved an appropriate wage structure reflecting (1) individual skills and (2) additional rewards, based on the success of the enterprise, to be shared by all employees and management.

In almost all the cases with which we are familiar, companies implement this philosophy of participation with a committee system made up of departmental production committees and an overall screening or steering committee. However, in very small plants, one plantwide committee may be sufficient.

Production Committees

Departmental production committees are made up of two or more employees, depending on the size of the department, and one or two management members. The management members are appointed by the company, and experience has shown that it is very important to have whoever is heading the department or area (such as a foreman, office manager, or chief engineer) take an active part as chairman of the committee. Employee members are usually elected by the employees in the department; in some cases they are appointed by the union leadership.

Committees meet regularly and discuss suggestions for improvements. The employee members must be allowed a certain amount of time to contact other employees to obtain new suggestions and to discuss the action taken on pending suggestions. In one very successful application of the plan which is reported later in this article, a company has broadened the duties of employee members to make them responsible for chasing down the results of pending suggestions. This job usually belongs to the foreman, but the company has found that putting the responsibility on the shoulders of employee members stimulates employee interest in general and facilitates getting rapid action on suggestions. This company has maintained a record for getting action on suggestions that is as good as any we have seen.

Is committee work time-consuming? Experience in all three of the companies to be reported shows that the amount of time employee members lose from their regular jobs, either in attending meetings or in contacting employees, is surprisingly low. The production committee gets together formally once a month. At this meeting its members:

1. Make sure that they have recorded each suggestion that has been submitted during the month and any action which has been taken. (Usually, one of the employee members has the responsibility for seeing that all suggestions have been recorded and sent to the person or department in the company that types up the minutes of all production committees and returns a copy to each committee member.)

2. Process all suggestions, attend to previous suggestions on which action has not been completed, and then take up any other business considered important to the department's performance. (Such discussion may take many forms. Often a foreman or other member presents a departmental problem which he wants the committee to evaluate in the hope of achieving a solution. These problems range all the way from the layout of new equipment to cost factors on specific products.)

Although the majority of suggestions are approved by committees, the committees do not have the right to accept or reject ideas presented. That right is reserved by management. Moreover, there is one area of business that the production committee must *not* get into. This has to do with union business, grievances, wages, and so forth. The committee deals exclusively with operating improvements.

If the production committee has been functioning properly during the month and is doing its job thoroughly, the meetings described may take approximately one hour or slightly longer. If the production meeting is over in 15 minutes, it is clear that the committee is functioning strictly as a suggestion committee and probably is not getting sufficient management leadership and direction.

Screening Function

The minutes of the production committee are forwarded as quickly as possible to the screening committee, which meets once each month—as soon as the accounting department can make available the figures reporting the performance of the previous month. The chairman of this committee is usually a top executive who serves along with other top executives from the various departments of the company. The president, steward, or other officer of the local union or unions involved usually serves, too, and employee members represent various areas. In some cases the employee member may represent two or more production committee areas; in other cases there may be an employee member from each production committee area. As at the production committee level, the employee members are usually elected by their constituents, but in some cases they may be appointed by the union. The screening committee members proceed as follows:

1. Their first order of business is to go over the performance of the previous month and analyze the reasons why it was favorable or not so favorable, as the case might be. One of the most important functions of each member is to understand fully the economic variables that affect the bonus result, so that he or she can impart such information to other employees. Employees must understand the results and have complete confidence in the method of measurement which is employed. In each of the three situations to be discussed, the company faced periods (sometimes of many months) when economic conditions offered little or no bonus opportunity. Yet, during such periods, participation and employee interest remained at a high level. The results attained during these periods of hardship, in our judgment, provide the real proof of how well Scanlon's philosophy was being implemented.

2. Their second function is to take up any company problems or matters of interest which management wants to communicate to all employees. For example, we have seen the sales department bring a competitor's product into the meeting, so that members could analyze the kind of competitive problems that they were facing. Again, samples of new products which the company has developed are often the topic of discussion, thus giving employees a chance to visualize the production problems they will eventually be facing. Usually an area of great interest at every screening meeting is the sales and economic outlook—the opportunities and possible problems that lie ahead.

3. They discuss and take care of any suggestions which have not been resolved at the production committee level. Hopefully, a vast majority of suggestions will have been handled at the lower level. However, there are certain areas (e.g., capital expenditures and new equipment) which involve the company as a whole, and problems in these areas must go to a higher level to be resolved. In a sense, the screening committee is also considered a kind of "court of higher appeal" for suggestions which have not met with approval at the production committee level but which the suggestor would like to have considered further.

In all cases there is no voting by the committee on suggestions, but there is thorough discussion of all points of view when there is disagreement. After careful consideration, management makes the final decision.

Measurement of Rewards

From the standpoint of employees, the payoff of a Scanlon Plan is in dollars and cents. How is the amount of reward determined?

Companies employing the Scanlon Plan follow widely-differing methods of measuring the amounts of bonus payments to employees. In some of Scanlon's early work, profit sharing was the basis of bonus rewards. In recent years the most commonly used type of measurement is what is loosely termed a sales value of production ratio, where the ratio of total payroll to sales value of production (net sales plus or minus the change in inventory) in a prior base period is compared with the ratio in the current period.[3] Any improvement in this ratio provides a bonus pool. Part of this pool is set aside in a reserve against deficit months (months when the ratio goes above that of the base period). The amount set aside is determined by analysis of past fluctuations in the ratio.

After removing the reserved amount from the bonus pool each month, the remainder is divided. Usually 25 percent is the company's share, and 75 percent is paid out to all employees as that month's performance bonus. Participation usually encompasses everyone in the company up to and including the president, or, in the case of a very large, multiplant company, everyone employed in the facility in which the plan is in effect. The bonus is distributed as a percentage of the employee's gross income during that accounting period, so that the bonus paid reflects differentials in wages or salaries paid for differences in job content. (Federal Wage and Hour Law provisions require that Scanlon bonuses be reflected in any overtime premiums which the employee earns. For this reason "gross income" must include overtime premiums.)

At the end of a "Scanlon Year" the reserve pool remaining after providing for any offsetting deficits is split up in the same manner as the monthly bonuses. The company retains its share, and the remainder is paid out as a year-end bonus (in the same proportions as the monthly bonuses).

Other types of measurements that have been used are for the most part similar to the one just described in that the total payroll of the participants comprises the numerator of the ratio. Variations in the denominator have entailed the use of:

1. Net sales without adjustments for changes in inventory.
2. Sales value added, where purchased materials are subtracted from sales value of production.
3. Physical production count, on which sales dollars are imputed (this is limited to the manufacture of a single product, and has some severe drawbacks).

Each of the three companies to be discussed employs a sales-value-of-production type of measurement. In one case, only finished-good inventory is included in the calculations; it is priced at sales value. In a second case, work-in-process and finished-good inventories are included, and they are factored to a conservative sales valuation. In the third case, all inventories are included, valued at cost in the same manner as on the company's financial statements.

Case Studies

Now let us look at the Scanlon Plan in practice. We shall take three cases, each representing problems and conditions different from the others, the one common characteristic being that the plan has been in effect ten or more years. The variety of these cases demonstrates how flexible the Scanlon Plan is; it can be tailored to fit a multitude of situations. For a summary of some of the company facts, see table 1.

Atwood Vacuum Machine Co.

This family-owned company, with its corporate headquarters located in Rockford, Illinois, has had the Scanlon Plan for 14 years. Six plants are covered. Total employment is in excess of 2,000 people. Everyone participates in the program, including the president of the company. At the time the Scanlon Plan was implemented, an individual incentive system was dropped.

Atwood is a supplier of automotive parts hardware to all of the major automobile manufacturers. It also has a general product division which manufactures proprietary products, such as trailer hitches, brake actuating systems, and trailer hot-water heaters. Each of the plants bargains individually with an independent union.

With a major share of its volume going to the automotive industry, the company is faced with the possibility of going out of business each model year. The fact that the company is making a certain component for the auto industry in 1969, for instance, certainly does not guarantee that it will be making it in 1970.

Each plant has its own Scanlon production committees. These committees are composed of employee, union, and management representatives. However, there are only two plants holding monthly screening committee meetings; the plants located within a 55-mile radius of Rockford attend the screening committee meeting held there, while at the same time the other two plants, located over 200 miles away, join in holding a screening committee meeting. The company sends at least one executive from the main plant to attend the latter meeting.

TABLE 1
Three Companies Using Scanlon Plans

	Atwood	*Parker*	*Pfaudler*
Number of employees	2,000	1,000	750
Number of plants	6	1	1
Union affiliations	3 (independent)	2 (AFL-CIO)	2 (AFL-CIO)
Product	Automotive hardware	Writing instruments	Project engineering, glassteel equipment, stainless steel equipment, food-filling equipment
Type of production	High volume; competitive	High volume consumer item	Custom as well as standard fabricating
Type of bonus measurement	Payroll/sales value of production	Payroll/sales value of production	Payroll/sales value of production
Frequency of reviewing measurement	Annually	Periodically	Periodically
Prior incentive plans	Individual incentive	Individual incentive	No incentives

Top management feels it is imperative that all of these plants operate under one plan. Depending on how severe the model changeover may be in a given year, one plant may very well be affected more than another is. Having them all together provides much-needed stability. It also facilitates the transfer of jobs from one plant to another.

Turning now to the record of incentive payments under the plan, the most important facts are these:

1. During the 14 years of the Scanlon Plan at Atwood, annual bonuses have ranged from a high of approximately 20 percent of the payroll to a low of approximately 5 percent.

2. In the 187 periods of operation (the company's accounting year consists of 13 four-week periods), bonuses have been earned in 163 periods.

3. The highest monthly bonus was approximately 26 percent.

4. There has been a close correlation between annual profits and bonuses paid.

In terms of suggestions received under the Scanlon Plan, Atwood has no peer. Over 25,000 suggestions have been turned in by employees.

A significant indicator of the efficacy of an incentive plan is whether sales or production grows in proportion to payroll. If payroll grows proportionately larger over the years, that is a *sign* (not necessarily an absolutely correct one) that incentives are not as effective as they should be. What is Atwood's experience in this connection? The measurement of performance used is total payroll to sales value of production; this ratio today is within 0.5 percent of the ratio at the time the plan was started 14 years ago. This is evidence of increased worker efficiency combined with willing acceptance of the technological changes introduced by management. Because of the volatility of the Atwood business, the method of measurement is evaluated every year.

Parker Pen Co.

In this company the Scanlon Plan is used solely in the Manufacturing Division, located in Janesville, Wisconsin. There are approximately 1,000 employees covered by the plan; it has been in operation for 14 years. There are two international unions involved; one is the United Rubber Workers of America, AFL-CIO, Local No. 663, covering the production workers, and the other is the International Association of Machinists, AFL-CIO, Lodge No. 1266, covering the tool room group. The company manufactures superior-quality writing instruments which are sold domestically and exported throughout the world. The Janesville plant also supplies component parts to Parker subsidiaries located throughout the world.

Management installed the plan after disposing of an individual incentive system. That system had been in effect for many years, and both management and the union felt it had outlived its usefulness. Under the system, the company had had trouble introducing automated or mechanical changes. Moreover, by 1954, costs had risen so that approximately 50 percent of the company product was being made outside of Janesville, and the Janesville plant was gradually becoming an assembly operation.

Probably one of the greatest benefits the company has received from the plan has been the acceptance of automation by the people involved. Partly as a result, the company now manufactures better than 80 percent of the product in the Janesville operation.

Unlike the other two companies described in this section, Parker makes a consumer product and hence gets locked in to certain price categories. For instance, the current Jotter ball pen, an important part of the company line, had a price of $1.98 established in 1955. The same price is in effect today. (How many other things can you buy today that have the same sales price as they had 14 years ago?)

As for bonuses paid, some of the salient facts are these:

1. The highest yearly average has been approximately 20 percent, and the lowest, 5½ percent.

2. During the 168 months of operation, bonuses have been paid in 142 months. The highest monthly bonus was approximately 30 percent.

3. The correlation between bonuses paid and division profits has been excellent.

If one were to ask management what it feels is the most important asset that the Scanlon Plan has brought to the company, the answer probably would be willingness to accept change. Out of this cooperative spirit have developed more jobs, whereas the trend was to fewer jobs prior to installation of the plan. As for the ratio of payroll to sales which is used for measuring bonuses, it is slightly in excess of one percentage point of what it was back in 1954. This fact is evidence of increased worker efficiency along with willing acceptance of technological changes introduced by management.

Pfaudler Co.

This company, a division of Sybron Corporation, is located in Rochester, New York. It produces chemical, pharmaceutical, food-manufacturing, and brewery equipment. The Scanlon Plan has been in existence at Pfaudler's for 17 years; the number of employees covered by the plan is approximately 750, and they work in the Manufacturing Division. There are two unions involved, the United Steelworkers of America, AFL-CIO, Local No. 1495, and the Coppersmithing Branch of Sheet Metal Trades, Local No. 356.

On many occasions we have heard executives at Pfaudler describe it as a "large job shop." By that they mean that much of its product is scientifically engineered and tailored to fit a specific application of a customer company in the chemical industry. Sales are highly volatile. For instance, because Pfaudler supplies in excess of 70 percent of the world's needs for glass-lined chemical equipment, it is faced from time to time with either a substantial backlog of orders or a pronounced lack of orders. The company's manufacturing cycle—the period from the time when an order is booked to the first delivery on the order—is generally 12 weeks.

The plan has been most effective in dealing with either an overabundance of orders or a lack of them. As a result of the work of the various production committees and the screening committee, these ups and downs the company faces have been shortened on the downward cycle; the cooperation of the people involved has very often brought in work that otherwise would have gone to someone else.

The type of activity that the screening and production committees have engaged in has been very broad in range. For example:

> Several years ago a major chemical company had a disastrous explosion at one of its operations. The company was desirous of placing the entire order of approximately 20 large units with Pfaudler, but was hesitant to do so because of the length of time before delivery could be expected. The Pfaudler management got the screening and production committees together for a series of meetings and discussed the order with them. It meant producing the equipment in a 7-week cycle rather than the normal 12-week cycle for this type of equipment. In these discussions, ways for doing the work were considered which demanded extreme flexibility in the plant. The discussions were fruitful, and the production time was shortened. Pfaudler was awarded the entire order and went on to meet the delivery deadline. Significantly, other work scheduled to be completed during this time was also kept on schedule.

During each rebuilding and expansion program that the company has undertaken, production committees in the areas affected have had an opportunity, prior to the program getting under way, to pore over the blueprints of the work to be done. Committee members have raised questions concerning the layout of the equipment and recommended changes to ensure the best possible utilization of the new facilities.

Thousands of suggestions for change and improvement have been studied. Many of the ideas have produced substantial savings in cost or have brought improved quality.

As for the bonuses paid to employees participating in the plan, the highlights of the past 17 years are as follows:

1. The highest annual bonus year was 17½ percent of wages for the year, and the lowest was approximately 3 percent of wages.
2. Over the 204 months of operation, bonuses have been paid in 179 months.
3. The highest bonus earned during a given month was approximately 22 percent.

Major Findings

It is interesting to note that two of the three situations discussed had individual incentive systems in effect prior to installation of the Scanlon Plan. Both companies were (as they are today) high-volume producers of standard products—situations which would be expected to lend themselves very well to the use of standards and individual incentive arrangements. However, in both cases it was found that a Scanlon-type plan achieved better results than individual incentives did. In this respect, the cases are typical of many others in corporate experience. Why does the Scanlon approach lead to better results? Reasons like the following are important:

1. Working under the Scanlon Plan, an employee finds it more natural to take a broader view of the company's problems.
2. Management finds it easier to stress quality production, if that is important, in a Scanlon Plan environment than where the direct worker is paid according to his specific operation.
3. Getting the cooperation and support of the indirect servicing groups—i.e., total room, maintenance, and materials handling—is much easier when these groups receive incentive earnings.
4. Through their committee activity, managers are able to discuss company objectives with employees and attain a response that is not possible under an individual incentive system. It is very important that the participants look on the success of the enterprise as being the basis for their own individual success. When this attitude is present, the entire organization responds to problems—such as quality problems, stepped-up schedules, and customer delays—in a way calculated to get them solved as quickly as possible.

The third company—Pfaudler—did not have individual incentives prior to adopting Scanlon. It had never felt that its type of production lent itself to incentive systems other than the plant-wide type. Its experience under the Scanlon Plan has been much the same as at Atwood and Parker in terms of employee interest in better job methods, better quality, and better productivity generally.

Acceptance of Change

One of the most interesting aspects of the experience of these companies (and of numerous others) concerns employee attitudes toward technological change and new equipment. While there is a natural human reluctance to change, employees in Atwood, Parker, and Pfaudler are now pushing management to bring in new equipment and to get it operating properly for the benefit of all. In one case, the company had introduced a substantial amount of equipment which was not functioning up to expectations. At production and screening meetings, employee members pointedly and vociferously kept suggesting how the equipment could be utilized to better advantage.

In the three companies, managers devote a portion of the time at production and screening meetings to discussion of future plans with respect to plant expansion and new equipment. Pfaudler has had excellent results in the plant expansion programs it has undertaken in Rochester by submitting the detailed blueprints of equipment layout and other matters to the production committees that would eventually be located in the areas of expansion. Suggestions made by employees have sometimes led to modifying or changing the layout, which has resulted in a smoother flow of work through the department.

Management finds that discussing plans well in advance creates an interest in the organization and minimizes fears that might otherwise develop. Its experience has shown that thorough discussion of planned changes enables members of the organization (management as well as employees) to realize that the new technology is not going to bring with it all sorts of ills that cannot be solved satisfactorily.

Measuring Performance

The three companies in the case studies take different approaches to the question of how best to measure performance and review the measurements used:

1. At Atwood, management feels it must review performance measurements at the end of each automotive model year. The new product mix and its effect on normal labor content in the sales dollar becomes a fundamental part of this review, along with the other economic variables which might affect the equities of the parties in the plan.

An interesting aspect of this review is that the accounting services have been set up so that a computer can execute the very voluminous computations needed to determine whether a very complicated new product mix has a different average direct labor content than did the previous one (differences are based on the volume projections which have been supplied by the automotive companies). Although the ratio of labor to sales may change from year to year, it has never changed much more than one percentage point at a time, and it is currently within one half of a percentage point from where it started 15 years ago.

2. At Parker, management began by changing the basic labor-sales ratio every time a measurable change occurred which might affect the norm. During the first year the ratio was changed twice. Then it was determined that a complete review would be made once each year and the ratio changed only at that time, if need be. After several years of such studies, it was decided that the situation had shown such stability that an annual review was not needed. Since then, the norm has been reviewed only when major changes in conditions have occurred.

As has been mentioned, prices for the company's products have been extremely "sticky" during the recent years of general price inflation. At the same time, the company has negotiated regularly with its two unions and has increased wages in line with area and national patterns. Hence, with little price relief available, the company has had to work very hard in the area of technological change in order to maintain the ratio of payroll to sales prices within one and one-half percentage points of where it was 15 years ago. The cooperation and interest of employees has been a key ingredient in the success of this effort.

3. The approach at Pfaudler has been to leave the measurement ratio alone unless changing conditions require a new norm. Management feels that prices of company products can follow wage increases, thus allowing a good degree of stability in the

ratio. However, management does maintain a constant watch on the labor content in the product mix, as it bids repeatedly on large contracts.

Over the years, the corporation has experienced a great degree of growth as a result of mergers and acquisitions. Corporate personnel have been moved from the plant to a new corporate headquarters and are no longer part of the Scanlon Plan. Consequently, the labor-sales ratio at Pfaudler is substantially lower today than it was 17 years ago.

Impact on Efficiency

One highly significant conclusion that emerges from corporate experience with the Scanlon Plan concerns the relationship between the kind of production process involved and the quality of employee participation. The nature of the production process may influence the *direction* that participation and suggestions take, but the general quality of participation can be equally high *regardless* of the type of operation. The three cases described are one demonstration of this finding.

At Atwood the volatility of the product mix and the rigorous demands of the auto industry exert a great deal of pressure on management to evaluate suggestions immediately and apply them (if they are useful) as soon as possible. A vast majority of the suggestions are processed within one month of the time of submission. Because of high production runs, a small saving per unit of product cost can add up to a substantial saving in total if the timing is right. For instance, at the beginning of production of a new model, an improvement in tooling may be very profitable. Toward the end of the model run, however, improved tooling may not be feasible because the costs cannot be amortized over a large enough volume of production.

At Parker Pen, as at Atwood, a suggestion affecting a high-volume product can produce a substantial saving. However, the relationship of the company to its market makes the situation quite different. Whereas Atwood may be concerned with the approval of only one customer, Parker's customers number in the thousands. Where a suggestion involves changing the aesthetic appeal of a particular writing instrument, a very difficult judgment must be made concerning the impact on sales. Suggestions may take longer to be resolved in this kind of operation, and the technical evaluation may be further removed from the eyes of the employee.

Management has found that where a marketing decision is involved, it is very important to get a complete answer back to the employee so that he maintains his interest in further participation. If the employee feels that his suggestion got short shrift from someone "on the hill," it is difficult to get another idea from him.

At Pfaudler the value of one unit of product is so high that one failure can be costly. Also, the technology of glassteel makes the production problem an interesting challenge. While there is great emphasis on implementing new ideas so that they can be utilized on the current equipment in the plant, suggestions may run into technical ramifications that require a year or longer to resolve.

In short, the success of the Scanlon Plan is measured by the ability of the organization to tackle and solve the problems posed by production. In spite of the wide differences in operations in the three companies described here, they all have experienced a high degree of participation which has contributed to production efficiency.

Union Reactions

How do unions react to the Scanlon Plan? Do they benefit as employees do? In each of the three situations described, the unions have negotiated regularly and have attained increases in wages and fringe benefits in line with patterns established in the labor market, the industry, or the nation generally. In none of these companies, nor in others we know that are using the Scanlon Plan, has there been less employee interest in the results of negotiation or in the union generally. Moreover, having been involved daily with the company's situation as a result of Scanlon Plan participation, union officials find themselves approaching the bargaining table with much more knowledge of the company's situation; thus they are better able to tell fact from fiction in management's statements. By the same token, the company has a better understanding of the union's problems and needs.

In many union-management relationships the most difficult problem for the union leader is to get top management to sit down and discuss the various problems that are plaguing the union and its membership. A basic prerequisite for success with the Scanlon approach is that management be "willing to listen." Where the plan is in operation, therefore, it should not be surprising that the number of written grievances has dropped markedly. This does not imply that there are no longer any problems or that the unions play a lesser role in solving problems. The significance is that mutually satisfactory solutions were developed without going through four stages of grievance procedure and on to arbitration.

As every international union representative knows, the local which is most difficult to satisfy is the one which deals with a company that says *no* to everything. If the Scanlon approach eases such a relationship, it will surely result in a membership that is better satisfied with the efforts of the international union.

Conclusion

The three situations described in this article pose just about all of the kinds of *problems* that most industrial plants are facing today. What may distinguish the three companies more is that they all have good management. If you talk to the president or other managers in the companies, you find one common characteristic: they all know there is no substitute for good management. It is also important to note that in each of the companies the union is ably directed. In other words, the Scanlon Plan is not used as a crutch for good leadership.

Each of the companies described has gone through business cycles, through good times as well as bad. Executives in the plants will tell you that the value and strength of a Scanlon Plan is just as good when the going is rough as when business is good.

Probably most important to the success of a Scanlon Plan is that everyone in the organization knows management wants to work with employees to improve operations. This should be made very clear to all personnel from top to bottom. The message of the Scanlon Plan is simple: operations improvement is an area where management, the union, and employees can get together without strife. Collaboration is part of the job. In applying a Scanlon Plan, a company in essence says to its employees, "Look, we can run the company—we have run it for a number of years—we can run it well. But we think we can run it much better if you will help us. We're willing to listen."

Notes

1. See *Scofield et al.* v. *National Labor Relations Board et al.* (Wisconsin Motors), U.S. Supreme Court, No. 273, April 1, 1969.

2. For a full discussion of the work of Joseph N. Scanlon, see *The Scanlon Plan: A Frontier in Labor Management Cooperation*, edited by Fred G. Lesieur (Cambridge, The M.I.T. Press, 1958), Chapter I.

3. Ibid., pp. 65-79.

CHAPTER **8**

Job and Work Satisfaction

For years many in industrial psychology held to the belief that job satisfaction causes job performance. Now, after decades of research, it is known that this is not generally true. In fact, as Lawler points out in his article in this chapter, the opposite relation may hold: performance may cause satisfaction. Even though they may not cause performance, job satisfaction and job attitudes are important. First, the degree of satisfaction and fulfillment that people derive from their work life is an important consideration in itself. And, as Lawler points out, a theory of job satisfaction is necessary to the understanding of the processes involved in producing satisfaction and dissatisfaction. Second, job dissatisfaction is apparently a cause of absenteeism and turnover, as the review of research evidence by Porter and Steer clearly indicates. An understanding of these processes, therefore, is an important prerequisite for managerial success.

Satisfaction and Behavior

E. E. LAWLER

Compared to what is known about motivation, relatively little is known about the determinants and consequences of satisfaction. Most of the psychological research on motivation simply has not been concerned with the kinds of affective reactions that people experience in association with or as a result of motivated behavior. No well-developed theories of satisfaction have appeared and little theoretically based research has been done on satisfaction. . . . Most of the research on the study of satisfaction has

From *Motivation in Work Organizations,* by E. E. Lawler. Copyright © 1973 by Wadsworth Publishing Company, Inc. Reprinted by permission of the publisher, Brooks/Cole Publishing Company, Monterey, California.

been done by psychologists interested in work organizations. This research dates back to the 1930s. Since that time, the term "job satisfaction" has been used to refer to affective attitudes or orientations on the part of individuals toward jobs. Hoppock published a famous monograph on job satisfaction in 1935, and in 1939 the results of the well-known Western Electric studies were published. The Western Electric studies (Roethlisberger & Dickson, 1939) emphasized the importance of studying the attitudes, feelings, and perceptions employees have about their jobs. Through interviews with over 20,000 workers, these studies graphically made the point that employees have strong affective reactions to what happens to them at work. The Western Electric studies also suggested that affective reactions cause certain kinds of behavior, such as strikes, absenteeism, and turnover. Although the studies failed to show any clear-cut relationship between satisfaction and job performance, the studies did succeed in stimulating a tremendous amount of research on job satisfaction. During the last 30 years, thousands of studies have been done on job satisfaction. Usually, these studies have not been theoretically oriented; instead, researchers have simply looked at the relationship between job satisfaction and factors such as age, education, job level, absenteeism rate, productivity, and so on. Originally, much of the research seemed to be stimulated by a desire to show that job satisfaction is important because it influences productivity. Underlying the earlier articles on job satisfaction was a strong conviction that "happy workers are productive workers." Recently, however, this theme has been disappearing, and many organizational psychologists seem to be studying job satisfaction simply because they are interested in finding its causes. . . .

The recent interest in job satisfaction also ties in directly with the rising concern in many countries about the quality of life. [Editors note: The concept of "quality of work" or "quality of life" is receiving a large amount of emphasis in speeches made by industrial psychologists, labor leaders, and managers. We believe it will become an important issue of concern for personnel managers in the very near future.] There is an increasing acceptance of the view that material possessions and economic growth do not necessarily produce a high quality of life. Recognition is now being given to the importance of the kinds of affective reactions that people experience and to the fact that these are not always tied to economic or material accomplishments. Through the Department of Labor and the Department of Health, Education, and Welfare, the United States government has recently become active in trying to improve the affective quality of work life. Job satisfaction is one measure of the quality of life in organizations and is worth understanding and increasing even if it doesn't relate to performance. This reason for studying satisfaction is likely to be an increasingly prominent one as we begin to worry more about the effects working in organizations has on people and as our humanitarian concern for the kind of psychological experiences people have during their lives increases. What happens to people during the work day has profound effects both on the individual employee's life and on the society as a whole, and thus these events cannot be ignored if the quality of life in a society is to be high. As John Gardner has said,

> Of all the ways in which society serves the individual, few are more meaningful than to provide him with a decent job. . . . It isn't going to be a decent society for any of us until it is for all of us. If our sense of responsibility fails us, our sheer self-interest should come to the rescue [1968, p. 25].

As it turns out, satisfaction is related to absenteeism and turnover, both of which are very costly to organizations. Thus, there is a very "practical" economic reason for organizations to be concerned with job satisfaction, since it can influence organizational effectiveness. However, before any practical use can be made of the finding that job dissatisfaction causes absenteeism and turnover, we must understand what factors cause and influence job satisfaction. Organizations can influence job satisfaction and prevent absenteeism and turnover only if the organizations can pinpoint the factors causing and influencing these affective responses.

Despite the many studies, critics have legitimately complained that our understanding of the causes of job satisfaction has not substantially increased during the last 30 years (for example, see Locke, 1968, 1969) for two main reasons. The research on job satisfaction has typically been atheoretical and has not tested for causal relationships. Since the research has not been guided by theory, a vast array of unorganized, virtually uninterpretable facts have been unearthed. For example, a number of studies have found a positive relationship between productivity and job satisfaction, while other studies have found no evidence of this relationship. Undoubtedly, this disparity can be explained, but the explanation would have to be based on a theory of satisfaction, and at present no such theory exists. One thing the research on job satisfaction has done is to demonstrate the saying that "theory without data is fantasy; but data without theory is chaos!"

Due to the lack of a theory stating causal relationships, the research on job satisfaction has consistently looked simply for relationships among variables. A great deal is known about what factors are related to satisfaction, but very little is known about the causal basis for the relationships. This is a serious problem when one attempts to base change efforts on the research. This problem also increases the difficulty of developing and testing theories of satisfaction. Perhaps the best example of the resulting dilemma concerns the relationship between satisfaction and performance. If satisfaction causes performance, then organizations should try to see that their employees are satisfied; however, if performance causes satisfaction, then high satisfaction is not necessarily a goal but rather a by-product of an effective organization.

Why has the research on job satisfaction developed so slowly and in such an atheoretical way? One important reason seems to be the lack of attention paid to job satisfaction by psychologists interested in learning, development, and other traditional psychological topics. In marked contrast is the area of motivation where . . . a number of theories have been stated. Motivation theories from other areas of psychology have proven very helpful in understanding motivation in organizations and have formed the basis for our approach to thinking about motivation in organizations.

Unfortunately, no similar set of theories exists in the area of satisfaction. What little theory there is comes almost entirely from the research of industrial psychologists. In some cases this theory is not explicit but is implied by the way satisfaction is measured. For example, although Porter (1961) has never presented an actual theory of satisfaction, a particular manner of defining satisfaction is implicit in his approach to measuring need satisfaction. His approach indicates that he sees satisfaction as the difference between what a person thinks he should receive and what he feels he actually does receive. Before examining in detail any of the theories of job satisfaction, it is important to distinguish between the concepts of facet or factor satisfaction and overall job satisfaction. Facet satisfaction refers to people's affective reactions to particular aspects of their job. Pay, supervision, and promotion opportunities are frequently studied facets. Job satisfaction refers to a person's affective reactions to his total work role. . . .

Theories of Job Satisfaction

Four approaches can be identified in the theoretical work on satisfaction. Fulfillment theory was the first approach to develop. Equity theory and discrepancy theory developed later, partially as reactions against the shortcomings of fulfillment theory. Two-factor theory, the fourth approach, represents an attempt to develop a completely new approach to thinking about satisfaction.

Fulfillment Theory

Schaffer (1953) has argued that "job satisfaction will vary directly with the extent to which those needs of an individual which can be satisfied are actually satisfied" (p. 3). Vroom (1964) also sees job satisfaction in terms of the degree to which a job provides the person with positively valued outcomes. He equates satisfaction with valence and adds "If we describe a person as satisfied with an object, we mean that the object has positive valence for him. However, satisfaction has a much more restricted usage. In common parlance, we refer to a person's satisfaction only with reference to objects which he possesses" (p. 100). Researchers who have adopted the fulfillment approach measure people's satisfaction by simply asking how much of a given facet or outcome they are receiving. Thus, these researchers view satisfaction as depending on how much of a given outcome or group of outcomes a person receives. . . .

Discrepancy Theory

Recently, many psychologists have argued for a discrepancy approach to thinking about satisfaction. They maintain that satisfaction is determined by the differences between the actual outcomes a person receives and some other outcome level. The theories differ widely in their definitions of this other outcome level. For some theories it is the outcome level the person feels should be received, and for other theories it is the outcome level the person expects to receive. All of the theoretical approaches argue that what is received should be compared with another outcome level, and when there is a difference—when received outcome is below the other outcome level—dissatisfaction results. Thus, if a person expects or thinks he should receive a salary of $10,000 and he receives one of only $8,000, the prediction is that he will be dissatisfied with his pay. Further, the prediction is that he will be more dissatisfied than the person who receives a salary of $9,000 and expects or thinks he should receive a salary of $10,000. . . .

Equity Theory

Equity theory is primarily a motivation theory, but it has some important things to say about the causes of satisfaction/dissatisfaction. Adams (1963, 1965) argues in his version of equity theory that satisfaction is determined by a person's perceived input-outcome balance in the following manner: the perceived equity of a person's rewards is determined by his input-outcome balance; this perceived equity, in turn, determines satisfaction. Satisfaction results when perceived equity exists, and dissatisfaction results when perceived inequity exists. Thus, satisfaction is determined by the perceived ratio of what a person receives from his job relative to what a person puts into his job. According to equity theory, either under-reward or over-reward can lead to dissatisfaction, although the feelings are somewhat different. The theory emphasizes that over-reward leads to feelings of guilt, while under-reward leads to feelings of unfair treatment. . . .

Two-factor Theory

Modern two-factor theory was originally developed in a book by Herzberg, Mausner, Peterson, and Capwell (1957), in which the authors stated that job factors could be classified according to whether the factors contribute primarily to satisfaction or to dissatisfaction. Two years later, Herzberg, Mausner, and Snyderman (1959) published the results of a research study, which they interpreted as supportive of the theory. Since 1959, much research has been directed toward testing two-factor theory. Two aspects of the theory are unique and account for the attention it has received. First, two-factor theory says that satisfaction and dissatisfaction do not exist on a continuum running from satisfaction through neutral to dissatisfaction. Two independent continua exist, one running from satisfied to neutral, and another running from dissatisfied to neutral (see Figure 1). Second, the theory stresses that different job facets influence feelings of satisfaction and dissatisfaction. Figure 2 presents the results of a study by Herzberg et al., which show that factors such as achievement recognition, work itself, and responsibility are mentioned in connection with satisfying experiences, while working conditions, interpersonal relations, supervision, and company policy are usually mentioned in connection with dissatisfying experiences. The figure shows the frequency with which each factor is mentioned in connection with high (satisfying) and low (dissatisfying) work experiences. As can be seen, achievement was present in over 40 percent of the satisfying experiences and less than 10 percent of the dissatisfying experiences.

Satisfied	Neutral

Dissatisfied	Neutral

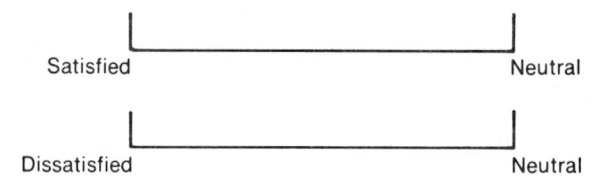

Figure 1. Two-factor Theory: Satisfaction Continued

Perhaps the most interesting aspect of Herzberg's theory is that at the same time a person can be very satisfied and very dissatisfied. Also, the theory implies that factors such as better working conditions cannot increase or cause satisfaction, they can only affect the amount of dissatisfaction that is experienced. The only way satisfaction can be increased is by effecting changes in those factors that are shown in Figure 2 as contributing primarily to satisfaction. . . .

Equity Theory and/or Discrepancy Theory

Equity theory and discrepancy theory are the two strongest theoretical explanations of satisfaction. Either theory could be used as a basis for thinking about the determinants of satisfaction. Fortunately it is not necessary to choose between the theories, since it is possible to build a satisfaction model that capitalizes on the strengths of each theory. . . . We will try to build such a model. In many ways, equity theory and discrepancy theory are quite similar. Both theories stress the importance of a person's perceived outcomes, along with the relationship of these outcomes to a second perception. In discrepancy theory, the second perception is what the outcomes should be or what the person wants the outcomes to be; in equity theory, the second perception is what a person's perceived inputs are in relation to other people's inputs and outcomes. Clearly, it could be argued that the two theories are talking about very similar concepts when they talk about perceived inputs and the subject's feeling about what his outcomes should be. A person's perception of what his outcomes should be is partly determined by what he feels his inputs are. Thus, the "should be" phrase from discrepancy theory and the "perceived inputs relative to other people's inputs and outcomes" phrase from equity theory are very similar.

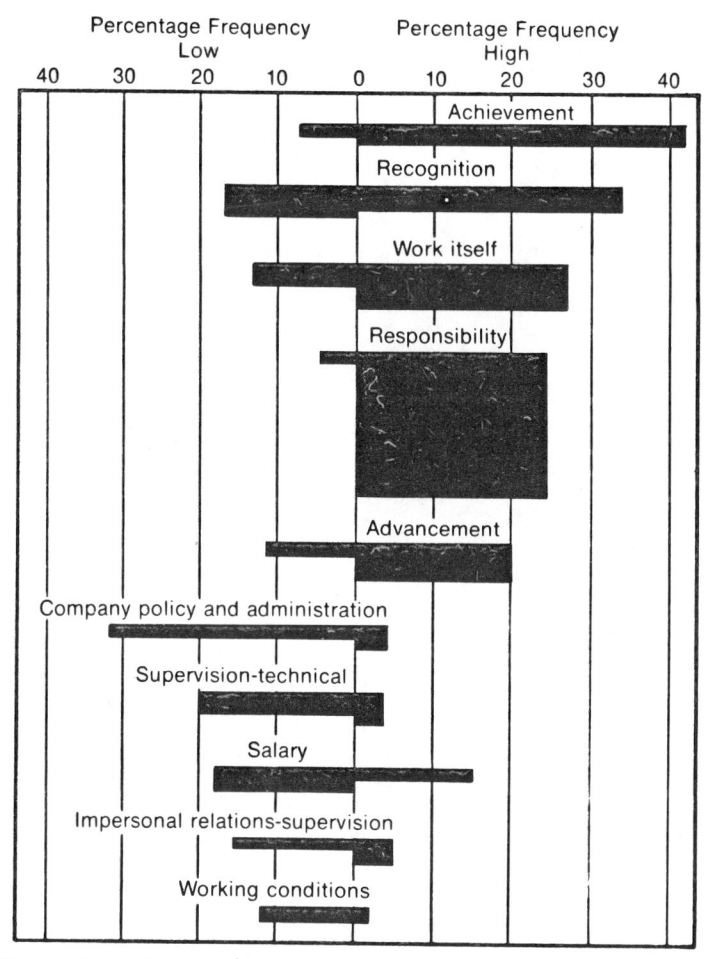

Figure 2. Comparison of Satisfiers and Dissatisfiers (Adapted from Herzberg et al., *The Motivation to Work*, 2nd ed., copyright ©1959 by John Wiley & Sons, Inc., reprinted by permission.)

Determinants of Satisfaction

The research on the determinants of satisfaction has looked primarily at two relationships: (1) the relationship between satisfaction and the characteristics of the job, and (2) the relationship between satisfaction and the characteristics of the person. Not surprisingly, the research shows that satisfaction is a function of both the person and the environment. These results are consistent with our approach to thinking about satisfaction . . . that personal factors influence what people feel they should receive and that job conditions influence both what people perceive they actually receive and what people perceive they should receive. . . .

The evidence on the effects of personal-input factors on satisfaction is voluminous and will be only briefly reviewed. The research clearly shows that personal factors do affect job satisfaction, basically because they influence perceptions of what outcomes should be. . . . The higher a person's perceived personal inputs—that is, the greater his education, skill, and performance—the more he feels he should receive. Thus, unless the high-input person receives more outcomes, he will be dissatisfied with his job and the rewards his job offers. Such straightforward relationships between inputs and satisfaction appear to exist for all personal-input factors except age and seniority. Evidence from the study of age and seniority suggests a curvilinear relationship (that is, high satisfaction among young and old workers, low satisfaction among middle-age workers) or even a relationship of increasing satisfaction with old age and tenure. The tendency of satisfaction to be high among older, long-term employees seems to be produced by the effects of selective turnover and the development of realistic expectations about what the job has to offer.

Consequences of Dissatisfaction

Originally, much of the interest in job satisfaction stemmed from the belief that job satisfaction influenced job performance. Specifically, psychologists thought that high job satisfaction led to high job performance. This view has now been discredited, and most psychologists feel that satisfaction influences absenteeism and turnover but not job performance. However, before looking at the relationship among satisfaction, absenteeism, and turnover, let's review the work on satisfaction and performance.

Job Performance

In the 1950s, two major literature reviews showed that in most studies only a slight relationship had been found between satisfaction and performance. A later review by Vroom (1964) also showed that studies had not found a strong relationship between satisfaction and performance; in fact, most studies had found a very low positive relationship between the two. In other words, better performers did seem to be slightly more satisfied than poor performers. A considerable amount of recent work suggests that the slight existing relationship is probably due to better performance indirectly causing satisfaction rather than the reverse. Lawler and Porter (1967) explained this "performance causes satisfaction" viewpoint as follows:

> If we assume that rewards cause satisfaction, and that in some cases performance produces rewards, then it is possible that the relationship found between satisfaction and performance comes about through the action of a third variable—rewards. Briefly stated, good performance may lead to rewards, which in turn lead to satisfaction; this formulation then would say that satisfaction rather than causing performance, as was previously assumed, is caused by it.
>
> [Figure 3] shows that performance leads to rewards, and it distinguishes between two kinds of rewards and their connection to performance. A wavy line between performance and extrinsic rewards indicates that such rewards are likely to be imperfectly related to performance. By extrinsic rewards is meant such organizationally controlled rewards as pay, promotion, status, and security—rewards that are often referred to as satisfying mainly lower-level needs. The connection is relatively weak because of the difficulty of tying extrinsic rewards directly to performance. Even though an organization may have a policy of re-

warding merit, performance is difficult to measure, and in dispensing rewards like pay, many other factors are frequently taken into consideration.

Quite the opposite is likely to be true for intrinsic rewards, however, since they are given to the individual by himself for good performance. Intrinsic or internally mediated rewards are subject to fewer disturbing influences and thus are likely to be more directly related to good performance. This connection is indicated in the model by a semi-wavy line. Probably the best example of an intrinsic reward is the feeling of having accomplished something worthwhile. For that matter any of the rewards that satisfy self-actualization needs or higher-order growth needs are good examples of intrinsic rewards [p. 23-24].[1]

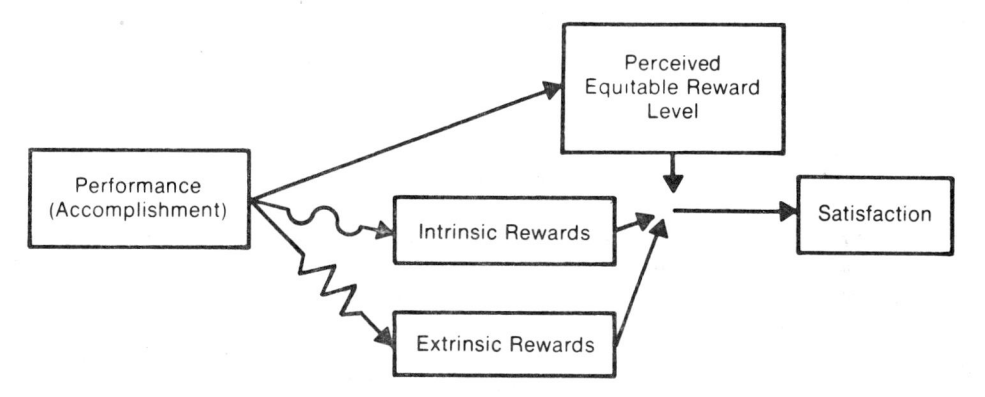

Figure 3. Model of the Relationship of Performance to Satisfaction (From Lawler, E. E., and Porter, L. W., "The Effect of Performance on Job Satisfaction," (in *Industrial Relations*, 1967, 7, 20-28. Reprinted by permission of the publisher, Industrial Relations.)

Figure 3 shows that intrinsic and extrinsic rewards are not directly related to job satisfaction, since the relationship is moderated by perceived equitable rewards (what people think they should receive). The model in Figure 3 . . . shows that satisfaction is a function of the amount of rewards a person receives and the amount of rewards he feels he should receive.

Because of the imperfect relationship between performance and rewards and the important effect of perceived equitable rewards, a low but positive relationship should exist between job satisfaction and job performance in most situations. However, in certain situations, a strong positive relationship may exist; while in other situations, a negative relationship may exist. A negative relationship would be expected where rewards are unrelated to performance or negatively related to performance.

To have the same level of satisfaction for good performers and poor performers, the good performers must receive more rewards than the poor performers. The reason for this, as stressed earlier, is that performance level influences the amount of rewards a person feels she should receive. Thus, when rewards are not based on performance —when poor performers receive equal rewards or a larger amount of rewards than good performers—the best performers will be the least satisfied, and a negative satisfaction-performance relationship will exist. If, on the other hand, the better performers are given significantly more rewards, a positive satisfaction-performance relationship should exist. If it is assumed that most organizations are partially successful in relating rewards to performance, it follows that most studies should find a low but positive relationship between satisfaction and performance. Lawler and Porter's (1967) study was among those that found this relationship; their study also found that, as predicted, intrinsic-need satisfaction was more closely related to performance than was extrinsic-need satisfaction.

In retrospect, it is hard to understand why the belief that high satisfaction causes high performance was so widely accepted. There is nothing in the literature on motivation that suggests this causal relationship. In fact, such a relationship is opposite to the concepts developed by both drive theory and expectancy theory. If anything, these two theories would seem to predict that high satisfaction might reduce motivation because of a consequent reduction in the importance of various rewards that may have provided motivational force. Clearly, a more logical view is that performance is determined by people's efforts to obtain the goals and outcomes they desire, and satisfaction is determined by the outcomes people actually obtain. Yet, for some reason, many people believed—and some people still do believe—that the "satisfaction causes performance" view is best.

Turnover

The relationship between satisfaction and turnover has been studied often. In most studies, researchers have measured the job satisfaction among a number of employees and then waited to see which of the employees studied left during an ensuing time period (typically, a year). The satisfaction scores of the employees who left have then been compared with the remaining employees' scores. Although relationships between satisfaction scores and turnover have not always been very strong, the studies in this area have consistently shown that dissatisfied workers are more likely than satisfied workers to terminate employment; thus, satisfaction scores can predict turnover.

A study by Ross and Zander (1957) is a good example of the kind of research that has been done. Ross and Zander measured the job satisfaction of 2680 female workers in a large company. Four months later, these researchers found that 169 of these employees had resigned; those who left were significantly more dissatisfied with the amount of recognition they received on their jobs, with the amount of achievement they experienced, and with the amount of autonomy they had.

Probably the major reason that turnover and satisfaction are not more strongly related is that turnover is very much influenced by the availability of other positions. Even if a person is very dissatisfied with his job, he is not likely to leave unless more attractive alternatives are available. This observation would suggest that in times of economic prosperity, turnover should be high, and a strong relationship should exist between turnover and satisfaction; but in times of economic hardship, turnover should be low, and little relationship should exist between turnover and satisfaction. There is research evidence to support the argument that voluntary turnover is much lower in periods of economic hardship. However, no study has compared the relationship between satisfaction and turnover under different economic conditions to see if it is stronger under full employment.

Absenteeism

Like turnover, absenteeism has been found to be related to job satisfaction. If anything, the relationship between satisfaction and absenteeism seems to be stronger than the relationship between satisfaction and turnover. However, even in the case of absenteeism, the relationship is far from being isomorphic. Absenteeism is caused by a number of factors other than a person's voluntarily deciding not to come to work; illness, accidents, and so on can prevent someone who wants to come to work from actually coming to work. We would expect satisfaction to affect only voluntary absences; thus, satisfaction can never be strongly related to a measure of overall absence rate. Those studies that have separated voluntary absences from overall absences have, in fact, found that voluntary absence rates are much more closely related to satisfaction than are overall absence rates (Vroom, 1964). Of course, this outcome would be expected if satisfaction does influence people's willingness to come to work.

Organization Effectiveness

The research evidence clearly shows that employees' decisions about whether they will go to work on any given day and whether they will quit are affected by their feelings of job satisfaction. All the literature reviews on the subject have reached this conclusion. The fact that present satisfaction influences future absenteeism and turnover clearly indicates that the causal direction is from satisfaction to behavior. This conclusion is in marked contrast to our conclusion with respect to performance—that is, behavior causes satisfaction. . . .

The research evidence on the determinants of satisfaction suggests that satisfaction is very much influenced by the actual rewards a person receives; of course, the organization has a considerable amount of control over these rewards. The research also shows that, although not all people will react to the same reward level in the same manner, reactions are predictable if something is known about how people perceive their inputs. The implication is that organizations can influence employees' satisfaction levels. Since it is possible to know how employees will react to different outcome levels, organizations can allocate outcomes in ways that will either cause job satisfaction or job dissatisfaction.

Absenteeism and turnover have a very direct influence on organizational effectiveness. Absenteeism is very costly because it interrupts scheduling, creates a need for over-staffing, increases fringe-benefit costs, and so on. Turnover is expensive because of the many costs incurred in recruiting and training replacement employees. For lower-level jobs, the cost of turnover is estimated at $2000 a person; at the managerial level, the cost is at least five to ten times the monthly salary of the job involved. Because satisfaction is manageable and influences absenteeism and turnover, organizations can control absenteeism and turnover. Generally, by keeping satisfaction high and, specifically, by seeing that the best employees are the most satisfied, organizations can retain those employees they need the most. In effect, organizations can manage turnover so that, if it occurs, it will occur among employees the organization can most afford to lose. However, keeping the better performers more satisfied is not easy, since they must be rewarded very well. . . . Although identifying and rewarding the better performers is not always easy, the effort may have significant payoffs in terms of increased organizational effectiveness.

Note

1. Lawler, E. E., and Porter, L. W. The effect of performance on job satisfaction. *Industrial Relations*, 1967, 7, 20-28.

References

Adams, J. S. Toward an understanding of inequity. *Journal of Abnormal Psychology*, 1963, 67, 422-436.

Adams, J. S. Injustice in social exchange. In L. Berkowitz (Ed.), *Advances in experimental social psychology.* Vol. 2. New York: Academic Press, 1965.

Gardner, J. W. *No easy victories.* New York: Harper & Row, 1968.

Herzberg, F., Mausner, B., Peterson, R. O., & Capwell, D. F. *Job attitudes: Review of research and opinion.* Pittsburgh: Psychological Service of Pittsburgh, 1957.

Herzberg, F., Mausner, B., & Snyderman, B. *The motivation to work.* (2nd ed.) New York: John Wiley & Sons, 1959.

Hoppock, R. *Job satisfaction.* New York: Harper & Row, 1935.

Lawler, E. E., & Porter, L. W. The effect of performance on job satisfaction. *Industrial Relations,* 1967, 7, 20-28.

Locke, E. A. What is job satisfaction? Paper presented at the APA Convention, San Francisco, September 1968.

Locke, E. A. What is job satisfaction? *Organizational Behavior and Human Performance,* 1969, 4, 309-336.

Porter, L. W. A study of perceived need satisfactions in bottom and middle management jobs. *Journal of Applied Psychology,* 1961, 45, 1-10.

Roethlisberger, F. J., & Dickson, W. J. *Management and the worker.* Cambridge, Mass.: Harvard University Press, 1939.

Ross, I. E., & Zander, A. F. Need satisfaction and employee turnover. *Personnel Psychology,* 1957, 10, 327-338.

Schaffer, R. H. Job satisfaction as related to need satisfaction in work. *Psychological Monographs,* 1953, 67 (14, Whole No. 364).

Vroom, V. H. *Work and motivation.* New York: John Wiley & Sons, 1964.

Organizational, Work, and Personal Factors in Employee Turnover and Absenteeism

LYMAN W. PORTER
RICHARD M. STEERS

To those concerned with studying the behavior of individuals in organizational settings, employee turnover and absenteeism represent both interesting and important phenomena. They are relatively clear-cut acts of behavior that have potentially critical consequences both for the person and for the organization. It is probably for this reason that turnover and absenteeism have been investigated in a relatively large number of studies to date and are likely to remain a key focus of personnel research by psychologists. . . .

In the past, there have been some four reviews of the literature dealing with turnover and absenteeism. Three of these (Brayfield & Crockett, 1955; Herzberg, Mausner, Peterson, & Capwell, 1957; Vroom, 1964) are now somewhat dated in relation to all of the research carried out during the past decade or so, and the fourth (Schuh,

Reprinted by permission of the author and the publisher from *Psychological Bulletin,* vol. 80 (1973), no. 2, pp. 151-76. The research was supported by a grant from the Office of Naval Research, Contract No. N00014-69-A-0200-9001, NR 151-315.

1967) represents a highly specialized review of only a portion of the available literature. Before proceeding to our own analysis of the recent literature, it will be helpful to summarize briefly what was uncovered by these previous reviews.

Brayfield and Crockett (1955) and Herzberg et al. (1957) both found evidence of a strong relationship between employee dissatisfaction and withdrawal behavior (i.e., both turnover and absenteeism). Brayfield and Crockett went further, however, to point out major methodological weaknesses in a number of the studies, such as the failure to obtain independent measures and the use of weak or ambiguous measurement techniques. In fact, such flaws were so prevalent that they questioned whether methodological changes alone would substantially alter the magnitude of direction of many of the obtained relationships. In general, then, Brayfield and Crockett pointed as much to a need for increased rigor in research techniques as toward the acceptance or rejection of an attitude-withdrawal relationship.

Several years later, Vroom (1964) again reviewed the literature pertaining to job satisfaction and withdrawal. The results of his analysis generally reinforced the earlier conclusions. Vroom reported that the studies he reviewed showed a consistent negative relationship between job satisfaction and the propensity to leave. In addition, he found a somewhat less consistent negative relationship between job satisfaction and absenteeism. Vroom interpreted the findings concerning job satisfaction and withdrawal as being consistent with an expectancy/valence theory of motivation; namely, workers who are highly attracted to their jobs are presumed to be subject to motivational forces to remain in them, with such forces manifesting themselves in increased tenure and higher rates of attendance.

Schuh's (1967) review focused primarily on studies of the prediction of turnover by the means of personality and vocational inventories and biographical information. From his review, he concluded that there was not a consistent relationship between turnover and scores on intelligence, aptitude, and personality tests. On the other hand, some evidence was found that vocational interest inventories and scaled biographical information blanks could be used to fairly accurately predict turnover. Moreover, a very small number of older studies pertaining to job satisfaction were cited in the review, and these too seemed predictive of turnover. . . .

Job Satisfaction and Withdrawal

Subsequent to the publication of the earlier reviews, a number of new investigations have appeared concerning the relationship of overall job satisfaction to turnover and absenteeism. These findings are briefly summarized here in order to determine how they relate to the earlier findings as previously reviewed.

In two related predictive studies of particular merit, Hulin investigated the impact of job satisfaction on turnover among female clerical workers. Using the Job Descriptive Index as a measure of job attitudes, Hulin's (1966) first study matched each subject who subsequently left the company over a 12-month period with two "stayers" along several demographic dimensions. Significant differences were found between the stayer and leaver groups on mean satisfaction scores. Hulin concluded that at least in this sample, subsequent leavers *as a group* could be accurately distinguished from stayers based on a knowledge of the workers' degree of job satisfaction up to 12 months prior to the act of termination.

These findings raised the question as to the possibility of reducing this turnover by increasing a worker's degree of satisfaction on the job. Toward this end, the company instituted new policies in the areas of salary administration and promotional opportunities. Approximately 1-1½ years after these changes, Hulin (1968) again administered the Job Descriptive Index to a sample similar to the previous one. Subsequent leavers were matched with two stayers each, and again it was found that termination decisions were significantly related to the degree of worker satisfaction. Equally important was the finding that satisfaction scores with four of the five Job Descriptive Index scales rose significantly between the first and second studies. Simultaneously, the department's turnover rate between these two periods dropped from 30 percent during the first study period to 12 percent during the second.

Other important studies have yielded essentially the same results among life insurance agents (Weitz & Nuckols, 1955), male and female office workers (Mikes & Hulin, 1968), retail store employees (Taylor & Weiss, 1969a, 1969b), and female operatives (Wild, 1970).

Taking a somewhat different approach to the topic, Katzell (1968) and Dunnette, Arvey, and Banas[1] investigated the role of employee expectations at the time of hire as they related to later job experiences and turnover. In both studies, no significant differences were found to exist at the time of entry between the expectation levels of those who remained and those who later decided to leave. However, as time went on, significant differences did emerge; those who remained generally felt their original expectations were essentially met on the job, while those who left felt their expectations had not been met.

Also relevant to the role of met expectations in the participation decision are the field experiments of Weitz (1956), Youngberg (1963), and Macedonia (1969). These studies (described in greater detail below) found that where individuals were provided with a realistic picture of job environment—including its difficulties—prior to employment, such subjects apparently adjusted their job expectations to more realistic levels. These new levels were then apparently more easily met by the work environment, resulting in reduced turnover.

Many studies, therefore, point to the importance of job satisfaction as a predictor of turnover. However, it appears that expressed intentions concerning future participation may be an even better predictor. In a large scale investigation of managerial personnel, Kraut[2] consistently found significant correlations between expressed intent to stay and subsequent employee participation. Such findings were far stronger than relationships between expressed satisfaction and continued participation. And, in a study of turnover among Air Force pilots, Atchison and Lefferts (1972) found that the frequency with which individuals thought about leaving their job was significantly related to rate termination. Based on these preliminary findings, an argument can be made that an expressed intention to leave may represent the next logical step after experienced dissatisfaction in the withdrawal process.

While considerable investigation has been carried out since the previous reviews concerning the relation of job satisfaction to turnover, only two studies have been found considering such satisfaction as it relates to absenteeism. Talacchi (1960), using the Science Research Associates' Employee Inventory, found a significant inverse relation between job satisfaction and absenteeism among office workers. He did not, however, find such a relation concerning turnover. And Waters and Roach (1971), using the Job Descriptive Index with clerical workers, found significant inverse relations between job satisfaction and both turnover and absenteeism.

In summary, the recent evidence concerning the impact of job satisfaction on withdrawal (especially on turnover) is generally consistent with the findings as reviewed by Brayfield and Crockett (1955), Herzberg et al. (1957), and Vroom (1964). (These new findings are summarized in Table 1.) It appears, however, that the major asset of these more recent findings is not simply their confirming nature but rather their increased methodological rigor over those studies reviewed previously. Most of the earlier studies contained several design weaknesses (see, e.g., the discussion by Brayfield & Crockett) which the more recent studies have overcome to a significant degree. For example, 12 of the 15 new studies reviewed here were predictive in nature. In addition, several of the research instruments used in the more recent studies (e.g., the Job Descriptive Index) appear to be more rigorously designed in terms of validity, reliability, and norms. Thus, these newer studies go a long way in the direction of providing increased confidence in the importance of job satisfaction as a force in the decision to participate.

TABLE 1
STUDIES OF RELATION OF JOB SATISFACTION TO TURNOVER AND ABSENTEEISM

Investigator(s)	Population	n[1]	Type of withdrawal studied	Relation to withdrawal
Weitz & Nuckols (1955)	Insurance agents	990	Turnover	Negative
Weitz (1956)	Insurance agents	474	Turnover	Negative
Talacchi (1960)	Departmental workers	NA	Turnover	Zero
			Absenteeism	Negative
Youngberg (1963)	Insurance salesmen	NA	Turnover	Negative
Hulin (1966)	Female clerical workers	129	Turnover	Negative
Hulin (1968)	Female clerical workers	298	Turnover	Negative
Katzell (1968)	Student nurses	1852	Turnover	Negative
Mikes & Hulin (1968)	Office workers	660	Turnover	Negative
Dunnette et al.	Lower level managers	1020	Turnover	Negative
Macedonia (1969)	Military academy cadets	1160	Turnover	Negative
Taylor & Weiss (1969a, 1969b)	Retail store employees	475	Turnover	Negative
Kraut	Computer salesmen	Varied	Turnover	Negative
Wild (1970)	Female manual workers	236	Turnover	Negative
Waters & Roach (1971)	Female clerical workers	160	Turnover	Negative
			Absenteeism	Negative
Atchison & Lefferts (1972)[2]	Air Force pilots	52	Turnover	Negative

Note. NA = not available.

[1] Sample sizes reported here and on the following tables reflect the actual number of subjects used in the data analysis from which the reported results were derived.

[2] Both Kraut, and Atchison and Lefferts found that an expressed intention to leave represented an even more accurate predictor of turnover than job satisfaction.

Specific Factors Related to Withdrawal

While consideration of the role of overall job satisfaction in the decision to participate is important, it tells us little about the roots of such satisfaction. Knowing that an employee is dissatisfied and about to leave does not help us understand *why* he is dissatisfied, nor does it help us determine what must be changed in an effort to retain him. For the answer to these critical questions, it is necessary to look more closely at the various factors of the work situation as they potentially relate to the propensity to withdraw. We begin our discussion with those factors that are generally organization-wide in their impact on employees and move toward those factors that are more unique to each individual.

Organization-wide Factors

Organization-wide factors for purposes of this discussion can be defined as those variables affecting the individual that are primarily determined by persons or events external to the immediate work group. Under this rubric would fall such factors as pay and promotion policies and organization size. . . .

The results of . . . investigations relating organizational environment factors to withdrawal, are summarized in Table 2.

Pay and promotional considerations often appear to represent significant factors in

TABLE 2
STUDIES OF RELATIONS BETWEEN ORGANIZATION-WIDE FACTORS
AND TURNOVER AND ABSENTEEISM

Factor	Population	n	Type of withdrawal studied	Relation to withdrawal
Satisfaction with pay and promotion				
Patchen (1960)	Oil refinery workers	487	Absenteeism	Negative
Friedlander & Walton (1964)	Scientists and engineers	82	Turnover	Negative
Knowles (1964)	Factory workers	56	Turnover	Negative
Saleh et al. (1965)	Nurses	263	Turnover	Negative
Bassett (1967)[1]	Engineers	200	Turnover	Negative
Ronan (1967)	Administrative & professional personnel	91	Turnover	Negative
Hulin (1968)	Female clerical workers	298	Turnover	Negative
Dunnette et al.	Lower level managers	1020	Turnover (pay)	Zero
			Turnover (promotion)	Negative
Kraut	Computer salesmen	Varied	Turnover	Negative
Telly et al. (1971)	Factory workers	900	Turnover	Zero[2]
Conference Board (1972)	Salesmen; management trainees	Varied	Turnover	Negative
Participation in compensation plan design				
Lawler & Hackman (1969)	Custodians	83	Absenteeism	Negative
Scheflen et al. (1971)	Custodians	NA	Absenteeism	Negative
Organization size				
Ingham (1970)	Factory workers	8 units	Turnover	Zero
			Absenteeism	Positive

Note. NA = not available.

[1] Bassett posited such a relationship but did not specifically test for it.

[2] This relation was explained by the nature of the union contract, which standardized pay and promotion procedures based essentially on seniority.

the termination decision. While several of the recent studies reviewed simply confirmed such a conclusion, other studies investigated the reasons behind such a relationship. These studies fairly consistently pointed out the importance of perceived equity and met expectations as important forces in such a decision. The size of the pay raise or the rate of promotion, while important in and of themselves, are, in addition, weighed by an employee in the light of his expectations, given his level of self-perceived contribution. The resulting determination of his degree of satisfaction or dissatisfaction then apparently inputs into his decision to remain or to search for preferable job alternatives.

The results of one study indicated that turnover rates appear to be fairly constant among organizations of varying sizes, while absenteeism is significantly higher in larger firms than in smaller ones. Some theoretical considerations were offered to explain this variance but were not effectively substantiated by empirical data.

Immediate Work Environment Factors

A second set of factors instrumental in the decision to withdraw centers around the immediate work situation in which the employee finds himself. In previous reviews, Brayfield and Crockett (1955) found that negative employee attitudes toward their job context (especially at the lower levels) were significantly related to absenteeism and, to a lesser extent, to turnover. And Herzberg et al. (1957) found that such factors as the nature of the social work group were of particular importance in the decision to participate.

Since these reviews were published, significant research has been carried out which tends to supplement existing knowledge concerning the importance of immediate work environment factors in withdrawal. Factors to be considered here include *(a)* supervisory style, *(b)* work unit size, and *(c)* the nature of peer group interaction. . . .

These findings, summarized in Table 3, provide a relatively clear picture of the relation of at least three immediate work environment factors to an employee's decision to participate or withdraw. Several studies have pointed to the importance of supervisory style as a major factor in turnover. Apparently, when one's expectations concerning what the nature of supervision should be like remain substantially unmet, his propensity to leave increases. No studies, however, have been found relating supervisory style to absenteeism. This neglect of absenteeism studies is rather surprising considering the widely accepted notion of the centrality of the supervisor as a factor in such withdrawal.

The size of the working unit has been shown to be related to both turnover and absenteeism among blue-collar workers; however, insufficient evidence is available to draw conclusions concerning such influence on managerial or clerical personnel.

Finally, most of the research in the area of co-worker satisfaction demonstrates the potential importance of such satisfaction in retention. Such findings, however, are not universal. A possible explanation for the divergent findings is that some people have a lower need for affiliation than others and may place less importance on satisfactory co-worker relations. Alternatively, it is possible that some organizational settings provide for a greater degree of peer group interaction, thereby increasing the probability that one's level of expectations would be met in this area. In either event, co-worker dissatisfaction cannot be overlooked as a possible cause of attrition.

Job Content Factors

It has long been thought that the duties and activities required for the successful performance of an individual's particular job can have a significant impact on his decision to remain with and participate in the employing organization. Such job require-

TABLE 3
STUDIES OF RELATIONS BETWEEN IMMEDIATE WORK ENVIRONMENT FACTORS AND TURNOVER AND ABSENTEEISM

Factor	Population	n	Type of withdrawal studied	Relation to withdrawal
Satisfaction with supervisory relations				
Fleishman & Harris (1962)	Production workers	NA[1]	Turnover	Negative (curvilinear)
Saleh et al. (1965)	Nurses	263	Turnover	Negative
Ley (1966)	Production workers	100	Turnover	Negative
Hulin (1968)	Female clerical workers	298	Turnover	Negative
Skinner (1969)	Production workers	85	Turnover	Negative (curvilinear)
Taylor & Weiss (1969a, 1969b)	Retail store employees	475	Turnover	Zero
Telly et al. (1971)	Production workers	900	Turnover	Negative
Receipt of recognition and feedback				
Ross & Zander (1957)	Female skilled workers	507	Turnover	Negative
General Electric Company (1964a)	Engineers	36	Turnover	Negative
Supervisory experience				
Bassett (1967)	Technicians and engineers	200	Turnover	Negative
Work unit size				
Kerr et al. (1951)	Production workers	894	Turnover	Positive
			Absenteeism	Positive
Acton Society Trust (1953)	Factory workers	91	Absenteeism	Positive
Hewitt & Parfitt (1953)	Factory workers	179	Absenteeism	Positive
Metzner & Mann (1953)	Blue-Collar workers	251	Absenteeism	Positive
	White-collar workers	375	Absenteeism	Zero
Mandell (1956)	Clerical workers	320	Turnover	Positive
Argyle et al. (1958)	Production departments	86	Turnover	Zero
			Absenteeism	Positive (curvilinear)
Revans (1958)	Factory workers	Varied	Absenteeism	Positive
Baumgartel & Sobol (1959)	Blue- and white-collar workers	3900	Absenteeism	positive
Indik & Seashore (1961)	Factory workers	NA	Turnover	Positive
			Absenteeism	positive
Satisfactory peer group interactions				
Evan (1963)[2]	Management trainees	300	Turnover	Negative
Hulin (1968)	Female clerical workers	298	Turnover	Negative
Taylor & Weiss, (1969a, 1969b)	Retail store employees	475	Turnover	Zero
Farris (1971)	Scientists and engineers	395	Turnover	Negative
Telly et al. (1971)	Production workers	900	Turnover	Negative
Waters & Roach (1971)	Clerical workers	160	Turnover	Zero
			Absenteeism	Negative

Note. NA = not available.

[1] A total of 56 foremen plus approximately 3 subordinates of each foreman took part in the study; specific *N* not reported.

[2] Inference based on study results.

ments are presumed to represent for the individual either a vehicle for personal fulfillment and satisfaction or a continual source of frustration, internal conflict, and dissatisfaction. In recent years, several new investigations have appeared which provide added clarity to the role of such job-related factors in the withdrawal process. Four such factors will be discussed here: (*a*) the overall reaction to job content, (*b*) task repetitiveness, (*c*) job autonomy and responsibility, and (*d*) role clarity. . . .

In general, turnover has been found to be positively related to dissatisfaction with the content of the job among both blue- and white-collar workers. Insufficient evidence

TABLE 4
STUDIES OF RELATIONS BETWEEN JOB CONTENT FACTORS AND TURNOVER AND ABSENTEEISM

Factor	Population	*n*	Type of withdrawal studied	Relation to withdrawal
Satisfaction with job content				
Saleh et al. (1965)	Nurses	263	Turnover	Negative
Hulin (1968)	Clerical workers	298	Turnover	Zero
Katzell (1968)	Student nurses	1852	Turnover	Negative
Dunnette et al.	Lower-level managers	1020	Turnover	Negative
Taylor & Weiss (1969a, 1969b)	Retail store employees	475	Turnover	Negative
Kraut	Computer salesmen	Varied	Turnover	Negative
Wild (1970)	Female manual workers	236	Turnover	Negative
Telly et al. (1971)	Production workers	900	Turnover	Negative
Waters & Roach (1971)	Clerical workers	160	Turnover	Negative
			Absenteeism	Negative
Task repetitiveness				
Guest (1955)	Automobile assembly line workers	18	Turnover	Positive
Kilbridge (1961)	Production workers	568	Turnover	Zero
		331	Absenteeism	Positive
Lefkowitz & Katz (1969)	Factory workers	80	Turnover	Positive
Taylor & Weiss (1969a, 1969b)	Retail store employees	475	Turnover	Positive
Wild (1970)	Female manual workers	236	Turnover	Positive
Job autonomy and responsibility				
Guest (1955)	Automobile assembly line workers	18	Turnover	Negative
Ross & Zander (1957)	Female skilled workers	507	Turnover	Negative
Turner & Lawrence (1965)	Blue-collar workers	403	Absenteeism	Negative
Taylor & Weiss (1969a, 1969b)	Retail store employees	475	Turnover	Negative
Hackman & Lawler (1971)	Telephone operators and clerks	208	Absenteeism	Negative
Waters & Roach (1971)	Clerical workers	160	Turnover	Negative
Role clarity				
Weitz (1956)	Insurance salesmen	474	Turnover	Negative
Youngberg (1963)	Insurance salesmen	NA	Turnover	Negative
Macedonia (1969)	Military academy cadets	1260	Turnover	Negative
Lyons (1971)	Nurses	156	Turnover	Negative

Note. NA = not available.

is available, however, to draw any such conclusions concerning absenteeism, but initial investigations point to a similar relationship. More specifically, the available data tend to indicate that both absenteeism and turnover are positively associated with task repetitiveness, although such a conclusion may represent an oversimplification of the nature of the relationship (see, e.g., Hulin & Blood, 1968). Finally, a strong positive relation has been found consistently between both forms of withdrawal and a perceived lack of sufficient job autonomy or responsibility.

The degree of role clarity on the part of the individual can apparently affect turnover in two ways. First, an accurate picture of the actual tasks required by the organization can function to select out, prior to employment, those who do not feel the rewards offered justify doing such tasks. And, secondly, accurate role perceptions can serve to adjust the expectations of those already employed to more realistic levels as to what is expected of them in terms of performance. The resulting increased congruence between expectations and actual experience apparently can serve to increase satisfaction and continued participation. No conclusions can be drawn concerning the effect of role clarity on absenteeism due to a lack of investigations on the subject.

The results of those studies relating to job content are summarized in Table 4.

Personal Factors

Factors unique to the individual also appear to have a significant impact on the problems of turnover and absenteeism. Such factors include (*a*) age, (*b*) tenure with the organization, (*c*) similarity of job with vocational interest, (*d*) personality characteristics, and (*e*) family considerations. While often overlooked by investigators, the inclusion of such items are central to developing a comprehensive model explaining the dynamics of work participation. . . .

The findings concerning personal factors in withdrawal are summarized in Table 5. Age is strongly and negatively related to turnover, while being somewhat positively (though weakly) related to absenteeism. Similarly, increased tenure appears to be strongly related to propensity to remain. One possible explanation here may be that increases in tenure result in increases in personal investment on the part of the employee in the organization (i.e., after a while, he may not be able to "afford" to quit). No solid conclusions can be drawn concerning the impact of tenure on absenteeism, however, due to conflicting results.

From limited studies, turnover appears to be related positively to the similarity between job requirements and vocational interests. No studies were found that related such interests to absenteeism, however. Predicting turnover or absenteeism from interest inventories (assuming they are properly validated) represents an important possibility for organizations because such data can be collected *prior* to employment. Such an advantage does not exist for most predictors of withdrawal.

The majority of studies investigating the relationship between personality traits and withdrawal center around turnover so no conclusions can be drawn about their relation to absenteeism. Apparently, the possession of more extreme personality traits may lead to an increased tendency to leave the organization. While further investigation is definitely in order here, a tendency exists for employees manifesting very high degrees of anxiety, emotional instability, aggression, independence, self-confidence, and ambition to leave the organization at a higher rate than employees possessing such traits in a more moderate degree. The implications of such a phenomenon, if borne out by further research, need also to be investigated for their effects on organizational efficiency and effectiveness. That is, if such a pattern really exists, research is needed as to the desirability for the organization of accepting a higher turnover rate in exchange for

TABLE 5
STUDIES OF RELATIONS BETWEEN PERSONAL FACTORS AND TURNOVER AND ABSENTEEISM

Factor	Population	n	Type of withdrawal studied	Relation to withdrawal
Age				
Minor (1958)	Female clerical workers	440	Turnover	Negative
Naylor & Vincent (1959)	Female clerical workers	220	Absenteeism	Zero
Fleishman & Berniger (1960)	Female clerical workers	205	Turnover	Negative
de la Mare & Sergean (1961)	Industrial workers	140	Absenteeism	Positive
Shott et al. (1963)	Male office workers	561	Turnover	Zero
	Female office workers		Turnover	Negative
Cooper & Payne (1965)	Construction workers	392	Absenteeism	Positive
Ley (1966)	Factory workers	100	Turnover	Negative
Bassett (1967)	Technicians and engineers	200	Turnover	Negative
Downs (1967)	Public service organization trainees	1736	Turnover	Positive
	Public service organization employees (after training)		Turnover	Negative
Stone & Athelstan (1969)	Clerical workers	453	Turnover	Negative
Farris (1971)	Scientists and engineers	395	Turnover	Negative
Robinson (1972)	Female clerical workers	200	Turnover	Negative
Tenure				
Hill & Trist (1955)	Factory workers	289	Absenteeism	Zero
Baumgartel & Sobol (1959)	Male blue-collar workers	3900	Absenteeism	Negative
	Female blue-collar, male and female white-collar workers		Absenteeism	Positive
Fleishman & Berniger (1960)	Female clerical workers	205	Turnover	Negative
Shott et al. (1963)	Male and female office workers	561	Turnover	Negative
Knowles (1964)	Factory workers	56	Turnover	Negative
Robinson (1972)	Female clerical workers	200	Turnover	Negative
Congruence of job with vocational interests				
Ferguson (1958)	Insurance salesmen	520	Turnover	Negative
Boyd (1961)	Engineers	326	Turnover	Negative
Mayeske (1964)	Foresters	125	Turnover	Negative
"Extreme" personality characteristics[1]				
Cleland & Peck (1959)	Ward attendants	54	Turnover	Positive
Hakkinen & Toivainen (1960)	Miners	135	Turnover	Positive
MacKinney & Wolins (1960)	Male production foremen	175	Turnover	Positive
Meyer & Cuomo (1962)	Engineers	1360	Turnover	Positive
Sinha (1963)	Industrial workers	110	Absenteeism	Positive
Farris (1971)	Technical personnel	395	Turnover	Positive
Family size				
Naylor & Vincent (1959)	Female clerical workers	220	Absenteeism	Positive
Knowles (1964)	Male factory workers	56	Turnover	Negative
Stone & Athelstan (1969)	Female physical therapists	453	Turnover	Positive
Family responsibilities				
Guest (1955)	Male auto assembly line workers	18	Turnover	Positive
Minor (1958)	Female clerical workers	440	Turnover	Positive
Fleishman & Berniger (1960)	Female clerical workers	205	Turnover	Positive
Saleh et al. (1965)	Nurses	263	Turnover	Positive
Robinson (1972)	Female clerical workers	200	Turnover	Positive

[1] See text for more detailed description.

possible resulting increases in performance from such mobile employees. No research has been found that demonstrates that low-turnover employees (those possessing more moderate personality traits) are in fact better performers. Thus, reduced turnover may be an undesirable goal if it is bought at the price of reduced work-force effectiveness.

Finally, family size and family responsibilities were generally found to be positively related to turnover and absenteeism among women, while their impact on men appears to be mixed.

Summary and Discussion

The foregoing review clearly shows that a multiplicity of organizational, work, and personal factors can be associated with the decision to withdraw. It is possible, however, to summarize briefly those factors for which sufficient evidence exists to draw meaningful conclusions concerning their relation to withdrawal.

In general, very strong evidence has been found in support of the contention that *overall* job satisfaction represents an important force in the individual's participation decision. In addition, based on preliminary evidence, such satisfaction also appears to have a significant impact on absenteeism. These trends have been demonstrated among a diversity of work group populations and in organizations of various types and sizes. Moreover, the methodologies upon which these findings are based are generally of a fairly rigorous nature.

However, as noted earlier, it is not sufficient for our understanding of the withdrawal process to simply point to such a relationship. It is important to consider what constitutes job satisfaction. Under the conceptualization presented here, job satisfaction is viewed as the sum total of an individual's met expectations on the job. The more an individual's expectations are met on the job, the greater his satisfaction. Viewing withdrawal within this framework points to the necessity of focusing on the various factors that make up the employee's expectation set.

We have proposed four general categories, or "levels" in the organization, in which factors can be found that affect withdrawal. Sufficient evidence exists to conclude that important influences on turnover can be found in each of these categories. That is, some of the more central variables related to turnover are organization-wide in their derivation (e.g., pay and promotion policies), while others are to be found in the immediate work group (e.g., unit size, supervision, and co-worker relations). Still others are to be found in the content of the job (e.g., nature of job requirements) and, finally, some are centered around the person himself (e.g., age and tenure). Thus, based on these findings, the major roots of turnover appear to be fairly widespread throughout the various facets of organizational structure, as they interact with particular types of individuals.

On a more tentative level, initial findings indicate that role clarity and the receipt of recognition and feedback are also inversely related to turnover. However, not all of the possible factors reviewed here have been found to be clearly or consistently related to termination. For example, conflicting data exist concerning the influence of task repetitiveness and of family size on such withdrawal.

Much less can be concluded about the impact of these factors on absenteeism due to a general lack of available information. Sufficient evidence does exist, however, to conclude with some degree of confidence that increased unit size is strongly and directly related to absenteeism. In addition, tentative evidence suggests that opportunities for participation in decision making and increased job autonomy are inversely related to such behavior.

One further point warrants emphasis here concerning the turnover studies reviewed above. To a large extent, there is an underlying assumption, often inferred but sometimes stated, that the reduction of all turnover is a desirable goal. Such an assumption may be questioned on several grounds. First, from the individual's point of view, leaving an unrewarding job may result in the procurement of a more satisfying one. Second, from the organization's standpoint, some of those who leave may be quite ineffective performers, and their departure would open positions for (hopefully) better performers. The important point here is that a clear distinction should be made in future research efforts between effective and ineffective leavers. The loss of an effective employee may cost far more than the loss of an ineffective one, and the costs of efforts to retain the latter may well exceed the benefits. Third, given the present state of technological flux, turnover may in some ways be considered a necessary evil. It may be necessary to simply accept certain levels of turnover as the price for rapid change and increased efficiency. . . .

References

Acton Society Trust. *Size and morale.* London: Author, 1953.

Argyle, M., Gardner, G., & Cioffi, I. Supervisory methods related to productivity, absenteeism and labor turnover. *Human Relations,* 1958, *11,* 23-40.

Atchison, T. J., & Lefferts, E. A. The prediction of turnover using Herzberg's job satisfaction technique. *Personnel Psychology,* 1972, *25,* 53-64.

Bassett, G. A. *A study of factors associated with turnover of exempt personnel.* Crotonville, N.Y.: Behavioral Research Service, General Electric Company, 1967.

Baumgartel, H., & Sobol, R. Background and organizational factors in absenteeism. *Personnel Psychology,* 1959, *12,* 431-443.

Boyd, J. B. Interests of engineers related to turnover, selection, and management. *Journal of Applied Psychology,* 1961, *45,* 143-149.

Brayfield, A. H., & Crockett, W. H. Employee attitudes and employee performance. *Psychological Bulletin,* 1955, *52,* 396-424.

Cleland, C. C., & Peck, R. F. Psychological determinants of tenure in institutional personnel. *American Journal of Mental Deficiency,* 1959, *64,* 876-888.

Conference Board. *Salesmen's turnover in early employment.* New York: Author, 1972.

Cooper, R., & Payne, R. Age and absence: A longitudinal study in three firms. *Occupational Psychology,* 1965, *39,* 31-43.

de la Mare, G., & Sergean, R. Two methods of studying changes in absence with age. *Occupational Psychology,* 1961, *35,* 245-252.

Downs, S. Labour turnover in two public service organizations. *Occupational Psychology,* 1967, *41,* 137-142.

Evan, W. M. Peer-group interaction and organizational socialization: A study of employee turnover. *American Sociological Review,* 1963, *28,* 436-440.

Farris, G. F. A predictive study of turnover. *Personnel Psychology,* 1971, *24,* 311-328.

Ferguson, L. W. Life insurance interest, ability and termination of employment. *Personnel Psychology,* 1958, *11,* 189-193.

Fleishman, E. A. A leader behavior description for industry. In R. M. Stogdill & A. E. Coons (Eds.), *Leader behavior: Its description and measurement.* (Ohio Studies in Personnel; Research Monograph No. 88) Columbus: Ohio State University, Bureau of Business Research, 1957. (a)

Fleishman, E. A. The Leadership Opinion Questionnaire. In R. M. Stogdill & A. E. Coons (Eds.), *Leader behavior: Its description and measurement.* (Ohio Studies in Personnel; Research Monograph No. 88) Columbus: Ohio State University, Bureau of Business Research, 1957. (b)

Fleishman, E. A. *Revised manual for Leadership Opinion Questionnaire.* Chicago: Science Research Associates, 1968.

Fleishman, E. A., & Berniger, J. One way to reduce office turnover. *Personnel*, 1960, *37*, 63-69.

Fleishman, E. A., & Harris, E. F. Patterns of leadership behavior related to employee grievances and turnover. *Personnel Psychology*, 1962, *15*, 43-56.

Friedlander, F., & Walton, E. Positive and negative motivations toward work. *Administrative Science Quarterly*, 1964, *9*, 194-207.

General Electric Company, Behavioral Research Service. *Attitudes associated with turnover of highly regarded employees.* Crotonville, N.Y.: Author, 1964. (a)

General Electric Company, Behavioral Research Service. *A comparison of work planning program with the annual performance appraisal interview approach.* Crotonville, N.Y.: Author, 1964. (b)

Guest, R. H. A neglected factor in labour turnover. *Occupational Psychology*, 1955, *29*, 217-231.

Hackman, J. R., & Lawler, E. E., III. Employee reactions to job characteristics. *Journal of Applied Psychology*, 1971, *55*, 259-286.

Hakkinen, S., & Toivainen, Y. Psychological factors causing labour turnover among underground workers. *Occupational Psychology*, 1960, *34*, 15-30.

Herzberg, F., Mausner, B., Peterson, R. O., & Capwell, D. F. *Job Attitudes: Review of research and opinion.* Pittsburgh: Psychological Service of Pittsburgh, 1957.

Hewitt, D., & Parfitt, J. A note on working morale and size of group. *Occupational Psychology*, 1953, *27*, 38-42.

Hill, J. M., & Trist, E. L. Changes in accidents and other absences with length of service. *Human Relations*, 1955, *8*, 121-152.

Hulin, C. L. Job satisfaction and turnover in a female clerical population. *Journal of Applied Psychology*, 1966, *50*, 280-285.

Hulin, C. L. Effects of changes in job-satisfaction levels on employee turnover. *Journal of Applied Psychology*, 1968, *52*, 122-126.

Hulin, C. L., & Blood, M. R. Job enlargement, individual differences, and worker responses. *Psychological Bulletin*, 1968, *69*, 41-55.

Indik, B., & Seashore, S. *Effects of organization size on member attitudes and behavior.* Ann Arbor: University of Michigan, Survey Research Center of the Institute for Social Research, 1961.

Ingham, G. *Size of industrial organization and worker behaviour.* Cambridge: Cambridge University Press, 1970.

Kahn, R., Wolfe, D., Quinn, R., Snoek, J., & Rosenthal, R. *Organizational stress: Studies in role conflict and ambiguity.* New York: Wiley, 1964.

Katz, D., Maccoby, E., Gurin, G., & Floor, L. *Productivity, supervision and morale among railroad workers.* Ann Arbor: University of Michigan, Survey Research Center, 1951.

Katz, D., Maccoby, N., & Morse, N. *Productivity, supervision and morale in an office situation.* Ann Arbor: University of Michigan, Institute for Social Research, 1950.

Katzell, M. E. Expectations and dropouts in schools of nursing. *Journal of Applied Psychology*, 1968, *52*, 154-157.

Kerr, W., Koppelmeier, G., & Sullivan, J. Absenteeism, turnover and morale in a metals fabrication factory. *Occupational Psychology*, 1951, *25*, 50-55.

Kilbridge, M. Turnover, absence, and transfer rates as indicators of employee dissatisfaction with repetitive work. *Industrial and Labor Relations Review*, 1961, *15*, 21-32.

Knowles, M. C. Personal and job factors affecting labour turnover. *Personnel Practice Bulletin*, 1964, *20*, 25-37.

Lawler, E. E., III. *Pay and organizational effectiveness: A psychological view.* New York: Mcgraw-Hill, 1971.

Lawler, E. E., III, & Hackman, J. R. Impact of employee participation in the development of pay incentive plans: A field experiment. *Journal of Applied Psychology*, 1969, *53*, 467-471.

Lefkowitz, J., & Katz, M. Validity of exit interviews. *Personnel Psychology*, 1969, *22*, 445-455.

Ley, R. Labour turnover as a function of worker differences, work environment, and authoritarianism of foremen. *Journal of Applied Psychology*, 1966, *50*, 497-500.

Lyons, T. Role clarity, need for clarity, satisfaction, tension and withdrawal. *Organizational Behavior and Human Performance,* 1971, *6,* 99-110.

Macedonia, R. M. Expectation-press and survival. Unpublished doctoral dissertation, Graduate School of Public Administration, New York University, June 1969.

MacKinney, A. C., & Wolins, L. Validity information exchange. *Personnel Psychology,* 1960, *13,* 443-447.

Mandell, M. *Recruiting and selecting office employees.* New York: American Management Association, 1956.

March, J. G., & Simon, H. A. *Organizations.* New York: Wiley, 1958.

Mayeske, G. W. The validity of Kuder Preference Record scores in predicting forester turnover and advancement. *Personnel Psychology,* 1964, *17,* 207-210.

Metzner, H., & Mann, F. Employee attitudes and absences. *Personnel Psychology,* 1953, *6,* 467-485.

Meyer, H., & Cuomo, S. *Who leaves? A study of background characteristics of engineers associated with turnover.* Crotonville, N.Y.: General Electric Company, Behavioral Science Research, 1962.

Mikes, P. S., & Hulin, C. Use of importance as a weighting component of job satisfaction. *Journal of Applied Psychology,* 1968, *52,* 394-398.

Minor, F. J. The prediction of turnover of clerical employees. *Personnel Psychology,* 1958, *11,* 393-402.

Naylor, J. E., & Vincent, N. L. Predicting female absenteeism. *Personnel Psychology,* 1959, *12,* 81-84.

Patchen, M. Absence and employee feelings about fair treatment. *Personnel Psychology,* 1960, *13,* 349-360.

Porter, L. W., & Lawler, E. E., III. Properties of organization structure in relation to job attitudes and job behavior. *Psychological Bulletin,* 1965, *64,* 23-51.

Porter, L. W., & Lawler, E. E., III. *Managerial attitudes and performance.* Homewood, Ill.: Irwin, 1968.

Revans, R. Human relations, management and size. In E. M. Hugh-Jones (Ed.), *Human relations and modern management.* Amsterdam: North-Holland Publishing, 1958.

Robinson, D. D. Prediction of clerical turnover in banks by means of a weighted application blank. *Journal of Applied Psychology,* 1972, *56,* 282.

Ronan, W. W. A study of some concepts concerning labour turnover. *Occupational Psychology,* 1967, *41,* 193-202.

Ross, I. C., & Zander, A. Need satisfaction and employee turnover. *Personnel Psychology,* 1957, *10,* 327-338.

Saleh, S. D., Lee, R. J., & Prien, E. P. Why nurses leave their jobs—An analysis of female turnover. *Personnel Administration,* 1965, *28,* 25-28.

Scheflen, K. C., Lawler, E. E., III, & Hackman, J. R. Long-term impact of employee participation in the development of pay incentive plans: A field experiment revisited. *Journal of Applied Psychology,* 1971, *55,* 182-186.

Schuh, A. The predictability of employee tenure: A review of the literature. *Personnel Psychology,* 1967, *20,* 133-152.

Shott, G. L., Albright, L. E., & Glennon, J. R. Predicting turnover in an automated office situation. *Personnel Psychology,* 1963, *16,* 213-219.

Sinha, A. K. P. Manifest anxiety affecting industrial absenteeism. *Psychological Reports,* 1963, *13,* 258.

Skinner, E. Relationships between leadership behavior patterns and organizational situational variables. *Personnel Psychology,* 1969, *22,* 489-494.

Stogdill, R., & Coons, A. (Eds.) *Leader behavior: Its description and measurement.* Columbus: Ohio State University, Bureau of Business Research, 1957.

Stone, T. H., & Athelstan, G. T. The SVIB for women and demographic variables in the prediction of occupational tenure. *Journal of Applied Psychology,* 1969, *53,* 408-412.

Talacchi, S. Organization size, individual attitudes and behavior: An empirical study. *Administrative Science Quarterly,* 1960, *5,* 398-420.

Taylor, K., & Weiss, D. Prediction of individual job termination from measured job satisfaction and biographical data. (Research Report No. 30) Minneapolis: University of Minnesota, Work Adjustment Project, October 1969. (a)

Taylor, K., & Weiss, D. Prediction of individual job turnover from measured job satisfaction. (Research Report No. 22) Minneapolis: University of Minnesota, Work Adjustment Project, May 1969. (b)

Telly, C. S., French, W. L., & Scott, W. G. The relationship of inequity to turnover among hourly workers. *Administrative Science Quarterly,* 1971, *16,* 164-172.

Turner, A. N., & Lawrence, P. R. *Industrial jobs and the worker: An investigation of response to task attributes.* Boston: Harvard University Press, Division of Research, 1965.

Vroom, V. *Work and motivation.* New York: Wiley, 1964.

Walker, C. R., & Guest, R. H. *The man on the assembly line.* Cambridge: Harvard University Press, 1952.

Waters, L. K., & Roach, D. Relationship between job attitudes and two forms of withdrawal from the work situation. *Journal of Applied Psychology,* 1971, *55,* 92-94.

Weitz, J. Job expectancy and survival. *Journal of Applied Psychology,* 1956, *40,* 245-247.

Weitz, J., & Nuckols, R. C. Job satisfaction and job survival. *Journal of Applied Psychology,* 1955, *39,* 294-300.

Wild, R. Job needs, job satisfaction, and job behavior of women manual workers. *Jounral of Applied Psychology,* 1970, *54,* 157-162.

Youngberg, C. F. An experimental study of "job satisfaction" and turnover in relation to job expectancies and self expectations. Unpublished doctoral dissertation, New York University, 1963.

CHAPTER **9**

Union Constraints on Personnel Actions

In the early days, unions capitalized on worker dissatisfaction in order to attract new members. Today a large number of new members join unions automatically as required under a union shop contract. In the first reading in this chapter, Bok and Dunlop examine the history and nature of the bargaining relationship which has resulted from the unionization of employees. The reading by Stagner and Rosen examines the types of disputes which generally result between management and organized workers today. These disputes may result in strikes, worker slowdowns, and worker grievances. Stagner and Rosen examine the dynamics of labor-management conflicts and offer principles to the personnel or labor relations specialist that can be applied in settling these disputes.

The last reading in this chapter—that by Kleingartner—discusses how collective bargaining among professionals in the public sector works, examining how traditional definitions of collective bargaining found in the private sector, especially among blue-collar employees, cannot work for public sector, professional employees, since while private sector employees tend to seek better working conditions, public sector professionals tend to bargain for more authority.

Collective Bargaining in the United States: An Overview

D. C. BOK
J. T. DUNLOP

The democratic character of labor organizations and the nature of their internal operations have aroused particular interest in the United States.[1] If unions were largely devoted to political action or social reform, rather than collective bargaining, their internal affairs might have attracted no more attention than those of the American Medical Association or the National Association of Manufacturers. But unions have traditionally been preoccupied with collective bargaining, and this preoccupation has given labor organizations a significance that has stimulated interest in almost every phase of union activity and has created a series of problems for employers and for the economy as a whole.

Although the practice of collective bargaining has been known for more than one hundred fifty years, the term itself seems to have been first used in 1891 by Mrs. Sidney Webb, the Fabian writer and, in collaboration with her husband, historian of the British labor movement.[2] As the Webbs stated, "In unorganized trades the individual workman, applying for a job, accepts or refuses the terms offered by the employer without communication with his fellow workmen. . . . But if a group of workmen concert together, and send representatives to conduct bargaining on behalf of the whole body, the position is at once changed."[3] Individual bargaining is thus transformed into collective bargaining.

The Special Character of Collective Bargaining in the United States

Collective bargaining is carried on within a framework of law, custom and institutional structure that varies considerably from one country to another. The framework of bargaining in the United States has certain characteristics that sharply distinguish it from that of most other industrial democracies.

Decentralization

Perhaps the most significant characteristic of the American collective-bargaining system is that it is highly decentralized. There are approximately 150,000 separate union-management agreements now in force in the United States. A majority of union members work under contracts negotiated by their union with a single employer or for a single plant. Only 40 percent of employees covered by collective agreements involve multi-employer negotiations, and the great bulk of these negotiations are confined to single metropolitan areas.

In Europe and Australia, on the other hand, the great majority of union members are covered by general agreements negotiated for large groups of employees on a multi-

Copyright © 1970, by the Rockefeller Fund Inc. Reprinted by permission of Simon and Schuster.

employer basis. Collective bargaining in Sweden, for example, is normally carried out within the framework of a national agreement negotiated by the central conferedation of labor unions and its counterpart on the management side. Subsidiary agreements then are hammered out in negotiations conducted on an industrywide basis. Additional negotiation takes place at the plant level. Since each of these levels of negotiation may cover some of the same subjects, such as wages, the bargaining arrangements may be said to consist of three tiers, in contrast to the single tier that is more typical in the United States. In Great Britain, there are normally two separate tiers, an industrywide negotiation followed by bargaining at the plant level.[4] In France the dominant pattern of bargaining is initially regional. In the typical case, a general agreement covering a large section of the country is negotiated by an association representing a group of loosely related industries. Thus, a key French negotiation takes place within the greater Paris region involving the metalworks sector—a group which includes a variety of industries ranging from steel plants and automobile factories to jewelry shops and repair establishments. In addition to regional negotiation, bargaining may also take place at the plant level, usually with individual workers but sometimes through regular plantwide negotiations with the unions.

The prevalence of plant and company negotiations in the United States is a natural outgrowth of the patterns of organization among employers and unions, the great size of this country, and the highly competitive character of its economy. National negotiations, along Scandinavian lines, are hardly feasible, since the AFL-CIO has much less authority over its affiliates than the central confederations in most other industrial democracies (with the possible exception of Great Britain), and managements also are less centralized in their decisions on labor-relations issues. The manager in America has been strongly inclined to act independently in working out his labor and personnel policies. To be sure, multi-employer bargaining associations are not unknown; they are quite common on the local level and exist on a nationwide basis in a few industries, as in railroads. Nevertheless, it is difficult to envisage American employers following the example of their Swedish counterparts by forming a single national confederation with power to veto any important bargaining concession by a member firm or to compel any member to join in a lockout. Nor is it likely that American employers will follow the lead of those abroad in forming powerful bargaining associations in virtually all major industries.

Exclusive Jurisdiction

In the United States, unlike most countries in Western Europe, one union serves as the sole representative for all the employees in a plant or other appropriate bargaining unit. [Note: Government employment, however, provides some exceptions to exclusive representation. Executive Order 10988 provided for more than one form of recognition by a government agency, so that two or more unions may legitimately be recognized in federal employment. In New York City government, different unions may represent the same worker for different purposes, one for grievances and another for wages and benefits.] This practice conforms to the American political custom of electing single representatives by majority vote. It also can be traced back to the tradition of conflict among the autonomous international unions. To restrain such conflict, the American Federation of Labor—as far back as the 1880s—developed the concept of exclusive jurisdiction. Under this principle, only one union was authorized to represent employees in a particular occupation, a group of jobs, or, occasionally, an industry. Employers generally accepted exclusivity since it stabilized labor relations by diminishing disputes among competing unions. It was natural, therefore, for the principle to be embodied in public policy when the government began to develop detailed regulation over collective bargaining. Thus, during World War I and under the Railway Labor Act of 1926, a system of elections was adopted to enable groups of employees to select a single representative by majority vote. The same procedures were subsequently carried forward on a broader scale in the National Labor Relations Act of 1935 and its subsequent amendments.

A different system of representation prevails in most other industrial democracies.[5] In a few countries, as in West Germany, the federation is made up of unions neatly divided along industrial lines so that there is less need for an explicit doctrine of exclusive jurisdiction in order to curb union rivalries. There also are a number of nations where the labor movement is split along political or religious lines that reflect fundamental ideological cleavages in the society. Under such circumstances, there are obvious objections to any system that would give one union exclusive rights over its rivals. In France, for example, neither employers nor the political parties in power would accept a system that would allow the Communist-controlled unions to win exclusive bargaining rights wherever they could enlist a majority of employees against the opposing Socialist and Catholic organizations. Instead, each of the rival unions is simply given the right to represent its members, and collective bargaining normally takes place through uneasy coalitions among the three major labor federations.

Individual Bargaining

Under almost any system, collective bargaining leaves room for a degree of individual negotiation over certain terms and conditions of employment. Even in the United States, the law explicitly provides that an employee can discuss individual grievances with representatives of management.[6] And in a few fields—for example, the performing arts—agreements typically leave employees free to bargain individually for salaries above the minimum. For the most part, however, collective agreements in the United States specify the actual wages and terms of employment which in fact govern the workers in the bargaining unit, and individual employees do not negotiate different terms on their own behalf.

In most other industrial democracies, the scope for individual or small-group bargaining is much greater. Collective agreements generally do no more than provide minimum wages and conditions. In the tight labor markets that have prevailed in so many of these countries, actual wages have drifted well above the contract rates in the great majority of plants. As a result, though negotiated pay increases put upward pressure on wage levels, the actual rates of pay are largely fixed by individual bargaining, often initiated by employers seeking to keep their work force from going elsewhere.[7]

Collective agreements in the United States also tend to specify many more conditions of employment than is the case in other countries. In Western Europe, for example, a union contract normally obliges the employer to observe little more than a minimum-wage scale and a few basic provisions relating to working conditions and perhaps a few fringe benefits. In this country, on the other hand, agreements are extremely detailed and far-reaching in their content. Collective bargaining typically regulates standards for discipline, promotion criteria, transfers and layoffs, priorities for determining who will be laid off and recalled, shift schedules, procedures for resolving grievances and a wide variety of other matters.

The decentralized structure of the American industrial-relations system does much to explain the greater reach of the collective agreement and the more restricted role for individual and small-group bargaining and unilateral action by the employer. In Europe, where negotiations normally embrace entire industries or groups of related industries in particular regions and where so many diverse employers participate in the negotiations, it is extremely difficult to write a detailed set of contract rules applicable to each participating firm. As a result, the parties have been content to negotiate contracts containing only a limited number of minimum terms and conditions.

In this country, on the other hand, the pattern of plant and companywide bargaining enables unions to negotiate contracts specifying a detailed system of wages and working conditions to be observed at each workplace. Even in industries where multiemployer bargaining has prevailed, unions have been sufficiently organized at the plant level to negotiate supplementary provisions to take account of special conditions in particular plants. But in most European countries, where plant locals scarcely exist, this process has been much slower to develop. Lacking strong organizations at the workplace, unions have left many terms of employment to be resolved through individual bargaining or by consultation with workers' councils,[8] which often are established by law and are not formally a part of the union hierarchy.

The Role of Law in Fixing Conditions of Employment

Just as individual bargaining plays a part, along with collective negotiations, in setting terms and conditions of employment, so also does the law have a role in the process. In every industrialized country, legislation has been passed to perform such functions as fixing minimum wages or maximum hours, or providing safety requirements, or requiring payroll deductions for social security and other welfare programs. In at least one respect, however, the law performs a broader function abroad than it does in the United States. In other industrial democracies, outside the Scandinavian bloc, legislation has been passed that can be used to extend the terms of collective agreements to nonunion enterprises in the same industry. In a few countries, the extension of the collective agreement is ordered by a labor tribunal or a regular court. More often, either the union or the employers' association can petition a designated public official who has descretion to extend the terms of the agreement throughout the industry in question. In the United States, however, no comparable procedure exists. [Note: One consequence of the arrangements in the United States is that the economically weak—agricultural labor and those employed in small retail establishments, for example—have relatively little protection. They are excluded from much social legislation and do not enjoy the benefits of collective bargaining. The Davis-Bacon Act does, however, specify that the Secretary of Labor shall predetermine the wage rates and benefits to be paid to workers employed on construction projects under federal government contract; and the Walsh-Healy Act empowers the Secretary to prescribe the prevailing minimum wages in connection with the government's purchases. In Great Britain the Wages Councils, and in Australia the arbitration courts, provide more egalitarian conditions of employment for the unorganized without bargaining power; they extend to such workers benefits comparable to those developed by parties to collective bargaining.]

The absence of any authority in law to extend a collective-bargaining contract to others who have not accepted the agreement is rooted in the structure of the American industrial-relations system. It is comparatively easy to extend a contract containing a few minimum terms and conditions, particularly when the contract has been negotiated by an association representing a large and representative group of firms. In the United States, however, where rival unions may coexist in a single industry, where contract terms set actual rather than minimum requirements, and where provisions are highly complex and often vary from one firm to another, it would be very difficult to find a single set of terms that would be suitable for all firms in the industry.

In another respect, the structure of bargaining in this country has caused the law to play a more ambitious role in collective negotiations than it does abroad. Although we rely less heavily on legislation to fix the substantive terms of employment, there is much more regulation in the United States over the tactics and procedures of bargaining.

This difference largely reflects the special tensions and pressures that arise in a highly decentralized system of bargaining. Under plantwide or companywide negotiations, the individual employer must confront the union in his enterprise, instead of leaving negotiations to his employer association to be conducted on a regional or industrywide basis. The bargaining process reaches into the details of his business, seeking to regulate every aspect of working conditions in his plant. The contract terms do not merely set minimum standards but also fix the actual conditions to be observed. Above all, the institution of bargaining threatens to subject him to contract obligations that may put him at a disadvantage with his nonunion competitor or even other organized enterprises. Under these circumstances, the bargaining process is accompanied by greater tension, and the employer often resists the union more strenuously than is common abroad. In turn, the law responds to these strains and seeks to contain antagonisms within reasonable bounds. Thus, law in the United States defines the subjects that must be bargained about. It requires the parties to "bargain in good faith" and clothes this obligation with detailed rules proscribing stalling tactics, withholding of relevant information, and other forms of behavior that are considered unfair. The net result is a complex of regulations that greatly exceeds anything to be found in other industrialized countries.[9]

The Role of the Parties in Determining the Structure of Bargaining

These special characteristics help to define the framework of the American system of collective bargaining. Within these contours, several types of negotiation go on. The most familiar aspect of bargaining involves the discussions between the parties over the terms and conditions of employment for the workers involved. But a vital part of the bargaining process has to do with determining the structure and the procedures through which these discussions will take place.

One question of structure has to do with the level at which different issues should be resolved. This problem is particularly significant in any negotiation that affects more than one place of work. In a situation of this kind, the parties must decide which issues should be agreed upon at the negotiating table and incorporated into a master agreement and which should be left for labor and management representatives to settle at the company, plant, or departmental level.[10] Agreements made at these subsidiary levels are called local supplements. Sometimes the interdependence between the two settlements creates problems. Is one settlement contingent upon the other, and is a failure to conclude one a basis for a strike or lockout in all units? Which settlement will be made first?

These questions are often difficult to resolve. In a multi-plant company, for instance, such matters as the amount of time allowed for wash-up before the end of a shift or the allocation of parking facilities might be best handled at the plant level. But it is also clear that policies or precedents on these matters at one plant may influence decisions elsewhere. Considerations of bargaining power and market competition may also influence the level at which particular issues are treated. As technological and market changes take place, it may be necessary to alter these arrangements and provide for more centralization on some issues, as with the introduction of containers in the East Coast longshore industry, and greater decentralization in other instances, such as the determination of the number of trainmen in a crew on the railroads. Since conditions vary widely from one plant or industry to another, there is little uniformity among collective-bargaining relationships in the pattern of centralization and decentralization in negotiations.

A second problem in arranging negotiation procedures concerns the range of jobs, territory, and employees to be governed by the ensuing agreement. Several illustrations may be helpful. The basic steel companies took major strikes in 1946 in part to achieve separate negotiations for their fabricating facilities from their basic steel operations. As a result, separate agreements with different expiration dates and different wage scales now are negotiated at different times, reflecting the different competitive conditions that affect these two types of operations. In view of differing market conditions for the different products involved, the major rubber companies have on occasion insisted on differential wage increases for tire plants and those plants making rubber shoes and other rubber products. Conversely, twenty-six cooperating international unions sustained an eight-month strike in the copper negotiations of 1967-68 in an effort to obtain collective-bargaining agreements with the same expiration dates and identical wage increases for all employees of a company.

A third set of structural problems has to do with the relations among different craft unions bargaining with a common employer. In recent years, the newspaper printing industry, the West Coast shipbuilding industry, and the construction industry have suffered many strikes growing out of disagreements over the wage pattern or sequence of settlements among a group of interrelated crafts agreements. For example, the 114-day New York newspaper strike of 1962-63 was fought by Bertram Powers, president of Local 6 of the International Typographical Union, largely to change a system of bargaining which had existed since the early 1950s. Under the prior agreement, wage settlements had been made with the Newspaper Guild and then extended to other newspaper unions. As a result of the strike, contract expiration dates were negotiated which removed the five-week lead the Guild had previously held and thus eliminated its ability to impose an industrywide pattern on the other unions before they ever got to the bargaining table. Thus, the strike enabled Powers to put an end to a follow-the-leader pattern that had deprived his union of any real power to negotiate its own wage agreements.[11]

Serious questions may arise also in deciding which subjects should be encompassed within the scope of collective bargaining. The subjects that are dealt with vary widely, reflecting in each contract the problems of the relevant workplace and industry. Some maritime agreements specify the quality of meals and even the number of bars of soap, towels, and sheets that management is to furnish to the crew. Such provisions are natural subjects for negotiation, since they are vital to men at sea, but they would make no sense in a normal manufacturing agreement. In some contracts in the ladies' garment industry, companies agree to be efficient and to allow a union industrial engineer to make studies of company performance. These provisions would be regarded as ludicrous in the automobile industry. Detailed procedures respecting control over hiring are central to collective bargaining in industries with casual employment, where employees shift continually from one employer to another, as in construction and stevedoring; but in factory and office employment, new hiring typically is left to the discretion of management. In this fashion, the topics raised in collective bargaining tend to reflect the problems of the particular workplace and industry.

The law also plays a part in deciding the subjects for negotiation, since the National Labor Relations Act (Section 9a) requires the parties to bargain in good faith over "rates of pay, wages, hours of employment, or other conditions of employment." Pursuant to this Act, the National Labor Relations Board and the courts have decided which subjects are mandatory topics for collective bargaining and which are optional. In some instances, particular subjects or bargaining proposals have been held to be improper or illegal and hence nonnegotiable, such as a union's insistence on a closed shop or an employer's demand that the union bargain through a particular form of negotiating committee or take a secret ballot prior to calling a strike. On the whole, however, the Board and the courts have steadily broadened the scope of mandatory bargaining to include Christmas bonuses, pensions, information on plant shutdowns, subcontracting, provisions for checkoff of union dues, and many other topics.

The provisions of the National Labor Relations Act would appear to make legal rulings decisive as to the scope of bargaining. And on a few issues, such as pension plans, litigation undoubtedly played a significant role. In the main, however, although the law may help to define the outer limits of bargaining, the actual scope of negotiations is largely decided by the parties themselves.

The Process of Bargaining: Negotiation, Administration, and Consultation

In common parlance, "collective bargaining" is used to refer to three separate forms of labor-management activity: negotiations for a new contract, administration of an existing agreement, and informal consultation on matters of common interest to the parties.

Negotiation

The process of negotiating a new agreement varies widely from one firm to another. In a number of industries, for example, the smaller firms will usually follow the pattern set by a larger competitor; bargaining for them will mean little more than seeking to make a few minor adjustments in the pattern-setting agreement to take account of special conditions. In larger firms—and particularly in the pattern-setting companies—bargaining will be a much more elaborate and difficult process.

When bargaining involves more than simply accepting a standard agreement, there will normally be much preparation on both sides. The union will develop a series of demands through local meetings, consultation among officials, and sometimes the use of surveys and questionnaires. Management will likewise develop its position through meetings among its officers and staff. Both parties will normally arm themselves with research data; for example, they may study the nature of prior grievances, draw upon studies of market and employment trends, and analyze the financial and competitive position of the firm itself.

Once these preparations are complete, the process of bargaining often proceeds through a series of stages. At the outset, the union customarily presents a long and extravagant list of demands. In many instances, the company will respond by submitting its own proposals, which are typically far apart from those of the union. Although this exchange may seem as irrelevant and ritualistic as the mating dance of the great crested grebe, it can serve a variety of purposes. By putting forward many exaggerated demands, the parties create trading material for later stages of negotiations. They disguise their real position and thus give themselves room for maneuver as bargaining progresses. They explore a wide range of problems that may have been bothering each side, and they have the opportunity to explain concerns to each other. They manage to satisfy their constituents or principals by seeming to back numerous proposals, only to scale down many of the demands or abandon them altogether later on in the negotiations when it is more expedient to do so. A proposal may be advanced and explored, only to be put aside for more serious negotiation in subsequent years.

After the initial presentations, there normally is a period of exploration in which each side tries to clarify the proposals of the other and marshal arguments against them. At this stage of negotiation, little change can be expected in the positions of the parties. As bargaining progresses, each side will begin to formulate a combination of proposals, or "package," which it considers an appropriate basis for settlement. The package offered by each side gives the other party a clearer sense of the priorities attached to various items and the possible concessions to be gained. In this process, more than one package may be put forward by either side.

Eventually, before or after a stoppage, an agreement will be reached. The meeting of the minds will normally be arrived at first during informal talks between key negotiators, and the proposed settlement will then be discussed before the full negotiating committees on either side. Thereafter, the tentative agreement must be reduced to contract language, usually with the advice of lawyers and after much further discussion over details of wording.

After the agreement is reduced to writing, ordinarily it must be ratified or approved by the principals involved. On the union side, ratification may be required by the membership of the union, by a specified group of elected delegates, or by an elected wage policy committee, as in the case of the basic-steel agreement. Management negotiators in a single company will need the approval of the president or the board of directors. In association bargaining, the approval of the elected directors or the full membership of the association is typically required.

The ratification of settlements by union members serves a variety of purposes. By obtaining an explicit vote of approval for the settlement, subsequent enforcement of the agreement by management, by union officers, or by an arbitrator is made easier. Ratification also requires union negotiators to explain and "sell" the agreement to the membership. In doing so, ratification provides a check to insure that the negotiators keep in touch with the rank and file and reflect their interests in the bargaining process.

The quality of union leadership and its influence on the membership are subtly reflected in collective bargaining and ratification. In many bargaining relationships, ratification on the union side is a formality. The negotiators, by common consent, are in touch with the membership or wage policy committee with power to ratify; the negotiators are highly respected, and their views and recommendations carry great weight. In other instances, the union leaders occupy a more tenuous position; they lack the influence and prestige to guarantee acceptance even of a satisfactory contract.

As previously observed, there has been a marked increase in the proportion of settlements that have been rejected in the ratification process. According to federal mediators, the most common reasons for rejection are dissatisfaction with the size of wage and fringe benefits, lack of understanding by the leaders of the real desires of the members, internal political rivalries, and inadequate ratification procedures that give undue weight to the views of dissident members. At times, however, a rejection can be a deliberate tactic in the bargaining process. Union representatives may take a management offer to the members to demonstrate the unity and the sentiments of the rank and file. They may appear to accept a proposal and later oppose ratification in order to extract further concessions from management. Such stratagems normally are harmful to bargaining relationships. Management is unlikely to make its best offer at the bargaining table once it has been burnt by the use of a rejection as a tactical maneuver; it will save its best offer for a later date, thus causing the agreement-making process to become more difficult.

Administration of The Contract

Although many of the most important issues concerning the terms of employment will be settled explicitly in the collective agreement, controversies will continue to arise over its meaning and application. Such disputes are inevitable. Most collective agreements are highly complex documents covering a multitude of problems Typically, they are negotiated within a limited period of time, often in an atmosphere of rush and crisis. As a result, certain problems are bound to be overlooked. Others arise from changing circumstances that could not possibly have been foreseen when the contract was signed. Still others reflect ambiguities which were deliberately created by the parties with the thought that not every controversy could be settled in negotiations if the agreement was ever to be signed within the time available.

Almost all collective agreements contain procedures to be used in resolving "grievances," or disputes over the application of the contract. In some cases, the procedures are very simple. In the construction industry, for example, where many contractors have a work force that changes constantly from one job to another, it is often not feasible to operate an elaborate grievance machinery. Hence, disputes often are settled at the workplace through informal discussions between the union representative and the employer. Similarly, grievances in small establishments often are resolved by having the aggrieved employee get in touch with the union representative, who then may take up the matter directly with the employer. Where larger numbers of employees are involved, however, the grievance machinery tends to become more elaborate.

Most contracts for larger plants provide several stages at which a grievance can be considered. Typically, the aggrieved employee will first present his complaint to the foreman or supervisor, with or without the assistance of a union representative. The great majority of grievances are settled at this stage; were it otherwise, higher management and union officials could easily become overwhelmed with the task of reviewing complaints. But where an accommodation cannot be reached at this early stage, the contract will provide one or more levels of appeal at which disputes can be considered by progressively higher echelons within the union and management hierarchy. If no settlement can be reached through this process, the agreement will typically provide for presentation to an outside arbitrator, who will issue a final and binding decision following a hearing of the parties.

Today, arbitration procedures can be found in an estimated 94 percent of all collective-bargaining agreements. Nevertheless, not all disputes are made subject to this procedure, even in contracts with fully developed grievance machinery. For example, contracts signed by the major automobile companies expressly provide that the arbitrator shall not decide disputes involving production standards used in the measured day-work system; in some of these firms, matters involving health and safety and rates of new jobs are likewise excluded from arbitration.[12] Despite such exceptions, it is fair to say that arbitration represents the dominant method for resolving grievances that the parties cannot settle by themselves. Through this procedure, a peaceful and impartial resolution of disputes is obtained without the delay and formality that might result from taking such matters to court or making the dispute a test of economic power.

In light of the experience in countless plants, it is clear beyond dispute that an effective, well-administered grievance procedure can play an indispensable role in improving labor relations and providing a measure of industrial due process to the workers involved. The advantages to be gained have been summed up in the following terms by a distinguished panel of labor relations experts:

> A major achievement of collective bargaining, perhaps its most important contribution to the American workplace, is the creation of a system of industrial

jurisprudence, a system under which employer and employee rights are set forth in contractual form and disputes over the meaning of the contract are settled through a rational grievance process.... The gains from this system are especially noteworthy because of their effect on the recognition and dignity of the individual worker. This system helps prevent arbitrary action on questions of discipline, layoff, promotion, and transfer, and sets up orderly procedures for the handling of grievances. Wildcat strikes and other disorderly means of protest have been curtailed and effective work discipline generally established. In many situations, cooperative relationships marked by mutual respect between labor and management stand as an example of what can be done.[13]

Joint Consultation

In many labor-management relationships, the parties have fashioned machinery to consult with one another during the term of the collective agreement. Such arrangements may involve high-level officials from both sides or specialists concerned with particular technical problems. They may or may not include impartial representatives.

Many purposes can be served by discussions of this kind. A study committee may be useful in exploring some special question, such as a pension program or a new job evaluation plan, which is too complex to be handled satisfactorily in the limited time available for regular contract negotiations. In other cases, a committee may be needed to construct and administer special machinery for dealing with a large, continuing problem such as the displacement of personnel through automation or the closing of a plant. Regular consultation may be employed to develop information and exchange ideas with a view to narrowing the range of issues to be taken up in subsequent contract negotiations. In a strike-torn firm or industry, a committee may also be formed to search for ways of resolving underlying problems or redesigning bargaining procedures in order to eliminate the sources of controversy.[14]

These three processes—negotiation, administration, and joint consultation—are not always readily disentangled in practice. Discussions between representatives of the parties may be of a mixed character. They may talk over a particular grievance and in so doing agree to exchange letters which embody the solution of a more general problem. The administrative and the legislative functions are here closely intertwined. A joint study committee may, on occasion, find a resolution for some pending grievances, agree on some new provision in the contract, or simply provide an exchange of information and opinion. Nonetheless, it is helpful to distinguish these three types of interaction between labor and management organizations even though general usage may employ the term "collective bargaining" to describe them all.

The Social and Economic Functions of Collective Bargaining

If society is to evaluate the institution of collective bargaining and compare it with alternative procedures, its social and economic functions must be clearly perceived. Five functions seem particularly important.

Establishing the Rules of the Workplace

Collective bargaining is a mechanism for enabling workers and their representatives to participate in establishing and administering the rules of the workplace. [Note: Some writers have contended that collective bargaining is a process of joint decision making or joint management. It is true that many rules are agreed to by the parties and written into the collective agreement. But many other functions are left exclusively to management. Moreover, labor agreements typically specify areas within which management takes the initiative, with unions being left to file grievances if they feel that management has violated the contract. Although management may consider it wise to consult with the union before taking certain types of action, it is normally not obligated to seek advance consent from the union. It is misleading to equate collective bargaining with joint management by unions and employers.] Bargaining has resulted in the development of arbitration and other safeguards to protect the employee against inequitable treatment and unfair disciplinary action. More important still, the sense of participation through bargaining serves to mitigate the fear of exploitation on the part of the workers. Whether or not wages would be lower in the absence of bargaining, many employees would doubtless feel that their interests would be compromised without the presence of a union or the power to elect a bargaining representative. In view of these sentiments, collective bargaining may well serve as a substitute for sweeping government controls over wages as a device for insuring adequate, visible safeguards to protect the interests of employees.

Choosing the Form of Compensation

Collective bargaining provides a procedure through which employees as a group may affect the distribution of compensation and the choices between money and hours of work. One of the most significant consequences of collective bargaining over the past two decades has been the growth of fringe benefits, such as pensions, paid holidays, health and welfare, and vacations with pay. If unions had not existed, it is unlikely that individual workers would have spent added income in exactly the same way; indeed, it is doubtful whether, in the absence of collective bargaining, health and pension plans at present prices would have grown widespread. Moreover, though speculations of this kind are treacherous, the history of social-insurance legislation in the United States suggests that, under a system where the government was responsible for setting wages and terms of employment, fringe benefits would not have grown to the extent they have.[15]

These fringe benefits have had a significant impact upon the whole economy. There can be little question that collective bargaining played a major role in focusing priorities and attention upon medical care in the past decade. With the growth of health and welfare plans, information about medical care has been widely disseminated and developed; a body of experts in business and labor have arisen, and the pressures for public programs in the medical field have been accelerated. In much the same way, the extent of expansion in vacation-oriented industries—motels, resorts, transportation, boating, and leisure goods—must be partly attributed to the emphasis in collective bargaining on greater vacation benefits for employees.

Standardization of Compensation

Collective bargaining tends to establish a standard rate and standard benefits for enterprises in the same product market, be it local or national. Labor contracts in the ladies' garment industry seek to establish uniform piece rates (and labor costs) for all companies that produce the same item within the same general price brackets; all the firms in the basic steel industry confront virtually the same hourly wage schedule for all production and maintenance occupations; and all construction firms bidding on contracts in a locality confront known and uniform wage schedules.

Such uniformity is naturally sought by unions. As political institutions, they desire "equal pay for equal work" in order to avoid the sense of grievance that results when one group of members discovers that another group is performing the same job in another plant at a higher wage. Thus, unless there are stong economic reasons for maintaining wage differentials, unions will normally push hard for standardization.

From the standpoint of employers, it should be observed that uniform wage rates do not necessarily imply uniform labor costs. Firms paying the same hourly rates may have varying wage costs as a result of differences in equipment and managerial efficiency. But competition tends to remove these differences and promote more uniform labor costs among close rivals. In highly competitive industries, employers often have a keen regard for such standardization; it protects the enterprises from uncertain wage rate competition, at least among firms subject to the collective agreement.

From the standpoint of the economy as a whole, the effects of standardization are mixed. In some instances, wage uniformity may be broadened artificially beyond a product market area, as when the wage rates in a tire company are extended to apply to its rubber-shoe-work. The effect is to produce a less efficient use of economic resources. The resulting premium over the wages paid in other rubber-shoe plants eventually will compel the tire companies to give up doing business in the rubber-shoe field. In a more important sense, however, the effect of uniformity has been positive in that it has favored the expansion of more profitable, more efficient firms. In a country like France, on the other hand, bargaining establishes only minimum rates, so that backward companies can often survive by paying lower wages than their competitors if they can somehow manage to retain the necessary work force.

Determining Priorities on Each Side

A major function of collective bargaining is to induce the parties to determine priorities and resolve differences within their respective organizations. In the clash and controversy between the two sides, it is easy to assume a homogeneous union struggling with a homogeneous management or association of employers. This view is erroneous and mischievous. In an important sense, collective bargaining consists of no less than three separate bargains—the agreement by different groups within the union to abandon certain claims and assign priorities to others; an analogous process of assessing priorities and trade-offs within a single company or association; and the eventual agreement that is made across the bargaining table.

A labor organization is composed of members with a conglomeration of conflicting and common interests. The skilled and the unskilled, the long-service and the junior employees, the pieceworkers and the day-rated workers, and those in expanding and contracting jobs often do not have the same preferences. A gain to one of these groups often will involve a loss to another. Thus, in George W. Taylor's words, "To an increasing extent, the union function involves a mediation between the conflicting interests of its own membership."[16]

Similarly, corporate officials may have differing views about the negotiations, even in a single company. The production department and the sales staff may assess differently the consequences of a strike. The financial officers may see an issue differently from the industrial-relations specialists. These divergences are compounded where an association of companies bargains with a union, for there are often vast differences among the member firms in their financial capacity, vulnerability to a strike, concern over specific issues, and philosophy toward the union.

One of the major reasons that initial demands of both parties often diverge so far from final settlements is that neither side may have yet established its own priorities or preferences, or assessed the priorities of the other side. In many cases, these relative priorities are established and articulated only during the actual bargaining process. (This view of the bargaining process helps to explain the sense of comradeship that labor and management negotiators often develop through the common task of dealing with their respective committees and constituents.)

This process of accommodation within labor and management is central to collective bargaining. It should not be disparaged as merely a matter of internal politics on either side. In working out these internal adjustments in a viable way, collective bargaining serves a social purpose of enormous significance. The effective resolution of these problems is essential to the strength of leadership and to the continued vitality of both the company and the union.

Redesigning The Machinery of Bargaining

A most significant function of collective bargaining in this country is the continuing design and redesign of the institution itself. While it is true that the national labor policy—as reflected in legislation, administrative rulings, and court decisions—has a bearing on some features of collective bargaining, the nature of the institution is chiefly shaped by the parties themselves. As previously noted, the collective-bargaining process largely determines the respective roles of individual bargaining and union-management negotiations. It defines the subjects to be settled by collective bargaining. It determines the structure of bargaining relationships. It establishes the grievance procedures and prescribes the uses of arbitration and economic power in the administration of an agreement. It decides the degree of centralization and decentralization of decision making. It influences the ratification procedures of the parties. The results are seldom fixed. The bargaining parties must reshape their bargaining arrangements from time to time in response to experience and emerging new problems. Thus, the design of collective bargaining and its adaptation to new challenges and opportunities have much to do with its capacity to fulfill its social functions effectively and without undue cost to the public.

Five Major Issues

In certain respects, collective bargaining is being subjected to a closer scrutiny than in the past, because of the special circumstances in which the country now finds itself. On the one hand, it is plain that society is becoming more critical of its institutions and more demanding in the performance it expects of them. Collective bargaining must now be judged in the light of the American position in the world, which has created new demands for economic progress and monetary stability. The consequences of labor negotiations must be viewed in the light of more insistent demands for full employment. And though labor and management have grown more professional in their dealings with each other and more successful in avoiding strikes, Secretary of Labor Willard Wirtz could still observe that ". . . neither the traditional collective-bargaining procedures nor the present labor-dispute laws are working to the public's satisfaction, at least as far as major labor controversies are concerned."[17]

At the same time, the climate in which collective bargaining must operate has also become more trying. In recent years, bargaining has been spreading rapidly into the field of public employment, where the parties are often inexperienced in labor relations and the problems involved are in many respects more difficult than in the private sector. Full employment has also placed new strains upon the bargaining process. With jobs so plentiful employees are less amenable to discipline and control. Their demands have grown larger, particularly in an economy where the cost of living has been creeping upward. Labor shortages have likewise created difficulties by forcing managers to hire less-experienced and less-qualified employees.

From these pressures have emerged five groups of questions that have been debated increasingly in recent years. . . .

1). Economic strife and dispute settlement. What can be done to protect the public interest when the parties to collective bargaining engage in economic warfare? Is the exertion of economic and political pressure an appropriate way to resolve bargaining disputes? Would not compulsory arbitration be a superior procedure, substituting facts and reason for power? What can the parties themselves and the government do to improve the performance of collective bargaining?

2). Efficiency and productivity. What is the impact of collective bargaining upon managerial efficiency? How extensive and serious are restrictive work practices, and what can be done about them? Does the rule-making character of collective bargaining necessarily stifle management in its quest for reductions in labor costs? When is a rule of collective bargaining an appropriate protection of the health, safety, or convenience of a worker, and when is it an undue limitation of efficiency? How can uneconomic work practices be eliminated in the future?

3). Inflation. What are the consequences of collective bargaining for inflation? The experience of many Western countries since World War II, including our own, raises the question whether free collective bargaining, continuing high employment, and price stability are compatible. What can be done to make collective bargaining less conducive to inflation or to reduce its inflationary bias at high levels of employment?

4). Public employees. In recent years, the process of negotiations has been spreading rapidly to many sectors of public employment. Are the procedures of private bargaining appropriate to public employment? Is the strike a suitable means to induce agreement in the public sector? What is the proper relation between negotiations in the public sector and legislative bodies and civil service? What machinery is appropriate to resolve disputes in public employment?

5). New opportunities for bargaining. What are likely to be the new subjects of collective bargaining in the private sector in the years ahead? What are the new needs and opportunities to which collective bargaining procedures can fruitfully be applied?

Notes

1. The literature on the theoretical analysis of collective bargaining includes the following: Sidney and Beatrice Webb, *Industrial Democracy* (London: Longmans, Green, 1914); Sumner H. Slichter, *Union Policies and Industrial Management* (Washington, D.C.: Brookings Institution, 1941); Neil W. Chamberlain, *Collective Bargaining* (New York: McGraw-Hill, 1951); Allan Flanders, *Industrial Relations: What Is Wrong with the System?* (London: Faber and Faber, 1965); Sumner H. Slichter, James J. Healy, and E. Robert Livernash, *The Impact of Collective Bargaining on Management* (Washington, D.C.: Brookings Institution, 1960); John T. Dunlop, *Industrial Relations Systems* (New York: Henry Holt, 1958).

2. Webb, *op. cit.*, p. 173, n. 1. The reference to the writing of Mrs. Webb, Beatrice Potter, is *The Cooperative Movement in Great Britain* (London, 1891), p. 217.

3. Webb, *op. cit.*, p. 173.

4. See *Royal Commission on Trade Unions and Employers' Associations,* Minutes of Evidence 2 and 3, Ministry of Labour (London, Her Majesty's Stationery Office, 1966), "We have to face that in many areas we have effectively two tiers of negotiation at the present time, the national bargaining and the bargaining on the factory floor on bonuses and piece rates," p. 47.

5. For a discussion of some other Western industrial-relations arrangements, see *Royal Commission on Trade Unions and Employers' Associations,* 1965-1968 (London: Her Majesty's

Stationery Office, 1968); Val R. Lorwin, *The French Labor Movement* (Cambridge: Harvard University Press, 1954); J. E. Issac and G. W. Ford, eds., *Australian Labour Relations Readings* (Melbourne: Sun Books, 1966); Adolf Sturmthal, ed., *White-Collar Trade Unions, Contemporary Developments in Industrialized Societies* (Urbana: University of Illinois Press, 1966); *The Trade Union Situation in Sweden,* Report of a Mission from the International Labour Office (Geneva: International Labour Office, 1961); Walter Galenson, *Trade Union Democracy in Western Europe* (Berkeley: University of California Press, 1964).

6. Labor-Management Relations Act, 1947, Section 9 (a).

7. See D. J. Robertson, *Factory Wage Structures and National Agreements* (Cambridge, England: University Press, 1960).

8. See Adolf Sturmthal, *Workers Councils, A Study of Workplace Organization on Both Sides of the Iron Curtain* (Cambridge: Harvard University Press, 1964).

9. See Robben W. Fleming, "The Obligation to Bargain in Good Faith," in *Public Policy and Collective Bargaining,* Joseph Shister, Benjamin Aaron, and Clyde W. Summers, eds. (New York: Harper and Row, 1962), pp. 60-87.

10. E. Robert Livernash, "Special and Local Negotiations," in *Frontiers of Collective Bargaining,* John T. Dunlop and Neil W. Chamberlain, eds. (New York: Harper and Row, 1967), pp. 27-49.

11. See A. H. Raskin, "The Great Manhattan Newspaper Duel," *Saturday Review,* May 8, 1965, p. 8.

12. See John T. Dunlop, "The Function of the Strike," in *Frontiers of Collective Bargaining, op. cit.,* pp. 103-21.

13. *The Public Interest in National Labor Policy* (New York: Committee for Economic Development, 1961), p. 32.

14. H. A. Clegg and T. E. Chester, "Joint Consultation," in *The System of Industrial Relations in Great Britain,* Allan Flanders and H. A. Clegg, eds. (Oxford, England: Basil Blackwell, 1954), pp. 323-64; James J. Healy, ed., *Creative Collective Bargaining: Meeting Today's Challenges to Labor-Management Relations* (Englewood Cliffs, New Jersey: Prentice-Hall, 1965); William Gomberg, "Special Study Committees," in *Frontiers of Collective Bargaining, op. cit.,* pp. 235-51.

15. See *The Princeton Symposium on The American System of Social Insurance* (New York: McGraw-Hill, 1968).

16. "The Public Interest: Variations on an Old Theme," *Proceedings of the Eighteenth Annual Meeting of the National Academy of Arbitrators,* 1965 (Washington, D.C.: B.N.A. Incorporated, 1965), p. 195.

17. W. W. Wirtz *Labor and the Public Interest* (New York: Harper and Row, 1964), p. 49.

Forms and Methods of Settling Industrial Disputes

R. STAGNER
H. ROSEN

In the coalition that is the industrial enterprise, many kinds of conflicts can and do occur. . . . Disputes occur because of differences in goals or in perceived pathways to goals. Disputes may increase in number and intensity because of organizational structures. They are also profoundly affected by economic influences, an area with which we [will not deal] except to point out that acceptable economic returns to the parties will depend to some extent upon perception—there is no economic formula to determine a "fair day's work" or a "fair day's pay." Controversies are also affected by the supply of alternative jobs (the labor market), by perceived wage levels elsewhere, and by customary profit ratios.

We are concerned with disputes between organized managers (the employer) and organized workers (the union). There are many other kinds of industrial disputes, of interest to various kinds of social scientists, that will not be explored here. However, so that the student can place union-management disputes in a context of other kinds of disputes, we present Table 1 to show the many other possibilities. Some of these other kinds of disputes have little or no impact on union-management controversy and, hence, are dismissed from further examination—particularly the management-government category, which is relevant only when it grows out of a union-management dispute (e.g., when the union charges unfair labor practices and appeals to the National Labor Relations Board). Similarly, the union-government category may grow out of a union-management dispute (e.g., when the union tries to pressure an employer to sign a contract by picketing the stores to which he sells his output or to which his trucks deliver merchandise).

TABLE 1
VARIETIES OF INDUSTRIAL DISPUTES

Parties	Example
Management-Government	Antitrust action
Intermanagement	Price competition between companies; disputes over patents and fulfillment of contracts
Interunion	Jurisdictional disputes, as between carpenters and millwrights over installation of factory equipment
Union-Government	Prosecution for secondary boycotts; collusion with employers against customers
Intramanagement	Factions within management striving for control of company
Intra-union	Factions within union striving for control of union
Union-Management	Union and company debate over division of earnings between wages and profits

From *Psychology of Union-Management Relations*, by R. Stagner and H. Rosen, Copyright © 1965 by Wadsworth Publishing Company, Inc. Reprinted by permission of the publisher, Brooks/Cole Publishing Company, Monterey, California.

Conflicts within management, such as *factionalism*, or between management and a rebel stockholder group usually have no significant tie with labor relations. Occasionally, one faction within management advocates a "tough line" with the union and the other group is more conciliatory; but even this connection is rare. Intramanagement disputes are most often related to the desire for personal power on the part of leaders of factions within the executive organization.

Interunion disputes occasionally cause union-management problems, and the manager is often the innocent victim. If he signs with one union, the other may picket him—even though it has no members on his payroll. During the hectic early days of the national space program, contractors sometimes paid two groups of workers to do the same job, to avoid the delays inherent in jurisdictional disputes.

The major psychological factor involved in jurisdictional disputes is job security. Since workers develop certain expectations about what work is properly theirs, giving this work to another group (brother unionists or not) threatens their job security. A second factor is the desire of union officers for power. If the two competing ship-officers unions were merged into a single organization, many disputes would be eliminated; however, many men would lose prestige and power, as well as their salaries, from the resulting abolition of duplicated offices. Leaders of one union raid another for members because added membership fattens the union treasury and strike fund, raises the bargaining power to a higher level, and inflates the ego of the leader. Jurisdictional disputes may result from the desire of either the leader or the members to protect traditional jobs and perhaps to add new job opportunities.

Intra-union disputes may occasionally precipitate a union-management controversy, because the leaders of union factions vie with each other to demonstrate to the rank-and-file their ability to win concessions from the boss. Thus, a competition arises similar to that in presidential election campaigns in which the major candidates try to outdo each other in boasting of their toughness toward Communists. (Such competition at the national level is far more dangerous, since it exacerbates tensions that could precipitate a nuclear catastrophe; but the intraplant friction caused by union leaders is also an unpleasant reality.)

Management sometimes contributes to union factionalism. Some executives believe—without much evidence—that divided unions are weak unions and therefore less of a threat. Covertly, they may encourage a continuing split; e.g., by making concessions to one side while refusing similar settlements requested by an opposing faction.

Other inter- and intra-union feuds may be based on ideological and other considerations. The Reuther-Addes fight within the UAW, just after World War II, was at least partly motivated by the Reuther group's anticommunist feelings. The conflict between the AFL-CIO and such groups as the Teamsters and the Longshoremen arises in part from the public reaction to reports of racketeering in these two unions, which was hurting honest unions by the association of ideas.

Having mentioned various kinds of industrial disputes that occasionally affect our central interest, let us now turn to disputes between the management of a company and the union that represents a group of employees of that company. This type of dispute probably accounts for over 90 percent of disputes affecting unions, and it is the kind we wish to examine in greater detail.

Union-management disputes may be classified in at least two ways: (a) by the occasion of the dispute, and (b) by the form it takes. By *occasion* we mean whether the dispute occurs in a union-organizing campaign, in negotiating a contract, or in the grievance procedure under an existing contract; and by *form* we mean the use of verbal weapons (such as hearings and table-pounding), of slowdowns and interferences with production, or of picketing and strikes. Our primary interest will be in the interlocking relationship between motivation, perception, organization, and leadership, as basic variables, and in the occasion and form of the overt dispute.

"Dispute" or "Conflict"?

We have rather carefully adhered to the term *industrial dispute* . . . because of the negative emotional tone associated with the word *conflict*. When one reads of a conflict, he thinks of uninhibited violence and bloodshed. Although such manifestations occur (consider the Perfect Circle strike of 1957 or the Essex Wire strike of 1964), this kind of occurrence was much commoner at the turn of the century and in the period of active unionization from 1935 to 1940.

The concept of dispute used here is a generic one, including within its compass both *competitive* behavior (which in our society is approved, at least in fields other than labor relations) and *conflict* behavior. A dispute is said to occur when two or more parties are striving toward goals which are (or are perceived to be) mutually exclusive or when the means used by one party to achieve its goal negate (or are perceived to negate) the goal-directed behavior of the other party. Thus, the desire of workers and management for more money represents mutually exclusive goals, at least in the short run; i.e., if workers get more, managers and stockholders get less. Promotion by seniority is perceived by the unionists as instrumental to a goal of security, but it is perceived by executives as blocking efficiency. Workers and managers agree that security and efficiency are desirable goals, but the tactics they utilize are in opposition (see Fig. 1).

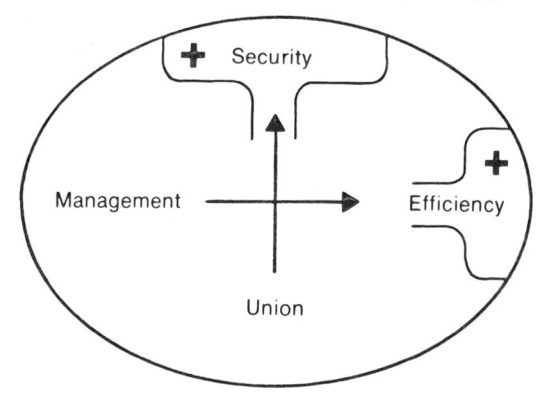

Figure 1. Situation when Worker Goals are Perceived as Blocking Management Goals.

A distinction between competition and conflict may be based on whether *rules* are perceived to be applicable: disputes under agreed-upon rules, as in price competition, would ordinarily not be called conflict; bombing the shop of a competitor, on the other hand, is conflict, not competition. In some cases the rules are ambiguous, and perceptions often differ; what businessmen call "cutthroat competition" and economists call a "game of ruin" occurs when rules are not perceived to be applicable.

It is not always easy to decide which rules apply—or whether any rules apply—to a given dispute. However, the kind of distinction we propose can be made, in most cases. To take a familiar illustration, two heavyweight boxers meet in the ring under clearly defined rules; they have mutually exclusive goals (only one can win); violence and bloodshed are very likely; yet we call this *competition,* not *conflict.* Tactics and circumstances are clearly laid down, and negative sanctions are provided if either breaks the rules. Suppose these same two men get into an argument in a bar and go into the alley to settle their dispute. They may well end up in a police station, charged with disturbing the peace, although their physical behavior is almost identical with that in the prize ring. Their behavior is *conflict,* because it flouts the rules laid down by society.

The rules that govern a dispute define the *expectations* which we discussed earlier. When rules get out of step with established expectations, as in the case of the Prohibition Act, they are difficult to enforce. The Civil Rights Act of 1964 codified expectations about which many people differed, and the enforcement of the act over the next few years will encounter many difficulties. When Congress passed the Wagner Act in 1933, many businessmen found that the rules did not fit their expectations and they rebelled against this law for some years.

Rules governing union-management disputes are laid down in a written contract. As in the instances just cited, such a contract may incorporate rules which do not fit the established expectations; and conflict may result. When a company that has fought unions for years finally signs an agreement with one, many supervisors have trouble adjusting; they go on firing union activists and ignoring seniority clauses until their expectations gradually become modified in conformance with the rules.

The written contract builds upon, but does not eliminate, what we have called the "psychological contract," the relationship of reciprocity in expectations of employer and employee. No contract can spell out just what the executive expects of the worker; job descriptions give only a small portion of the picture. Neither can any contract tell what treatment the employee expects from the company. Nevertheless, putting the contract in writing eliminates some ambiguity, clears up some confusions, and makes possible a gradual adjustment of expectations toward a common set of rules. As both sides agree on these, the relationship moves from conflict to competition, a dispute under rules.

Disputes at Contract Negotiation

The rules under which bargaining takes place are fuzzy and ambiguous. Although the NLRB requires both parties to bargain "in good faith," nobody knows what this means. It clearly does not mean that the union must abandon a claim whenever it is rejected by management, nor does it mean that management must yield when the union persists. The most we can say is that the rules require the parties to keep talking for a "reasonable" period of time; but even the word *reasonable* is subject to wide differences in interpretation. Given these ambiguities, it is not surprising that conflict is more likely to occur at contract-negotiating time than on other occasions.

Both parties bring certain expectations to the negotiations. It is general practice for each group to write its own expectations into proposals for the new contract. Thus management may try to write in that all promotions are based on ability alone. Unionists, knowing how hard it is to define ability with precision, fear discrimination and try to write in that all promotions are based on seniority alone. The likely compromise is one that attempts to incorporate both factors.

Similarly, each side is likely to have, at the beginning of negotiations, an idea of the limit beyond which it will make no concessions. This limit results in a *bargaining zone* for each side, with the preferred solution at one end and the tolerance limit at the other.

On a specific issue, such as union security, the union's desire may be a union shop with dues checkoff and superseniority for officers; the lowest acceptable settlement may be a union shop with an escape clause for a few present employees. The employer's wish may be for no union-security clause at all, and his tolerance limit may be compulsory union membership after a ninety-day probationary period. As the parties bargain, they explore these limits and, hopefully, find an area in which a compromise is possible. For both sides, there is a *bargaining zone* between the employer's tolerance limit and the union's tolerance limit. This conception is diagrammed in Figure 2.

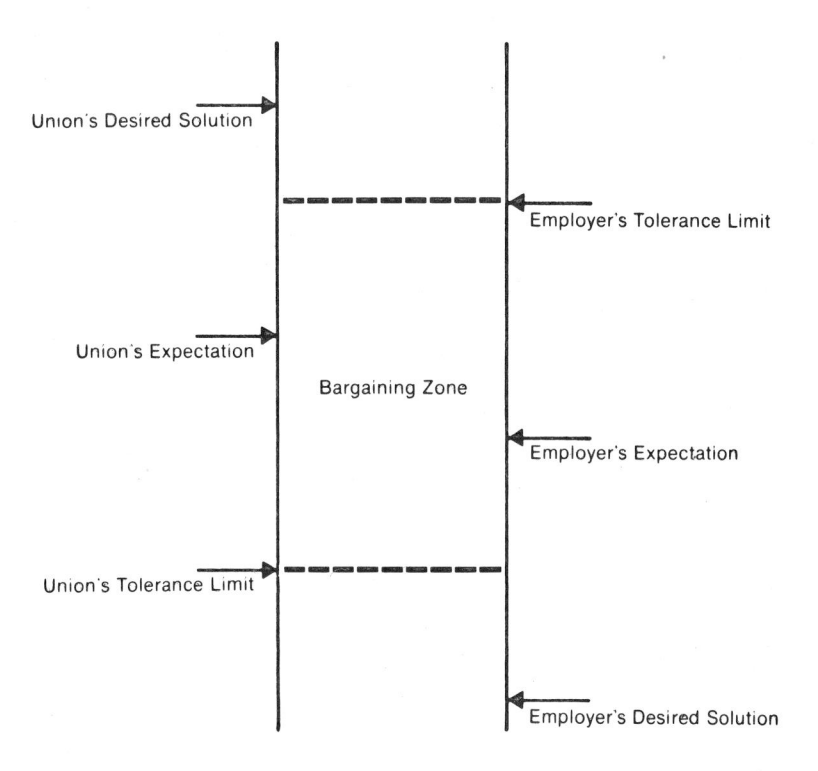

Figure 2. Desires, Expectations, and Tolerance Limits that Determine the Bargaining Zone

What factors determine the bargaining zone? . . . A contract clause that is unprecedented may seem completely unacceptable, whereas a familiar one is easily agreed to. In 1939, when rubber-workers in Akron were earning about 75c per hour, they did not demand an increase to $2.00; they asked for 90c and settled for 80c. Today no employer would resist a wage demand for 90c an hour (if anyone asked for it!). His range of acceptability is far above this point. This illustration shows that what is perceived as an unreasonable demand under one set of circumstances may look quite sensible under other conditions.

Standards of acceptability in bargaining are likely to be anchored to three sets of data: (a) industry practices, (b) community practices, and (c) recent trends. Thus, if one rubber company has granted extra vacations to employees of fifteen years' service, unions expect the same concession to be granted elsewhere in the industry (and executives in other companies are prone to feel that they must match the competition). Wage and other benefits are tied to the community average also. Workers in a low-paying industry who live in a community where wages are high will be keenly discontented, whereas, if they live in a low-income community, they will feel less severely frustrated. Finally, rising or falling trends in prices and wages affect our standards of expectation.

Conflicting parties, however, will select from among the data available only those items that fit their purposes. The union does not cite low-wage companies when making a case for an increase; and the company does not point to competitive practices when these are more generous than what it desires to grant. Each side can always find some instances to support the "wished-for" solution; and each side will tend to ignore the evidence presented by the opposition. Nevertheless, communication does take place; each takes some cognizance of the data, and the level of acceptability shifts. Management moves up a little, and the union down a little, until an acceptable point for both is identified. . . .

Disputes and the Grievance Procedure

Although disputes in contract bargaining draw more public attention, disputes about the behavior of the parties under a contract are more frequent. The *grievance procedure* is written into a contract to provide a set of rules under which such disputes can be settled in an orderly way, without an overt conflict. No contract can be written in such a way that every participant will agree on its meaning; just as contracts between businessmen can be taken to court or to arbitration, so union agreements must have a provision for settling disputes about whether the parties are living up to the contract.

When a worker files a grievance with his union steward, he is simply complaining that he is not receiving his rights (as he sees them) under the contract. Union spokesmen will sometimes heatedly say, "The company has violated this contract five hundred times in the past year," in reference to the number of grievances filed. This emotional way of stating the case implies that the worker is always right and the foreman is always wrong. But this implication is not easy to prove, and, as a rule, the foreman believes just as sincerely that he was interpreting the contract fairly.

In American firms, the grievance procedure usually provides for four steps. At first, the worker simply talks with his foreman. If the foreman modifies the situation to the employee's satisfaction, nothing is put into writing. This is the most efficient way to handle personal-grievance problems.

Second, if the worker is not satisfied, he writes out a grievance and files it with his committeeman or steward. As a result, the two may go together and talk with the foreman. Large numbers of grievances (in the typical company, over half of those written down) are settled at this first session. Often the steward convinces the worker that the contract does not cover the point at issue. However, if the steward wants to be re-elected, he may put up a show of a fight with the foreman and then resignedly say to the worker, "Well, I tried hard but couldn't get him to see reason."

Third, the steward may pass unsettled grievances, which he thinks involve contract violations, to a local committee of the union, which meets with production and labor-relations-staff people. Most of the remaining grievances are settled at this level. Unless arbitration is provided for, this is the final step before a strike. (In a multiplant company there may be one more level, in which the international-union representative sits down with the corporation official in charge of labor relations and tries to negotiate a settlement.)

Fourth, is *arbitration*, the last level for many union-management agreements. . . .

A grievance may be almost anything the employee wants to complain about, though his complaint must be tied to a clause in the contract. Because of the flexibility of the perceptual process, however, tying complaints to contracts is not as difficult as it might seem. For example, the employee who accuses his foreman of favoritism in the assignment of overtime work "sees" the foreman's actions in terms of his own desires. The worker may need the extra money; he may dislike a fellow worker who got the overtime work and extra pay; he may be annoyed with the foreman and want to get him in trouble with his boss by harassing him. But the foreman may "see" someone else as needing the money more; or that seniority should rule; or that an alphabetical procedure is fair; or that he is free to select anyone he wishes. Out of such divergent perceptions it is easy to build an industrial dispute.

Tactics Other Than Strikes

Management is in a position to stand pat on most of these controversies. The decision has been made and the action taken; it is up to the union to protest the unfulfilled conditions.

What shall the union leader do if the union's protest is ignored? There are a number of tactics other than a strike that he may utilize. Of these, we shall consider first some of the tactics used by workers themselves, whether organized or not.

The Slowdown

It is probable that even slaves used the *slowdown* against their masters. As far back as any records go in modern industry, this tactic has been used to pressure the employer to resolve a grievance. Mathewson (6) describes a food-packing plant in which workers learned that they could get some relief from work pressures by jamming the assembly line.

Some workers learn that if they obey all company rules in a blind, routine fashion, it slows down operations tremendously. The transit workers on the New York subway system, for example, can paralyze the system by observing all the obsolete safety rules on the books. Bus and truck drivers frequently take the same opportunity. Workers also make use of the device of reporting in sick. A big metropolitan dairy once had approximately four thousand drivers call in sick on the same day. Without considering the statistical probability that this coincidence represented real illness, we can see that the pressure on the employer was tremendous.

Some observers think that slowdowns will be more difficult for the worker with automated machinery. This does not seem probable. On the contrary, it is safe to predict that if workers have an unresolved grievance, they will find ways to stop the automated production line at irregular intervals and force the employer to act on their complaints.

Sabotage

The term *sabotage* is very instructive, because it is derived from the French *sabot*, meaning a wooden shoe; the term became popular through the practice of French factory workers of allowing a wooden shoe to fall into the machinery when they were discontented about working conditions. Management ultimately found this argument very persuasive in convincing them that they had better listen to worker grievances.

Sabotage is not always organized. One automobile executive told us of an operation in which production had been increased from 2,000 to 3,000 units per day by modification of a drill-press layout. However, the worker on this job resented the fact that he got no pay increase (the change was purely mechanical), and he discovered that by bumping the sheet metal against the drill as he removed the finished piece he would eventually break the drill and have to wait for it to be replaced. By some curious accident, the average production continued around 2,000 units per day. We do not know whether this message got through to top management, but if such breakdowns happen on a whole series of machines, it is understood rather promptly.

Legal Harassment

The union leaders have options such as filing charges against the employer with the NLRB on various disputed issues. Although these charges, in most cases, are eventually rejected by the Board, they require that the employer fill out forms, send witnesses to testify, and hire a lawyer or assign a member of his legal staff. Therefore, the nuisance value of the charges may be considerable, which sometimes contributes to accelerated settlement of disputes. The threat of legal harassment, however, is a two-edged sword. Employers may harass the union by NLRB charges, and they may even sue the union for damages under the Taft-Hartley Act. Few such suits ever come to trial and even fewer lead to collection of damages; usually the employer succeeds in convincing the union that a specific tactic must be abandoned, and when it is, the employer drops the suit.

Group Solidarity

In informal actions, as in the strike, the solidarity of the workers is very important. The sick-call technique depends on its use by a substantial majority of workers. If only a few cooperate in a slowdown, the employer is not under pressure.

We shall have something to say later about the problem of employee loyalty and group allegiance. At this point, the effectiveness of such tactics for putting pressure on the employer depends on the attitudes of the workers and on their willingness to take some individual risks in behalf of group goals.

The Strike

The reader may be perplexed by the fact that strikes, which monopolize newspaper reports on union-management relations, receive so little space here. The explanation is fairly simple. Strikes, like wars and other disastrous social conflicts, are similar to the visible part of an iceberg—they attract our attention to a danger. The vastly more significant portion (about nine-tenths) is hidden from view—yet the damage is done by the hidden portion of the iceberg. Strikes, therefore, serve a useful purpose when they call our attention to the fact that *unresolved industrial disputes* are in progress.

The Strike as Work Stoppage

In its simplest form, the strike is simply a concerted refusal to work. The employer has sales plans (or perhaps sales) that call for a given amount of production; the workers refuse to produce unless their demands are met. This refusal is a straightforward form of economic pressure, like that of a customer who refuses to buy unless the terms of trade are altered or that of a supplier who refuses to deliver raw materials unless the price is raised. The employer has the option of yielding or going—at least temporarily—out of business.

The Strike as an Information Device

The strike may often act primarily as a device to communicate to the public the fact that the workers are discontented and feel maltreated. In Italy and France, for example, many strikes are limited to twenty-four hours or even less. The unions do not have financial resources to help members through a long strike. Thus the strike is a technique for trying to mobilize the sympathy of the public and of the government. This kind of strike happens occasionally in the United States. A union may call a strike, which it has no hope of winning in terms of economic strength, in the hope that (a) it may get support from other unions, (b) it may get support from the public, or (c) it may induce the government to put pressure on the employer to settle.

Picketing is an important aspect of this public-information tactic; it is protected under the free-speech provision of the Bill of Rights. Pickets may succeed not only in communicating issues to the public, they may also embarrass management so that a settlement will be made that the union could not win on economic strength alone.

Public Perception of the Strike

The average citizen gets his information about a strike from newspaper headlines (regrettably, most people never read the stories under the headlines). Thus, the impression is usually one of unleashed violence and aggression. One sees headlines like these: "Union pickets jailed for overturning car"; "Union leader accuses plant guards of brutality"; "National Guard mobilized to keep peace"; "Six injured as shotgun blast cuts into picket line"; "Company guarantees protection to all who want to work"; "Plant damaged from brick-throwing unionists"; "Transportation workers refuse to cross picket line." When the strike involves the public more directly, we find these kinds of headlines: "Food rots as longshoremen refuse to unload"; 'Community terrorized as violence flares"; "Gasoline rationing feared as strike goes into fourth week"; "Strike imperils national security, says high official."

Psychoanalysts argue that most of us have repressed hostilities, which, we are afraid, may erupt if we are off guard; thus, we are intensely stimulated by outbursts of aggressive action in the environment. There seems to be some truth in this observation, as witness the morbid sightseers around a big fire, a catastrophic tornado scene, or a riot. Whether or not this theory is correct, the occurrence of violence in a strike induces anxiety, and people begin to demand government action. Since (on the surface, at least) the union precipitated the strike, the demand is likely to be for action against the union.

Dynamics of the Strike

It is precisely because of the adverse public view of strikes that we have presented our analysis of industrial disputes so methodically. If the reader is conscious of the vast background of motivational and perceptual factors that are involved in the causal process that results in the strike, perhaps he may realize that no simple explanation and no simple placing of blame on either side is going to be adequate.

The strike is inevitably tied in with *collective bargaining*—the attempt of both parties to establish a set of mutually acceptable expectations about each other. Insofar as both parties in bargaining hope to *optimize* (get the most gratification from the other party with the least loss to themselves), the bargaining relationship becomes one where both parties attempt to determine the consequences of various courses of action. [Elsewhere we have] discussed how the SEU model, utilizing motivational and perceptual factors, operated for the single person or group. In collective bargaining, the model applies to a two-group situation.

Collective bargaining is a sort of poker game. If a given course of action is undertaken, the expected utilities of the consequences, and the probability of their occurring, must be determined by a party in the dispute not only for itself but for the opposing party as well. Thus, the parties must attempt to put themselves in the "others' shoes." Interestingly enough, both company and union leadership are aware of a need for such mutual understanding, and have quite recently formalized the procedure both in role-playing and prebargaining approaches. For example, Table 2 indicates that it is essential for the union to make an estimate of whether management considers Alternative 1 or Alternative 2 more acceptable. Union tactics will be governed in considerable degree by the intensity of management opposition anticipated; and the firmness of the company negotiators will depend upon management's estimation of union strength and persistence.

TABLE 2

ILLUSTRATION OF UNION AND COMPANY ALTERNATIVES AND RELATED CONSEQUENCES

Company	*Union*
ALTERNATIVE 1:	ALTERNATIVE 1:
Giving in to union demands Perceived *Consequences:* 1. Lessening of investor return 2. Loss of competitive standing 3. Setting bad precedent 4. Avoiding costly strike 5. Avoiding government and public ill will	Accepting company counteroffer Perceived *Consequences:* 1. Loss of membership support 2. Loss of status within union movement 3. Setting bad precedent 4. Avoiding costly strike 5. Avoiding government and public ill will
ALTERNATIVE 2:	ALTERNATIVE 2:
Refusing to accede to union demands Perceived *Consequences:* 1. Due to potential strike, loss of investor return 2. Due to potential strike, loss of competitive standing 3. Loss of government and public good will 4. Maintenance of company prerogatives 5. Breaking union power	Sticking to original demands Perceived *Consequences:* 1. Prove strength and determination of union to members 2. Due to potential strike, loss of member income 3. Due to potential strike, loss of member support 4. Loss of government and public good will 5. Teach company a "lesson"

In major negotiations, such as those of the UAW with the "Big Three" auto companies, an almost formal ritual has been established. "Trial balloons" are released, either at the bargaining table or in the newspapers, and the vigor of the reaction to these proposals is carefully assessed. Each side asks for considerably more than it expects to get (see Fig. 2) and is constantly on the alert for cues to the issues on which the opponent is willing to fight to the finish. Since both teams are composed of professionals who have dealt with each other for years, the chances steadily improve that this information exchange will be accurate and that a settlement without serious disruption of the economy will result.

The Losses from Strikes

"If man were the rational economic animal postulated by classical economic theory, strikes would long since have disappeared from the American scene" (10, p. 439). Workers as well as employers lose heavily in any kind of extended strike. If both sides calculated long-run gains and injuries realistically, the necessary compromises would be reached without a strike. Note, for example, that the average worker puts in about two thousand hours a year on his job. Thus, a gain of 5c an hour over a prestrike offer gains him $100 a year. At current wage levels, this means that he has to work a year just to recoup the loss of one week on strike; hence, on a five-week strike, it takes five years just to get back even, before any net gain in earnings is experienced. From the union viewpoint, other losses must also be considered. These include the decrease of membership, expenditures for emergency aid to striker families, and possible political backlash in the form of restrictive legislation against unions.

The losses to the employer are harder to determine but substantial. During strikes, white-collar workers are usually kept on salary, and maintenance costs and interest charges continue. Customers may be lured away by competitors who can promise immediate delivery, and the public image of the firm may suffer substantially, especially if trouble occurs during the strike. Considering the sums spent to "improve the image," such losses may be costly to recoup.

Losses to consumers, and to the economy as a whole, are sometimes important. Hardships result from interference with normal marketing procedures; in a transportation tie-up, food may spoil. Thus, when work stoppages occur, there are other losses, beyond the major ones to workers and employers.

Violence in Strikes

Not the least of the costs of strikes is the occurrence of violence. Pickets marching around a plant recite their grievances and reinforce one another's hostilities. They may impulsively block the owner or top executives from getting in, or start throwing rocks to express their feelings. If the employer violates the strikers' expectations by hiring strike-breakers and attempting to operate his plant, he is likely to trigger extreme hostility. In the Essex Wire strike of 1964 nonstrikers' cars were forced off the road and the occupants beaten, plant windows were broken with bricks, and a plant guard was hit by shotgun fire. Although such incidents are rare as compared with the period 1935-1939, they are still deplorably frequent.

How can men who would not dream of beating up another man to take 5c from him beat up strangers in the course of an effort to gain a pay raise of 5c per hour? Several psychological factors operate in such behavior: the feeling of *social approval* for violence (since the other fellows do the same thing, it can't be wrong); reduced fear of punishment, because of *anonymity* (there are so many strikers that the police can't identify anybody to arrest, and witnesses won't testify anyway); the *excitement* of the situation; *displacement* of aggression from other frustrations; and the *stimulation* from belligerent leaders—all these motives contribute to irrational outbursts of violence on the part of strikers.

Whereas violence is rarely initiated by employers, *provocative* actions among them are common. Hiring additional guards, setting up barricades, and displaying armaments are employer actions not conducive to peaceful arbitration. Other employers, in their public comments on a strike, suggest that theirs is a righteous cause, in which they are justified in lashing out with all force available. However, because of a similar self-righteousness, millions of people have been killed in the many religious wars of this planet's history; there is a grave danger when an aggressive man feels that the improper behavior of unionists justifies his resort to uninhibited violence.

Lockouts

The manager also has an outlet for his annoyance, or simply a tool for imposing economic power, in the *lockout*. This outlet takes the form of saying, "If you don't conform to our demands, we'll close the plant." Thus the worker's concern over his job security is mobilized against his other motives, such as the desire for money, or some other goal he was seeking.

The employer may use the threat of a lockout to put the pressure of a majority of workers upon a minority which has a grievance. Where several employers bargain as a group with a single union, the threat of the union to strike a single employer can be countered by the threat of the association to close down every plant. Thus the complaining workers are faced with pressure from their fellow union members, who have no desire to be without paychecks while the dispute is being settled.

Principles of Dispute Settlement

Union-management disputes may be separated into those that arise from negotiations of new contracts and those that arise from disagreements over the meaning of contracts already signed. The latter are usually called *grievance cases,* and the former *contract cases.* Although the basic principles for settling these controversies are the same, some techniques (such as voluntary arbitration) that are widely used for grievance cases are rarely if ever used for contract cases. Despite this technical difference, we shall discuss the psychological principles of dispute settlement as if the two cases were the same—which, for our purposes, is almost always true.

Psychologists find their basic principles for guiding settlement of disputes in the laws of human behavior—specifically in the phenomena of perception, motivation, emotion, and frustration. These principles are the same, whether the disputes are between husband and wife, parent and child, Catholic and Protestant, Jew and anti-Semite, or Negro and white-supremacist.

Group disputes arise for only two reasons. One is that group A prevents group B from obtaining some sort of goal, and the second is that group A is perceived by group B as blocking its goal attainment, even though independent observers may agree that no such blockage occurs. The two reasons thus resolve into one: group A is perceived as threatening the goal achievement of group B.

... At this time, we wish to concentrate on the settlement of disputes that have already developed. Let us first identify three basic principles, and then see how they apply to some concrete instances of industrial disputes.

A Higher Loyalty

Parties to a dispute will settle their differences fairly readily if members of both groups acknowledge a *higher loyalty* to some more inclusive group. Unionists and executives share a loyalty to the nation which often plays a significant role in settling controversies. This loyalty was most conspicuously displayed during World War II, when the no-strike pledge of unions cut lost time from work stoppages to a minute fraction of its former total. But it has also operated in many other instances, such as in the acceptance by railroad unions of the compulsory arbitration of work rules, and the submission by employers to governmental orders to cease operations or to rehire discharged unionists. The importance of this psychological factor can best be demonstrated by quarrels between nations, in which case there is no higher loyalty, and in which it is considered a man's patriotic duty to kill off as many of the enemy as possible. Should either management or union lose confidence in the impartiality of the government, a similar kind of open warfare might be resorted to in union-management conflicts.

Superordinate Goals

Disputes may be settled with little difficulty when both parties recognize some goal above the one they are fighting about. In union-management disputes, this common goal is likely to be the necessity to keep the enterprise going, since profits and wages alike depend on production and sales. The goal of "mutual survival" is in the background of all discussions, and neither party—except under extreme emotional pressure—is likely to try to destroy the other. In the 1930s, many corporate executives still thought they could destroy unions, and, consequently, mutual considerations were less effective than they are today; but that particular belief has virtually disappeared.

A Common Frame of Reference

Disputes may be controlled when the parties can come to a reasonable agreement regarding the facts. When the twelve-hour day in industry was standard, managers could not "see" that it placed a heavy strain on workers. Today, there is general agreement that an eight-hour day is the most that should be demanded except under emergency conditions. A common frame of reference means that events in the enterprise will be perceived in a similar way.

We can illustrate in many ways the importance of similarity in perception. For example, the image held of the opposing party is important in dispute settlement. If the executive perceives the union as irresponsible and violent, he will be suspicious of its proffered agreements, and will try to hedge his promises with all kinds of reservations. This action will arouse the suspicions of the union leaders, who will interpret it as evidence that he intends to weaken or nullify the agreement.

Established expectations have their role to play. The manager has the belief that he alone has the right to determine the speed of operation of the machines. If the union challenges this belief, the manager may lose sight of the issue and he becomes more concerned with inroads upon his prerogatives. He may feel personally injured if his freedom of action is restricted beyond what he considers proper.

It has often been urged that negotiators for each side try to state the case for the other side, to be sure they understand it. Thus, the head of the management team would try to verbalize what the union is asking for, to the satisfaction of the union committee; the unionists in turn would have to show that they can put in words what management is asking, to the satisfaction of the management group. Such devices help in developing a common frame of reference; or, more precisely, they help in attaching verbal labels to events in the same pattern, so that communication becomes possible. However, this process does not guarantee that both sides have equal knowledge of the positions taken. Blake and Mouton (1) found that when two teams of managers competed to solve a problem, each group might meet the test of verbalizing the opposed position, although, on a test of information, they still knew more about their own solution than about the competing solution. Thus, this technique, though helpful, is no panacea.

It would probably be beneficial if more managers had work experience at the factory level. Current practice, however, is to hire recent college graduates as junior executives, and the only factory-work experience they get is of an observational variety. This management-hiring trend may make mutual understanding even more difficult in the future.

Applying the Principles

The basic principles for settling disputes operate in various specific devices such as bargaining, mediation, and arbitration. Since, in a sense, all union-management relations begin with the bargaining of a contract to cover the responsibilities of the parties to each other, let us discuss the bargaining process, to see how our basic principles operate in specific areas of disputes.

The Bargaining Process

Bargaining begins when one side attempts to communicate to the other its perception of the work situation and to induce a change in this situation. Bargaining may be directed toward higher wages, toward less loafing on the job, toward elimination of safety hazards, or toward any other goals that either management or union desires.

Bargaining is necessary because the situation as seen by management does not coincide with that seen by workers and union officers. If the two percepts agreed, joint action would be almost automatic. For example, if unionists agreed that workers were taking excessive time off, they would not object to its elimination. The controversy is over what is "excessive." Similarly, if managers saw a four-hour stretch on the assembly line as intolerable, they would quickly change the work rules. In this case, the controversy relates to an operational definition of "intolerable."

The bargaining process is a kind of learning situation for the members of each committee. Percepts of the work situation, expectancies, and levels of aspiration are built up over a period of many years, and the usual work situation tends to reinforce these established images. When managers talk only to managers, they are not contacting other views on any issues. Similarly, when unionists talk only to their fellows, they reinforce one another's version of the facts. The bargaining session is different, in that the union requires managers to take a look at some evidence that they have previously ignored, and management insists that the union representatives examine some information that is not compatible with their fixed opinions.

Over a period of time, the participants begin to see the facts in a slightly different light. Perhaps most of this change is in the estimate of the opponent's bargaining limit. The union spokesmen decide that if they push beyond a certain point, management will take a strike. The company team concludes that if they do not yield up to a specified level, the union will walk out. As each party modifies its demands, the discussion moves into the bargaining zone, and a peaceful settlement becomes possible. Graphic examples of this change will be found in Douglas (3). Although the cases Douglas describes are contract negotiations, the generalizations apply equally well to settling grievances. The only difference is that the written contract provides certain clauses which define the limits of the bargaining zone.

A major change that bargaining may produce is in the frame of reference, or the managers' standards set by "what other firms are doing." The union may bring in evidence—which management has preferred to ignore—to the effect that a certain change in work rules has been accepted by much of the industry. Management may present data on wage scales in the community that vitiate the union plea of inequity. Thus each side is, to some extent, compelled to assess data that it had previously ignored. This process may induce a shift in the bargaining zone.

In bargaining sessions, both sides usually make ritualistic avowals of their desire for mutual survival: the union denies any wish for the ruin of the company, and managers disavow any hope to break the union. Each also proclaims its loyalty to the welfare of the community and the nation. Whether these assertions are more than rituals is not clear. They may serve to remind each group of its dependence upon the other, if only to a limited extent, and this reminder favors peaceful settlement of the dispute. . . .

The Grievance Machinery

Normally, after a contract has been negotiated, procedures are established for settling disputes about the application of the contract. This procedural machinery serves mainly to bring the dispute within rules, so that it can be handled in an orderly fashion (through "competition" rather than "conflict").

Grievance hearings, at the first stage, require that both sides try to get all the relevant facts (but, naturally, each gathers evidence to support its contention). In some cases, it appears that either the worker or the foreman was misinformed, and the grievance is quickly cleared up. In other instances, there is a basic disagreement over the meaning of the contract. Such disputes may result in strikes, if the contract does not provide for arbitration.

We must not be surprised if the foreman (or the worker) is unclear about the interpretation of the union contract. In one study (2), even top union and management officials—those who had negotiated the agreement—gave different answers to questions about contract clauses.

The existence of established grievance machinery is probably the most important single factor for reducing the intensity and frequency of union-management conflicts. It prevents tensions from building up and assures the worker of an orderly procedure for handling his case. Because of the participation of union officials in it, to defend his position, he feels more willing to accept a verdict, even if unfavorable.

The use of bargaining officials, who are somewhat removed from the specific irritation, serves two purposes. First, distance lends perspective; thus, the more emotional elements of the worker-foreman interaction become diluted, or even disappear, at higher levels of the grievance procedure. Second, higher officials are more acutely aware of superordinate goals, which are very important to them. The foreman cannot know much about customer relations, but the vice-president for labor relations may be well aware that labor peace is very important at the moment. Further, he may know that this issue involves others that have implications beyond the ken of the foreman. Likewise, the international-union representative may abandon the worker's grievance, because he sees implications detrimental to union welfare (e.g., when resolving the grievance might arouse factional controversy inside the union).

Machinery for Dispute Settlement

Many controversies go beyond the level of in-plant grievance and the problems of negotiating new contracts. In some disputes, one or both parties may feel that their basic interests have become involved, and in others, emotional intensity may become so high that settlement at lower levels is impossible. We shall consider some of the techniques that are applicable to such disputes.

Government Intervention

When strikes or threats of strikes imply enough violence and hazards to third parties, government intervention may be required. For example, in 1962, after it had installed diesel locomotives and other advanced equipment, railroad management began a campaign to reduce the number of workers in freight service. Because this campaign threatened the jobs of many thousands of *operating* employees, the *operating* brotherhoods threatened a nationwide strike if the freight-service layoffs went into effect. Faced with this frightening possibility, Congress voted its first compulsory-arbitration law. Under this law, a panel was set up to hear the arguments of both sides and to render a verdict that could be enforced by the courts.

Government intervention, however, can be effective only when both sides are convinced of the impartiality of the arbitration panel, and its success depends to some extent on the patriotism of managers and unionists. If a radical union rejects the basic value of national unity, or if the arbitrators appear biased, the arbitration is likely to fail. Open violence, or continued hostility, if violence is suppressed, is likely to follow.

The railroad arbitration of 1962 was government intervention in its extreme form, *compulsory arbitration*. More common is *government mediation*, in which government representatives persuade (or press) both sides to sit down and negotiate when private talks have proved unsuccessful. However, before we explore this kind of settlement, let us consider *private arbitration*.

Private Arbitration

Many union-management contracts include a clause that provides for binding arbitration of disputes that occur over the meaning of the contract's terms. In practice, these disagreements involve different ways of perceiving situations. For example, a contract may list "sleeping on the job" as a ground for discharge. Without visual evidence, however, a foreman may decide that a man who was away from his post for forty-five minutes was sleeping, and fire him. The arbitrator may be required to decide whether the contract has been violated.

Similar ambiguous situations arise in connection with decisions about the proper amount of overtime pay, the pension rights of a retired employee, the right of a worker to refuse to enter a hazardous workplace, and many others. The worker and his representatives "see" the evidence in a way favorable to him; the manager may "see" something quite different. The arbitrator, as an outsider with a specialized knowledge of factory conditions, is asked to decide which percept is justified in terms of the relevant contract clause.

Establishments which have few cases going to arbitration are likely to hire an arbitrator when occasion requires; large corporations, such as the automobile companies, retain a *permanent umpire,* who is always available to hear disputes that cannot be settled at lower levels. In either case, it is customary for the cost to be split equally between management and union, and, after any settlement, either side can terminate the arbitrator's employment. If the arbitrator is a permanent umpire, the terminating party must pay *all* of his salary for the remainder of the year, a requirement that discourages impulsive actions.

Why do most large corporations, jointly with the unions, hire permanent umpires to hear arbitration cases and render decisions? The answer to this goes back to our discussion of perception. There is no way of knowing the "real" facts in any industrial dispute, because they differ according to the observer involved. A worker (and his steward) may honestly assert that he is working at a high output while the foreman alleges, with equal sincerity, that he is slowing production deliberately. A safety hazard that looks trivial to a safety engineer may look quite threatening to the worker who is in the situation for several hours a day. In short, there will always be disagreements about whether the facts support the position of management or the position of the union.

It would be possible to have wildcat strikes over such disagreements and, thus, to settle them by sheer economic force. But wildcat strikes are messy procedures, and they disrupt the activities of people not directly involved. The grievance and arbitration procedures provide an orderly way of handling disputes under an existing contract without resorting to picket lines and sit-downs at every turn. As long as both parties have confidence that the arbitrator is impartial, they will accept his decision as final. Any decision, even an unfavorable one, is often preferred to a continuing state of ambiguity and tension.

Mediation of Disputes

To accelerate the settlement of labor disputes, *outside mediation*—generally from the federal or state mediation service—may be necessary. The mediator may be invited in by the parties, when bargaining seems about to break down, or, more often, he may offer his assistance when a strike is dragging on and the parties have developed so much hostility that they refuse to speak to each other.

Unlike the arbitrator, the mediator has no power to impose a binding solution within an existing contract. He is usually brought in when a new contract is up for discussion and there are no agreed rules to apply. Thus, he is a kind of technical consultant to both sides, helping them find a solution, rather than a judge deciding who is right. He has only such tools as his prestige as an official mediator, his persuasiveness, his knowlege of union contracts, his sense of humor, and his ability to see the facts as they appear to each of the parties.

One of the mediator's main contributions is his opportunity to break the communications barrier between the parties. In a long strike—especially if there is any violence—tempers rise, each side calls the opposing leaders unpleasant names, and the parties may simply refuse to sit down together and bargain. Thus, the request from the mediator, in the name of the federal or state government, that the parties meet with him for talks on the problem is, in many cases, important to industrial peace.

Spokesmen for union or management sometimes become committed to positions from which it is embarrassing to retreat. For instance, a company president may state publicly, "We will never sign a contract with this union." Later he may discover that it will be economically wise to sign the contract. A request from a federal or state mediator to resume negotiations now helps to save face. If the president can point to a request from the White House, or even from the governor of his state, that he resume negotiations, he avoids an appearance of defeat.

The mediator can make other important contributions. He usually has a much wider range of experience with contract clauses than either the local management or the local union have. If he is experienced, he has learned to perceive the issues as they are perceived from both sides of the table. When he finds the parties deadlocked, he may be able to introduce a new way of defining the situation or an alternative way of phrasing a clause that will fall within the "bargaining zone" and, hence, be acceptable to both sides. In some disputes, he may simply keep calling meetings; since neither side is willing to take the public responsibility for breaking off these talks, the negotiators may become worn down to the point where they will reach agreement rather than continue the wearying routine.

Virtually the only sanction that the mediator has is public opinion, and even this weapon is not always reliable. Unless a strike causes great inconvenience, the public pays little attention, so that neither party will anticipate severe public censure if the mediator blames it for breaking off discussions. To a large extent, the mediator must rely upon persuasion and the ultimate operation of economic pressures on both sides to open the road to a settlement.

The Hidden Agenda

A basic requirement for mediating disputes is to find out what the parties *really* want. Unfortunately, their goals are not always discernible in their verbalized demands. We have noted elsewhere that some union demands are primarily punitive in character, as when it is impossible to eliminate unpleasant working conditions but possible to punish the company by demanding higher wages and other concessions. Aside from such cases, we find many examples of poorly verbalized or unstated goals which are sought in the dispute.

Consider the case of an impending reduction in the work force due to automated machinery. The union may demand that the coming layoffs be based solely on seniority, whereas management may demand that only those workers be kept on who have demonstrated their ability to do the new jobs. On the surface, such demands appear irreconcilable. However, closer inspection may indicate that the union is basically concerned with favoritism and bias in layoffs and wants a guarantee that no one will be laid off because of his union activity. It may happen that management wants to keep a few technically trained, valuable men who have not been on the job long enough to meet the standard of seniority that would have to be applied. Under these conditions, the mediator can propose a compromise that gives union officers superseniority as protection or that gives management the right to keep some workers without regard to seniority.

The average person is not always capable of giving an accurate account of his motives. Each of us has many desires that he prefers not to acknowledge even to himself. One role of the professional unionist is to verbalize the desires of workers, who perhaps find self-expression difficult or dangerous; but executives are not exempt from this phenomenon. Observations by McMurry (7), Eliasberg (4), and others indicate that successful industrialists may have unconscious desires for power and unacknowledged aggressive impulses that drastically limit their ability to negotiate intelligently with labor unions. The work of Muench (8, 9) suggests that the methods of clinical psychologists for making unconscious material conscious can make important contributions to mutual understanding—which is the first step in dispute settlement.

The Widened Agenda

Just as unrevealed goals may need to be brought into the open, so unintended consequences or wider implications of the controversy may need consideration. An arbitrator is barred from widening the dispute; he must rule within limits set by a contract. The mediator, however, can ask for a broader frame of reference. He may inquire of the union leaders whether they may not split their union by introducing a new seniority policy; he may call the attention of management to possible public displeasure with a plan to finance "paid" vacations through state unemployment insurance. The mediator can be very flexible; he may seek to rule out discussion of anything but the narrow point at issue, or he may insist on widening the agenda to include unintended consequences of a debated proposal. The skilled mediator is the person who knows when to adopt one tactic or the other.

The Public Interest

It would seem that the superordinate goal or higher good that disputing parties should seek, above their own advantage, is the *public interest*. Unfortunately, objective definitions of the public interest are hard to find. Each partisan sees his own goals as representing "the public welfare." Management spokesmen say, "It is in the public interest to keep prices down and avoid inflation," and union leaders retort, "It is in the public interest to keep purchasing power up and avoid recessions." What is the public interest? Obviously, it includes both of these alternatives, and many others.

Some would argue that the government is in the best position to determine the public interest. But when we observe the regional and interest blocs that exist within Congress, each asserting that his group's welfare is in the public interest, we lose enthusiasm for such a criterion. We are not accusing the labor and management leaders of cynical hypocrisy. Each man can truthfully and honestly say that, *as he sees it*, the national welfare will be best served if his side wins the victory. Perceptual distortions operate so effectively that he cannot see the arguments on the other side.

For the near future, decisions will probably continue to be made on the basis of political or economic strength. If the public sufficiently dislikes such decisions, a new coalition will probably develop enough political power to reverse the policies.

The Role of the Irrational

Executives and workers often hold to certain positions because of emotional involvement rather than "rational" self-interest in the economic sense. For example, an executive may say that he would simply refuse a demand for a profit-sharing clause on the ground that "it is not right." He would consider the probability and cost of a strike, but his decision would not be based on economic grounds. Similarly, workers may strike over excessive and arbitrary controls over workplace behavior, even though they will lose a great deal of money because of their action.

Perhaps it is fortunate that people sometimes act irrationally. Life could become pretty dull if everyone cooly calculated costs and made decisions on a purely economic basis. In evaluating industrial-relations problems, we must avoid the error of assuming that economics has the final or even the larger portion of the answer. A keen awareness of human emotions and of the variety of goals sought is thus important.

It is equally necessary that we recognize the valuable contributions to industrial harmony made by mediators and arbitrators. By their very detachment from the immediate conflict situation, they are able to view the problem in a larger perspective and see it without the distorting influences of personal emotion and motivation. Such perception makes for judicious and realistic problem solutions.

References

1. Blake, Robert R., and Mouton, Jane S. Reactions to intergroup competition under win-lose conditions. *Mgt. Sci.*, 1961, 7, 420-435.

2. Derber, M., Chalmers, W. E., and Stagner, R. The labor contract: Provision and practice. *Personnel*, 1958, 34, 19-30.

3. Douglas, Ann. *Industrial peacemaking*. New York: Columbia Univ. Press, 1962.

4. Eliasberg, W. A study in psychodynamics of the industrial executive. *J. clin. Psychopathol.*, 1949, 10, 276-284.

5. Ford, Henry, II. Bargaining and economic growth. Address to American Society of Corporation Secretaries, June 22, 1964.

6. Mathewson, S. B. *Restriction of output among unorganized workers*. N.Y.: Viking, 1931.

7. McMurry, R. N. The clinical psychology approach. In A. Kornhauser (Ed.), *Psychology of labor-management relations*. Champaign, Ill.: Industrial Relations Research Assn., 1949.

8. Muench, George A. A clinical psychologist's treatment of labor-management conflicts. *Personnel Psychol.*, 1960, 13, 165-172.

9. Muench, George A. A clinical psychologist's treatment of labor-management conflicts: A four-year study. *J. hum. Psychol.*, 1963, I, 92-97.

10. Stagner, R. *Psychology of industrial conflict.* New York: Wiley 1956.

Collective Bargaining Between Salaried Professionals and Public Sector Management

ARCHIE KLEINGARTNER

This article represents an analysis of one of the rather more troublesome areas accompanying the expansion of collective bargaining among professionals in the public sector, namely, the problem of defining the appropriate scope of negotiations. In the public sector, disputes over the proper subject matter for the bargaining process (to be distinguished from disputes over the disposition of subjects which the parties agree are properly on the bargaining table) tend to be more prevalent among professional occupations than among clerical and manual workers. That is, it is more likely that unions of teachers, social workers, nurses, and librarians will experience conflict with management over the proper subjects for negotiations than such groups as clerks, hospital orderlies, school bus drivers, and park employees. Unions which bargain for this second category of occupations tend to base their negotiating demands on the well-established bargaining subjects in the private sector. Public management generally accepts this arrangement.

Among professional and semi-professional employees we find unions wanting to bargain over matters different in both substance and implication from prevailing patterns among manual workers in the private or public sectors. Teachers wish to negotiate over class size and text materials used by students; social workers want a strong voice in the standards of service they provide to the clients; and librarians want to participate in determining policy on book selection. Decisions about these kinds of issues are at the core of the mission of the public agencies where these professionals are generally employed. A good deal of self-interested behavior on both the union and management sides helps insure that conflicts lead with some regularity to proceedings before employee relations boards and occasionally the courts.

The central hypothesis of this article is that there is embodied in the idea of professionalism a logic which imposes on those occupations which aspire to professional standards or are already characterized by them certain imperatives in bargaining and in the employment relationship. Thus, this article represents an attempt to analyze certain

Reprinted from *Public Administration Review*, March-April 1973, with permission.

aspects of the impact of occupational and professional factors on the scope of negotiations in the public sector. The frame of reference for this analysis is derived mainly from research which has been carried out on such salaried professional groups as teachers, social workers, nurses, and engineers. Between them they probably reflect most of the characteristics to be found among other professional groups.[1] To that extent, this analysis is intended to apply to all groups and occupations that operate within the orbit of professional standards and behavior.

The Goals of Professional Employees

Research into the literature reveals no general agreement on any authoritative statement on the meaning of the terms profession and professionalism. Nor is it necessary to attempt such a statement here. Yet, it is apparent that recognition as a profession has important social and economic consequences for the members of the occupation, and for the society. For some professions their professional character is explicitly recognized in legislation, giving them certain privileges and responsibilities that are denied other occupations.

In our society, to be recognized as a profession carries for its members an important assignment of differential prestige. Thus, for many occupations, the label rather than the substance of professionalism may become the end sought.

William J. Goode, in a recent analysis of the theoretical limits of professionalization, reached the conclusion that many aspiring occupations and semi-professions will never become professions in the full sense.[2] He included among the occupations inherently incapable of achieving full professional status those of school teaching, nursing, and librarianship. Social work, marital counseling, and perhaps city planning were identified by Goode as occupations that will achieve professionalism over the next generation. Dentistry, certified public accounting, clinical psychology, and aeronautical engineering are examples of occupations that have become professions in the last decade. If we assume a continuum ranging from occupations characterized by little or no professionalism at one end to full professionalism at the other, the concern of this analysis is with those occupations which in a relative sense tend toward the side of full professionalism.

Professionalism is a matter of degree, for the self-employed as well as for the salaried professional. It is not something which can be established once and for all, even for a single occupation. A cursory glance at the publications of the American Medical Association and the American Bar Association shows that even doctors and lawyers are deeply concerned with insuring their professional status and growth.

In many respects what professionals hope to derive from their work experience is not different from what all employees want. However, the intensity with which the former seek certain goals, the particular "mix" of work-related values that will provide optimum satisfaction and the hierarchy of these goals, tends to distinguish professionals from other groups.[3] Just as there exist differences between professionals and non-professionals, so many differences exist between occupations within the professional category. In general, however, professionals as a group have a stronger attachment to their work and expect to derive more from it than do the nonprofessional categories.[4] Clearly, for most professionals, work is more than "just a job." They expect to give a good deal of effort to their work and careers, and they expect to obtain a high level of reward for their efforts.

In order to link this discussion more closely to issues involving the scope of negotiations, it is helpful to separate the goals that professionals seek to achieve in their jobs and careers into two categories, which we can call level I and level II goals.

Level I Goals

Level I goals may be defined as those relating to fairly short-run job and work rewards. These goals are common to all categories of workers, irrespective of education, function, status, and related qualities. They have a relatively short time horizon in the sense that they have a "now" focus. It would be a great mistake, however, to underestimate the importance of adequate satisfaction of these goals for all employees, professional and nonprofessional alike. The fundamental concern that all employees seem to have with satisfactory wages or salaries, suitable working conditions, fair treatment on the job, fringe benefits, and a measure of job security are illustrative of level I goals.

The phrase found in many statutes and ordinances providing for collective bargaining under which the parties are required to negotiate in good faith on matters relating to "wages, hours, and working conditions," has as its frame of reference what is meant by level I goals. Wherever collective bargaining exists in the public sector, there is the recognition that level I goals are appropriate subjects to be brought to the bargaining table. While conflicts do develop over the employers' obligation to meet employees' specific demands with respect to these goals, the principle is rarely questioned that these matters are a proper and legitimate part of the collective bargaining process.[5] The distinguishing feature of level I goals in collective bargaining is that they are pursued in the expectation that a fairly immediate, closely job-centered gain will result for the persons covered by the agreement.

Level II Goals

Level II goals may be defined as the longer-run professional goals. These goals are not generally held by manual workers as realizable objectives; they are viewed as highly desirable and may play an important part in their fantasy lives, but they are seldom translated into concrete objectives. These goals relate importantly to long-range career and professional objectives. For professional workers level II goals are centrally related to the mission and content of the functions performed by members of the profession. In practice they rarely become concrete objectives (although much discussed) at the level of professional ideology until level I goals are adequately met.[6]

It seems that much of the substance of level II goals can be encompassed by the concepts of (1) autonomy, (2) occupational integrity and identification, (3) individual satisfaction and career development, and (4) economic security and enhancement. An illustrative definition of each concept follows:[7]

1. *Autonomy* — In part, autonomy may be defined as the right to decide how a function is to be performed. It suggests the professional's right, indeed, obligation, to practice in his work that which he knows. He expects to be trusted — not judged — by those to whom he makes available his specialized knowledge. Once admitted to full membership in the profession, he expects to adhere to a code of conduct formulated by the profession and binding on all its members. He desires an authority structure which recognizes the characteristics of the professional role.

2. *Occupational Integrity and Identification* — A professional occupation tries to delimit its boundaries in its dealings with clients and employees and to gain public recognition. With respect to internal organization, the occupation will take a position on whether to follow a policy of open or restricted entry. It will take action to protect itself from what it perceives as threats to its prerogatives and status. Salaried professionals are frequently subjected to a good deal of pressure to transfer their primary loyalty away from the profession to the goals of the organization which

employs them, as for example, when management tells the engineer that he is really part of management.

3. *Individual Satisfaction and Career Development* — Professionals want a good deal of direct control over decisions affecting their work and careers. The hierarchical authority structure of most organizations interposes a screen between the professional employees and management, with the latter making most of the critical decisions regarding the deployment of professional staff and rewards for performance.

Specific phrases commonly used in the literature to describe this area of professional interest include: "to be recognized as an expert in his field, especially by his employer," "to be protected from unqualified outsiders," "to do satisfying and socially useful work," "to have a predictable line of career development without leaving the profession," "a chance for social and economic mobility," etc. In part, professionals are conditioned by their training to want these things, but perhaps also, because some professions have achieved them, their achievement by members of the less successful professions become pressing occupational imperatives.

4. *Economic Security and Enhancement* — All employees want economic security and enhancement. In the context of level II goals, what makes that category important is the notion that the level of reward should be pegged not so much to the contribution made to the employing organization directly, or the need for having adequate income to sustain a certain standard of living, but rather that rewards bear a direct relationship to the quality of service rendered. Thus, for example, the quality of classroom teaching rather than the number of students taught or seniority would be the basis from which to measure professional worth.

Several observations may be made by way of comparing level I and level II goals. Whereas level I goals were defined as being more "now" oriented than level II goals, at some point the level II goals may become just as compelling for professionals as level I goals.[8] In collective bargaining, level I kinds of issues may involve greater dollar cost to the employer than level II issues. On the other hand, level I issues are less frequently disputed as appropriate subjects for bargaining. The level II issues, while clearly having economic consequences, are from the employer's point of view of greatest concern because they may provide a fundamental challenge to managerial authority. For that reason, level II goals are frequently more intractable in terms of conflict over whether they are appropriate subject for collective bargaining.[9]

Salaried professionals, to achieve both their level I and level II goals, must enter into a direct relationship with the employer. This can be done on an individual or on a group basis. Because the employer has many of his own goals to achieve, there may develop conflict at various points between the goals of the employees and the employers' own definition of his imperatives for success and survival.[10]

Unions and Associations among Salaried Professionals

All salaried professions establish protective organizations to advance the interests of the occupation as a whole and of its individual members.[11] Historically, there emerged two main patterns of protective organizations among the salaried professions. The dominant pattern consisted of broadly based professional associations and societies with fairly open membership policies. The National Education Association, the National Social Work Association, and the American Nurses' Association are illustrative of these types of organizations. A number of these organizations very early assumed the responsibility to advance the full range of job and professional interests of their members. In practice, they paid relatively little attention to immediate job matters, concentrating instead on broad professional objectives such as developing codes of ethics, establishing standards for professional practice, and publishing professional journals. Frequently, leadership posts and the dominant influence within these organizations were in the hands of persons well placed in the management heirarchy. They adopted an attitude of full cooperation with the employer on the assumption that there exists a fundamental identity of interest between their own professional goals and the goals of the employer. In this view there was little possibility that conflict could not be resolved through improved communication and education. The collective bargaining model which developed among industrial workers was viewed as quite unnecessary and unprofessional.[12]

The second general pattern of organization was that of independent and affiliated unions. The American Federation of Teachers, for example, was chartered by the AFL in 1917. What distinguished these organizations most critically from the various societies and associations was their early acceptance of the concept of direct negotiations with the employer. Characterized by varying degrees of militancy and success, they were vigorously opposed by the associations and employers. To the employers they represented an irritant rather than an effective force. The unions were handicapped by the associations' enormous edge in membership, influence, and prestige.

For a variety of reasons, the 1960s saw a marked movement in the direction of convergence in the goals, tactics, and strategies of the two kinds of protective organizations around a common set of job and professional problems. This convergence has advanced farther among some salaried professions (e.g., teachers and social workers) than among others (e.g., engineers and scientists).

Overall there has occurred a marked increase in the militancy and commitment to collective bargaining of both unions and professional associations in the public sector to achieve the full range of job and professional goals of their members. What we may see more of in the future are mergers of the two kinds of organizations into one inclusive type. In any event, the day of the primacy of the pure professional organization, shying away from confrontation with employers and unwilling to admit the need for collective action at the work place level, is drawing to a close.[13]

Management Response to Professional Unionism

Public management generally enters a bargaining relationship with salaried professional organizations with reluctance and apprehension. Management in both the private and public sectors is concerned about unions becoming involved in nonlabor issues for fear of losing control and reducing operating efficiency. In the private sector, management's defense against union demands for more participation in decision making has been that: (1) it is primarily accountable to the owners or the board of directors from whom it receives its authority, and (2) management needs the flexibility to insure that it achieves its profit goals. In the private sector the source of authority is downward from the owners or board of directors. In the public sector there is an upward flow of authority from the public-at-large to elect or appoint managers. As such, decisions made or contemplated by the manager are open to public debate and scrutiny. While the public manager has no profit goals which he is expected to achieve, his performance may be judged in part on his ability to stay within his budget or his skill in locating new sources of revenue. Ultimately, the public manager's performance is evaluated in terms of what the legislative bodies and the public decide best serves their interests. Both can be very demanding and discriminating. Resisting union encroachment on their prerogatives may be one of the expectations that they have of the public manager.[14]

Additionally, we should not underestimate the shock effect on many public entities that is generated by the requirement of meeting at the bargaining table to negotiate about matters which management had previously always determined on a unilateral basis. Widespread collective bargaining in the public sector is not much more than 10 years old. Many public managers have little knowledge about the law, the art, or process of bargaining. It is natural to expect defensiveness and caution in the initial bargaining encounters.

An employee demand which in an established relationship appears routine and nonthreatening may in a new relationship appear radical and destructive. Public management has perhaps not fully considered the unique aspects of managing a public enterprise or the opportunities for innovation and social invention through the dynamics of a bargaining relationship. There is need for trial and error in the public sector as there was in the private sector.

Perhaps a major step forward is taken when public management starts thinking less in terms of defending established managerial prerogatives and authority and more in terms of how to structure a relationship where the end result will be the most efficient service to the public at the lowest possible cost.

In some jurisdictions, public managers are prohibited by statute and civil service rules from participating definitively in negotiations on a wide variety of matters which are of central interest to employee organizations and to management. From a practical standpoint, advantages might accrue from greater uniformity among the various states on the matters which affect the employment relationship that are prescribed by law. However, the fact that certain matters are precluded from direct negotiations does not alter what salaried professional organizations try to achieve for their members; it may alter the methods they need to use in achieving them.

The hypothesis may be suggested that the more salaried professional organizations are thwarted in channelling both level I and level II goals through the bargaining machinery, the more they will attempt to achieve these goals through other methods — the legislative and lobbying processes, for example. An important public policy issue therefore is the extent to which employee-management relations in the public sector are to be structured so as to indicate a clear bias in favor of maximum reliance on collective bargaining.

When we consider the array of methods that salaried professionals have used to achieve their goals, collective bargaining has been, in a historical sense, one of the least used. Some methods employed in the past are being discarded as ineffectual, while others, such as informal consultation with management, lobbying, mutual aid, publication of professional journals, and promulgation of codes of ethics, continue to serve a useful purpose. Most salaried professionals recognize that professionalism must in its concrete aspects be obtained primarily from the employer.[15] However, what salaried professionals are ultimately committed to is not the bargaining process per se, but to achieve predictability about continuing adequate satisfaction of level I goals and to work toward achievement of the level II goals, which in the final analysis define what professionalism is all about.

In my view, the dominant pattern in negotiations between salaried professional organizations and public sector management is that in the early stages of the relationship the employee organization will typically focus primarily on achievement of level I goals.

However, the logic of professionalism will not allow the protective organization to ignore for long the level II goals of its members. The more professional the orientation of the salaried occupation involved, the sooner it will begin focusing on level II types of concerns. Employee organizations will constantly confront the problem of reconciling what is doable in the short run and what they are really trying to achieve in the long run. Ida Klaus' description of the evolution of the bargaining relationship between the United Federation of Teachers and the Board of Education in New York provides partial verification of this hypothesis. She viewed the relationship as having moved through four stages between 1962 and 1969.[16] The first stage, which commenced in 1962, she labelled the stage of "Exploration and Experimentation." It covers the initial bargaining encounter between the school board and the union. The end result of the negotiations was a 38-page collective bargaining agreement covering various aspects of salaries, hours, and working conditions, as well as the taking of some tentative steps toward union involvement in sharing decision making on more purely policy or managerial features of public school system administration.

The second stage of the relationship she called one of "Crisis and Turning Point." This stage commenced in early 1963, when negotiations got underway for the second agreement. Here it is instructive to quote her at some length:

> The main field of conflict during the second year concerned an extremely grave and difficult area in public education: the proper scope and boundaries of collective bargaining. Where is the line between what is primarily within the sphere of working conditions and hence subject to negotiation and bilateral decision, and what is essentially within the realm of educational policy and hence within the exclusive authority of the Board or the Superintendent and not subject to negotiation and agreements. The Union sought to extend collective bargaining to new aspects of educational administration, and the Board rejoined that such matters were reserved exclusively to the discretionary professional judgment and policy-making authority of the Board and of the Superintendent.[17]

The outcome of the second round of negotiations produced an agreement, 18 pages longer than the first, and included that the parties would "meet and consult" once a month during the school year "on matters of educational policy and development." One of the specific subjects of joint consultation was the development of a program for the improvement of "different schools."[18]

In 1965 when negotiations started for a third contract, the parties moved into the third stage of their relationship. By this time collective bargaining as the method for determining the salaries and working conditions of the teachers was firmly established. In addition,

> the process of regular joint consultation on a year-round basis added a new and broader dimension to the teacher-Board relationship. Through this process the Union became a truly powerful force in school administration. . . . It participated in planning the Board's internal procedures for administering the provision of the collective bargaining agreement. . . . On several occasions, the Board withdrew items appearing on the calendar for action at a public meeting upon the Union's insistence that the matter was a proper subject for collective bargaining and that "prior consultation and negotiation" had not taken place.[19]

Negotiations in 1967 for the fourth agreement between the parties and the agreement in effect at the time Ida Klaus published her analysis signified entry into still another stage of the relationship, which she called "The Emergence of Public Interest Issues Peculiar to the Enterprise." It would appear that in those negotiations the board sought to regain some of the authority it had agreed to share with the union in earlier contract negotiations. The union sought an additional extension of its role. After protracted negotiations, involving a special mediation panel and the longest strike in the history of the city, a settlement was reached in which the union achieved most of its final substantive demands directly affecting teacher working conditions. However, the union also made important concessions on the extension of its role in what the board considered to be policy matters.

It appears that over the period of time covered in Mrs. Klaus' analysis there occurred a steady expansion in the depth and variety of topics that became subject to bargaining. Many topics originally viewed by management as completely within its discretion gave way to joint determination. From Klaus' analysis, it can be seen that the initial major thrust of the union was on economic and job items, that is, level I issues. Over the years there has not been a lessening of the union's concern with these matters. However, it also seems clear that there has been a substantial measure of union penetration into the level II types of issues.

In presenting this much detail on teacher bargaining in New York City I do not mean to imply that it should be viewed as a model of what should or will occur in bargaining relations with teachers (or other professional groups) in other parts of the country. Each relationship tends to develop within a somewhat unique set of circumstances and will evolve somewhat differently. Yet, the overall direction of bargaining relationships for salaried professional employees will probably conform to the movement from level I to level II types of issues. The details of the timing, the path followed, and the problems that must be overcome will vary from situation to situation.

Public Policy Considerations

This article suggests that there is embodied in the idea of professionalism a certain logic which, to those occupations characterized by or aspiring to its substance, inevitably propels their protective organizations to move into areas of decision making including, but also going beyond, the collective bargaining goals of nonprofessional worker unions in the public or private sector.

Long before collective bargaining became prominent among professional employees, public employers and salaried professional organizations engaged in discussion and consultation on a wide range of level II or policy issues, as they are more commonly known. This kind of informal negotiation, which does not have a written agreement as its objective, is perhaps still the dominant pattern in public jurisdictions. The outcome of this consultation does not result in a redistribution of basic function or power. Part of the recent growth in collective bargaining stems from the unwillingness of public employers to take seriously the goals and aspirations of their salaried professional employees in these discussions.

Collective bargaining will probably have the effects of curtailing the importance and attractiveness of informal consultation, even in those public jurisdictions in which bargaining is not required because employers fear that informal negotiations could under certain circumstances be quickly transformed into an adversary bargaining relationship.

The general analysis put forward here does not suggest any easy or quick solutions by way of guidance for public management and legislative bodies in deciding how to deal with questions of scope of negotiations for professional employees. There are alternative approaches and assumptions which have been relied on in the search for a workable model.

There is one view which holds that legislation should attempt to specify with some precision the matters which must be kept out of the bargaining process. Alternatively there may be attempts to specify a narrow band of mandatory subjects of bargaining, leaving everything else either illegal or up to the discretion of management. In practical terms, management would probably give the language covering negotiable items a narrow construction. Whether or not prohibited from doing so, management would undoubtedly resist negotiating over most of what has been called here level II issues.

An alternative and perhaps more realistic approach to defining scope of negotiations is to take into account the particular circumstances surrounding the bargaining relationship. Except at the extremes, this approach does not look to ideology, legal philosophy, or tradition for guidance. In the public sector, it would mean looking beyond what has worked in the private sector to a consideration of the unique features of public sector management, and to the specific goals and capabilities of the employees and their organizations.

Public management, operating with this orientation, recognizes that it is neither possible nor wise arbitrarily to delimit the scope of negotiations. It will appreciate that a universal definition does not provide the various occupational subgroupings equal and adequate opportunity to bring to the negotiating table those benefits and rights associated with the expectations of the occupation and which lend themselves to the bargaining mechanism. In determining where authority and responsibility are to be located, management would not look so much to who has the right, or who has done it in the past, as to what the consequences of a change are likely to be. Will it make the agency more efficient? Will it improve the quality of service which it provides to the public?

A Concluding Note

A prominent complaint of professionals and their organizations has been that they are saddled with a lot of professional responsibility but without commensurate professional authority. Salaried professionals have made it clear that they want real authority to make decisions affecting not only their own status and career aspirations but the basic character, quality, and amount of services provided to the recipients of their professional services. We can expect for example, that increasingly teachers will be involved in deciding the content of the courses they teach, the textbooks they use, all of the learning activities within the classroom, overall curricular planning, recruiting of new colleagues, and promotion and tenure decisions. Parallel kinds of decisions exist for such groups as nurses, social workers, engineers, architects, and district attorneys in the public service.

We are rapidly moving from an era of unilateralism in public sector activity to one of bilateralism. This trend will undoubtedly continue at an accelerated rate. Consultation, negotiation, and bargaining which result in a genuine redistribution of authority are becoming part of everyday management in the public sector. The groups on the cutting edge of this revolution are the salaried professions. The implications of this revolution are a tall challenge to public management employee organizations alike.

Notes

1. There is a substantial literature that deals with the salaried professions. I have completed studies on a number of different salaried professional occupations. In part this paper represents an interim report on a much longer-term study of various aspects of collective action among the salaried professions. Much of the literature especially relevant to the theme being developed here is treated in the following two books: Sigmund Nosow and William H. From (eds), *Man, Work and Society* (New York: Basic Books, Inc., 1962), and Howard M. Vollmer and Donald L. Mills (eds.), *Professionalization* (Englewood Cliffs: Prentice Hall, Inc., 1966).

2. William J. Goode, "The Theoretical Limits of Professionalization," in *The Semi-Professions and Their Organizations*, Amitai Etzioni (ed.) (New York: The Free Press, 1969), pp. 266-313.

3. See, for example, Everette M. Kassalow, "White-Collar Unionism in the United States," in Adolf Sturmthal (ed.), *White-Collar Trade Unions* (Urbana: University of Illinois Press, 1966), pp. 359-360.

4. A classic study of this point is Robert Dubin's "Industrial Workers' Worlds: A Study of 'Central Life Interest' of Industrial Workers," *Social Problems*, Vol. III (January, 1956), pp. 131-142, in which as many as three-fourths of the industrial workers in his sample turned out to be basically non-job oriented. Several years later Louis Orzack used Dubin's questionnaire and methodology among a group of nurses to attempt to verify his prediction that work is more likely to be a "central life interest for professionals than for industrial workers." Orzack summarized the overall results of the two studies as follows: "Dubin reported that '. . . for almost three out of every four industrial workers studied, work and the workplace *are not* central life interests.' In contrast, for four of every five nurses studied, work and the workplace *are* central life interests. We may infer that these professional nurses are much more interested in their work than Dubin's factory workers were in theirs." See Louis Orzack, "Work as a 'Central Life Interest' of Professionals," *Social Problems*, Vol. 7 (Fall, 1959), p. 126. A number of other studies have come up with similar results.

5. For a very helpful discussion of a number of these points, see Russel A. Smith, "State and Local Advisory Reports on Public Employment Labor Legislation: A Comparative Analysis," *Michigan Law Review*, Vol. 67 (March, 1969), pp. 904-908. Also relevant to this point is Irving H. Sabghir, *The Scope of Bargaining in Public Sector Collective Bargaining* (Albany: State University of New York, 1970), *Passim*.

6. The hypothesis being expressed in this paragraph has its root in various treatments of the concept of professionalism and in ideas about the requirements for effective performance of professional jobs. This is expressed, for example, in such statements as, "The professional claims *autonomy*, the right to decide how his function is to be performed and to be free from lay restrictions," from George Strauss, "Professionalism and Occupational Associations," *Industrial Relations*, Vol 2 (May, 1963), p. 8. Also implicit in this formulation is Maslow's development of the idea that the basic human needs are arranged in a hierarchy of prepotency. See A. H. Maslow, "A Theory of Human Motivation," *Psychological Review*, Vol. 50 (1943), pp. 370-396.

7. These definitions draw liberally on material contained in Archie Kleingartner, *Professionalism and Salaried Worker Organization* (Madison, Wis.: Industrial Relations Research Institute. University of Wisconsin, 1967), especially Chapter III.

8. See Chapter 8 in Vollmer and Mills, *op. cit.*, pp. 264-294, for discussion of the importance of level II type goals to professionals.

9. See, for example, Sabghir, *op. cit.*, p. 114.

10. For an excellent theoretical development of this point, see Jack Barbash, "The Elements of Industrial Relations," *British Journal of Industrial Relations*, Vol. II (March, 1964), pp. 66-78.

11. Occupational associations tend to emerge almost simultaneously with the occupation itself. Harold L. Wilensky, "The Professionalization of Everyone," *The American Journal of Sociology*, Vol. LXX (September, 1964), p. 143.

12. Bernard Goldstein, "Some Aspects of the Nature of Unionism Among Salaried Professionals in Industry," *American Sociological Review*, Vol. 20 (April, 1955), pp. 201-202.

13. Garbarino, writing in 1968, concluded that ". . . organizations of professional employees — both those which call themselves unions and those which do not — will increasingly . . . do their best to look and sound like professional societies, but, if necessary, will act more like unions." Joseph W. Garbarino, "Professional Negotiations in Education," *Industrial Relations,* Vol. 7 (February, 1968), p. 106.

14. For additional treatment of various aspects of this issue see Michael H. Moskow, *et al., Collective Bargaining in Public Employment* (New York: Random House, 1970), pp. 208-209, and Paul H. Appleby, "Government Is Different," in Dwight Walso (ed.), *Ideas and Issues in Public Administration* (New York: McGraw-Hill Book Co., 1953), p. 61.

15. It seems to me that the important shift which has occurred here in recent years is that salaried professionals no longer derive much satisfaction from the rhetoric of professionalism. They increasingly want its substance. By rhetoric of professionalism I mean such things as being told that you are "part of management," that "unionism is incompatible with professionalism," and that professionals must never forget "to live up to their high professional calling and to the expectation of the community," and so forth.

16. Ida Klaus, "The Revolution of a Collective Bargaining Relationship in Public Education: New York City's Changing Seven-Year History," *Michigan Law Review,* Vol. 67 (March, 1969), pp. 1036-1065.

17. *Ibid.,* pp. 1042-1043.

18. *Ibid.,* p. 1046.

19. *Ibid.,* p. 1049.

CHAPTER **10**

Current Issues in Personnel: Women, Minorities, and the Disadvantaged

Starting a decade ago with the 1964 Civil Rights Act, this nation committed itself to eliminating job discrimination and to upgrading the economic and employment status of minorities and the disadvantaged. How well have we succeeded? Silberman, writing in 1970, states that much progress has been made; he presents evidence that both the absolute and relative economic status of blacks has improved. The view that Thurow has, looking backward six years later, is much less optimistic. He finds that progress has been limited, slow in coming, and fitful. Silberman feels that the government can create jobs for minorities and the disadvantaged by effectively stimulating and managing the economy. Thurow feels that this approach will never lead to full employment and that minorities will not make progress in closing the income gap with whites unless the government directly provides publicly-funded jobs to minorities on a massive scale. Silberman represents the optimism of the '60s; Thurow, the somber outlook of the '70s.

Reverse discrimination charges grow out of certain situations in which minorities compete directly with majority group members for available jobs. The study by Hall and Saltzstein makes clear, however, that minority groups compete for jobs not only with majority group members, but also with other minority groups. Hall and Saltzstein show that problems created by this kind of competition can also be complex and difficult.

Personnel departments today are charged with responsibility of assuring top management that every step possible will be taken to give women equitable treatment in all personnel decisions. This is no small responsibility; in fact many traditional beliefs and practices would seem to make it an almost impossible task. Difficulties begin even prior to the decision to hire. The studies by Bem and Bem show that the wording of job announcements and recruiting advertisements dramatically affect the sex composition of the group likely to apply for a given job. Their results indicate that sex-biased wording in job advertisements and in help-wanted ads are particularly likely to discourage women from applying for many jobs for which they might be qualified.

The Rosen and Jerdee research study indicates that, once on the job, men and women employees are apt to be treated differently—and in ways not necessarily beneficial to women's long-term career prospects. The Rosen and Jerdee research is interesting and enlightening for what it reveals about sex stereotypes. But it is also useful for another purpose: it reveals how behavioral scientists can sometimes slip into faulty thinking and adopt questionable assumptions. For example, consider the task of the manager-respondents in evaluating the male and female candidate for the job of purchasing manager—a job which requires extensive travel. Both candidates have four children, ages 4, 7, 8, and 11. The managers were not told whether the candidates had made arrangements for child care. Now consider the factual prior probabilities existing in our society. If a male candidate has four young children, the prior probability is very high that he has a wife who stays home with the children. In the case of a female candidate with four young children, the chances are much lower that her husband stays home and cares for the children. Thus the managers have a factual reason, based on knowledge of practices in our society, for preferring the male over the female candidate. They are not necessarily relying on "preconceived attitudes or role stereotypes" at all. The case of the male and female candidates for promotion to personnel director is similar. Supposedly, both candidates have "identical competing family demands." But are these demands really "identical" in our society, even if both candidates state them in the same way?

The article by Pogrebin focuses once again on one of the more common themes of the recession-ridden '70s: the competition between different social groups for scarce jobs. In many businesses, women and minorities were not hired in significant numbers until recently. Layoffs during recessionary times are usually based on seniority, and thus women and minorities are the first to go. Is this legal? Is it fair? Both questions are much more difficult than they appear at first glance. Pogrebin provides a thorough exploration of the complexities of this issue. Finally, Maureen Kempton provides an interesting personal note on the feelings of one policewoman whose career has been disrupted by the last-in first-out system.

Section A
Minorities and the Disadvantaged in Personnel Decisions

Black Economic Gains—Impressive But Precarious

CHARLES E. SILBERMAN

. . . Some students of the racial problem argue that only a relative handful of blacks have been able to move into the economic mainstream. Dr. Andrew Brimmer, the first and only black member of the board of governors of the Federal Reserve System, speaks of a "deepening schism between the able and the less able, between the well prepared and those with few skills" and suggests the schism may be widening.

In fact, job barriers have been coming down for all blacks, not only those with a college degree. The number of Negro families earning less than $3,000 a year decreased by one-third between 1960 and 1968, after adjusting for changes in the purchasing power of the dollar, as high-school graduates—and even "dropouts"—have been able to move into jobs from which Negroes traditionally have been barred, or to which they have had little access. Since 1960 the number of Negroes holding clerical jobs has more than doubled, and the number of Negro sales workers has risen 61 percent. In the blue-collar sector, the number of Negro craftsmen and foremen increased by 70 percent, of semiskilled workers by 41 percent. Equally important, a substantial proportion of the increase in semiskilled jobs occurred in comparatively well-paying durable-goods industries such as autos and steel.

As more Negroes found better-paying and/or higher-status jobs, their numbers decreased in the kinds of low-paying and low-status jobs to which Negroes traditionally have been confined. Thus the number of Negro domestic household workers dropped 28 percent, the number of nonfarm laborers by 8 percent, and the number of farmers and farm laborers by no less than 56 percent. And while the number of Negro service workers did increase, more of them graduated to more prestigious service jobs, such as firemen, policemen, guards, and watchmen.

The consequence of all this has been a rapid increase in the returns Negroes receive from investment in education, an increase already being reflected in the statistics of Negro income. In sharp contrast to the situation of only a few years ago, the gap between median Negro and white incomes is now smaller for Negroes with a year or

Reprinted from the July, 1970 issue of *Fortune* magazine by special permission; © 1970 Time Inc.

more of college than it is for those with no more than a high-school education (and smaller for those with a high-school education than for those with only an elementary-school diploma). Actually, current statistics understate the situation, since they take no account of the fact that a large proportion of better-educated Negroes are men and women who got their schooling recently and are just starting out in life.

The discrepancy between blacks and whites is likely to narrow still more in the near future, since the experience of other ethnic groups who have encountered discrimination indicates that there tends to be a lag of one or two decades between gains in educational attainment and their translation into increased income and occupational status. The same thing appears to be happening now to black Americans. And as the returns from education increase, so does the incentive to stay in school longer. The combination of more education and more job experience in turn is laying the base for a new period of catching up.

But Negroes will not be able to catch up unless the economy returns to a rapid rate of growth. Indeed, a rate of growth fast enough to keep the economy at full employment for an extended period of time is a prerequisite for any Negro progress at all. Full employment is the most effective solvent of discrimination in the labor market, because the alchemy of labor shortage turns people previously classified as unemployable into highly desirable employees. Since 1963, when it began intensive recruiting efforts, Chase Manhattan Bank has hired half of its new employees from minority groups. In part, of course, this reflects management's growing social consciousness, in part its desire to avert racial violence, but the overriding reason is that the bank's traditional supply of white clerical help has largely dried up. As one bank officer explains, "We need people. They're people. It's as simple as that."

Moving down the Queue

It is not quite as simple as that. But, allowing for some rhetorical exaggeration, the bank officer has provided a concise explanation of what economists call "the queue theory of the labor market." According to this theory, the available supply of labor is arrayed in order of workers' desirability, and employers choose job candidates from as far up the queue as they can. As aggregate demand for labor increases, employers have to move further and further down the line, taking people they previously had found unacceptable.

Since Negroes are heavily concentrated at the bottom of the queue, it takes a sustained period of expansion before employers begin reaching into the black labor pool. In part, this is because Negroes do have poorer qualifications. But only in part. While employers do move down the queue in an orderly sequence, the criteria for rating workers are highly subjective and frequently quite irrational.

A large element of irrationality is introduced by employers' lack of knowledge about the relation between entrance requirements—amount and quality of education, age, score on qualifying tests, etc.—and actual performance on the job. Since personnel men cannot admit their ignorance, still less admit that hiring is arbitrary and irrational, they feel bound to rest their judgments on such so-called "objective" criteria. Yet there is considerable evidence that the correlation between job performance and length of schooling or grades is quite low for a broad range of occupational categories. In some occupations there may even be an inverse correlation between education and job performance: the more education employees have, the higher their rate of turnover and, in some instances, the lower their productivity.

Just how senseless many "objective" standards really are was revealed during the past few years when, under the pressures of an apparent labor shortage, corporate managers took a hard look at their personnel practices. The experience of New York's First National City Bank is typical of a great many corporations, manufacturers as well as financial companies. Robert Feagles, a senior vice president, recalls that, when he was put in charge of personnel in 1965, turnover was abnormally high, with about 500 jobs going begging in a work force of 12,000. More important, supervisors were hanging on to incompetent people for fear that they would be replaced only by even less competent people—or not at all. Feagles' first move, therefore, was to create a personnel-research group, which proceeded to analyze the nature of the work performed in the job categories that accounted for the largest proportion of new hires.

The results were discomfiting, to say the least. By and large, the researchers found that the qualifications the bank required for a broad range of jobs bore little relationship to the actual requirements of the job. For example, supervisors all over the bank had been complaining that the young people hired as pages rarely stayed more than three months or thereabouts. The reason, Feagles' researchers found, was that the personnel department, which gave a battery of entry tests, had set a score of 130 on the Wonderlic I.Q. test as the minimum for a job as a page. But youths with that degree of intelligence found they could not stand the monotony for more than a few months.

For most entry jobs a high-school diploma was required, yet the jobs could be performed just as well, and in the case of particularly monotonous routine tasks, perhaps better, by people with substantially less education. A high degree of literacy was essential in other jobs, not because of the intrinsic nature of the work but because of the way it had been structured. By breaking the work down in different ways, dropouts could do the job without difficulty.

The labor shortage, in brief, was the product of the bank's unrealistic requirements. By lowering job requirements to those actually needed to perform the work in question, and by substituting a newly created set of aptitude tests for the old ones, First National City was able to tap a completely new source of supply in the city's predominantly black and Puerto Rican neighborhoods. At first, the flow of applicants was small; on the basis of past experience, many blacks and Puerto Ricans did not bother to apply since they took it for granted that they would not be hired. "We had to make ourselves believable in the labor market," Feagles puts it. To do so, the bank began active recruiting in minority neighborhoods, advertising in Negro and Spanish newspapers, contacting church groups and antipoverty agencies, and visiting high schools. As a result, the minority complement went from 12 percent to 24 percent of the work force in four years; it is now above 30 percent.

When the "Hard Core" Softens

Many of the factors corporate managers used to cite as compelling reasons for their inability to find or hire many Negro employees have turned out to be a lot less compelling when the supply of white workers dried up. Many blacks, to be sure, do lack the necessary job skills, but when labor is in short enough supply, it pays employers to incur substantial costs to teach the skills. There is reason to believe, in fact, that a substantial proportion of the "new" jobs which members of the National Alliance of Businessmen claim to have created for the so-called "hard core" unemployed are filled by men the companies would have hired even if there had been no special program.

A prolonged period of full employment softens the hard core in another way. For most jobs the most important kind of intellectual capital is what has been learned on the job rather than what has been learned in school. Negroes have been caught up in a vicious circle; the fact that so many jobs were barred to them in the past left many blacks poorly equipped for the jobs that began to open up in the Sixties. All the more so, since workers need two kinds of knowledge: specific work skills, and social skills—i.e., punctuality, acceptance of discipline and work rules, and so on. Lack of these social skills has constituted the biggest disadvantage of Negroes who previously had been limited to casual labor or other transient jobs. But social skills are learned on the job in much the same way that specific work skills are acquired. Hence the boom of the late Sixties—by providing steady jobs for previously unemployable blacks—equipped them with the social and other skills they need to compete for employment in the future.

The Zero-Sum Game

A further reason why rapid economic growth helps the Negro is that it reduces white resistance to black gains. Some of this resistance stems from deep-rooted racial hatred, but a great deal of it, though cloaked perhaps in anti-Negro rhetoric, grows out of a real conflict of interest. The harsh fact is that if Negroes gain a larger share of the "better" jobs, whites, by definition, will be left with a smaller share. More black foremen will mean proportionately fewer white foremen; more black school principals will mean fewer white principals; more black corporate vice presidents will mean fewer white vice presidents.

What this means is that the struggle to achieve Negro equality is, in the parlance of game theorists, a "zero-sum game," in which one group's gains are offset by another group's losses. Not entirely so; to some degree, whites' losses in terms of jobs and income are offset by less tangible gains—greater social peace (or less social disruption), a sense of satisfaction that justice is being achieved. What a good many civic leaders have sometimes failed to recognize, however—the Urban Coalition is a prime example—is that the people who enjoy the intangible or psychic gains are not necessarily the ones who bear the brunt of the losses, e.g., white blue-collar workers, whose chances of becoming foremen are diminished.

But if job opportunities are growing for everyone, whites are likely to be less resentful of the fact that Negroes are taking a larger share of the better jobs. If the number of foremen, craftsmen, plant managers, corporate executives, and school principals is growing, the absolute *number* of whites holding such jobs can increase even though the white *proportion* declines. Rapid economic growth can reduce white resentment still more, by making it possible for whites to move into other occupations. And if their real income is growing, whites are less likely to object to the fact that their tax dollars are being used, in part, to provide compensatory education and job training for Negroes.

Government has a large role to play, therefore, both in overcoming discrimination and in keeping the economy expanding rapidly. Governmental policy is important, too, as a means of influencing the composition of economic output, since the opportunites for upgrading black occupations and incomes vary widely from industry to industry.

Construction, for example, is a labor-intensive industry with a wage scale well above average, which means that increased employment of Negroes there would have a greater impact on black income than increases in almost any other blue-collar industry. And since the potential demand for construction will grow substantially over the next ten years, the number of blacks employed can be increased without threatening the jobs of whites. The degree to which the industry will be able to meet the projected demand will be strongly influenced by what the government does to stimulate housing and urban renewal. The degree to which that demand leads to greater employment of blacks depends on what government does to break down racial discrimination, which is more intense in construction than in most industries.

While rapid economic growth is a prerequisite for Negro progress, it is not enough; it must be supplemented by a direct attack on all forms of discrimination. The changes of the past five or ten years have reduced and occasionally eliminated some forms of discrimination. As is usually the case, however, solving one set of problems creates another set, or brings old problems into sharper focus. The more that overt discrimination in hiring recedes, the more important other kinds of discrimination become. Eliminating the disparities between blacks and whites is a two-stage process: giving Negroes equal access to initial employment, and giving them an equal crack at advancement. . . .

The Executive as Educator

. . . It is not enough for presidents or executive vice presidents to decree an end to discrimination within the company. Such decrees frequently are nullified by what one black executive calls "the not-in-my-department syndrome," whereby department managers express agreement in principle but find all sorts of reasons to explain why the decree cannot be put into practice "in my department." Hence top executives must act as educators, persuading supervisors—plant managers, foremen, etc., down the line—to change their ways.

Executives will be unable to educate their subordinates, however, unless they first educate themselves. There is no particular reason to assume that managers are any freer from racial prejudice than the rest of us; it is virtually impossible to have grown up in the U.S. without having absorbed *some* sense of superiority or distaste toward blacks. But executives have been quicker than most to recognize the high stakes that are involved for business and for the whole society in overcoming prejudice and discrimination. Businessmen made considerable progress in that direction in the Sixties. There is reason to hope that they will find the courage and strength to do what needs to be done in the Seventies.

The Economic Progress of Minority Groups

LESTER C. THUROW

While there are many statistics that could be used to explore the economic position of any minority group, the essential nature of a group's position can be captured in the figures that answer four basic questions. First, relative to the majority group, what is the probability of the minority's finding employment? Second, what are the earnings of employed minority group members, compared with those of the majority? Third, are minority group members making a breakthrough into the high-income jobs of the economy? And fourth, what is the group's general level of economic welfare as measured by its average family income compared to that of the majority?

In each case it is necessary to look not just at current data but at the group's economic history. Where has it been in terms of employment and earnings opportunities? Where is it going and how fast is it progressing? The current recession or depression is so severe that it has radically different impacts from those of previous post-World War II recessions. Data will therefore be presented on the progress or retrogression of groups through 1973, and then a separate analysis of the current recession will follow.

The data on family incomes according to ethnic origin reveal only three major groups with incomes below average—blacks, people of Spanish heritage, and American Indians. Of the almost 100 million Americans who think of themselves as having an ethnic origin, all have incomes above those of people who consider themselves native Americans. It is interesting to note that the groups with the highest average family incomes in 1972 were Russians ($13,929), Poles ($12,182), and Italians ($11,646). "Ethnic" Americans may talk as if they are economically deprived, but on average they have approached the top of the economic ladder.

Blacks versus Whites

Since World War II there has been no significant change in the ratio of employment probabilities for blacks and for whites (Table 1). No matter when you measure them—in good times or bad—black unemployment rates are approximately twice as high as those for whites. This was true prior to the civil rights and poverty decade of the sixties, and it is true now. The monthly data for early 1976 are not included, but the latest figures available show that the black unemployment rate, month by month, has held constant at twice that of whites.

While the current relative employment opportunities for blacks are no worse than they have been since World War II, there is no comfort in that. Absolute unemployment rates for both whites and blacks are the highest they have been since the Great Depression. Relative to the sizes of their respective populations, two black men or women are thrown out of work for every white man or woman during a period of rising unemployment.

Reprinted from *Challenge*, March-April 1976, copyright © 1976 by International Arts and Sciences Press, Inc. Reprinted by permission of International Arts and Sciences Press, Inc.

TABLE 1
Relative Unemployment
(Blacks/Whites)

Time	Ratio
1950-1959	2.0
1960-1969	2.1
1970-1975*	1.9

Source: Council of Economic Advisers, *Economic Report of the President, 1975*, GPO, Washington, D.C., p. 279.
*Based on data for the first ten months of 1975.

Our analysis indicates a long-run, deeply embedded structural relationship in the economy. The rapidly escalating black unemployment rates of this recession or depression are not a temporary phenomenon. They are exactly what the structure of the economy would lead us to expect. Nothing has changed in the past 30 years. No progress has been made.

TABLE 2
Relative Earnings of Full-Time Full-Year Workers
(Blacks/Whites)

Year	Males	Females
1955	.56	.56
1960	.59	.68
1968	.61	.77
1969	.62	.81
1970	.65	.83
1971	.65	.87
1972	.65	.88
1973	.66	.86

Source: U.S. Bureau of the Census, *Current Population Reports: Consumer Income*, Series P-60, GPO, Washington, D.C., various years.

While there is a wide variety of earnings statistics for blacks and whites, the earnings of full-time, full-year workers are the best summary measure for those who have escaped the problems of unemployment. The relative employment probabilities for blacks have not improved in the period since World War II, but relative earnings have (Table 2). Between 1955 and 1973, earnings of black males rose from 56 percent to 66 percent of those of white males, and earnings of black females rose from 56 percent to 86 percent of those of white females. (Over the period under consideration, white female earnings fell relative to those of white males [Table 3].) While there have been improvements for blacks—both male and female—the relative gains for females have been three times those of males.

It is interesting to note, however, that the rate of gains for blacks was no faster in the 1960s than it was in the 1950s. The civil rights and poverty programs of the 1960s might have been necessary to sustain the rate of increase started in the previous decade, but they did not serve to accelerate it.

More to the current point, however, are the data since 1970 or 1971. Since 1970 there has been little evidence of any advance in the relative earnings of black males, and since

TABLE 3
PROBABILITY OF HOLDING A JOB IN TOP 5 PERCENT OF EARNINGS DISTRIBUTION RELATIVE TO THAT OF WHITE MALES

	1960	1973
Black males	9.0%	19.00%
Black females	0.0	0.06
White females	6.0	4.00

Source: U.S. Bureau of the Census, *1960 Census of the Population, U.S. Summary*, p. 573 and *Current Population Reports, Consumer Income*, 1974, p. 145.

1971 the relative earnings of black females have shown scant improvement. These data are interesting because they antedate the current recession, which started in the first quarter of 1974. While there is enough sampling error in the data to make us refrain from calling a three-year hiatus in gains a trend, the pattern is nonetheless disturbing. The movement of the 1960s toward greater equality in earnings seems to be broken.

I would also predict that we will see a fall in the ratio of black to white full-time full-year earnings over the course of the current depression. Most of the progress in past years has been achieved not by altering the relative earnings of those already embedded in the labor force, but by altering the earnings of individuals just coming into the labor force. Thus the greatest relative gains have been made among young blacks. As far as an employer is concerned, this type of change causes the fewest disruptions. Young whites "lose" the traditional earnings edge of whites over blacks, but in concrete terms they have lost something that they did not yet have. To alter the relative position of older members of the labor force, it is necessary to reshuffle existing jobs or expected promotions. In any case, white employees are aware of the fact that they have lost something and are in a position to exert countervailing power.

But in a recession the whole process is reversed because of seniority provisions (formal and informal) in hiring and firing. The youngest workers are apt to be the first to lose their jobs and they are at a level where the ratio of black to white earnings is most likely to be near parity. Therefore a recession shifts the statistical balance: those remaining fully employed tend to be older groups with larger relative earnings differences between blacks and whites.

TABLE 4
RATION OF BLACK TO WHITE FAMILY INCOMES

Year	Ratio	Year	Ratio
1947	51%	1961	53%
1948	53	1962	53
1949	51	1963	53
1950	54	1964	56
1951	53	1965	55
1952	57	1966	60
1953	56	1967	62
1954	56	1968	63
1955	55	1969	63
1956	53	1970	64
1957	54	1971	63
1958	51	1972	62
1959	52	1973	60
1960	55		

Source: *Consumer Income*, 1974, p. 30.

Regardless of whether you believe that the current hiatus is significant, the gap in relative earnings, especially for black males, is also a manifestation of a long-run structural problem. If current progress were to continue, black females would achieve parity with white females in about ten years, but black males would not reach parity for another 75 years. Since there is no trend toward parity between white males and females, parity between black and white females is an achievement but it scarcely marks the end of the economic problem.

If we examine the job pattern in the top 5 percent of the earnings distribution curve, we will find some improvement in the relative position of black males. In 1960, black males were approximately 9 percent as likely to hold a job in the top percent of the earnings distribution, but by 1973, they were 19 percent as likely to do so. Black females held none of the top jobs in 1960 and only a handful in 1973. The white female group actually experienced a decline during this period: in 1960 they were 6 percent as likely as white males to hold a job at the top; in 1973, this figure had fallen to 4 percent.

Black family incomes have risen and fallen relative to white family incomes, depending upon the phase of the business cycle. Between 1947 and 1952, black family incomes rose from 51 percent to 57 percent of white family incomes at the peak of the Korean War, declined again to 51 percent with the recession of 1957-58, rose to 64 percent under the pressures of the Vietnam War and the civil rights movement, and then once again started to fall, reaching 60 percent in 1973 (Table 4). The most recent decline was not, however, caused by the business cycle, but by a reduction in the proportion of black families with two or more workers and an increase in the proportion of white families with two or more workers. The proportion of white families in this category now exceeds that of blacks, and will probably continue to rise, thus widening the gap between average family incomes of blacks and whites.

Families of Spanish Heritage

Extensive time series data are not available for Americans of Spanish heritage, but it is possible to report on their economic position in 1969 and to note a few changes between 1969 and 1973. This has been a period during which families of Spanish heritage have risen from a position of inferiority to both black and white families to one of economic superiority to black families. In 1969 the average black family's income was 63 percent of the average white family's, but the average family of Spanish heritage earned only 58 percent as much as the average white family. By 1973, the income of the average black family had dropped to 60 percent of that of the average white family, but the average family of Spanish heritage had risen to 69 percent of the income level of the average white family. Among Hispanic families the most spectacular gains were made by the Cuban, Central and South American, and Spanish segments (Table 5). Mexican Americans, however, have also made sharp gains in a rather limited period of time.

Rising relative family incomes can be caused by falling relative unemployment rates, rising relative earnings, or rising family labor force participation rates. While it is not possible to trace with precision the sources of Hispanic family income gains, some of the causes can be determined.

In 1970, unemployment rates were similar for black and Hispanic workers, with males showing a slightly lower rate and females a somewhat higher one. By 1974, female unemployment rates were still slightly higher, but male rates were 25 percent lower. The falling relative unemployment rates for male Hispanic workers thus contributed substantially to improved family income among people of Spanish heritage.

TABLE 5
Hispanic Relative to White Family Incomes

	1969	1973
Total	58%	69%
Mexican-American	56	67
Puerto Rican	51	64
Other	65	89

Source: U.S. Bureau of the Census, *Current Population Reports, Persons of Spanish Origin,* Series P-60, No. 213, p. 34 and No. 267, p. 7.

While Hispanic female unemployment rates have not fallen relative to those of whites or blacks, the rates of female participation in the labor force have been rising, keeping pace with those of whites and increasing faster than those of blacks. In 1970, participation rates were 9 percentage points lower for Hispanic than for black females, and approximately equal to those of white females. By 1974, Hispanic female participation rates had accelerated along with those of white females and had reached approximate parity with those of black females. Males of Spanish heritage maintained their position of parity with white males and their participation rates were approximately 8 percentage points higher than those of black males.

Higher male participation rates have a greater payoff for families of Spanish heritage than they do for black families, since fully employed male Hispanic workers are much closer to parity in income with fully employed white workers. In 1969, the average full-time, full-year Hispanic male worker earned 80 percent as much as the corresponding white, while the average fully employed Hispanic female earned 89 percent as much. Hispanic females, like blacks, were closer than Hispanic males to income parity with whites, but the income gap for males was much smaller. Similarly, Hispanic males are much more likely to hold high-paid jobs. In 1969, a black male was only 12 percent as likely as a white male to hold a job paying $25,000 or more per year, but a male of Spanish heritage was 38 percent as likely to hold such a job. This situation deteriorated slightly between 1969 and 1973, however, since by 1973 Hispanic males were only 21 percent as likely to hold higher-paid jobs. There was little change among women in this area: black and Hispanic women were half as likely as white women to hold high-paid jobs; but white women, in turn, were only 8 percent as likely to hold such jobs as were white men.

The figures show a substantial difference in economic progress between blacks and Hispanic workers in the 1970s. Black Americans have experienced a period of relative economic stagnation, while Hispanic Americans have made rapid gains. Falling relative unemployment rates for Hispanic males and rising relative participation rates for Hispanic females have been responsible for those gains.

American Indians

The smallest and poorest of all of America's ethnic groups are the American Indians. They are also the most poorly described and tracked by U.S. statistical agencies. Despite the existence of the Bureau of Indian Affairs, only the roughest estimates of the economic situation of American Indians are available. According to reports from approximately half of all the Indian reservations to the Economic Development Administration, the median family income of American Indians was $3,300 in 1969, with a range from $1,000 on several reservations to $15,000 on one reservation. This means that the median income of an Indian family is something on the order of one-third that of a white family.

Given the lack of data and the range of error, no one is in a position to say whether the population of American Indians is making any economic progress. However you look at it, when it comes to economic deprivation, American Indians are in a class by themselves. . . .

[Effects of the 1974 Recession]

. . . Members of minority groups . . . continue to suffer from a higher probability of being unemployed, but, surprisingly, the 1974 recession hit the earnings of year-round full-time white male workers the hardest. The real incomes of fully employed white males declined by 5 percent, while those of fully employed black and Hispanic males declined by 1.5 percent. Among fully employed females, whites experienced a cut in income of 4 percent, while, on the other hand, the incomes of black and Hispanic women both increased, the former by 3 percent and the latter by 0.5 percent. The increase in incomes for women of Spanish heritage was almost completely concentrated among those who work part-time or part of the year. Since overtime was slashed sharply during 1974, the decline in earnings for fully employed whites must be traced to the disappearance of overtime. Evidently, other groups receive little overtime and therefore have less to lose when overtime disappears. . . .

The Options

When one looks at the economic position of minority groups, one finds a mixed bag of small pluses and minuses. But it would be difficult to argue that our society was on the road toward narrowing income gaps between the majority and the minorities. The major policy tool for equalizing incomes—transfer payments—is working, but payments must go up very rapidly to hold the poor even with the rest of the population, and the existing transfer payments systems are not suited to helping those who are in the labor force or want to be there. For minority groups, the basic problem is lack of jobs. Millions of people give every indication that they are able and willing to work, but they are unable to find work.

This problem is not peculiar to the current recession or depression. Lack of jobs has been endemic in peacetime during the past 50 years of American history. Review the evidence: a depression from 1929 to 1940, a war from 1941 to 1945, a recession in 1949, a war from 1950 to 1953, recessions in 1954, 1957-58, and 1960-61, a war from 1965 to 1973, a recession in 1969-70, and a depression or severe recession in 1974-75. This was hardly an enviable economic performance.

As I was growing up professionally, I was constantly taught the received wisdom that there were no technical reasons why macroeconomic policies could not be used consistently to generate jobs for everyone who really wanted to work. I now believe those teachings to be technically correct, but irrelevant. Macroeconomic policies could be used to hold the economy at a point where there were jobs for everyone who wanted work, but they will not in fact be used for that purpose. The reasons for this are many: time lags in the decision process; fears of inflation; incompetence. Whatever the reasons, we need to face the fact that our economy and our institutions as they now stand will not provide jobs for all who want work. They never have done so, and they never will.

As a result, the principal way to narrow income gaps is to restructure the economy so that it will in fact provide jobs for everyone. Since we regard the United States as a "work ethic" society, this restructuring should be a moral duty as well as an economically desirable effort. We consistently preach that work is the only "ethical" way to receive income. We cast aspersions on the "welfare" society. Therefore we have a moral responsibility to guarantee full employment. Not to do so is like locking the church doors, and then saying that people are not virtuous if they do not go to church.

Since private enterprise is incapable of guaranteeing jobs for everyone who wants to work, then government, and in particular the federal government, must institute the necessary programs. No one should attempt to deny that a real, open-ended, guaranteed job program would constitute a major restructuring of our economy. Patterns of labor market behavior and the outputs of our economy would be fundamentally altered. It would be a move toward socialism, because the government would own the means of production for those who participated in the guaranteed job program, and the government would assume the social responsibility of making sure that everyone who wanted to work had an opportunity to work.

It should be pointed out, however, that real economic competition would almost certainly increase. If the guaranteed jobs are to be real jobs, then any guaranteed job program must produce some economic outputs. These outputs might consist of street cleaning in competition with public sanitation departments, or rebuilding railway roadbeds in competition with private industry. The problem is not in finding worthwhile things to do. The President's Automation Commission Report in the mid-1960s listed millions of potential public service jobs, and anyone with even a little imagination can think of many things that could be done to make this society a better one. If the option is between idleness and work, the choice is simple. As long as any useful output is produced, a work project takes precedence over involuntary unemployment.

A guaranteed job program must have several characteristics in order to achieve the objectives for which it is intended. First, it cannot be a program of employment at minimum wage rates. The objective is to open to everyone a structure of economic work opportunities equivalent to those open to fully employed white males. Thus, the program would have to structure earnings and promotion opportunities in the same way as they are structured for fully employed white males. There would be some low-wage jobs and some high-wage jobs, but most jobs would be in the middle. Some or all of the workers might be unionized. Second, the program must be open-ended, providing jobs to everyone who is able and willing to work regardless of age, race, sex, education, etc. Abilities and talents will play a role within the distribution of job opportunities, but no one who desires full- or part-time work will be denied it. Third, the program should not be viewed as a temporary antirecessionary measure. The lack of employment opportunities is not a temporary, short-run aspect of the U.S. economy. It is permanent and endemic. Even if this were not true, the program would still need to be permanent, since no industry could be expected to go in and out of business over the course of the business cycle and still operate efficiently. There is no reason, however, why there could not be temporary, short-run jobs for people who, for a limited period, are unable to find work in the conventional private or public sectors of the economy.

What would such a program cost? Payments for labor, materials, and capital might be high but as with all economic projects, the costs would depend upon the difference between the value of output produced and the payments made to factors of production. If care is shown in project selection, there is no reason why the projects could not generate substantial net benefits. If you are employing idle economic resources (workers without jobs), the real economic costs (opportunity costs) would be substantially less than the monetary costs.

How many people would need to be employed in a guaranteed job program? At the moment, when we have 8 million unemployed, the answer is obviously many millions. I would be willing to bet, however, that if a guaranteed job program were actually instituted, the performance of macroeconomic policymakers would improve. For if they did not implement fiscal and monetary policies to insure that private industry would want to hire most of the U.S. labor force, then they (i.e., governments) would be forced to hire directly all the people who were left over. I suspect that interest in maximizing private employment opportunities would suddenly arise. Thus, the number who needed employment would be large, but still much smaller than the current number of unemployed persons.

One of the subsidiary benefits of a guaranteed job program is that it would eliminate the endless sterile debates about what fraction of the unemployed are lazy and unwilling to work. Instead of arguing about it, let's put it to the test and see once and for all how many people really want to work and how many people are in fact lazy.

Conclusions

Historically, one of the interesting things about our economy and political structure is that we find it much easier to set up welfare programs to give people money than we do to set up work programs to give people jobs. Our public rhetoric would lead one to believe the opposite, even though people on welfare almost universally say that they would prefer work to welfare. In 1974, transfer payments totaled $140 billion. At the same time we are not willing to give enough money to really narrow the income gaps. If an equitable distribution of economic resources is ever to be achieved, it will require the provision of jobs for everyone who wants to work.

Politically, we are reluctant to give jobs, because to do so would require a major restructuring of the economy. A new source of competition would arise for both public agencies and private firms. To the extent that we were unable or unwilling to hold the private economy at the full employment level, we would have a socialized economy.

The time has come, however, to admit that the pursuit of equity and equal economic opportunity demands a fundamental restructuring of the economy. Everyone who wants to work should have a chance to work. But there is no way to achieve that situation by tinkering marginally with current economic policies. The only solution is a socialized sector of the economy designed to give work opportunities to everyone who wants them but cannot find them elsewhere.

Equal Employment in Urban Governments: The Potential Problem of Interminority Competition

GRACE HALL
ALAN SALTZSTEIN

Concern for equal employment in municipal government has heightened recently as a consequence of increased pressure from minority and women's organizations and, more directly, the placement of municipalities under Equal Employment Opportunity Commisssion (EEOC) jurisdictions by the 1972 Equal Employment Opportunity Act. Such pressures have been a part of federal-level personnel concerns for years, and a small body of knowledge dealing with resulting problems that personnel managers face is present.[1] Application of these same concerns to the city scene, however, presents personnel policymakers with a set of different and more perplexing problems. City governments are more directly involved in the daily lives of minority residents than are most state and federal agencies. Hence, pressures upon these governments for altered hiring patterns may be more intense than those at higher levels. Cities are also expected to hire in accordance with local workforce proportions of women and minorities. They may, therefore, be subject to differing pressures from the community, depending on the size and extent of political activity on the part of each group. Pressure from the community to hire certain kinds of employees, hence, may vary from community to community depending on the kind of city and the proportion of the work force of a given minority group. Further, the relative proximity of city hall to the living area of a particular group may affect the city's efforts in attracting minorities. Suburban cities, for instance, which are subject to county-wide hiring standards, may have more difficulty accomplishing their goals than would a central city in the same county, and some cities within a metropolitan area may have closer proximity to the residences of members of one ethnic group than another.

Factors embedded in the histories of different ethnic and racial groups and racial biases within the white majority community may also result in different minority hiring patterns in different cities. While authors tend to assume that the problems of minority recruitment are similar, a substantial body of literature suggests that one ought to expect pronounced hiring differences among different groups. Grebler, et al., for instance, has noted that the relative employability of Mexican-Americans and blacks in federal and local service varies considerably in different states.[2] A recent study by Rosenbloom also implies that competition among minority groups may result in certain agencies being dominated by one group at the expense of others.[3]

If different patterns of employment for various minority groups occur, personnel policy leading to equal employment would require different procedures and practices for each group. One group may be more recruitable than others, suggesting that a policy of equal employment ought to concentrate more resources on the excluded group. It is also

---

From *Public Personnel Management*, November-December 1975, pp. 386–93. Reprinted by permission of the International Personnel Management Association, 1313 East 60th Street, Chicago, Illinois 60637.

possible that control of important organizational components by one group excludes other minorities from recruitment. If so, diluting that group's influence on hiring would be required if a more equitable employment policy was sought.

Hence, several problems of relevance to today's urban public personnel manager are raised by equal employment pressures. Efficient urban personnel management requires an assessment of these questions. Where guidelines require several kinds of minority groups be hired, are some groups more readily recruited through normal personnel processes than others? Are some minorities more frequently hired in certain kinds of employment? Do minority or majority groups act to restrict minority employment in certain positions or kinds of employment? An answer of "yes" to any of these implies that personnel resources ought to be allocated in such a way as to overcome prejudicial patterns. If any of these patterns are present, the manner in which personnel resources are allocated may be a more important question than the extent of the effort.

This study is a pioneering attempt to examine these areas of inquiry. Employment of blacks and Mexican-Americans in 26 of the 27 Texas cities larger than 50,000 in population is examined to determine the incidence of employment of both groups and suggest explanations for various workforce configurations. Data on minority employment were obtained from the cities for 1973, the first year they were required to report this data to the EEOC. Because of the large and varying concentrations of blacks and Mexican-Americans in these cities and the detailed breakdown of the EEO4 forms by rank and functional unit, examination of the relative employability of these two groups proved to be feasible.[4]

Another product of this research is a simple methodology for examining minority hiring patterns within an organization which can be applied by personnel officers on their own organizations. Hopefully, this will assist in making more rational allocations of resources.

A concentration on Texas cities was chosen because of several problems associated with the topic. Because of the statutory requirements concerning the reporting of this data, the EEOC cannot disclose to an organization the information contained in the EEO4 forms which each municipality submitted to EEOC.[5] Texas, however, has an open-records law which requires that muncipalities make such information available to the public, thus facilitating the collection of the data.[6] Additionally, Texas is one of seven states which does not have any fair employment practices laws, thus eliminating the need to account for the effects of such laws on current employment patterns.[7] The most important justification for confining the study to Texas municipalities, however, is a desire to limit analysis of the Spanish-surname population to those persons of Mexican descent. The purpose here is in part to examine the interrelationships between employment of a particular Spanish-surname population (*i.e.*, Mexican-American) and the black population, which to some extent assumes employment to be affected by cultural characteristics of the minority group in question. Clearly, this cannot be examined with any accuracy if the Spanish-surname population were to include significant numbers of Puerto Rican- Cuban-Americans in addition to Mexican-Americans, as would be the case if a national sample of municipalities were utilized. Hence, the refinement in analysis is considered to justify the limitation in scope.

The Nature of Minority Hiring

Analysis of aggregate personnel totals by race revealed that Mexican-Americans are more frequently employed in Texas cities irrespective of the numbers or percentages of blacks or Mexican-Americans in the workforce. This is the case for different categories of total employment and for each major subunit of a municipal organization. Table 1 contrasts several different indicators of minority employment in these cities. The mean figure of a use index, which combines measures of a minority's representation in an organization or a subunit of that organization and its distribution across salary levels within the organization, is presented for the entire organization and the four basic subunits of a municipal organization—public works, finance, police, and fire. Also presented are percentage black and Mexican-American of the municipality's total workforce and the total number of professional employees. In all cases, the mean or percent for Mexican-American employees is higher than for blacks. The difference in means of the use indices for the two groups is statistically significant in all cases and fairly similar from one subunit to the next. The difference in the percentage of professional employees (11.2% Mexican-American, 2.1% black) between the two groups is particularly large.

TABLE 1
INDICATORS OF RATES OF EMPLOYMENT FOR BLACKS AND MEXICAN-AMERICANS

	Blacks Mean	Blacks Standard Deviation	Mexican-Americans Mean	Mexican-Americans Standard Deviation
All departments use index	*.397	.242	.585	.227
Public works departments use index	*.590	.350	.881	.224
Finance departments use index	*.351	.295	.522	.314
Fire departments use index	*.137	.217	.338	.334
Police departments use index	*.333	.264	.556	.313
Percent workforce	11.2	6.8	15.8	3.9
Percent of professional employees	2.1	2.4	11.2	21.2

*Difference of means test significance at .01.

The generality of this inference may be influenced by the workforce precentages of blacks and Mexican-Americans in the population of the cities. High use indices may be recorded in cities where one group nearly monopolizes the workforce or where the workforce percentage of either or both is so low that a random minority employee will significantly affect the index. This situation potentially occurred in three cities, two with a dominant Mexican-American workforce (Laredo and Brownsville) and one with low percentages of both groups (Amarillo). Eliminating these three cities leaves 23 cities with each minority comprising at least 5% of the workforce and neither group totaling more than 70% of the workforce. Since the use indices are related to the relevant work forces, one would expect that both groups would have similar use indices assuming no comparative advantage. Table 2 demonstrates clearly the relative recruitment advantage of the Mexican-American. In 17 of the 23 cities, the Mexican-American use indices are higher than the black indicators. Most pointedly, in 11 of the 17 cities with higher Mexican-American than black use indices, the black workforce is actually greater than the Mexican-American. Hence, Mexican-Americans enjoy a comparative advantage in securing and retaining municipal jobs regardless of their relative proportions in the labor force.

TABLE 2
COMPARISON OF USE INDICES AND WORKFORCE PERCENTAGES IN CITIES WHERE INTERMINORITY COMPETITION WAS EXPECTED

Workforce Percentage	Mexican-American Higher Than Black	Black Higher Than Mexican-American	No Difference
Mexican-American Greater than black	6	1	2
Black Greater than Mexican-American	11	2	1
Totals	17	3	3

Interminority Competition in Employment

Several authors have concluded that achieving equal employment in government is complicated by the presence of competition among minority groups for the same positions, or "territorial struggles" among groups to secure control of the hiring process.[9] Unions in the private sector, for instance, often developed as enclaves for the employment of particular ethnic groups, and in many cities only recently has this control been altered. If blacks and Mexican-Americans are recruited to city government in a similar pattern, one would expect that one group would be hired to the exclusion of the other in those cities where both groups compete for jobs. The data permitted the testing of this hypothesis both for aggregate city workforce totals and for organizational components.

Table 3 correlates three general employment indicators of black and Mexican-American employment—the percentage of the city workforce, the percentage of professional employees, and the percentage of maintenance employees. All correlations are negative, implying that higher proportions of one minority group coincide with lower proportions of the other group. (These correlations were compiled only for the 23 cities where interminority competition was expected.) This suggests that higher rates of employment of one group occurs along with exclusion of the other.

TABLE 3
CORRELATIONS OF INDICATORS OF BLACK AND MEXICAN-AMERICAN EMPLOYMENT

	% Workforce Black	% Professional Black	% Maintenance Black
% Workforce Mexican-American	—.587	—.296	—.657
% Professional Mexican-American	—.158	—.158	—.601
% Maintenance Mexican-American	—.238	—.296	.159

A more detailed look at those departments more commonly hiring minority members revealed the extent to which dominance of one group within departments was present. Utilities and Transportation, Streets and Highways, and Sanitation and Sewerage are departmental classifications common to all cities in the survey, and the frequent locations of large numbers of minority employees. These three were thus selected for a detailed look at the minority composition.

A typology based on comparative minority employment percentages was developed to assess hiring and retention practices in each of these departments in the 24 competitive cities. An "exclusive employer" was defined as one where departmental percentages of both groups were less than the city workforce proportion. A "segregated employer" is one where one group's departmental percentage is at least twice the city workforce percent while the other group is hired at a rate less than the workforce percentage. An "integrated employer" employment situation occurs when both groups are employed in numbers between the workforce percentage and twice that percentage. A "good" employer is one where the unit contains twice the workforce percentage of one group and between the workforce percentage and twice that percentage of the other. A "minority employer" is one where both groups are hired at twice their occurrence in the workforce.

Table 4 reveals the frequency of each of these patterns in the departments of these cities. The segregated case with one group hired in vastly greater numbers than the other is the most frequent, suggesting that capture of the recruitment process by one racial group is a very common occurrence in municipal employment. Frequently, the type of employer varies within the same city. In only four of the cities did the same pattern occur in all three departments. Rarer still, however, were variations in the advantage gained by one group over the other. The common pattern was for one group to dominate one or two departments, and have at least equal influence in the third. In most cities, the minority group and the white majority dominated the recruitment process and of the two minority groups, Mexican-Americans were more frequently the dominant group.

TABLE 4
FREQUENCY OF OCCURRENCE OF VARIOUS MINORITY EMPLOYMENT PATTERNS

	N	Total
Exclusive Employer	12	17.40%
Segregated Employer	28	40.70
Biased Employer	9	13.70
Integrated Employer	4	5.70
Good Employer	12	17.40
Minority Employer	4	5.70
Totals	69	100.00%

Conclusion and Implications

The analysis of the minority composition of city employment in Texas reveals several sources of difficulty for personnel policy makers in their attempt to promote and accomplish equal employment of blacks and Mexican-Americans. The analysis conclusively demonstrates that Mexican-Americans are more frequently employed in these cities than are blacks. Personnel officials may be making an incorrect assumption that relative success with one group can make up for a failure to hire another. It is more likely, however, that Mexican-Americans in Texas are more readily accepted by employers and clients than are blacks. Several authors have noted that the extent of prejudice against those of Mexican descent is less than that experienced by blacks.[10] If this is the case, successful equal employment policy requires the spending of greater efforts in hiring black employees. Budgetary decisions on personnel matters, therefore, ought to consider the relative success of past hirings and make future allocations accordingly.

In these cities, organizational components are frequently dominated by one minority group, often at the expense of the other. The presence of such patterns places additional burdens on a personnel policy designed to increase minority representation. To increase employment of the excluded group, internal organizational changes may be necessary to break the control of the dominant group. Withstanding the strains of potential minority-group conflict as old patterns are altered may be an important cost the organization will have to undergo if equal employment is accomplished.

This paper also presents a simple methodology that should be helpful in determining potential problems associated with equal employment implementation in cities. As equal employment opportunity pressures increase, it is important for personnel officers to discover sources of potential difficulty in hiring and retention of minority employees and allocate their resources accordingly. If one minority group controls the personnel process and acts to exclude the other, internal organizational change may be a more efficient use of resources than further recruitment efforts. What is urgently needed, therefore, are analyses of successful and unsuccessful attempts to deal with these problems in different kinds of organizations.

Notes

1. See N. Joseph Cager, *Public Personnel Administration in the United States* (1975, St. Martins), pp. 128-138; "Mini-Symposium on Affirmative Action," *Public Administration Review*, May/June, 1974, pp. 234-246; "Symposium on Social Equity and Public Administration," *Public Administration Review*, Jan.-Feb., 1974, pp. 1-50.

2. Leo Grebler, Joan Moore and Ralph C. Guzman, *The Mexican-American People: The Nation's Second Largest Minority* (Free Press, New York, 1970), pp. 222-226.

3. David H. Rosenbloom, "A Note on Interminority Competition for Federal Positions," *Public Personnel Management*, Jan.-Feb., 1973, pp. 43-48.

4. The EEO4 forms were obtained directly from the cities. We are indebted to the personnel directors for their cooperation. The missing city is Garland, whose forms were not received until after the analysis was completed.

5. The Equal Employment Opportunity Act of 1972 states that "It shall be unlawful for any officer or employee of the Commission to make public in any manner whatever any information obtained by the Commission pursuant to its authority . . ." (Sec. 709[e]).

6. Texas House Bill 6 states that the following category of information be specifically made available to the public: "the names, sex, ethnicity, salaries, title, and dates of employment of all employees and officers of governmental bodies." All the data contained on the EEO4 forms falls within these boundaries and hence is open to public scrutiny. In spite of the law, however, some difficulty in securing the forms occurred. Several were obtained only after a site visit. Local contacts were also needed in a few of the cities. Thanks to our persistence, perseverance, and endurance, however, we collected forms for all but one city.

7. Only Alabama, Louisiana, Mississippi, North Carolina, Tennessee, Texas, and Virginia have no fair employment practices laws.

8. The use index is a method developed by Professor Robert McKersie of the University of Chicago to measure minority employment status in an organization. The method has been employed by the U.S. Department of Labor in measuring its own in-house employment record as regards minorities and women (see U.S. Department of Labor, Secretary's EEO Task Force, "Final Report on the Status of Minorities and Women in the Department of Labor," Washington, D.C., October, 1971). As utilized here, the use index is simply the numbers of each group in a given municipal department as a proportion of that group's representation in the area workforce (penetration rate)

multiplied by the average salary for each group in a department as a proportion of the average salary for the entire department (distribution rate). If a minority group is employed in a department in numbers corresponding to their representation in the workforce and at salary levels on a par with the other department members, the use index for that group in that department would be 1.0. Each of the two measures is constrained at 1.0 so that a penetration rate exceeding that required for equity cannot make up for a low distribution rate or vice versa. The measures for each department are aggregated to provide a measure for the entire municipal government.

9. Rosenbloom, *op. cit.*

10. Paul Bullock, in "Employment Problems of the Mexican-American," *Industrial Relations*, May, 1964, states that "The Mexican-American, typically, is better off than the Negro and worse off than the Anglo in terms of income and rate of employment," but can only conjecture that a possible cause is the greater penetration of Mexican-American males into the craftsmen category. Leo Grebler, *et al., op. cit.*, notes that Spanish-surname individuals are over-represented in state and local public employment, while Negroes are greatly under-represented, but says these differences "are difficult to explain without further research," particularly since the educational attainment of Mexican-Americans in Texas is lower than that of Negroes.

Section B
Women and Personnel Decisions

Does Sex-biased Job Advertising "Aid and Abet" Sex Discrimination?

SANDRA L. BEM
DARYL J. BEM

Title VII of the 1964 Civil Rights Act forbids discrimination in employment on the basis of race, color, religion, national origin—and sex. Although the sex provision was treated as a joke at the time . . . the Equal Employment Opportunities Commission (EEOC)—charged with enforcing the Act—discovered in its first year of operation that 40 percent or more of the complaints warranting investigation charged discrimination on the basis of sex. According to a report by the EEOC, nearly 6,000 charges of sex discrimination were filed with that agency in 1971 alone, a 62 percent increase over the previous year.

Title VII extends as well to practices which aid and abet discrimination. For example, the Act forbids job advertisements from indicating a preference for one sex or the other unless sex is a bona fide occupational qualification for employment. In interpreting this provision, the EEOC has ruled that even the practice of labeling help-wanted columns as "Male" or "Female" should be considered a violation of the law.

Nevertheless, a large number of employers continue to write advertisements which specify a sex preference, and many more write advertising copy clearly intended to appeal to one sex only. Moreover, many newspapers continue to divide their help-wanted advertisements into sex-segregated columns. [Editor's note: Ms. Carmen R. Mayni, Director of the Women's Bureau of the U.S. Census Bureau ordered in November 1973 that all job title listings be "de-sexed"; e.g., "fireman" to "firefighter," in "Job Titles De-sexed," *The State Journal*, Lansing, Mich., Sunday, Nov. 25, 1973, p. E7.]

Do these advertising practices aid and abet discrimination in employment by actually discouraging applicants of one sex or the other from applying for jobs for which they are otherwise well qualified? The two studies reported in this article sought to answer this question empirically. Both were conducted and presented as part of legal testimony, the first in a suit filed by the EEOC against American Telephone and Telegraph Company, the second in a suit filed by the National Organization for Women against *The Pittsburgh Press*.

Experiment I

As part of an investigation into sex and race discrimination at the American Telephone and Telegraph Company, the EEOC discovered a pervasive sex bias in AT&T's job advertisements and recruiting brochures. For example, advertisements for the jobs of lineman and frameman were clearly written to appeal only to men (even the job titles

Reprinted with permission from the *Journal of Applied Psychology*, vol. 3 (1973), no. 1, pp. 6-18.

are male), whereas advertisements for the jobs of operator and service representative were written to appeal only to women. The EEOC therefore asked us to conduct a study to determine whether or not this sex bias acts to discourage applicants of the opposite sex. Accordingly, Experiment I was designed to answer the following three questions:

1. Do sex-biased job advertisements discourage men and women from applying for "opposite-sex" jobs?

2. Would more men and women be interested in applying for such "opposite-sex" jobs if the advertisements were unbiased; that is, if the advertisements did not seem to prefer one sex or the other either in their job titles, pronouns, or overall tone?

3. Would even more men and women be willing to apply for such "opposite-sex" jobs, if sex-reversed, "affirmative-action" advertisements were specifically written to appeal to them?

Method

Subjects

One-hundred twenty seniors from a racially integrated high school in the San Francisco Bay area served as subjects. Half were male and half were female. Few planned to go on to any 4-year college. Students who were not planning to go on to college were purposely sought as subjects so that they might be both appropriate for and interested in jobs like those advertised by the telephone company. (As seniors, many would even be preparing for jobs like these in the near future.)

Procedure

Each student was given a booklet containing 12 job advertisements and was asked to indicate on a 6-point scale how interested he or she would be in applying for each job. The scale ranged from "very uninterested" to "very interested" and was labeled at each point. The 12 advertisements included four telephone jobs and eight nontelephone jobs. In order of appearance, the jobs were: appliance sales, telephone operator, photographer, travel agent, telephone frameman, dental assistant, taxicab driver, telephone service representative, assistant buyer, keypunch operator, telephone lineman, and public relations/advertising.

The cover sheet introduced all 12 jobs as follows: "All of the jobs have a starting salary of between $100 and $120 per week with regular raises after that. None of the jobs require any previous training or experience beyond high school graduation; all of them provide paid on-the-job training." The phrase, "An Equal Opportunity Employer m/f," appeared at the end of every job advertisement.

Sex-biased job advertisements. One-third of the booklets advertised the telephone jobs in the sex-biased format used by AT&T. In other words, these ads were copied verbatim from AT&T ads and brochures furnished to us by the EEOC. The four sex-biased telephone advertisements were worded as follows:

Telephone Operator:
WHO SAYS IT'S A MAN'S WORLD?
Behind every man's telephone call, there is a woman. She's a smart woman. She's efficient. She has to be. She places the complex long distance calls people cannot place themselves or helps them locate telephone numbers.

Hers is a demanding job. But we make it worth her while. We can make it worth your while too. Not only do we pay a good salary to start, but also offer group life insurance, group medical coverage, good vacations with pay and free pensions.

 A stepping stone to management positions.
Pacific Telephone
An Equal Opportunity Employer m/f

Telephone Service Representative:
IF WE WERE AN AIRLINE, SHE'D BE OUR STEWARDESS!

 She is the telephone company. At least to most of our customers, she is. When someone wants a special service, an extra phone, or if there's been a billing problem—this is the girl they talk to.

 Her job is to help them.

 That's why she sits at a desk. Her own desk. And that's why she doesn't have to type or take shorthand. It's a lot easier to be helpful when you have good working conditions.

 She's been to our special Service Representative School. Seven weeks' worth. So she knows her job. And she knows how to handle people. Which is why we need her.

 Is it any wonder we think she's special?
Pacific Telephone
An Equal Opportunity Employer m/f

Telephone Frameman:

 The telephone frameman plays a vital role in telephone communications. This skilled craftsman connects cables and wires with equipment in our central office in order to provide telephone service. He also works with other craftsmen to correct troubles in wiring.

 A frameman should have mechanical aptitude, a liking for technical study, and an interest in electrical circuitry.

 Receive full pay during your full-time classroom training.
Pacific Telephone
An Equal Opportunity Employer m/f

Telephone Lineman:
WE'RE LOOKING FOR OUTDOOR MEN!

 If sitting at a desk or working indoors is not for you, Pacific Telephone will train you as a lineman, and we'll pay you while you learn.

 This job requires manual dexterity, pole-climbing ability, and the desire to work outdoors.

 It's smart to look into this opportunity because we are offering more than ever in pay and benefits to get linemen. And we will give raises and chances for promotion to keep you.
Pacific Telephone
An Equal Opportunity Employer m/f

Unbiased job advertisements. One-third of the booklets advertised the telephone jobs in sex-unbiased form, that is, in a form which did not seem to prefer one sex more than the other. This involved altering the tone of the advertisements, as well as eliminating all sex-related job titles and pronouns. However, in all other respects, these unbiased advertisements match AT&T job descriptions exactly. The four unbiased telephone advertisements were worded as follows:

Telephone Operator:

We need calm, coolheaded men and women with clear friendly voices to do that important job of helping our customers. They must be capable of handling emergency calls quickly and competently. They also place the complex long distance calls people cannot place themselves or help them locate hard-to-find telephone numbers.

Theirs is a demanding job. But we make it worth their while. We can make it worth your while too. Not only do we pay a good salary to start, but also offer group life insurance, group medical coverage, good vacations with pay and free pensions.

A stepping stone to management positions.

Pacific Telephone
An Equal Opportunity Employer m/f

Telephone Service Representative:

BE OUR AMBASSADOR TO THE PUBLIC!

You are the telephone company. At least to most of our customers, you would be. When someone wants a special service, an extra phone, or if there's been a billing problem—you are the man or woman they talk to.

Your job is to help them.

You're cool. You know how to handle people in a variety of situations. Yours is a key customer relations job with great opportunities for raises and promotions into management.

Start right off earning a full salary while you attend our special Service Representative School for seven weeks.

Pacific Telephone
An Equal Opportunity Employer m/f

Telephone Frameworker:

WHERE A JOB MEANS MORE
THAN JUST GOING TO WORK!

Just ask frameworkers Susan Frey or Roger Dowling: "We've got a good supervisor. If we run into problems, we can always expect a helping hand. Our supervisor will spend a couple of hours showing us something we don't understand sometimes. We help each other around here.

It's as good an outfit as there is around. If we've got to work for a living, this is the place."

The frameworker plays a vital role in telephone communications. Working in our central office, this skilled craftsperson connects cables and wires with equipment in order to provide telephone service for our customers. The frameworker also works with other craftspeople to correct troubles in wiring.

Receive full pay during your full-time classroom training.

Pacific Telephone
An Equal Opportunity Employer m/f

Telephone Lineworker:
WE'RE LOOKING FOR OUTDOOR PEOPLE!

Are you a man or woman who likes fresh air and exercise? If sitting behind a desk isn't for you, stay physically fit as a lineworker working in the great outdoors for Pacific Telephone.

You can start right off earning a full salary while we train you to do the job.

The lineworker's job requires manual dexterity, pole-climbing, and the desire to work outdoors. Modern power tools and efficient machines help the lineworker do the job, but his or her primary aids are intelligence and a pair of good hands.

It's smart to look into this opportunity because we are offering more than ever in pay and benefits to get lineworkers. And we will give raises and chances for promotion to keep you.

Pacific Telephone
An Equal Opportunity Employer m/f

Sex-reversed "affirmative-action" advertisements. One-third of the booklets advertised the telephone jobs in sex-reversed format. In other words, these ads were worded so as to appeal specifically to that sex not normally recruited for these jobs. Once again, however, the advertisements remained true to AT&T job descriptions. The four sex-reversed advertisements were worded as follows:

Telephone Operator:

We need calm, coolheaded men with clear masculine voices to do that important job of helping our customers. He must be capable of handling emergency calls quickly and competently. He also places the complex long distance calls people cannot place themselves or helps them locate hard-to-find telephone numbers.

His is a demanding job. But we make it worth his while. We can make it worth your while too. Not only do we pay a good salary to start, but also offer group life insurance, group medical coverage, good vacations with pay and free pensions,

A stepping stone to management positions.

Pacific Telephone
An Equal Opportunity Employer m/f

Telephone Service Representative:
IF WE WERE A GOVERNMENT,
HE'D BE OUR AMBASSADOR!

He is the telephone company. At least to most of our customers, he is. When someone wants a special service, an extra phone, or if there's been a billing problem—this is the man they talk to.

His job is to help them.

He's cool. He knows how to handle people in a variety of situations. His is a key customer relations job with great opportunities for raises and promotions into management.

Start right off earning a full salary while you attend our special Service Representative School for seven weeks.

Pacific Telephone
An Equal Opportunity Employer m/f

Telephone Framewoman:
WHERE A JOB MEANS MORE
THAN JUST GOING TO WORK!

Just ask framewoman Susan Frey: "I've got a good supervisor. If I run into problems, I can always expect a helping hand. My supervisor will spend a couple of hours showing me something I don't understand sometimes. We help each other around here.

It's as good an outfit as there is around. If I've got to work for a living, this is the place."

The framewoman plays a vital role in telephone communications. Working in our central office, this skilled craftswoman connects cables and wires with equipment in order to provide telephone service for our customers. She also works with other craftspeople to correct troubles in wiring.

Receive full pay during your full-time classroom training.

Pacific Telephone
An Equal Opportunity Employer m/f

Telephone Linewoman:
WE'RE LOOKING FOR OUTDOOR WOMEN!

Do you like fresh air and exercise? If sitting behind a desk isn't for you, stay slim and trim as a linewoman working in the great outdoors for Pacific Telephone.

You can start right off earning a full salary while we train you to do the job.

The linewoman's job requires manual dexterity, pole-climbing, and the desire to work outdoors. Modern power tools and efficient machines help the linewoman do her job, but her primary aids are her intelligence and her own two hands.

It's smart to look into this opportunity because we are offering more than ever in pay and benefits to get linewomen. And we will give raises and chances for promotion to keep you.

Pacific Telephone
An Equal Opportunity Employer m/f

Summary of procedure. The same four telephone jobs were thus presented in three different formats: the sex-biased format used by AT&T, a sex-unbiased format, and a sex-reversed "affirmative-action" format. All 8 nontelephone ads were worded in sex-unbiased fashion and remained constant in all booklets. In other words, only the wording of the telephone jobs changed from condition to condition. For purposes of analysis, a subject was defined as "interested in applying" for a job if he or she checked any of the following three categories: "slightly interested," "moderately interested," "very interested." A subject was defined as "not interested" if he or she checked "slightly uninterested," "moderately uninterested," or "very uninterested."

Results

Do sex-biased job advertisements discourage men and women from applying for "opposite-sex" jobs? As shown in Figure 1, our results clearly suggest this to be the case.

Consider first the results for women. When the jobs of lineman and frameman were advertised in a sex-biased format, no more than 5 percent of the women were interested. When these same jobs were advertised in a sex-unbiased format, 25 percent of the women were interested. And when the ads for lineman and frameman were specifically written to appeal to women, nearly half (45%) of the women in our sample were interested in applying for one or the other of these two jobs ($X^2 = 8.53, p < .01$, one-tailed). In other words, sex-biased advertisements do discourage women from applying for so-called male jobs; more women would be interested in applying for such jobs if the ad's sex bias were removed; and even more women would be interested if affirmative-action ads were specifically written to recruit them.

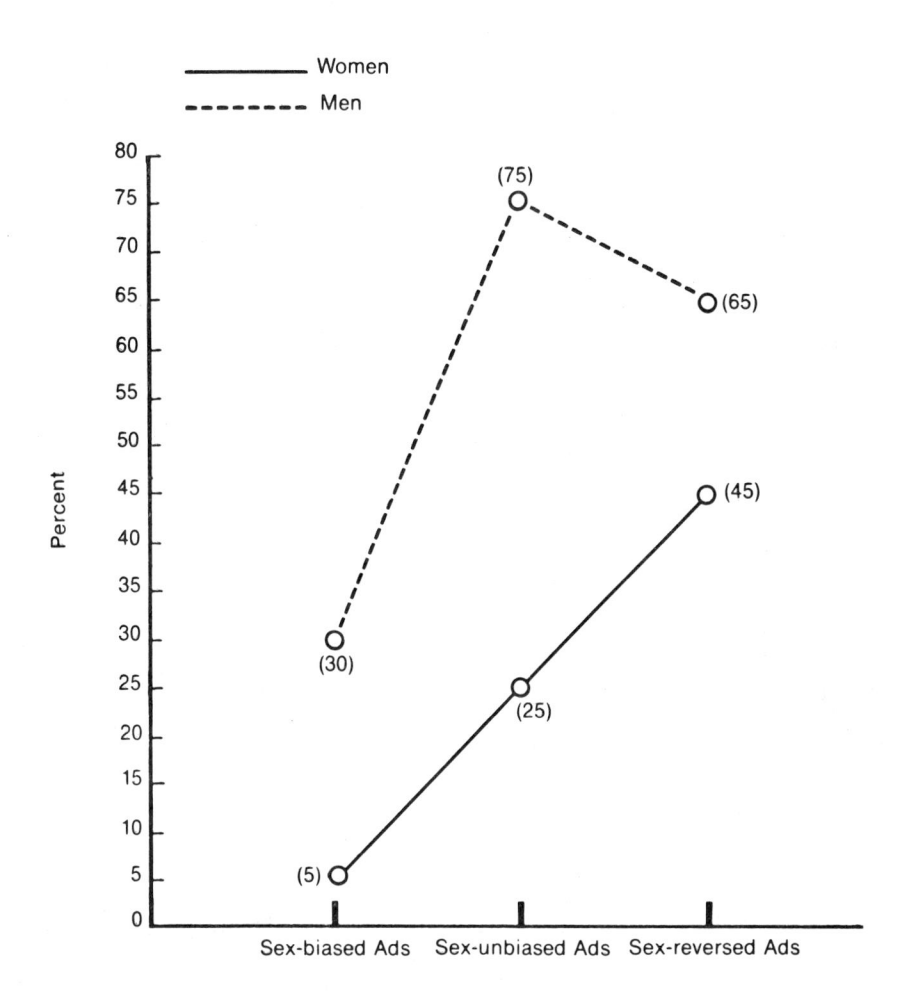

Figure 1. Percent of men and women who were interested in applying for either of the "opposite-sex" jobs. (Each data point represents 20 subjects.)

The results for men show a similar, but not identical, pattern. As can be seen in Figure 1, men are generally more interested in the jobs of operator and service representative than women are in the jobs of lineman and frameman. (This difference may be due, in part, to the fact that Pacific Telephone does employ male operators in the Bay Area.) Despite this fact, the results clearly indicate that sex-biased job advertisements still tend to discourage men from applying for jobs as operator and service representative ($X^2 = 9.09, p < .01$, one-tailed). For when the sex bias is removed, the percentage of men interested in applying for one or the other of these jobs jumps from 30 percent to 75 percent. Wording these ads in sex-reversed "affirmative-action" format does not further increase the percentage of men who are interested. [Neither does it significantly reduce it, however ($X^2 < 1$, n.s.)]. It may be that 75 percent is the maximum one can expect for any particular job and that a sex-reversed format *would* serve to further increase male interest for "female" jobs with lesser initial interest.[2]

The results of Experiment I thus indicate that sex bias in the content of a job advertisement does serve to aid and abet discrimination by discouraging both men and women from applying for "opposite-sex" jobs. Experiment II addresses itself to a second form of sex bias: the segregation of job advertisements into "Male" and "Female" columns.

Experiment II

Method

Fifty-two women attending Carnegie-Mellon University in Pittsburgh were asked to rate each of 32 jobs which had been advertised in Sunday editions of *The Pittsburgh Press*. Sixteen of the ads had been drawn from the "Male" column and 16 had been drawn from the "Female" column. Each woman was given a booklet containing all 32 ads. She was asked to read each ad and to rate it on a 6-point scale which ranged from "definitely unwilling . . ." to "definitely willing—to apply for the job." The women were told to assume that they had the necessary prerequisites for each job: "We are only interested in your preferences, not your skills."

Segregated want ads. Half of the booklets listed the ads in a sex-segregated format identical to that used by *The Pittsburgh Press*. The 16 male jobs were listed in alphabetical order in a column labeled "Jobs-Male Interest." The 16 female jobs were listed in alphabetical order in a column labeled "Jobs-Female Interest." Of these, half listed the male jobs first and half listed the female jobs first. In addition, the following disclaimer, quoted verbatim from *The Pittsburgh Press,* appeared on every other page of the booklet:

NOTICE TO JOB SEEKERS

"Jobs are arranged under Male and Female classifications for the convenience of our readers. This is done because most jobs generally appeal more to persons of one sex than the other.

"Various laws and ordinances—local, state and federal, prohibit discrimination in employment because of sex unless sex is a bona fide occupational requirement. Unless the advertisement itself specifies one sex or the other, job seekers should assume that the advertiser will consider applicants of either sex in compliance with the laws against discrimination.

Integrated want ads. Half of the booklets listed the identical 32 ads in alphabetical order with no sex labeling. The disclaimer again appeared on every other page of the booklet, but with its first paragraph deleted.

Results

Do sex-segregated want ads discourage women from seriously considering those jobs which appear in a "male interest" column? The results show this to be the case. When jobs were segregated and labeled on the basis of sex, as they are in many newspapers, only 46 percent of the women in this study were as likely to apply for "male interest" jobs as for "female interest" jobs. In other words, a majority of the women did prefer "female interest" jobs. But does this really reflect a true preference on the part of women for so-called "female interest" jobs? No, it does not. For when these same jobs appeared in an integrated alphabetical listing with no reference to sex, fully 81 percent of the women preferred the "male interest" jobs to the "female interest" jobs ($X^2 = 6.60$, $p < .02$, two-tailed).[2]

For example, the job of newspaper reporter fell in popularity from 7th place when it appeared in the integrated listing to 19th place when it was segregated and labeled as a "male interest" job. It seems clear that the newspaper editor who wishes to hire only male reporters—in violation of the law—can place his ad in the "Male Interest" column, secure in the knowledge that this will effectively discourage female applicants. It is in this way that sex-segregated want ads can "aid and abet" discrimination in employment on the basis of sex.

Discussion

What can we infer from these studies about the effects of sex-biased advertising on actual job applicants? Can we generalize these results to the actual job-seeking situation? It is our view that, if anything, these studies actually *under*estimate the extent to which sex-biased job advertisements discourage both men and women applicants from applying for jobs for which they are otherwise qualified.

First, we required the men and women in our studies to rate *every* ad regardless of how it was worded. Despite the fact that the instructions on the cover of the booklets stated this specifically and despite the fact that we emphasized the point verbally, spontaneous comments and questions indicated that both the men and the women were highly resistant to reading and rating job advertisements obviously biased as appropriate for the opposite sex. We therefore suspect that most men and women never even bother to read, let alone seriously consider, "opposite-sex" advertisements.

Second, we asked the men and women in our study only to indicate whether or not they would be interested in applying for each job. They did not, in fact, have to expose themselves to the risk of encountering discrimination—or ridicule—by actually applying for jobs which had already been designated by an employer as inappropriate for their sex. Clearly it is easier to say you will apply for a job than to actually apply.

Third, the newspaper study employed the relatively benign form of sex-segregated want ads used by *The Pittsburgh Press*. But most newspapers do not contain the disclaimer and they adhere to the more explicit headings of "Male Help Wanted" and "Female Help Wanted."

In sum, one cannot justify sex-biased advertising on the grounds that men and women have different job preferences. These studies clearly show that sex-biased advertising helps to create and to perpetuate those preferences and, furthermore, that unbiased advertising can serve to alter those preferences. Thus, for an employer to advertise as if there were "male" jobs and "female" jobs is to produce a self-fulfilling prophecy.

Postscript

As noted earlier, the two studies presented here were conducted and presented as part of legal testimony, the first in a suit filed by the Equal Employment Opportunities Commission (EEOC) against AT&T, the second in a complaint filed by the National Organization for Women (NOW) with the Pittsburgh Human Relations Commission against *The Pittsburgh Press*.

When it first became clear to *The Pittsburgh Press* that the pressures from NOW were serious and might lead to successful legal action, the newspaper changed the format of its classified advertising headings from the more blatant "Male Help Wanted" and "Female Help Wanted" to the more benign "Jobs—Male Interest" and "Jobs—Female Interest." In addition, they added the disclaimer reproduced earlier. This alteration of format did not succeed, and the Commission still ruled against them, agreeing with the contention of NOW that sex-segregated advertising columns did, in fact, aid and abet discrimination in employment. Since then the *Press* has lost appeals in the lower courts and the United States Supreme Court has now agreed to hear the case.

The EEOC action against AT&T was filed with the Federal Communications Commission, one of the few federal regulatory agencies with antidescrimination provisions in its guidelines. The occasion for the complaint was a request from AT&T to the FCC for a rate increase. The EEOC investigation of AT&T was a massive one and resulted in their conclusion that AT&T was the country's "greatest oppressor of women." The case has now been settled, and in a letter to us, William H. Brown III, Chairman of the EEOC, stated:

> The agreement which we reached with AT&T was a milestone in the history of civil rights. In addition to an unprecedented back pay award and greatly increased job mobility for women and minorities throughout the Bell System, the companies are committed to recruit and hire or promote females until they hold at least 38 percent of the inside craft jobs and 19 percent of the outside craft jobs. Males will have to be recruited and hired into at least 10 percent of the operator jobs and 25 percent of the other clerical jobs. In the long run, this means that about 100,000 or more persons will be in jobs traditionally held by the opposite sex. These commitments go well beyond any current or previous programs by any company and they have been obtained largely because of your work. . . . Since AT&T's principal justification for its sex-segregation of jobs was lack of interest by females, your experiment provided the spearhead of our argument on that issue.

In addition, AT&T has now directed that all of its advertising and recruiting materials be rewritten to remove sex bias, and a nationwide advertising campaign has been launched in the mass media featuring sex-reversed "affirmative-action" ads for traditionally sex-typed telephone jobs.

For example, an ad has recently appeared in *Life, Newsweek,* and other national magazines which shows an attractive young woman atop a telephone pole. The accompanying text reads:

THE PHONE COMPANY WANTS MORE INSTALLERS
LIKE ALANA MACFARLANE

Alana MacFarlane is a 20-year-old from San Rafael, California. She's one of our first women telephone installers. She won't be the last.

We also have several hundred male telephone operators. And a policy that there are no all-male or all-female jobs at the phone company.

We want the men and women of the telephone company to do what they want to do, and do best.

For example, Alana likes working outdoors. "I don't go for office routine," she said. "But as an installer, I get plenty of variety and a chance to move around."

Some people like to work with their hands, or, like Alana, get a kick out of working 20 feet up in the air.

Others like to drive trucks. Some we're helping to develop into good managers.

Today, when openings exist, local Bell Companies are offering applicants and present employees some jobs they may never have thought about before. We want to help all advance to the best of their abilities.

AT&T and your local Bell Company are equal opportunity employers.

A similar ad is now recruiting male telephone operators. It shows a young man, blonde, casually dressed, sitting at a switchboard, wearing a headset.

THE PHONE COMPANY WANTS MORE OPERATORS LIKE RICK WEHMHOEFER

Rick Wehmhoefer of Denver, Colorado, is one of several hundred male telephone operators in the Bell System.

Currently, Rick is a directory assistance operator. "So far, my job has been pleasant and worthwhile," he says. "I enjoy assisting people."

We have men like Rick in a lot of different telephone jobs. Both men and women work as Bell System mechanics, truck drivers, installers and engineers.

We want the men and women of the telephone company to do what they want to do, and do best.

Today, when openings exist, local Bell Companies are offering applicants and present employees some jobs they may never have thought about before. We want to help all advance to the best of their abilities.

AT&T and your local Bell Company are equal opportunity employers.

When we were being cross-examined at the FCC hearings, our sex-reversed "affirmative-action" ads were criticized and ridiculed by AT&T attorneys. We leave it as an exercise for the reader to compare our ads with those now appearing in the mass media. (Perhaps we should sue for plagiarism.)

Notes

1. Parametric analyses based on subjects' numerical ratings yield the same conclusions reported here.

2. Surveys have shown that jobs listed in "male interest" columns are preferable in terms of objective features like salary, fringe benefits, opportunity for advancement, etc.

Sex Stereotyping in the Executive Suite

BENSON ROSEN
THOMAS H. JERDEE

Women's liberationists often complain that even the most sophisticated and sympathetic male managers cannot easily shed deeply ingrained attitudes regarding the proper roles of women in business. They argue that these attitudes creep into a variety of decisions in which a person's sex is not an obvious issue. Most often these are not straightforward decisions to give favored treatment to a man over a woman, but rather decisions that result in specific ways of treating women, without any thought as to how men would be treated in identical circumstances. For example, a manager might hesitate to send a female to a meeting in another city, while as a matter of course he would send a similarly situated male employee.

These subtle forms of differential treatment could have an important cumulative impact on the self-image and career progress of the disenfranchised female. The degree to which this sort of phenomenon occurs has, however, up to now been a matter of conjecture. To determine the extent to which unintended bias can creep into the decisions of managers, we conducted a survey-experiment with the participation of [Harvard Business Review] subscribers in management positions. (For a description of the survey method, see table 1.)

The participating managers were asked to respond to a questionnaire designed to sample executive decision making. What they received was a series of brief incidents that required them to evaluate and choose between alternative courses of action with regard to an employee of a fictitious organization. The experimental feature of the survey was that the questionnaire had two versions. The respondents received either Form 1 or Form 2, which differed only in the sexes of the employees involved in the 11 incidents. Each version of the questionnaire featured men and women in an approximately equal number of cases, so the respondent had no way of knowing that other participants in the survey were evaluating the identical incidents with employees of the opposite sex in the key roles. (The [seven] cases presented in this article were taken from both Forms 1 and 2 of the questionnaire and are presented exactly as they were sent to the participants.) In this way it is possible to determine whether, when salience of sex is not an obvious factor and when all other factors are constant, HBR readers as a group tend to make different evaluations and decisions depending on the sex of the employee.

We sent either Form 1 or Form 2 to 5,000 HBR subscribers; 30% (or 1,500) responded, returning nearly equal numbers of Form 1 and Form 2. The readers who did respond are similar to those described in past HBR studies and are representative of most major industries and job functions. Exhibit I gives a profile of the participants.

When we analyzed the responses separately on the basis of age, geographic region, industry, and job function, we found no significant pattern of differences in stereotyping. There are, however, some interesting differences for male and female respondents, which are discussed later in the article. But it is important to remember that female respondents comprise only 5.3% of the sample. Thus male/female differences must be interpreted with caution.

Reprinted by permission from *Harvard Business Review*, vol. 52 (1974), pp. 45–48; copyright © 1974 by the President and Fellows of Harvard College; all rights reserved.

TABLE 1
THE SURVEY APPROACH

In this HBR survey, subscribers were given a brief history of a hypothetical organization and asked to assume the role of an important official in the organization. In this role, they encountered a series of 11 memos, letters, reports, and other communications, and were asked to respond to each incident by recommending appropriate managerial action. The questionnaire/exercise was developed according to the following procedure:

1. A hypothetical organization, The Miller Clothing Company, was described, and participants were instructed to take the role of the executive vice president.

2. Incidents depicting Miller Clothing Company employees in situations involving selection, promotion, development, supervision, discipline, and various kinds of personal conflicts were written in letter or memo form.

3. There was a *male* and *female* version for each of the 11 incidents. For example, some of the participants evaluated the qualifications of an applicant named Mrs. Karen Wood for the purchasing manager's position, and others evaluated Mr. Carl Wood for the same position. The applicants' qualifications and all other details of the incident, with the exception of the name, were identical.

4. Two complete questionnaires were assembled. Form 1 had a male employee in the first incident, a female employee in the second incident, and so forth. Form 2 had a female employee in the first incident, a male employee in the second incident, and so on.

5. For each item, alternative approaches were offered. The respondents were asked to evaluate *each* of the alternatives, as well as, in some cases, to determine the appropriateness of the question in general. The evaluations were on a 6-point scale ranging from extremely favorable to extremely unfavorable. (The percentages reported are summed over the three favorable categories.)

6. Analyses of the influence of sex-role stereotypes on personnel decisions were made by comparing responses to Form 1 with responses to Form 2, for each of the 11 incidents.

The incidents require decisions comparable to administrative decisions on the job. Each decision is made for only one employee (sometimes a male and sometimes a female). This is more realistic than confronting managers simultaneously with both a male and a female employee for promotion, supervisory assistance, or discipline. If the latter approach were employed, managers would more likely try to act in a fair and impartial way, because the potential for sex discrimination would be obvious.

In most organizations, administrative questions like the ones in the survey usually occur as single events. In the survey situations, where the possibility of discrimination is not an obvious factor in the decision process, the inherence of sex-role stereotypes would be expected to have a greater impact. The use of two forms of the exercise permitted experimental manipulation of the sex variable and provided an interesting approach for investigating the influence of sex-role stereotypes on managerial decisions.

Survey Findings

The responses to survey incidents indicate greater organizational concern and support for male employees than for female employees. We conclude:

Managers expect male employees to give top priority to their jobs when career demands and family obligations conflict. They expect female employees to sacrifice their careers to family responsibilities.

If personal conduct threatens an employee's job, managers make greater efforts to retain a valuable male employee than the equally qualified female.

In selection, promotion, and career-development decisions, managers are biased in favor of males.

The first group of incidents compares the sacrifices expected of the families of career men to those of career women.

EXHIBIT 1
CHARACTERISTICS OF PARTICIPATING HBR SUBSCRIBERS

Relative Size of Organization	Age	Marital Status	Sex
Among largest...56.7%	Under 30....18%	Married.....85.0%	Male.......94.7%
About average...27.7	30-34......20	Single......11.3	Female......5.3
Small..........15.6	35-39......17	Other....... 3.7	
	40-44......15		
	45-49......13		
	50-54...... 9		
	55-59...... 5		
	60-65...... 2		
	Over 65...... 1		

The Lady Doth Protest too Much?

Three of the . . . incidents examine the conflicts between career demands and family responsibilities. The relationship between an employee and the organization can be conceived of as a psychological contract that has specific work expectations of the employee and more subtle ones of the employee's family. Here we portray situations where executives might hold quite different expectations regarding how male and female employees should resolve home-career conflicts. The first incident presents a problem where social requirements associated with the job create family tensions.

MEMORANDUM
TO: FROM:
Executive   Jack Garrison,
Vice President   Marketing Staff—
                                Bennett Division

I appreciate the discussion we had the other evening. It was comforting to learn that the problem I am having with my wife is not unusual in managerial ranks. I have taken your suggestion and written up a recent conversation between me and my wife, for your use in your human-relations seminar in Chicago. This is, of course, with the understanding that the source of this case will not be revealed to anyone.

I would really appreciate it if you would let me know how you think this situation should be resolved. I'll also be looking forward to hearing from you about the discussion in Chicago.

I have entitled the attached case "The cocktail party."

The Cocktail Party

Jack and Judy Garrison have been married three years. Jack is an aspiring business executive and Judy is a very successful free-lance writer. Below is a part of their conversation after attending a cocktail party at the home of an executive in Jack's division.

Judy: Oh, boy, what a bunch of creeps. Do we have to go to these parties, honey?

Jack: Judy, honey, you know we have to. These things mean a lot to me. Tonight I had a chance to talk to Mr. Wilson. On the job it would take a week to get an appointment with him. I was able to get across two good ideas I had about our new sales campaign, and I think he was listening.

Judy: Is Wilson that fat slob who works in marketing, the one with the dull wife? I spent

ten minutes with her and I nearly died! She's too much. Jack, the people there tonight were so dull I could have cried. Why did I major in English lit, anyhow? I prefer to talk to people who know what is going on in the world, not a bunch of half-wits whose main interests are their new cars and spoiled kids. I tried to talk to one guy about Virginia Woolf and he didn't even know who she was. These people are incredible. Do we have to go to another cocktail party again next week? I'd like see *Look Back in Anger* instead. I've got the tickets. One of my wifely duties is to give you culture. What an uncouth bunch in the business world.
Jack: One of my husbandly ambitions is to get ahead in the business world. You know that these parties are required for bright junior executives coming up in the organization. And I'm a bright junior executive. If we don't go, who knows which of the other junior execs will get to Wilson with their good ideas.
Judy: Can't you relax and work a 40-hour week? That's what they pay you for.
Jack: I guess I'm too ambitious to relax.
Judy: I'd still like to go to the play. At least we could think about real problems.
Jack: And I'd be a mediocre, lower-management nobody for the rest of my career.
Judy: I want you to be a success, Jack. But the idea of spending more evenings talking to idiots is too much!

(The alternative form of this incident has Judy Garrison as the aspiring manager and Jack Garrison as the free-lance writer.)

Percent Approving	Spouse should go to parties and stop making it an issue	Junior executive should attend parties alone	Junior executive should stop attending parties
Female junior executive	~50	~40	~20
Male junior executive	~70	~25	~15

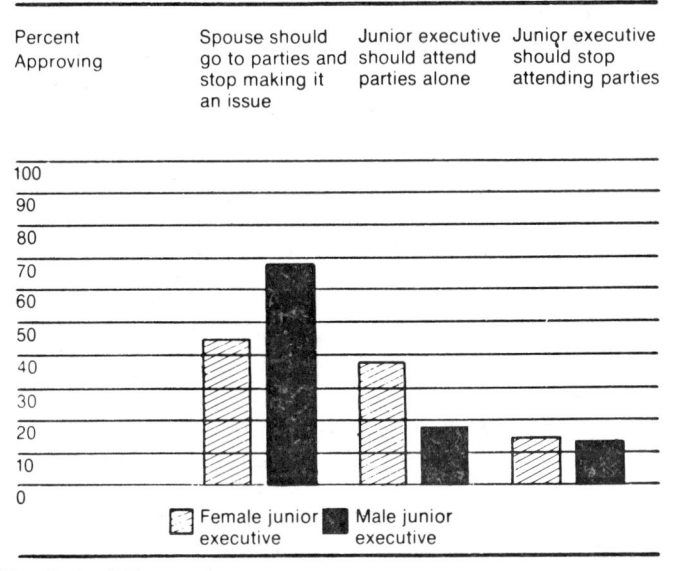

Exhibit II. The Cocktail Party

Respondents were asked to evaluate three alternative approaches for resolving the problem: (1) the spouse should go to the parties and stop making such an issue of it; (2) the junior executive should attend the parties alone; or (3) the junior executive should stop attending the parties. Exhibit II compares the participants' evaluations of the three alternatives.

The conclusion we draw from this is quite clear: managers consider that women are obliged to participate in the social activities associated with their husbands' careers; much less in the way of career support is expected from the husbands of working women. The difference in expectations could make it easier for men to combine their professional and social lives, and thus give the appearance of complete dedication to their work. Career women might find it more difficult to combine their work and social lives, and, therefore, might be seen as less dedicated to their work, even though they spend just as much time and energy on the job.[1]

The next situation illustrates how sex discrimination might work in *favor* of female employees who experience home-career conflicts. The working woman is often viewed as having legitimate competing demands and obligations in her dual role as housewife and career woman, and is, therefore, seen as deserving certain forms of preferential treatment that would be considered inappropriate for male employees. Consider the [following incident].

MEMORANDUM
TO: FROM:
Executive   Richard Bell,
Vice President   Accounting Manager
SUBJECT:
Request for Leave of Absence

Ruth Brown, an accountant in the main office, has requested one month's leave beginning next week. She has already taken her vacation this year. She wants the leave in order to take care of her three young children. The day care arrangements the Browns had made for the period covered by her request suddenly fell through, and they have been unable to make other arrangements satisfying their high standards. Ruth's husband is principal of the junior high school and he cannot possibly get time off during the next month.

The problem is that Ruth is the only person experienced in handling the "cost" section in the accounting department. We would either have to transfer an accountant with the same experience from the Richardson Division or else train a replacement for only one month's work. I have urged Ruth to reconsider this request, but she insists on going ahead with it.

I have also checked with the legal department and we do not have to hold the position open for Ruth if she insists on taking the whole month off.

I would appreciate it if you could give me your decision on this as soon as possible.

(Form 2 of this exercise concerns a request from a male accountant, Ralph Brown, whose wife is principal of the junior high school.)

Respondents were first instructed to evaluate the appropriateness of the leave request, and then they were asked to decide whether leave should be granted with or without pay. Responses are shown in Exhibit III.

Here we have a situation where the male stereotype of complete dedication to the job seems to influence recommendations. Managers think it is less appropriate for males than for females to take time off because of family obligations. These findings illustrate an interesting dilemma for husbands of career women. Their wives may expect them to share many family responsibilities that have previously been considered the female's province, while their boss expects their complete dedication to the job. This suggests a need for changes in attitudes with regard to the appropriate roles for *both* males and females, in both professional and private life.

The last incident in this group involves a direct clash between the professional careers of a husband and wife.

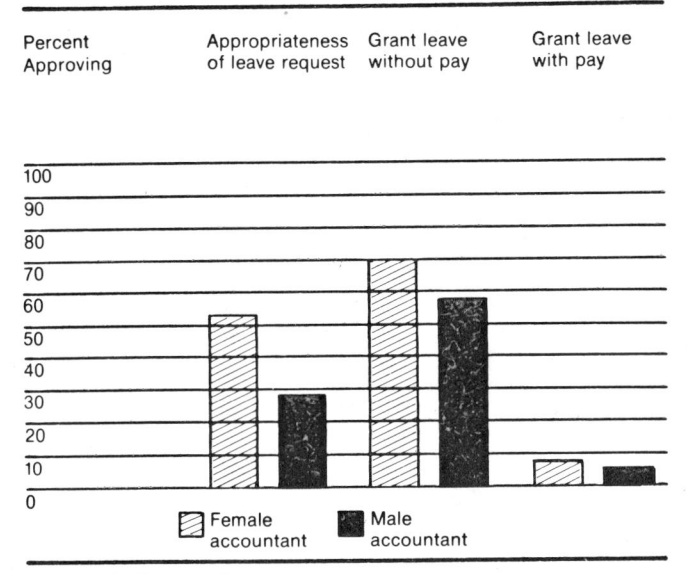

| Percent Approving | Appropriateness of leave request | Grant leave without pay | Grant leave with pay |

Exhibit III. Request for Leave of Absence

MEMORANDUM
TO:
Executive
Vice President

FROM:
Joseph Schmidt,
Computer Operations

As you know, Ronald Cooper is a computer operator in my section. He has played a key role in computerizing our inventory system. Recently, Ronald's wife was offered a very attractive managerial position with a large retail organization on the West Coast. They are seriously considering the move. I told Ronald that he has a very bright future

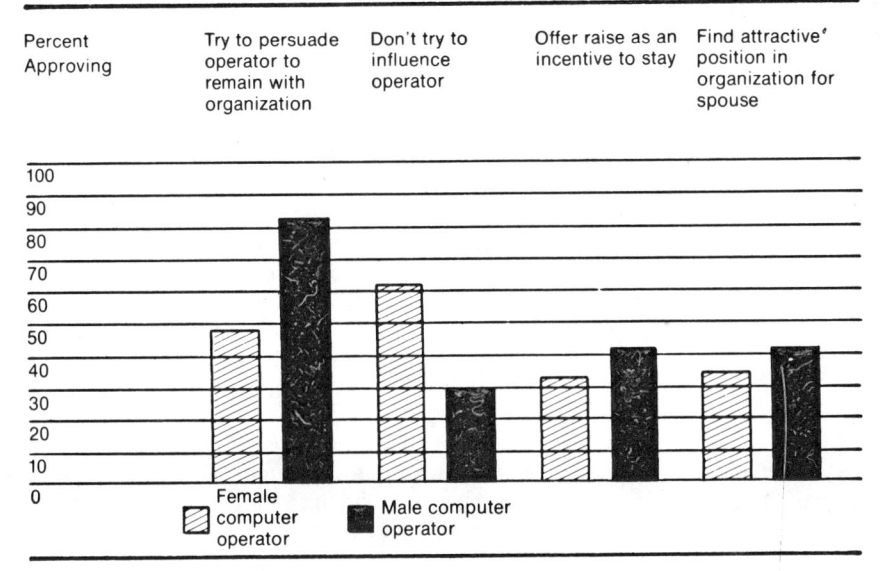

| Percent Approving | Try to persuade operator to remain with organization | Don't try to influence operator | Offer raise as an incentive to stay | Find attractive position in organization for spouse |

Exhibit IV. "Valuable" Computer Operator

with our organization and it would be a shame for him to pull out just as we are expanding our operations. I sure would hate to lose him now. What do you think we should do about the situation?

(The alternative form features a female computer operator whose husband is offered a position on the West Coast.)

We offered four alternative courses of action to deal with the computer operator: (1) try to convince the computer operator that too much has been invested in his (her) career to leave now; (2) don't try to influence the computer operator; (3) offer the computer operator a sizable raise as an incentive to stay; or (4) try to find an attractive position for the employee's spouse in the organization. The ratings shown in Exhibit IV indicate significantly greater organizational efforts to retain valuable male employees than female employees.

The responses to these three incidents show a pattern of greater managerial support for male employees and greater demands on their families. The next two cases from the survey show this same pattern of less organizational concern for female employees in disciplinary decisions.

Frailty, Thy Name Is Woman!

Are male and female employees accorded similar treatment in situations where the employee has violated company policy or engaged in off-the-job behavior that could interfere with performance and prove embarrassing to the organization? In previous research on factors influencing disciplinary judgments, we have found that supervisors are hesitant to impose penalties on "highly valued" employees. If male employees are considered more "valuable" than female employees, we thought this might be reflected in differential disciplinary treatment.

The first of the two disciplinary cases concerns an employee whose tardiness is a problem.

MEMORANDUM
TO: FROM:
Executive   David Jennings,
Vice President   Chief Design Engineer

I have a problem and I don't see how to solve it. It concerns one of the design engineers, Jill Diller, who has worked for me for the past 15 months. Jill persists in arriving late every morning. She is always 10 minutes late, more usually 15 minutes to a half hour. I am at my wit's end. I have tried everything I can think of—private discussions, written reprimands, threats, sarcasm, and more. She is still late every morning.

When Jill walks into the office, the work stops and everyone watches. Some of the designers are even joking that Jill's coming in late has something to do with her recent engagement. I don't like to get too tough with a creative girl like Jill, but her behavior is bound to hurt morale in the department.

(In Form 2 of the exercise, a tardy *male* engineer is described.)

Respondents' evaluations of the different strategies for handling the situation are shown in Exhibit V. Most participants recommend the more severe alternatives—"warn employee that if she (he) continues to come in late, she (he) will be given a one week suspension," or "threaten to fire the engineer if she (he) continues to come in late, and follow through with the threat if necessary." These strong disciplinary actions are favored

Women, Minorities, and the Disadvantaged 463

| Percent Approving | Suspend for one week for continuing tardiness | Threaten to fire and follow through if necessary | Don't make an issue of tardiness |

□ Female design engineer ■ Male design engineer

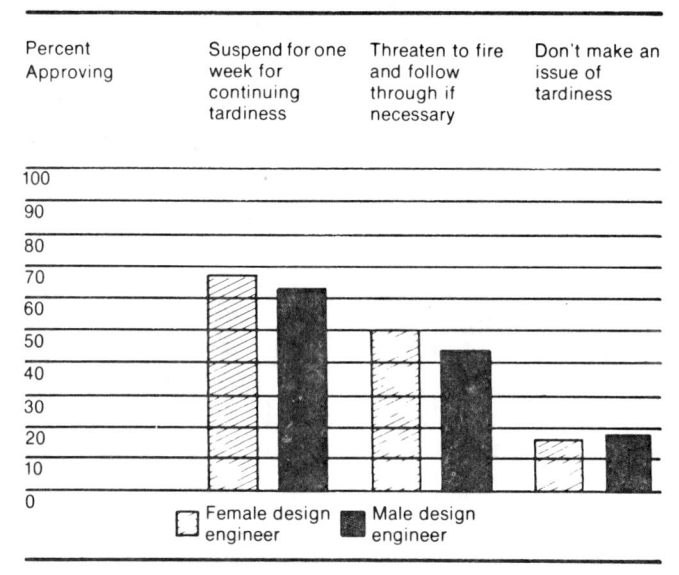

Exhibit V. Chronically Late Design Engineer

somewhat more for the female compared with the male employee. The mild disciplinary action, "don't make an issue of the tardiness," is considered inappropriate for both the male and the female engineer.

The second incident involving a discipline issue is a situation where the personal activities of a junior executive might interfere with job performance.

MEMORANDUM   CONFIDENTIAL
TO: FROM:
Executive   Frank Williams,
Vice President   Comptroller

I would like to get your advice on a matter of great sensitivity involving one of the junior executives in our organization. It has been brought to my attention by an unimpeachable source that Renée Holman, assistant comptroller in my division, is having an affair with a prominent young playboy. I understand it has reached the point where any day now Renée's husband will publicly denounce the young playboy as a homewrecker. I have been reluctant to bring this up, but I know that Renee's marital problems will hurt her work. I would appreciate any advice you could give me on this.

(Form 2 describes a male junior executive and a prominent socialite.)

Exhibit VI compares the participants' evaluations of three alternatives for dealing with this situation. The choices are: (1) do nothing unless the junior executive raises the issue; (2) advise the junior executive to see a marriage counselor; or (3) confront the junior executive and threaten termination unless the affair stops.

The findings indicate that respondents are less likely to raise the issue with a female employee and are more likely to recommend marriage counseling for a male employee in this situation. Perhaps the predominately male sample of respondents felt that it was inappropriate to approach a female employee on such a sensitive issue, regardless of the organizational consequences.

| Percent Approving | Do nothing unless junior executive raises the issue | Advise junior executive to see a marriage counselor | Confront employee and threaten termination unless affair stops |

Female junior executive / Male junior executive

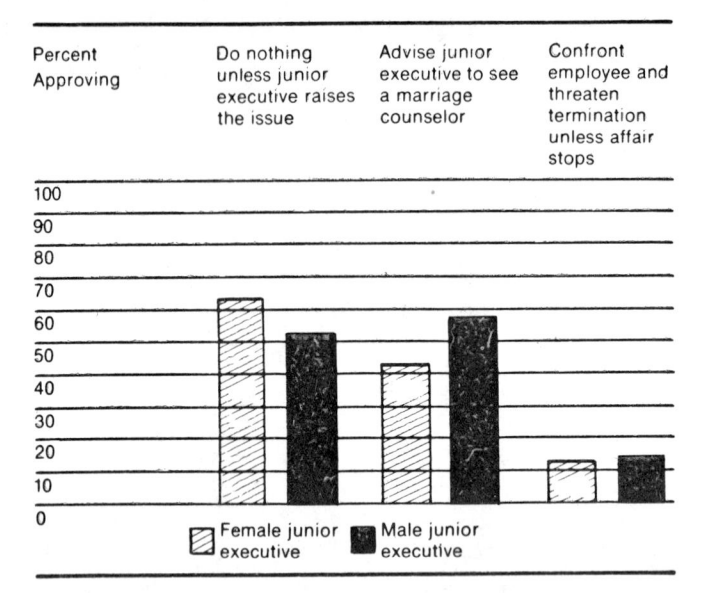

Exhibit VI. Philandering Junior Executive

When the disciplinary incidents are considered together, an interesting pattern of bias in dealing with the problems can be seen. Where the disciplinary problem involves a clear-cut rule infraction, as depicted in the first disciplinary incident, more severe disciplinary action is recommended for a female employee than for a male employee. The difference is small, however (only 5%); this might indicate that when there are clear guidelines, it is easier for managers to make face-value evaluations which do not call on the manager's preconceived notions.

In the more ambiguous situation illustrated in the second incident, where an employee's private life interferes with the job demands, greater deference is shown to the female employee. We might speculate that a female employee's on-the-job behavior is closely scrutinized; however, unlike her male counterpart, her personal life is considered beyond the domain of organizational control. Perhaps managers feel less concern about preserving the female's employability.

Get Thee to a Nunnery!

The remaining incidents are concerned with sex discrimination in various kinds of personnel decisions. In recent years there have been considerable social and legal pressures to provide equal employment opportunities for women. In response to these pressures, organizations have established new goals and policies for the selection, training, and promotion of women employees. In spite of these efforts to remove bias from personnel decisions, we find that subtle forms of sex discrimination still occur in decisions to . . . select and promote employees. . . .

Selection and Promotion Decisions. The last two case incidents examine the influence of sex-role stereotypes on the selection and promotion of males and females to managerial positions.

It has frequently been alleged that managerial jobs requiring extensive travel are considered inappropriate for females. Therefore, in one case readers were asked to evaluate the resume of either a male or a female applicant (with identical family backgrounds, work histories, and so on) for a managerial position involving travel.

MEMORANDUM
TO:
Executive
Vice President

FROM:
Corporate Recruiting
Office

Pursuant to our recent discussion with you about the need to recruit a purchasing manager for the new operation, we have developed a set of brief job specifications and have located some candidates who may be suitable for the opening. Will you please review the attached resume and give us your evaluation?

Job Requirements for Purchasing Manager

The major responsibilities of the new purchasing manager will be to purchase fabrics, materials, and clothing accessories (buttons, belts, buckles, zippers, and so on) for the production of finished goods.

For the most part, the purchasing manager will have to travel around the country visiting wholesalers and attending conventions and showings. The person hired for this position should have a knowledge of the quality of raw materials and have the ability to establish a "fair" price for goods purchased in large quantities. The person selected for this position will have to travel at least 20 days each month.

RESUME
NAME:
Mrs. Karen Wood
POSITION APPLIED FOR:
Purchasing Manager
PLACE OF BIRTH:
Cleveland, Ohio
MARITAL STATUS:
Married, four children ages 11, 8, 7, and 4
EDUCATION:
B.S. in Business Administration,
Ohio State University
RELEVANT WORK EXPERIENCE:
One year as purchasing trainee,
Campbell Textiles, Inc.
Ten years' experience
in various retail clothing stores,
in sales, buying,
and general management.
INTERVIEWER'S REMARKS:
Good personal appearance; seems earnest
and convincing.
Good recommendations from
previous employers

(Form 1 of the exercise has a resume of Carl Wood as candidate for purchasing manager.)

Exhibit VII shows how the male and female candidates fared in selection, suitability, and potential to remain on the job. Clearly, the majority of HBR respondents feel it is quite inappropriate to hire a woman for a managerial position requiring extensive travel. In

| Percent recommending selection and percent rating applicant favorably | Recommend Selection | Favorable rating of applicant's suitability for the job | Favorable rating of applicant's potential to remain on the job |

□ Female applicant   ■ Male applicant

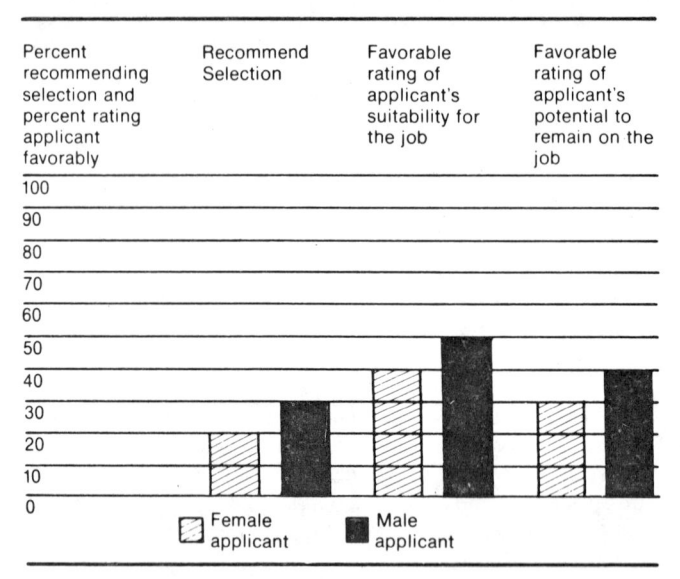

Exhibit VII. Selection of Purchasing Manager

addition, the woman applicant is seen as less suitable for the job and less likely to remain with the organization.

In the last case, we present a candidate for promotion who has a possible conflict between job demands and family responsibilities.

MEMORANDUM
TO:
Executive
Vice President

FROM:
Mark Taylor—
Corporate
Personnel Office

SUBJECT:
Promotion of Gerald Adams

We are at the point where we must make a decision on the promotion of Gerald Adams of our personnel staff. Gerald is one of the most competent employees in the corporate personnel office, and I am convinced that he is capable of handling even more responsibility as Bennett Division Personnel Director. However, I am not altogether certain that he is willing to subordinate time with his family to time on the job, to the extent that may be required with Bennett. I have had the opportunity to explore with him the general problem of family versus job, and he strongly believes in a healthy balance between them. He believes that he should very rarely stay late at the office or participate in weekend meetings.

He believes that his first duty is to his family, and that he should manage his time accordingly. This viewpoint has not affected his performance in the past, but it could be a problem in the more demanding position as head of personnel with the Bennett Division.

What do you think we should do?

(Form 2 has the identical memo; however, the candidate is a woman.)

Exhibit VIII shows the responses to the three alternative courses of action: (1) do not

| Percent recommending promotion and favorably rating actions | Do not promote | Persuade candidate to make stronger job commitment prior to promotion | Base promotion on past experience |

Exhibit VIII. Promotion to Personnel Director

promote; (2) persuade candidate to make stronger job commitment prior to promotion; or (3) base the promotion on past experience.

In this situation, respondents clearly favor promotion for the male candidate, but not for the female candidate in identical circumstances. The statement, "My first duty is to my family," and the general reluctance to work overtime are interpreted quite differently when attributed to a male employee compared with a female employee. In this incident, the male candidate is more frequently given the "benefit of the doubt" and given the promotion.

These two cases provide further evidence of bias in favor of males. In both cases, identical competing family demands are apparently seen as less compelling for males than for females. Employment and promotion in the face of these demands is supported for males but not for females.

Nevertheless, indications of discrimination in selection and promotion practices are *not* found in two other case examples not given here. When the job requirements are exact and the applicant does not match them, respondents reject both a male and a female for the position of corporate finance officer. Similarly, when applicant and job match, both a male and a female candidate for promotion to a marketing director's position are evaluated highly. This suggests that it may be relatively easy to make unbiased decisions in situations where a candidate's qualifications are clearly unacceptable or clearly acceptable. A lack of ambiguity in making a decision also overwhelms any sex biases in the remaining case. Respondents strongly disapprove of a tough-sounding memo from both a male (87%) and a female (80%) shipping manager.

On the other hand, in situations where available information is ambiguous or contradictory, decision makers may fall back on preconceived attitudes (sex-role stereotypes in this instance) to arrive at their ultimate decision. In a sense, respondents may be providing more information for themselves by filling in their own prejudices or some widely held societal expectations.

Vive la Difference?

We also examined differences between male and female respondents in dealing with the items. Although these findings should be accepted with caution, as only 5.3% of the respondents were female, we think they are of interest and should be included here.

In one situation we found a kind of reverse discrimination. Whereas males are somewhat more severe in determining the appropriate disciplinary action for a chronically tardy female engineer compared with that for a tardy male engineer, our female participants are more harsh with a male engineer. At the same time, however, 40% of the female participants approve of the most lenient choice—"don't make an issue of it"—for the tardy female employee. This finding is contrary to the widely held belief that women supervisors tend to be particularly tough in dealing with rule infractions by their female subordinates.

The female participants are considerably less influenced by the person's sex than are male respondents in responding to three of the cases. They see a request for a leave of absence as equally appropriate from either a male or a female accountant. Perhaps some of the female respondents had experienced a problem similar to what we depicted in this incident and had developed an appreciation for the husband's help in coping with this type of family problem. The female respondents are also less influenced by sex-role stereotypes in making decisions regarding the promotion of a candidate in the marketing department and the organizational effort to retain a valuable computer operator. In the latter case, the female respondents who received Form 1 recommend that the organization exert the same effort to retain the male employee as the respondents who received Form 2 do for the female employee.

But the pattern of sex discrimination is quite similar for both male and female participants in four other situations. Both male and female respondents discriminate against women in cases involving the following: (1) selecting a purchasing manager; (2) nominating an employee to attend a training conference; (3) giving advice to a philandering junior executive; and (4) resolving a conflict over workrelated social obligations. In these incidents, it seems that males and females share common perceptions and expectations about what is appropriate behavior for men and women in organizations and in family life. It appears that, in some situations, women are likely to be the victims of discriminatory decisions made by not only male but also female managers.

Conclusions

Frequently, there is a time lag between the statement of a managerial policy and its implementation. This phenomenon appears to be particularly true with regard to the acceptance of women in management positions. According to our survey findings, social and psychological barriers to women interested in a management or professional career still exist despite recent changes in policies on the employment of women.

The responses we received to the case examples reflect two general patterns of sex discrimination: (1) there is greater organizational concern for the careers of men than there is for those of women, and (2) there is a degree of skepticism about women's abilities to balance work and family demands.

Beneath these patterns of discrimination there is an underlying assumption that is not at first apparent from the survey findings: it would seem to be the women who are expected to change to satisfy the organizational expectations. For example, written comments from participating managers often suggest that women must become more assertive and independent before they can succeed in some of the case examples in the survey. These managers do not see the organization as having any obligation to alter its attitudes toward women. Neither, apparently, are organizations about to change their expectations of men. Perhaps because it is expected that the job will eventually "win out" over the family, a man is given the time and opportunity to resolve home-career conflicts on the job. This in itself says a great deal about how organizations might conceive of a man's relationship with his family—second place.

Another conclusion we can draw from this survey is that when the information is scant and the position ambiguous, managers tend to fall back on traditional concepts of male and female roles. This was clear in the case of the cocktail party and the request for leave of absence. Only when there are clear-cut rules and qualifications do both women and men stand a chance of breaking out of the stereotyped parts written for them.

In a survey of this magnitude each percentage point represents quite a number of individual decisions. When the results are extrapolated to the entire population of American managers, even a small bias against women could represent a great many unintentional discriminatory acts, which potentially affect thousands of career women. The end result of these various forms of bias might be great personal damage for individuals and costly underutilization of human resources.

Finally, if managers are sincere in wanting to encourage all employees equally, they ought to examine their own organization's implicit expectations of both men and women to see if they reflect some of the same traditional notions revealed in the survey. Identification of these biases might assist managers in moving toward the goal of equal employment opportunity.

Note

1. See Cynthia F. Epstein, "Encountering the Male Establishment: Sex-Status Limits on Women's Careers in the Professions," *American Journal of Sociology*, 1970, vol. 75, p. 965.

Who Shall Work?

BERTRAND B. POGREBIN

Before 1965, the Continental Can plant in Harvey, Louisiana, followed a white-only hiring policy—although two blacks had been hired during the labor shortage of World War II. When Title VII of the Civil Rights Act banned sex and race discrimination in employment in 1965, Continental Can began hiring black workers as well as whites. By 1971, out of 400 employees, 50 were black.

Reprinted from *Ms. Magazine*, November 1975, with permission.

Two years later the recession forced the company to lay off about 250 employees. Following the provisions of the company's contract with the Steelworkers Union, workers were let go on the basis of seniority (length of service). In other words: last hired, first fired.

Because they had been among the most recently hired, all the black employees, except the wartime two, were laid off. Moreover, 138 of the laid-off whites had more seniority and were thus entitled to come back to work before the first black could be recalled. Given the state of the economoy and the company's business outlook, it might be a decade before another black could be employed at that plant.

Last December, as a result of a court order, Karen Pioch was hired as a police officer by the City of Detroit. She was one of 100 women cops that the city was required to immediately employ to remedy such discriminatory hiring practices as: different educational requirements (high school degree for men; two years of college for women); age (18 for men; 21 for women); frequency of qualifying exams (weekly for men; annually for women); and assignments (unrestricted for men; limited for women).

Karen Pioch had testified that she would have applied to the police force sooner if not for the extra educational requirement. In 1972, after completing two years of college, she did take and pass the annual exam, but there was no opening for her until two years later when the Court ordered the city to hire 100 new women. At the time of the order, women comprised 2.1 percent of the Detroit force. The 100 new hires brought the proportion to 6 percent.

Then last June, in a drastic economy move, Detroit announced the layoff of 825 police officers, among them 210 women. All of the 100 court-ordered new hires were dismissed. And Karen Pioch had to turn in her badge.

The stories of Karen Pioch and Continental Can point up the issues that have split traditional labor allies and thus far defied a resolution that is fair to all sides.

In both cases, and in dozens more, the aspirations of minorities and women toward equal employment opportunity had begun to be realized. (The phrase "minorities and women" has become common usage in Title VII cases. However, it should be clear that "minorities" include women and "women" refers to *all* women.) However, since the national economic crunch, and wherever there are layoffs, newly hired women and minority employees have been set on a collision course with the labor unions and their basic contract protection of the senior employee.

Defining the Issues: Who Gets Fired First?

The dilemma is deceptively simple to state: a cutback; two employees for one job. Who goes? Who stays?

Is it, as in Harvey, Louisiana, the older, long-term white worker whose job security is honored? Or should the recently hired black worker retain the job that it took legislation to open? Is it, as in Detroit, the male police officer who is kept on after years of service? Or must there be job protection for a Karen Pioch, who's been on the job only a few months though effectively excluded from the force for decades?

The questions get knottier: does it make any difference if the particular blacks laid off are the same blacks who actually applied for the job years earlier and had been refused? If they had not been turned away, wouldn't they now have the necessary seniority to stay on the job despite layoffs? Should they be penalized twice—once at their earlier rejection and now because that very act of discrimination prevented them from having seniority?

Should they be given "fictional seniority" to make up for the past discrimination? Should white workers relinquish their job rights and thus bear the brunt of society's past generic racism— whether or not they are individual racists?

Similarly, if the woman being laid off in Detroit was not actually rejected because she never applied for work in prior years, does she then have no claim to job preference now? What if she never applied earlier because she knew of the police department's antiwomen policies? Should any weight be given to the chilling effect of this known sex bias? Should Karen Pioch be given "fictional seniority" from the date she would have applied to the force had women's applications been treated fairly?

Finally, since both the senior white males and the junior female or minority employees are all innocent victims of the employers' discriminatory practices, should any of the workers lose their jobs? Instead, why not put the onus on the responsible party: let the employers pay for their past evils.

The "Front Pay" Concept: Fair or Futile?

One answer, formulated by the United Auto Workers, is "front pay," which asks the employer to pay victims of its past bias, who are subsequently hired and then laid off, the wages and fringe benefits they would have received. "Victims" include not only those who applied for jobs and were rejected but also those who were *discouraged* from applying at all because they knew of the employer's negative policies. The front pay concept provides economic redress; it does not, however, provide for "phantom" or "fictional seniority." The relative seniority of the employees continues to be based on true length of service.

Unfortunately, our current economic system has all but ruled out the front pay solution, however innovative and appealing it might appear. First, it is unlikely that the courts will impose on the employer an economic obligation that could be unlimited. Second, front pay can be economically self-defeating because it saddles an employer with pay for two workers to fill one shrinking job. Since it is supposed to be paid for as long as the employee *would have* worked, there is an incentive for the employer to cut back, relocate, or close to eliminate that job, and thus limit his double costs. If the employer is forced out of business, we may not have the problem of two workers for one job, because there may be no job for either worker. Finally, if some employees are going to earn front pay by staying home, doesn't that raise the specter of the older employee working for what the newer employee earns for nothing?

Divide and Conquer

As long as we posit a profit-motivated economy, a company's financial health determines just how many jobs are available. The inevitable result has been to pit women against male minority workers and both groups against white males in the battle for whatever jobs do exist. Ironically, such divisions reestablish the same lines previously drawn by the discriminating employer whose policies created the problem in the first place.

Another irony is that the conflict lines up the beneficiaries of Title VII—women and minority workers—against the very unions that so strongly lobbied for enactment of Title VII back in 1964.

Although the Equal Employment Opportunity Commission (EEOC) is entrusted with the enforcement of Title VII, the Commission, at this writing, has been unable or unwilling to issue guidelines on layoffs to assist employers and labor unions in resolving the conflict. Meanwhile, unions insist that seniority rights remain inviolate. Companies are unenthusiastic about alternate solutions to layoffs. And senior employees are refusing to relinquish privileges for the benefit of their junior brother and sister workers. With no federal guidelines and no willingness to compromise, the issue has been thrown into the courts.

Plant-wide Seniority Systems: Are They Sex and Color-blind?

In our two earlier examples, the Detroit police case *(Schaefer* v. *Tannian)* and the Continental Can case *(Watkins* v. *Steelworkers),* the union contracts provided for layoffs solely on length of service with the company, i.e., plant seniority. In *Watkins,* the union and employer, as joint parties to the contract, reminded the court that Title VII exempts "bona fide" seniority systems from its reach. They argued that Continental Can's plant seniority *is* bona fide because it is blind to race and sex. It is not based on length of service in certain departments which may have been restricted, but on total length of service in the company as a whole. Therefore, they argued, plant seniority is a neutral and objective criterion for layoffs. But the judge, citing the company's 20 years of lily-white hiring, ruled that even plant-wide seniority cannot be valued "where blacks were, by virtue of prior discrimination, prevented from accumulating relevant seniority."

The Watkins Solution: Proportional Layoffs

The judge ordered the company to rehire a sufficient number of blacks to restore the ratio of blacks that existed in the company's work force as of the date the last new employee was hired. He decreed that no one, black or white, was to be laid off at that time. But if future layoffs were necessary, they would be allocated among whites and blacks to maintain that ratio.

Many courts have followed this *Watkins* reasoning. In New York the court ordered the Board of Education to lay off school principals according to the existing ratio of black and Puerto Rican principals to the total number, the supervisors' contracts' seniority terms notwithstanding.

In Cleveland, the city was enjoined from laying off a disproportionate number of junior women police officers.

In Georgia, the Carling Brewing Company was ordered to take affirmative action so that newly hired blacks were not regularly laid off from four to six months every year because of seasonal layoffs.

The judge did some creative remedy-making in *Schaefer,* the Detroit police case. Here he followed the *Watkins* reasoning and found that seniority could not be allowed to govern the order of layoffs because it would wipe out the court's ordered hiring of women. Then he took notice of the fact that the wages of a number of the newly hired employees— including the 100 women—happened to be paid for by federal funds. Laying them off didn't save Detroit any money—it only satisfied the seniority provision of the contract.

What the city wanted was to reach the senior work force that *was* paid with city funds. Therefore, the judge departed from the *Watkins* ratio layoff remedy and simply ordered all federally funded employees to be retained—Karen Pioch included.

Despite the popularity of its reasoning, the *Watkins* case was reversed on appeal and the *Watkins* approach has hardly been universally accepted. In New Jersey *(Jersey Central Power and Light Co.* v. *IBEW Local Unions)*, a district court judge ordered that a huge layoff be done on a ratio basis to retain the spirit of the company's affirmative action plan for women and minorities. The decision was reversed on appeal on the narrow grounds that the affirmative action plan was subordinate to the contract seniority system.

The Controversy over "Fictional Seniority"

The *Watkins* decision has also been criticized for adopting the concept of "fictional seniority," a concept which William Kilberg, Solicitor of the Department of Labor, calls "alien to American jurisprudence." Kilberg points out that since none of the *Watkins* plaintiffs were old enough to have suffered discrimination by the company before 1965, their claim was based on the denial of rights to other blacks who never did work for the company. And it resulted in the layoffs of middle-aged white workers who put in more than 10 years working for the company.

In two other cases, *Franks* v. *Bowman Transportation Co.* and *Waters* v. *Wisconsin Steel Works,* the laid-off black employees actually had been the same people who had been rejected in earlier years. However, both courts refused to credit the black employees with "fictional seniority." Instead, these courts held that *any* plantwide seniority system is acceptable for layoff determination, regardless of its effect on minorities and women. The Supreme Court will review the *Franks* case in its present term. [*Ed. note:* In this case the Court granted retroactive seniority to all women and minority group members who can prove prior discrimination.]

The Case for Strict Seniority: A Neutral Measure

The Court will be asked to weigh the rights of two innocent parties. The pro-seniority forces argue that seniority distinguishes employees on a nondiscriminatory basis—time on the job. They say that to strike down a seniority system that is race and sex neutral and to create "fictional seniority" for a worker, who didn't log the time on the job is to engage in reverse discrimination. They cite no less a champion of civil rights than Supreme Court Justice William O. Douglas, who said in another context: "There is no constitutional right for any race to be preferred . . . a white is entitled to no advantage by reason of that fact; nor is he subject to any disability, no matter what his race or color."

Many union women worry about the long-term effect of the *Watkins* ratio solution. "We fought for years to eliminate separate seniority lists for women," says a union official. "To argue for percentage layoffs by sex just segregates us all over again."

It's the Basis for Job Security
Pro-seniority advocates point out that workers' length of service is their only investment in their jobs. Like any investment, it grows day by day. Diluting "real" seniority with "fictional" seniority becomes particularly troublesome when applied to allow women employees to displace slightly senior black and Chicano males (as it does in many

cases where hiring policies reflected the entry of once-excluded groups: white males, oldest; minority men, newer; women, newest).

Besides, "fictional seniority" for new women and minority employees doesn't necessarily aid the *actual* victims of the previous discrimination. It is a remedy for a *class* of people, not for specific aggrieved individuals. The answer, say the pro-seniority forces, is full employment, not an attack on seniority.

The Case Against Seniority: It Preserves Past Wrongs

The counterargument centers on practical effects. Honoring strict seniority can institutionalize past discrimination. What good does it do to say we won't discriminate from now on if promotions, transfers, and order of layoffs are all based on length of service? If white males argue that diluting their seniority punishes them for the employer's past discrimination, females and minorities can argue that crediting the white male with the fruits of that discrimination *continues* the burden on the traditional victims. As between the two groups, shouldn't the burden now move on to those who have, however innocently, enjoyed the benefits of the illegal policies?

Seniority Shouldn't Be Considered Immutable
More important, the concept of seniority must not be regarded as sacrosanct or inviolate. In its industrial context, it is a creature of collective bargaining, that is, a union-negotiated contract provision. The *kind* of seniority negotiated, i.e., plant-wide or departmental or job classification, can make for widely different results depending on economic chance. For example, if a product line is being closed in a company with departmental seniority, the senior employees working on the ill-fated product line may be laid off while the junior employees in another department remain.

Since collective bargaining agreements are periodically renegotiated, seniority rights may be changed or diluted for any number of reasons: to call for a different seniority system; or to negotiate for superseniority for union officers. (Interestingly, there are no cries of "fictional seniority" when those officers get top seniority regardless of actual length of service.) For decades, the National Labor Relations Board has awarded "fictional seniority" to workers who were discriminated against for engaging in union activity. Workers discriminated against for reasons of race or sex would seem entitled to the same treatment.

There are other erosions of the seniority "guarantee": if the employer sells or closes, seniority may be lost. If the company is merged, seniority lists may either be dovetailed with the merged company's or end-tailed (with acquired employees going to the bottom of the list); or—as in airline mergers of two pilot groups—seniority may be decided by arbitration. Finally, employees may lose seniority upon their promotion or transfer to a new job.

Thus, even aside from Title VII cases, seniority embraces a variety of rights that are always subject to change and are different from company to company and industry to industry. They are not "rights" in the sense that they are fixed and immutable. They represent an employee's present expectations about her or his status relative to other employees.

Seniority Provisions Affect only Unionized Workers

We should view the concept of seniority rights in its nationwide setting. Since seniority is almost exclusively a product of collective bargaining, it is not even a factor in nonunion jobs—which is where a majority of Americans work. So, for most of the workers in this country, there is no formal seniority protection. Presumably, for nonunion workers, no conflicting interest stands in the way of Title VII and enforcement of affirmative action. By contrast, union-negotiated seniority systems allow the discriminating company and its preferred workers to insulate themselves by private agreement from out national equal employment policy.

How can these diverse interests be reconciled? As one union attorney put it, "I hate these Title VII layoff cases because there's no right side."

The EEOC has failed to provide any leadership. Last spring it indicated that it would not regard as bona fide any seniority system resulting in displacement of a "disproportionate number of female or minority employees." The agency was about to issue guidelines requiring employers to consider work sharing, elimination of overtime, voluntary retirement, reduction in hours or rotating layoffs, instead of disproportionate layoffs. Eventually the EEOC backed off under unified criticism from the AFL-CIO, the U.S. Chamber of Commerce, and from other federal agencies that cited conflicting court rulings.

Some private lawsuits have tried to protect all sides. In *Bales* v. *General Motors Corp.*, California women employees tried to enjoin GM from dismissing them. At the same time the women asked the court to explore alternatives to layoffs (the EEOC guidelines were to propose such alternatives). The injunction was denied and the matter is pending.

Thus far, innovative solutions have been left to the ingenuity of private parties and individual judges. As in the Detroit police case, judges should be free to weigh the practical effects and set aside seniority when it works to no one's advantage. In some cases, ignoring seniority should be seen as temporary means of correction. Certainly, ignoring seniority altogether should prove more difficult for the courts than awarding "fictional seniority" to those originally denied employment.

Unless the Supreme Court resolves all these questions at once, the possibility of huge damage suits fixing back-pay liability on the employer and the union may make compromise attractive. They may voluntarily seek a form of shared work coupled with unemployment compensation in their new contracts. Since they could lose all in a court case, unions may bargain for modified seniority protection—justifying "half a loaf" to their membership.

At this writing, the unemployment rate is at its highest level in 35 years. It seems unlikely to change in the immediate future. The time has come for the government to commit itself to a national policy of full employment rather than leave the issue of "who works?" to individual stopgap solutions. The prospects, however, do not seem bright.

All We Want for Christmas Is Our Jobs Back

MAUREEN KEMPTON

Before the layoffs in the New York City Police Department, we had 618 women on the force. Then came the squeeze; 3,000 officers were let go, and of them approximately 375 were women. Our group, the Committee of Female Police Officers, has decided we're going to publicize our fight for our jobs. Sure, the laid-off men are in just as bad shape as we are. Some even need the money more than we do. But the situation is different where the laid-off women are concerned.

It took so long for policemen, their wives, and the public to learn to accept women on patrol. It took so long for us to prove ourselves capable of doing the job. Now we're losing all that ground. And they're telling us it will be two years before we're recalled to work—if at all. By that time, all the gains will be forgotten, and we'll have to fight the battle for acceptance all over again.

We're not the only ones suffering. Society will feel the absence of women police officers. For instance, the rape prevention squad is gone. If a woman gets raped today in certain precinct areas, it could be up to 72 hours before she'd ever speak to a trained woman officer.

How do you measure how important it is to have a woman officer in a rape case? In my precinct when I came back to headquarters after a seminar on rape, the guys teased me with stuff like, "Here she comes to hold some dizzy dame's hand." I said, "I hope it never happens to your wife." They answered, "It would never happen to *my* wife." Most of the men still see rape victims as women on the prowl—not as decent, innocent victims of a crime. A rape victim has to deal with guys like that—guys without the kind of training that women officers have.

Only 10 precincts out of 73 in New York City still have women—and they're only on matron duty; they search women prisoners and guard female cells in detention centers. But on patrol, there are few women left, if any at all. So you're missing the calming influence that women police have been found to have in family disputes and street fights.

Early in my career, my partner and I came on a fight in the street. Other officers were having trouble breaking it up. I went up to one of the fighters, held his hand, and asked if he'd like to go home. He said yeah, if I'd go with him. So I walked him to the corner and cooled the whole scene.

Ken McFeeley, president of the Patrolman's Benevolent Association, was elected on a platform of taking women off patrol. He failed to add that he was taking 2,600 men with us. We've picketed with those men, but we've also decided to form our own group to take the soft route. We want to let people know what's going on and what they're missing when women are let go from the force.

I was on the force for 26 months, after graduating in the top 5 percent of my police academy class. Before I became a cop, I raised three kids, taught school part-time, was a census interviewer and a part-time matron. After I passed my test, I was on the list for five years before I was appointed. Now I really want that job.

What kills me is that there were 4,000 officers appointed after I was. Since only 3,000 had to be laid off, I should still have my job, and I would have it—except for veteran's preference. That's what gives ex-servicemen, whether draftees or enlisted, 30 months

Reprinted from *Ms. Magazine*, November 1975, with permission.

automatic extra seniority and five bonus points on the police exam score.

Last January, before the layoffs, the mayor asked the police to give up something or he would have to fire people. We agreed to work five extra days so the new rookies who were on probation would be kept; and they were hired. Many got their 30 months veteran's preference credit and thereby gained seniority on me and lots of other people who let them in by working those extra five days. It burns me up.

What do you do with your knowledge when you can't use it? I no longer carry a weapon. But I call 911 [the emergency telephone number] a lot, because I'm tuned in to crimes-in-progress and crimes-about-to-happen. A lot of laid-off cops have been turning in the alarm and then giving the collar [credit for arrest] to a working cop. We can't afford to spend the time in court for a citizen's arrest, because we're not being paid and we're looking for a job.

When I'm driving, I find myself looking at inspection stickers on cars. You get used to working 24 hours a day when you're a police officer. It's hard to turn that off.

CHAPTER **11**

Current Problems in Personnel: Employee Well-Being in the World of Work

Many studies have been reported that have shown that the work environment can affect worker fatigue and productivity. (See for example J. W. Griffith, W. A. Kerr, T. B. Mayo, and J. R. Topal, "Changes in Subjective Fatigue and Readiness for Work During the Eight-Hour Shift," *Journal of Applied Psychology,* 1950, *34,* 163-66.) Behavioral scientists are currently raising questions about the potential effect of the work environment on drug abuse rates, injury rates, alcoholism, and employee mental health.

The Occupational Safety and Health Act (OSHA) passed by Congress in 1971, has forced organizations to modify the work environment so that effective accident control can be maintained. As the first reading in this chapter points out, many workers and managers are complaining about the way the government is enforcing the Act. The reading does much to explain why OSHA has a bad image within U.S. industry.

In the next article, King, a freelance reporter, works with and interviews employees in the sanding department of a Ford Motor Company plant. The employees discuss the work environment in their department and explain why they feel "stuck" in their jobs. Relating this article to the one by Hall and Morgan on career development (chap. 5) and the one by Dowling on improving manufacturing jobs (chap. 7), along with the fact that the federal government under OSHA is attempting to improve the physical environment of jobs, we could conclude that these workers may not be as "stuck" as they think. Management and the federal government in many countries are attempting to improve the quality of work life of employees like those described by King.

The article by Levinson shows that it is not only blue-collar manufacturing employees who are frustrated. Many executives today are frustrated, traumatized, or bored with their jobs. Failure among executives has caused many executives to escape through suppression, alcoholism, aggression, low self-esteem, and even suicide. Levinson shows how awareness of our vulnerability to failure can keep us from resorting to such unhealthy means of adjustment.

The last reading in this chapter, that by Trice, outlines how alcoholism has become a major problem among executives and workers alike in organizations today. Trice examines the work-world behavior of alcoholics and demonstrates how the work setting can either contribute to alcoholism or lead to a truly effective means of identifying and treating the problem.

Protecting People on the Job:
ABC's of a Controversial Law

Important changes are taking place in the government's costly and much-criticized program to make workplaces in America safer and more healthful.

For 4½ years the Occupational Safety and Health Act, known widely as "OSHA," has affected about 5 million firms as well as most federal and State agencies—about 3 of every 4 workers.

Almost every phase of the law's implementation has stirred controversy. It has embittered employes as well as employers. Some detractors call OSHA "a four-letter obscenity."

Now, under pressure, changes are coming. For a look at what is in the works—and for answers to some questions that are being asked—*U.S. News & World Report* went to top authorities.

First of all, What Is OSHA?

It's a law requiring virtually all employers to make sure that their operations are free of hazards to workers.

OSHA was enacted in July, 1970, after two years of all-out lobbying for it mainly by the AFL-CIO and some other labor-union groups. Proponents wanted sweeping action by Washington to reduce on-the-job injuries, illnesses and deaths, which they claimed had reached shocking dimensions.

The Act, 31 pages in length, went into effect on April 28, 1971. The Occupational Safety and Health Administration was formed in the Labor Department to issue and enforce standards, which now fill 450 pages.

Why Do Workers Complain about OSHA?

Some claim that new rules are silly and that they cramp work styles. Others fear the government's power to shut down their workplace if it's considered unsafe.

The complaint of labor-union chieftains is different. They say that the Administration enforces the regulations halfheartedly and has moved too slowly in setting additional standards for health and safety.

What Irks Businessmen about OSHA?

Many things. Businessmen say the law has added vastly to equipment expenses, administrative tasks and management headaches.

Further, many executives complain that the law is stacked against their firms and has been carried out in an irrational, often harassing, manner. They also complain of overwhelming red tape and paper work. An official of the National Association of Manufacturers maintains that soon "there will not be enough medical, clerical and industrial-hygiene personnel within this country to perform the duties required by the standards."

The sheer bulk and complexity of rules torments many businessmen. Even the Federation of American Scientists found the language of these edicts "convoluted beyond recognition."

Reprinted from *U.S. News & World Report*, November 24, 1975. Copyright 1975 U.S. News & World Report, Inc.

One set of OSHA rulings goes on page after page, using trigonometric equations, to define "ladder" and "exit."

Among other gripes heard from businessmen:

The OSHA agency is heavily staffed with labor-union sympathizers.

Government officials could use OSHA's broad powers as a lever for extracting political contributions. Allegations of such tactics emerged in the course of the Watergate hearings.

Is the Government Doing Anything to Respond to these Complaints?

The word has come down from the top at the Labor Department: Stop being so rough on businessmen. Try to co-operate more with companies that are really trying to improve working conditions.

In the wake of this policy, some OSHA officials have been replaced.

On November 8, the Labor Department even issued a press release praising some firms for "going beyond" OSHA standards.

OSHA officials must now accompany any new standards they devise with a statement on how it is likely to affect the nation's economy, especially inflation. The aim is to make OSHA standards more realistic.

Improvements in current regulations are also being promised.

When OSHA was getting started, the Government adopted en masse several thousand assorted rules, regulations, standards and codes with little regard as to whether they were outmoded, suitable or simply some group's version of what would be ideal.

Revising standards will be a slow process. This past summer the agency held hearings for five weeks with more than 100 witnesses and 1,200 prehearing comments on proposed noise standards. Those standards are not expected to be issued before early next year.

Is Anything Being Done about the Unions' Complaint that Enforcement Isn't Stiff Enough?

Yes. There will be more inspections—from about 225,000 this year to 300,000 in 1976.

And inspectors will pay more attention to health perils. Special targets: high noise levels and dangers in handling toxic substances, particularly asbestos, cotton dust, carbon monoxide, silica and lead. Policy, until recently, emphasized accident prevention.

The Labor Department in mid-October proposed new standards to cut employe exposure to trichlorethylene, a degreasing solvent, and beryllium, a metal used in aerospace products.

What Would Businessmen Like to See?

Some continue to fight for outright repeal of the Act. They claim that the U.S. for decades has had excellent safety records compared with the rest of the industrialized world and that these records were getting still better long before OSHA arrived.

But most businessmen would be glad just to get OSHA modified. They think:

OSHA officers should be permitted to consult with them prior to inspections so that the employers can correct problem areas.

Penalties should be eliminated for minor violations that are found on a first inspection.

Equipment that already is installed should be exempted unless it is a serious hazard.

Interested parties should be notified 90 days before new standards are imposed.

Is Congress Moving to Amend the Law?

Not very fast. There are about 70 bills on Capitol Hill to rescind the Act or limit its scope. Only one is given much chance of getting out of labor committees. It would temporarily allow OSHA officials to consult with managers who wonder whether their work conditions are up to snuff—without immediately subjecting the firm to citations for any violations that are found during the consultation.

Considered most likely to pass: bills to switch the safety of mines and railroads out of other departments and into the Labor Department.

Congress has been watching OSHA. In fact, investigators of the Senate Labor Committee and the General Accounting Office, an arm of Congress, have accused OSHA administrators of severe ineptitude and of devoting "an inordinate amount of time to nonserious violations."

Is OSHA Worth Its Cost?

Proponents of strong safety laws argue that any cost is small when it saves lives and limbs. But OSHA's program is expensive—and it's getting more so.

The Occupational Safety and Health Administration spent 293.3 million dollars from April, 1971, through fiscal 1975. It has requested 116 million for the fiscal year that began July 1. That's small potatoes compared with what OSHA regulation is costing business. One estimate put corporate expenses for compliance at 3.12 billion dollars for this year alone. Much bigger costs are expected once new noise standards are proclaimed.

Businessmen say little of this expense adds to efficiency and that much of it will have to be passed to customers through higher prices.

What Good Has OSHA Done in Its 4-1/2 Years of Existence?

OSHA officials say it's impossible to tell whether the incidence of job-related accidents and illnesses has declined much since the law took effect.

They suspect that employers suddenly became more careful about reporting accidents once the Federal Government entered the picture. This tended to inflate accident rates and thus tossed safety statistics into turmoil.

Firms at least have become more safety-conscious. Most businessmen acknowledge that.

The definite beneficiaries: bureaucrats, lawyers, publishers of newsletters and journals about safety, holders of safety seminars and makers of safety equipment.

Some equipment firms advertise products as "OSHA-required" or "OSHA-approved." Confused corporate purchasers have spent thousands of dollars on such products, only to find some were neither needed nor required.

What Are the Functions of the Safety Agency?

It sets standards and rules, conducts inspections, issues citations for violations and imposes fines.

Safety officials can issue charges without indictments from grand juries or without even consulting a lawyer.

A businessman can receive a citation and a proposed penalty even if there is no existing standard dealing with a particular hazard spotted by an inspector.

Who Does the Inspecting?

The OSHA agency recruited the best people it could get when it was formed. The early corps of inspectors was composed mostly of experienced professionals from industry.

But more and more compliance officers are trainees, getting on-the-job experience. Businessmen usually feel they know more about safety in their shops than any outsider. They also complain that federal inspectors barge into offices and plants without prior notice or warrants and waste a lot of time and effort on trivial tasks, such as measuring the height of toilet partitions and checking to see if OSHA posters are properly displayed.

Inspectors are told not to cozy up to businessmen. They are not allowed to advise employers on compliance. Nor can they give dispensation to a manager who corrects a violation immediately after it is pointed out to him.

Businessmen say inspectors become overzealous and petty in an effort to please their superiors.

"They are like traffic cops who feel they have to make out a certain number of tickets or they won't be doing their jobs," comments Charles J. Pilliod, Jr., chairman of Goodyear Tire & Rubber Company.

Can the Agency Issue Citations to Workers for Violations?

No. Even though a safety violation is caused entirely by a careless or disgruntled worker, OSHA still places blame on the employer.

What Are the Penalties?

The maximum fine is $1,000 per day per violation, but the average imposed for some 900,000 violations reported to date has been only $25. And fewer than a third of these charges have withstood appeals from employers. However, employers still must pay all their own legal expenses, even when the charges brought by the Government are later found to be groundless.

In addition, there are the costs of altering practices or equipment to satisfy OSHA. Some of the corrections seem to the businessmen to be unnecessary—or even harmful.

What Provision Is there for Appeals from Rules or Citations that Seem to Be Unreasonable?

The executive branch—which serves as prosecutor, judge and jury in its safety-and health cases—also controls the Occupational Safety and Health Review Commission. That's the agency created to hear appeals in such cases.

Even the chairman of the appeals commission, Robert D. Moran, has asked that his agency be put under the judicial branch in order to assure its impartiality.

The Review Commission frequently has socked employers with higher penalties than were assessed against them originally.

"This has a chilling effect on an employer's exercise of his right to appeal and is thus a blatant denial of fundamental fairness," complains Richard B. Berman, director of labor law for the United States Chamber of Commerce.

The Review Commission typically takes from 7½ months to two years to decide on an employer's formal objection to an OSHA action.

These periods are expected to stretch out still further as the Commission takes on cases regarding noise levels and toxic chemicals—cases requiring testimony by expert witnesses.

Who Has Been Hit Hardest by Policing So Far?

Safety officials have given special attention to longshoring, meat packing, lumbering, construction, roofing, sheetmetal work and the manufacture of transportation equipment, especially snowmobiles and other types of recreational vehicles.

A higher percentage of inspections have been made of companies having more than 250 employes than of smaller firms. Still, the agency frequently is accused of picking on small companies.

The National Federation of Independent Business charges OSHA administrators with using small firms as "guinea pigs" to establish legal precedents and to build up a record of successful cases.

Overburdened small businessmen, the group contends, would rather pay fines than hire attorneys and travel to far-off hearings before review boards.

Does OSHA Apply to the Government Itself?

Yes. Government workplaces are required to meet OSHA standards. But the Government's own safety record is not impressive.

The General Accounting Office found that a quarter of the violations reported in four federal agencies were "of such a severe nature that, had they been found in private business, the employer would have been assessed substantial monetary penalties."

More than 300 hazardous conditions were discovered in the OSHA agency's own building in Washington, D.C. Example: The cabinet of a fire extinguisher had no handle and was sealed shut with paint.

Inspections also showed that an OSHA office in Cincinnati had several safety hazards, including blocked fire exits and a collapsing ceiling.

Such revelations have added to OSHA's bad image within American industry. That image—more and more people in Washington are concluding—must be improved if the law is to be a successful avenue for assuring wholesome and safe places to work for America's growing labor force.

In the Sanding Booth at Ford

RICK KING

It's a cold, windy morning in January 1974. The recession is getting worse, and manufacturing plants all over the San Francisco Bay area are laying off. A steel plant has closed. International Harvester and Raytheon have laid off a shift. But the Milpitas Ford plant is hiring a swing shift to make more Pintos and Mustangs. It is the only plant in the United States actively hiring.

I'm 24, unemployed, and trying to avoid going to law school. At 6:30 there are already 20 people in line. By the time the office opens at 8:00, the line has tripled in size. Most of the applicants are black or Chicano and half are women.

Reprinted with permission from *The Washington Monthly*, January 1976. Copyright by The Washington Monthly Co., 1028 Connecticut Ave., N.W., Washington, D.C. 20036.

It is the same mix you see in unemployment offices. Men in platform shoes and construction boots, Coors beer tank tops and neatly ironed, flowered shirts. The only difference is that all the women wear pants, as if to point out that they are ready for manual labor. Everyone waits patiently. Already there are six applications for every place. The pay is over $5 an hour (by 1976 it will be over $6). No one talks.

At 9:00 I am sitting across from my interviewer, a black in his middle thirties. I notice his Boalt Law School ring and then look into his eyes. I promise myself I won't look down until he does. We stare at each other through the whole interview. I point out that I will do anything to get the job: stand in line again, fill out another application. He is impressed by my enthusiasm and assures me that one application is enough.

"Usually, we like people to stand outside longer," he confides, adjusting his tie. "If it rains and people stay in line, we think that's a good sign. Shows they really want the job." For the first and only time, I look away and then back to see if he is serious. He is.

Three months later, I take a physical and am ready to work. Another 14 days and I am sitting at a seminar table with 20 other new hires. Five are women. Our group leader from Labor Relations, who looks like Rocky Marciano, is passing out forms: medical insurance, forms for Detroit and the union local. He advises that we take Blue Cross instead of Kaiser health insurance. All 20 of us dutifully follow his advice.

I look around the table. Most of the women are big, and everybody is healthy. There is none of the fat that would distinguish 20 randomly chosen Americans. I am one of the few who is not married. There is only one man over 30. He has worked previously making Mack trucks.

We watch a movie, "Don't Paint It Like Disneyland." The film consists of interviews with Ford workers at River Rouge. The message is clear: the work is hard but the pay is good. Our group leader turns off the projector and announces that he worked on the line for ten years.

"If you don't have any guts, you'll quit the first day. I almost did. And you'll want to quit, I promise you that." I became convinced that if this behemoth almost quit, I'll never last five minutes.

"You're going to hate that job so bad during the first few weeks. You're going to hate Ford, this plant, your foreman. If you get through the first week, you have a chance."

He pauses and drops his voice. "But folks, let's face it. There's no place in the country, no place in the world, that's going to hire people like you, without any skills, and pay them over $5 an hour." I look at the man next to me, a young Chicano in an army jacket with Sanchez stenciled over the left pocket. He raises his eyes in an expression of resignation and agreement.

Carefully we put on our safety glasses, file out of the room, and walk through a door that says "Safety Equipment Required Beyond This Point." Moving from the quiet of the office, we are assaulted by a noise level like that of an airport runway. Everywhere there are cars of all different colors, lines of cars moving in different directions. Cars extend as far as can be seen.

We follow the group leader through the plant, respectful and wide-eyed as if in a cathedral for the first time. Conveyor belts hanging from the ceiling carry tires and parts. People hurry by in blue overalls or aprons. The foremen's neat shirts, ties, and slacks are a stark contrast. Everyone wears a watch.

Within the confusion I notice a few specific jobs. A young woman with a huge afro jams gas nozzles into cars as they pass by. Two men grab tires off a rack, bounce them on the floor, deftly catch them, secure them to each car, and bolt them tight.

As we walk workers stare at us and grin. Many are yelling. My ears gradually adjust to the din. "Don't do it," the workers are yelling. "You'll be sorry." I grin at the people pointing at us and realize that we new hires are the only ones wearing safety glasses.

Eight hours later, I drive home despondent. My hands are bleeding and I feel like an idiot. I am supposed to be a block sander. Unfortunately, I am only able to do about one-fifth of the work assigned me. Lew, who is teaching me the job, assures me that it is all right. "You'll learn," he says. "Don't worry. At least you hustle. As long as you kill yourself for them, they'll keep you." I arrive home, drink two beers, eat a steak, and go to bed four hours early.

The Closer You Look . . .

Within a few weeks, everything is more familiar. I drive to work with Denny, a block sander who was hired on the same day I was. We pass by alternating orchards, factories, trailer parks, and billboards. WHAT IS A BULLFROG? asks one. The answer is Smirnoff and lime. Just before you get to the plant, the Galaxy bar is full of people trying out bullfrogs before work. Similarly, the liquor stores do a rush business on beer. Many cars pulling into the plant parking lot give off the odor of marijuana.

The executive parking lot is uniformly populated by late model Fords. The employees lot is crowded with '56 Chevies, Toyotas, Datsuns and some exquisite, hand-painted motorcycles. People who have worked at both GM and Ford say that GM puts a little extra time into building its cars.

A huge banner over the employees' entrance proclaims, "The closer you look, the better we look."

Before work I walk slowly toward the time clock, relishing the few moments of freedom. If there's time, I wander around the plant. Under one roof, it has a floor space of ten football fields. The roof is two stories high. In some places the assembly line goes up in the air or crisscrosses over itself. A private railroad brings in parts from the Midwest and divides the plant in half. On the west side, cars are made. On the east, small pickup trucks.

A few minutes before 4:30, I clock in, drink two cartons of chocolate milk for energy, go to the bathroom (no chance again until break), hop over two lines, and walk into the booth. I work in the paint department in an enclosed booth. The cars enter and exit through a narrow opening at either end. Our job is to sand the car smooth before it receives its final coat of colored paint.

The booth is hazy with dust from the shift before. The primer coat is lead-based and I wear a surgeon's mask that I bought in San Francisco. Ford provides masks, but they are uncomfortable. Art, who works across from me, uses the mask I give him. Denny, next to me, doesn't; it makes it too hard to breathe.

I hold a ten-pound air sander in my right hand and a handful of sandpaper in my left. My responsibility is the right-hand half of the trunk, roof, and hood. I open the passenger door and sand quickly inside with the sandpaper in my left hand. Then I sand the whole surface area with the air sander. Any large metal burrs or blobs of paint have to be removed with a scraper I carry in my apron pocket. The many paint runs, grease spots, or specks of dirt have to be ground down to bare metal and smoothed out. Also, the small grill in front of the windshield has to be sanded over three times. Since the line speed is usually between 55 and 58 cars per hour, I have to perform my job within 67 seconds.

After a few months, the work is routine. I've learned which parts of the job I can skip when I get tired. One day, however, a Frederick Taylor efficiency expert appears with a stopwatch and lurks behind pillars hoping we won't notice him. Even the foreman, Stan, hates him. If the expert thinks fewer workers are needed, the responsibility for enforcing an increased workload falls on Stan.

The word is quickly spread and the whole line slows down. Jobs that a worker used to be able to finish with a few seconds to spare suddenly become unbearable. In our case the acting is to no avail. Two people are taken out of the booth and the four remaining are given extra work. In addition to my normal job, I now have to sand around the tail and headlights, and help Denny, in front of me, with the sides.

Coping

The four of us adjust. The work is always physically exhausting, like playing a game of football or soccer. But the real punishment is the inevitability of the line. I want to take a walk, go to the bathroom, have a Mr. Goodbar. It doesn't matter. There's always another car

Someone shows me a *Newsweek* article with a picture of an autoworker playing a guitar while the line rolls by. The implication is that the work is so easy it's possible to take time off to play a little blues. I have to plan ahead to get a drink of water: five seconds to the fountain, five seconds for the drink, five seconds back into the booth.

The monotony of the line binds us together. Small gaps, usually a few car lengths, happen almost every day. We constantly peer down the line to see if any are coming. The big hope is that a gap won't appear during your break.

Occasionally, the line breaks down. This is what we all wait for. The plant is turned upside down. Foremen in ties appear from nowhere and furiously try to figure out what has happened. It is the only time they do physical work. At the same time, we stand around grinning and give specious advice. For once, Ford is paying us to do nothing.

Yet, such moments are rare. Within the booth, we rely on each other for entertainment. We yell at each other or speculate about whether we'll go home early. Ron and Denny trade statistics from the *Guinness Book of World Records*. We invent a form of basketball using a trashcan as a basket and play fast games during gaps. The other three constantly exchange cigarettes. We tell each other about our lives before we joined Ford.

The booth is our world. Because we have to see any spots on the paint, the booth is white and brightly lit by neon lights. It is three car lengths long and 15 feet wide. The booth is enclosed to prevent the dust from escaping. There is a coating of dust on everything. The noise of the sanders makes it necessary to shout to be heard.

While working, although we may be immersed in our own thoughts, there is always an unconscious awareness of the other three. Unused to repetitive work, I am the most absent-minded. Once, I find my foot caught on the line. The next car is proceeding normally and will run over my foot in a few seconds. I scream. Instantaneously, without need for explanation, Ron, Denny, and Art snap out of their private thoughts. They push the moving car back up the line and then free my foot. The whole incident takes five seconds.

I also have the least capacity to endure the frustration. One day, hating myself and hating Ford, I smash my $150 sander into a hunk of twisted metal. I look up at my friends. They are amazed. To steal from Ford or to sabotage a car is understandable. But to destroy a tool is simply childish.

Our reliefman, who studied four years to be a Jesuit, gives me another sander. He switches parts among a few old sanders and is able to disguise the fact that my sander was ever destroyed. What I have done is no big deal, just odd.

You Die in Little Ways

Sabotage against the cars themselves is common. As a matter of course, we used to force the trunks closed in a way that ensured the cars couldn't be painted properly. But most sabotage takes place in the trim department, where dashboards, mirrors, inside panels, windows, and extras are installed. Because so many items are installed in this section, it is difficult to trace the saboteur. Every day, mirrors are smashed and quarter panels are ripped. The art lies in sabotaging in a way that is not immediately discovered. As work is done further down the line, it becomes progressively more difficult to repair the original problem. Another form of sabotage is to ignore work. There is a legendary trim worker whose job is to install six screws. He never puts in more than four.

Sometimes the results are artistic. For a week, cars would periodically come down our line with a huge, sculpted penis where the gear shift was to be installed. Workers came from all over the plant to look at these wonders. Gradually they grew larger and larger until the last was at least four feet long. Then they mysteriously ceased.

Usually the day passes with few such diversions. After conversation has lost its appeal, one slips inevitably, reluctantly, into daydreams. Ron mostly dreams about sex. Art hears music. Denny builds and rebuilds fantasy motorcycles or thinks of his ex-girlfriend and their little girl. I imagine going to South America and learning Spanish.

The fantasies on the line are replaced by nightmares of the line slowly devouring them or of falling further and further behind. One friend installs dream quarter panels into his girlfriend's back. She wakes him up, but the minute he falls asleep, he starts all over again.

Faced with the daytime prospect of working on 400 cars, it's nice to have a little artificial energy. The plant seems to be fueled by "crossroads"—little white benzedrine pills with a cross imprinted on them.

Speed is sold openly, when it's available. Dealers walk through the plant on a half-hour break and sell 20 bags. Sections of the line buy a couple of $5 or $10 bags and split them up over a week. However, there is never enough to fill the demand.

One day the painters in the booth next to us drop acid. Luis, who has two kids and a condominium on time, paints sitting down, can't talk, and skips lunch. The pass rate on their paint jobs is normal.

Drugs, no matter how strong, provide no anesthesia for certain conditions. The ventilation in the paint booth never seems to work too well. The painters complain of being unable to breathe and of getting headaches. One day they carry Luis out of their booth unconscious. He has been overcome by the paint fumes.

Another time, Denny comes back from his break and announces a big gap coming up. Half an hour later, when the gap arrives, we hear there has been a walkout in the arc welding booth. "Just a little labor problem," mutters our foreman. "I don't know any more about it than you do." I start to walk over to Body. "Got to keep to the area, Rick," Stan tells me. "General foreman wants it that way."

A taper comes back from break and says the welders are back at work. It was something about gloves and safety equipment, but she isn't sure. Three hours later, another rumor arrives. This time the welders have walked out of the plant. The four of us in the booth look at each other. We let two cars go by.

What was happening? Why had they walked out? If we joined them, would we be the only ones leaving the plant? "I'll do it if you do it." "I'll do it if *you* do it." Ron's wife has just had a baby. Art is getting married in a week. We start working again. You die in little ways.

Why the Welders Walked Out

The arc welders who walked out had been trained together in a federally financed manpower program in San Jose. They had been hired directly from the program. By the time they got to Ford, they already knew and trusted each other. Arc welding is one of the dirtiest, most painful jobs in the plant. The torches and general heat in Body Section combine to make the area like an oven. At the same time, the welders have to wear bulky protective clothing. Despite protective gloves, welders' arms are crisscrossed with scars from the sparks thrown up by their torches.

Their foreman, Becker, had been brought from St. Louis, where a Mercury shift had been laid off. Discipline in the St. Louis plant is reputed to be the tightest in the Ford organization. In the summer it gets so hot that workers have to tie wet towels around their heads to keep from overheating. One time, St. Louis workers stayed on the line with a foot of water on the floor. California employees shake their heads in disbelief when they hear such stories.

Becker thought his young California workers were chicken. They kept asking for replacements of the long gloves that protected their arms. He wouldn't provide them; they're expensive and he wanted to make them last longer. The welders called their union rep. He told them things would be all right.

Becker continued to supervise their work. They asked for the gloves again. "They're coming." Everybody knows that safety equipment is kept in lockers close to the work area. Becker was playing with them. They stopped work.

Instantly, they were surrounded by UAW representatives, Labor Relations department bigwigs, and foremen. They demanded that the foreman be transferred and that they get their gloves. The gloves were produced. It was promised that the foreman would be replaced during lunch.

When the welders came back from lunch, the foreman was still there. One welder put down his tools and started walking out. Another later told me, "Hell, I didn't want to walk out right then. But when he's walking out of the plant, what can you do?" They all walked out.

Ten welders and two other workers left the plant. They were all fired. The UAW assured them that the problem was being handled. But nothing happened. Some of the welders appeared at the plant gates and passed out leaflets asking people to come to the next union meeting. A few days later, the company rehired three of the welders who were not considered "ringleaders." Anybody passing out leaflets was, of course, a ringleader.

At the union meeting it took two of the three hours and a challenge to the chair to bring up the question of the arc welders. A member of the International happened to be at the meeting and counseled against any type of action. Someone was finally able to move that the Union put out an informational leaflet about the incident. Union official after union official warned that a leaflet would upset the delicate balance of negotiations. When asked what negotiations, they replied that they could not say.

People who supported the welders were baited as college agitators (as indeed some were). When it came to a vote, all the workers from the line voted unsuccessfully for the welders. Almost all the UAW officials voted against them.

United Against Workers

Ford won the battle of attrition. Without the support of the union, unable to muster a significant following inside the plant, the welders became increasingly discouraged. Gradually, Ford hired back the welders who had lost heart, the ones who stopped passing out leaflets at the plant gates. In the end, only the two or three most militant welders kept passing out leaflets and trying to organize legal help. They were never rehired.

What makes the assembly line work efficiently is fear, not engineering. There have been no significant technological breakthroughs since Henry Ford first designed the line. The system is based on forcing men and women to produce as much per minute as possible. Once inside the factory, the fear system is immediately apparent. Every problem becomes a crisis, because it threatens to disrupt the smooth flow of the line.

Each department (Body, Paint, Trim, Chassis, and Pre-Delivery) has a quota to meet. In Paint, for example, 75 percent of the cars are supposed to pass inspection. Because the departments are competitive, there is a reluctance to admit mistakes. When a department supervisor has a problem he can't solve, he often just hides it.

Before the cars come to us to be sanded, they are dipped in an ionized paint solution called "E" coat. This coat of paint actually penetrates the metal and prevents rust. One day we noticed there was no E coat on the cars. We called Stan and he went to talk to the department supervisor.

A few minutes later Stan returned and told us to keep sanding. I counted at least 75 cars that passed without any E coat. The supervisor made sure they were duly inspected and passed. Once outside the paint section, the paint job would never be inspected again. Most people on the line estimated that the cars would rust out within a year. "They'll ship 'em to Boston and blame it on the rock salt," was the general prognosis

If the department supervisor is displeased with a foreman under him, he will do anything to frighten him into performing better. Brutal tonguelashing is common. Foremen work under the constant threat of being returned to the line (foremen cannot be fired, they have the opportunity to start over as workers). While ulcers are a common problem among foremen, heart attacks are also frequent. Many new foremen quit in disgust and go back to the line.

The ones who remain are the most brutal and competitive. Strangely enough, their drive to extract the utmost from the workers carries over to the machines, which are used until they break. Obviously, it would be cheaper to replace them as they wear out, but the mentality doesn't allow it.

If management is harsh, at least it doesn't pretend to help you. But the union does, and some of the worst contempt is reserved for union officials. UAW stands for United Against Workers, a friend tells me.

Typically, union officials seem more at home with Labor Relations executives than with workers. The atmosphere is one of smoke-filled back rooms and secret bargains. It is hard to find a union official in the plant. When you have a problem, you have to telephone and then wait for your representative. Sometimes he comes and sometimes he doesn't.

Of course, all locals are different. Local 560 can be characterized by my own representative, who spent ten minutes one day delineating the problems of the auto industry to me. The root of the problem, he explained, is that workers are lazy. If people would just come to work faithfully and work a little harder, we'd all be better off.

A few years ago, someone was killed in Body Section. A piece of machinery fell on him. The story is that the chairman of the Health and Safety Committee presented his regular report at the next meeting a few weeks later. He didn't mention the dead man. When asked why not, he pointed out that the man hadn't filed a grievance. Consequently, he couldn't investigate the problem.

Staying Human

From what I've said, working at Ford must seem like a circle in Hell. That's mostly the way I remember it. The work is trivial and the conditions poor. Intense discipline is combined with poor planning. The UAW, one of the most liberal unions in the country, constantly proves itself unresponsive to workers' needs. Aside from a few isolated ex-student revolutionaries, there are no political movements.

Each worker seemingly stands alone. Some want to work for a few years and then go to school. Most want to last 30 years and retire with a full pension. As Jerry, our reliefman, says, "I may have been born here, but I'm not going to die here."

But the atmosphere is not one of total defeat. Among workers there is a strong, unstated feeling of trust. It manifests itself in little ways. On a break, a complete stranger will tell you about his deepest marital problems or his feelings of despair, simply because you too are wearing overalls. After five minutes, he'll look at his watch, wave goodbye, and rush back to the job.

Although opposition to Ford is not organized, it is constant. Militancy on an individual level is high. Overly tough foremen find their work sabotaged and are subject to continual verbal harassment. Efficiency experts are forced to hide while doing their inspections. Workers are united in one thing — hating Ford.

Still, 30 years is a very long time. Sabotage helps relieve frustration, but without some type of political context it becomes an empty gesture. So, the worker settles into a slow, cynical wait for retirement. After all, it's a steady job.

During the wait, there remains the dignity of not joining management. There is a clear distinction between exploiter and exploited. The refusal to become one of the exploiters is the constant, steadfast expression of humanity in the face of Ford's regime.

One of my clearest memories of Ford is walking down the chassis line one afternoon. One part of the line runs above the workers who assemble the undercarriage. All day they stand in a narrow concrete trench working on the cars passing over their heads. They have no room to move around and can't see anything.

I hear a strange noise suddenly, like the beat of jungle drums in a Tarzan movie. It gathers force and grows louder, drowning out the sound of the rest of the plant.

Every worker beneath the line is beating on the bottom of the cars with his wrenches. All around, above ground, people laugh and walk in rhythm to the percussion.

Sometimes, on the line, I fantasize about that sound, and the rhythm spreads and spreads.

On Executive Suicide

HARRY LEVINSON

In recent months two corporate executives have made headlines across the nation by committing suicide. One in New York City leaped to his death from his office window. A routine check following his death disclosed that he had authorized a bribe to a foreign official in order to prevent an increase in export taxes which would have harmed his company. In Texas a top executive shot himself. He left behind a note that alleged he had been involved in political wrongdoing on behalf of his superiors.

In each case it was easy to conclude that the man had taken the only way out to avoid the intolerable consequences of guilt. That conclusion, however, is too glib; behind such incidents lie complex mechanisms that make certain executives particularly vulnerable to suicide, especially in times of economic distress. In self-interest, the special nature of these factors should be widely understood in management ranks.

Suicide always raises the question, "Why?" The question is especially important during a recession, when the suicide rate always rises. Both of these men were very successful, as their top-ranking positions indicate. Both had strong consciences, or their behavior would not have troubled them. What intense pressures for achievement or approval forced these men to comply with actions that violated their consciences? What rigid self-demands made them think that death was the only way out of their dilemmas? Why do some executives attach so much importance to their roles? Why are their aspirations so high and crucial to them that if they face business reverses, their only solution is to punish themselves with long hours of fatiguing work and perhaps eventually with death?

In this article I want to explore some of these questions, to examine the character of the executive likely to be vulnerable to suicide, and to suggest why suicide can appear as a way out to a dynamic individual. Then I shall discuss ways in which people can recognize the symptoms of severe depression in themselves and in others, thereby, perhaps, preventing suicide.

The reader should appreciate the limitations of a brief presentation. All we can do here is try to understand a little about a very complex phenomenon and hope that understanding may cause someone to cry for help instead of escape to death.

High Aspirations, Low Self-image

A bright, aggressive, middle-aged corporate controller thought himself to be in line for the position of vice president of finance. He approached the company president and asked whether he would be appointed to that position. The president said that he would not, whereupon the controller left the company and became financial vice-president at another company. On the first day in his new post he jumped from the eighteenth-story offices of the company. His suicide was inexplicable. Many years after the event his former employer still blamed himself for refusing the controller his promotion.

Reprinted by permission from *Harvard Business Review*, July-August 1975, pp. 118–22; copyright © 1975 by the President and Fellows of Harvard College; all rights reserved.

In this example are some of the common elements surrounding suicidal behavior: intelligence, ambition, disappointment (and, for those who were close to the person, uncomprehending guilt). These elements are particularly germane for executives.

Executives are men and women of high aspiration. As a rule, they are very ambitious, seeking power, prestige, and money, and nearly always they are competing intensely against other executives. In psychological jargon, they have extremely high ego ideals that revolve around power. They have deep-seated, unconscious pressures for attainment; their conscious goals are merely the tip of the iceberg. People who have such high levels of aspiration are frequently nagged by the feeling of being a long way from achieving their goals. No matter what their achievement, it never seems to be enough. As a result, they always view themselves as inadequate.

All of us try constantly to narrow the gap between the ego ideal and the self-image. The failures of a person with irrationally high self-demands lower his self-image and thereby increase his anger at himself. We experience self-directed anger as depression. While depression is widespread and is usually amenable to treatment, in its extreme form, as we have seen, it often leads to suicide.

Early Traumas

The problems of high aspiration, high ego ideal, and low self-image start very early in life and contain significant components of irrationality. Some infants react to frustrations as the product of a hostile world and take a fighting stance toward it. Others interpret pain and frustration as a product of their own inadequacies and therefore are prone to blame themselves. This is a depressive position and becomes a context for self-flagellation when later frustrations or failures confirm already established belief. Regardless of any achievements, such persons always see themselves as deficient and, according to their logic, deserving of self-punishment.

Among those particularly subject to depression are people who early in life lose one parent or both. And if the parents of a person who attempts suicide were separated from him when he was a child, the separation is more likely to have been intentional (such as through divorce) than natural (such as through death).[1] The consequent loss of love and support in childhood results in anger at the loss. Through primary-process thinking (explained in a moment) the child becomes angry with the lost parent for deserting him—which the child thinks is his fault because he is unlovable or inadequate. Irrationally, he becomes enraged with himself. Although the rage in time subsides, it leaves a psychological bruise, and new losses—such as business losses—can stir up the rage again. The person is now more vulnerable to self-punishment.

A second element of irrationality often underlying depression in later life lies in what is called primary-process thinking. In this state the child equates thinking and feeling with doing. When the child is frustrated, his anger mounts and his wish to attack the frustrating object frightens him. In his anger with his parents or others, the child fears that his thoughts alone will destroy them. Simultaneously he feels he is bad for having such thoughts.

In an effort to cope with these feelings, the child frequently develops a pattern of behavior in which he controls the expression of feelings so that they do not show. They become unconscious; he is no longer aware of them. He tries to be so good and so competent that nobody will ever believe he has harbored bad thoughts. This pattern underlies the elevation of ego ideal aspirations to unrealistically high levels; the consequent pressures to achieve perfection follow the person through life, though he does not know why.

Dr. Margaret Prouty, former chief of pediatrics at Jackson Clinic in Madison, Wisconsin, has reported cyclical occurrences of depression among a selected group of children from seven to nine years old. Her profile of these youngsters corresponds strikingly to the problems of the ambitious, depressive adult: "The majority are perfectionists, have a poor self-image and find that their classmates, parents, and teachers cannot measure up to their expectations. They have much need of affection and approbation, trying hard to please and be good. They have a high incidence of anxiety and dependence and poor ability to express antagonism. . . . One of their chief personality defects is an almost total lack of sense of humor. Life is indeed real and earnest and they have no ability to laugh at themselves or others."[2] The future will find many of these children, and children like them, in managerial roles and other positions of responsibility and power, where their intensity, seriousness, and drive to perform well will make them high achievers and superior workers.

Through adolescence and adulthood the ego ideal demands are stimulated further by external pressures for achievement, by the expectations of parents and other influential figures, by competition for preferred places on athletic teams, in colleges, for professional training and preferred jobs, and by competition within organizations. In short, those who may be coping with repressed childhood rage this way demand much of themselves, and much is demanded of them.

Threat of Failure

When scholastic, professional, or organizational achievement is a cherished dream, the threat of failure, real or imagined, is a constant companion. By the time they reach middle age, many persons, especially ambitious executives, feel defeated by a lifetime of competition and still others feel constantly burdened by the threat of failure. Intently pursuing high aspirations, they are vulnerable to defeats that move their self-images farther away from their ego ideals, increasing their disappointment in themselves. As this gap increases, they get angry at themselves, become highly self-critical, feel inadequate, guilty, and depressed. These feelings may finally lead some to self-destruction.

For the corporate executive, this depressive pattern is reinforced by a career demanding that he absorb his frustrations and control his emotions ("Don't make waves"), carry on with equanimity regardless of what storms may come his way or be stirred up within him. He must not admit to having problems and must not under any circumstances give way or seek help. In fact, to seek help from a friend or the company doctor is considered a sign of weakness or failure to cope. Moreover, if he seeks help from a psychiatrist or psychologist, he is either weak or crazy or both. When a conscientious executive with tremendous self-demands recognizes that he is failing to cope effectively with a situation under circumstances in which he must control intense negative feelings, he may see limited alternatives. If he does not seek professional help, escape from an apparently hopeless situation can seem possible only by developing psychosomatic symptoms, by attacking himself in the form of accidents, or, in the extreme, by committing suicide.

In an effort to avoid the attack on self, some managers may attack and sabotage their organizations quite unconsciously. They make "stupid" mistakes. They provoke and discharge competent people, reorganize without reason, or go off on what prove to be tangents of diversification. Some try to overcontrol their organizations with rigid systems that allow them to "whip people into line" and punish those who don't "shape up." Sometimes these managers plunge their organizations into bitter, unnecessary strikes or provoke community attacks that ultimately result in their defeat. They ascribe the failure, however, not to themselves but to the organization or someone else.

But people can destroy themselves in many ways other than the physical. Some manage repeatedly to jeopardize or set back their careers, some ruin their marriages or damage their children. Some undermine their own best-laid plans; we have recently witnessed the example of Richard Nixon who, if he had planned it, could not have engineered his destruction more effectively than did his own unconscious will. Even accidents can be psychological in origin.[3] These self-destructive events cannot be ascribed only to those who are "pathological," mentally ill, or crazy. As every clinician knows, these experiences are commonplace. When people are under heavy stress from self-criticism, they may atone unconsciously for their fantasied sins by punishing themselves.

Prevention of Suicide

How can one recognize and cope with threats to the self-image that may precipitate depression and, eventually, self-destructive behavior? Here are some recommendations:

Self-directed aggression occurs with greater intensity in the person who is very conscientious and who has overidentified with his or her profession, business, occupation, or major life interest. The more the person has circumscribed his sources of ego gratification and organized his life around one activity, the more vulnerable he is. Defeat or loss in that area can be cataclysmic. Therefore one should cultivate a range of interests to which he can devote himself. He cannot be equally competent in all of them, but when things go badly in one area, he can always turn to another for gratification.

Accurate, honest, and frequent performance appraisal is important to enable the executive to maintain a perspective on himself. Everyone needs confirmation from others of his performance; statistics do not satisfy this need. While the person who is not performing well may suffer a temporary decline in his self-image, the appraisal opens up alternatives to failure. Information from outside the organization may provide some input; it is useful, for example, for an executive to learn from another company that his peers have similar problems.

The chief executive officer is usually exempt from realistic appraisals, though he may often be criticized. A committee of outsiders on the board of directors, who have the necessary knowledge and detachment, may serve the purpose. In my judgment, a major function of the board is to help the CEO cope with the stress that comes with the job. Of course, board members who view anxiety over problems as reflection of weakness are of no help to him.

When a problem seems insurmountable, it should be broken down into components so that they can be tackled one at a time. Frequently, the advice and consultation of others is helpful in this task. Spouses and good friends have served such a function, and sometimes colleagues in trade associations or other outsiders can help with business-related problems.

In reporting relationships, senior executives should try to relieve irrational pressures of guilt or responsibility that people express—but not by dismissing their expression with words like "Don't let it bother you" or "Forget it." One constructive way to avoid a buildup of pressures is through clarification of what is and is not the subordinate's responsibility. Job descriptions usually include the former but not the latter. It may be helpful if the superior recounted his own past problems and failures in order to help his subordinate accept the human quality of imperfection in himself and others.

Be alert to signs of depression. These include loss of appetite and substantial weight loss, sleeplessness or excessive fatigue, heavy drinking, excessive use of tranquilizers or energizers, inability to complete work because of mental paralysis or reverie, increasing irritability, slowness and dull quality in speech, physical symptoms that have no physical basis, repeated deep sighing, and talk of suicide.

An executive who suspects that a subordinate is depressed should not urge him or her to take a vacation or take time off to "rest." The subordinate would only have greater freedom to punish himself and heighten the depression. The person whose depression does not require hospitalization needs to have an atmosphere in which he can work on his problems, with the support of his superiors and preferably with the involvement of others. Above all, a seriously depressed person must be treated professionally. His superiors, peers, and subordinates may think that the problem is not serious, or that the person will "snap out of it." But such optimism is unfounded unless substantiated by a diagnostician.

Point of Vulnerability

When a person suffers a loss or defeat and becomes depressed, he usually does one of five things:

1. He acts positively to narrow the gap between his goals and his present position. This is the best course to follow, obviously, but also the most difficult, especially in cases of serious depression.

2. He becomes more irritable. He turns his anger against others—wife, children, subordinates, friends, and even against his business. (Child abuse has reportedly increased as a consequence of the recession.[4])

3. He seeks to escape his feeling of futility and find solace in religion, counsel, or good works. If these avenues fail to bring relief, he may flee to alcohol and drugs. Some people flee by "copping out" or withdrawing in some fashion, others by engaging in a frenzy of social activity or by plunging into work.

4. He tries to control or deny his feelings on the assumption that ultimately they will somehow go away or that he can overcome his problems.

5. He atones for his supposed failures or sins. He can punish himself by having accidents or by making "stupid mistakes" in which he sets himself back. If driven to extremes, he can kill himself.

A person's greatest asset, the wish to succeed, can become his point of greatest vulnerability if a significant loss or defeat triggers a torrent of self-criticism. As a matter of self-preservation, each of us must try to temper the irrationality of that torment while at the same time capitalizing on its motivational power—the push to reach high goals. Awareness of these factors will help us remain alert to the danger to ourselves and to others. Executives, whose self-images are always at risk, are especially vulnerable.

Notes

1. Thomas Crook and Allen Raskin, "Association of Childhood Parental Loss with Attempted Suicide and Depression," *Journal of Consulting and Clinical Psychology*, April 1975, p. 277.

2. Margaret Prouty, "Juvenile Ulcers," *American Family Psysician/GP*, September 1970, p. 66.

3. See Karl A. Menninger, *Man Against Himself* (New York: Knopf, 1938).

4. *Time*, March 17, 1975, p. 88.

Alcoholism and the Work World

HARRISON M. TRICE

In the United States, the relationship of alcoholism to the work world has received increasing attention over the past decade. Government and voluntary groups have been encouraging the cooperation of management and labor in the development of programs to fight this difficult health problem. The Federal government has begun serious work on a program to aid employees who suffer from alcoholism. Even labor unions, which understandably view such programs as anti-labor in character, are showing a willingness to deal openly with the problem. The advances, however, are slow.

The question is often asked: Why should management and labor be concerned about alcoholism? First, there can be a direct increase in operating costs as a result of the alcoholic's inefficiency and absenteeism. Second, alcoholics can generate personnel problems such as lowered worker morale or employer involvement in family problems. Third, the expedient solution of discharge can both deprive the employer of needed experience and aggravate the alcoholic's drinking problem. Fourth, alcoholism is a disease, and each member of society, even business, has an obligation to fight any disease when he can.

The work world has the potential to do something truly effective about alcoholism. Based on a summary of available data concerning alcoholism and the job, I will set forth several reasons for increasing the effort devoted toward stimulating management and labor to constructive action. I will also discuss the major problems encountered in any preventive program and the unique potential of the work world for recognizing the problem drinker, the first step toward prevention or cure.

Prevention programs must be aimed at the three general development stages of alcoholism. In the early development stage, symptoms are almost nonexistent. The prevention strategy is to eliminate the forces leading to alcoholism before it fully develops. The second stage can be called "disrupted but normal." Symptoms start becoming visible. Early recognition, however, can still prevent alcoholism from developing completely. The third stage is fully developed alcoholism. The only action now possible is to provide treatment that will stop or cure the physical and psychological damage caused by the disease.

Who Is the Alcoholic?

Many people have a preconceived image of the "average alcoholic" as a sloppy, staggering drunk with no visible means of support. This inaccurate image suggests the need for a working definition of alcoholism. Problem drinking and alcoholism are behavioral disorders centered around the employee's family and job which cause him to deviate from his expected role. From the standpoint of the work world, alcoholism can be defined as repeated disruption of job performance due to the consumption of alcohol which impairs the expected role.

Reprinted with permission from *Sloan Management Review*, Fall, 1970, no. 2, pp. 67-75.

The alcoholic is generally a man. Available statistics show the male to female ratio of alcoholics to be five to one over recent years; it should be noted, however, that the female alcoholic is more difficult to identify. The alcoholic is generally middle aged. Studies repeatedly show alcoholism to be concentrated in the mature years of the forties and early fifties, when work productivity is at a peak, when experience and judgment have matured, and when there is still energy for sustained contributions to the organization. Were alcoholism spread more evenly over the age groups, its impact on productivity would clearly be lessened.

The alcoholic is most likely to be recognized in lower-status occupations, although present research suggests that the distribution remains much the same throughout the entire industrial complex. Alcoholism appears among professional, managerial, and white collar employees in proportions roughly similar to those in blue collar and operative jobs. Thus, the risk of losing managerial and professional employees through alcoholism is equal to the risk of losing workers in the lower ranks.

Specific Job Behaviors

Both the quality and quantity of work decline sharply as alcoholism progresses. One study, conducted over a three-year period, compared the work performance of employees who had been diagnosed as alcoholic, psychoneurotic, or psychotic. The results showed the alcoholic employee to be the most impaired.[1] Another study indicated that the "manner" in which the work efficiency declined varies with the occupational type. Higher status employees, such as professionals and managers, tend to appear consistently on the job in spite of the ill effects of drinking.[2] They seem to rationalize their drinking by proving they can continue to work, although in fact their work suffers. A form of on-the-job absenteeism occurs as efficiency declines. Freedom from supervision allows them to continue unchallenged for a relatively long time. In contrast, lower status employees who are more closely supervised engage in much stay-away absenteeism, but do a substantial day's work when on the job. Poor work and absenteeism constitute two of the main impacts of the problem drinker on the organization.

The typical problem drinker continues to work at a full-time job during most of his developing alcoholism, with about 3 percent of a normal work force probably affected. Among higher status employees, the figure is closer to 5 percent. These percentages fluctuate with sex, age, ethnic makeup, and locality.

On-the-job accidents are not significantly characteristic of the alcoholic employee. Studies of both A.A. members and of accident records kept by specific companies deny the popular notion that the alcoholic on the job is accident prone. Four factors seem to account for this finding. First, the developing alcoholic becomes extra cautious, thereby reducing both his effectiveness and his risk of accident. Second, when accident risk runs high, the alcoholic resorts to absenteeism, leading to accidents off the job rather than at work. Third, alcoholics generally work out a routine for controlling the effects of alcohol. Finally, the cooperation of fellow workers, and occasionally supervisors, helps protect a drinker from accident exposure.

The off-the-job accident rate of alcoholics, on the other hand, is three to four times higher than that of non-alcoholics. This increases the cost of stay-away absenteeism as well as the direct cost of sick pay and other employee benefits. There is some evidence to suggest that persons with other behavioral disorders also show high off-the-job accidents rates, but not in such a chronic pattern. Therefore, the amount of sick pay due to absenteeism is probably higher for alcoholics than for employees with other emotional disturbances.[3]

Available evidence indicates that problem drinkers do not show an unusual turnover rate. Following the same pattern as non-alcoholics, they change jobs frequently in lower status occupations, and remain relatively longer in professional and managerial positions. The job-hopper stereotype of the alcoholic is generally untrue, especially in high status occupations.

The alcoholic actively works to conceal his problem, frequently with aid from work associates, subordinates, and occasionally the supervisor. About 20 percent experience little or no help in concealing their drinking. Here again, occupational status governs, with more help being offered to the higher ranks. Lower status workers often receive no aid from either supervisors or fellow workers. Camouflage efforts in any rank are only temporarily successful, but are more successful in the higher positions where freedom from visibility and supervision conceals the problem for much of the development process. In the final stage, the alcoholic can no longer remain hidden from his associates, subordinates, or supervisors.

The effect of the alcoholic on the morale of other employees gives cause for concern to both union and management. In the lower ranks, the alcoholic's fellow workers become disgusted and concerned when forced to pick up part of his work. Supervisors faced with unpredictable scheduling must allot extra time to the problem. The union shop steward must cope with grievances which are likely to embarrass the union. In managerial and responsible professional positions, the alcoholic can clearly lower the morale of all employees on his level and below. It is difficult to respect and follow a leader driven toward incompetence by alcoholism.

Recognizing Alcoholism on the Job: The Problems

Motivating people to recognize alcoholics and insuring accurate identification are the major problems. The motivation problem is the less obvious and the more interesting of the two. The immediate supervisor of the developing alcoholic is often deeply disturbed by the need to work in direct contact with him. As one supervisor reported painfully, "If I had two like *him* in this group of machinists, I'd apply for early retirement." Presently, there are only two studies of supervisor reaction to the problem drinker. Both rate alcoholics as greater supervisory problems than employees with other emotional difficulties.[4] However, even when the supervisor can identify an employee as being an alcoholic, he is hesitant to take action. This reflects the general cultural ambivalence about alcoholism in the United States. Several forces cause the supervisor to vacillate between taking action and treating the problem as part of his normal duties. Among the forces pushing him toward action are the unpredictable performance and the absenteeism of the alcoholic. In addition, the supervisor's work record suffers when the alcoholic does not produce his share or when worker morale deteriorates, reducing production efficiency.

Acting against these forces is the difficulty of recognizing the problem drinker. The early symptoms are characteristic of several other problems and are thus difficult to classify. The supervisor is not a professional psychiatrist or social worker. Without some training, attempts at early classification would be of questionable value due to the risk of premature labeling and the concurrent danger of establishing a self-fulfilling prophecy

There is also the supervisor's fear that passing his problems to someone else will reflect poorly on his own ability as a supervisor. In addition, such an action can create a form of credibility gap between himself and the employee. Should his action result in the firing of that employee, the supervisor is faced with the more difficult problem of replacing an experienced worker. His reluctance to take action is intensified when he knows the alcoholic's family or has worked closely with the alcoholic for several years. Finally, the supervisor runs some risk of not being supported "upstairs" or of creating a union problem greater than a mere grievance.

In dealing with white collar employees another factor becomes apparent. Warkov and Bacon have shown that supervisors of white collar workers seem unwilling to make the same connection between poor worker performance and alcoholism which they make with lower status employees. Supervisors are less prone to recognize problem drinking among members of their own class. However, the study concludes that once the white collar deviant drinker is recognized, the supervisor is less tolerant of him than those of lower status.[5]

A unique problem exists within a union shop situation. Union officials are reluctant to participate with management in joint prevention programs, regardless of the potential benefits for the alcoholic and for improved union-management relations through cooperation on such programs. Cooperation could lead to charges of collusion from the membership or build conflicts within the union. Moreover, the union has a legal obligation to represent its members in challenging any policy by management, which could include programs aimed at alcoholism.

Recognizing Alcoholism on the Job: The Potential

To demonstrate the superiority of the work place as a setting for preventive and therapeutic action against alcoholism, it is necessary to consider the obstacles which any such program must hurdle. First, the lack of a satisfactory definition of alcoholism tends to make the disease seem unreal. In the work world, however, a definition such as the one presented earlier is more obvious. Second, established social values recognize alcohol as an integral part of everyday life, a symbol of sophistication, a social facilitator.[6] The work world can help keep the use of alcohol in proper perspective by confronting the potential alcoholic with the effects his drinking has on job performance. Third, prevention programs inevitably invade the personal life of the individual. Observing and helping the individual in the work environment could eliminate the need for a social worker, for example, to visit the individual's home. Fourth, premature labeling of an alcoholic may tend to drive him further into the disease. Training supervisors to recognize symptoms and to provide some counseling would allow close observation without labeling the individual or sending him to a clinic. Fifth, rehabilitation processes regarding alcoholism are not yet sufficiently understood. Treatment in the third stage of development is not always effective. Recognition of the problem in the second stage or early in the third stage can eliminate the need for intensive treatment. Sixth, preventive schemes are difficult to integrate into the pivotal institutions of society such as business, the professions, the church, and the family. Yet, preventive efforts cannot remain outside these institutions and be effective. Since the job is one of the pivotal institutions in the employee's life, efforts in this environment are a necessary part of any preventive scheme.

The work world has a greater potential than the family, or even the clergyman or doctor, for overcoming these obstacles. Supervisors, unlike wives and relatives, are not emotionally involved with the problem drinker. Supervisors work under pressure to produce and are therefore more objective about the alcoholic's behavior. They have the highest readiness to act of any of the people close to the alcoholic and have the potential for action. It is they who must cope with the problems of poor job performance, absenteeism, and perhaps eventual replacement.

Potentials for genuine social controls exist in the job situation. The job becomes the key factor in the life of most workers and in this the alcoholic is no exception. For him the job is often his last bastion, and so long as it is intact he sees nothing wrong with his drinking. Consequently, a confrontation for poor job performance may well create the crisis that will open the door for therapy and prevent further development of the disorder. Only the work world has this potential for constructive confrontation.

Management Action

What specific actions can management take to fight alcoholism? The answer lies in supervisor training and realistic company policies. Training of supervisory personnel within a supportive company policy can provide a means of speeding up the recognition process. Four criteria for an effective training program have been suggested.[7] First, training must be relevant to the work world of the supervisor. Specific symptoms should be examined in the order of their appearance. These symptoms include hand tremors, intense nervousness, mood changes, avoidance of associates, and absenteeism. Learning to recognize the symptoms will increase the supervisor's ability to identify an incipient alcoholic. Second, the training should point out the work problems created by the alcoholic. Recognition of such problems as poor morale, lowered efficiency, and increased need of supervision will decrease the tolerance level of the supervisor and result in earlier referral and treatment of the disease. Third, to increase their receptiveness, supervisors should be introduced to the subject prior to formal training. Last, a variety of training techniques, such as films, lectures, case work, and reading, should be employed. This will ensure that at least one method meets with success.

Employers should establish an explicit company policy incorporating the following points: alcoholism is a health problem; the company health plan will include those addicted to the use of alcohol without discrimination; alcoholism is recognized as a unique health disorder which must be confronted with a crisis to effect either prevention or treatment. The policy should call for such confrontation whenever poor performance occurs. If the condition continues, the drinker should be offered unhesitating support in seeking rehabilitation on condition of cooperation. Finally, if the preliminary steps fail, stringent disciplinary methods should be used such as curtailment of fringe benefits, layoffs, and finally discharge. Unless the threat of final separation remains real, the alcoholic will discount the danger and any therapy will fail. Such action removes his last defense, that of an intact job, and acts to offset the emotional rewards of drinking. The confrontation thus reduces the value of alcohol to the alcoholic. Policies based on this approach produce high rehabilitation rates.

Union Action

What specific action can the union take? Early recognition of the problem opens many ways in which the alcoholic can be helped by the union before company discipline becomes necessary. The union can communicate to the worker information about company programs or policies. Coming from a union source, such information is more likely to be believed than if it comes from management. If the drinker has gone beyond the first stages and nears confrontation with the company for his unsatisfactory work, the union can help convince the alcoholic that the company is serious and can suggest that he attend the clinic regularly. The steward can provide aid and counsel to both the alcoholic and his family, helping them through the crisis and back into the work world. He can also persuade fellow workers to welcome the alcoholic back into the old groups.

If the problems of union-management cooperation can be overcome, a joint program against alcoholism can be established. Stewards could be trained along with supervisory personnel to recognize the problems and behaviors of alcoholic workers. Joint observations will help to avoid premature labeling of employees as problem drinkers. The steward should be closely tied to the overall program by making him the link between the alcoholic and his family and job. He should also maintain clear lines of communication with management and higher union officials to simplify joint action. With the union handling most of the personal contact with the member, a joint program should prove possible.

If union-management cooperation is difficult to establish, the union can run its own program on alcoholism. It could: enlist the aid of various community facilities such as A.A., AFL-CIO community service organizations, or information seminars; set up an effective training program for stewards and other union officials; and work toward obtaining management cooperation. Nevertheless, a unilateral program staged by either management or labor will be less effective than a jointly sponsored program.

Conclusion

The greatest possibilities for preventing alcoholism lie in the crisis confrontation strategy growing from natural forces surrounding the job. Unfortunately, this avenue is not yet sufficiently traveled and is often neglected for less promising ways. Management and unions are two pivotal institutions in American life which can be more potent in an enlightened community effort against alcoholism than welfare agencies, medical facilities, or jails. Most alcoholics do belong to the work world and when lost through alcoholism deprive the organization and society of an investment in training, experience, and special knowledge. By recognizing the alcoholic's existence in their own world and treating him there, unions and management can insure a high recovery rate. When business acts on the assumption that alcoholism is a treatable disease and follows through with carefully considered programs, the potential success of constructive programs outside, as well as within, the work world is increased. The strategy is to attack the problem where and when there is a reasonable chance of success, that is, on the job.

Notes

1. See Trice (5).
2. See Trice (4).
3. See Maxwell (3).
4. See Trice (5) and Warkov and Bacon (6).
5. See Warkov and Bacon (6).
6. See Lemert (2), pp. 18-21.
7. See Belasco and Trice (1).

References

1. Belasco, J., and Trice, H. M. *The Assessment of Change in Training and Therapy.* New York, McGraw-Hill, 1969.
2. Lemert, E. *Human Deviance, Social Problems and Social Control.* Englewood Cliffs, N.J., Prentice-Hall, 1967.
3. Maxwell, M. "A Study of Absenteeism, Accidents, and Sickness Payments in Problem Drinkers in One Industry," *Quarterly Journal of Studies on Alcohol,* Vol. 20 (1959), pp. 302-308.
4. Trice, H. M. "The Job Behavior of Problem Drinkers." In: D. Pittman and C. Snyder (eds.), *Society, Culture and Drinking Patterns.* New York, Wiley, 1962.
5. Trice, H. M. "Reaction of Supervisors to Emotionally Disturbed Employees," *Journal of Occupational Medicine,* Vol. 7 (1965), pp. 177-189.
6. Warkov, S., and Bacon, S. "Social Correlates of Industrial Problem Drinking," *Quarterly Journal of Studies on Alcohol,* Vol. 26 (1965), pp. 58-71.

CHAPTER **12**

A Look into the Future

The future is capricious and it delights in defying would-be prophets, but predictions and projections must be made if there is to be intelligent planning. Our final articles attempt to extrapolate present trends into the future to provide a glimpse of some of the major changes that may take place. The authors' conclusion is that an increased emphasis on education, social service occupations, and highly sophisticated attempts to integrate the poor and the disadvantaged into U.S. work-life will be the three major developments to come. What we are seeing, of course, is that federal, state, and local governments are putting pressure on organizational leaders to increase the quality of work-life of employees while continuing to increase productivity. That, it seems, is the direction in which we are moving and will continue to move.

Can We Legislate the Humanization of Work?

WILLIAM A. STEIGER

No politician worth his salt gives a speech that doesn't contain a caveat in it somewhere. To be fair, I'm going to begin with mine.

It must be noted that concerns with the quality of work are somewhat cyclical. In times of high employment, we turn to considering the value and meaning of our jobs. In times of employment crisis we turn most of our attention simply to *jobs*, to finding employment.

In the field of employment it is the creation of jobs, the effort to maintain high employment, which has always been our major governmental concern. It will continue to be so. It is fair to say that if we in government don't bend our greatest efforts to improving the economy, and thus the job market, we not only can't humanize work, we can't even assist our citizens to maintain a humanized existence.

Reprinted by permission of Congressman Steiger.

I put this sense of priority to you so strongly, not because I do not feel there is a role for government in the humanization of work, but because it must be understood that given a financial choice, government must and will first spend to assist employment. Priorities are a pain maybe, but they are real.

To begin with, I find I must redefine the topic given to me. The question is clearly not, "Can we legislate the humanization of work?" In the broad sense of humanization, the government has been active for years. The question rather is to what extent and in what directions can and should government become involved in this issue?

For the most part, government has historically affected the work place by the passage of broad, philosophical measures, and has left the details of work modes, methods, and various technicalities to labor and business. For this reason I will leave the questions of improvement of assembly lines, etc., to the experts—since for the most part this has not been government's historic role, nor do I believe it should be.

Past examples of government efforts are well known but worth noting. Child labor laws in the early twentieth century clearly affected the work place, the workers, and the community in a positive and long-range fashion. The Fair Labor Standards Act in the '30s established our current pattern of an 8-hour work day, 40-hour week, cutting down abuses of health and safety.

The Walsh-Healy Act in 1936 imposed restrictions on government contractors in terms of hours, wages, and working conditions.

These are examples of direct impact legislation in the field of work condition improvement. In a real sense, they are only the tip of the iceberg. Other legislative measures have had indirect byproducts of tremendous importance to the work force.

Standards for interstate trade, such as the many laws involving food processing and handling, the tough federal meat law of the '60s is one example, clearly were aimed at consumer protection. But surely the inevitable improvement in plant conditions brought the side benefit of improved humanized working conditions.

In the same way various state and local laws for health checks of employees, again designed to protect the consumer, have had the secondary benefit of safeguarding the health of the worker.

Workmen's Compensation, clearly a work humanizer in its efforts to protect the job-injured employee, has had enormous impact in the identification and improvement of conditions leading to such injury or illness. Once such problems must be reported, a part of the battle is over.

These are only a few examples of what we can call the spin-off effect of legislative programs on the work force. One more recent piece of legislation will have a great effect in years to come.

Women's Rights, opening up countless job categories for women, is bound to result in changes in the work place, work conditions, and hours. Whether its effect will be to reverse completely past protective efforts remains to be seen. But change the work place it will!

It must be noted that in two specific areas in the past ten years, government has gone directly and in detail into the work place.

The Williams-Steiger Occupation Health and Safety Act of 1970 is the single most important step by government to deal with the work environment beyond wages and hours. It is a qualitative, not quantitative, bill in that it concerns upgrading work conditions by promulgation of standards for machinery, noise levels, toxic materials and general job safety and health.

It is aimed at insuring every worker a safer and, therefore, in my opinion, more humane place of work.

OSHA covers 57 million workers, 4.1 million places of business and coupled with the Coal Mine Safety Bill of '69, the Metal and Nonmetallic Mine Act passed earlier, and the Longshoreman's Act, covers almost every worker in the United States.

The need was indisputable. According to the Survey of Working Conditions (August 1971, U.S. Dept. of Labor), "the labor's standards problems against which most workers wanted protection were first, work-related illness or injury." .... and for good reason.

Such injuries and illness cost the U.S. economy in 1970 9.1 billion dollars in lost wages, hospital insurance costs, workmen's compensation, and the like. Most important, 14,200 lives were lost.

While OSHA has only been in existence one year, it is, I believe, already having an impact on the work place. While its major impact at the moment is in the area of job safety, the long-range significance of OSHA will be, in my judgment, in the health field. This problem is more complex than safety because it does not deal with immediate and visible problems—a lost life, or limb—but with the insidious diminution of a life—the slow creeping, often unknown and unnoticed degeneration of the health of a worker who handles various materials over a span of time. Hopefully, the establishment of standards and revision of these standards based on new and constantly gathered data for the use of such materials will protect the current work force far better than we have ever done before.

For the first time, through the Department of Labor, we hope to have: first, accurate data on work place accidents and deaths, and second, an ability to measure previously little noticed dangers.

(Coal Mine Safety Director says, "No black lung—humanization at the most basic level!")

The second area of direct impact legislation is the field of manpower. Here government again went into the work place, not to affect work conditions, but to affect training, retraining, and job availability.

Manpower training legislation was born in response to the worker's fear of automation. The federal government became an active partner in answering the need for retraining the man replaced by machine. A further step followed later as the fear of automation receded. The federal government began an effort to train or retrain the so-called underemployed or unemployed, to assist the man or woman at the lowest rungs of the employment ladder to move upward to more rewarding and meaningful work. The intent was clearly the humanizing of labor for those in the least rewarding, most monotonous jobs.

Since the passage of the Manpower Development and Training Act in 1962 (MDTA), the concept has broadened significantly to include programs for the disadvantaged, public service employment, and the new careers program. New careers is perhaps the program most directed toward work humanization since it seeks to break down artificial barriers to upward mobility in a variety of public sector employment areas such as health, recreation, police and fire protection, parks, sanitation; the intent is to provide more meaningful work.

So far our efforts in the field of upward mobility have been limited for the most part to the public sector. The federal government has not, as yet, done a good job in attempting to expand this concept of upward mobility to the private sector. A few surveys and some demonstration projects are about the extent of our efforts to date.

Today we spend 3.6 billion dollars on various manpower programs. This is likely to be expanded. The future, in my judgment, will bring an even greater emphasis on the upgrading of those currently employed and will contribute to an acceleration of the growth of public employment.

Where does the federal government's future role lie in the humanization of work?

Every study of work problems has a common thread. There is the constant refrain of the meaningless quality of much employment and the workers' dissatisfaction with it. Improvement is imperative.

As President Nixon noted in his Labor Day [1971] speech, . . . "the work ethic in America is undergoing some changes.

"It means that business, labor, and government should explore the new needs of today's wage earners: We must give the individual worker more responsibility—more of the feeling that his opinion counts.

"We must find ways to better recognize and reward the extra effort a worker puts into his job.

"We must open up new and equal opportunities to allow a person to grow in his job.

"In our quest for a better environment, we must always remember that the most important part of the quality of life is the quality of work. And the new need for job satisfaction is the key to the quality of work."

Let me suggest a few potential areas for the government to assist in this quest for job satisfaction.

Direct impact efforts are easiest to define and some are already in the works. Continuing education and career education together offer one of the best hopes for increasing work opportunities and a satisfied work force.

Career education in the form of vocational technical education has expanded and will continue to do so.

Youngsters must have more options than they do today. In part it is a question of emphases. We must have elementary and secondary counseling in career choices. No child in the United States should ever feel that a college education is the only way to meaningful work and status. Over 40 percent of high school graduates enter colleges and less than half of those ever earn a 4-year degree. Yet in 1970 the federal government spent approximately 14 dollars for college and university education for every dollar spent for vocational technical education. Something is seriously out of balance about this, and every parent in this country should be up in arms.

And so should you. Because until all of us take note of occupational education needs, and support them, we will never impart to employment in technical fields the very status necessary to give it meaning and dignity.

Vocational Education Amendments of 1968 and the unpassed Career Education Act of 1970 are both aimed at giving new life to this educational stepchild. Specifically, the effort is to: *one*, provide guidance counselors in career education starting in 4th, 5th, and 6th grades; *second*, to expand career education in the high school in an effort to change, if not abolish, what has normally been called general education; *third*, to recognize that one does not teach in secondary school a specific skill since evidence indicates a man changes his job many times in a work lifetime. What is needed is a *foundation* for learning specific skills and undertaking future retraining.

If we don't succeed in this effort, I have little hope for work humanization.

A second direct impact effort is in the field of government-funded research. We could and probably should do more.

Neal Herrick has proposed joint government-foundation research into "the identification of bad jobs and the application of technology to eliminate or improve them." Such an effort could supplement the work already started in the private sector in this field and the results of the research should be disseminated.

This suggests a related direct effect approach in the form of tax incentives. We could assist those using newly discovered methods to improve work by granting tax benefits.

Granted, there is a real hesitancy about using this incentive approach insofar as the worker is concerned. We seem to have little problem in giving tax breaks for capital investment and machine depreciation, but meet great resistance at suggestions of tax incentives for employee training and job upgrading. It is, however, an option which should be explored.

Indirect efforts can also have significant impact, as legislative history shows. It is my assumption that almost any effort which increases a worker's positive options humanizes his work. On this assumption, let me suggest some federal legislation which could so increase options.

First and perhaps most significant is any of a variety of federally funded day-care center plans—one of which is sure to pass in the near future. Clearly this vastly increases options for two-job families, and will have tremendous impact on the labor force. Whether we have sufficiently considered the social implications of such centers is another question. However, the potential for job choice clearly increases if two parents can work. One wage earner might, for example, elect to work at less wages temporarily in order to pursue further education and thus attain better employment. Mobility becomes easier.

Tax write-offs for child care for working parents, recently passed, will also clearly increase the chances for mothers to work.

We can also push for upgraded employment services. Jerome Rosow, former Assistant Secretary of Labor, suggests such a simple measure as keeping employment service offices open evenings and Saturdays would greatly improve the opportunities for job hunting for those workers seeking other employment options.

We can remove various legislative and administrative barriers which now exist to experimentation in work hours and schedules.

For example, the Walsh-Healy Act and Contract Work Hours Standards Act of 1962, both of which regulate firms with government contracts over $10,000, prevent such firms from going to a 4-day, 40-hour work week because they require overtime pay for hours worked in excess of 8 hours in one day.

I've introduced legislation which would amend these acts so as not to inhibit those who wish to try a new workweek concept.

It may or may not be viable, but it is an option, and a potentially life-enriching one for the work force.

Finally, maybe business, labor and government should join in a continuing education effort. It is not just the quality of work itself which grows meaningless in our society. We also face grave problems with the satisfying and meaningful use of leisure time which is bound to grow.

Our local schools are under-used and in financial difficulties. They close for summer months and stand empty in the evening. Why not identify first, the schools' capacities to offer a variety of adult educational programs, and second, survey the communities' labor force to determine their interest not just singly, but as family units in such offerings; thirdly, with the help of federal and private business funds on a percentage basis, offer courses to the community's work force.

It would seem to me that the business which enriches the general life of its worker's family in such a way would take a giant step toward humanizing his work life as well.

I suggest the last possibility because I wonder in part if we are not missing the forest for the trees. Indeed much can be done to humanize work. Our society is surely capable of countless technical achievements to eradicate the most objectionable features of almost any work.

But it seems to me that even if we succeed in that area, we have not answered the need that lies behind job dissatisfaction. As our society has advanced, it has become nearly impossible for the individual to see his single small efforts as significant and meaningful to our society. It is not simply work which needs humanizing, but our very lives.

I believe in education, and in its power to enrich man's existence. No man has too much of it, and the society which offers such enrichment must offer, too, hope of an increase in the meaning of each individual life.

Work and Nonwork: Merging Human and Societal Needs

MARVIN D. DUNNETTE
LEAETTA HOUGH
HENRY ROSETT
EMILY MUMFORD
SIDNEY A. FINE

Merging Work and Nonwork

Is it too much to expect that in the future man's capacity for work will be fully integrated with his capacity for pleasure? [Here we will trace] the meager beginnings, the feeble first steps man has taken toward that goal and offer some thoughts on further actions to speed the process.

Perhaps in the year 2001 we will no longer suffer from alienation and apathy; quality of life rather than a sense of needing to belong will provide unity of purpose, and we will have learned to build constructively on our differences rather than waste our efforts in group conflict. Human values and organizational goals in the world of tomorrow will stress autonomy, diversity, and acceptance. Achievement, though still important, no longer will be Western man's central aim. Production of goods and services will be planned toward the broad goal of providing pleasure and improving the quality of each person's life. The worlds of work and nonwork will have merged. Man's capacity for joy and his search for self-actualization will find easy and open expression.

A big order? Yes. Even so, its realization seems within reach, though far from easy to attain. So far, society's maladaptive use of its human and natural resources has been counter to the hope of providing a better life for all. Future efforts to improve the physical and environmental well-being of people, however, will yield millions of new job opportunities—new careers to use fully the human resources available in society.

From *Work and Nonwork in the Year 2001*, by M. D. Dunnette. Copyright © 1973 by Wadsworth Publishing Co., Inc. Reprinted by permission of the publisher, Brooks/Cole Publishing Co., Monterey, Calif.

A Resource Conservation Industry

Technology

In the broadest sense, the age of technology has generated new needs, needs so great and so important that already a new industry—the resource conservation industry—is developing to meet them. Consider, for example, the needs created by just one segment of technology, the invention and mass production of the automobile. Vast numbers of cars and drivers have led to new jobs in driver education, automobile inspection, traffic control, building and maintenance of roads, air pollution control, noise pollution control, recycling junked automobiles, and so on. Other areas affected by the technological revolution are education, urban and rural development, recreation, community services, health care, and pollution control. Needs for improving the quality of our environment and the quality of life create countless new job opportunities.

Education

Only 50 percent of American high schools today provide professional counseling and vocational guidance to students. Increasing the number of counselors—through para-professional training, which will provide new careers—can result in bringing resource conservation job opportunities to the attention of more high school students, encouraging them to enter this field. Better utilization of human resources requires such earlier and greater emphasis on how those resources may be best utilized and directed in the world of tomorrow.

Urban and rural development

Urban-development legislation has a long history; yet, it is estimated that over eight million substandard housing units still exist in the United States. These must be replaced or rehabilitated at prices people can afford. Such work will help to provide jobs and incomes for the unemployed and may also serve as excellent training for such skilled trades as carpentry, plastering, painting, papering, masonry, and glazing.

Rural America also faces the severe problems of low income, few jobs, and substandard education. Extension agents who understand both administrative problems and agricultural development and marketing must train local people. Experts in technical and leadership training could begin to develop the resources of particular rural areas, and trained aides could make significant strides toward improving rural educational systems.

Recreation

Recreational services provide stimulating activities in all phases of human living —educational, social, cultural, and physical—and many new jobs in recreation are created each year. Total employment in the management of public and private recreation areas is expected to reach 1.4 million by 1980. For young people in rural areas, the creation of recreational services provides job opportunities in their own communities.

Within both urban and rural communities, there is already a demand for recreation workers who can perform in many capacities. More personnel are needed to organize and supervise individual and group activities and to direct physical, social, and cultural programs for all ages at hospitals, community centers, and playgrounds. Para-professionals can easily supervise special activities such as tennis, basketball, and even arts and crafts. Many recreational workers today are para-professionals who assist social workers in correctional and welfare institutions as well as in schools and hospitals. Opportunities exist also in industrial settings where recreational activities are provided for company employees. There are shortages of trained recreation workers in hospitals, local government projects, and youth organizations throughout the country. Employment opportunities in these fields grow each year.

Community services

Modern cities demand broader and more comprehensive community services, including law enforcement, day care centers, employment services, and family guidance and counseling services. For example, in the United States today, nearly 400,000 children under 12 are unsupervised during their working mothers' absence from their homes. As more women move into the labor force in the years ahead, these numbers will increase. The establishment of day-care centers will create new jobs as well as answer the direct need for child supervision. The personnel working in these centers may also be able to teach children about such things as home management, nutrition, textiles, clothing, furnishings, buying goods and services, use of leisure time, and economic responsibility.

Health

Cities and rural areas are in serious need of trained medical personnel. Many people do not go to clinics or hospitals for care because of family responsibilities, the lack of accessible facilities, or simply fear of institutional complexities. Para-professional medical workers are needed to teach out-patients to recognize symptoms of common disorders, do follow-up studies on patients, provide transportation to and from clinics, care for children and older people, allay patients' anxieties, and to listen to complaints. And these medical workers need to be in accessible locations. Hospitals, also, need more personnel to orient and interview incoming patients and, in general, to give patients more attention.

Pollution control and conservation

Nearly every major river system is polluted. Air in urban areas is contaminated. Man's natural environment needs immediate attention to remain habitable.

Yet pollution is as complex as it is widespread. Smog and soot make our cities dirty but also irritate our eyes, injure our lungs, and affect paint, metals, and even the stone of our buildings. Insecticides and fungicides can contaminate both crops and soils and, eventually, the waterways. The environmental crisis demands intensive efforts to combat and control pollution; thousands of workers are needed to help reverse the ecocidal process. For example, sanitation and health workers, testers, inspectors, environmental educators, research personnel, demonstration agents, and people who function as agents for change are desperately needed.

New Careers for the Poor

Clearly, society's needs dictate an increase in job and career opportunities in education, health care, environmental renewal, personnel services, and recreational activities. These new careers can provide greater personal fulfillment for the nearly 21 million poor people in the United States while also leading to improvement in the overall quality of life for everyone. In a word, wisdom in using the forces and innovations of technology to create a resource conservation industry should reduce the waste and destructive exploitation of human and natural resources.

Job training programs have been tried in the past, but unfortunately they have not been uniformly successful.

Man-job Adaptation: Organizational Accommodation

To make good use of his functional skills in meeting the specific demands of any job, adaptation and accommodation must take place between an individual and the work organization. An individual's functional skills will ordinarily be most efficiently applied and utilized when his adaptive skills are closely attuned to specific organizational conditions and requirements; they will be least effective when his adaptive skills are incompatible with specific organizational demands. Hence effective worker performance and good job training and career development demand an alert organizational system sensitive to the adaptive as well as functional and specific content skills of employees and, most important, a readiness to accommodate its own nature and functioning to the adaptive capabilities and/or potentials of its employees.

Sociologists, child development specialists, and educators have studied the influence of family, social class, and early childhood experiences in school on the acquisition of adaptive skills. Findings from research in all of these areas indicate that differential socialization yields differential adaptive skills, or that differential adaptive skills are a result of the social class, and early childhood and family experiences of individuals.

Successful adaptation seems to require not only conformity to, or the acceptance of, societal norms but also positive and flexible interaction with the environment. Moreover, successful adaptation implies responsiveness not only to society's expectations and rules but also to its novel demands. A person may fit into a particular environment—that is, conform—but when he moves to a different environment, his previously adaptive behaviors may be maladaptive. Consequently, successful adaptation demands behavioral change even though the new behavior is contrary to previous values and attitudes.

Difficulties encountered by most new careers programs flow directly from their unfortunate attachment to bureaucracies. Complex bureaucracies have usually been rigid rather than accommodative, and they have demanded of target participants behaviors that ignore the participants' generally very limited adaptive skills. Program courses have been designed to teach mainly functional skills and impart information about things, data, people, and information processing. Even the on-the-job training and apprenticeships have dealt mainly with specific content. Stresses induced by adaptive breakdowns are regarded frequently as sources of personal and value conflict, not as stimuli for creating adaptive skill training procedures. Program directors are not entirely at fault; their negligence is due in part to the absence of available adaptive skills training methods.

Considerations for Teaching Adaptive Skills

Adaptive skills training is likely to be complex and costly; it cannot be implemented successfully in a series of one- or two-week orientation programs. If adaptive skills are to be learned by adults whose present skills are maladaptive to technological situations, the problem will require nothing less than a total approach. In a sense, society must be willing to make the effort similar to that used in some institutions with persons with mental and emotional problems who are dealt with intensively in a program combining hospitalization and treatment in a normal environment setting.

First, new methods must be developed to assess systematically the level of a person's adaptive skills and, in particular, the relevance of those skills to different job or career assignments. Second, current training and development programs, such as the Job Corps and residential halfway houses, should be evaluated to ascertain what conditions are more or less suitable for different types of persons. Learning conditions simulating early childhood, family, and peer group situations may prove most effective for altering adaptive skill levels to fit specific social and technological conditions. Third, it will be necessary to learn the best way for reinforcing positive adaptive skills in young adults. Can adaptive skills be taught apart from functional and specific content work skills? What is the proper mix and/or emphasis in a work situation? If adaptive skills training is to lead to competence in specific content skills, specific skill training probably should be integrated from the beginning with the more basic skills training.

The emphasis in vocational training should be shifted from teaching a specific skill to teaching functional abilities useful in a variety of settings. Learners should be exposed to a variety of contexts in which they can try out their newly acquired skills and knowledges. This can be done by providing relevant shop or laboratory work situations supplemented by field trips and demonstrations. Company training should, of course, not be the only agency for imparting adaptive skills; schools should continue as important training sites. Curricula should focus not only on subject matter and work-relevant knowledge and skills but also on such adaptive dimensions as attitudes, values, and work habits. Teaching methods should include field trips to places of work, films depicting work and nonwork activities, visits, talks, demonstrations, and role playing. Such activities would allow the students to explore different styles of successful work adaptation. Both teachers and vocational counselors need to be aware of and reinforce a variety of adaptive behavior and attitudes that will be needed in work situations.

Costs of adaptive skills training programs will often exceed the costs of broad content-oriented educational programs. Nonetheless, it is crucial to undertake such training if we are to follow the technological imperative for improving the quality of life through broadening the scope of job and career possibilities. On the other hand, the costs of neglecting such teaching programs would certainly be very high if measured in terms of continued financial dependency, delinquency, criminality, and similar social upheaval for increasing segments of our society.

Prognosis and Hope

Highly efficient and accurate communication between individuals and organizations will be the critical glue in the merged worlds of work and nonwork in the year 2001. Through better communication, adaptation and accommodation will be assured and sustained, and the role conflict and role ambiguity so prevalent in current job training and career programming will have long since disappeared. Ambiguity and conflict in work settings have inevitably led to emotional tension, anxiety, fear, anger, hostility, and finally apathy. But the emergence of new careers is now fully conceded to be a complex social process involving massive change in social arrangements and redefinitions of existing occupations. Creating each new job category means an emergence of a new group, shifts in relationships between colleagues, patterns of economic rewards, and redistribution of autonomy, power, and prestige. It is our hope that the adaptive skills of our present industrial and educational institutions are sufficient to allow them to move flexibly and creatively toward the adaptive skill training programs such as we have discussed above. Only then can the development of a great new industry—a resource conservation industry devoted to giving men and women full opportunities for pleasurable self expression in the world of tomorrow—be certain. . . .

New Approaches for New Careers—Strategic and Technical Considerations

How have poor planning, faulty coordination, and role definition problems affected most new career program efforts? An examination of the basic conditions of difficulty is essential if society is to move beyond the present shambles by the year 2001. Broadly speaking, there are two points of view—strategic and technical.

From a strategic point of view, it must first be ascertained how new careers can fit into existing personnel structures. Such structures are arenas of individual aggrandizement for status, power, or careerism. These structures do, therefore, reflect the basic needs of people for recognition, response, and self-realization, as well as their ability, or inability, to exercise good will and good intentions.

Most present career employees have, over the course of time, worked out personal strategies for getting ahead. They are obviously not willing to step aside for incoming new careerists who operate under different sets of rules. If new rules are indeed more advantageous, they should be administered for the existing work force either before or at least at the same time as their introduction for new careerists. For example, if performance standards are going to be changed for new careerists, they should also be changed for present career employees. If new careerists are to receive transportation assistance, special training courses, or other support services, these same benefits should accrue to present employees, too. Although the need for such equal treatment may seem obvious, it has been, surprisingly, widely ignored.

On the technical level, the implementation of new policies must be examined. In general, persons in charge of public service agencies, especially those agencies concerned with human services, are ignorant of specific role requirements. They know little of how an employee's actions may or may not contribute to specific goals, or how to achieve certain standards of performance; they know little of the technology of the work or how the work should be supervised. Managers at all levels, from the lowest to the highest, must thus learn to define their job goals. Though under constant review, the goals at any time must be firm and explicit. They must, of course, reflect the values and beliefs of the organization but state them explicitly in terms of time, cost, manpower, location, and user (consumer or client). This explicitness is essential for assessing work performance, especially in human service organizations, where bureaucracies tend to shift their focus to record keeping and maintenance activities and away from their essential service roles. Employees can easily outguess the bureaucratic mechanism to learn exactly how to beat the system—to catch on to where the payoff is and then respond accordingly.

Second, task behaviors must accomplish the objectives of the organization. Each employee must know exactly how his contribution relates to overall objectives. In addition, specific job behavior must be explicitly defined; words such as "assists," "prepares," "develops," and "directs" are too general to have effective operational meaning. Job descriptions must outline in specific detail the sources of information, nature of instruction, tools, equipment, methods, and guidelines so that for any job one can draw reliable inferences about the degree of complexity of the task, its relation to things, data, and people, the relevant performance standards, and the general education and specific training required to perform according to standard. Not until these conditions, attainable through existing knowledge, are implemented can an effective personnel management base be laid for the year 2001.

What will happen if these conditions for improving job analyses and job descriptions are met? Four valuable outcomes are likely: accountability, self-selection, team identification, and payment according to achievement and usefulness to the team. All four outcomes have favorable implications for both productivity and personal growth.

Accountability means that every task performance will be capable of evaluation, both intrinsically, according to an employee's behavior, and organizationally, according to the relative contribution toward achieving objectives. Both descriptive standards for the whole performance and numerical standards for specific service or behavioral output will be useful. Given the setting, organization, and resource limitations, it will be possible to trace failure in achieving objectives back to the constituent tasks themselves; thus it can be determined whether failure is due to the objectives set, the methods available, the state of the art, the skills and training applied, or to some combination of these.

Self-selection may be the most important and powerful force in bringing worker and work together. It is certainly the most widely ignored and distrusted, but need it be? Is it possible that self-selection hasn't worked only because of inadequate and imprecise job information, as described above? For example, it has been my experience in the recruitment and promotion situations where task information, delineated in terms of the dimensions described above, was presented to potential candidates, that most of them eliminated themselves for one reason or another. When adaptive skill requirements were also provided, further self-selection took place. Why not learn to control the process of self-selection, a process that passes the option to the workers and makes self-selection part of their own growth? It should be emphasized that every aspect of self-selection as described here is job related.

Team identification is an alternative to job identification. Instead of filling job slots, people would participate in fulfilling overall organizational objectives. Objectives would be the responsibility of teams of workers. A team leader would fulfill several managerial functions such as serving as a channel of communications between team members and higher levels of management for routine organizational information, providing training support for new team members, and acting as a major source of technological and methodological information relevant to objectives and an arbiter in coordinating assignments to team members.

Workers would enter the team largely through self-selection and team acceptance and be taught the more elementary tasks by team members. Workers could progress at their own speed and in accordance with the availability of other team members to train and give support for more and more difficult tasks. They could choose to specialize in some tasks, share obligations for others, or learn all the tasks necessary to achieve the objective. Teams would rotate tasks, including technical and janitorial maintenance. With the learning of each task, the worker would grow in flexibility and in functional capability. Training support would take place both on and off the job. Two observations are in order: (a) much work is now done this way, but not properly acknowledged and rewarded as such, and (b) teamwork is not appropriate for really creative (not innovative) work, nor are really creative individuals usually good team members.

Although lip service is often given to the idea that pay scales are based on merit, they rarely are. For the most part, people are paid on the bases of formally negotiated or informal arrangements (collective bargaining, salary surveys, labor market agreements), seniority, status, and monopolistic practices. Even within a single labor market area, there exist wide pay discrepancies for any given job. Collective agreements tend to establish employment uniformity for those workers included in the agreements, but, even when quality of performance is accounted for, there is still considerable discrepancy between workers inside and those outside the agreement. Too often, workers must bargain for salaries on the basis of their position in the organization or their title, rather than on the basis of job performance. A homemaker is one of the most notorious examples of unfair practices. Well-organized assembly line workers and semi-automatic machine workers performing work that could easily and possibly be performed better (as the work is designed) by a robot are paid three or four times as much as the workers to whom they entrust the care and well-being of their children and who must exercise considerably more discretion and perform a much greater variety of tasks.

Workers employed in the year 2001 would be paid a basic rate for performing a basic core of entry tasks. Then, following a reasonable period of probation, they would receive additional increments. From the start, they would be assigned to a team and allowed to learn additional tasks as they became ready for them until they had learned all the tasks relating to the objectives of the team. They would then earn a team rate. They would carry no job titles, but would be identified with the team and the particular job to be done. There would be no specific educational requirements for achieving pay rates, although functional and specific training would be available and encouraged to enhance the worker's ability. There would be additional increments within pay rates for achieving higher standards. Team leaders and team members would determine who deserved such special merit increases on the basis of task performance standards. However, special merit increases should be quite exceptional, since team participation would recognize a wide range of effective performance.

References

Fine, S. A. *Guidelines for the employment of the culturally disadvantaged.* Washington, D.C.: The Upjohn Institute for Employment Research, September 1969.

Hallowitz, E., & Riessman, F. The role of the indigenous nonprofessional in a community mental health neighborhood service center program. *American Journal of Orthopsychiatry,* 1967, *37,* 766-788.

Roman, M. Community control and the community mental health center: A view from Lincoln Bridge. In *Community Control: Realities and Possibilities.* New Haven: Yale University Press, 1971.

Appendix

Federal Executive Agency Guidelines on Employee Selection Procedures

Introduction

The Equal Employment Opportunity Coordinating Council, which is composed of the Department of Labor, the Equal Employment Opportunity Commission, the Civil Rights Commission, the Civil Service Commission and the Department of Justice, is charged by law (sec. 715 of the Civil Rights Act of 1964, as amended, 42 U.S.C. 2000e-14) to eliminate inconsistency among the operations of the agencies and departments responsible for enforcement of Federal equal employment opportunity law. Pursuant to that mandate, the Coordinating Council began work on proposed uniform guidelines on employee selection procedures early in 1973. A proposed draft of August 23, 1973, was circulated for comment pursuant to the procedures continued in OMB circular A-85. Later drafts also received wide circulation and have been the subject of written and oral comments.

Based upon these comments, the case law, and the American Psychological Association's Standards for Educational and Psychological Tests (1974), the Staff Committee of the Council, working pursuant to decisions made by the Council at its November, 1974, meeting, undertook a redraft of the proposed uniform guidelines.

A draft "Staff Committee Proposal, Sept. 24, 1975, Uniform Guidelines on Employee Selection Procedures" was agreed upon by the designated representatives on the Staff Committee of the four agencies having operational responsibility—the Department of Labor, the Equal Employment Opportunity Commission, the Civil Service Commission and the Department of Justice—for purposes of Council consideration, and for circulation for analysis and comments.

The Equal Employment Opportunity Commission reviewed the Staff Committee Proposal, Sept. 24, 1975, and determined that it did not represent the position of that agency, and for that reason opposed circulating the Staff Committee Proposal for prepublication comment pursuant to the A-85 procedure.

However, a majority of the Council believed that the Staff Committee Proposal, September 24, 1975, should be widely circulated for comment, as a step toward achievement of the goal of Uniform Guidelines on Employee Selection Standards.

The Staff Committee Proposal, Sept. 24, 1975, was accordingly circulated for prepublication comment pursuant to the A-85 procedure. Substantial additional comments were received, and modifications of the proposal were made.

A majority of the Coordinating Council believed that the proposed guidelines, as modified, should be published in the *Federal Register* for formal comment as a step toward achievement of the goal of uniformity in guidelines on employee selection procedures. Accordingly, the revised proposed uniform guidelines on employee selection procedures were published for comment in the *Federal Register* on July 14, 1976. 41 Fed. Reg. 29016. Many additional comments were received, and additional modifications in the proposed guidelines have been made.

On October 13, 1976, at a meeting of the Coordinating Council, the Equal Employment Opportunity Commission, determined that the resulting draft continued not to represent the views of that agency and opposed the adoption of the proposed guidelines and any action to recommend adoption of the proposed guidelines.

It has become clear that the Coordinating Council has not been successful in achieving a uniform federal position on the issue of employee selection procedures at this time.

The three undersigned have, however, determined to adopt and endorse the guidelines which were developed under the auspices of the

Coordinating Council. We do so in the issuances set forth below. Because unanimity does not appear feasible at this time, the term uniform has been deleted from the title, and the guidelines are now referred to as "Federal Executive Agency Guidelines on Employee Selection Procedures." We have determined to adopt and endorse the Federal agency guidelines for the following reasons:

1. One of the most important functions of federal guidelines in this area is to represent "professionally acceptable methods" for demonstrating whether a selection procedure has validity for a particular job. *Albemarle* v. *Moody,* 422 U.S. 405, 425. The American Psychological Association has described the proposed guidelines as being "essentially consistent with the Standards for Educational and Psychological Tests and with the best available knowledge concerning effective use of selection procedures in employment decisions" and as "concise, realistic and much-needed." We believe that the proposed guidelines better represent professionally accepted standards for determining validity than any existing set of guidelines.

2. While existing federal agency guidelines have been granted "great deference" by the courts, and have been of assistance in litigation, the most recent of them is more than five years old. They therefore are based upon the American Psychological Association's 1966 "Standards" rather than their 1974 "Standards," and do not take into account subsequent developments in the field of industrial psychology. Similarly, they do not take into account the judicial decisions, most of which were rendered after their publication. Accordingly, the federal agency guidelines set forth below are, in our judgment, more consistent with the Supreme Court and the authoritative decisions of the other appellate courts, than any set of existing guidelines.

3. Because federal agency guidelines are applicable to the Federal Government itself as well as to those employers doing business with the Federal Government and others subject to federal law, any apparent anomaly of applying a lesser standard to the Federal Government than it demands from others will be removed.

4. The federal agency guidelines provide practical guidance which will enable those users who seek to do so to bring themselves into compliance with Federal law. They are, in our judgment, more practical and realistic and will do more to provide actual equality of opportunity on a widespread basis, than any existing set of guidelines.

5. At present there are at least three sets of federal guidelines: the Regulations of the Civil Service Commission, and instructions which may be applicable to state and local governments as well as to the federal government itself; the regulations of the Secretary of Labor concerning selection procedures (41 CFR Part 60-3); and the guidelines on employee selection procedures of the EEOC (29 C.F.R. Part 1607). The adoption of the federal agency guidelines will therefore be a step toward achievement of a uniform federal position and uniform guidelines.

For the above reasons, we also recommend the adoption of the proposed Federal Executive Agency Guidelines by each Federal agency having responsibility for enforcement of Federal law prohibiting discrimination on the grounds of race, color, religion, sex and national origin. Such adoption will lead to the achievement of a uniform federal position and uniform guidelines in this vital area.

Harold R. Tyler, Jr.,
Deputy Attorney General.
Michael H. Moskow,
Under Secretary of Labor.
Robert E. Hampton,
Chairman, Civil Service Commission.

Federal Register, vol. 41, no. 227, Nov. 23, 1976

Part I—General Principles

§1 Statement of Purpose

a. These guidelines are intended to be a set of principles which will assist employers, labor organizations, employment agencies, and licensing and certification boards in complying with equal employment opportunity requirements of Federal law with respect to race, color, religion, sex and national origin. They are designed to provide a framework for determining the proper use of tests and other selection procedures consistent with Federal law. These guidelines do not require a user to conduct validity studies of selection procedures where no adverse impact results. However, all users are encouraged to use selection procedures which are valid, especially users operating under merit principles. Nothing in these guidelines is intended or should be interpreted as discouraging the use of procedures which have been properly validated in accordance with these guidelines for the purpose of determining qualifications or selecting on the basis of relative qualifications. Nothing in these guidelines is intended to apply to persons not subject to the requirements of Title VII, Executive Order 11246, or other equal employment opportunity requirements of Federal law. These guidelines are not intended to apply to any responsibilities an employer, employment agency or labor organization may have under the Age Discrimination Act of 1975 not to discriminate on the basis of age, or under section 504 of the Rehabilitation Act of 1973 not to discriminate on the basis of handicap. Nothing contained in these guidelines is intended to interfere with any obligation imposed or right granted by Federal law to users to extend a publicly announced preference in employment to Indians living on or near an Indian reservation in connection with employment opportunities on or near an Indian reservation.

§2 Scope

a. These guidelines will be applied by the Department of Labor to contractors and subcontractors subject to Executive Order 11246 as amended by Executive Order 11375 (hereinafter "Executive Order 11246"); and by the Civil Service Commission to federal agencies subject to Sec. 717 of the Civil Rights Act of 1964, as amended by the Equal Employment Opportunity Act of 1972 (hereinafter "the Civil Rights Act of 1964") and to its responsibilities toward state and local governments under Section 208(b) (1) of the Intergovernmental Personnel Act; by the Department of Justice in exercising its responsibilities under Federal law; and by any other Federal agency which adopts them.

b. These guidelines apply to selection procedures which are used as a basis for any employment decision. Employment decisions include but are not limited to hire, promotion, demotion, membership (for example in a labor organization), referral, retention, licensing and certification, to the extent that licensing and certification may be covered by Federal equal employment opportunity law. Selection for training is also considered an employment decision if it leads to any of the decisions listed above.

c. These guidelines do not apply to the use of a bona fide seniority system within the meaning of Title VII of the Civil Rights Act of 1964, as amended, as defined by Federal appellate court decisions, for any employment decision. These guidelines do not call for the validation of such a seniority system used as a basis for such employment decisions, and the use of such a seniority system as a basis for such employment decisions is consistent with these guidelines.

d. These guidelines do not apply to the entire range of Federal equal employment opportunity law, but only to selection procedures which are used as a basis for making employment decisions. For example, the use of recruiting procedures designed to attract racial, ethnic or sex groups which were previously denied employment opportunities or which are presently underutilized may be necessary to bring an employer into compliance with Federal law, and is frequently an essential element to any effective affirmative action program; but the subject of recruitment practices is not addressed by these guidelines because that subject concerns procedures other than selection procedures.

§3 Relationship between Use of Selection Procedures and Discrimination

a. The use of any selection procedure which has an adverse impact on the members of any racial, ethnic or sex group with respect to any employment decision will be considered to be discriminatory and inconsistent with these guidelines, unless the procedure is validated in accordance with the principles contained in these guidelines or unless use of the procedure is warranted under §3b.

b. There are circumstances in which it is not feasible or not appropriate to utilize the validation techniques contemplated by these guidelines. In such circumstances, the user should utilize selection procedures which are as job related as possible and which will minimize or eliminate adverse impact. (i) When an unstandardized, informal or unscored selection procedure which has an adverse impact is utilized, the user should seek insofar as possible to eliminate the adverse impact, or, if feasible, to modify the procedure to one which is a formal, scored or quantified measure or combination of measures and then to validate the procedure in accord with these guidelines, or otherwise to justify continued use of the procedure in accord with Federal law. (ii) When a standardized, formal or scored selection procedure is used for which it is not feasible or not appropriate to utilize the validation techniques contemplated by these guidelines, the user should either modify the procedure to eliminate the adverse impact or otherwise justify continued use of the procedure in accord with Federal law.

c. Generally where alternative selection procedures are available which have been shown to be equally valid for a given purpose, the user should use the procedure which has been demonstrated to have the lesser adverse impact. Accordingly, whenever a validity study is called for by these guidelines, the user should make a reasonable effort to investigate suitable alternative selection procedures which have as little adverse impact as possible, for the purpose of determining the appropriateness of using or validating them in accord with these guidelines. If a user has made a reasonable effort to become aware of such alternative procedures and a validity study for a job or group of jobs has been made in accord with these guidelines, the use of the selection procedure may continue until such time as it should reasonably be reviewed for currency. Whenever the user is shown a suitable alternative selection procedure with evidence of at least equal validity and less adverse impact, the user should investigate it for the purpose of determining the appropriateness of using or validating it in accord with these guidelines. This subsection is not intended to preclude the combination of procedures into a significantly more valid procedure, if such a combination has been properly validated.

§4 Information on Impact

a. Each user should have available for inspection records or other information which will disclose the impact which its selection procedures have upon employment opportunities of persons by identifiable racial, ethnic or sex groups in order to determine compliance with the provisions of §3 above. Where there are large numbers of applicants and procedures are administered frequently, such information may be retained on a sample basis, provided that the sample is appropriate in terms of the applicant population and adequate in size. The records called for by this section are to be maintained by sex, and by racial and ethnic groups as follows: Blacks (Negroes), American Indians (including Alaskan Natives), Asians (including Pacific Islanders), Hispanic (including persons of Mexican, Puerto Rican, Cuban, Central or South American, or other Spanish origin or culture regardless of race), whites (Caucasians) other than Hispanic and totals. The classifications called for by this section are intended to be consistent with the Employer Information (EEO-1 et seq.) series of reports. The user should adopt safeguards to insure that records of race, color, religion, sex, or national origin are used for appropriate purposes such as determining adverse impact, or (where required) for developing and monitoring affirmative action programs, and that such records are not used for making employment decisions.

b. The information called for by this section should be examined for possible adverse impact. If the records called for by this section indicate that the total selection process for a job has no adverse impact, the individual components of the selection process need not be evaluated separately for adverse impact. If a total selection process does have adverse impact, the individual components of the selection process should be evaluated for adverse impact.

A selection rate for any racial, ethnic or sex group which is less than four-fifths (4/5) (or eighty percent) of the rate for the group with the highest rate will generally be regarded as evidence of adverse impact, while a greater than four-fifths rate will generally not be regarded as evidence of adverse impact. Smaller differences in selection rate may nevertheless be considered to constitute adverse impact, where they are significant in both statistical and practical terms. Greater differences in selection rate would not necessarily be regarded as constituting adverse impact where the differences are based on small numbers and are not statistically significant, or where special recruiting or other programs cause the pool of minority or female candidates to be atypical of the normal pool of applicants from that group.

c. Federal agencies which adopt these guidelines for purpose of the enforcement of the equal employment opportunity laws or which have responsibility for securing compliance with them (hereafter referred to as enforcement agencies) will consider in carrying out their obligations the general posture of the user with respect to equal employment opportunity for the job classification or group of classifications in question. Where a user has adopted an affirmative action program, the Federal enforcement agencies will consider the provisions of that program, including the goals and timetables which the employer has adopted and the progress which the employer has made in carrying out that program and in meeting the goals and timetables. These guidelines recognize that a user is prohibited by Federal law from the making of employment decisions on the basis of race and color and (except for bona fide occupational qualifications) on the basis of sex, religion and national origin; and nothing in this subsection or in these guidelines is intended to encourage or permit the granting of preferential treatment to any individual or to any group because of the race, color, religion, sex or national origin of such individual or group.

§5 General Standards for Validity Studies

a. For the purpose of satisfying these guidelines users may rely upon criterion related validity studies, content validity studies or construct validity studies, in accordance with the standards set forth in Part II of these guidelines, §12 *infra*.

b. These guidelines are intended to be consistent with generally accepted professional standards for evaluating standardized tests and other assessment techniques, such as those described in the *Standards for Educational and Psychological Tests* prepared by a joint committee of the American Psychological Association, the American Educational Research Association, and the National Council on Measurement in Education (American Psychological Association, Washington, D.C. 1974) (hereinafter "*APA Standards*"), and standard text books and journals in the field of personnel selection.

c. For any selection procedure which has an adverse impact each user should maintain and have available such documentation as is described in Part III of these guidelines, §13 *infra*.

d. Selection procedures subject to validity studies under §3a above should be administered and scored under standardized conditions.

e. In general, users should avoid making employment decisions on the basis of measures of knowledges, skills or abilities which are normally learned in a brief orientation period, and which have an adverse impact.

f. Where cut off scores are used, they should normally be set so as to be reasonable and consistent with normal expectations of acceptable proficiency within the work force. Where other factors are used in determining cut off scores, such as the relationship between the number of vacancies and the number of applicants, the degree of adverse impact should be considered.

g. Selection procedures may be used to predict the performance of candidates for a job which is at a higher level than the job for which the person is initially being selected if a majority of the individuals who remain employed will progress to the higher level within a reasonable period of time. A "reasonable period of time" will vary for different jobs and employment situations but will seldom be more than five years. Examining for a higher level job would not be appropriate (1) if the majority of those remaining employed do not progress to the higher level job, (2) if there is a reason to doubt that the higher level job will continue to require essentially similar skills during the progression period, or (3) if knowledges, skills or abilities required for advancement would be expected to develop principally from the training or experience on the job.

h. Users may continue the use of a selection procedure which is not at the moment fully supported by the required evidence of validity, provided: (1) the user can cite substantial evidence of validity in accord with these guidelines and (2) the user has in progress, when technically feasible, studies which are designed to produce the additional data required within a reasonable time.

If the additional studies do not produce the data required to demonstrate validity, the user is not relieved of or protected against any obligations arising under federal law.

i. Whenever a validity study has been made in accord with these guidelines for the use of a particular selection procedure for a job or group of jobs, additional studies need not be performed until such time as the validity study is subject to review as provided in §3c above. There are no absolutes in the areas of determining the currency of a validity study. All circumstances concerning the study, including the validation strategy used, and changes in the relevant labor market and the job should be considered in the determination of when a validity study is outdated.

§6 Cooperative Validity Studies and Use of Other Validity Studies

a. It is the intent of the agencies issuing these guidelines to encourage and facilitate cooperative development and validation efforts by employers, labor organizations and employment agencies to achieve selection procedures which are consistent with these guidelines.

b. Criterion-related validity studies conducted by one test user, or described in test manuals and the professional literature, will be considered acceptable for use by another user when: (1) the weight of the evidence from studies meeting the standards of §12b below shows that the selection procedure is valid; (2) the studies pertain to a job which has substantially the same major job duties as shown by appropriate job analyses and (3) the studies included a study of test fairness for those racial, ethnic and sex subgroups which constitute significant factors in the borrowing user's relevant labor market for the job or jobs in question. If the studies relied upon satisfy (1) and (2) above but do not contain an investigation of test fairness, and it is not technically feasible for the borrowing user to conduct an internal study of test fairness, the borrowing user may utilize the study until studies conducted elsewhere show test unfairness, or until such time as it becomes technically feasible to conduct an internal study of test fairness and the results of that study can be acted upon.

If it is technically feasible for a borrowing user to conduct an internal validity study, and there are variables in the other studies which are likely to affect validity or fairness significantly, the user may rely upon such studies only on an interim basis in accord with §5h, and will be expected to conduct an internal validity study in accord with §12b below. Otherwise the borrowing user may rely upon such acceptable studies for operational use without an internal study.

c. Selection procedures shown by one user to be content valid in accord with §12c will be considered acceptable for use by another user for a performance domain if the borrowing user's job analysis shows that the same performance domain is present in the borrowing user's job. The selection procedure may be used operationally if the conditions of §12c(3) and §12c(6) are satisfied by the borrowing user.

d. The conditions under which findings of construct validity may be generalized are described in §12d(4).

e. If validity evidence from a multiunit or cooperative study satisfies the requirements of subparagraphs b, c or d above, evidence of validity specific to each unit or user usually will not be required unless there are variables in the units not studied which are likely to affect validity significantly.

§7 No Assumption of Validity

a. Under no circumstances will the general reputation of a selection procedure, its author or its publisher, or casual reports of its validity be accepted in lieu of evidence of validity. Specifically ruled out are: assumptions of validity based on a procedure's name or descriptive labels; all forms of promotional literature; data bearing on the frequency of a procedure's usage; testimonial statements and credentials of sellers, users, or consultants; and other non-empirical or anecdotal accounts of selection practices or selection outcomes.

b. Professional supervision of selection activities is encouraged but is not a substitute for documented evidence of validity. The enforcement agencies will take into account the fact that a thorough job analysis and careful development of a selection procedure enhances the probability that the selection procedure is valid for the job.

§8 Employment Agencies and Employment Services

a. An employment agency, including private employment agencies and State employment agencies which agrees to a request by an employer or labor organization to devise and utilize a selection procedure should follow the standards for determining adverse impact and, if adverse impact is demonstrated, show validity as set forth in these guidelines. An employment agency is not relieved of its obligation herein because the user did not request such validation or has requested the use of some lesser standard of validation than is provided in these guidelines. The use of an employment agency does not relieve an employer or labor organization of its responsibilities under Federal law to provide equal employment opportunity or its obligations as a user under these guidelines.

b. Where an employment agency or service is requested to administer a selection program which has been devised elsewhere and to make referrals pursuant to the results, the employment agency or service should obtain evidence of the absence of adverse impact, or of validity, as described in these guidelines, before it administers the selection program and makes referrals pursuant to the results. The employment agency must furnish on request such evidence of validity. An employment agency or service will be expected to refuse to make referrals based on the selection procedure where the employer or labor organization does not supply satisfactory evidence of validity or lack of adverse impact.

§9 Disparate Treatment

The principle of disparate or unequal treatment must be distinguished from the concepts of validation. A selection procedure—even though validated against job performance in accordance with the guidelines in this part—cannot be imposed upon members of a racial, sex or ethnic group where other employees, applicants, or members have been denied the same employment, promotion, transfer or membership opportunities as have been made available to other employees or applicants. Those employees or applicants who have been denied equal treatment, because of prior discriminatory practices or policies, must at least be afforded the same opportunities as had existed for other employees or applicants during the period of discrimination. Thus, the persons who were in the class of persons discriminated against and were available in the relevant job market during the period the user followed the discriminatory practices should be allowed the opportunity to qualify under the less stringent selection procedures previously followed, unless the user demonstrates that the increased standards are required for the safety or efficiency of the operation. Nothing in this section is intended to prohibit a user who has not previously followed merit standards from adopting merit standards; nor does it preclude a user who has previously used invalid or unvalidated selection procedures from developing and using procedures which are validated in accord with these guidelines.

§10 Retesting

Users should provide a reasonable opportunity for retesting and reconsideration. The user may however take reasonable steps to preserve the security of its procedures. Where examinations are administered periodically with public notice, such reasonable opportunity exists, unless persons who have previously been tested are precluded from retesting.

§11 Affirmative Action

The use of selection procedures which have been validated pursuant to these guidelines does not relieve users of any obligations they may have to undertake affirmative action to assure equal employment opportunity. Nothing in these guidelines is intended to preclude the use of selection procedures (consistent with Federal law — see §4c) which assist in the achievement of affirmative action objectives.

Part II—Technical Standards

§12 Technical Standards for Validity Studies

The following minimum standards, as applicable, should be met in conducting a validity study. Nothing in these guidelines is intended to preclude the development and use of other professionally acceptable techniques with respect to validation of selection procedures.

a. Any validity study should be based upon a review of information about the job for which the selection procedure is to be used. The review should include a job analysis except as provided in §12b(3) below with respect to criterion related validity. Any method of job analysis may be used if it provides the information required for the specific validation strategy used.

b. Criterion-related Validity

(1) Users choosing to validate a selection procedure by a criterion-related validity strategy should determine whether it is technically feasible (as defined in Part IV) to conduct such a study in the particular employment context. The determination of the number of persons necessary to permit the conduct of a meaningful criterion-related study should be made by the user on the basis of all relevant information concerning the selection procedure, the potential sample and the employment situation. These guidelines do not require a user to hire or promote persons for the purpose of making it possible to conduct a criterion-related study; and do not require such a study on a sample of less than thirty (30) persons.

(2) There should be a review of job information to determine measures of work behaviors or performance that are relevent to the job in question. These measures or criteria are relevant to the extent that they represent critical or important job duties, work behaviors or work outcomes as developed from the review of job information. The possibility of bias should be considered both in selection of the measures and their application. In view of the possibility of bias in subjective evaluations, supervisory rating techniques should be carefully developed. All criteria need to be examined for freedom from factors which would unfairly alter scores of members of any group. The relevance of criteria and their freedom from bias are of particular concern when there are significant differences in measures of job performance for different groups.

(3) Proper safeguards should be taken to insure that scores on selection procedures do not enter into any judgments of employee adequacy that are to be used as criterion measures. Criteria may cor ɔist of measures other than work proficiency including, but not limited to length of service, regularity of attendance, training time or properly measured success in job relevant training. Measures of training success based upon pencil and paper tests will be closely reviewed for job relevance. Whatever criteria are used should represent important or critical work behaviors or work outcomes. Job behaviors including but not limited to production rate, error

rate, tardiness, absenteeism and turnover, may be used as criteria without a full job analysis if the user can show the importance of the criterion to the particular employment context. A standardized rating of overall work performance may be utilized where a study of the job shows that it is an appropriate criterion.

(4) The sample subjects should insofar as feasible be representative of the candidates normally available in the relevant labor market for the job or jobs in question, and should insofar as feasible include the racial, ethnic and sex groups normally available in the relevant job market. Where samples are combined or compared, attention should be given to see that such samples are comparable in terms of the actual job they perform, the length of time on the job where time on the job is likely to affect performance and other relevant factors likely to affect validity differences; or that these factors are included in the design of the study and their effects identified.

(5) The degree of relationship between selection procedure scores and criterion measures should be examined and computed, using professionally acceptable statistical procedures. Generally, a selection procedure is considered related to the criterion, for the purposes of these guidelines, when the relationship between performance on the procedure and performance on the criterion measure is statistically significant at the .05 level of significance, which means that it is sufficiently high as to have a probability of no more than one (1) in twenty (20) to have occurred by chance. Absence of a statistically significant relationship between a selection procedure and job performance should not necessarily discourage other investigations of the validity of that selection procedure.

Users should evaluate each selection procedure to assure that it is appropriate for operational use. Generally, if other factors remain the same, the greater the magnitude of the relationship (e.g., correlation coefficient) between performance on a selection procedure and one or more criteria of performance on the job, and the greater the importance or number of aspects of job performance covered by the criteria, the more likely it is that the procedure will be appropriate for use. Reliance upon a selection procedure which is significantly related to a criterion measure, but which is based upon a study involving a large number of subjects and has a low correlation coefficient will be subject to close review if it has a large adverse impact. Sole reliance upon a single selection instrument which is related to only one of many job duties or aspects of job performance will also be subject to close review. The appropriateness of a selection procedure is best evaluated in each particular situation and there are no minimum correlation coefficients applicable to all employment situations. In determining whether a selection procedure is appropriate for operational use the following considerations should also be taken into account: the degree of adverse impact of the procedure, the availability of other selection procedures of greater or substantially equal validity; and the need of an employer, required by law or regulation to follow merit principles, to have an objective system of selection.

(6) Users should avoid reliance upon techniques which tend to overestimate validity findings as a result of capitalization on chance unless an appropriate safeguard is taken. Reliance upon a few selection procedures or criteria of successful job performance, when many selection procedures or criteria of performance have been studied, or the use of optimal statistical weights for selection procedures computed in one sample, are techniques which tend to inflate validity estimates as a result of chance. Use of a large sample is one safeguard; cross-validation is another.

(7) Fairness of the Selection Procedure

i. When members of one racial, ethnic, or sex group characteristically obtain lower scores on a selection procedure than members of another group, and the differences are not reflected in differences in measures of job performance, use of the selection procedure may unfairly deny opportunities to members of the group that obtains the lower scores.

ii. Where a selection procedure results in an adverse impact on a racial, ethnic or sex group identified in accordance with the classifications set forth in §4 above and that group is a significant factor in the relevant labor market, the user generally should investigate the possible existence of unfairness for that group if it is technically feasible to do so.

The greater the severity of the adverse impact on a group, the greater the need to investigate the possible existence of unfairness. Where the weight of evidence from other studies shows that the selection procedure is a fair predictor for the group in question and for the same or similar jobs, such evidence may be relied on in connection with the selection procedure at issue and may be combined with data from the present study; however, where the severity of adverse impact on a group is significantly greater than in the other studies referred to, a user may not rely on such other studies.

iii. Users conducting a study of fairness should review the APA *Standards* regarding investigation of possible bias in testing. An investigation of fairness of a selection procedure depends on both evidence of validity and the manner in which the selection procedure is to be used in a particular employment context. Fairness of a selection procedure cannot necessarily be specified in advance without investigating these factors. Investigation of fairness of a selection procedure in samples where the range of scores on selection procedures or criterion measures is severely restricted for any subgroup sample (as compared to other subgroup samples) may produce misleading evidence of unfairness. That factor should accordingly be taken into account in conducting such studies and before reliance is placed on the results.

iv. If unfairness is demonstrated through a showing that members of a particular group perform better or poorer on the job than their scores on the selection procedure would indicate through comparison with how members of other groups perform, the user may either revise or replace the selection instrument in accordance with these guidelines, or may continue to use the selection instrument operationally with appropriate revisions in its use to assure compatibility between the probability of successful job performance and the probability of being selected.

v. In additional to the general conditions needed for technical feasibility for the conduct of a criterion-related study (see §14(j), below) an investigation of fairness requires the following:

(1) A sufficient number of persons in each group for findings of statistical significance. These guidelines do not require a user to hire or promote persons on the basis of group classifications for the purpose of making it possible to conduct a study of fairness; and do not require a user to conduct a study of fairness on a sample of less than thirty (30) persons for each group involved in the study.

(2) The samples for each group should be comparable in terms of the actual job they perform, length of time on the job where time on the job is likely to affect performance, and other relevant factors likely to affect validity differences; or such factors should be included in the design of the study and their effects identified.

vi. If a study of fairness should otherwise be performed, but is not technically feasible, the use of a selection procedure which has otherwise met the validity standards of these guidelines will be considered in accord with these guidelines, unless the technical infeasibility resulted from discriminatory employment practices which are demonstrated by facts other than past failure to conform with requirements for validation of selection procedures. However, when it becomes technically feasible for the user to perform a study of fairness and such a study is otherwise called for, the user should conduct the study of fairness.

c. Content Validity

(1) There should be a definition of a performance domain or the performance domains with respect to the job in question. Performance domains may be defined through job analysis, analysis of the work behaviors or activities, or by the pooled judgments of persons having knowledge of the job. Performance domains should be defined on the basis of competent information about job tasks and responsibilities. Performance domains include critical or important work behaviors, work products, work activities, job duties, or the knowledges, skills or abilities shown to be necessary for performance of the duties, behaviors, activities or the production of work. Where a performance domain has been defined as a knowledge, skill or ability, that knowledge, skill or ability must be used in job behavior. A selection procedure based on inferences about psychological processes cannot be supported by content validity alone. Thus content validity by itself is not an appropriate validation strategy for intelligence, aptitude, personality or interest tests. Content validity is also not an appropriate strategy when the selection procedure involves knowledges, skills or abilities which an employee will be expected to learn on the job.

(2) If a higher score on a content valid selection procedure can be expected to result in better job performance the results may be used to rank persons who score above minimum levels. Where a selection procedure supported solely by content validity is used to rank job candidates, the performance domain should include those aspects of performance which differentiate among levels of job performance.

(3) A selection procedure which is a representative sample of a performance domain of the job as defined in accordance with subsection (1) above, is a content valid procedure for that domain. Where the domain or domains measured are critical to the job, or constitute a substantial proportion of the job, the selection procedure will be considered to be content valid for the job. The reliability of selection procedures justified on the basis of content validity should be a matter of concern to the user. Whenever it is feasible to do so, appropriate statistical estimates should be made of the reliability of the selection procedures.

(4) A demonstration of the relationship between the content of the selection procedure and the performance domain of the job is critical to content validity. Content validity may be shown if the knowleges, skills or abilities demonstrated in and measured by the selection procedure are substantially the same as the knowledges, skills or abilities shown to be necessary for job performance. The closer the content of the selection

procedure is to actual work samples, behaviors or activities, the stronger is the basis for showing content validity. The need for careful documentation of the relationship between the performance domain of the selection procedure and that of the job increases as the content of the selection procedure less resembles that of the job performance domain.

(5) A requirement for specific prior training or for work experience based on content validity, including a specification of level or amount of training or experience, should be justified on the basis of the relationship between the content of the training or experience and the performance domain of the job for which the training or experience is to be required.

(6) If a selection procedure is supported solely on the basis of content validity, it may be used operationally if it represents a critical performance domain or a substantial proportion of the performance domains of the job.

d. *Construct Validity.* Construct validity is a more complex strategy than either criterion related or content validity. Accordingly, users choosing to validate a selection procedure by use of this strategy should be careful to follow professionally accepted standards, such as those contained in the APA *Standards* and the standard text books and journals.

(1) There should be a job analysis. This job analysis should result in a determination of the constructs that underlie successful performance of the important or critical duties of the job.

(2) A selection procedure should be selected or developed which measures the construct(s) identified in accord with subparagraph (1) above.

(3) A selection procedure may be used operationally if the standards of subparagraphs (1) and (2) are met and there is sufficient empirical research evidence showing that the procedure is validly related to performance of critical job duties. Normally, sufficient empirical research evidence would take the form of one or more criterion related validity studies meeting the requirements of §12b. See also second sentence of §12.

(4) Where a selection procedure satisfies the standards of subsections (1), (2) and (3) above, it may be used operationally for other jobs which are shown by an appropriate job analysis to include the same construct(s) as an essential element in job performance.

Part III—Documentation of Validity Evidence

§13a. For each selection procedure having an adverse impact (as set forth in §4) the user should maintain and have available the data on which the adverse impact determination was made and one of the following types of documentation evidence:

(1) Documentation evidence showing criterion related validity of the selection procedure (see §13b. *infra*).

(2) Documentation evidence showing content validity of the selection procedure (see §13c. *infra*).

(3) Documentation evidence showing construct validity of the selection procedure (see §13d. *infra*).

(4) Documentation evidence from other studies showing validity of the selection procedure in the user's facility (see §13e. *infra*).

(5) Documentation evidence showing what steps were taken to reduce or eliminate adverse impact, why validation is not feasible or not appropriate and why continued use of the procedure is consistent with Federal law.

This evidence should be compiled in a reasonably complete and organized manner to permit direct evaluation of the validity of the selection procedure. Previously written employer or consultant reports of validity are acceptable if they are complete in regard to the following documentation requirements, or if they satisfied requirements of guidelines which were in effect when the study was completed. If they are not complete, the required additional documentation should be appended. If necessary information is not available the report of the validity study may still be used as documentation, but its adequacy will be evaluated in terms of compliance with the requirements of these guidelines.

In the event that evidence of validity is reviewed by an enforcement agency, the reports completed after the effective date of these guidelines are expected to use one of the formats set forth below. Evidence denoted by use of the word "(ESSENTIAL)" is considered critical and reports not containing such information will be considered incomplete. Evidence not so denoted is desirable, but its absence will not be a basis for considering a report incomplete.

b. *Criterion-related validity.* Reports of criterion related validity of selection procedures are to contain the following information:

(1) *User(s), and Location(s) and Date(s) of Study.* Dates of administration of selection procedures and collection of criterion data and, where appropriate, the time between collection of data on selection procedures and criterion measures should be shown (ESSENTIAL). If the study was conducted at several locations, the address of each location, including city and state, should be shown.

(2) *Problem and Setting.* An explicit definition of the purpose(s) of the study and the cir-

cumstances in which the study was conducted should be provided. A description of existing selection procedures and cut-off scores, if any, should be provided.

(3) *Review of Job Information or Job Analysis.* Where a review of job information results in criteria which are measures other than work proficiency (see 12b(3)), the basis for the selection of these criteria should be reported (ESSENTIAL). Where a job analysis is required, the report should include either: (a) the important duties performed on the job and the basis on which such duties were determined to be important, such as the proportion of time spent on the respective duties, their level of difficulty, their frequency of performance, the consequences of error, or other appropriate factors; or (b) the knowleges, skills, abilities and/or other worker characteristics and bases on which they were determined to be important for job performance (ESSENTIAL). Published descriptions from industry sources or Volume I of the *Dictionary of Occupational Titles* Third Edition, United States Government Printing Office, 1965, are satisfactory if they adequately and completely describe the job. If appropriate, a brief supplement to the published description should be provided.

If two or more jobs are grouped for a validity study, a justification for this grouping, as well as a description of each of the jobs, should be provided (ESSENTIAL).

(4) *Job Titles and Codes.* It is desirable to provide the user's job title(s) for the job(s) in question and the corresponding job title(s) and code(s) from United States Employment Service *Dictionary of Occupational Titles* Volumes I & II. Where standard titles and codes do not exist, a notation to that effect should be made.

(5) *Criteria.* A full description of all criteria on which data were collected, including a rationale for selection of the final criteria, and means by which they were observed, recorded, evaluated and quantified, should be provided (ESSENTIAL). If rating techniques are used as criterion measures the appraisal form(s) and instructions to the rater(s) should be included as part of the validation evidence (ESSENTIAL).

(6) *Sample.* A description of how the research sample was selected should be included (ESSENTIAL). The racial, ethnic and sex composition of the sample should be described, including the size of each subgroup (ESSENTIAL). Racial and ethnic classifications should be those set forth in §4a above. A description of how the research sample compares with the racial, ethnic and sex composition of the relevant labor market is also desirable. Where data are available, the racial, ethnic and sex composition of current applicants should also be described. Descriptions of educational levels, length of service, and age are also desirable.

(7) *Selection Procedure.* Any measure, combination of measures, or procedures used as a basis for employment decisions should be completely and explicitly described or attached (ESSENTIAL). If commercially available selection procedures are used, they should be described by title, form, and publisher (ESSENTIAL). Reports of reliability estimates and how they were established are desirable. A rationale for choosing the selection procedures investigated in the study should be included.

(8) *Techniques and Results.* Methods used in analyzing data should be described (ESSENTIAL). Measures of central tendency (e.g., means) and measures of dispersion (e.g., standard deviations and ranges) for all selection procedures and all criteria should be reported for all relevant racial, ethnic and sex subgroups (ESSENTIAL). Statistical results should be organized and presented in tabular or graphical form, by racial, ethnic and/or sex subgroups (ESSENTIAL). All selection procedure-criterion relationships investigated should be reported, including their magnitudes and directions (ESSENTIAL). Statements regarding the statistical significance of results should be made (ESSENTIAL).

Any statistical adjustments, such as for less than perfect reliability or for restriction of score range in the selection procedure or criterion, or both, should be described; and uncorrected correlation coefficients should also be shown (ESSENTIAL). Where the statistical technique used categorizes continuous data, such as biserial correlation and the phi coefficient, the categories and the bases on which they were determined should be described (ESSENTIAL). Studies of test fairness should be included where called for by the requirements of Section 12b(7) (ESSENTIAL). These studies should include the rationale by which a selection procedure was determined to be fair to the group(s) in question. Where test fairness has been demonstrated on the basis of other studies, a bibliography of the relevant studies should be included (ESSENTIAL). If the bibliography includes unpublished studies, copies of these studies, or adequate abstracts or summaries, should be attached (ESSENTIAL). Where revisions have been made in a selection procedure to assure compatibility between successful job performance and the probability of being selected, the studies underlying such revisions should be included (ESSENTIAL).

(9) *Uses and Applications.* A description of the way in which each selection procedure is to be used (e.g., as a screening device with a cut-off score or combined with other procedures in a

battery) and application of the procedure (e.g., selection, transfer, promotion) should be provided (ESSENTIAL). If weights are assigned to different parts of the selection procedure, these weights and the validity of the weighted composite should be reported (ESSENTIAL).

(10) *Cut-off Scores.* Where cut-off scores are to be used, both the cut-off scores and the way in which they were determined should be described (ESSENTIAL).

(11) *Source Data.* Each user should maintain records showing all pertinent information about individual sample members in studies involving the validation of selection procedures. These records (exclusive of names and social security number) should be made available upon request of a compliance agency. These data should include selection procedure scores, criterion scores, age, sex, minority group status, and experience on the specific job on which the validation study was conducted and may also include such things as education, training, and prior job experience. If the user chooses to include, along with a report on validation, a worksheet showing the pertinent information about the individual sample members, specific identifying information such as name and social security number should not be shown. Inclusion of the worksheet with the validity report is encouraged in order to avoid delays.

(12) *Contact Person.* It is desirable for the user to set forth the name, mailing address, and telephone number of the individual who may be contacted for further information about the validity study.

c. *Content Validity.* Reports of content validity of selection procedures are to contain the following information:

(1) *Definition of Performance Domain.* A full description should be provided for the basis on which a performance domain is defined (ESSENTIAL). A complete and comprehensive definition of the performance domain should also be provided (ESSENTIAL). The domain should be defined on the basis of competent information about job tasks and responsibilities (ESSENTIAL). Where the performance domain is defined in terms of knowledges, skills, or abilities, there should be an operational definition of each knowledge, skill or ability and a complete description of its relationship to job duties, behaviors, activities, or work products (ESSENTIAL).

(2) *Job Title and Code.* It is desirable to provide the user's job title(s) and the corresponding job title(s) and code(s) from the United States Employment Service *Dictionary of Occupational Titles* Volumes I & II. Where standard titles and codes do not exist, a notation to that effect should be made.

(3) *Selection Procedures.* Selection procedures including those constructed by or for the user, specific training requirements, composites of selection procedures, and any other procedure for which content validity is asserted should be completely and explicitly described or attached (ESSENTIAL). If commercially available selection procedures are used, they should be described by title, form, and publisher (ESSENTIAL). Where the performance domain is defined in terms of knowledges, skills or abilities, evidence that the selection procedure measures those knowledges, skills or abilities should be provided (ESSENTIAL).

(4) *Techniques and Results.* The method by which the correspondence between the content of the selection procedure and the job performance domain(s) was established and the relative emphasis given to various aspects of the content of the selection procedure as derived from the performance domain(s) should be described (ESSENTIAL). If any steps were taken to reduce adverse racial, ethnic, or sex impact in the content of the procedure or in its administration, these steps should be described. Establishment of time limits, if any, and how these limits are related to the speed with which duties must be performed on the job, should be explained. The adequacy of the sample coverage of the performance domain should be described as precisely as possible. Measures of central tendency (e.g., means) and measures of dispersion (e.g., standard deviations) should be reported for all selection procedures as appropriate. Such reports should be made for all relevant racial, ethnic, and sex subgroups, at least on a statistically reliable sample basis.

(5) *Uses and Applications.* A description of the way in which each selection procedure is to be used (e.g., as a screening device with a cut-off score or combined with other procedures in a battery) and the application of the procedure (e.g., selection, transfer, promotion) should be provided (ESSENTIAL).

(6) *Cut-off Scores.* The rationale for minimum scores, if used, should be provided (ESSENTIAL). If the selection procedure is used to rank individuals above minimum levels, or if preference is given to individuals who score significantly above the minimum levels, a rationale for this procedure should be provided (ESSENTIAL).

(7) *Contact person.* It is desirable for the employer to set forth the name, mailing address and telephone number of the individual who may be contacted for further information about the validation study.

d. *Construct Validity.* Reports of construct validity of selection procedures are to contain the following information:

(1) *Construct Definition.* A clear definition

of the construct should be provided, explained in terms of empirically observable behavior, including levels of construct performance relevant to the job(s) for which the selection procedure is to be used (ESSENTIAL).

(2) *Job Analysis.* The job analysis should show how the constructs underlying successful job performance of important or critical duties were determined (ESSENTIAL). The job analysis should provide evidence of the linkage between the construct and the important duties of the job and how this linkage was determined (ESSENTIAL).

(3) *Job Titles and Codes.* It is desirable to provide the selection procedure user's job title(s) for the job(s) in question and the corresponding job title(s) and code(s) from the United States Employment Service *Dictionary of Occupational Titles*, Volumes I and II. Where standard titles and codes do not exist, a notation to that effect should be made.

(4) *Selection Procedure.* The selection procedure used as a measure of the construct should be completely and explicitly described or attached (ESSENTIAL). If commercially available selection procedures are used, they should be identified by title, form and publisher (ESSENTIAL). The evidence demonstrating that the selection procedure is in fact a proper measure of the construct should be included (ESSENTIAL). Reports of reliability estimates and how they were established are desirable.

(5) *Anchoring.* The empirical evidence showing that performance on the selection procedure is validly related to performance of critical job duties should be included (ESSENTIAL).

(6) *Uses and Applications.* A description of the way in which each selection procedure is to be used (e.g., as a screening device with a cut-off score or combined with other procedures in a battery) and application of the procedure (e.g., selection, transfer, promotion) should be provided (ESSENTIAL). If weights are assigned to different parts of the selection procedure, these weights and the validity of the weighted composite should be reported (ESSENTIAL).

(7) *Cut-off Scores.* Where cut-off scores are to be used, both the cut-off scores and the way in which they were determined should be described (ESSENTIAL).

(8) *Source Data.* Each user should maintain records showing all pertinent information about individual sample members in studies involving the validation of selection procedures. These records (exclusive of names and social security number) should be made available upon request of a compliance agency. These data should include selection procedure scores, criterion scores, age, sex, minority group status, and experience on the specific job on which the validation study was conducted and may also include such things as education, training, and prior job experience. If the user chooses to include, along with a report on validation, a worksheet showing the pertinent information about the individual sample members, specific identifying information such as name and social security number should not be shown. Inclusion of the worksheet with the validity report is encouraged in order to avoid delays.

(9) *Contact Person.* It is desirable for the user to set forth the name, mailing address, and telephone number of the individual who may be contacted for further information about the validity study.

e. *Evidence of Validity from other Studies.* When validity of a selection procedure is supported by studies not done by the user, the evidence from the original study or studies should be compiled in a manner similar to that required in the appropriate section of this §13 above. In addition, the following evidence should be supplied:

(1) *Evidence from Criterion-related Validity Studies*

(i) *Job Information.* A description of the important duties of the user's job and the basis on which the duties were determined to be important should be provided (ESSENTIAL). A full description of the basis for determining that these important job duties are sufficiently similar to the duties of the job in the original study (or studies) to warrant use of the selection procedure in the new situation should be provided (ESSENTIAL).

(ii) *Relevance of Criteria.* A full description of the basis on which the criteria used in the original studies are determined to be relevant for the user should be provided (ESSENTIAL).

(iii) *Other Variables.* The similarity of important applicant pool/sample characteristics reported in the original studies to those of the user should be described (ESSENTIAL). A description of the comparison between the race and sex composition of the user's relevant labor market and the sample in the original validity studies should be provided (ESSENTIAL).

(iv) *Use of the Selection Procedure.* A full description should be provided showing that the use to be made of the selection procedure is consistent with the findings of the original validity studies (ESSENTIAL).

(v) *Bibliography.* A bibliography of reports of validity of the selection procedure for the job or jobs in question should be provided (ESSENTIAL). Where any of the studies included an investigation of test fairness, the results of this investigation should be provided (ESSENTIAL). Copies of reports published in journals that are not commonly available should be described in detail or attached (ESSENTIAL). Where a user is relying upon unpublished studies, a reasonable effort should be made to obtain these studies. If these unpublished studies are the sole source of validity evidence they should be described in detail or attached (ESSENTIAL). If these studies are not available, the name and address of the source, an adequate abstract or summary of the validity study and data, and a contact person in the source organization should be provided (ESSENTIAL).

(2) *Evidence from Content Validity Studies*

(1) *Similarity of Performance Domains.* A full description should be provide of the similarity between the performance domain in the user's job and the performance domain measured by a selection procedure developed and shown to be content valid by another user (ESSENTIAL). The basis for determining this similarity should be explicitly described (ESSENTIAL).

(3) *Evidence from Construct Validity Studies*

(i) *Uniformity of Construct.* A full description should be provided of the basis for determining that the construct identified as underlying successful job performance by the user's job analysis is the same as the construct measured by the selection procedure (ESSENTIAL).

Part IV—Definitions

§14 The following definitions shall apply throughout these guidelines:

(a) Ability: The present observable competence to perform a function.

(b) Adverse Impact: Defined in §4 of these guidelines.

(c) Employer: Any employer subject to the provisions of the Civil Rights Act of 1964, as amended, including state or local government and any Federal agency subject to the provisions of Sec. 717 of the Civil Rights Act of 1964, as amended, and any Federal contractor or subcontractor or federally assisted construction contractor or subcontractor covered by Executive Order 11246, as amended.

(d) Employment agency: Any employment agency subject to the provisions of the Civil Rights Act of 1964, as amended.

(e) Enforcement agency: Any agency of the executive branch of the Federal Government which adopts these guidelines for purpose of the enforcement of the equal employment opportunity laws or which has responsibility for securing compliance with them.

(f) Labor organization: Any labor organization subject to the provisions of the Civil Rights Act of 1964, as amended, and any committee controlling apprenticeship or other training.

(g) Racial, sex or ethnic group: Any group of persons identifiable on the grounds of race, color, religion, sex or national origin.

(h) Selection procedure: Any measure, combination of measures, or procedure, other than a bona fide seniority system, used as a basis for any employment decision. Selection procedures include the full range of assessment techniques from traditional paper and pencil tests, performance tests, training programs or probationary periods and physical, educational and work experience requirements through informal or casual interviews and unscored application forms.

(i) Selection Rate: The proportion of applicants or candidates who are hired, promoted or otherwise selected.

(j) Technical feasibility: The existence of conditions permitting the conduct of meaningful criterion related validity studies. These conditions include: (a) an adequate sample of persons available for the study to achieve findings of statistical significance; (b) having or being able to obtain a sufficient range of scores on the selection procedure and job performance measures to produce validity results which can be expected to be representative of the results if the ranges normally expected were utilized; and (c) having or being able to devise unbiased, reliable and relevant measures of job performance or other criteria of employee adequacy. See §12b(1). With respect to investigation of possible unfairness, the same considerations are applicable to each group for which the study is made. See §12b(7).

(k) Unfairness of Selection Procedure (differential prediction): A condition in which members of one racial, ethnic, or sex group characteristically obtain lower scores on a selection procedure than members of another group, and the differences are not reflected in differences in measures of job performance. See §12b(7).

(l) User: Any employer, labor organization, employment agency, or licensing or certification board, to the extent it may be covered by Federal equal employment opportunity law which uses a selection procedure as a basis for any employment decision. Whenever an employer, labor organization, or employment agency is required by law to restrict recruitment for any occupation to those applicants who have met licensing or certification requirements, the licensing or certifying authority to the extent it may be covered by Federal equal employment opportunity law will be considered the user with respect to those licensing or certification requirements. Whenever a state employment agency or service does no more than administer or monitor a procedure as permitted by Department of Labor regulations, and does so without making referrals or taking any other action on the basis of the results, the state employment agency will not be deemed to be a user.